Organizational Careers

Organizational Careers

A Sourcebook for Theory

Barney G. Glaser, editor

Routledge
Taylor & Francis Group

LONDON AND NEW YORK

First published 1968 by Transaction Publishers

Published 2017 by Routledge
4 Park Square, Milton Park, Abingdon, Oxon OX14 4RN
605 Third Avenue, New York, NY 10017

Routledge is an imprint of the Taylor & Francis Group, an informa business

Library of Congress Catalog Number: 2027024161

Library of Congress Cataloging-in-Publication Data

Organizational careers : a sourcebook for theory / Barney G. Glaser, editor.
    p. cm.
    Includes bibliographical references and index.
    ISBN 978-0-202-36162-8
     1. Occupations. 2. Professions. 3. Vocational guidance. I. Glaser, Barney G.

HB2581.G58 2007
306.3'6--dc22

              2007024161

ISBN 13: 978-0-202-36162-8 (pbk)

For Lila, Jill, and Bonnie

ACKNOWLEDGMENTS

For his general advice and constant encouragement, I am indebted to my friend, colleague and collaborator, Anselm L. Strauss. I wish also to extend my appreciation to Howard S. Becker and Fred Davis for their support when generating the idea for this reader. Lastly, my abiding interest in "things" organizational was generated in Robert K. Merton's classic seminar on organizational theory at Columbia University.

Contents

Organizational Careers

Introduction

In general, organizations obtain work from people by offering them some kind of career within their structures. The operation of organizations, therefore, depends on people's assuming a career orientation toward them. To generate this orientation, organizations distribute rewards, working conditions, and prestige to their members according to career level; thus these benefits are properties of the organizational career. To advance in this career is to receive more or better of all or some of these benefits. Generally speaking, therefore, people work to advance their organizational careers. But also, generally speaking, people do not like to talk about their careers or to be asked about them in everyday conversations with many or unknown people. In this sense, a person's own organizational career is a sensitive or "taboo topic." Discussions with others about one's career occur only under the most private, discreet conditions. As a result, while people may talk abstractly and generally about careers, these discussions are typically based on a combination of the little they know of their own career and much speculation. They often have very little particular or general knowledge based on actual careers. These observations apply also to a large sector of the sociological community, as indicated by a brief perusal of the table of contents of sociological monographs and readers on organizations. The topic of careers is seldom discussed and almost never concertedly focused upon.

Several sociologists, however, have written on careers in general in their focus on problems of work and professions. Many of their discussions, of course, clearly refer to organizational careers, though these sociologists are writing on the general topic of occupational careers. There is a difference between these two topics. An occupational career is a very general category referring to a patterned path of mobility wherever it may take people geographically, organizationally, and socially while following a certain type of work. An organizational career, in contrast, is a specific entity offered by an organization to people working in it, using its services, or buying its goods.

PURPOSES OF THIS READER

Since so much of what we all do is linked with organizations, it is very important to consider an organizational career as a special entity and develop our understanding of it. We hope to achieve this purpose partially by bringing

1

together many articles on careers that fit the category of organizational work careers. This act of itself will initiate much general understanding.

We also wish to start the generation of a formal, grounded theory of organizational careers by initial comparative analysis of these articles.[1] In its beginning operation, a comparative analysis for generating theory starts with the general understandings gained by reading about the same problem from the perspective of several different organizational careers. Pursuit of the comparative analysis brings out several other purposes of this reader.

For the interested reader, whether sociologist or non-sociologist, this book brings together a very rich body of comparative knowledge, experience, and thought on organizational careers. The general understandings, concepts, and strategies gained by merely reading it will aid the reader in "making it" in his own career. This is important to so many of us whose work life is tied up with an organizational career. With little information on which to base our decisions, we are continually trying to decide and manage how to move through the organization to some advantage. The comparative analysis afforded by this book just naturally leads one to an applied sociological perspective.

For the sociologist, this reader may have several benefits. Teachers may use it simply as a body of information on work careers. But they may also use it for teaching students the techniques of comparative analysis and of generating theory from data.[2] Sociologists (students and teachers alike) will find the comparative materials a stimulant and guide to scholarship and research on organizational careers. The comparisons will lead the sociologist to develop relevant categories, hypotheses, and problems and to discover important gaps in our knowledge of particular organizational careers and in our budding theories. The end result, we trust, will be the stimulation to develop more formal theory for various aspects of organizational careers.

Lastly, this reader will indicate how, in many instances, the analysis of organizations can be usefully accomplished through a theory of the careers of its members. The properties of their organizational careers are prime determinants of the behavior of the people who man the organization. This is, however, a neglected topic in most sociological analyses and descriptions of organizations. The focus of explanations of behavior is typically upon goals and work expectations, authority and power structures, rational decision-making, efficiency demands, and working conditions. Organizational careers appear to be too sensitive or taboo a topic to acknowledge as a determinant of a man's behavior, with its subsequent effect on the organization. Perhaps the self-interest it implies as the motivation behind behavior, which is presumably in the service of the organization, is not supposed to be acknowledged.

---

[1] Barney G. Glaser and Anselm L. Strauss, *The Discovery of Grounded Theory* (Chicago: Aldine Publishing Company, 1967), Part I.

[2] For the latter two purposes, we suggest that it be used in conjunction with Glaser and Strauss, *ibid.*

Furthermore, the articles published in this volume only describe, by and large, various aspects of a career. The concept of "organizational career" is itself seldom used in them as a way of describing the organization as a social structure or explaining organizational behaviors, problems, or facts. If employed in this way, a theory of organizational careers would itself be a very relevant tool by which to analyze organizations.[3]

FROM SUBSTANTIVE TO FORMAL THEORY[4]

By substantive theory we mean that developed for a substantive or empirical area of sociological inquiry, such as patient care, race relations, professional education, delinquency, or financial organizations. By formal theory we mean that developed for a formal or conceptual area of sociological inquiry, such as stigma, deviant behavior, socialization, status congruency, authority and power, reward systems, social mobility, organizations, or organizational careers. Both types of theory may be considered as "middle-range." They fall between the "minor working hypotheses" of everyday life and the "all-inclusive" grand theories.[5]

Substantive and formal theories exist on distinguishable levels of generality, which differ only in terms of degree. Therefore, in any one study each type can shade at points into the other. The analyst, however, should focus clearly on one level or the other, or on a specific combination, because the strategies vary for arriving at each one. For example, in my analysis of the organizational careers of scientists, the focus was on the substantive area of scientists' careers, not on the formal area of organizational careers. With the focus on a substantive area such as this, the generation of theory can be achieved by a comparative analysis between or among groups within the same substantive area. In this instance, I compared the career stages of junior investigator, senior investigator, and supervisor within two different promotional systems of the organization. The substantive theory also could be aided in its generation by comparing the organizational careers of scientists with other substantive cases within the formal area of organizational careers, such as those of lawyers or military officers. The comparison would illuminate the substantive theory about scientists' careers.

However, if the focus of level of generality is on generating formal theory, then the comparative analysis would be made among different kinds of substantive cases and their theories which fall within the formal area, without relating the resulting theory to any one particular substantive area. The focus

---

[3] For an example of this type of organizational analysis, see Anselm Strauss, Leonard Schatzman, Rue Bucher, Danuta Ehrlich, and Melvin Sabshin, *Psychiatric Ideologies and Institutions* (New York: Free Press of Glencoe, 1964).

[4] The next four sections to this introduction draw heavily on Chapters 2, 3, 4, and 5 in Glaser and Strauss, *op. cit.* I wish to thank Anselm Strauss for permission to reproduce this material.

[5] See Robert K. Merton, *Social Theory and Social Structure* (rev. ed.; New York: Free Press of Glencoe, 1957), 5–10.

of comparisons is now on generating a formal theory of organizational careers from several substantive theories, not on generating a theory about a single substantive case of an organizational career. This is the approach used to generate formal theory in this volume. We have discussed other approaches to generating grounded formal theory in *The Discovery of Grounded Theory*, for example, one substantive area formal theory which uses "rewriting-up" techniques, direct formulation from data when no substantive theory exists, and expanding a single, existing substantive theory with comparative data. Combinations of these approaches are quite appropriate. The approach one uses depends on the prior substantive research and theory development applicable to the formal area. Comparative analysis of substantive theories is perhaps the most powerful of these approaches. In our area of formal theory, the current state of knowledge and theory on many substantive organizational careers is at a stage which allows this reader to be attempted.

Both substantive and formal theories must, we believe, be grounded in data; that is, systematically discovered and generated from the data of social research. Substantive theory faithful to the empirical situation cannot, we believe, be formulated merely by applying a few ideas from an established formal theory to the substantive area. To be sure, one goes out and studies an area with a particular sociological perspective, and with a focus, a general question or a problem, in mind. But he can (and we believe should) also study an area without a preconceived theory that dictates, prior to the research, relevancies in concepts and hypotheses. It is presumptuous to assume that one begins to know the relevant categories and hypotheses until after a few days of exploratory research. A substantive theory must first be generated from data in order to see which of a number of diverse formal theories may be applicable for generating additional substantive formulations.

Ignoring this first task—discovering substantive theory relevant to a given substantive area—is the result, in most instances, of believing that formal theories can be applied directly to a substantive area and will supply most or all of the necessary concepts and hypotheses. The consequence is often a forcing of data, as well as a neglect of relevant concepts and hypotheses that may emerge. On the other hand, the approach of allowing substantive concepts and hypotheses to emerge on their own enables the analyst to ascertain which, if any, existing formal theory may help him generate his substantive theories. He can then be more faithful to his data, rather than forcing it to fit a theory. He can be more objective and less theoretically biased. Of course, this also means that he cannot merely apply Parsonian or Mertonian categories at the start, but must wait to see whether they are linked to the emergent substantive theory concerning the issue in focus.

Substantive theory helps, in turn, to generate new formal theories and to reformulate previously established ones. In several ways it becomes a strategic link in the formulation and development of formal theory based on data. A substantive theory may have important general relevance and become, almost automatically, a springboard or stepping stone to the development of a grounded formal theory. For example, a substantive theory on the comparative failure of scientists leads directly to the need for a theory of comparative failure in work or even more generally in all facets of social life.

Other aspects of the link between research data and grounded formal theory provided by substantive theory involve the development of an initial direction for choosing relevant conceptual categories, conceptual properties of categories, and hypotheses relating these concepts, and the choice of possible modes of integration for the theory. We emphasize "initial," since the formal theory is generated from comparing many substantive theoretical ideas from many different cases, initially relevant categories, and properties, and hypotheses can change in the process. Also, in integrating formal theory, formal models of process, structure, and analysis may be useful guides to integration, along with models provided by the comparatively analyzed substantive theories. Suffice it to say that our approach to grounding under-lines the point that the formal theory we are talking about is induced by comparative analysis and must be contrasted with "grand" theory that is generated by logical deduction from assumptions and speculations about the "oughts" of social life.

Within these relations between social research, substantive theory and formal theory is a design for the cumulative nature of knowledge and theory. The design involves a progressive building-up from facts through substantive to formal grounded theory. To generate grounded substantive theory, we need many facts for the necessary comparative analysis; ethnographic studies and direct data collection are required. Ethnographic studies, substantive theories, and direct data collection are all, in turn, necessary for building up by comparative analysis to formal theory. This design, then, locates the place of each level of work within the cumulation of knowledge and theory, and thereby suggests a division of labor in sociological work.

This design also suggests that besides ethnographic studies *multiple* substantive *and* formal theories are needed to build up, through discovering their relationships, to more inclusive formal theories. Such a call for multiple theories is in contrast to the directly monopolistic implication of logico-deductive theories whose formulators talk as if there is only one theory for a formal area, or perhaps only one formal sociological theory for all areas. The need for multiple substantive theories to generate a formal theory may be obvious, but it is not so obvious that multiple formal theories are also necessary. One formal theory never handles all relevancies of an area, and by comparing many we can begin to arrive at more inclusive, parsimonious levels of formal theory. Parsimonious grounded formal theories are hard won by this design. The logico-deductive theorist, proceeding under the license and mandate of analytic abstraction and deduction from assumptions and conjecture, engages in a premature parsimony of formulation. He is not bothered by the theoretical comparative analysis of data and substantive theories required to achieve a theory that fits and works in explaining and interpreting a formal area of inquiry.

SELECTION OF ARTICLES

The method of advancing from data to substantive theories to a grounded formal theory used here to generate a beginning formal theory of organizational careers has dictated the criteria for choosing and excerpting the articles for this volume. The present state of the sociological study of careers is that we have many substantive theories on similar and diverse problems for many different kinds of organizational careers. Thus, according to our method, our state of knowledge is at the point where a sufficient number of grounded substantive theories have been developed. The next step is to put them together for a comparative analysis that will generate formal (but partial) theories on aspects of organizational careers. This step is the task of this book.

The principal criterion for the selection of articles for this reader is *ideational*—to provide as broad and diverse a range of substantive, theoretical ideas on organizational careers as possible. *This range of ideas may be contrasted to, and does not mean, a broad range of data or of authors.* Thus, the articles have been chosen to provide as many categories, properties, hypotheses, and problems on careers as space permits—which will, in turn, provide the initial elements for developing formal theory on organizational careers. While the raw data on careers is abundant, the writings with substantive theoretical ideas grounded in data are far fewer. Thus our range of authors and data is not great, and it need not be. Further, the grounded theory from one author's work may be used in several places, since ideas that fit theoretical areas or problems are the criterion of placement—*not how much of an author or of a kind of data is used.*

Following our ideational criterion, the articles here have been carefully excerpted from the originals to bring out general ideas, accompanied by sufficient data to understand their grounding. Remaining discussions of methods and tables and lengthy descriptions have been left out. The reader may refer to original sources if these additional data are necessary to him. They are no longer necessary for comprehending the idea, once it has been grounded. This method of extracting has resulted in a continuous flow of theoretical ideas on careers, uninterrupted by the normal tedium of many research presentations. Footnotes which considerably overlap each article have been deleted unless they provide a useful bibliography for the whole book.

Most articles come from exploratory qualitative research, since in this form of research we usually find an abundance of general categories, hypotheses, and problems, in contrast to their sparseness in quantitative research. Also, qualitative research discussions are easier and richer to read, especially for interested readers outside of sociology.

It will be readily apparent to the reader that the ideas in many of the articles are applicable to several parts of the book. But each is put in the section in which it will contribute the most, ideationally, to the generation of theory. The reader may, however, read articles in another section for the section he is studying. For example, he may read articles on promotion for more comparisons to the ones on succession. In each article, the categories of relevance may be clearly focused on or only mentioned; they may be categories of careers or categories which vary by careers; they may be focused on a particular career or focused on a different topic that happens to mention careers. In some articles the organizational structure is explicitly woven into the analysis, and in others it is only implicit. When the goal is finding categories and problems for generating formal theory, abstract shifts from the author's focus and emphasis are in order.

The reader will notice the social-psychological and social-interaction tendency of these articles. This is probably accounted for by the tendencies of the Chicago School which initiated the study of careers (see Part I). It would appear that further studies should weave more of the organizational structure into career studies.

GENERATING FORMAL THEORY BY COMPARATIVE ANALYSIS

The term comparative analysis—often used in sociology and anthropology—has grown to encompass several different meanings and thereby to carry several different burdens. Many sociologists and anthropologists, recognizing the great power of comparative analysis, have employed it for achieving their various purposes. To avoid confusion we must, therefore, be clear as to our own use for comparative analysis—generating of theory—in contrast to its other uses—achieving either accurate evidence, empirical generalizations, specification of a concept, or verifications of a hypothesis. Generation of theory both subsumes and assumes these other uses, but only to the extent that they are in the service of generation. Otherwise they are sure to stifle it.

In our use, comparative analysis is considered as a general method, just as are the experimental and statistical methods: all use the logic of comparisons. Comparative analysis can, like these other methods, be used for social units of any size. Some sociologists and anthropologists customarily use the term comparative analysis to refer only to comparisons between large-scale social units, particularly organizations, nations, institutions, and large regions of the world. But such a reference restricts a general method to use with only one specific class of social units to which it has frequently been applied. As a general method for generating theory, comparative analysis takes on its fullest generality when one realizes its power applied to social units of any size, large or small, ranging from men or their roles to nations or world regions. It can also be used to compare conceptual units of a theory or theories (as we do in this book), such as categories and their properties and hypotheses. In our case, this results in generating, densifying, and integrating the theories into a formal theory by discovering a more parsimonious set of concepts with greater scope.

The basic criterion governing the selection of comparison groups for generating theory is their *theoretical relevance* for furthering the development of emerging categories, properties, hypotheses, and integration of the theory. Any groups may be selected that will help generate these elements of the theory. Rules of comparability of groups used in descriptive and verificational studies do not apply in generating theory because *group comparisons are conceptual.* Conceptual comparisons are made by comparing diverse or similar evidence from different groups which indicate the same conceptual categories and properties, not by comparing the evidence for its own sake. Or, they are made by comparing theoretical concepts grounded in each group or by comparing evidence for a concept from one group to a concept already developed from another. Comparative analysis of concepts and/or their indicators takes full advantage of the "interchangeability" of indicators and develops, as it proceeds, a broad range of acceptable indicators for categories and properties.[6]

The articles are arranged in each part to facilitate these processes. The reader begins with the first article. By the second or third article, the reader is thinking about and comparing different data and ideas within the broad category designating the part, such as demotion. Second, in trying to understand all these data and ideas, he is forced to develop theoretical notions that subsume them in an orderly fashion. For example, he might specify under what conditions demotion is clear or ambiguous. Third, he may then end up thinking in terms of categories, properties, and hypotheses that are very different and more general than any one article considered (as well as using the categories within the articles which are of sufficient generality), such as a typology of demotion. Last, these categories and properties begin to relate to each other, thereby integrating into a dense, formal theory. At this point one also discovers clear gaps in the theory and directions for new research. (We have indicated in the introductions to each part where the analysis of each article fits by placing the author's name in parentheses.)

Two typical rules of comparability are especially irrelevant when generating theory is the goal. One rule states that to be included within a set of comparison groups, a group must have enough features in common with them. Another rule is that to be excluded it must show a fundamental difference from the others. These two rules for verificational and descriptive studies attempt to hold constant strategic facts or to disqualify groups where the facts either cannot actually be constant or would introduce more unwanted differences. In sum, one hopes that in this set of purified comparison groups spurious factors will not influence the findings and relationships and render them inaccurate.

[6] Paul F. Lazarsfeld and Wagner Theilens, Jr., *The Academic Mind* (New York: Free Press of Glencoe, 1958), 402–408.

These rules hinder the generation of theory. Weeding out spurious factors is not important in generating, since spurious factors are just one more theoretical idea to be included in the theory. Indeed, concern with these rules to avoid spuriousness and inaccuracy diverts the analyst's attention away from the important sets of fundamental differences and similarities among groups which, upon analysis, become important qualifying conditions under which categories and properties vary. These conditions should be made a vital part of the theory. Further, these two rules hinder the use of a wider range of groups for developing categories and properties. Such a range, necessary for the categories' fullest possible development, is achieved by comparing any group, irrespective of differences or similarities, as long as the data indicate a similar category or property.

When theoretically sampling for comparison groups, several matters must be kept in mind. The analyst must be clear on the basic *types* of groups he wishes to compare in order to control their effect on the generality of both population *scope* and *conceptual level* of his theory. The simplest comparisons are made among different groups of exactly the same substantive type; for instance, different federal bookkeeping departments. These comparisons lead to a substantive theory that is applicable to this one type of group. Somewhat more general substantive theory is achieved by comparing different types of groups; for example, different kinds of federal departments in one federal agency. The scope of the theory is further increased by comparing different types of groups within different larger groups (different departments in different agencies). Generality is further increased by making these latter comparisons for different regions of a nation, or, to go further, different nations. *The scope of a substantive theory can be carefully increased and controlled by such conscious choices of groups.*

The sociologist may also find it convenient to think of subgroups within larger groups, of internal and external groups to the substantive area or to a larger group, and of created or natural groups as he broadens his range of comparisons and attempts to keep tractable his substantive theory's various levels of generality of scope. Creating groups, it must be mentioned, is as equally applicable to qualitative data as it is to quantitative. For instance, when using interviews, a researcher can study comparison groups composed of respondents grouped in accordance with his emergent analytic framework.

As the sociologist gradually shifts the degree of conceptual generality from substantive to formal theory, he must keep in mind the *class* of groups he selects. While the logic and process of comparative analysis remains the same, the process becomes more difficult because of the more abstract conceptual level and wider range of groups. For substantive theory, the sociologist can select groups within the same substantive class regardless of where he finds them. He can, thus, compare the "emergency ward" to all kinds of medical wards in all kinds of hospitals both in the United States and abroad. But he may also conceive of the emergency ward as a subclass of a larger class of organizations, all designed to render immediate assistance in the event of accidents or breakdowns of any kind. For example, fire, crime, riots, automobile breakdowns or accidents, and plumbing problems have all given rise to emergency organizations that are on 24-hour alert. In taking this approach to choosing dissimilar, substantive comparative groups, the analyst must be clear about his purpose. He may use groups of the more general class to illuminate his substantive theory of, say, emergency wards. He may wish to begin generating a formal theory of emergency organizations. He may desire a mixture of both: for instance, he may want to bring out his substantive theory about emergency wards within a context of some formal categories about emergency organizations.

When the sociologist's purpose is to discover formal theory, he will definitely select dissimilar, substantive groups from the larger class for increasing his theory's scope. And he will also find himself comparing groups that seem to be non-comparable on the substantive level, but which on the formal level are conceptually comparable. Non-comparable on the substantive level here implies a stronger degree of apparent difference than does dissimilar. For example, while fire departments and emergency wards are substantially dissimilar, the conceptual comparability is still readily apparent.

Since the basis of comparison between substantively non-comparable groups is not readily apparent, it must be explained on a higher conceptual level. For example, one could start developing a formal theory of social isolation by comparing four apparently unconnected monographs: *Blue Collar Marriage, The Taxi-Dance Hall, The Ghetto,* and *The Hobo.*[7] All deal with facets of "social isolation," according to their authors. For another example, Goffman has compared apparently non-comparable groups when generating his formal theory of stigma.[8] Anyone who wishes to discover formal theory, then, should be aware of the usefulness of comparisons made on high-level conceptual categories among the seemingly non-comparable. He should actively seek this kind of comparison, do it with flexibility, and be able to interchange the apparently non-comparable comparison with the apparently comparable ones. The non-comparable type of group comparison can greatly aid him in transcending substantive descriptions of time and place as he tries to achieve a general, formal theory.

Theoretical Formulation

It is important in this closing section to suggest how we believe the generated theory may usefully be formulated. Grounded theory may take different forms. And although we consider the process of generating theory to be inextricably related to its subsequent use and effectiveness in research

---

[7] Respectively, Mirra Komarovsky (New York: Random House, 1962); Paul Cressey (Chicago: University of Chicago Press, 1932); Louis Wirth (Chicago: University of Chicago Press, 1962 edition); and Nels Anderson (Chicago: University of Chicago Press, 1961).

[8] *Stigma* (Englewood Cliffs, N.J.: Prentice-Hall, 1963).

and application, the form in which the theory is presented can be (but is best not) independent of the process by which it was generated. Grounded theory may be presented either as a well-codified or axiomatically developed set of propositions, or in a running theoretical discussion, using conceptual categories and their properties as elements in the hypotheses, which are the generalized relations between them.

We have chosen the discussional form for several reasons.[9] Our strategy of comparative analysis for generating theory puts a high emphasis on *theory as process*; that is, theory as an ever-developing entity, not as a perfected product. The discussional form renders this emphasis best. To be sure, theory as process must be presented at times in publications as a momentary product, but it is written with the assumption that it is still developing. Theory as process, we believe, renders quite well the reality of social interaction and its structural context. The discussional form of formulating theory gives a feeling of "ever-developing" and "modifiability" to the theory, allows it to become quite rich in complexity and density, and makes its fit and relevance to reality easy to comprehend.

In contrast, to state a theory in propositional form, except perhaps for a few scattered core propositions, would make it less complex, dense, and rich and more laborious to read. It would also, by implication, tend to "freeze" the theory instead of giving the feeling of a need for continued development. When necessary for a verificational study, parts of a theoretical discussion can, at any point, be rephrased as a set of propositions. This rephrasing is simply a formal exercise—usually required of students—since the concepts are already related in the discussion.

Also, with either a propositional or discussional grounded theory, the sociologist can then logically deduce further hypotheses. Deduction from grounded theory, as it develops, is the method by which the researcher directs his theoretical sampling for more comparative groups.

Making a distinction between category and property indicates a systematic relationship between these two elements of theory. A category stands by itself as a conceptual element of theory—for example, a demotion. A property, in turn, is a conceptual aspect or element of a category—for example, the degree of clarity of a demotion. Both are concepts indicated by the data, and not the data itself. Once a category or property is conceived, change in the evidence that indicated it will not destroy it. The change in data can only modify or clarify it, if any effect is warranted. Conceptual categories and properties have a life apart from the evidence that gave rise to them.

Categories and properties vary in degree of conceptual abstraction. Synthesis and integration of the theory may occur at many levels of

---

[9] This choice is not new, since most theory is written this way, whether grounded or logico-deductive. But we have noted this decision, on the request of several colleagues, to fend off the criticism that the only true theory is the one written, by the numbers, as an integrated set of propositions. The form in which a theory is presented does not make it a theory; it is a theory because it explains or predicts something.

conceptual and hypothetical generalization, varying from the substantive to the formal level of abstraction. This is one aspect of the density of generated grounded theory; another aspect is how densely a category is developed in terms of its theoretical properties; and another is how well the theory is integrated within its full range of conceptualization. We believe that a generated theory takes much densification so that it will fit a multitude of situations in the area it purports to explain. A dense theory lends itself to ready modification and reformulation to handle new qualifications required by changing conditions in what is "going on."

Several kinds of theoretical ideas are useful in generating a dense property development of a category. The analyst is literally forced by comparative analysis to think in terms of the full range of types, degree, or continua of a category, its dimensions, the conditions and contingencies under which it exists or is pronounced or minimized, its major consequences, its structural context, social and structural processes that bring it about or maintain it, strategies people use to control or handle it, its relationship to other categories and their properties. Examples of these ideas are found woven into the theoretical introductions to each part of this volume.

There follow nine parts to this volume. Each is devoted to opening up the topic and the task of generating a formal theory of that aspect of organizational careers under focus. Each part is introduced with a formal theoretical statement generated by comparative analysis of the ensuing articles. The introductions are an example of the formal theory which can be generated by comparative analysis of the articles, how to comparatively analyze for this purpose, and what directions are useful to take in generating more theory from the articles and from further study and research.

PART I

Toward a Theory of Organizational Careers

A general theory of organizational careers can be aided by initial formulations from the "classic" articles in this section on careers in general. These articles come from successive generations of sociologists who, because of their training and/or teaching at the University of Chicago, have been stimulated to take up the topic of careers in their research, scholarship, and thought. In these articles we find many basic dimensions and problems of careers which provide a general perspective helpful to guiding the comparative analyses necessary to generating and integrating the various aspects of a theory of organizational careers. Further, they provide a general focus on careers of all kinds which show the context for our more delimited focus on "organizational careers."

An organizational career is one type of status-passage (Hughes). It is a passage from one status to another through the type of social structure frequently called by sociologists either an "organization," a "formal organization," a "complex organization," or a "bureaucracy." This career is linked with the organization either by a job in which the person does the work of the organization or by a client position provided by the organization in which the person receives the work of the organization—patient, customer, consumer, and so on. In this reader, we consider only articles on job-related organizational careers, with one exception (Glaser) in Part VIII.

A formal theory of organizational careers should consider several interrelated central units of analysis: the person having the career, other people associated with the person, the career itself, the organization, and the society (or its sector) in which the organization exists. Consideration of these units in analyzing a particular career is always, of course, subject to their particular relevance. However, the formal theory must consider them in order to guide analyses that make any particular unit relevant.

From the point of view of the person, several basic aspects of organizational careers emerge in the articles of this section. Some organizational careers advance persons to different—usually more skilled—work; some merely advance the career while the work stays the same; and some make the work easier or less skilled while advancing the career. There is no necessarily direct relation between the career and the kind of work involved at each stage. It depends on the type of career offered by the type of organization. Organizational careers guide the person into kinds of interpretations, perspectives, or meanings of his work and his performance of it, his responsibility, his powers, rights, and privileges, and his identity, and they guide others' appraisals of the person on these dimensions (Hughes). Further, the organizational career structures, at each stage, the various people within and outside the organization that a person will work and associate with. At each stage of his career the person faces new organizational (and family) concerns which tend to vary his motivation for continuing the career and his loyalty and commitment to the organization. At each stage of the career the person faces a turning point in his work life and identity, some being relatively incidental and some being traumatic, requiring transitional periods and occasioning choices about leaving the organization or taking an alternative career direction within the organization.

The organizational career literally moves the person through the organizational structure or freezes him in one place. Thus several facets of organizational mobility must be considered for a theory of organizational careers (Becker and Strauss). To what degree is the career clearly ordered, and stages and rates of advancement and promotions routinized? Sometimes the career must literally be created by the person having it as he goes along. Careers will vary in the clarity of definition of each stage or rank and how people are led to expect the next direction in their career—they may be moved up, down, sideways, or kept in place. These attributes of career vary in terms of the size of the organization, its general stability, whether and how it is changing, and whether it moves people along individually or by cohorts (all together) at one's particular stage or for one's group. We must discover theory for how people start their careers moving when blocked, stimulate promotions, prevent or refuse changes in their position, avoid undesirable positions or demotions when they cannot "keep up," gauge their career timetables (Roth) and compare them to other people's, handle the uncertainties of movement through the organizational career, become sponsored, give up the career, develop possessiveness or proprietary rights over positions which they must sometimes be talked or forced into vacating, switch careers on the wave of their movements, move between organizations, and so forth.

From the point of view of the organization, the following articles highlight several basic concerns linked with organizational careers. In order to keep itself manned, the organization must continually fill positions through recruitment and replacement. Recruitment usually refers to filling positions at the beginning of the career, but it can also refer to bringing in people from the outside to all levels. "Recruitment programs" refer to the beginning and highlight the continual need of organizations for new, young people, ranging from those who are highly trained to severely unskilled. Replacement usually refers to the filling of vacated positions, which occurs for several reasons that relate to movements of people in their careers. The organizational problem is how to manage existing turnover, how to plan, generate, and procedurally order succession between positions, and, once people are moved between positions, how to train and help them take over their new responsibilities. The organization must also establish procedures (however codified or surreptitious) for filling highly skilled positions, positions of power, undesirable positions, lower rank positions, and for severing people from the organizational career—retiring or firing them. In resolving these problems in some fashion, the organization provides a broad shape and style of career for its people, several patterns of interdependence between careers, a context (often shifting) for these careers, and a ground for routinizing careers, for starting new careers, and for differentiating old careers into several new ones.

The organizational career has several relationships with society (Wilensky). Many people in various sectors of society are untouched by organizational careers in their own work. Some people just find non-organizational work as their condition. Others vehemently look for these sectors of society and work in them exclusively. But since ours is a society whose principal institutions are run by complex organizations, these people must in their current, daily rounds deal of necessity with others in the midst of their own organizational career—a contingency strongly influencing many dealings.

The organizational career provides for people a stability in life plan, style, and cycle, engendering their motivation to work. This stability is one of the sources of a stable organization and thus leads to stability in the organizational sectors of society. This stability is clearly seen in the continuity of employment, style, and plan of life in the governmental sectors of civil service and the military. It is also felt in the instability effects on society of transient and temporary work and of undesirable workers for which careers are non-existent. The educational institutions of our society are devoted to providing stable numbers of people to fill career positions of importance to organizations that firmly integrate society. Organizational careers also, however, force upon vast numbers of people a residential mobility that generates problems of stability for many facets of society, such as transportation, record-keeping, ownership, financial responsibility, community involvement, and so forth.

Clearly the facets of organizational careers that relate to society are in need of much research and theory development. This reader does not provide much on this subject.

To move toward a formal theory of organizational careers we must generate many theories on the many aspects of organizational careers in relation to people, the organization, and society. As these are developed they become integrated, however tightly or loosely, and represent a general formal theory. The articles in this section merely open up pathways to research and theory development.

The remainder of the book presents articles on several of the current foci of studies of organizational careers: recruitment, motivation, loyalty, promotion, demotion, succession, moving between organizations, and career patterns. These articles provide the beginning grist for a comparative analysis designed to generate formal theory for these problems. However central these problems are, there are doubtless many more of high relevance upon which we have little or no research and theory. The articles in this book provide many leads to these other relevant areas of organizational careers by their text and, importantly, by their lack of generality of scope which indicate the neglected gaps in our knowledge of subjects relevant to the study and theory of organizational careers. The task remains for sociologists to start discovering grounded theories on aspects of organizational careers for integration into a formal theory.

1

Career and Office

EVERETT C. HUGHES

Organizational careers guide the person into kinds of interpretations, perspectives, or meanings of his work—his competence, his responsibility, his powers, rights, and privileges, and his identity. They also guide other people's appraisals of the person on these dimensions of careers. Professor Hughes develops these problems in terms of the stages of a career.

In any society there is an appropriate behavior of the child at each age. Normal development of personality involves passing in due time from one status to another. Some stages in this development are of long duration; others are brief. While some are thought of as essentially preparatory, and their length justified by some notion that the preparation for the next stage requires a set time, they are, nevertheless, conventional.

In a relatively stable state of society, the passage from one status to another is smooth and the experience of each generation is very like that of its predecessor. In such a state the expected rate of passage from one status to another and an accompanying scheme of training and selection of those who are to succeed to instituted offices determine the ambitions, efforts, and accomplishments of the individual. In a society where major changes are taking place, the sequence of generations in an office and that of offices in the life of the person are disturbed. A generation may be lost by disorder lasting only for the few years of passage through one phase.

However one's ambitions and accomplishments turn, they involve some sequence of relations to organized life. In a highly and rigidly structured society, a career consists, objectively, of a series of status and clearly defined offices. In a freer one, the individual has more latitude for creating his own position or choosing from a number of existing ones; he has also less certainty of achieving any given position. There are more adventurers and more failures; but unless complete disorder reigns, there will be typical sequences of position, achievement, responsibility, and even of adventure. The social order will set limits upon the individual's orientation of his life, both as to direction of effort and as to interpretation of its meaning.

Subjectively, a career is the moving perspective in which the person sees his life as a whole and interprets the meaning of his various attributes, actions, and the things which happen to him. This perspective is not absolutely fixed

Excerpted, with permission, from "Institutional Office and the Person," *American Journal of Sociology*, 43 (November, 1937): 404–413.

either as to points of view, direction, or destination. In a rigid society the child may, indeed, get a fixed notion of his destined station. Even in our society he may adopt a line of achievement as his own to the point of becoming impervious to conflicting ambitions. Consistent lines of interest and tough conceptions of one's destined role may appear early in life.

Whatever the importance of early signs of budding careers, they rarely remain unchanged by experience. The child's conception of the social order in which adults live and move is perhaps more naïve than are his conceptions of his own abilities and peculiar destiny. Both are revised in keeping with experience. In the interplay of his maturing personality and an enlarging world the individual must keep his orientation.

Careers in our society are thought of very much in terms of jobs, for these are the characteristic and crucial connections of the individual with the institutional structure. Jobs are not only the accepted evidence that one can "put himself over"; they also furnish the means whereby other things that are significant in life may be procured. But the career is by no means exhausted in a series of business and professional achievements. There are other points at which one's life touches the social order, other lines of social accomplishment—influence, responsibility, and recognition.

A woman may have a career in holding together a family or in raising it to a new position. Some people of quite modest occupational achievements have careers in patriotic, religious, and civic organizations. They may, indeed, budget their efforts toward some cherished office of this kind rather than toward advancement in their occupations. It is possible to have a career in an avocation as well as in a vocation.

Places of influence in our greater noncommercial organizations are, however, open mainly to those who have acquired prestige in some other field. The governors of universities are selected partly on the basis of their business successes. A recent analysis of the governing boards of settlement houses in New York City shows that they are made up of people with prestige in business and professional life, as well as some leisure and the ability to contribute something to the budget.

It would be interesting to know just how significant these offices appear to the people who fill them; and further, to whom they regard themselves responsible for the discharge of their functions. Apart from that question, it is of importance that these offices are by-products of achievements of another kind. They are prerogatives and responsibilities acquired incidentally; it might even be said that they are exercised ex officio or *ex statu*.

The interlocking of the directorates of educational, charitable, and other philanthropic agencies is due perhaps not so much to a cabal as to the very fact that they are philanthropic. Philanthropy, as we know it, implies economic success; it comes late in a career. It may come only in the second generation of success. But when it does come, it is quite as much a matter of assuming certain prerogatives and responsibilities in the control of philanthropic institutions as of giving money. These prerogatives and responsibilities form part of the successful man's conception of himself and part of the world's expectation of him.

Another line of career characteristic of our society and its institutional organization is that which leads to the position of "executive." It is a feature of our society that a great many of its functions are carried out by corporate bodies. These bodies must seek the approval and support of the public, either through advertising or propaganda. Few institutions enjoy such prestige and endowments that they can forego continued reinterpretation of their meaning and value to the community. This brings with it the necessity of having some set of functionaries who will act as promoters and propagandists as well as administrators. Even such a traditional profession as medicine and such an established organization as the Roman Catholic church must have people of this sort. By whatever names they be called, their function is there and may be identified.

Sometimes, as in the case of executive secretaries of medical associations, these people are drawn from the ranks of the profession. In other cases they are drawn from outside. University presidents have often been drawn from the clergy. In the Y.M.C.A. the chief executive officer is quite often not drawn from the ranks of the "secretaries." But whether or not that be the case, the functions of these executive officers are such that they do not remain full colleagues of their professional associates. They are rather liaison officers between the technical staff, governing boards, and the contributing and clientele publics. Their technique is essentially a political one; it is much the same whether they act for a trade association, the Y.M.C.A., a hospital, a social agency, or a university. There is, indeed, a good deal of competition among institutions for men who have this technique, and some movement of them from one institution to another. They are also men of enthusiasm and imagination. The institution becomes to them something in which dreams may be realized.

These enthusiastic men, skilled in a kind of politics necessary in a philanthropic, democratic society, often come to blows with the older hierarchical organization of the institutions with which they are connected. Therein lies their importance to the present theme. They change the balance of power between the various functioning parts of institutions. They change not only their own offices but those of others.

Studies of certain other types of careers would likewise throw light on the nature of our institutions—as, for instance, the road to political office by way of fraternal orders, labor unions, and patriotic societies. Such careers are enterprises and require a kind of mobility, perhaps even a certain opportunism, if the person is to achieve his ambitions. These ambitions themselves seem fluid, rather than fixed upon solid and neatly defined objectives. They are the opposites of bureaucratic careers, in which the steps to be taken for advancement are clearly and rigidly defined, as are the prerogatives of each office and its place in the official hierarchy.[1] It may be that there is a tendency for our social structure to become rigid, and thus for the roads to various positions to be more clearly defined. Such a trend would make more fateful each turning-point in a personal career. It might also require individuals to cut their conceptions of themselves to neater, more conventional, and perhaps smaller patterns.

However that may be, a study of careers—of the moving perspective in which persons orient themselves with reference to the social order, and of the typical sequences and concatenations of office—may be expected to reveal the nature and "working constitution" of a society. Institutions are but the forms in which the collective behavior and collective action of people go on. In the course of a career the person finds his place within these forms, carries on his active life with reference to other people, and interprets the meaning of the one life he has to live.

[1] Mannheim would limit the term "career" to this type of thing. Career success, he says, can be conceived only as *Amtskarriere*. At each step in it one receives a neat package of prestige and power whose size is known in advance. Its keynote is security; the unforeseen is reduced to the vanishing-point ("Über das Wesen und die Bedeutung des wirtschaftlichen Erfolgsstrebens," *Archiv für Sozialwissenschaft und Sozialpolitik*, LXIII [1930], 458 ff.).

2

Careers, Personality, and Adult Socialization

HOWARD S. BECKER and ANSELM L. STRAUSS

The organizational career literally moves the person through the organizational structure, or freezes him in one place. Professors Becker and Strauss consider several facets of organizational mobility, such as the degree to which a career is clearly ordered or created en route; its stages, rates of advancement, and other temporal aspects; the method and organizational contexts in which promotions and demotions are routinized; and alternative career routes in the organization.

In contradistinction to other disciplines, the sociological approach to the study of personality and personality change views the person as a member of a social structure. Usually the emphasis is upon some cross-section in his life: on the way he fills his status, on the consequent conflicts in role and his dilemmas. When the focus is more developmental, then concepts like career carry the import of movement through structures. Much writing on career, of course, pertains more to patterned sequences of passage than to the persons. A fairly comprehensive statement about careers as related both to institutions and to persons would be useful in furthering research. We shall restrict our discussion to careers in work organizations and occupations, for purposes of economy. . . .

CAREER FLOW

Organizations built around some particular kind of work or situation at work tend to be characterized by recurring patterns of tension and of problems. Thus in occupations whose central feature is performance of a service for outside clients, one chronic source of tension is the effort of members to control their work life themselves while in contact with outsiders. In production organizations somewhat similar tensions arise from the workers' efforts to maintain relative autonomy over job conditions.

Whatever the typical problems of an occupation, the pattern of associated problems will vary with one's position. Some positions will be easier, some more difficult; some will afford more prestige, some less; some will pay better than others. In general, the personnel move from less to more desirable positions, and the flow is usually, but not necessarily, related to age. The pure case is the bureaucracy as described by Mannheim, in which seniority and an

Excerpted, with permission, from *American Journal of Sociology*, 62 (November, 1956): 253–63.

age-related increase in skill and responsibility automatically push men in the desired direction and within a single organization.[1]

An ideally simple model of flow up through an organization is something like the following: recruits enter at the bottom in positions of least prestige and move up through the ranks as they gain in age, skill, and experience. Allowing for some attrition due to death, sickness, and dismissal or resignation, all remain in the organization until retirement. Most would advance to top ranks. A few reach the summit of administration. Yet even in bureaucracies, which perhaps come closest to this model, the very highest posts often go not to those who have come up through the ranks but to "irregulars"— people with certain kinds of experiences or qualifications not necessarily acquired by long years of official service. In other ways, too, the model is oversimple: posts at any rank may be filled from the outside; people get "frozen" at various levels and do not rise. Moreover, career movements may be not only up but down or sideways, as in moving from one department to another at approximately the same rank.

The flow of personnel through an organization should be seen, also, as a number of streams; that is, there may be several routes to the posts of high prestige and responsibility. These may be thought of as escalators. An institution invests time, money, and energy in the training of its recruits and members which it cannot afford to let go to waste. Hence just being on the spot often means that one is bound to advance. In some careers, even a small gain in experience gives one a great advantage over the beginner. The mere fact of advancing age or of having been through certain kinds of situations or training saves many an employee from languishing in lower positions. This is what the phrase "seasoning" refers to—the acquiring of requisite knowledge and skills, skills that cannot always be clearly specified even by those who have them. However, the escalator will carry one from opportunities as well as to them. After a certain amount of time and money have been spent upon one's education for the job, it is not always easy to get off one escalator and on another. Immediate superiors will block transfer. Sponsors will reproach one for disloyalty. Sometimes a man's special training and experience will be thought to have spoiled him for a particular post.

RECRUITMENT AND REPLACEMENT

Recruitment is typically regarded as occurring only at the beginning of a career, where the occupationally uncommitted are bid for, or as something which happens only when there is deliberate effort to get people to commit themselves. But establishments must recruit for all positions; whenever personnel are needed, they must be found and often trained. Many higher positions, as in bureaucracies, appear to recruit automatically from aspirants

[1] Karl Mannheim, *Essays on the Sociology of Knowledge*, ed. Paul Kecskemeti (New York: Oxford University Press, 1953), 247–49.

at next lower levels. This is only appearance: the recruitment mechanisms are standardized and work well. Professors, for example, are drawn regularly from lower ranks, and the system works passably in most academic fields. But in schools of engineering young instructors are likely to be drained off into industry and not be on hand for promotion. Recruitment is never really automatic but depends upon developing in the recruit certain occupational or organizational commitments which correspond to regularized career routes.

Positions in organizations are being vacated continually through death and retirement, promotion and demotion. Replacements may be drawn from the outside ("an outside man") or from within the organization. Most often positions are filled by someone promoted from below or shifted from another department without gaining in prestige. When career routes are well laid out, higher positions are routinely filled from aspirants at the next lower level. However, in most organizations many career routes are not so rigidly laid out: a man may jump from one career over to another to fill the organization's need. When this happens, the "insider-outsider" may be envied by those who have come up by the more orthodox routes; and his associates on his original route may regard him as a turncoat. This may be true even if he is not the first to have made the change, as in the jump from scholar to dean or doctor to hospital administrator. Even when replacement from outside the organization is routine for certain positions, friction may result if the newcomer has come up by an irregular route—as when a college president is chosen from outside the usual circle of feeding occupations. A candidate whose background is too irregular is likely to be eliminated unless just this irregularity makes him particularly valuable. The advantage of "new blood" versus "inbreeding" may be the justification. A good sponsor can widen the limits within which the new kind of candidate is judged, by asking that certain of his qualities be weighed against others; as Hall says, "the question is not whether the applicant possesses a specific trait . . . but whether these traits can be assimilated by the specific institutions."[2]

Even when fairly regular routes are followed, the speed of advancement may not be rigidly prescribed. Irregularity may be due in part to unexpected needs for replacement because a number of older men retire in quick succession or because an older man leaves and a younger one happens to be conveniently present. On the other hand, in some career lines there may be room for a certain amount of manipulation of "the system." One such method is to remain physically mobile, especially early in the career, thus taking advantage of several institutions' vacancies.

THE LIMITS OF REPLACEMENT AND RECRUITMENT

Not all positions within an organization recruit from an equally wide

[2] Oswald Hall, "The Stages in a Medical Career," *American Journal of Sociology*, LIII (March, 1948), 332.

range. Aside from the fact that different occupations may be represented in one establishment, some positions require training so specific that recruits can be drawn only from particular schools or firms. Certain positions are merely way stations and recruit only from aspirants directly below. Some may draw only from the outside, and the orbit is always relevant to both careers and organization. One important question, then, about any organization is the limits within which positions recruit incumbents. Another is the limits of the recruitment in relation to certain variables—age of the organization, its relations with clients, type of generalized work functions, and the like.

One can also identify crucial contingencies for careers in preoccupational life by noting the general or probable limits within which recruiting is carried on and the forces by which they are maintained. For example, it is clear that a position can be filled, at least at first, only from among those who know of it. Thus physiologists cannot be recruited during high school, for scarcely any youngster then knows what a physiologist is or does. By the same token, however, there are at least generally formulated notions of the "artist," so that recruitment into the world of art often begins in high school.[3] This is paradoxical, since the steps and paths later in the artist's career are less definite than in the physiologist's. The range and diffusion of a public stereotype are crucial in determining the number and variety of young people from whom a particular occupation can recruit, and the unequal distribution of information about careers limits occupations possibilities.

There are problems attending the systematic restriction of recruiting. Some kinds of persons, for occupationally irrelevant reasons (formally, anyway), may not be considered for some positions at all. Medical schools restrict recruiting in this way: openly, on grounds of "personality assessments," and covertly on ethnicity. Italians, Jews, and Negroes who do become doctors face differential recruitment into the formal and informal hierarchies of influence, power, and prestige in the medical world. Similar mechanisms operate at the top and bottom of industrial organizations.[4]

Another problem is that of "waste." Some recruits in institutions which recruit pretty widely do not remain. Public caseworkers in cities are recruited from holders of bachelor's degrees, but most do not remain caseworkers. From the welfare agency's point of view this is waste. From other perspectives this is not waste, for they may exploit the job and its opportunities for private ends. Many who attend school while supposedly visiting clients may be able to transfer to new escalators because of the acquisition, for instance, of a master's degree. Others actually build up small businesses during this "free time." The only permanent recruits, those who do not constitute waste, are

---

[3] Cf. Strauss's unpublished studies of careers in art and Howard S. Becker and James Carper, "The Development of Identification with an Occupation," *American Journal of Sociology*, LXI (January, 1956), 289–98.

[4] Cf. Hall, *op. cit.*; David Solomon, "Career Contingencies of Chicago Physicians" (unpublished Ph.D. thesis, University of Chicago, 1952). . . .

those who fail at such endeavors.[5] Unless an organization actually finds useful a constant turnover of some sector of its personnel, it is faced with the problem of creating organizational loyalties and—at higher levels anyhow—satisfactory careers or the illusion of them, within the organization.

TRAINING AND SCHOOLS

Schooling occurs most conspicuously during the early stages of a career and is an essential part of getting people committed to careers and prepared to fill positions. Both processes may, or may not, be going on simultaneously. However, movement from one kind of job or position or another virtually always necessitates some sort of learning—sometimes before and sometimes on the job, sometimes through informal channels and sometimes at school. This means that schools may exist within the framework of an organization. In-service training is not only for jobs on lower levels but also for higher positions. Universities and special schools are attended by students who are not merely preparing for careers but getting degrees or taking special courses in order to move faster and higher. In some routes there is virtual blockage of mobility because the top of the ladder is not very high; in order to rise higher, one must return to school to prepare for ascending by another route. Thus the registered nurse may have to return to school to become a nursing educator, administrator, or even supervisor. Sometimes the aspirant may study on his own, and this may be effective unless he must present a diploma to prove he deserves promotion.

The more subtle connections are between promotion and informal training. Certain positions preclude the acquiring of certain skills or information, but others foster it. It is possible to freeze a man at given levels or to move him faster, unbeknownst to him. Thus a sponsor, anticipating a need for certain requirements in his candidate, may arrange for critical experiences to come his way. Medical students are aware that if they obtain internships in certain kinds of hospitals they will be exposed to certain kinds of learning: the proper internship is crucial to many kinds of medical careers. But learning may depend upon circumstances which the candidate cannot control and of which he may not even be aware. Thus Goldstein has pointed out that nurses learn more from doctors at hospitals not attached to a medical school; elsewhere the medical students become the beneficiaries of the doctors' teaching.[6] Quite often who teaches whom and what is connected with matters of convenience as well as with prestige. It is said, for instance, that registered nurses are jealous of their prerogatives and will not transmit certain skills to practical nurses. Nevertheless, the nurse is often happy to allow her aides to relieve her

---

[5] Cf. unpublished M.A. report of Earl Bogdanoff and Arnold Glass, "The Sociology of the Public Case Worker in an Urban Area" (University of Chicago, 1954).

[6] Rhoda Goldstein, "The Professional Nurse in the Hospital Bureaucracy" (unpublished Ph.D. thesis, University of Chicago, 1954).

of certain other jobs and will pass along the necessary skills; and the doctor in his turn may do the same with his nurses.

The connection between informal learning and group allegiance should not be minimized. Until a newcomer has been accepted, he will not be taught crucial trade secrets. Conversely, such learning may block mobility, since to be mobile is to abandon standards, violate friendships, and even injure one's self-regard. Within some training institutions students are exposed to different and sometimes antithetical work ideologies—as with commercial and fine artists —which results in sharp and sometimes lasting internal conflicts of loyalty.

Roy's work on industrial organization furnishes a subtle instance of secrecy and loyalty in training.[7] The workers in Roy's machine shop refused to enlighten him concerning ways of making money on difficult piecework jobs until given evidence that he could be trusted in undercover skirmishes with management. Such systematic withholding of training may mean that an individual can qualify for promotion by performance only by shifting group loyalties, and that disqualifies him in some other sense. Training hinders as well as helps. It may incapacitate one for certain duties as well as train him for them. Roy's discussion of the managerial "logic of efficiency" makes this clear: workers, not trained in this logic, tend to see short cuts to higher production more quickly than managers, who think in terms of sentimental dogmas of efficiency.

Certain transmittable skills, information, and qualities facilitate movement, and it behooves the candidate to discover and distinguish what is genuinely relevant in his training. The student of careers must also be sensitized to discover what training is essential or highly important to the passage from one status to another.

RECRUITING FOR UNDESIRABLE POSITIONS

A most difficult kind of recruiting is for positions which no one wants. Ordinary incentives do not work, for these are positions without prestige, without future, without financial reward. Yet they are filled. How, and by whom? Most obviously, they are filled by failures (the crews of gandy dancers who repair railroad tracks are made up of skid-row bums), to whom they are almost the only means of survival. Most positions filled by failures are not openly regarded as such; special rhetorics deal with misfortune and make their ignominious fate more palatable for the failures themselves and those around them.[8]

Of course, failure is a matter of perspective. Many positions represent failure to some but not to others. For the middle-class white, becoming a caseworker in a public welfare agency may mean failure; but for the Negro from

[7] Donald Roy, "Quota Restriction and Goldbricking in a Machine Shop," *American Journal of Sociology*, LVII (March, 1952), 427–42.
[8] Cf. Erving Goffman, "On Cooling the Mark Out: Some Aspects of Adaptation to Failure," *Psychiatry*, XV (November, 1952), 451–63.

the lower-middle class the job may be a real prize. The permanent positions in such agencies tend to be occupied by whites who have failed to reach anything better and, in larger numbers, by Negroes who have succeeded in arriving this far. Likewise, some recruitment into generally undesirable jobs is from the ranks of the disaffected who care little for generally accepted values. The jazz musicians who play in Chicago's Clark Street dives make little money, endure bad working conditions, but desire the freedom to play as they could not in better-paying places.[9]

Recruits to undesirable positions also come from the ranks of the transients, who, because they feel that they are on their way to something different and better, can afford temporarily to do something *infra dig*. Many organizations rely primarily on transients—such are the taxi companies and some of the mail-order houses. Among the permanent incumbents of undesirabe positions are those, also, who came in temporarily but whose brighter prospects did not materialize; they thus fall into the "failure" group.

Still another group is typified by the taxi dancer, whose career Cressey has described.[10] The taxi dancer starts at the top, from which the only movement possible is down or out. She enters the profession young and good-looking and draws the best customers in the house, but, as age and hard work take their toll, she ends with the worst clients or becomes a streetwalker. Here the worst positions are filled by individuals who start high and so are committed to a career that ends badly—a more common pattern of life, probably, than is generally recognized.

Within business and industrial organizations, not everyone who attempts to move upward succeeds. Men are assigned to positions prematurely, sponsors drop protégés, and miscalculations are made about the abilities of promising persons. Problems for the organization arise from those contingencies. Incompetent persons must be moved into positions where they cannot do serious damage, others of limited ability can still be useful if wisely placed. Aside from outright firing, various methods of "cooling out" the failures can be adopted, among them honorific promotion, banishment "to the sticks," shunting to other departments, frank demotion, bribing out of the organization, and down-grading through departmental mergers. The use of particular methods is related to the structure of the organization; and these, in turn, have consequences both for the failure and for the organization.

ATTACHMENT AND SEVERANCE

Leaders of organizations sometimes complain that their personnel will not take reponsibility or that some men (the wrong ones) are too ambitious. This complaint reflects a dual problem which confronts every organization.

[9] Howard S. Becker, "The Professional Dance Musician and His Audience," *American Journal of Sociology*, LVII (September, 1951), 136–44.
[10] Paul G. Cressey, *The Taxi-Dance Hall* (Chicago: University of Chicago Press, 1932), 84–106.

Since all positions must be filled, some men must be properly motivated to take certain positions and stay in them for a period, while others must be motivated to move onward and generally upward. The American emphasis on mobility should not lead us to assume that everyone wants to rise to the highest levels or to rise quickly. Aside from this, both formal mechanisms and informal influences bind incumbents, at least temporarily, to certain positions. Even the ambitious may be willing to remain in a given post, provided that it offers important contacts or the chance to learn certain skills and undergo certain experiences. Part of the bargain in staying in given positions is the promise that they lead somewhere. When career lines are fairly regularly laid out, positions lead definitely somewhere and at a regulated pace. One of the less obvious functions of the sponsor is to alert his favorites to the sequence and its timing, rendering them more ready to accept undesirable assignments and to refrain from champing at the bit when it might be awkward for the organization.

To certain jobs, in the course of time, come such honor and glory that the incumbents will be satisfied to remain there permanently, giving up aspirations to move upward. This is particularly true when allegiance to colleagues, built on informal relations and conflict with other ranks, is intense and runs counter to allegiance to the institution. But individuals are also attached to positions by virtue of having done particularly well at them; they often take great satisfaction in their competence at certain techniques and develop self-conceptions around them.

All this makes the world of organizations go around, but it also poses certain problems, both institutional and personal. The stability of institutions is predicted upon the proper preparation of aspirants for the next steps and upon institutional aid in transmuting motives and allegiances. While it is convenient to have some personnel relatively immobile, others must be induced to cut previous ties, to balance rewards in favor of moving, and even to take risks for long-run gains. If we do not treat mobility as normal, and thus regard attachment to a position as abnormal, we are then free to ask how individuals are induced to move along. It is done by devices such as sponsorship, by planned sequences of positions and skills, sometimes tied to age; by rewards, monetary and otherwise, and, negatively, by ridicule and the denial of responsibility to the lower ranks. There is, of course, many a slip in the inducing of mobility. Chicago public school teachers illustrate this point. They move from schools in the slums to middle-class neighborhoods. The few who prefer to remain in the tougher slum schools have settled in too snugly to feel capable of facing the risks of moving to "better" schools. Their deviant course illuminates the more usual patterns of the Chicago teacher's career.

TIMING IN STATUS PASSAGE

Even when paths in a career are regular and smooth, there always arise problems of pacing and timing. While, ideally, successors and predecessors should move in and out of offices at equal speeds, they do not and cannot. Those asked to move on or along or upward may be willing but must make actual and symbolic preparations; meanwhile, the successor waits impatiently. Transition periods are a necessity, for a man often invests heavily of himself in a position, comes to possess it as it possesses him, and suffers in leaving it. If the full ritual of leavetaking is not allowed, the man may not pass fully into his new status. On the other hand, the institution has devices to make him forget, to plunge him into the new office, to woo and win him with the new gratifications, and, at the same time, to force him to abandon the old. When each status is conceived as the logical and temporal extension of the one previous, then severance is not so disturbing. Nevertheless, if a man must face his old associates in unaccustomed roles, problems of loyalty arise. Hence a period of tolerance after formal admission to the new status is almost a necessity. It is rationalized in phrases like "it takes time" and "we all make mistakes, when starting, until. . . ."

But, on the other hand, those new to office may be too zealous. They often commit the indelicate error of taking too literally their formal promotion or certification, when actually intervening steps must be traversed before the attainment of full prerogatives. The passage may involve trials and tests of loyalty, as well as the simple accumulation of information and skill. The overeager are kept in line by various controlling devices: a new assistant professor discovers that it will be "just a little while" before the curriculum can be rearranged so that he can teach his favorite courses. Even a new superior has to face the resentment or the cautiousness of established personnel and may, if sensitive, pace his "moving in on them" until he has passed unspoken tests.

When subordinates are raised to the ranks of their superiors, an especially delicate situation is created. Equality is neither created by that official act, nor, even if it were, can it come about without a certain awkwardness. Patterns of response must be rearranged by both parties, and strong self-control must be exerted so that acts are appropriate. Slips are inevitable, for, although the new status may be fully granted, the proper identities may at times be forgotten, to everyone's embarrassment. Eventually, the former subordinate may come to command or take precedence over someone to whom he once looked for advice and guidance. When colleagues who were formerly sponsors and sponsored disagree over some important issue, recrimination may become overt and betrayal explicit. It is understandable why those who have been promoted often prefer, or are advised, to take office in another organization, however much they may wish to remain at home.

MULTIPLE ROUTES AND SWITCHING

Theoretically, a man may leave one escalator and board another, instead of following the regular route. Such switching is most visible during the schooling, or preoccupational, phases of careers. Frequently students change their line of endeavor but remain roughly within the same field; this is one way for less desirable and less well-known specialties to obtain recruits. Certain kinds of training, such as the legal, provide bases for moving early and easily into a wide variety of careers. In all careers, there doubtless are some points at which switching to another career is relatively easy. In general, while commitment to a given career automatically closes paths, the skills and information thereby acquired open up other routes and new goals. One may not, of course, perceive the alternatives or may dismiss them as risky or otherwise undesirable.

When a number of persons have changed escalators at about the same stage in their careers, then there is the beginning of a new career. This is one way by which career lines become instituted. Sometimes the innovation occurs at the top ranks of older careers; when all honors are exhausted, the incumbent himself may look for new worlds to conquer. Or he may seem like a good risk to an organization looking for personnel with interestingly different qualifications. Such new phases of career are much more than honorific and may indeed be an essential inducement to what becomes pioneering.

Excitement and dangers are intimately tied up with switching careers. For example, some careers are fairly specific in goal but diffuse in operational means: the "fine artist" may be committed to artistic ideals but seize upon whatever jobs are at hand to help him toward creative goals. When he takes a job in order to live, he thereby risks committing himself to an alternative occupational career; and artists and writers do, indeed, get weaned away from the exercise of their art in just this way. Some people never set foot on a work escalator but move from low job to low job. Often they seek better conditions of work or a little more money rather than chances to climb institutional or occupational ladders. Many offers of opportunities to rise are spurned by part-time or slightly committed recruits, often because the latter are engaged in pursuing alternative routes while holding the job, perhaps a full-time one providing means of livelihood. This has important and, no doubt, subtle effects upon institutional functioning. When careers are in danger of being brought to an abrupt end—as with airplane pilots—then, before retirement, other kinds of careers may be prepared for or entered. This precaution is very necessary. When generalized mobility is an aim, specific routes may be chosen for convenience sake. One is careful not to develop the usual motivation and allegiances. This enables one to get off an escalator and to move over to another with a minimum of psychological strain.

Considerable switching takes place within a single institution or a single occupational world and is rationalized in institutional and occupational terms, both by the candidates and by their colleagues. A significant consequence of this, undoubtedly, is subtle psychological strain, since the new positions and those preceding are both somewhat alike and different.

CLIMATIC PERIODS

Even well-worn routes have stretches of maximum opportunity and danger. The critical passage in some careers lies near the beginning. This is especially so when the occupation or institution strongly controls recruitment; once chosen, prestige and deference automatically accrue. In another kind of career the critical time comes at the end and sometimes very abruptly. In occupations which depend upon great physical skill, the later phases of a career are especially hazardous. It is also requisite in some careers that one choose the proper successor to carry on, lest one's own work be partly in vain. The symbolic last step of moving out may be quite as important as any that preceded it.

Appropriate or strategic timing is called for, to meet opportunity and danger, but the timing becomes vital at different periods in different kinds of careers. A few, such as the careers of virtuoso musical performers, begin so early in life that the opportunity to engage in music may have passed long before they learn of it. Some of the more subtle judgments of timing are required when a person wishes to shift from one escalator to another. Richard Wohl, of the University of Chicago, in an unpublished paper has suggested that modeling is a step which women may take in preparation for upward mobility through marriage; but models may marry before they know the ropes, and so marry too low; or they may marry too long after their prime, and so marry less well than they might. Doubtless organizations and occupations profit from mistakes of strategic timing, both to recruit and then to retain their members.

During the most crucial periods of any career, a man suffers greater psychological stress than during other periods. This is perhaps less so if he is not aware of his opportunities and dangers—for then the contingencies are over before they can be grasped or coped with: but probably it is more usual to be aware, or to be made so by colleagues and seniors, of the nature of imminent or current crises. Fortunately, together with such definitions there exist rationales to guide action. The character of the critical junctures and the ways in which they are handled may irrevocably decide a man's fate.

INTERDEPENDENCE OF CAREERS

Institutions, at any given moment, contain people at different stages in their careers. Some have already "arrived," others are still on their way up, still others just entering. Movements and changes at each level are in various ways dependent on those occurring at other levels.

Such interdependence is to be found in the phenomenon of sponsorship, where individuals move up in a work organization through the activities of older and more well-established men. Hall has given a classic description of sponsorship in medicine. The younger doctor of the proper class and acceptable ethnic origin is absorbed, on the recommendation of a member, into the informal "inner fraternity" which controls hospital appointments and which is influential in the formation and maintenance of a clientele. The perpetuation of this coterie depends on a steady flow of suitable recruits. As the members age, retire, or die off, those who remain face a problem of recruiting younger men to do the less honorific and remunerative work, such as clinical work, that their group performs. Otherwise they themselves must do work inappropriate to their position or give place to others who covet their power and influence.

To the individual in the inner fraternity, a protégé eases the transition into retirement. The younger man gradually assumes the load which the sponsor can no longer comfortably carry, allowing the older man to retire gracefully, without that sudden cutting-down of work which frightens away patients, who leap to the conclusion that he is too old to perform capably.

In general, this is the problem of retiring with honor, of leaving a life's work with a sense that one will be missed. The demand may arise that a great man's work be carried on, although it may no longer be considered important or desirable by his successors. If the old man's prestige is great enough, the men below may have to orient themselves and their work as he suggests, for fear of offending him or of profaning his heritage. The identities of the younger man are thus shaped by the older man's passage from the pinnacle to retirement.

This interdependence of careers may cross occupational lines within organizations, as in the case of the young physician who receives a significant part of his training from the older and more experienced nurses in the hospital; and those at the same level in an institution are equally involved in one another's identities. Sometimes budding careers within work worlds are interdependent in quite unsuspected ways. Consider the young painter or craftsman who must make his initial successes in enterprises founded by equally young art dealers, who, because they run their galleries on a shoestring, can afford the frivolity of exhibiting the works of an unknown. The very ability to take such risk provides the dealer a possible opportunity to discover a genius.

One way of uncovering the interdependence of careers is to ask: Who are the important *others* at various stages of the career, the persons significantly involved in the formation of one's own identity? These will vary with stages; at one point one's agemates are crucial, perhaps as competitors, while at another the actions of superiors are the most important. The interlocking of careers results in influential images of similarity and contrariety. In so far as the significant others shift and vary by the phases of a career, identities change in patterned and not altogether unpredictable ways.

THE CHANGING WORK WORLD

The occupations and organizations within which careers are made change in structure and direction of activity, expand or contract, transform purposes. Old functions and positions disappear, and new ones arise. These constitute potential locations for a new and sometimes wide range of people, for they are not incrusted with traditions and customs concerning their incumbents. They open up new kinds of careers, to persons making their work lives within the institution and thus the possibility of variation in long-established types of career. An individual once clearly destined for a particular position suddenly finds himself confronted with an option; what was once a settled matter has split into a set of alternatives between which he must now choose. Different identities emerge as people in the organization take cognizance of this novel set of facts. The positions turn into recognized social entities, and some persons begin to reorient their ambitions. The gradual emergence of a new speciality typically creates this kind of situation within occupations.

Such occupational and institutional changes, of course, present opportunity for both success and failure. The enterprising grasp eagerly at new openings, making the most of them or attempting to; while others sit tight as long as they can. During such times the complexities of one's career are further compounded by what is happening to others with whom he is significantly involved. The ordinary lines of sponsorship in institutions are weakened or broken because those in positions to sponsor are occupied with matters more immediately germane to their own careers. Lower ranks feel the consequences of unusual pressures generated in the ranks above. People become peculiarly vulnerable to unaccustomed demands for loyalty and alliance which spring from the unforeseen changes in the organization. Paths to mobility become indistinct and less fixed, which has an effect on personal commitments and identities. Less able to tie themselves tightly to any one career, because such careers do not present themselves as clearly, men become more experimental and open-minded or more worried and apprehensive.

CAREERS AND PERSONAL IDENTITY

A frame of reference for studying careers is, at the same time, a frame for studying personal identities. Freudian and other psychiatric formulations of personality development probably overstress childhood experiences. Their systematic accounts end more or less with adolescence, later events being regarded as the elaboration of, or variations on, earlier occurrences. Yet central to any account of adult identity is the relation of change in identity to change in social position; for it is characteristic of adult life to afford and force frequent and momentous passages from status to status. Hence members of structures that change, riders on escalators that carry them up, along, and down, to unexpected places and to novel experiences even when in some sense foreseen, must gain, maintain, and regain a sense of personal identity. Identity "is never gained nor maintained once and for all."[11] Stabilities in the organization of behavior and of self-regard are inextricably dependent upon stabilities of social structure. Likewise, change ("development") is shaped by those patterned transactions which accompany career movement. The crises and turning points of life are not entirely institutionalized, but their occurrence and the terms which define and help to solve them are illuminated when seen in the context of career lines. In so far as some populations do not have careers in the sense that professional and business people have them, then the focus of attention ought still to be positional passage, but with domestic, age, and other escalators to the forefront. This done, it may turn out that the model sketched here must undergo revision.

[11] Erik H. Erikson, *Childhood and Society* (New York: W. W. Norton & Co., 1950), 57.

3

The Study of the Career Timetables

JULIUS A. ROTH

Professor Roth takes up at length the discussion of the temporal aspects of organizational careers begun by Professors Becker and Strauss. He considers the conditions for timetable norms provided by the structural context in which they occur, the splitting-up of careers into blocks of time, reference points to judge the timing of career movements, shifting time perspectives, bargaining over differential timetables, and handling the temporal aspects of failure.

People will not accept uncertainty. They will make an effort to structure it no matter how poor the materials they have to work with and no matter how much the experts try to discourage them.

One way to structure uncertainty is to structure the time period through which uncertain events occur. Such a structure must usually be developed from information gained from the experience of others who have gone or are going through the same series of events. As a result of such comparisons, norms develop for entire groups about when certain events may be expected to occur. When many people go through the same series of events, we speak of this as a career and of the sequence and timing of events as their career timetable.

The illustrations of career timetables that I have used in this book are for the most part ones that were selected *because* they were relatively easy to analyze and present to the reader. They were ones on which relatively detailed information was available and on which the career timetable was most clearly structured. I have briefly speculated on a few areas where a timetable structure is not at all clear-cut—for example, horizontal movements in occupational careers and consumption timetables. In these cases there is insufficient information available to make an analysis of a career sequence, and we cannot even be sure they fit the criteria of career timetables used in this book. For example, there has been considerable study of consumption patterns in relation to the life cycle, especially the family life cycle, but such studies have been almost entirely of the gross statistical relationship type—that is, what quantity of given products or services is purchased at given stages of the life cycle. There has been virtually no study of the process of decisions and actions of consumer purchase of given families over an extended period of time. But it is this type of study that is needed if a timetable of consumership with its many complexities and interrelationships is to be revealed.

I contend that it may be worthwhile to study career timetables in a variety of areas (in most cases probably as part of a broader study of a career), including areas where a timetable structure now seems obscure. In this chapter I review the dimensions and issues of such a study, note some cautions and qualifications that one might watch for, and make a tentative effort to point out the definitions and boundaries of career timetables.

CONDITIONS FOR TIMETABLE NORMS

From an examination of the careers illustrated in this book, the following conditions appear to be necessary for timetables to develop:

1. The series of events or conditions under scrutiny must be thought of in terms of a career—a series of related and definable stage or phases of a given sphere of activity that a group of people goes through in a progressive fashion (that is, one step leads to another) in a given direction or on the way to a more or less definite and recognizable end-point or goal or series of goals. This means that there must be a group definition of success or attainment of a goal. Such definitions may be provided by movement through an institutional hierarchy (business executive careers, academic careers); through a series of contingencies moving in a given direction (the private practice physician getting a better clientele, better office location, better hospital appointments; the schoolteacher getting better school assignments or more desirable courses to teach); escape from an undesirable situation (the patient getting out of a hospital, the prisoner getting out of jail, the draftee getting out of the army); or development in a given direction (children developing toward independent adulthood).

2. There must be an interacting (not necessarily face-to-face) group of people with access to the same body of clues for constructing the norms of a timetable.

A CULTURE-BOUND PHENOMENON

Anthropologists, in their reports on primitive groups, have in many cases pointed out that the concept of time of the people they studied is quite different from our own. Although ideas about the nature and structuring of time are quite diverse, they seem to fall into two main patterns:

Epochal time . . . may be seen as a vast continuum of progress and catastrophe or it may be interpreted as a great cyclic system featuring the restoration of virtue to government after each inevitable fall, as in the Chinese sense of history. The metaphors commonly used by speakers of English—the stream of time, Father Time, the pressure of time—are not those of other languages, and time often is not personified at all. Time may be relatively so unimportant to a people that their sense of history does not even include knowing one's own age. On the other hand, it may dominate a people's thought to such an extent that the measurement of time may become a preoccupation. To such a society, time is a commodity to be spent, lost, invested, saved, wasted, thrown away, or employed to best advantage. Its passage is marked in terms of very fine distinctions and past time is studded with memorial days, anniversaries, and foundings.[1]

These two orientations toward time are dealt with specifically in Murray Wax's comparison of the world view and time perspectives of the Pawnee Indians and the Bible-era Hebrews.[2]

In his analysis of Pawnee mythology and way of life Wax notes the lack of attention to accurate measures of time. Often the Pawnees do not even keep track of the calendar month. Life is seen as a series of repetitions or cycles —day and night, one season to another and return, misfortune and blessing, poverty and wealth. They search for turning points, for example, for a movement from a condition of being hungry, cold, wet, and poor to being sated, warm, dry, and rich. But such a change is not a progression; it merely turns attention to an expectation of a change back to the former condition. There is no need to plan for the future—good fortune is not the culmination of planning and labor, but the consequence of a blessed relationship with the supernatural.

The examination of the writings of the Hebrews of the Biblical era shows the development of a quite different time perspective. The Old Testament, according to Wax, is written with "a linear sense of history—a conception of time as the dimension along which action moves simply and straightforwardly, in an immutable sequence of cause and effect." The religion did not celebrate the birth and death and rebirth of the gods with the passage of the seasons as the religions of agricultural societies often do. Yahweh never died. He was not the god of the yearly round, but of crucial events, and his rewards and punishments could be extended into the future. In the Old Testament, history is progress. One version of this history even has a clear-cut final goal—the coming of the Kingdom of God—and the events along the way may be regarded as bench marks of progress.

Wax names the Pawnee-type view the "closed time system" and the Biblical Hebrew view the "open time system." The closed time system seems to be found in most primitive cultures and in many of the older civilizations that do not stem from the ancient Hebrew. The open time system became part of the cultural heritage that passed from ancient Judaism to early Christianity and has come to dominate the more "advanced" parts of the present-day world.

In the closed system people do not know their ages in years, but deduce their ages from their development. In the open system, development is thought of as time-serving—so many years of age, school, etc. In the closed

[1] Robert J. Smith, "Cultural Differences in the Life Cycle and the Concept of Time," in *Aging and Leisure*, ed. Robert W. Kleemeier (New York: Oxford University Press, 1961), 85.
[2] Murray Wax, "Time, Magic and Asceticism: A Comparative Study of Time Perspectives" (Ph.D. dissertation, University of Chicago, 1959), especially Chaps. 3, 6, 8, 9.

system work is regulated by conditions—weather, hunger—and one rests when he is supplied with his needs or when the weather prevents work. In the open system work and leisure are regulated by the clock and calendar.

It is obvious that my definitions of careers and the conditions under which timetable norms develop correspond to Wax's open time system. This same time perspective is implicit throughout my discussion of the timetable of tuberculosis treatment and the structuring of time in my other examples. In fact, the structuring of events into a career can occur *only* when one thinks in terms of such an open time system. The career timetable with its attendant phenomena is, therefore, a culture-bound concept.

It is, however, a culture-bound concept whose area of application is apparently spreading and becoming more pronounced. In our society the segment of the population that tends to adhere to the open time system in its more extreme form is the professional and executive middle class, and this is precisely the segment that is increasing proportionately in the total population and whose values dominate our major institutions. The English language, which expresses the open time system more explicitly than any other major language, is spreading rapidly throughout the world as a second language and in many areas as the first language of the educated class. The Communist world has long been dominated by the concept of a timetable of progress, a timetable of winning out over capitalism. In fact, Communism as a political and philosophical ideology has perhaps carried the idea of a historical march of events toward an inevitable goal to the most extreme form in which it has yet appeared. The newly independent "underdeveloped" nations are concerned with "catching up" with the more economically advanced nations. The plans for social and economic improvement that they have been issuing in recent years are essentially timetables of the catching-up process. The populations in which the closed time system holds sway grow steadily smaller.

Allowing, then, for such a cultural limitation, what issues must be considered in the study of a career timetable? In the remainder of this chapter I deal with those issues which had an important place in the analysis of the tuberculosis treatment career and the other careers that served as illustrations in this book. Of course, further study may considerably add to and modify this scheme of analysis.

SPLITTING UP BLOCKS OF TIME

Everyone, even the backward mental hospital patient, makes use of various devices to break up the days, weeks, months, and years of his life into smaller units. Such division of large masses into smaller blocks occurs not only in relation to time. We divide books into chapters, chapters into sections, sections into subsections and paragraphs. We divide academic disciplines into specialty areas, topics, and courses so that the subject matter may be viewed a little at a time. When a long series of digits must be memorized, people invariably break the series up into groups of a few digits each and memorize the digits in these groups rather than as an undifferentiated series of digits. These examples are perhaps all different aspects of the same psychological phenomenon.

However, although the splitting of time periods into smaller units probably always goes with the development of timetable norms, this process in itself does not make a career timetable. The units into which the chronic patient breaks up his days and weeks show no discernible direction or movement toward discharge from the hospital or other goal. The life prisoner can look forward to Sunday as a welcome break in a dreary routine, but the succession of Sundays does not lead him anywhere. The division of time into units with recurring markers may make one's life more psychologically manageable, but it does not in itself make a career timetable. For such a timetable to develop, the reference points must move in some definable direction or toward some recognizable goal.

THE MEANING OF REFERENCE POINTS

In all timetables we find dividing points for events that serve as signposts for progress in a given direction (toward discharge or graduation or adulthood, attaining family security or racial equality or a certain occupational position). In retrospect, such signposts may also serve as reference points from which one may predict and measure further progress.

Reference points may be more or less clear-cut and stable. If they are prescribed in detail and rigidly adhered to, as in the career of pupils in our school system, one's movement through the timetable is almost completely predictable. As the reference points become less rigid and less clear-cut, they must be discovered and interpreted through observation and through interaction with others of one's career group. The more unclear the reference points are, the harder it is for members of a career group to know where they stand in relation to others and the more likely it is that they will attend to inappropriate clues and thus make grossly inaccurate predictions concerning future progress. The degree of stability is related in part to the changes in timetables through time. Such changes may be gradual and almost imperceptible or they may occur quickly, as in military careers in time of war, occupational careers during economic expansion or depression, and disease careers at a time of drastic changes in treatment methods.

The meanings of such reference points are learned by members of the group through observation of the experience of other members and through the communication of experiences, ideals, myths, and hopes among the members of the group. During a time of rapid change in the timetable when the changes are not made explicit, such information will contain many contradictions and thus make the construction of stable and reliable timetable norms more difficult. We may conceive of an extreme situation where rapidity of change and lack of explicit information may make the development of group timetable norms impossible. Not that members of the group will not keep trying, but that their judgments will so often be so far wrong that they lose confidence in their ability to make predictions of the future. None of the careers we have used as illustrations approaches this extreme, and it is difficult to invent a realistic group traversing the same career line without some fairly accurate norms of progress. In any case, the stability of norms is relative. They are more stable (and more accurately predictive) for Valentine Hospital TB patients than for Dover Sanatorium patients, for railroad firemen and engineers than for airline pilots; but in no case do they seem to be completely absent.[3]

When career contingencies change as a result of adding alternative career lines to an existing traditional career structure, the problem of estimating norms is often dealt with by equating the reference points for the new lines to the old ones. A good example is the present-day development of academic and quasi-academic careers. The traditional career signposts have been blurred in recent years by the enormous increase in university nonfaculty research appointments and the employment of academic research people by industry, foundations, and government agencies. The pressure of researchers to know where they stand in relation to their fellows has often been met by making their positions equivalent to positions in the traditional system. The industrial research organization imitates the university graduate department in its table of organization (while borrowing the labels from business); heads of government research agencies informally equate a given GS rank to an academic rank; the university research associate becomes "research associate (assistant professor)."

The reference points and stages of a timetable do *not* necessarily describe what a person is actually doing at a given stage of the timetable, but serve only as symbols of such activity. A "bed rest" patient who is promoted to an "exercise" classification may already have been as active as an exercise patient is supposed to be while he was still on bed rest. The promotion is important in letting him know where he stands on the road to discharge even though it tells us nothing at all about the amount of activity that this patient engaged in before or after his promotion. With the slow promotions in the peacetime army, it is not unusual for a captain, let us say, to carry out the tasks that the table of organization prescribes for a major for a long period of time before he is actually promoted to major. The promotion is an extremely important

---

[3] Where we have professional-client or boss-subordinate relationships, it is not only the underdog, but also his superior, who is confused by sharp changes in timetable contingencies. When treatment methods undergo a sudden shift, not only do the patients have greater difficulty anticipating their future careers, but the physicians also become much more doubtful about when patients should be given privileges or be discharged—until a new set of norms to accompany the new treatment has been worked out. When a corporation is drastically reorganized, not only is the junior executive's timetable thrown into temporary confusion, but his bosses also have much greater difficulty deciding when their subordinates are "ready" for promotion under the new circumstances.

point in his career—especially for a regular army officer—even though it may not make the slightest difference in the work that he performs. It is important to study just how close the formal definitions of timetable reference points or stages are to the actual activity of the participants at those points or stages. The greater the discrepancy between the two, the greater will be the discrepancy between status and function in that particular career line and the more "unrealistic" will be the status distinctions.

The Search for a Reference Group

Career lines may be divided between those where each participant starts running as soon as he comes to the track (continuous system) and those where the participants have to wait for a bunch to collect before starting off (cohort system). Of the illustrations used in this book, only the draftee army and the school system use a cohort system. With this system there can be no doubt what the appropriate reference group is for measuring one's progress—one starts off and travels with the same group all the way.

With a continuous belt, on the other hand, it is not so clear who one's closest colleagues are. Not only does each begin at a different time, but each moves ahead at a different rate. The participant must not only "dope out" the nature and sequence of the bench marks; he must also construct an appropriate subgroup from among his potential colleagues to serve as a primary model for his own career expectations or hopes—a model group that contains at least some members who are slightly ahead of him in the timetable so that he may use their experience to anticipate his own future. Thus, parents compare the development of their children mainly with that of others in the social circle with which they identify. TB patients compare themselves primarily with other patients receiving the same type of treatment and having the same kind of disease condition so far as the patients can tell. The academic man compares himself with others aiming for the same type of institution. Business executives compare themselves primarily with colleagues with similar ambitions working in the same type of organization.

The way in which the member of a career group decides which subgroup to identify himself with for timetable purposes might be thought of as the sociological side of what psychologists call "level of aspiration." A person attaches himself to a faster or a slower moving subgroup depending upon what set of expectations he thinks he can meet.

Not everyone climbs on a given career belt and sticks to it. Changing career belts is common in our society—perhaps far more common than our bias for studying conceptually static situations would lead us to believe. The patient may recognize that his condition is markedly better or worse than he first thought or that his treatment program has been drastically altered; and, therefore, he seeks new models to help predict a newly conceived future. A physician may start out his career as a general practitioner and later decide to restrict his practice to a specialty, or—as is increasingly becoming necessary in order to make such a shift—to take off a period of time for the training and supervised work required for entering a specialty. A family may move for a time in line with the expectations of a given social class and then decide to set its sights on moving into a higher stratum. The factory worker whose primary job interest was union politics may decide that he would rather try for a supervisory position with the company.

Whenever such a career shift is made, the participant must figure out a new timetable with new reference points. The old one, if not shucked off, may only lead him astray. The academic man who has succeeded in making a shift from a small teachers college to a major university must take on a new set of expectations including some important differences in his career timetable norms. The issues are no longer such things as the time when he gets a chance at summer and evening teaching, is able to determine class schedules, or obtains a foothold in the administrative hierarchy, but rather the timing of publications, research projects, and the right to organize seminars for select students. His models are no longer fellow college faculty members, but a nationwide professional colleague group from similar institutions. Unless the person can shift his career norms to fit the new setting, his predictions of his career timetable will not be useful to him.

Of course, the academic man making such a shift is likely to have prepared himself for it in advance. In many career areas, however, such preparation is less likely to occur. Students of social mobility, for example, have noted that people attempting to switch their identification to a higher social class often do so with great naïveté and make mistakes in their timing of given kinds of interaction with others that reduce the chances of their being accepted into the status to which they aspire. Important dimensions in the study of career timetables, therefore, are the readiness or the difficulty with which a given shift in a career may be accomplished and the characteristics of careers that make such shifts more or less difficult.

Shifting Time Perspectives

Another aspect of a career timetable that deserves attention is the change that may occur in timetable perspectives during the course of the career. We have seen in the case of the long-term hospital patient how the timetable norms lengthen with increasing duration of hospitalization, at least up to a certain point. The patient frequently starts out identifying himself with those who are in for a short time. Only after he himself has passed this stage does he begin to think of himself as staying the "average" time, and then he even advances the average somewhat when he stays longer until it becomes obvious that he is being kept "overtime."

We may wonder whether the same process occurs in other careers. The new executive trainee fresh out of college fancies himself, let us say, a department head by age 30 and revises this expectation upward only when he reaches age 30 without being near this goal. The average, he finds from observation, seems to be between ages 35 and 40, so he still has plenty of time. When he has not reached this level by age 40, he may note that in a number of cases other men did not reach the department-head level until age 45, so he still has a chance. Only when he is approaching age 50 without making the grade does he finally admit that he is clearly behind schedule.

Do such shifts in perspectives occur in occupational groups, with parents observing and directing their children's development, with families trying to keep pace with the social and economic advancement of their social circle, or on the part of politicians striving to work their way up through a hierarchy of public offices? And what is the attitude toward those who are very far ahead or very far behind the timetable norms? Do such attitudes have the effect of moving the actual careers of individuals closer to the group norms as they do in the case of tuberculosis and polio patients?

Shifting perspectives are probably more common in some types of careers than in others. We may expect a lag in the norms when a career timetable is changing rapidly, as with the airline pilots whose career stages are being slowed up or with middle-class children whose developmental timetable is being speeded up. Perhaps a lack of explicitness in timetable bench marks also makes such shifting of perspectives during the course of one's career more likely.

HANDLING FAILURE

A career timetable is, as I mentioned earlier, a tight production schedule which not all those following the career path can keep up with. Some fall so far behind and have so little chance of catching up—either in the reasonably near future, or ever—that the normal timetable no longer applies to them except to show how much they have fallen by the wayside.

The proportion of such "failures" varies widely from one career line to another. In some—for example, public school pupils—it is a small proportion of the total; in others—for example, nursing home inmates—it is a majority. In some cases the definition of failure is sharp and unmistakable and is symbolized by shifting the person to a different social and/or geographical location—for example, the patient moved from an intensive treatment unit to a chronic service. In other cases, failure to keep up to the mark in the promotion system is never clearly established, and there is an accumulation of borderline cases who may or may not be considered failures depending upon slight differences of interpretation of their career experiences—for example, business executive careers, where it is often not clear whether many of the men in intermediate positions have been left behind or are still in the running, but on the slow side of the norm.

There must be some provision in every career line for those who cannot keep up to the mark, especially those who are being left hopelessly behind to the point where they become a class apart. In some career lines, the failures may be uncompromisingly shucked off—airline piloting seems to approach this extreme. In other career lines, however, the total society or some organized part of it has made a commitment to a given category of its members that cannot easily be rejected. Care and treatment of the ill and education of the young are typical of such career lines in the United States. Those who cannot possibly approach the normal timetable of recovery or learning must still be cared for, but in a different way and with a different set of expectations. A "chronic sidetrack" is created for them. They are still pupils, but in an ungraded class or a special school. They are still patients, but receiving largely maintenance care rather than active treatment. They are still part of the domain occupied by their career group, but no longer part of the forward-moving promotion system.

There are intermediate ways of dealing with timetable failures. In many universities and in large, well-established businesses there is often an obligation to provide a job for the professor or executive even when he is no longer considered useful to the organization. Because of the nature of the relationship, the unwanted incumbents cannot be moved off to a dead-end sidetrack in as blatant a manner as can the public hospital patient or the public school pupil who is considered hopeless. (However, systems of compulsory retirement with loopholes for excepting individuals who are still wanted sometimes operate as such a sidetrack at the upper age range.) The sidetracking in such cases must operate more subtly, often with the notion of failure or rejection denied or obscured by a consolation prize.

An important issue to investigate, then, in any study of a career timetable is the manner in which failure is handled, both by those who suffer the failure and by others who play a part in the control of their career timetables. When a number of studies dealing with this issue has been made, we may be able to specify in more detail the conditions under which different modes of handling failure are applied. For example, does a firm commitment by a public agency to provide long-term service to a given category of people invariably lead to the development of chronic sidetracks? Under what conditions can an organization frankly reject those who cannot be maintained in the promotion system? (For instance, does obvious danger in a career activity, such as piloting aircraft, give the authorities the right to be ruthless in getting rid of the unwanted?) On the other hand, under what conditions must the indications of failure be more indirect and subtle? In what ways can the definition of failure be affected and manipulated by the person whose career is directly involved? When, for example, can a person dodge being sidetracked by switching to a different social or organizational career line—different job, different social class aspirations, different institutional treatment program?

BARGAINING OVER THE TIMETABLE

When a career is part of a service or authority relationship, each of the two (or more) groups concerned attempts to structure the same series of events. If the nature of the relationship is more than a unique or fleeting one, each party to the relationship will develop timetable norms that are somewhat different from each other because their goals, their criteria of success or progress, and their conceptions of proper timing are more or less different from each other. If the relationship is to continue, bargaining and accommodation must take place. The two parties inevitably influence each other's timetables, often simply as a result of anticipating the reactions of the other to given decisions, procedures, rules, or other actions.

Thus, the parent attempts to some extent to impose upon his children his conception of the proper timetable of development, but he must make compromises in response to the spoken and unspoken pressures from his children and his anticipation of how they will feel about the demands that he will make on them. At the same time, children are trying to do some things before they are expected to or allowed to and are trying to avoid doing some other things at the time when they should. The children too modify some of their behavior and some of their pressures so as to avoid conflict with the parents. Thus both parents and children are constantly making compromises about the times when they believe certain events or stages of development should occur.

Of course, there are limiting cases where the room for bargaining over the timetable is narrowed to the vanishing point. Where we have the imposition of a standardized timetable as a massive bureaucratic procedure—as in compulsory military service—this limit is approached. Under what conditions does the highly standardized timetable appear? Certainly, the degree of control plays a part. The controlling authority must have the power to impose a timetable without compromise. Not only must the draftee serve his time whether he likes it or not, but his superiors usually have no power to modify the total time or its sequence except under certain specific circumstances (e.g., certain kinds of illness). Giving the underdogs' superiors discretionary power to modify their subordinates' career timetables immediately opens the door to wholesale bargaining.[4]

However, power to control the underdogs is certainly not the only factor leading to standardized timetables. The degree of uncertainty of outcome plays a part, but it is not clear just what that part is. If the outcome of

[4] This point is often recognized by hospital medical directors who try to reduce the pressure for concessions from patients by prohibiting their ward doctors from giving patients passes, privileges, or discharges other than those prescribed by a standardized timetable unless the exception is approved by the director or medical board. The difficulty with this solution for the physicians is that it poses another dilemma for them: it prevents the ward doctor from exercising his independent expert judgment in treating his patients and thus makes him somewhat less of a physician according to the values held by the medical profession. In fact, this solution can be used only when the ward doctors are interns or residents-in-training or unlicensed foreign physicians working under a restrictive contract.

treatment of disease, training for a job, control of sexual behavior, or the rehabilitation of criminals is highly uncertain, it may seem to be a good reason for considerable leeway in timing the sequence of events in each of these careers and thus promoting a wider area of bargaining between superior and subordinate, professional and client, or two parties engaged in a joint series of acts. However, sometimes the effect is quite the opposite—a standardized timetable is imposed or maintained as a way of avoiding the disruptive consequences of uncertainty and widespread bargaining. Thus, the outcome of academic education in terms of test performance of pupils is highly variable and uncertain, yet the public school system imposes one of the most rigid, unvarying timetables of progress in a career that we can find in our society. Hospital physicians, too, sometimes impose standard time points in areas where uncertainty is greatest: for example, the sequence of giving passes after admission or surgery. Perhaps standardization results from a combination of a high degree of uncertainty and a powerful authority to impose a timetable without compromise. However, this question can only be addressed with more assurance after there have been further studies of career timetables in a variety of areas differing in certainty, power of authority, and perhaps other factors. In any study of a career timetable, there should be an effort not only to determine to what extent and in what ways the timetable is or is not standardized, but also what there is about the career and bargaining situation that produces or prevents standardization.

Another aspect of the timetable that deserves attention is the use of testing points. These, too, must be imposed by an authority on subordinates or underdogs and thus become part of the bargaining relationship to the extent that the subordinates can influence the evaluation of their performance or the use to which information about their performance is put. The executive who knows he is being evaluated for a crucial decision about his future promotion potentialities may contrive to control the communication system in such a way that he makes his performance look better than it is to his bosses.

We must be careful, however, to see whether the apparent testing points perform a definite function in affecting the career timetable or whether they are merely empty formalities. A good example of the latter is our public school system, which, despite a standard series of scholastic testing points, promotes and graduates the vast majority of pupils "on time" regardless of performance, on the grounds that it would be psychologically damaging to the pupils to be separated from their age group. Occupations in which seniority reigns supreme may operate in a similar way.

This brings us to another important issue. In the long-term treatment of illness examined in this book, the bargaining process in every case tended to move the length of hospitalization of patients toward the average or norm. Pressure from patients for release increased as they were kept past the expected time, and even physicians came to think of prolonged hospitalization as a reason for considering discharge more favorably. The envy generated when a patient was far ahead of the expected timetable, as well as the physicians' doubts about the credibility of a rapid cure or improvement, had the effect of prolonging the stay of patients whose condition seemed to improve rapidly. The same process seems to be at work in the social and intellectual development of children—rapid developers are often held in check and slow developers are pushed ahead, making them all more "normal." Is this phenomenon common to many other career timetables, and what conditions promote or block such an "averaging" effect?[5]

Perhaps the most interesting and most important aspect of a study of bargaining over career timetables is the process by which the actual bargaining is conducted. Of course, we have instances where such negotiation is overt and explicit, as in the bargaining between white and Negro groups over a timetable of racial equality. In most cases the bargaining is sub rosa, often explicitly denied, as when a physician says he will not bargain with patients about treatment, a parent says he will not bargain with his children about freedom to go places alone, a prison commissioner says he will not bargain with rioting prisoners about the conditions of parole. In such cases the bargaining goes on without seeming to and sometimes must be hidden to be successful.

Such indirect bargaining becomes a complex process of social interaction. The client, the inmate, the subordinate, the controllee must accumulate information about the careers of others of his kind (and must decide who his kind are) so that he may develop a conception of what his expected timetable is. By observing and comparing notes with his fellows he can build up a dossier of precedents, pressures, and subversive actions that can be used against those who officially control the timetable in an effort to modify the timetable in accordance with his expectations and wishes (which are frequently simply a reflection of the norms of his colleague group). The amount and conditions of access to information about the experiences of his colleagues, the way in which he obtains information, and the use made of this information to modify the timetable are all major foci of the study of bargaining around the career timetable.

At the same time, the professional, the expert, the authority, the controller must decide what an appropriate timetable for his charges is and must defend his decisions against their pressures to change them. He must seem more certain than he really is. He must try to hold off special concessions while appearing to give consideration to special circumstances. He too must communicate with his colleagues in order to define "reasonable" points on a timetable, to make an effort to maintain a consistent front against pressure for changes and concessions, and to gain support for decisions that restrict the actions of those over whom he exercises control.

[5] Remember, too, that the underdogs in a bargaining relationship do not invariably want to speed up the timetable, although the selection of illustrations in this book may have given that impression. Sometimes an effort is made to slow it down either as a whole or, as in the case of the co-pilots putting off transition school, in selective part in order to increase the chances of success in the long run.

Both controller and controllee, however, must constantly modify their own inclinations in response to the reactions and anticipated reactions of the other party. Strictly unilateral action without regard to the reactions of others may lead to an outcome that is definitely not desired. The patient who pushes too hard to move toward discharge may end by being cut off from treatment; the employee who tries to force promotion may find himself out of a job; the child who tries to extort privileges may be cut off from the affection and protection of his parents. On the other side, the physician who ignores the demands of the patients may completely lose control over them; the employer who will not bargain over promotion may lose his best employees; the parent who tries never to give in to his child may lose the child's affection. Just what are the limits to which one may push one's side of the negotiation without endangering a greater value? This is one of the important decisions that must be made in the bargaining relationship, and the ways in which such decisions are reached can be an important focus for the study of bargaining over the timetable.

INTERACTION OF TIMETABLES

The timetable analyses I have presented in this book were directed toward specific areas or activities that included only part of the lives of many people. That is, they dealt in each case with the one thing that all the people in a group had in common—the treatment of TB or polio or mental disease, work as a pilot or auto assembly plant employee or teacher, getting an education through the school system, fighting for racial equality. The selection of career boundaries is to some extent arbitrary. We select those which suit our purpose. Child development, for example, is a rather broad career category, and for certain purposes we may want to focus on the timetable of subdivisions of child development—linguistic development, sexual development, development of social group formation—recognizing that they are to some degree related and will affect one another. Of course, the selection of career boundaries cannot be completely arbitrary. The category used must have meaning to the people whose behavior is being studied; otherwise, it could scarcely be used as an explanatory device for that behavior.

If one wishes to apply a timetable analysis to the whole of a person's life, he must realize that each person is operating on a number of timetables simultaneously. The amount of pressure the long-term patient brings to bear to influence his treatment timetable may depend on his occupational or family timetables. A man may be a parent concerned with measuring the development of his children in terms of the expectations about child development in his social group and at the same time be a professor measuring his success in his professional career by reference to the expectations of his occupational colleague group. His career stage will affect the school where he chooses to teach, which in turn will affect the kinds of schools, neighborhood, and companions to which his children will be exposed at a given stage of their development. (It may also work the other way around—the stage of development of the professor's children may determine his place of residence, which will partly determine the kind of occupational position he can obtain at a given point in his professional career.) If the focus is on individual development, the interactions between timetables may be of more interest than the separately analyzed career timetables.

A similar approach may be applicable to a process study of families or other small, homogeneous, ongoing social units. Families may have timetables of progress or development, commonly including such major bench marks as the birth, marriage, and death of individual members, social and geographical mobility, the purchase of a home and other major possessions. Developmental cycles of families have frequently been described by anthropologists in studies of primitive groups. The primitive family has usually been regarded as a unitary group, with the developmental timetables of the individual members a well-integrated part of the total family pattern. It is precisely this assumption, however, that will not hold up with regard to our own modern family. (Of course, it often does not hold up in the case of primitive societies either, but the discrepancy is much smaller and often unnoticeable.) For this reason, we must pay more attention to the career timetables of individual family members, the extent to and manner in which they conflict with the total family timetables, and the manner in which the conflicts are resolved. We might also examine the relative influence of the individual timetables on the total family timetable. We may expect, for example, that the husband's occupational timetable will have a major influence, but in many lines of work this may not be true. We may ask whether the housewife-and-mother role can have an important timetable which is not merely a reflection of that of the total family group. Do housewives, as such, have a career? And if so, do they have intercommunicating groups that develop timetable norms for their career role?

Does it make sense to speak of a consumption career, and do interacting groups of consumers develop norms of timetables of consumption? Are there careers of social participation with a timetable of statuses through which the participants expect to move? If so, how do such timetables interact with work and family career timetables? Do some groups of people operate on still other timetables that we have not yet teased out at all? Such issues can be effectively dealt with only when there has been more detailed longitudinal investigation of various spheres of human activity and of the interaction between the spheres.

It may well be possible, and for some purposes useful, to conceive of the life cycle as an interacting bundle of career timetables.

4

Careers, Life-Styles, and
Social Integration

HAROLD L. WILENSKY

The organizational career has several relationships with
society at large and the social units within society.
Professor Wilensky discusses the stability and integration
effect of organizational careers on society in general and
particularly on its government, educational and financial
institutions, and on the family with respect to its mobility
and life style.

Now we want to link work situation to leisure style and at the same time view
both in the context of changes over the life cycle. Consideration of "careers,"
with special attention to the "other-directed" Organization Man, can illustrate
an approach to the problem. . . .

Limited as the few systematic studies of job histories are, they leave no
doubt that modern adult life imposes frequent shifts between jobs, occupations, employers, and work-places, and that these moves often involve
status passage which is momentous for both the person and the social
structure. . . .

Let us look at career patterns and related career contingencies as a special
case in the analysis of work-life mobility. . . .

A career, viewed structurally, is a succession of related jobs, arranged in
a hierarchy of prestige, through which persons move in an ordered, predictable sequence. Corollaries are that the job pattern is instituted (socially
recognized and sanctioned within some social unit) and has some stability
(the system is maintained over more than one generation of recruits). The
proportion of the labour force in careers, so conceived, may be increasing,
but it is doubtful whether it is as yet more than a quarter or a third.

Careers, though they grip only a minority of the labour force, are a major
source of stability for modern society, as Weber, Mannheim, and many others
have noted. Every group must recruit and maintain its personnel and motivate
role performance. Careers serve these functions for organizations, occupational groups and societies. At the same time they give continuity to the
personal experience of the most able and skilled segments of the population—
men who otherwise would produce a level of rebellion or withdrawal which
would threaten the maintenance of the system. By holding out the prospect
of continuous, predictable rewards, careers foster a willingness to train and
achieve, to adopt a long view and defer immediate gratifications for the later

Excerpted, with permission, from *International Social Science Journal*, 12(4) (Fall, 1960):
553–58.

pay-off. In Mannheim's phrase, they lead to the gradual creation of a "life plan." It becomes important to ask, "What is happening to careers?"

It is likely that with continuing industrialization careers are becoming on average more discrete and are characterized by more numerous stages, longer training periods, less fluctuation in the curve of rewards (amount, timing, duration), a more bureaucratic setting and more institutionalization, but are less widely visible (fewer, smaller publics recognize them).

Each of these dimensions of career is related to life style and thus to the types and levels of integration of persons and groups into community and society. The point can be illustrated with references to the "other-directed" Organization Man celebrated in recent American literature. If we are specific in defining work role and career, we are able to view much of popular sociology in clearer perspective. Consider three dimensions of careers—number of ranks, career curve, organizational setting. Giving Riesman and Whyte[1] a sympathetic reading and putting their observations in this context, we may state the Organization Man theme as follows:

Certain attributes of a class of large, complex organizations and of one type of career shape the work behaviour and life style of middle managers and technicians.

At work, these men play it safe, seek security, cultivate smooth human relations. In the community they put down many but shallow roots; they pick up and drop friends the way they buy and trade cars and homes—speeding up the obsolescence of both.

This is a life style which is active, group-centred, conforming and fluid—a pseudo-community pattern, unguided by stable values. Behavior both at work and off work is characterized by expedient conformity ("If I don't do this, I'll get into trouble") and by other-direction, or conformity as a way of life whatever the content of values and norms conformed to ("A man should get along with the gang").

Now, the aspects of work organizations which permit us to call this fellow an organization man are those which necessitate residential mobility and provide stable careers with opportunity for climbing through many ranks. The following structural attributes of organizations and occupations seem to be at the root of this mobility and its accompanying way of life:

1. Organizations with tall hierarchies; careers with many stages, affording quick and steady climb. Mobility consequences: much career opportunity.
2. Organizations with a high ratio of managers to managed. Careers with administrative posts at the end. Mobility consequences: much career opportunity.
3. Organizations with history and prospect of continued growth. For example, organization of occupational group produces wide variety of products and services (diversification is a cushion against fluctuating

---

[1] D. Riesman, *et al., The Lonely Crowd* (New Haven: Yale University Press, 1959); W. H. Whyte, Jr., *The Organization Man* (New York: Simon & Shuster, 1956).

demand), or an indispensable service in continuous demand (e.g., education, breakfast cereal). Mobility consequences: stable career opportunity and expectations.

4. Long, prescribed training, e.g. executive development and/or rotation programmes, professional schools. Mobility consequences: stable career opportunity and expectations.

5. Multiple units, geographically scattered. Mobility consequences: career climb associated with residential mobility.

Long exposure to this type of work situation may indeed produce a pseudo-community style of life. The mobility—the cycle of arrival and departure—fosters shallow roots. The opportunity for stable careers both attracts and shapes men who value security and play it safe.

To test this idea, we are comparing middle-level executives or engineers in two large work-places with contrasting structure and growth potential.[2] It is my guess that the organization man flourishes only in the middle ranks of those organizations and occupational groups which approximate to the above description.[3]

It is obvious that only a tiny fraction of the population works in such organizations, and has such well-ordered work lives. There are millions, even

[2] A study of about 600 Detroit mothers illustrates how differences in work environment can be reflected in such matters as child-rearing philosophies and practices. Miller and Swanson found sharp contrasts between the child training of families whose heads work in large bureaucratic organizations and those whose heads were more free-enterprising or less used to urban living (self-employed, born on a farm or abroad, and so on). In general, parents exposed to low-risk work situations—wage-workers or salaried employees in big hierarchical organizations—put less accent on an active, independent approach to the world in their child training; they were also less concerned with "internalization," with development of strong "built-in" self-control. These "bureaucratic" parents encourage an accommodating, adjustive way of life. They were more concerned that their children learn to be "nice guys"—able to make numerous friends easily.

While this study does not permit specific links between child training "styles" and such attributes of organizational structure as those listed above, it is consistent with my hypotheses.

One can argue that the stable career in the growing, complex multi-unit organization produces the organization man; the style of life he develops is expressed in his child-rearing practices and in his demands upon the school system; the revamped family and school in turn shape college life in the appropriate mould. The colleges then produce a supply of young men on the make, who, through self-selection and recruitment, are distributed among jobs appropriate to their predisposition, reinforcing the pseudo-community pattern.

[3] Why in the middle ranks? (1) Men at the bottom are too close to the task and what it takes to get it done to become enamoured of procedure, or over-committed to sociability. Top executives have an overview of the whole enterprise. They also have to relate it and justify it to the community in terms of organizational purposes. Contrast the middle ranks: they are most insulated from both the day-to-day task and the overview of both enterprise and community. They are therefore more vulnerable to technicism, less likely to show initiative (encourage innovations that fit the organization's mission). (2) Jobs in the middle are less clearly defined, and the criteria of success are often vague. The top men are responsible for profit, survival and growth in the long run, but how much responsibility for enterprise success or failure can be assigned to anyone in the middle? Similarly, men at the bottom are more clearly accountable (with process prescribed and product inspected, quality-controlled, etc.). Yet, competition among the "comers" in the middle is keen. Strong competition for vaguely-defined jobs breeds insecurity. Insecurity breeds both overconformity and underconformity and encourages "politicking." The insecure fear change and seek safety in fixed rules (whether they fit organizational needs or not), or if sticking to useful rules makes the boss unhappy, they underconform. Cf. H. L. Wilensky and C. N. Lebeaux, *Industrial Society and Social Welfare* (New York: Russell Sage Foundation, 1958), 243 ff; R. G. Francis and R. C. Stone, *Service and Procedure in Bureaucracy* (Minneapolis: University of Minnesota Press, 1956), 162 ff; P. M. Blau, *The Dynamics of Bureaucracy* (Chicago: University of Chicago Press, 1955).

among the work-committed, who will never experience the joys of a life plan provided by a secure and growing organization of the right characteristics. Most men do not have careers; among those who do, career curves vary.

One can hold, with Riesman and Whyte, that these men of regular career, however few, provide a model for a life style which will diffuse throughout the population. But there are other counteracting tendencies that may carry the day.

For it is these very organizations (hierarchical, administration-heavy, multi-unit, steadily growing) and these very jobs and careers (middle management and staff) that will undergo the most drastic changes in coming years.

As with technological change in the past, white-collar automation means both upgrading and downgrading. The insurance adjuster finds himself attending only to troublesome, challenging cases; office mechanization takes care of the routine semi-clerical tasks which once burdened him. On the other hand, the office manager with 30 subordinates in a payroll department confronts an electronic brain programmed and run by others and has only two girls working under him. This is only the beginning. The high-speed computer takes over routine clerical work, but it also makes it possible to restructure and in effect downgrade a great many administrative and technical jobs.

If we combine the rapid handling of information by computers, the application of mathematics and statistics to administrative problems (mathematical programming and operations research), and the recruitment and training of better-educated managers who are smart enough to use the staff to put these methods to work, then we have a formula for revolution in the middle bureaucracy. As several observers suggest, the new "information technology" can routinize tasks once done in conference and committee by men skilled in human relations and the workings of the organizational machinery. It can allow the top to control the middle, as scientific management in the past allowed supervisors to control the workers.

In short, middle management may become highly structured and controlled. Innovation and planning would be centralized. Top executives, surrounded by programmers, research and development men, and other staff experts, would be more sharply separated from everybody else. The line between those who decide "What is to be done and how" and those who do it—that dividing line would move up. The men who once applied Taylor to the proletariat would themselves be Taylorized.

The implications seem plain enough: the execution of controllable routine acts does not require great job enthusiasm, sociable conformity, or any other character trait beyond reliability and disciplined work habits. The model of Organization Man, which I concede to be the vanguard model of mid-century America may, like our cars, be far from the model of the eighties.

Part II

Recruitment to Organizational Careers

There are two points of view to consider in generating theory on the recruitment of people to an organizational career. One is the view of the person recruited —how he appraises the organization, its career and his prospects within it. The other is that of the organization—how it proceeds to screen and decide upon what people to hire or otherwise bring into the organization and under what conditions it might try them out.

Recruitment begins with the process by which the organization or the recruit reaches the other (Marcson, Caplow and McGee, Smigel). The organization might actively go out looking for recruits, usually with an image of the "right type" of man (social background, values, style, education, and so forth) for the job and the organization. They might tap the resources of third parties (people or other organizations) that specialize in (as well as, perhaps, engage in for personal reasons—for example, a sponsor) mating recruits and organizations. The organization may go to employment agencies, placement bureaus, referral systems, alumni organizations, or noted sponsors; ask influential clients; seek recruits through personal contacts; and so forth. These third parties put them in touch with the "right" potential recruits, thus providing initial screenings and narrowing their field of choice (Sills). The needs of the organization for quantity and/or quality in recruits direct them to the various kinds of third parties. For example, sponsors put them in touch with the quality person, employment agencies with large numbers of lesser skilled people.

55

Organizations also develop their own programs for reaching recruits directly. They might advertise in journals and newspapers or other media. They may employ public relations firms to guide their advertising. They form hiring departments which start recruitment programs such as visiting college campuses or high schools, interviewing students, and inviting possible recruits with the appropriate social background to come to the organization for a talk (Smigel). They develop procedures for "baiting" recruits, at the right moment in their lives, with favorable images of the organizational career. They highlight its most socially favored, if not its most general goal, and its "great" working conditions. They use current myths to reinforce the prestige of belonging to the organization. They offer the recruit potential association with favored models—a general, a scientist, an outstanding executive, a famous lawyer—to encourage him with this form of subtle training for advancement. They may also offer him post-hiring education. They figure out limited ways of hiring the recruit, such as with one-year contracts, initial rotating assignments, options, clear temporary or try-out periods, or no commitments, in order to keep him in the recruiting process for a few years to see if he is really worth taking into the organization for a particular type of career. Thus the recruit may not just be hired, but brought into the organization gradually.

Recruitment is then a process going on for a period of time both inside and outside the boundaries of the organization. It is a process of screening, wooing, and eliminating before the career actually starts. It might vary from being a fairly simple process of solicitation and short test period to, as in the cases of academic organizations and law firms, a highly elaborated process, sometimes requiring time and effort seemingly far beyond what the particular requirements of the position and person would seem to demand.

Elaborate procedures of recruitment, focused on "choosing the right man" or making sure that no one who gets as far as an interview on organizational premises is later refused a job, have other vital consequences. These procedures involve large numbers of others in the organization, whose careers will be interdependent with that of the recruit (Caplow and McGee). These others will know that they have been consulted, have had some say and commitment to a decision, and can protest if comparative discrepancies in the organizational career offered to the recruit might cause personal or general morale problems. Other organizations, such as the army, simply ignore the wishes and problems of other members who will have interdependent careers with the recruit. Fitness for these positions is arrived at on the basis of objective, technical criteria, not on subtle, personal, and organizationally sensitive ones embodied in elaborate procedures.

Another condition affecting recruitment procedures is how easy will it be to get rid of people who do not work out. This condition influences how important it is to screen and try out recruits. Some organizations can never fire or "lay off" a person once the career has started. Other organizations can simply ask the man to leave. Yet others must go through an extended "edging out" process.

Organizations must also contend with their position among other organizations in the competitive market for recruits. Sometimes their procedures must work very fast to win out in intense competition. Other times they have months to decide, even if the competition is stiff.

The organization must also screen people for its future as well as its current requirements and provide images of careers that entice recruits into a long-range or short-range view of possible commitment. Thus some recruits will plan on becoming executives in later years, and others will plan on a short stint for experience and their record before moving on to a more permanent career.

The recruit might actively go out and seek entrance to organizational careers by applying at personnel offices and going to placement agencies. He may also ask friends, make visits to strategic people, and drop the word that he is available into the "right" grapevine or referral systems. Of course, finding the latter two might be difficult, impossible, or a simple matter, depending on the type of career of the recruit and his current location in the organizational world. It is often hard to negotiate a rise from lower prestige organizations to higher ones.

Recruits from educational institutions might be routinely listed in a placement bureau. This source of third party might be the approved method for becoming recruited. It also might be a residual source of poorer careers, and hinder receiving the best chances if they come only through private, informal sponsorship channels. Depending on his previous educational institution, the recruit may or may not have to be active in seeking a start in an organization. Graduates from the best universities might have to be active and gracious in putting off too many offers from recruiters that come to campus; graduates from other educational institutions might simply go through placement bureau channels with no stigma attached; or they might be just cast free to find a job (for example, trade school graduates).

After contact with an organization the recruit may have to jockey for and then negotiate his offer, if the organization allows such space. This "offer space" is usually found in organizations with higher skilled careers that compete with other organizations. Workers' careers usually start with a flat "take it or leave it" offer that the union has negotiated. The recruit may have to make a decision about his occupational career at the same time that he selects an organization, or his career status may automatically be fixed as a consequence of being hired for a job.

The decision to accept the organizational career will also include considering *anticipated consequences* for family life, ability to moonlight, kinds of colleagues and need for colleagues (stimulating, none, no chance for contact with them, etc. [Riesman]) and probable type of career (how routinized, how rapid advancement in position and salary can be). The recruit may anticipate consequences from the described working conditions, responsibilities, and kind of identity he will receive and feel; from juxtaposing organizational with personal goals; from the size, kind, and prestige of the organization; and so forth.

Many of these anticipations may be inaccurate because of lack of experience and knowledge both generally and specifically with the organization and because of belief in the "baiting" recruitment rhetoric of the organization. But, however accurate or inaccurate the anticipations, the recruit will usually find—some months after joining the organization—that because of the experience and knowledge he gains, the reasons for which he started the career are not the reasons he stays with the career.

Theory on recruitment processes of organizational careers may usefully begin being generated along the lines of these general categories and properties obtained from the comparative analysis of the following articles. Surely we must also discover the relationship of these processes to societies that depend upon the organizational careers of large numbers of people for its stability, growth, and change.

5

The Recruitment of Industrial Scientists

SIMON MARCSON

In discussing means of recruitment, Professor Marcson touches on the processes of reaching potential recruits and baiting them for the job while screening them. He then discusses managing the strains between what a potential recruit expects and what the organization actually is and provides regarding work and career.

As all major industrial research organizations, P.E.C. is faced with the problem of recruitment, selection, and training. In a sense this may be described as "the problem of creating new roles in old organizations, and of coordinating them with existing roles."[1] P.E.C. is faced, then, with the problem of not only finding the appropriate recruits, but also developing commitments on their part to the industrial research laboratory.

The Pacific Electronics Corporation maintains extensive machinery for the recruitment of scientists and engineers. Since the manpower need for engineers and scientists is ever present in its many engineering units in addition to the research laboratory, P.E.C. advertises continuously in newspapers and magazines, and over television from time to time. In this way scientists and engineers, both as members of the general public and as members of a specialized occupational group, come to be familiar with P.E.C.'s needs. In addition, the laboratory pursues its own specialized advertising campaign for recruits.

MEANS OF RECRUITMENT

The personnel office centers the recruiting activities of scientists for the laboratory in a staff member who specializes in Ph.D. recruiting.[2] At times this person has been a member of the technical staff serving a tour of duty in

[1] David N. Solomon, "The Sociology of Applied Science," *The McGill News* (Winter, 1958), XL, 22.

[2] The type of qualifications this specialist will frequently have is indicated in the following advertisement from *Chemical Engineering News* (February 22, 1960), 112:

University Relations

For large industrial laboratory in Northeast. Scientific and personnel relations at universities and professional societies. Emphasis on Ph.D. recruiting and educational trends. Travel about 30 per cent of the year. Ph.D. in chemistry or chemical physics with ten to fifteen years of academic experience preferred. Salary open. Reply to Box 75—L-2, C. & E. N., Easton, Pa.

this position. The staff recruiter establishes and maintains contact with universities and conducts the necessary correspondence between the laboratory and the recruit. Systematic visits are made to universities which produce graduates in the fields of research in which the P.E.C. laboratory is interested. These visits are invariably made by members of the scientific staff. A member of the professional staff described his recruiting in the following way:

In regard to recruiting, this is usually done in teams of two men. You are usually sent to a university where you have an "in." I have a relative at the particular university I am sent to so I am assured a warm welcome.

The mechanics of recruiting were set out as follows by the same scientist.

The purpose of the contacts made is to plant a seed with the young scientists who are nine months away from getting their degrees. The method is usually to contact the head of the department and tell him that you are going to be there during a certain period of time. You also try to contact professors whose students are working in certain areas of interest. It is through these professors that you make your first contacts with the students. In these interviews you do not attempt to screen too carefully. For the most part your job is to try to sell P.E.C. to the particular student.

As we see from the above interview, an attempt is made in the assignment of professional staff members to a university to select scientists who have alumni or other connections. This enables them to have well established relationships among members of the faculty, and facilitates their contacts with promising students.

If the recruiting visit turns up an eligible candidate for research in the laboratory, he is invited to come to the P.E.C. laboratory for extensive interviewing. There he meets selected members of the scientific staff drawn from the research areas in which he might work. They discuss his research experience and interests with him. He is given an opportunity to explain his thesis research work. At the end of this series of interviews with the scientific staff, the Ph.D. recruiter compiles all the recommendations on the candidate and they are presented to the salary committee. This committee is composed of technical staff, personnel people, and research management. It is this committee which determines the specific salary to be offered the recruit.

In the course of the interviewing process the recruit is told about the laboratory and the corporation. An attempt is made to impress upon the recruit that some fundamental research is being conducted at the laboratory. It is also pointed out that distinguished scientists who have made fundamental contributions are members of the scientific staff. Emphasis is placed on the fact that none of the five laboratories is engaged purely in applied research. It is for this and other reasons that all five laboratories are organized to include some fundamental research. It is the laboratory's means of recognizing the importance of fundamental research in the scientist's career expectations.

This is further emphasized in the recruiting problems the laboratory faces.

Industrial laboratories invariably have difficulty recruiting the best university graduates, and as a result are only able to attract the next to the very top of a graduating class. As a staff member explained:

The best university graduates go to the universities rather than come to the industrial research laboratories. This is so because they have more freedom to choose their research in the university.

The industrial laboratory counters this by emphasizing the important role fundamental research has in its laboratories. The recruit obviously is not convinced, for when he has a wide latitude of choice he chooses research and teaching in the university. When he does choose the industrial laboratory, he retains and carries over his interests in fundamental research; he expects to fulfill his expectations regarding fundamental research.

The recruitment of both recent university graduates and mature scientists does not occur outside the image the industrial laboratory has established for itself in the scientific world. This means that the papers read by P.E.C. laboratory people at scientific meetings and their publication influence and affect this image. This means that the verbal exchanges that take place at scientific meetings about types of research and degrees of latitude in research become part of the ingredients affecting the laboratory's image. A professional staff member explained these elements in some detail.

One can generally become aware of the framework within a particular company even if he is not an employee. That is, companies do a good deal of publishing and you can become aware of their orientation from this. More directly, the company can tell you what it wants, or you can tell the company what you think you want. Some things can be of interest to the company for different reasons. Another level of becoming aware is from your group leader. You come to know from him on the basis of his suggestions what the company's orientation is.

The questions that concern a scientist about an industrial laboratory are many and revolve about his professional aspirations regarding research. Is there an opportunity here for creative research, or is it just an engineering factory? Are individual contributions recognized? What is the manner of the recognition? Is it in the form of publications, promotions, and salary increases? Is it possible to build a professional reputation in these laboratories? Are there opportunities for association with scientific leaders? While these questions reflect the recruit's expectations, they are not without their influence on the industrial laboratory. The P.E.C. laboratory attempts to represent itself as a research organization where the recruit can find positive answers to these questions. This influences the laboratory in an attempt to live up to these representations.

The P.E.C. laboratory, in turn, has a number of questions it raises about a recruit. Are his recommendations strong enough and sound? How much of a risk are we taking in his appointment that he will turn out to be a productive creator of significant contributions? If he has a reputation for personality difficulties, do his abilities outweigh this? Will his research training and experience meet the particular needs of the laboratories? Is the recruit a creative and original person? Will he fit in as a working associate with a given set of supervisors? The answers to these questions determine the recruit's evaluation and the salary offer from the P.E.C. laboratory.

If these two sets of questions have been satisfactorily answered on the part of the recruit and the laboratory, the recruit comes to work. It is at this point, if he is a recent graduate, that he is introduced to the work rules of industrial research. He learns that he is expected to report to work at a given hour. He does not have to punch a clock, but he is expected to be on time. If his lateness is a matter of minutes, nothing is said about it. However, if it becomes a matter of a half hour or an hour, it will be brought to his attention by his superiors. Similarly, he learns there is a stated period for lunch as the laboratory cafeteria is only open during that period, and the closest restaurant is some distance away. He may work on after the five o'clock bell has announced the end of the work day, but he finds his associates gone and the supply room closed, and he falls into the pattern of leaving on time. He adopts quickly the requirements of industrial employment.

Immediately on reporting to work at P.E.C. a trainee with a B.S. is given three consecutive short-term assignments. Ph.D. recruits are permitted to engage in independent work. Frequently the recruit has had interests in working in research areas in association with a distinguished scientist he has heard of as being present in the laboratory. Often his interest is in research of a fundamental character.

There are people in the general research section who are given the privilege of working on non-commercial projects. However, there is the illusion when you are hired that this is the general case for all. One believes because one wants to. When I came to P.E.C. I believed I would be working in a different group, but I was given an assignment on a ghastly problem.

The laboratory persuades the B.S., and B.S.E. recruit that he has to accept the three short-term assignments before he is eligible for such consideration. These assignments are in different research areas of the laboratory, and are selected on the basis of both the recruit's background and the laboratory's needs. It is hoped, however, that one of these assignments will capture his interest sufficiently to keep him involved in that area of research for a number of years. The assigned research areas are invariably in applied problems of research, and the reason for this is to see how he will fit into an industrial research laboratory.

If the recruit performs acceptably on these assignments he is reappointed. Acceptable performance is judged not only on technical competence but also on adaptation to the applied research programs of industrial research. The laboratory has actually started on a program of retraining the individual to fit into the industrial laboratory, accept its goals, and contribute to them. Originally, the Ph.D. recruit might have had aspirations of undertaking some fundamental research problem that would make a profound scientific contribution. The laboratory's interests, however, are in an individual who will make contributions to its device inventions. In this it succeeds only partially in remolding his aspirations.

It is when the recruit has completed his first year of short-term assignments that he begins to realize there are gaps between his goals and the laboratory's objectives. At this point he is no longer a recruit on trial. He is now a technical staff member accommodating his expectations to the system of expectations of the laboratory. The function of assigned and trial research is to help the recruit adapt to the industrial laboratory.

EXPECTATIONS OF THE RECRUIT

The strains involved between these different systems of expectations does not encompass all the recruits. The main distinguishing line is between the physicist and the engineer. The physicist acquires his professional involvements and characteristics during his lengthy graduate training. Whether the engineer has had graduate training or not, the emphasis is on applied engineering problems rather than on theoretical ones. An engineer explained this as follows:

In my graduate work I had intended going into an industrial laboratory, and I am glad I came to P.E.C. P.E.C. has fulfilled all that I expected. It is a very satisfactory place to work because of its freedom and informality and especially because of its wide range of problems. P.E.C. is a good place to work because, while one can work on fairly sophisticated problems, they are not entirely theoretical ones. I am interested in the application of my work.

The engineer is usually less concerned about fundamental research than the physicist. It is the physicist, by and large, who expects to be engaged in fundamental theoretical or experimental research.

A physicist summed up this system of expectations with which the newcomer is imbued.

I had hoped when I first came here that I would be permitted to pursue a basic research program. I have come to the conclusion that the industrial laboratory is timid. It hesitates about the connection between fundamental research and applied research. It is, therefore, necessary and important that when a man comes in from the university with some experience and stature, that he try to educate research management of the laboratory to change its views and to adopt a more acceptable and fundamental approach.

Typically, as a physicist, he had looked forward to a career of basic research. Once he discovers that his expectations need reorganization, he undertakes a series of adaptations. As he sees it, initially he is engaged in changing the laboratory. In actuality, he also adapts to the requirements of the work situation. In adjusting to his new role he goes through a process of change that permits him to internalize selected aspects of his new environment.

Every formal organization attempts to utilize its human and technical resources as a means of attaining its goals. It formulates and creates rules, written and unwritten, which are intended to designate and prescribe acceptable behavior. The organization shores up its rules and expectations with its own system of rewards and punishments. However, the individual members who are within the organization resist being treated as a means to attain these goals. The organization's members define these expectations when they are able to discern them as pressures for conformity, but much of this they do not discern. They are therefore frequently in the position of not knowing how to define the strains and conflicts they are experiencing.[3]

When these strains are discerned, the research scientist recognizes the problem of the relation of the individual to the organization.

There is a constant conflict between the individual and the organization. The individual's self-centeredness is in conflict with the demands of the laboratory. The laboratory has its own needs and demands. There were some individuals who were not entirely self-reliant and accepted readily, sometimes too readily, suggestions which were made. There was, therefore, the problem of achieving balance between the interests of the individual and the interest of the laboratory.

The scientist at this point accepts the laboratory work situation as adaptation to demands and establishing an equilibrium.[4]

---

[3] Moore and Renck, "The Professional Employee in Industry," *Journal of Business* (January, 1955), 58. "Factors in the morale of professional employees revolve around a fundamental conflict which exists between the expectations and values of professional employees and the opportunities which they have to realize their ambitions and interests as professionals in the industrial setting," *ibid.*, 63.

[4] E. C. Hughes points out, "This leads to the problem of self-conception and discovery of self. A person's conception of himself is itself something of a stereotype, to which parents, teachers, siblings, peers, and his own dreams have contributed. Some people project themselves far into the future, others operate more or less in the present. But in either case, there come moments of necessary revision and adjustment of one's notions about what he can do and wants to do. One may say, then, that a young man thinking about himself as a physician is thinking about a young man as yet unknown to himself, doing work and playing roles not yet known, in situations he has never yet been in. This is not to underestimate the anticipatory playing of roles; but no matter how sensitive the individual's anticipation of himself in a future role, there is some gap between anticipation and realization." *Men and Their Work* (Glencoe, Ill.: Free Press, 1958), 126.

6

Recruitment to the Academic Career

DAVID RIESMAN

The decision to accept recruitment into an organizational career will include considering anticipated consequences on family life, ability to moonlight, kinds of colleagues and needs for colleagues, and the probable type of career. Professor Riesman also considers the social sources of recruits—their location in society and their values—and the changes of these sources over time.

Not very much is known about what happens in college (or, for that matter, prior to college) that might lead a young person to consider an academic career or to reject it. Two studies recently done by faculty members at Wesleyan University, however, give a rough and approximate sense as to which colleges and which types of colleges send people into graduate schools of arts and sciences and into more or less productive careers as scholars. These studies have surprised many educators, for they show that many of the leading and most distinguished universities (Harvard, Yale, and Princeton, for example) have turned out relatively few scientists in proportion to their graduates, whereas a number of small and often impoverished liberal arts colleges, primarily in the Middle West, have turned out, in proportion to their enrollments, a great many. Some of the colleges with distinguished records in this respect are well known for their educational venturesomeness—for example Antioch, Swarthmore, Reed, and the University of Chicago, But others included in this group, such as Grinnell, Hope, Linfield, Kalamazoo, and Wabash, are either not widely known or not in any way experimental; many still retain their ties with the Protestant churches under whose auspices they were founded. The Catholic colleges have a very poor record according to the criteria of the Wesleyan researches, as have the southern universities save in one or two fields.

There are problems in interpreting these data, especially concerning the records of the state universities, whose undergraduate bodies are not strictly comparable to those of most liberal arts colleges. Nevertheless, a few tentative conclusions can be drawn. In the first place, while the Bible Belt of the South has produced mathematicians and poets, it is from the Protestant but not Fundamentalist colleges of the North that a relatively large proportion of natural and social scientists have come. The affinity between some versions of Protestantism and scientific work has often been remarked. For the less hierarchical churches of Protestantism ask the individual to determine his own

Excerpted, with permission, from *Daedalus*, 88(1) (Winter, 1959): 147–67.

relation to God—to search out his own cosmology. As it becomes secularized, this search may take scholarly form, or indeed, as often happened in the sixteenth and seventeenth centuries, one may try to reconcile science and religion through scientific work or even to show the glory of God through the shape of the heavens. Correspondingly, as is well known, a number of men in the older generation of social scientists are the sons of ministers, who have found in a scientific career a way of sublimating or transcending some of the conflicts between the scientific world view and the Protestant one with which they grew up.

In the second place, if one looks again at the list of institutions that have produced notable scholars, one sees that these colleges often have drawn on rural and small-town constituencies and on the lower middle class in general. That is, they have drawn on people who, when they landed in college, did not have a very differentiated or complex idea of what the world offered. If they came from a farm, for example, they might have been able to see themselves getting away from a plow only by becoming tractor salesmen or county agents —and then they discovered in college that they could become botanists or biologists or teachers in the agricultural colleges. This opportunity proved to be a way of getting off the farm while still retaining a tie with rural life and its values. Similarly, a bright boy from an impoverished background might land in college without ever having heard that one can make a living as a physiologist or an astronomer. But he might have had the luck to encounter in college a teacher who was doing just that. If this teacher befriended him and offered him, so to speak, the key to the laboratory, the student might end up in his master's shoes—a captive of the field whose horizons were thus opened to him.

In other words, the very lack of cosmopolitanism of some of these colleges (especially perhaps in the Middle West), and the lack of cosmopolitanism of the students who in the past went there, meant that a teacher of even moderate quality and interest in his students could accumulate disciples quite readily. Conversely, the inferior record in the recruitment of scholars from the undergraduate population of the great cosmopolitan universities has in my judgment been partly due to the fact that students who went there have had many other choices in mind. (Likewise their social science professors, busy with graduate students, with consultantships, and with all the opportunities and temptations of a metropolis, have also had other alternatives to looking for disciples among their undergraduate students.) That is, such students have found other ways to spend their time, even other intellectual ways, than in the laboratory or in the office of the favorite professor. They could envisage themselves (assuming they eschewed business) becoming diplomats, journalists, or TV script-writers, along with a thousand other opportunities offered by the big city. Moreover, students coming from homes where the parents themselves attended college on the one hand might think of an academic career as a downward step in social mobility (as against the upward step that it was for the farmer's son or the person from the lower or the lower middle class), and on the other hand, having already been somewhat exposed to academic values, they might not be captured as readily by them through the medium of an exciting professor.

We can approach some of these same matters in another way by reminding ourselves of the experience many prospective scholars have had in their high school years. Except at a rare urban institution like Bronx Science or Hunter College High School in New York City, a boy or girl who is headed for science and scholarship feels out of place in high school. He is bookish when nobody is bookish, or he putters with chemicals when other boys are out on a date or at sports. He feels alienated and alone. He ends up as valedictorian, recognized only in that ambiguous way. Then he may be picked up by a recruiter from a college that is looking for a few scholars to balance its athletes and Good Time Charlies. At last he may find himself not alone; for the first time in his life he has allies and, in the person of a teacher or two, even models and sponsors. Moreover, the teachers can become allies against parents who have often felt troubled about their child's unworldliness or bookishness or "queerness." Henceforth the student may be set for life in a new mold and a new career, possibly discovering that the things that were regarded as vices in his high school years now turn out to be virtues.

The Wesleyan studies, and consequently the interpretation I have drawn of them here, are necessarily already out of date, since the scholars whose careers were sufficiently advanced for statistical follow-up mainly attended college in the period between the two world wars. As readers of Sinclair Lewis and Sherwood Anderson will remember, this was a period in which, in the smaller and especially in the Midwestern communities from which scholars came, there were often strong anti-intellectual currents; in which the dominant values were those of money, power, swank, Republican respectability, and practicality. In such a climate of opinion, it was understandable that professors should have been regarded as stuffy, as not quite manly, as occupants of an ivory tower that probably needed dusting. (Or alternatively, professors were regarded as radical cranks who could be trusted neither to teach the right brand of economics or theology nor to provide models for the success-prone student.) In that climate of opinion, the handful of alienated students would naturally find themselves sympathizing with their college professors; and conversely, the professors would themselves be looking for recruits among the students as hostages against the culture of Babbittry around them. For example, Veblen's comments on life in the state university town such as Columbia, Missouri, fifty years ago, reveal how eagerly such men would have greeted a student who shared their contempt for the childish snobbery and intellectual and emotional crudity of the local businessmen and of their friends at the School of Commerce. Indeed, in Veblen's book, *The Higher Learning in America*, one finds a picture of the professor as a genuine scholar whose interests and values are brutally overridden by businessmen, by trustees, and by their strong-arm representative in the president's chair.

In such a pattern of recruitment into academia, it was plain that not many would be "called"—that is, find so peripheral a calling to their liking. As a result, professors could and did spend their time with a few students and tried to deal with the rest by liberally distributing gentlemanly C's. And so it was that those boys from the lower or humbler strata who aspired to become professors would be slowly groomed for that recondite elite.

The Spread of "Collegiate" Values

The present situation is quite different. College faculties have been expanding too fast to permit the slow and careful grooming of a few hand-picked scholars. Indeed, in some fields men now may become professors at an age at which they would once still have been teaching assistants. A bright assistant professor today may be more sought out than a famous full professor even ten or fifteen years ago. The competition of the three state universities of Michigan is only an example of the raiding that goes on quite generally. A great many factors have cooperated to produce these changes. The country is richer, which means that it needs fewer people to tend its farms and factories and can locate more of them in the professions and in the other more or less intellectual careers such as communications, management, and teaching itself. It can also afford to keep people in school longer and to send many more of them to college. And people have more leisure in which to absorb some of the "cultural" values previously associated with attending college; the better large-circulation magazines and networks, paper books, and "art" movies spread intellectual values, at least sporadically. More people travel, visit Europe, read *Gourmet* magazine, and in general feel entitled to follow the style set by those who have attended college. In the process America has become not only more urbanized but also in many ways more urbane.

Correspondingly, I believe that the small liberal arts colleges of the Midwest may not show up as the great recruiting grounds for scholars twenty years from now. The sharpness of the conflict between science and religion is attenuated today; it seldom drives people into a creative tension that results in their becoming biologists or psychologists. Nor do the remaining Protestant colleges seem to me very ascetic. Moreover, there are fewer boys who want to get off the farm by becoming teachers; there are fewer farms, and those that remain are often large and complex businesses.

At the same time, I am inclined to think that the big cosmopolitan universities are no longer channeling their best students largely into such socially approved careers as law, medicine, business, and the diplomatic service, but are increasingly serving also to recruit scholars. This is in part because their student bodies have become less "social," and include many relatively poor boys who once would have gone to local and often to denominational colleges. For example, the Minneapolis *Star & Tribune* now sends small-town newsboys on scholarships to Yale and Harvard, boys who in an earlier day, if they had attended college at all, would have gone to Carleton or St. Olaf's or Gustavus Adolphus or the University of Minnesota. One result may be that in the future institutions such as Carleton and St. Olaf's will not show up quite so well as they did in the Wesleyan studies, while Harvard and Yale may show up somewhat better.

For the small-town newsboy skimmed out of the Midwest by the increasing talent hunts of the national universities, the transition from high school to college may still be very sharp and dramatic, even traumatic. But as I have implied, college is not so sharp a break from home as it once was for the many youngsters whose high schools have already anticipated college (as some of the wealthy suburban high schools do) and whose parents are themselves collegiate. It follows that, while youngsters who are entirely given over to intellectual or artistic values may still feel quite alone, those who have a partial but not exclusive interest in those values no longer need feel, either at home or in high school, that they belong to a minority culture. While, as we all know, a great deal has been said about anti-intellectualism in America during the McCarthy years and later, it is at least arguable that these very attacks on the intellectuals are, *inter alia*, a response to their rising power in a society that more and more requires intellectuals, or at least educated specialists, to get its work done. Whereas once bankers were hated and feared in part because they controlled the "mystery" of the gold standard, today scientists and intellectuals control the relevant mysteries, and, as Edward Shils points out in *The Torment of Secrecy*, give rise to analogous fears of domination and analogous opportunities for demogogic attack.

The increasing attention to intellectual values is especially striking among some businessmen. In recent years many large corporations have instituted executive training programs so that their middle-management people, who have often been trained as engineers or as business administration majors, can transcend narrow professional horizons and model themselves on the going version of the industrial statesman. And industrial statesmanship today takes a great interest in colleges, because increasingly businessmen do go to college (as the Warner and Abegglen studies show), use colleges for executive training and development purposes, and meet professors as consultants, market researchers, and social equals. The hope Justice Brandeis expressed before the First World War—that business would become a profession— approaches reality as managers become increasingly aware of the need to handle complex data in making decisions rather than playing hunches or following tradition. Despite ritualistic speeches on ceremonial occasions, big business—little business, including farming, is an entirely different story— has become much less Philistine and much less hostile to intellectual values.

This, of course, is not to say that sheer disinterested intelligence brought to bear on matters of national concern is everywhere welcome. While at present a general liberalism permeates the country at large, there are definite limits, and few voices are raised anywhere to attack nationalism as such or our own militarism. In fact, many universities are as much bases for fighting the Cold War as any S.A.C. outpost; they do research on weapon systems, or military-sponsored social science research on presumptive enemies and allies.

Another limit on academic liberalism occurs in the sphere of religion. Just as most professors are good patriots, so also, if they have not joined the general "return to religion," they are (whatever Fundamentalist senators may think) hardly ever atheistic. For good reasons as well as bad ones, the academy is less of a threat to certain basic values of the American community, and the outlook of the big businessman and of many a professor is not so different as either may still hopefully or sadly think. In contrast with the situation Veblen satirized, the leading universities are not dominated by small-town business values. Rather, a process of mutual infiltration has occurred.

These developments render somewhat paradoxical the attitudes I find among many of my own students and those at other leading colleges: namely, a posture of contempt for business and a belief that, in contrast, teaching offers respectability and even integrity. (I should make clear that this is not a political contempt, for these students are very rarely directly political; it is rather a cultural, moral, or intellectual contempt.) Some students come to this outlook because they harbor aristocratic values and look down on business-men as the English gentry traditionally looked down on people in trade. But others are themselves the children of small businessmen, and they have over-generalized from their parental occupations, with their often rapacious ethics and lack of intellectual range, to the large managerial businesses I have been describing. That is, small business is still competitive, still what Veblen would have called a "pecuniary" occupation, in the sense that it deals with bargains and mere tricks of trade, not with large engineering and industrial concep-tions. The result is that the younger generation, seeking not only social but also intellectual mobility away from the parental small business (and, in this group, increasingly coming from Jewish and Catholic families rather than Protestant ones), have their eye on the professions as the road to status and opportunity. Academic careers then become alternatives either as belated second choices—for instance, a student ending up as a biologist because he could not get into medical school—or as first choices, decided with the bless-ing of parents and peers.

Many of the parents of these young people, whose values contrast with those of an older day, do not want them in the business but rather out of the business—although, of course, still self-supporting. And many of the occupa-tions that once would have raised the parents' protest today may seem a golden opportunity. Van Cliburn may persuade them that the piano is not a road to ruin; Charles Van Doren may persuade them that one can make money as an English teacher. Less and less are professors regarded as mem-bers of a small, deviant but semi-elite group—although, as we shall see, those who teach the humanities often so consider themselves—but rather as people who have gone into a business that isn't business.

Certainly, as I have said, the life of the businessman and the life of the professor become less and less distinct. The professor is no longer to be regarded as a stuffy fellow. He has become a man of the world, perhaps traveling on an expense account, attending a conference in Washington one day and flying to a UNESCO meeting in Paris the next. In honor of his new status, the novels I mentioned now portray him as having sex appeal and even a lurid sex life. As universities become bigger and bigger, it is hard for them not to judge their output by business standards or at least bureaucratic ones (as I am told the Michigan legislature has recently been judging the educational institutions of that state). I have heard professors in the social sciences pass judgment on each other in terms that would not be different if they were engaged in production control. They speak of a man's "output" or his "productivity" as measurable and even quantifiable things, and yards of print take the place of foot-pounds or B.T.U. (Natural scientists, having the most money, are also exposed to these tendencies.)

Many professors in classics, in literature, in history, and in the humanities generally believe themselves to espouse the traditional academic values. But in the process of homogenization of values that I have been describing, this becomes more and more difficult, and we see the paradox that some of the embattled humanists engage in "selling" the humanities as good for whatever ails the U.S.A. with the same public-relations fervor that they deprecate in Madison Avenue. The social sciences stand somewhere between, trying to drag an uneasy foot out of the humanities while not quite managing to locate the other foot in the profitable camp of the natural sciences. But in fact, as I shall try to indicate, it is impossible to tell whether a man is a humanist or not by the label of his discipline; and I have seen a number of colleges where the anthropologists are more humanistic than the teachers of English, the physicists by far more humanistic than the economists or the sociologists.

As to these comparisons, however, I should add a word of caution against pushing them too far. One of the characteristics of any older generation, markedly of the present older generation in the universities, is to talk about the good old days. In general, it is safe to say that the old days were not so good and not so different as most of us believe. There were plenty of professors at the turn of the century who espoused business values, just as there were many ministers who did, and they did so with a vulgarity that one could hardly match today among businessmen. Correspondingly, there were other professors a generation ago who really were stuffy, pretentious without being literate, erudite without understanding, pedantic without being critical. Along with the general rise in standards of education, I believe college teachers have become brighter and better.

THE DISTAFF SIDE

So far, I have emphasized patterns of recruitment of college teachers in terms of the backgrounds from which they come and the collegiate atmospheres in which they are nurtured. Before turning to some of the reasons why I have chosen to be a teacher myself (in spite of all the misgivings implicit in what I have said), I want to say something about the problems posed for the college professor as a family man. Professors get many of the benefits of the academic culture while their wives are saddled with many of the drudgeries. In my observation, it is less the professors who suffer from low incomes than their wives and children—especially their wives; and, of course, the wives and children make the professor suffer. This is so in spite of the fact that many men who are teaching today and complaining about their salaries are doing ever so much better, even in financial terms, than their parents ever dreamed of doing. For the trouble is that their own rise, while considerable in absolute terms, is not great relative to the rise of others who have been equally mobile but have gone into different fields. Moreover, while the gap that once separated an instructor's salary from that of a full professor has been greatly reduced, there is still substantial difference in affluence within a university community, where the professors at the law school and at the medical school, and probably at the business school, may be getting as much as twice the salary of those in medieval history, while the professors of economics and sociology may be more than doubling their salaries with consulting fees—the academic form of moonlighting.

Such moonlighting, furthermore, represents another peril of the academic life: namely, that teaching less and less provides the traditional advantage of long vacations and much time to spend at home with wife and children. Wealthy lawyers, industrialists, or doctors, who work long hours and see little of their families, at least can feel that, after all, they bring home excellent salaries and fees, as well as high community status, even if they bring themselves home too little and too late. The professor, however, belongs to that stratum of society that has come to believe that the father should play a role in the home and in bringing up his family: it is one of his do-it-yourself activities. He is protected neither by his high salary nor by his traditional values against feeling himself inadequate as a parent when he can neither educate his children as he would like nor see as much of them as they might like. For increasingly his work is never done. His reading and research get crowded into the corners of the day. His position is vulnerable to all sorts of demands, and to protect himself he has to be more calculating or more incompetent than he knows how to be or cares to be or can afford to be. In addition, his wife shares his worries, and he must share hers. Hence, while in principle the professor still has more time than most professional men to spend at home, including the long summer vacation, much of this time in fact is spent either earning money to pay the plumber or working like a plumber. Indeed, the college professor must often feel that he is training his students for the "new leisure" while not enjoying much of it himself.

In the early years of married life, these problems may seem somewhat remote to the young graduate students whose wives are working at secretarial or other uninteresting jobs to help their husbands earn their degrees. Moreover, in the beginning years of teaching, at least at the major colleges and universities, a leveling of salaries has occurred, so that the pay of an instructor or assistant professor sometimes approaches a pinched white-collar subsistence level. But, correspondingly, in the later years when there are children one wants to send to good schools and colleges, a salary that might have seemed ample before World War I has been so depreciated by inflation as to require endless scrimping and anxiety. And by then one's investment in teaching may be too great to permit change to a more lucrative occupation. One may turn to writing profitable textbooks, surrendering earlier ideals of pioneering research and of a life of scholarly intellectual pleasures.

I emphasize these problems because I see a number of graduate students who doggedly insist on going into teaching because they feel that, if they entered business, they would condemn themselves to meanness and triviality. Yet in a number of such cases I am not sure that teaching is going to prove worth such sacrifices in comparison with other no less intellectual occupations that pay better. The teachers of these students, to justify their own sacrifices, have had to convince themselves that there is no life like the academic life, and they are thus tempted to impose these ideals on their students in turn. But I know men who are working in market research, in business consulting, in industrial psychology, who not only deal day after day with fascinating problems but are given a freedom of investigation and of choice of problems that is in the best sense academic. There are, perhaps, not many such openings, but neither are there many openings in universities that offer genuine freedom. Furthermore, judging from my own experience and from that of a number of others, there is much to be said for alternate bouts of teaching and of non-academic work. The occasional year in the field is one of the attractions of anthropology. Similarly, there are economists who would profit from a term in management, and some political scientists have realized that they might profit from a term in Congress or the state legislature or the state house. The broadest professions, after all, are specialties among other specialties; and one of the few ways in which, in the course of a lifetime, one can escape specialism is to move from one specialty or subspecialty to another. Even today, this sort of horizontal mobility remains one of the great opportunities of American life.

I have been told by many professors that I do not need to issue such caveats as these, since students today are out for the main chance and want only security and an easy corporate existence. This may perhaps be so in general, although I have my doubts about it. I am addressing myself now to the more serious and intellectual students who may not wear their idealism on their sleeves but whose contempt for business, though often misplaced and unfair, does represent an aspiration for a life not devoted only to making money and vendible disutilities.

THE SEARCH FOR COLLEAGUES

What is perhaps most characteristic in the work of the college professor is not his relatively low salary (that of schoolteachers, social workers, and ministers is often considerably lower) nor the fact that he grows older while his charges do not (for he shares this characteristic also with schoolteachers, pediatricians, policemen, and wardens), but rather that he sets his own goals; the goals are not given by an institution. This is certainly so in the penumbra of freedom beyond his regular teaching and other curricular duties, and even these duties, the higher one rises in the system, are defined in terms of one's own aims and definitions of the situation. It is this that makes the professor kin to the artist or writer, who is often seeking to create his own institutional norms; and it is this freedom, I am sure, that attracts many to the profession. It certainly attracts me.

But no one should underestimate the miseries of having to set one's own goals. It is much easier, in my observation, to meet a payroll or to try a case than to do research or to try to help students learn something. For creative intellectual work is never done, and it is certainly never done to one's own satisfaction. To be sure, professors and creative people, like other people, try to find outside judgments in order to avoid having to set their own goals. Sometimes these judgments are found in the tradition of work within the confines of a particular school. If one is a psychologist, for example, one may do work in the tradition of Hovland or that of Hull, adding a little bit to the enormous, expanding edge of what is known, and feeling that one is part of a cumulative process that is primarily colleaguial and collective. In this work one will be supported by the contemporaries of one's own school and tradition of work, and one will seldom have to ask oneself whether that tradition is itself worth while—especially since, guided by that tradition, one can keep turning out papers and graduate students.

Much useful work is done in this way by conscientious craftsmen, and some careful work by opportunists—in fact, the motives of most of us, for most of the time, are mixed and have very little to do with the truth of our discoveries. However, one is not better off if one does not belong to a school but finds an audience for one's work in the general intellectual public. For while the vice of the school-bound scholar is pedantry or a monopolistic out-look, the vice of the scholar oriented to the general public may be carelessness or flippancy. The public at large may be indiscriminate, its judgments vacil-lating and unreliable.

In this situation, it seems to me, the college teacher's real problem is to learn how to find his true colleagues. Let me take, for example, the situation of the man teaching sociology on a particular campus. He may assume, to start with, that his true colleagues are other sociologists there, and perhaps he will also assume that a cultural anthropologist and a social psychologist in the psychology department could be true colleagues. If he does not re-examine such judgments, he may find himself limited by the accidents that have brought these other people to the same institution in the same era. But if he looks beneath the surface of things, beneath the labels that people carry, he may find, for instance, that one of the historians (it could well be an economic historian) is closer to him and his way of thinking and feeling— while the historian himself has been suffering from the prison of the other historians. Thus it might turn out that the historian is more interested in generalization than historians are generally supposed to be, while the sociologist is more interested in history than his colleagues happen to be. And it may turn out that they share certain values that transcend the discipline. Similarly a particular chemist might find that his musical tastes are shared by a physicist and by a colleague in the art department, but not by the other chemists, let alone the chemical engineers. And this may help him see that the cast of mind of the physicist is closer to his own—more abstract, let us say—and that the man in the art department who plays in the same string quartet may be curious about styles of thought and have a lot to say that stimulates his thinking about symmetry in form, for example.

In my own experience, the very best and most imaginative people in any field are in some ways more like each other than they are like their mediocre department mates in the same field.

Such considerations about the nature of colleagueship were a factor in deciding me to shift from the law to social science. I was writing articles in the law reviews on the social-psychological aspects of legal and constitutional questions, and I found I was communicating more readily with sociologists and social psychologists than with people trained in the law. Certainly, as one grows and develops—and to grow and develop is the chief task and oppor-tunity of the scholar, as of those in other callings—one's true colleagues change, and one has to guard against too readily continuing membership in any one fraternity, no matter how pleasant and reassuring the company.

THE SEARCH FOR IDENTITY

The search for colleagueship is a lifelong matter. It begins before adoles-cence with the search for a chum, a confidant. It lends much of the energy and excitement to the life of the undergraduate. However, when college becomes too ardently vocational, the search may become truncated or curtailed in the rivalry of protoprofessional men. A similar attenuation often occurs when students move on from college into graduate and professional schools. Law students, for instance, often have had broad humanistic and scientific interests when they were in college, but when they come to law school they are apt to put such concerns behind them as preprofessional and to identify themselves or even to overidentify themselves with the law—that is, with their image of it, which is perhaps based on the small practice of an uncle or an acquaintance with a judge or some equally limited picture. Some of my former colleagues in law-school teaching, faced with such students, seek to persuade them to broaden their horizons, on the ground that they will become better and more statesmanlike and more civic-minded lawyers as a result—and possibly even more successful lawyers. But in combating the image students have of their future calling, there is always the danger that one will disorient them by presenting a vision of their career to which they cannot then live up. The problem is similar for professors in major medical schools, who may have ideals for the practice of medicine that can be fulfilled only in a big teaching hospital.

In comparison with teachers of law and medicine, the teachers of graduate students in the social sciences often worry because their field is not yet fully a profession. The sociologist is often at a loss to say clearly what it is that he does, what it is that distinguishes him from other academic people, while at the same time his students are in search of an unequivocal identity. It is tempting to provide the symbols of belongingness by insistence on a single pattern of methodology or a single vocabulary—one so patently complex that the layman is at first put off. Students, in fact, are apt to define the field even more narrowly than do their teachers, in the often vain hope that this will provide both psychological and career security. And, of course, since in the hierarchy of academic life it is the teachers of graduate students who in general have the highest prestige and the best working conditions, it is not surprising that research is accorded more distinction in graduate school than is ability or interest in teaching. At its best, the teaching of graduate students is like old-fashioned work with apprentices, but at its frequent worst it is a form of pseudo discipleship in which the student flatters the teacher in the hope of being recommended for scholarships and jobs—flatters him by using his terms, sharing his animosities, and working on his projects. In contrast, in my experience, the teaching of undergraduates has more to recommend it.

7

Procedures of Academic Recruitment

THEODORE CAPLOW and REECE J. McGEE

Elaborate procedures of recruitment focused on choosing the "right man" or making sure that no one who gets as far as an interview on organizational premises is later refused a job have several vital aspects and consequences. One consequence is that many other people whose careers will be interdependent with the recruit are involved for their own protection in the recruitment procedures. Another is negotiating the offer. Professors Caplow and McGee discuss the operation of such recruitment procedures in the academic marketplace.

The process of faculty recruitment cannot be understood or adequately described without attention to the details of hiring procedures, which turn out to be extraordinarily complex and elaborate. . . . The anlaysis of hiring procedures may clarify our general view of the values held in the academic profession.

OPEN AND CLOSED HIRING

A distinction must be made between the two kinds of recruitment in general use—"open," or competitive, hiring and "closed," or preferential, hiring. In theory, academic recruitment is mostly open. In practice, it is mostly closed.

In the theoretical recruiting situation, the department seeking a replacement attempts to procure the services of an ideal academic man. Regardless of the rank at which he is to be hired, he must be young. He must have shown considerable research productivity, or the promise of being able to produce research. He must be a capable teacher with a pleasing personality which will offend neither students, deans, nor colleagues. In order to secure the very best man available, the department simultaneously announces the opening in many quarters and obtains a long list of candidates named by their sponsors. When a sufficient number of high-caliber candidates have applied for the position, the department members sift and weigh the qualifications of each most carefully in order to identify the one who best meets their requirements. This is the model hiring situation. It is a stereotype of the profession, and it actually occurs in a small percentage of cases. Indeed, some elements of the model situation are present in almost every vacancy-and-replacement, but the outlines are blurred and distorted by a host of other factors.

The most common of these distorting factors is the preferential treatment of some candidates, based on an association between themselves and the hiring department. For want of a better term, it may be called nepotism, although the word is perhaps excessively strong. According to one of the dictionary definitions, it is the "bestowal of patronage by reason of relationship rather than merit." . . .

It is not difficult, despite the taboo, for a man with the appropriate disciplinary connections to go soliciting a position. The taboo, it would appear, is quite real (since there are statements that men who solicit positions are rejected from candidacy in some departments), but it can certainly be evaded if things are done discreetly. The technique is to solicit while avoiding the appearance of solicitation. . . .

The crucial factor here is possession of the appropriate acquaintances in the discipline to whom one's availability may be indicated. These are the connections by means of which one is freed of local institutional ties. . . .

Discrimination on racial or religious grounds is a luxury in the hiring process which seems to be practiced only when there is a surplus of candidates of quality. It is *always* institutional. We know of no instance of a disciplinary discrimination system. As suggested elsewhere, women tend to be discriminated against in the academic profession, not because they have low prestige but because they are outside the prestige system entirely and for this reason are of no use to a department in future recruitment.

With the exception of a few disciplines which enjoy the privilege of hiring in a truly international market (Spanish studies, for example), the importation of scholars from abroad is a sign of a very tight market in a specialty. The major universities may seek men from abroad before they will seek them from the minor league at home. Failing to discover a candidate to their taste in a foreign land, they may decide not to hire at all; or they may even hire a woman, who, being outside the prestige system, cannot hurt them. Not even as a last resort will they recruit from institutions with prestige levels much below their own.

THE PROCESS IN PRACTICE

If we turn from the model recruiting situation to examine what usually occurs, it may first be noted that there is considerable evidence that both vacancies and appointments are disturbing to academic departments and often result in a cumulative turnover of personnel. This is to say that the occurrence of a vacancy, especially when coupled with a search for a replacement, increases the probability of future vacancies in the same department. . . .

The apparent explanation of this circumstance is that the personnel process frequently provides an evaluation of either the departed man or a candidate which is inconsistent with the self-evaluation of some other member of the department, thereby turning his thoughts to greener, or less stony, pastures.

Another event which occurs frequently in the personnel process is the intrusion of outside influence upon the department. For example, a nepotistic appointment may be blocked when an outsider, usually the dean, requests the reopening of the field for further candidates. Factions within a department will often do the same thing, seldom opposing the man whom their rivals have put up for candidacy but muddying his inside track or obstructing it completely by the insistence that other candidates, better qualified, may be found if the search is extended somewhat.

We may also note that many academic men seem to be, as one respondent put it, "passively on the market" all the time. This is to say that they are not soliciting positions actively but will listen to any proposal which comes their way. This is, of course, one way for the individual professor to resist institutional authority, and it is sometimes cited as one of the academic substitutes for unionization. . . .

There is, as a matter of fact, a great deal of coyness in the recruiting process, but mostly on the side of the hiring parties, encouraged by higher administrators. It is very seldom seen in candidates. Ideally, both parties to the negotiation are supposed to be mutually friendly and ingratiating. The candidate usually is, and genuinely so. The university cannot be. It believes it has too much at stake, and the uncertainties of buying a less-than-perfectly-known quantity loom too large. This institutional anxiety can lead to coyness on a grand scale.

"His name had been brought to the attention of the President there. They met at the home of a friend of his, by accident, seemingly. The President then made him an offer when he went there to make a talk."

Festina Lente

When we examine the specific procedures of hiring in the American university, they turn out to be almost unbelievably elaborate. The average salary of an assistant professor is approximately that of a bakery truck driver, and his occupancy of a job is likely to be less permanent. Yet it may require a large part of the time of twenty highly-skilled men for a full year to hire him. The reader is invited to consider the following report:

"We had discussed the problem many times in staff meeting. We did a great deal of thinking on this. Our first step was to bring together a committee. They met a number of times trying to decide the qualities to be looked for and then to dig up suitable people to fill the role. After a number of meetings, it was boiled down to five men. One man notified us he couldn't be considered. The other four were brought here at intervals of a week or two. They met with each member of the staff and discussed their specialty. Lastly we invited each to give a paper. We brought in heads of other departments and members of the administration to hear them. They added their impressions to our own. We quickly centered on two men. It was difficult to decide, they had highly contrasting interests, abilities, and accomplishments. There were two or three staff meetings before the vote. The needs of the department were examined. We asked ourselves, 'Do we need glamour or promise?' "

"The four men who came each spent about half a week with us. The committee had got out an elegant and complete biography on each man prior to his visit. The vote was taken the week following the appearance of the last man. The Chairman saw the Dean the day afterward, and the Dean said, 'Go to it,' so the letter was sent that day. The level and approximate salary had been settled between the Chairman and the Dean previously, but it wasn't inflexible. The vote included the assistant professors, since it was made at that level."

Hiring procedures of approximately this complexity and duration are not the exception but the rule. Since they have no apparent ritual function in most cases, the best explanation we can offer is that these lengthy procedures reflect anxieties attendant upon the comparison of candidates by estimation of their disciplinary prestige. The appointment of an assistant professor or an instructor for two or three years does not seem to be of enough importance to the university to justify so complex a system on other grounds. . . .

Some Recruiting Agents

In many academic specialties within disciplines there are one or two men who are nationally recognized as leaders. These men sometimes become informal deans in their fields. Through their wide acquaintance, they can place almost anyone in the specialty, although they can seldom deny placement to anyone, since they do not control all the vacancies existing. . . .

The Slave Market, an inaccurate (although beloved) figure of speech in wide use among professors, refers in general to the academic labor market and is used in particular reference to professional meetings and conventions. It is a misnomer in most disciplines, for it suggests the sale of professor-flesh upon the block with particularly high value being placed upon muscles and endurance. It is specifically applicable only to a few fields, such as English, where there is a great deal of routine and unavoidable undergraduate instruction to be done.

Appearing only infrequently, but dramatically when it does, is an especially elaborate form of procedural elaboration which might be called the Puppet Show. It occurs when a department *really* wants a specific man and is uncertain about being permitted to hire him. In general, it seems to develop in colleges where deans exercise their authority capriciously, for in the cases reported there is no definite evidence that the dean would have opposed the appointment had it been broached directly to him. The department, however, took no chances.

"In the meantime we'd brought another man in as a Visiting Professor. In June, I talked to him to see if he'd be interested in staying on. He said 'No.' But he spent the summer with us and had a wonderful time. Well, by that time we'd picked out four more men including two we couldn't get at less than associate with $2,000 more than the Dean said we could have. We looked them all over and weren't particularly interested. Then one day this visiting man intimated it wouldn't be impossible to interest him in the permanent post. He asked what I thought the Dean might say. I wrote the Dean a letter, about the four men, only this time I headed the list with the weakest and worked up to the strongest of the four. Then I added a paragraph to this effect: 'If the administration should wish to do something outstanding for this department, to bring it once more into the ranks of the best in the country, they might be able to bring in our Visitor as a permanent member.' I saw the Dean about two weeks later. He said, 'That was a very clever letter. I wouldn't hire the first two people on your list and after finishing your letter I could come to only one conclusion.' " . . .

The role of the department chairman in the hiring process is an uncertain one. He may be a servant or a tyrant. . . .

[Interviewer]: "Was this an open vote?"
"Certainly the discussion was open. I think I may have requested closed ballots. I believe that's what I did. That's what we're doing now on promotions; they want that secret so if there's any complaint they can't say, 'The chairman didn't do it right.' I believe I have their votes in their own handwriting on file, in case there's an error or ever any cause to defend it before the Dean."

This example of closed but not secret balloting illustrates rather neatly the role of the chairman who is a servant of the servants. One other aspect of the chairman's role in the hiring process needs comment. In a good department, to concentrate the hiring in the hands of the chairman is often to allow him to build a feudal empire. Many medical school departments offer excellent examples. They may be, and often are, professionally excellent, but their members, whatever their private feelings toward the chairman, are never likely to forget they owe their positions and their prospects to him. To be the chairman of a bad department and to be solely responsible for hiring, on the other hand, is to be gray of hair and ulcerous of stomach from the constant and frustrating effort to secure suitable candidates or approval for unsuitable ones.

As far as the data of this study permit us to judge, the presence of a university committee in the hiring process is likely to impede the already complex procedures, sometimes to the point of breakdown. The situation is often recognized by the working professor. . . .

"The Dean has a committee that does these things [evaluation of candidates] all over again. It's a farce, in my opinion. It should work, but it doesn't. They've made some awful appointments. And they've made some mistakes and promoted the wrong people."

There seems to be no sure way for men who are members of one discipline to check their judgments of a man in another. Knowing neither the prestige nor the bases of judgment of the men recommending the candidate, the members of the committee must resort to their own friends in the discipline or to marginal persons in it (who are more likely to talk freely to outsiders) to arrive at an appraisal themselves. These appraisals will almost certainly be distorted (from the department viewpoint) by the pressure of interdisciplinary rivalries. . . .

The function of placement bureaus in the recruiting process of major universities can be summarized by saying that prestige is attached to the non-use of their services. This is less true of the university's own placement service than of commercial agencies (which exist somewhere in the darkness of an academic limbo beyond Siberia), but even these are mostly patronized by aspirants with degrees in education, a discipline which, in the view of many academic men, occupies a special Siberia of its own. The contamination of these users has passed to the bureau itself, for reasons which become evident upon analysis.

Recommendations are read primarily in the attempt to ascertain the disciplinary prestige of the candidate. The first consideration for any hiring department is to safeguard itself against a ridiculous choice, the public-knowledge of which could lower the departmental reputation at one blow. The unwritten, essential, and elemental rule of hiring, then, is that the candidate must be disciplinarily respectable before he will be considered at all. It is exactly this elemental respectability which no placement service can guarantee, unlike the private letter of recommendation which demonstrates the subject's respectability by the very fact of its existence. As a result, there is a tendency in most fields for only the weakest candidates to use the services of a placement agency. Only where the "slave market" prevails can the placement bureau safely be used by a major department. In such cases, the prestige of the department depends upon the senior men and is relatively unaffected by the juniors.

HIRING PROCEDURES IN PERSPECTIVE

When academic hiring procedures are viewed in perspective, their most striking feature is the time and effort which most departments devote to appointments, including the appointments of junior men, who tend to be transient and unimportant to the department. It has been noted that in most cases the procedure seems to have no ritual significance, although there are some instances of its being used to manipulate a dean. We should also note that if the procedure is too prolonged and agonized, it may pass the point of no return, and the department will find itself unable to make a replacement because any candidate suggested will be vetoed by a remark to the effect: "But is he as good as that young Smith whom we turned down three years ago?"

We have suggested that what the department attempts to do in hiring is to establish the candidate's prestige-potential—his value for future staff procurement. The elaboration of procedures is in part explained by the fact that there are no objective means by which future prestige can be measured. Prestige, it must be remembered, is subjective, consisting, in essence, of what other people think about a man. It may be more important to the department than the qualities of the man, observed in themselves. The academic labor market is an exchange where universities speculate in future prestige values, based on yet undone research. By attempting to hire men whose value will increase at more than the normal rate, they hope to purchase future institutional prestige below the market price. However, since most universities and most departments tend to get the candidates whom their actual prestige deserves, and since they are normally subject to the Aggrandizement Effect, they are very frequently dissatisfied with their purchases. . . .

The Merits of Candidates

As part of the hiring process often hidden within the overlapping layers of procedures is the actual evaluation of candidates on their merits. The following sensible nonsense is an excellent summary of the way the market for futures is viewed by many of its most active traders.

"We take a good look at their letters and then when they're down here we look at them and talk to them and then we take a good look into our crystal ball and pull out the best man. In other words, we're completely subjective about the whole thing.

"It's usually fairly simple. You can tell from a ten-minute conversation if a man will be a good teacher. The thing that is perturbing is trying to forecast what their scientific career is going to be like on the basis of the same conversation. What counts is drive and imagination. You can have pretty good luck, though, this way. We hired a man this way three years ago who has proved to be the outstanding man in the country of those who were available at that time.

"We can't afford to hire any other way. There is no other way of judging a man's research and scholarly capacities. It's extremely time-consuming, but it works."

Despite the occasional recognition that the process of evaluation is subjective, the overelaboration of procedures which characterizes the whole system of recruiting often represents a dogged attempt to achieve consensus at any price.

"We pass the recommendations and vita and stuff around to the whole staff—everyone on the full-time staff—and they look it over. If there are too many applicants, I may do a little weeding first and throw out the obviously unsuitable ones. Then we write and get opinions from the men we know we can trust with whom they've worked or in their home departments. Then we invite two or three of them down here in a rank order of preference, and everyone gets a chance to see them and talk to them, and we ask them to give a seminar paper for an hour at a staff seminar. Sometimes during the time they're here, a day or two, everyone gets a chance at them and really works them over, in particular with regard to what they have done and are doing in research, what their research attitudes are, that kind of thing. Of course, if they have publications, everyone reads those, or most of us do. And we have a party and pour a couple of drinks into them if they'll take them, and see how they are when they're loosened up a bit. Then we take them into the Deans of the College of Letters and the Graduate School and let them have a look at them. Then after they go home, we have a staff meeting and really chew them over and everyone gets a chance to have a say and contribute what he thinks of the man.

Every man in the department has the blackball privilege, although of course he has to be able to state his reasons. We respect them, too; doesn't matter who they come from if they make sense. We can't afford to have brawls within the department."

The blackball device, mentioned above, may help to insure department harmony, but it probably tends to favor men with neutral characteristics. This is not always an asset, even in a democratic department.

Throughout the information on candidate evaluation, the human element obtrudes in singular ways, sometimes comic, and often pathetic.

"We had one young woman come down here from one of the Big Ten. She had the M.A. and was working on her doctoral dissertation and we would have very much liked to have gotten her, but when she saw the Dean, he turned her down. He didn't like the way she was turned out, thought she was too stylishly dressed. We had thought she looked very lovely." . . .

One of the most time-honored of all of the evaluative devices in use is that of having all the staff members of the department above the rank at which the replacement is to be made meet to decide upon a man. This keeps the hierarchy hierarchical and reduces the probability of invidious comparison between the emoluments offered the new man and those of present members of the same rank.

Even under the best conditions, the evaluation of candidates is beset with uncertainty. If judgment is made on the basis of a visit, the judges get no view of that research ability which is chiefly sought. If the candidate is judged on the basis of his recommendations, the judge must not only determine what those recommendations really mean but must also evaluate the disciplinary prestige of the recommending scholars.

THE DECISION-MAKING PROCEDURE

As for the actual credentials used in decision making, it is not an over-generalization to say that departments do not, as a rule, consider teaching, academic records, or theses. Why theses are not read is a puzzling question, since the thesis is usually the only major work which a young man can show and probably represents the best current effort of which he is capable. But they are not read—in the same way that publications are not generally read in the course of his candidacy for a position. Of course, they may be taken out of the library and piled upon the chairman's desk so that anyone who wishes to do so may look at them.

The reason why publications, all protestations to the contrary, are not really *read* has been suggested before: because men are hired for their repute, and not for what that repute is purportedly based upon. Men are hired, to put it baldly, on the basis of how good they will look to others. It is assumed that the long, grueling training demanded for the Ph.D. guarantees a satisfactory quality of teaching and the quality, if not the quantity, of a man's research. There is very little point in trying to determine how good the man *really* is, or even how good the department opinion of him may be. What is important is what others in the discipline think of him, since that is, in large part, how good he *is*. Prestige, as we have remarked before, is not a direct measure of productivity but a composite of subjective opinion. . . .

It may also be said, in the light of the analysis above, that an academic man's career is pretty well determined by the time he has reached the age of forty. Opinions of him by then will have crystallized and will be so widely diffused that the possibilities of changing them will be slight. Disciplinary prestige is a feature of a social system, not a scientific measurement. It is correlated with professional achievement but not identical with it. A man may, for example, publish what would be, in other circumstances, a brilliant contribution to his field, but if he is too old, or too young, or located in the minor league, it will not be recognized as brilliant and will not bring him the professional advancement which he could claim if he were of the proper age and located at the proper university. Disciplinary prestige, then, has a social and institutional locus. There are men to whom this has happened in every discipline, and many readers will be able to supply specific examples.

A further illustration of the nature of the prestige order is that a man's prestige in his discipline is often measured by the number of citations he receives from other authors—yet the number of citations received is in part a consequence of high prestige. And lest the reader who is a physical scientist believe himself exempt, let it be pointed out that, although the scientist's prestige is presumed to depend upon the quality of his work, the quality is often a function of the equipment to which he has access—which is at least partly dependent on his prestige. High-energy accelerators are not available to unknown instructions.

The haunting uncertainties and anxieties of the selection process are reduced in a few specialties in which professional skill—and, hence, prestige—can be determined by audition. Music is such a field. In these areas we find none of the elaborate procedures which prevail elsewhere in the academic profession. . . .

A final point of interest is that many of the people most concerned with hiring do not seem to know precisely what the hiring procedures at their universities are. In the same department, procedures often vary from one appointment to the next. It is not unusual for the dean to initiate all personnel, actions for one department of his college and scarcely to be consulted in another. The formal procedures of appointments are often unfamiliar to people who make appointments.

Perhaps the precise method of selection makes so little difference to the university because all methods are used to measure, very imperfectly, the same variable, and none of them measures it well. . . .

The results . . . suggest that departments get the replacements to which their place in the prestige order entitles them.

HAZARDS OF THE MARKET

There is a ceremonial way of canvassing for a roster of candidates. It consists of seeking nominations from the big names, both human and institutional in the discipline. The ceremony is almost always carried out when time allows, but men are hired where they are found and contracts with them are made in such a variety of ways as to defy cataloguing.

We have spoken before of nepotism in the hiring process. Our data on the extent to which closed, or preferential, hiring occurs indicate that for the replacements made in the sample universities 40 per cent of instructors and assistant professors and 61 per cent of associate and full professors had some contact with the department before their candidacy. There is a statistically significant positive association between the two variables. This is to say that as the rank of the replacement increases, the probability that he has had some contact with the department to which he goes also increases. In a sense, of course, this is to be expected because the greater the rank, the greater the likelihood that the individual will at least have met someone from the hiring department before. However, in most of these cases, the reported contact was much more than casual acquaintance.

We also note in the interviews a steady insistence that prior contact does not make any difference—*i.e.*, does not unduly influence the selection of candidates. . . .

For purposes of formal evaluation, prior association between the candidate and the hiring department probably does not make much difference, since it does not affect his prestige; but, as we have already suggested, certain reasons exist why familiar candidates are preferred to unknowns. In departments rated high by their chairmen, 59 per cent of the candidates had prior contact before the replacement was hired, whereas in low-rated departments only 38 per cent had such contact. . . .

This is to be expected if our analysis of the rating process is correct; better departments seek men with more prestige; men with more prestige are better known and have a wider acquaintance in the discipline.

Prestige is not rank—which is definite and discrete. One has a given rank or one has not; there can be no ambiguity about it. Prestige, being a kind of average of opinions about a man, is, like any average, subject to distortion by extreme values. Hiring departments, therefore, are most sensitive to sharply negative opinions. A mildly critical opinion may be balanced by laudatory reports, but a sharply negative opinion from someone of high prestige is usually sufficient to destroy a candidate's chances. It is our impression, however, that negative opinions referring to personality factors are less likely to be fatal than those referring to professional ability.

The compilers of rosters are haunted by uncertainty about finding and evaluating men. We suggested earlier that disciplinary respectability is so urgent a requirement in a candidate that some canvassing techniques are not

used for the sole reason that they cannot assure this. The result of the uncertainty, of course, is often nepotism, since departments are apt to prefer
anyone who is at all familiar to someone who is totally unknown.

There is another uncertainty to be taken account of: the fear of the
"Bogie-man Replacement." There appear to be two kinds of bogie-men whom
departments fear. The first is the temperamental prima donna, who can wreck
a department by his mere presence. He is especially dangerous in the tenure
ranks since prima donnas—as visualized—will do anything to get what they
want. The second, and more conspicuous, bogie-man is the "man who won't
fit in." Among the most common qualities sought in candidates are "the
right personality," "someone whom we can live with," and the like. The
frequent reliance upon the blackball, or the senatorial courtesy principle, is
illustrated by one or two of the interviews that we have quoted previously.
This concern with getting replacements with whom the department can live,
and the rule that a candidate must be *persona grata* to everyone in the department, reflect the fear of the man who won't fit in. On the part of the candidate,
"fitting in" involves the acceptance of the values of the department as a peer
group and a willingness to defend it under attack from without, especially
from higher administrators, whom the department often regards as enemies.

This conception of the department as an embattled band is especially
strong in expanding disciplines, in which the process of professional growth
makes recurrent demands upon the administration for further funds for new
positions, promotions, and research support. The department must, in this
situation, be a conflict group, constantly striving to acquire a larger share
of the finite institutional budget at the expense of competitors. Such departments are especially wary of "traitors" who will betray departmental secrets
to the administration or to its disciplinary enemies. Equally dangerous is the
nonconformist, who cannot be assimilated into the defensive structure of the
department and who threatens its prestige by operating as a detachable
Achilles' Heel.

These threats are given the weight and worry which they receive from
professors because each man's prestige is linked to that of his department,
and anything which threatens the prestige of the department is experienced as
a threat to the individual's ego. There is seldom any feeling expressed that the
replacement must be a pal, a "good buddy," to the members of the department, or personally charming; but he must be a reliable member of the peer
group. If he is this, he may also be almost anything else he chooses.

So the poker game of personnel is haunted by uncertainty and anxiety.
We have several instances where this anxiety about the process has so
mounted within departments that even nontenured appointments are put on a
short-term basis in order to assure that there will be no problem of disposal,
should the replacement turn out to be a bogie-man. Thus we find the title of
"acting assistant professor" in increasing vogue at certain major universities.
The reader is asked to consider, if he will, the level of anxiety which makes a

two-year contract seem too long, so that junior staff must be hired on an "acting" basis in order to shorten their tenure to one academic year at a time. We even have one case of an acting instructorship.

Signing and Sealing

An examination of the techniques of offering also reveals situational stresses at work. In general, candidates do not delay acceptance of offers very long. Universities, on the other hand, are apt to withhold final word until the last possible moment, presumably in case a better candidate appears or something unseemly is learned about the one in hand. It is much easier for a candidate to make up his mind than it is for the institution. (He knows more about the institution than it knows about him.) . . .

In general, the candidate tends to abandon his hesitations at an earlier point in the sequence of events, whereas the department is often undecided up to the moment an offer is made, and even beyond. *The immediate outcome of the academic personnel process, in the typical case, is a happy candidate and a worried department.*

Despite their general reluctance to reach a final decision, universities tend to make initial offers rather early in the process in order to get candidates to commit themselves. The offers are often extremely discreet in their wording and detail. A very common proceeding, for example, is to ask the candidate to accept the position before the university has offered it:

> "I sent the nomination to the Dean, briefed him on what we wanted. The Dean recommended him to the Vice-President, the Vice-President to the President, and the President approved the nomination, so I called him to tell him so. I had, prior to that time, secured a letter from him saying that he would accept the position under the conditions stated if it were offered. That's S.O.P.—we always do that."

The candidate in this case, is ethically bound to accept the position and not to seek others while waiting. The university is not bound to make an offer, and the failure to do so can always be attributed to higher officials whom the candidate does not know. All questions of ethics aside, this procedure is a vestige of the buyer's market of an earlier era, and it can impose real handicaps on departments forced to operate in the seller's market of today.

8

Recruiting Volunteers

DAVID SILLS

Recruitment to an organization for work that is not financially compensated is the problem Professor Sills considers. He shows how the process of reaching the recruit and attracting him under this condition relies heavily on the use of social relationships which were established for other purposes. The personal contact based on a friendship or business relationship becomes part of our theory on how recruits are found, approached, and enticed into the organization.

In this chapter, attention is given to the problem of recruiting new members— a problem which is also endemic to all voluntary associations but which stems not from the process of delegation but rather from the inherent nature of organizations themselves. Since organizations are not *primary* associations like nations, churches, and families, which obtain many if not most of their numbers through natural reproduction, but rather *secondary* associations, they are dependent for their survival upon the continual incorporation of new individuals into their membership.

Practitioners in the fields of social work and community organization are of course generally aware of the fact that voluntary associations must actively recruit new members, as are the leaders and staff members of most organizations. But writers who have approached the topic of voluntary associations with an interpretative or theoretical orientation seem generally to have assumed that the members of voluntary associations join on their own initiative, since these associations are usually defined as "interest groups" which exist to further the interests of their membership.

An examination of the wide range of voluntary associations in America, however, reveals that the term "interest group" is much too narrow a definition. Consider, for example, the classification of associations developed by Sherwood Fox on the basis of his analysis of some 5,000 voluntary associations. By noting the functions which each association performed, Fox makes a distinction between *majoral, minoral*, and *medial* organizations. *Majoral associations* are those associations which serve the interests of the major institutions of society. Business, professional, scientific, educational, labor, and agricultural associations belong to this category. *Minoral associations*, on the other hand, are those which serve the interests of significant minorities in the

Excerpted, with permission, from *The Volunteers* (New York: Free Press of Glencoe, 1957; pp. 78–115).

population. Women's clubs, fraternal groups, hobby clubs, and various associations formed to protect the rights of different ethnic minorities in the population are all examples. Finally, *medial associations* mediate between major segments of the population. Social welfare organizations, which mediate between the community and the underprivileged population; veterans' groups, which mediate between war veterans and the government; and voluntary health associations, which mediate both between research scientists and the public, and between individuals suffering from a disease or disorder and the medical profession, are examples of medial associations.

These three broad types of associations, differ markedly in the way their members are characteristically recruited. Membership in majoral associations is for the most part merely an adjunct to the performance of an occupation. For this reason, active recruitment is either unnecessary or is limited to making the existence of certain facilities known to the occupational group. The recruitment of doctors into the American Medical Association, scientists into a professional society, farmers into a grange or marketing cooperative, and skilled workers into a trade union, for example, is generally of this character. Most eligible people join majoral associations either because they are compelled to or because it is a matter of self-interest, of establishing and maintaining good relationships with their occupational colleagues.

Membership in minoral associations, on the other hand, is more likely to be a matter of individual initiative. The purest case is perhaps that of the hobby group, whose members may only be in touch with each other through an organization publication, and who join and drop out as the intensity of their personal interest dictates. Most minoral associations conform closely to the image of a voluntary association as one in which membership is based upon "true" volunteering. Both majoral and minoral associations, accordingly, are examples of what are generally called "interest groups."

Finally, membership in medial associations, particularly voluntary health associations, comes about for the most part as a result of active recruitment on the part of the organization. The fundamental reason for this situation, as far as voluntary health associations are concerned, is that our society has developed other institutionalized methods of dealing with health problems. The family and the schools, for example, are charged with teaching children the basic tenets of hygiene; national and local governments are responsible for the maintenance of public health standards and practices; and the medical and nursing professions are responsible for restoring to health individuals who become ill. From the point of view of the individual, this allocation of responsibility means that, although concerned in a general way with the health of his community, he has no compelling obligation to do more than take the common-sense steps necessary to protect the health of himself, his family, and his community. From the point of view of a voluntary health association, this allocation of responsibility means that there is no specific mechanism which it can utilize in order to obtain new recruits. Unlike a church, for example, a voluntary health association cannot depend on natural reproduction or religious conversion as a source of new members; unlike a military organization, it has no such coercive mechanism as conscription legislation; unlike a government bureaucracy, a business firm or a professional or trade association, it cannot depend upon the occupational structure for recruits; unlike fraternal or social organizations, it does not have recreational facilities to offer as an inducement; and unlike automobile clubs or veterans' groups—to cite only a few examples of other types of voluntary associations—it cannot obtain new members from any clearly-defined segment of the population. As a result, a voluntary health association has two possible courses of action. It can either make a general, impersonal appeal for volunteers, or it can make use of relationships which were established for other purposes. Most voluntary health associations adopt both courses of action; as will presently be demonstrated, the Foundation relies strongly upon the latter. . . .

Information concerning the procedures utilized by the Foundation to recruit Volunteers could conceivably be obtained in three different ways. The recruiting procedures recommended in various manuals published by the Foundation for the guidance of Chapters might be examined; Volunteers could be asked to report how they normally went about the task of recruiting other Volunteers; and Volunteers could be asked to tell how they themselves were recruited.

The first of these techniques proved to be of little value in this research, since the manuals do not go into any detail concerning this topic, and in any case report only those procedures which are recommended, not those which are actually used. The second technique also proved to have limited utility, since most Volunteers who themselves had recruited others could not estimate which one procedure they had used most frequently. Accordingly, the data presented in this chapter were obtained by asking Volunteers how they themselves had become members of the Foundation.

TYPES OF RECRUITS: A SUMMARY

PRIOR EXPERIENCES	PERSONAL EXPERIENCE WITH POLIO		PARTICIPATION IN COMMUNITY ORGANIZATIONS	
Personal goals	"Other-oriented"	"Self-oriented"	"Other-oriented"	"Self-oriented"
Image of the Foundation:				
"People"	0	0	7	66
"Purposes"	11	31	21	98
TYPE OF RECRUIT	*Polio Veterans*		*Humanitarians*	*Good Citizens Joiners*
Number of recruits	42		28	66
				98
Per cent of all Volunteers	18		12	28
				42

Trigger Events

Although the delineation of four types of recruits has shed considerable light on the problem of why Volunteers joined the Foundation, one more category of reasons must be considered: the specific events which led to their becoming members. ...

For present purposes, the term "trigger event" is used as being most descriptive of what took place in most instances of joining the Foundation.

The most frequent trigger event was the occasion of being asked to join by a friend: 52 per cent of all Volunteers joined the Foundation in response to an invitation extended by someone whom they knew personally. Another 20 per cent were asked to join by some other member of the community; 8 per cent were asked to join by an organizational or occupational colleague; and 10 per cent volunteered on their own initiative. Polio Veterans are more likely than other Volunteers to have volunteered on their own initiative; Humanitarians and Joiners are more likely to have been asked by an organizational or occupational colleague; and Good Citizens are more likely to have been approached by a community member whom they may not have known personally. These inter-type variations reflect of course characteristic differences in the types of experiences which preceded membership in the Foundation. Of more significance than these differences, however, is the fact that in the case of 90 per cent of the Volunteers some trigger event was a necessary component of their joining the Foundation. The specific nature of these trigger events is discussed in the section, *Recruiting Volunteers*.

Volunteering

Although "volunteering" has been classified above as a trigger event, it is more accurately described as a residual category which includes all Volunteers who said that no one had asked them to join the Foundation, but who joined on their own initiative. Accordingly, it was necessary to inquire of these Volunteers what circumstances had led them to take this initiative; that is, what trigger event had taken place.

A total of twenty-four of the Volunteers interviewed joined without receiving a specific invitation. In the case of ten of these twenty-four "true" Volunteers it was the circumstance of having had polio in their family which triggered their decision—nine of these ten Volunteers had received financial aid from the Foundation, and sought to repay their local Chapter by participating as a Volunteer.

Five other Volunteers belonged to organizations which assumed responsibility for some phase of the March of Dimes; they heard about the project, became interested, and volunteered. A polio epidemic was the trigger event which tripped off the decision of three Volunteers—in every case they initially volunteered to serve as a Polio Emergency Volunteer in their local hospital. Finally, a number of chance events served to activate the predisposition of others. One man was told by his wife that the March of Dimes needed some help, so he telephoned the Chairman and offered his services. Another Volunteer, a young lawyer who had been stricken with polio during World War II, was spurred into the decision by the March of Dimes campaign itself; the campaign publicity reminded him of his sense of obligation, and he volunteered. One Volunteer became a Polio Emergency Volunteer when she substituted one day for her sister who could not visit the hospital. One woman resigned from her job as the secretary of the State Representative, and then became a Volunteer; another was lunching with friends and heard them discussing the need for assistance; and a wife "naturally helped out" when her husband was asked to be Campaign Director. In every case, then, some crucial event took place which activated the decision.

It cannot of course be concluded from this discussion of trigger events that individuals became Volunteers "because" they are asked, or "because" some event took place which led them to volunteer their services, since many invitations and other opportunities to join are bypassed. It is impossible to document this assertion with the data available, since all of the Volunteers interviewed in this research had (by definition) *not* refused this invitation. However, comments such as the following statement by a March of Dimes Chairman in Glass City indicate that invitations—although they may be necessary conditions for membership—cannot be viewed as sufficient conditions:

(*Are you active in other community organizations?*) No, I don't *aim* to volunteer. I say "no" as often as I can. Yes, the Red Cross as Chairman, and also our Military Fund. I am Co-Chairman—I believe it was for the USO. I turned the Cancer down. I don't think I've ever been asked for Heart. I've been getting three requests in a row—Red Cross, Polio, and Cancer.

Why did this Volunteer, as well as other Volunteers, not decline to join the Foundation when the opportunity presented itself? In large part, this question has been answered by the previous description of the four types of recruits. But part of the question remains unanswered, and must remain so, since many Volunteers are unclear in their own minds as to the exact nature of the relationship between what Kornhauser and Lazarsfeld call "factors in the individual and factors in the situation." As a result of their own uncertainty as to their "real" reasons for joining, many Volunteers relieved themselves of responsibility, and reported that they were "talked into it." The Campaign Director in Lumber City confided that he had been "sucked into it," and a March of Dimes Chairman in Pinetree County—using a colloquial expression more common in his part of the country—claimed that "they 'hornswoggled' me into it."

RECRUITING VOLUNTEERS

The Utilization of Role Relationships

It was noted in the Introduction to this chapter that a characteristic of all medial associations, and particularly of voluntary health associations, is that their members are not, for the most part, people who joined on their own initiative—they are recruited by the organization. In the case of the Foundation, only 10 per cent of the Volunteers studied joined without a specific invitation. It is accordingly of some interest to examine the ways in which Foundation Volunteers actually go about the business of recruiting new Volunteers.

Since relatively few people feel obligated to join the Foundation as a matter of course—in the same way, for example, that a doctor feels obligated to join his county medical society—Foundation Volunteers must make use of obligations which have been incurred in other ways. These other obligations are best described as "role relationships."

The concept "role relationship" is derived from a consideration of society as a system comprised of myriads of interpersonal relationships. A fundamental requirement of any social system is that people must "behave in given situational conditions in certain relatively specific ways, or at least within relatively specific limits." Individual participants in the system are thus guided in many of their actions by considerations which result from their membership in a particular interpersonal relationship; that is, they feel "a sense of obligation" to behave in a certain way. Because obligations of this kind apply only to behavior in certain situations, they differ from such obligations as those "to onself" or "to God," in that avoiding the disapproval of others is the underlying reason for taking steps to fulfill them.

From this point of view, a large proportion of social behavior can be described as the fulfillment of obligations which derive from various role relationships. In fact, it is generally difficult to persuade people to take any specific course of action, including joining a voluntary association, unless they view this action as a necessary component of the proper fulfillment of some role obligation. . . .

Attention will be given to those relationships which this research has revealed are most frequently utilized by Foundation Chapter and March of Dimes Volunteers in order to obtain new recruits: *friendship*, *community membership*, and *organizational membership*.

It will be recalled from the discussion presented earlier in this chapter that each Volunteer interviewed was asked to recount the circumstances under which he or she became a Foundation Volunteer, and that 90 per cent of the Volunteers reported that someone had asked them to join. These invitations were described as "trigger events," since they serve to activate the predispositions of Volunteers. These same responses, however, may be used as indicators of the role relationship which was utilized by the recruiter. Accordingly, if the person who extended the invitation was a friend, it was assumed that the obligations which result from interpersonal or friendship relations were utilized; if this person was a Volunteer whom he or she didn't know, or a State Representative, or any one else who approached the new Volunteer because of his reputation for civic-mindedness or some related reason, it was assumed that obligations stemming from community relationships were utilized; and if this person was a co-member of some other community organization, or a co-worker at his place of work, or a business or professional associate, it was assumed that organizational relationships were called upon. That is, the *role relationship* between the recruiter and the recruited was used in this analysis as an "indicator" of the *role obligation* utilized.

Interpersonal Relationships

The role relationship most frequently employed in recruiting is that of friendship: 58 per cent. . . .

Volunteers do not of course extend invitations to their friends indiscriminately; rather, they select people who have already demonstrated their competence and interest in community activities. Typically, this means that Volunteers select people with whom they have worked in other community volunteer activities. During the interviews, Volunteers repeatedly stressed the fact that taking part in one community activity leads to friendships which in turn lead to participation in other activities. March of Dimes Volunteers in particular are often recruited on an "exchange for services rendered" basis. That is, Volunteers frequently turn to people whom they have helped on other campaigns, and explicitly or otherwise use an obligation incurred in the past as the basis for expecting an acceptance at this time. "After all," confided the Chapter Chairman in Oil City, "some guy helps you out and then you can't turn him down. R—— now, he had helped me many times, so when he asked me to take this on, I didn't mind at all." Many Volunteers profess to regret this situation, complaining that "one thing leads to another," but there is no doubt that the utilization of obligations which originate in personal friendships is of crucial importance for maintaining a constant influx of new members into the Foundation.

Community Relationships

Community and organizational relationships were used with nearly equal frequency—in 22 and 20 per cent of all invitations, respectively.

In the case of invitations which invoke the obligations attendant upon community relationships, an appeal is made not to an individual's sense of duty toward his friends, or toward an organization, but rather toward the community at large. This type of approach is particularly effective among people who are self-consciously aware of their reputation as community leaders affiliated with all "good causes." The Campaign Director in South City, for example, explained his acceptance in these terms: "I think this is one way of fulfilling one's responsibility to the community."

Often obligation to the community is invoked by a Volunteer—or even a prestigeful non-Volunteer who is willing to help the Chapter out—by telephoning or calling upon a prospective recruit and asking if he will perform a community service by taking part in Chapter or March of Dimes activities. The Chairman of Women's Activities in Harbor City, for example, reported that as a newcomer to the city she was pressed into service by one of the community's social leaders. She couldn't refuse the invitation, she said, because "you'd be a cad if you didn't work in this town. I don't see how any woman has the time for bridge or relaxation—they don't leave you a minute."

A common method of making use of community membership obligations is to telephone or write to someone in the community who has had polio in the family recently, and who has received help from the Chapter, and ask if he would like to take part in the activities. A March of Dimes Chairman in College Town, for example, explained that "She got my name from the hospital and thought anyone who had gotten help would be able to help, a very good assumption. I was always surprised why no one had asked me before." And the Chapter Chairman in Payday Town reported his experiences as follows: "I was released from Warm Springs in July 1949. In the Fall of 1949 Mr. —— asked me to help. . . . I said, 'Yes, of course.' I was Chairman of the March of Dimes for three years . . . then I became Chapter Chairman."

But the most frequent invitation of all, accounting for two out of every three invitations which invoked the obligations of community membership, came from the State Representative, part of whose job it is to ensure that every Chapter in his jurisdiction is making full use of the volunteer resources of its community. Sometimes State Representatives approach people directly. The Chapter Chairman in Oldtown, for example, reported that the State Representative "went to the priest . . . and said he needed some active people to be on the Chapter. The priest referred him to me and I said I would like to help." More often, however, a Chapter or March of Dimes officer will learn of a potential Volunteer, and will ask the State Representative to extend the invitation, in the hope that his prestige as an official representative of the national organization will carry more weight.

Organizational Relationships

Invitations extended in the name of an organization, and which accordingly invoke the sense of obligation which people feel toward an organization, come about in a number of ways. Often a community organization is asked by the Chairman to assume responsibility for one phase of the March of Dimes, and individual members of the organization are subsequently asked by one of their co-members to carry out specific assignments. The American Legion Auxiliary, the Lions Club, the Junior Chamber of Commerce, and the P.T.A. are among the groups which most often adopt the March of Dimes as an organizational "project." Nearly half of all Volunteers whose relationship to an organization was utilized were approached in this way, but this proportion still does not fully reflect the importance of organizational activities as a mechanism for recruiting, since (as already related) many people who were approached by friends would not have made these friendships had they not participated in other organizational activities.

A third of the invitations which made use of the obligations of organizational membership were extended to business and professional associates, which reflects the fact that many business firms consider participation in community volunteer activities as an employee responsibility. In fact, during periods of intensive volunteer activity, such as the March of Dimes, some firms will ask an employee to serve as a full-time Volunteer, remaining, of course, on the payroll of the firm during this period.

Finally, many of the Volunteers who joined during the early years of the Foundation were asked by fellow Democrats to help out with the President's Birthday Ball. One-quarter of all Volunteers who were invited to participate by an appeal to their organizational loyalty (ten Volunteers in all) were asked by members of a local Democratic organization.

Recruiting as a Pattern of Informal Organization

It is very difficult for a voluntary health association to make explicit provisions in its various manuals for the recruitment of new members, since its local units have no legitimate claim over any specific individuals. Voluntary associations are generally defined as "interest groups," and the tacit assumption is generally made in the literature on interest groups that people having certain interests will seek out those groups most likely to serve them. As previously noted, however, voluntary health associations are faced with a particularly unstructured situation with respect to recruitment, since our society has developed institutionalized methods for dealing with health problems that do not necessarily include voluntary health associations. For these reasons—lack of guidance from the organization and the absence of institutionalized patterns—voluntary associations tend to develop informal patterns of recruitment.

The major informal pattern developed by Foundation Chapters and March of Dimes organizations—the utilization of role relationships which were established for other purposes—has constituted the major focus of this section. It has been shown that each of the three major role relationships utilized represents a pattern of informal organization. Interpersonal relationships, for example, often entail the pattern of reciprocity, in which the basic claim that the recruiter has over the recruit is the fact that he has helped him out in some similar activity in the past. When the obligations of community membership have been utilized, very often the basis for expecting an acceptance is the fact that the recruit has been helped by the Chapter in the past, and therefore feels some sense of unfulfilled obligation. And the obligations attendant upon organizational relationships have been put to maximum use by defining cooperation with Foundation activities as a responsibility of another community organization, and thereby enlisting the support of individuals whose primary obligation is to that organization. All of these patterns are best described as *informal* patterns, since no official provisions are made for them in the various manuals published by the Foundation.

It should not, however, be concluded from the foregoing that the utilization of role relationships is necessarily an approach to the problem of recruitment which is rationally planned by Chapter and March of Dimes leaders. On the contrary, Volunteers generally approach the problem of recruitment in an extremely pragmatic manner, and take advantage of any opportunity which presents itself. Although they are more or less conscious of the fact that role relationships are utilized, they certainly do not describe their behavior in these terms. It is only when information pertaining to a large number of specific instances of recruiting is gathered together and examined systematically that actual patterns emerge.

9

Recruitment of Wall Street Lawyers

ERWIN O. SMIGEL

Organizations develop, in some cases, intricate programs for reaching and attracting recruits. They may advertise in journals and newspapers or other media, employ public relations firms, or form hiring departments which search out recruits with appropriate backgrounds and education. They also develop myths about themselves as highly favorable places to work and have a career. While screening may appear objective, knowing someone in the organization usually helps a great deal. Professor Smigel discusses the various means by which law firms recruit young law students to their organizations.

MYTHS AND LAW OFFICE CHOICE

While opportunity seems to be the most significant factor in job choice, law students often base their choice of jobs, according to placement officers and the evidence obtained from interviews with seniors and individuals in the sample, on personal bias, half truths, myths, fads, and other factors not generally considered important in making such decisions. The recruiter must take these factors into account in a tight job market.

The most frequently heard "reputational myth" involves the notion that one or two firms work much harder and much longer than other large firms. There are legends about the kinds of clients a firm has. Associates in one firm supposedly play bridge all afternoon and then have to work all night. Some offices are known as "friendly" firms where everyone knows everyone else and social life continues outside the firm. Certain offices are known not to hire female or Italian lawyers. These myths can hamper—or help—a firm's recruiting from year to year.

Often a firm is given a "short-term halo" based on the report of a returning alumnus. A dean in charge of placement at one of the Ivy League law schools corroborates this finding:

At one time X firm couldn't get anyone, but now that isn't so. Y firm was going great, but now they can't get anyone. There's usually some student with leadership and he gets the rest to want to go where he goes. To some extent, their choice is based on impressions and sometimes law firms gang up on a firm like Z firm and run them down. Also, students' interests change from year to year—one year it was taxation, the next international law. They try to go to the firm where they can get this kind of work. I think the law student picks his job on the basis of feel—a

Excerpted, with permission, from *The Wall Street Lawyer* (New York: Free Press of Glencoe, 1964; pp. 50–65).

year later, all of them say their firm is the best in the world. They develop strong loyalties.

The interviews bear out the experience of the dean that some choice is based on how a recruit "feels" about an organization. Thus, one associate reported on a position he refused: "While they offered me a job, I didn't feel they wanted me"; and a student respondent, speaking of a partner who had just interviewed him, said, "He's the nicest fellow I've ever met." To the anxious recruit the hiring partner represents a symbol of things to come.

These findings are not intended to mean that law students are completely naive—they are not. Much of their information is correct, is partially correct, or was correct. There appears to be a correlation between the truth of a statement and how close a student is to law review men. Law review students usually get first chance at the best jobs. Their review colleagues from the previous year are already working at preferred positions and this gives the current review man an edge over his fellow student. It is difficult not to believe a persistent rumor especially when one's information comes from a brother student or alumnus, even though the information is second-hand.

Recruitment Techniques

The law firms try to cater to the wishes and stereotypes of the law student, and when appropriate they attempt to manipulate or change them. In a competitive market, with its scarcity of preferred men, students can be selective. Under these circumstances, the firms first sell the idea of practicing in the large organizations to the reluctant or ambivalent recruit. The firms then try to sell themselves individually, hoping that these devices will maximize their chances to attract preferred men.

Image-making Machinery

To change, maintain, or create attractive images, and to assure or reassure the recruit, the firms send notices to the placement offices of the law schools in which they plead innocent to certain detrimental charges and claim desirable attributes. This is part of their "image-making machinery." In order to determine the content of these notices, announcements sent to Harvard Law School were analyzed. Examples from these bulletins illustrate the main theme. Most of them are designed to bolster a desire or defeat a fear.

Some firms belittle students' anxieties about too-early specialization by statements that they are "not as rigidly departmentalized as some very large offices," or by reporting that "insofar as possible, law clerks are given an opportunity to work on problems in those fields in which they are most interested and are not required to select a speciality or confine their work to one field." Another firm emphasizes: "We are departmentalized only to a slight extent and none of our younger men specializes in a particular field unless he requests it."

This anxiety goes hand in hand with concern about not receiving "proper training," and attempts are made to allay both of these fears. Representative notices read:

Men coming with the firm directly out of law school are not assigned to a department of the office until they have been with the firm for one or two years. During this period conscious effort is made to see that these men have the opportunity to work with as many different partners in as many different fields of the law as possible. Emphasis is placed on broad general experience. This will include not only research work and preparation of memoranda of law but also drafting legal papers, participation in conferences and with clients, attendance at court hearings, and several weeks' experience in the managing clerks' department.

Some firms announce they do not use the pool system (through which a lawyer can be assigned to do anything for anybody), hoping this statement will help blunt the senior's fear that he will "get lost" in the large organization. To assure him of his independence one firm declares: "It is the purpose of our training to bring a man to the point where he can work independently as quickly as he is able to." To assure recruits of security, firms announce they do not place men from the outside over old associates; or that they receive requests from corporations for lawyers, so that if individuals are not admitted to partnerships their futures are nevertheless assured. For the shy, or the "consciousness of kind" graduates, one firm writes to Harvard that "30 per cent of our staff came from Harvard."

Other techniques designed to capture the fancy of the recruit are also used, although generally not by the large firms. These inducements are in the nature of extra benefits. They include communiques assuring work in an air-conditioned building, group life and disability insurance, and a contribution toward a hospitalization plan.

These promotional notices to the law schools make a difference. In addition to announcing opportunities, they may weaken the resolve of some men against the large law firm and strengthen favorable predisposition of others. Mainly, they make claims for their firms and assist in creating an image. Over a period of time, however, such promotional activities can have only limited effect. For if the claims are not implemented by commitments which correspond to the reality of the organizational experience, a seriously damaged public image spread by disaffected personnel is the result. In the long run, then, the credibility of the firms' claims depends to a great extent on their readiness to back up their statements by corresponding changes in organizational structure and functioning.

The law schools function not only as communicators of law firm images but also as employment middle-men. They bring together persons needing jobs and firms with positions to be filled. This is a very important function, for there are very few employment agencies which deal with the employment of lawyers. Dean Toepher of Harvard found that "36 per cent of the law school seniors received substantial help from the school's placement services." Occasionally an alumnus asks the placement office to find jobs, but they are rarely able to fill this kind of request. Their work is mainly with the graduating senior. The placement offices solicit firms for jobs, sometimes visit them, and occasionally investigate an employer. As an Ivy League employment official put it: "I don't want these boys to start on the wrong foot. They might get mixed up with some negligence lawyers." One placement officer prepared a list of 237 firms for his students after having circularized a larger list of 700 law firms.

Most law schools keep close contact with their alumni and as their alumni find themselves in positions of power they can be of help to the young graduate. The placement office sees to it that the new graduate and the old can get together. Sometimes they publish a list of alumni and their firms because alumni often give preference to applicants from their own school. Some law schools have local placement offices run by alumni. The men who come to these placement centers usually are not, academically at least, the best men. They are somewhat older and many are from the harder-to-place minority groups. These graduates generally are placed with the small law firms and corporations. Some few lawyers in this study, however, did get jobs with the large law firms through these New York alumni offices.

In addition, the Harvard Law School Association of New York City, Inc., has a placement smoker at the Harvard Club during the Christmas holidays, which is still the main job-hunting season. At one session, for example, former Justice David W. Peck (class of '25) presided and Walter R. Mansfield (class of '35) from Donovan Leisure Newton & Irvine, represented the large firms. He and some other Harvard alumni stated the benefits of different kinds of legal practice and in this way offered job hunters a belated orientation. Also present were a panel of alumni hosts, a number of them from large law firms. At this meeting Harvard, through its alumni, gave its graduates not only an orientation lecture but also job contacts.

At the various placement offices advice is given to both the law firms and the graduates. The firms are told which men the placement officers think best suited for them; the men are told which firms to apply to and how to behave in an interview situation. As we shall see later, this is part of the selecting-out and socialization process. For example, young men have been advised to talk about themselves: "within the realm of strictest modesty, colored to reach the law firm," or to "endeavor to reflect within limits, of course, the personality of the individual you are talking to. If he is conservative, be conservative. If he does all the talking don't interrupt him. If he expects you to talk, talk."

Law School Visits

The law firms send representatives to visit the law schools. More of these men go to Harvard and Yale than to the other schools. Competition, however, has forced some partnerships not only to advertise in the midwest and western national schools but also, to an increasing degree, to send representatives to the universities of Chicago and Michigan. An examination of the placement records at the University of Chicago reveals that few students are actually employed by the eastern large law offices; nor are the men who are hired necessarily at the top of their class. This may be due to a shortage of the types of lawyers the large firms prefer or to the fact that fewer lawyers from the University of Chicago want to go to these big firms. In a sample of the student body at Indiana University law school, no one stated that he wanted to go to Wall Street. Since few graduates from Midwestern law schools go to the large New York firms, and since face-to-face recruitment in this area is not as persistent as it is in the east, little desire has been developed for these firms. This makes it more difficult for the large firms to obtain the kind of men they want from the Midwest.

Interviewing Procedures

The representatives of law firms, when they visit the various universities, interview seniors who are interested in practicing with their firm. The interview takes between fifteen and twenty minutes and the weeding-out process continues. Only 6.1 per cent of the sample (interviewed for this study) were hired directly through school interviews. Another 7.1 per cent were invited to visit the law firms and then were employed.

The hiring partner is usually the man who sees applicants; sometimes he brings with him a recent and well-liked alumnus in the hope that school ties and still-warm contacts will influence the prospective employee. While at the law school, the various representatives of the firms may wine and dine the students they want most. There is a correlation between the difficulty of obtaining men and the efforts of a firm to get them. Each organization would like to obtain the best and most popular man. When a firm succeeds in getting this man, the impression left with the school is that this firm just takes the best men. This makes recruiting easier that year and the next. Seniors at the lower end of the first quarter of the class will then feel it an honor to be accepted by the firm which has hired the top man in the class. A former placement officer is unhappy with the hiring techniques used by the law firms. He reports that, except in their concern for grades, the:

People who hire do not do so as much on logic as on feeling. They have an image of themselves or some other ideal type. It is sort of like a blind date—if they don't like them, they are courteous, but not enthusiastic. If they like them, that's another story. These days they go to all sorts of lengths to get the man they want. They pick one man by first hiring his roommate. It's like fraternity rushing. They work up a lot of early enthusiasm. I don't think this is the right way to go about professional employment. They should proceed to walk handily and slowly. They're not being entirely frank. Their effort not to offend anyone is wrong. They never tell a man, "No, you won't do."—they string people along so as not to offend them. Now they take care of them for the summer—give them a delightful time—because the summer people carry the information back to the school and they may get their man. They also send the most personable junior partner to convince the best law student. I don't like it.

Although some high-pressure recruiting does go on (and reports from the case histories collected confirm this), most of the recruiting is more sedate. Most firms, for example, may interview a special possibility at lunch or dinner, paying his fare to New York and perhaps also the fare of his wife. Nevertheless, the recruitment techniques are not so high-pressure as those often associated with large corporations. Perhaps this will come about. At the moment, however, fancy courting is the exception rather than the rule.

In addition to the employment offices at the universities there are a few lawyer placement services. The two most effective placement offices are in New York and Chicago.

Mrs. Trainer, the former head of the placement office in New York, reports that two-thirds of their jobs were for experienced people and very few requests for men came from the large law firms. (Less than one per cent of the sample was recruited in this manner.)

Almost 29 per cent of our sample of lawyers said their appointments to the law firms were obtained at least in part through influence. This does not mean that they did not have some of the requirements the law offices desire. Because they did and because influence was generally defined by spokesmen for law firms as client pressure, which was relatively rare, the law offices deny this charge and say that influence plays only a very little part in recruitment.

Two per cent of the sample claimed, however, that they received their position because clients had requested it. Another 15.5 per cent reported that other outside contacts had intervened on their behalf. The intensity of the intervention varies from a pressure request for a favor to a more gentle nudge by a social contact. . . . Eleven per cent felt they had obtained their position because they knew someone in the firm.

LIMITS ON RECRUITMENT

Competition for lawyers among the large firms in New York City is limited in two major ways: the firms will not pirate an employee from another law office, and they maintain a gentlemen's agreement to pay the same beginning salary, commonly called the going rate. However, a small number of cases, mostly of editors of law reviews, have been reported in which these agreements were not strictly adhered to. Bargaining, however, was the exception for most members of the sample.

The going rate in 1963 was $7500 for a beginning lawyer, somewhat higher for a man who had been in service or had clerked for a judge or had some other kind of desirable experience. Beginning salaries for each succeeding year are set by a few representatives of the major large firms, usually, one respondent reported, informally at lunch. These people spread the word. Generally this is simple, for members of other firms call the ratemakers just before the hiring season begins and then continue to pass on the information. Eventually it becomes almost common knowledge both to firms and to recruits. The further (in geographical distance) the firm is from the decision as to the going rate, the less necessary it is for it to honor the agreement, unless it is competing for preferred men; then the necessity increases. The large Washington firms also pay the New York going rate; the Boston or Chicago firms pay somewhat less—but they know about the gentlemen's agreement.

The law firms justify standardizing the starting salaries, since they feel that it is best for professional people not to base a most important career decision on initial salaries. This does not mean money is not considered—it is, and in two ways. The competition among the Wall Street lawyers for the same kind of men tends to increase starting salaries. In 1953, for example, it was $4000; in 1963 it was $3500 higher. Ethically, the only real additional monetary inducement the recruiter can offer involves future income. Suggestions of large bonuses or indications that partnerships "are more possible in our firm" are sometimes made. Some of the middle size firms allow associates to bring their own clients into the office, with the right to a share of what is earned from these clients.

Although these basic agreements limit salary competition somewhat, they intensify competition in other respects. The firms compete by raising psychic as well as other kinds of relatively intangible "income." Competition for the preferred laywer is further pointed up by the willingness of law firms to hire some law school seniors, although they are scheduled to go into the armed forces before they can practice, in order to insure the firm of their services after they are discharged.

ORGANIZATIONAL ADAPTATION TO MEET RECRUITMENT NEEDS

Nevertheless, most of the firms studied are old and conservative, proud of both these attributes, and therefore reluctant to extend the limits of what they will do to attract attorneys. Since, however, it is necessary for the immediate and long-run survival of a firm to recruit "proper" legal talent, some changes in the organization of the law firms have been made to meet the demands of the recruit. This has occurred despite the resistance to such change especially on the part of the older, more conservative partners. These men, who often seem to think of themselves as akin to small-town general practitioners, do not like the notion of a segmented, departmentalized, hierarchical organization, regarding it as something not quite professional. They also resent the time reorganization may take away from the practice of the law, and make changes only when they believe that they must. When changes do take place they do not happen quickly.

The Hiring Partner

As previously suggested, law firms no longer believe they can afford to wait until the candidate comes to them. More and more, firms are sending lawyers to visit the major schools to look over the crop for the next year. Harvard, for example, which in 1947 did not have a placement office, was visited in 1950–51 by 64 firms, in 1955–56 by representatives of 185 law firms and corporations, and in 1956–57 by 194 prospective employers. This practice, and the tradition of seeing anyone who wants a job, have led to the formalization of the role of "hiring partner," who is generally one of the most attractive and personable of the partners. Creation of this position is an early attempt by a firm to put its best foot forward. The hiring partner is needed not only to attract graduates but also to save the valuable time of other partners. While visiting the various law schools, the hiring partner weeds out the poorer prospects and invites the better ones to visit the firm in New York. The hiring partner is also better able than his colleagues to evaluate the candidates, since he sees a good percentage of all applicants.

In addition to the men invited to visit firms, there is, each year, between the Thanksgiving and Christmas holidays, a mass migration of other young lawyers to Wall Street. Many third-year students making the rounds of the large law firms do not know all the firms; they tend to visit only the offices with the best reputations. Thus, these offices get the greatest number of applicants and presumably have a better chance of obtaining the best men. Thirty-six per cent of that portion of the sample who were asked how they obtained their job reported that they had come to the firm "off the street" during the hiring season and were interviewed and eventually employed. This figure, however, is misleading as an index of what most large law firms do since two firms account for 54 per cent of the "off-the-street recruiting." . . .

A lawyer who no longer works for a large firm sketches his job-hunting experiences. "It was pretty much a pavement-pounding proposition" and he continues to say that his choice was made "largely out of ignorance." He had friends who were scattered around the downtown firms but he found that the ideas he received from them and from the partners who interviewed him in the firms he went to see "turned out to be erroneous." He doesn't think you can really know much about a firm unless you are part of it. . . .

Graduating seniors report that they hear of firms not only through rumors or friends or acquaintances who work for them but also through an organization's famous client, or the reputation of some of its partners. The late Randolph Paul, for example, was a well-known and respected tax specialist and because of this (even though most of his time was spent in the firm's Washington office) he was able to attract some additional men to visit Paul, Weiss, Rifkind, Wharton & Garrison. There are many other examples.

Formalizing Office Interviewing Systems

Some firms—in self defense but also to maintain good will and a good reputation with the law schools and the legal profession, while at the same time continuing their work and recruitment—have set up elaborate systems to take care of the estimated three hundred to four hundred candidates seen during the year. One large office developed the following system:

Any lawyer who applies for a position is interviewed; no one is turned away. Ten to twelve associates are designated as interviewers. The receptionist tries to spread the work around. Each associate rates the candidate as a "one," "two," or "three." If rated "one," the candidate is sent to a partner who sits on the hiring committee. If rated "two," the applicant may be "all right" but the associate does not think him acceptable; but he is also sent to a partner—though generally he is given less time. A "three" rating means that the applicant is rejected; even rejected candidates, however, are sent to a partner, though not necessarily one who is a member of the hiring committee. The partner spends five minutes with a "three" and then sends him on his way—but he tries to leave the applicant with a favorable impression of the firm. If the partner disagrees with the associate, he refers the candidate to a member of the hiring committee. The man rated "one" is sent to this committee immediately, and at least three people on the committee see this applicant. If the candidate passes this test, then the hiring partners have him see other partners.

Not all firms have such an elaborate procedure. One law office assigns fourteen partners, three different ones each day, to do the screening. This procedure reflects the view that better public relations are maintained if partners rather than associates do the initial interviewing. If one of these partners passes favorably on an applicant, he is sent to two or more partners. Eventually he is interviewed by the hiring partner, who sees all candidates and compares them—a process which requires valuable time but is thought to be necessary and worth while.

Summer Boarders

Another device of the large law offices to further selective recruitment is to invite second-year law students to clerk with them during the summer. Six per cent of the sample had been "summer boarders" in the firms that finally employed them. Most firms do not really need these summer boarders as workers, but their value is threefold: the boarders get to know the firm; they provide the firm with a preview of their ability; if they are good and are liked, they are offered jobs when they graduate; in any event, they return to the law schools and report what they have seen—hopefully, reporting favorably.

When a firm makes a major revision in its organization because of recruitment, it does so to meet the demands of a number of candidates; generally, however, the change also satisfies other internal requirements.

The Firm as a Postgraduate Law School

One request most applicants make of law firms is that they provide opportunities for training, a request closely related to the seniors' fear that they will be forced into quick specialization. Candidates are told that diversified work will be available and the firms try to make good on this commitment. But when an associate who has been successful in one kind of work becomes known as "good" or "expert" in that particular area of law, more of his colleagues then send him work in his acquired "specialty," so that soon he becomes an expert in fact. Thus, it is costly for the firm to change his functions, and partners who have been relieved of this particular job are reluctant to take it on again. Consequently, the associate remains in his special area and does not get the broad training he desires. More and more firms, however, finding themselves committed to training their new men (because it is a good recruiting device, to be sure, but also because many partners think that it helps to make better lawyers and therefore benefits the firm), are beginning to further formalize their educational programs. In a sense these firms are becoming postgraduate vocational schools.

One of the largest law partnerships is more formalized than the others in this respect. The hiring partner in this office, who had devised the educational program, found that it was attracting candidates and was becoming known in law schools and throughout the "Street." . . .

Additional Adjustments

As they debate the merits of large firms, recruits often complain that "you don't get ahead fast enough—it takes forever to make partner." Some few firms assign the title "Junior Partner" to people who would normally be senior associates, perhaps creating the illusion that the associates are moving up faster than they actually are—and this illusion may aid the firm in its recruitment efforts. Many organizations have initiated rules and other changes to reassure ambitious recruits. For example, candidates fear competition from relatives of partners, and members of a firm may fear the possibility that a colleague's unqualified son may be taken into the firm as a partner. Hence the increasing adoptions of rules against nepotism.

Anxiety about being lost in the giant firm is often mentioned by both the applicant and the young associate. The pool system, although it functions formally as a training device, adds to that concern. In addition many associates do not feel that this plan for work assignment is "professional." Because of the disapproval of the assignment of bright young lawyers to more or less mechanical jobs, some offices are doing away with the pool system.

Increased Employment of Minority Groups

During World War II many large firms began to accept Jewish lawyers as associates at an accelerated rate. Those respondents I queried, when asked why this change occurred, most frequently said that it was due to the impetus of the Fair Employment Practice Act. That, however, is probably not the main reason, except as passage of such a law reflects changing public opinion. A dean from one of the Ivy League law schools suggests that the Jewish lawyers now coming in greater numbers from Ivy League colleges and the best law schools are in a different position from their predecessors. He points out that discrimination "is becoming less and less of a problem. In almost every case it is not being Jewish that throws a man back but lack of polish that accompanies anyone who is half a generation away from another country."

Jewish lawyers who are employed by these large offices usually come from the top of their classes in the Ivy League colleges and law schools, and the firms, initially at any rate, hired them mainly because competition made it difficult always to secure an attorney with all the preferred background factors. Employment of Jewish lawyers probably may continue to be a problem to both the Jewish law students and to the firms. The law students will want to know if some Jews will be promoted to partnership. And, although many large firms do have Jewish partners, the question will remain as to whether the giant firms plan to restrict this practice by some sort of quota system. . . .

Part III

Career Motivations
within the Organization

Career motivations never quite stand still. The shifting in direction and objects of motivations is accounted for by the changing conditions of organizational life and begins upon entering the organization. The career motivations that lead to recruitment may change once the person becomes involved in the organizational career. The major condition that changes the objects of career motivations is the person's stage of career with its associated problems and contingencies. He may be at the stage where many prospects for advancement stimulate him into working hard and striving for a better position. He may have arrived at "a" top or be leveled off before reaching this limit. This condition generates motivations to hold down a position until retirement, slow down work (if safe), or look elsewhere for a different career. When his performance is judged poor by others, he may lack advancement or be demoted, which is likely to undercut his motivation to work hard and continue pursuing the organizational career.

As the person advances, his motivations to achieve certain goals of the organization are continually being modified by current and changing associations with people in and outside the organization and by his increasing knowledge about the organization's activities and reward systems (Marcson). He revises the "best" goals to pursue for a person at his stage. For example, while young his goals may focus on the basic work of the organization. Later they may (and typically do) become administrative goals and perhaps empire building. New goals of work and career may be

111

literally forced on him, thus forcing a shift in motivations. Truly the person's motivations toward work, goals, and career levels and movements must keep up with his career as it changes. If they do not, he will be out of line with where he is and what is expected of him. This condition makes him liable to the dissatisfactions that come with discrepancies between what he expects and what he is supposed to expect and will, in fact, obtain among the alternative career directions and top levels available to him at his stage.

The diversity of kinds of specific careers and their associated work and goals varies with the size and kind of organization. The person's abilities, training, and sponsors condition how many of these career options he may be able to take. These factors, by providing opportunity, engender the motivation necessary to take them. The army, for example, has many diverse kinds of specific working careers for its members to pursue. There are, however, several kinds of general types of organizational careers with fairly distinctive, associated motivations, as admirably summarized by Kornhauser, which occur no matter what is entailed in the person's particular work and organization.

The person may be seeking an organizational career of *service* to people, organization, and/or country, whether he is a highly trained professional, an expert, or merely a willing worker. The service career may range from a missionary to fee-for-service career with consequent variation in motivations. The person may be a *careerist* (see Wilensky and Janowitz), seeking only to reach the top of the hierarchy, as constituted, as fast as possible in order to have power and control and to better his general social condition and rank. He may be motivated principally toward a *professional* career among colleagues, wherever they may be found in the world, using the organization as only a base of operations. He may seek a *simple organizational career* of constant work with financial and job security, whether white or blue collar. This career is trimmed with modest aspirations, if any, to lower or middle level supervisory positions, which motivations themselves can become easily cooled off by lack of promotion and opportunity (Chinoy). In these careers, seniority and its security benefits provide the movement and the motivated goals, unless seniority ends in loss of current position and salary in a particular organization (Seidman). The person may have *no career motivations* and simply flounder around between jobs within and between organizations, oblivious to or ignorant of the career each job might offer him.

Motivation toward these various types of careers may be initially generated from boyhood ambitions, current social values, religion, geographical regions linked with rural and urban values, more recognized kinds of success, and goals of various professional, educational, and trade schools, before being modified by colleagues and arrangements within the organization. Therefore, the modification that occurs after joining the organization is a result of past motivations and present shiftings occurring within the organizational career.

Since career motivations are ever-shifting, it is apparent to organizations that motivations can be molded to suit their requirements of a proportionate distribution of people into various types of careers. Their tool is to develop incentive or reward systems to keep the motivations for particular careers at constant levels of intensity. By this maneuver they maintain the division of labor relatively intact even as it is changing. Organizations may also carefully recruit people from a sector of society or particular educational institutions with the right motivation for careers (the sons of officers get commissions readily in the army). They also may develop indoctrination programs of a great variety to instill a necessary kind of motivation in the person beginning a career. Some organizations regularly send their men back to schools (colleges or in-service schools) for re-indoctrination on the prime goals of the organization and their associated career potentials.

Sometimes, as a way of controlling its members' motivations to work hard and thereby move ahead in the career, organizations will develop elaborate hierarchies for advancement (Dreyfuss). These hierarchies can even be artificial in the sense of not corresponding to the division of work and its relative evaluations on skill and prestige. This excessive gradation keeps employees scrambling in the competition for advances and benefits of the organizational career instead of relaxing and grouping for confrontations with higher management on working conditions. If employees realize what is happening, it dampens their motivation to pursue a career that gets them nowhere.

Another way of controlling its members' motivations (at the other end of the gradation range) is to offer to most employees a career at one organizational level with slight salary increases for seniority. Thus, from the start, their aspirations are cooled down and they learn to pursue the one goal of their job and hope they last long enough for the salary increments.

In any event, whether careers are spoken of in general or specific types, motivations toward career and work are intimately linked. Sometimes they are discernibly different and alternatively boost each other, with incentive systems for work that hold out career movements as rewards and career rewards that set the person up for new work. Sometimes they are virtually the same—to work for one's career is to do what the organization wants (for example, basic research). A formal theory of careers must lead to describing, understanding, and accounting for these relations in career and work motivations.

10

Professional Incentives in Industry

WILLIAM KORNHAUSER

Organizations offer many general types of careers and
develop incentive systems to motivate their employees to
follow these careers. An organization has various incentive
systems because it depends, for its effectiveness, on a
certain distribution of motivations toward its work.
However, while motivations toward career and work are
intimately linked, they may be either discernibly different
or virtually the same. Professor Kornhauser discusses the
difference between professional and organizational orientations and incentives and considers the variation in incentives in different organizational contexts.

As a professional, an individual acquires stature from his colleagues in the
profession. As an employee, he acquires status from his superiors in the
organization. A series of accomplishments and rewards in the profession
constitutes a "successful" professional career. A series of progressively
higher positions in the organization constitutes a "successful" bureaucratic
career. The contingencies of a professional career are not the same as those
of a bureaucratic career, and may conflict with them. Therefore, career
lines of professionals in large organizations influence their motivation for
professional work. The capacity of the work establishment to define the status
and career of its professional employees is at the same time a way of motivating them toward the organization's objectives. The capacity of the profession
to get its standards of performance incorporated into the organization's set
of rewards and incentives is a major way of sustaining these standards.
Organizational and professional incentives may be in part incompatible, so
that a problem of integration of incentive systems arises.

We shall first specify the distinction between professional and organizational orientations and incentives, and then consider their variations in
different kinds of organizations and professions.

WORK ORIENTATIONS, FUNCTIONS, AND INCENTIVES

A professional employee may be strongly oriented toward the profession
in which he has been trained, the organization for which he works, both the
profession and the organization, or neither of them. These types of orientation
have been distinguished in several organizational contexts. Reissman

Excerpted, with permission, from *Scientists in Industry* (Berkeley: University of California Press,
1962; pp. 117–56).

distinguished all four types in his study of civil service specialists in a state agency:

Functional Bureaucrat—One who is oriented towards and seeks his recognition from a given professional group outside of rather than within the bureaucracy. . . . He is active in his professional societies and seeks appreciation and recognition on the basis of his professional specialities.

Job Bureaucrat—He is immersed entirely within the structure. Professional skills only provide the necessary entrance qualifications and determine the nature of the work to be done. He seeks recognition along departmental rather than professional lines.

Specialist Bureaucrat—Though he resembles the first type in his professional orientations, he exhibits a greater awareness of and identification with the bureaucracy. He seeks his recognition from the department and the people with whom he works rather than from like-professionals who are privately employed.

Service Bureaucrat—He entered civil service primarily to realize certain personally-held goals which center about rendering service to a certain [nonprofessional] group. The bureaucracy offers a framework through which he can best function and his task is one of utilizing that mechanism to achieve his goals.[1]

Blau also distinguished between a professional and nonprofessional orientation among specialists in a state agency.[2]

Marvick distinguished three of the four types of orientation in his study of a military research agency:

Specialist orientation is one in which professional expertise is given primacy. Stress is placed on furthering a career in the profession, avoiding executive posts, and not being overly concerned whether professional employment is found in public or private organizations. Preoccupied with matters of skill gratification, this type tends to be indifferent and detached in respect to the material benefits and social life of the work establishment.

Institutional orientation is "place-bound"; gratifications are sought in the personal benefits available in the work establishment. Stress is placed on a career within the work establishment. This type tends to be indifferent to benefits that are derived from the application of skills to a task.

Hybrid orientation is neither "skill-bound" nor "place-bound." Rather, stress is placed on acquiring immediate personal advantages, such as power, prestige, and income. It is "opportunistic," in contradistinction to professional or organizational loyalty.[3]

In a study of scientists in a federal research agency, Marvick's distinction between "specialist" and "institutionalist" is related to scientific performance.[4]

Wilensky distinguished four types of staff specialists in trade unions:

[1] Leonard Reissman, "A Study of Role Conceptions in Bureaucracy," *Social Forces*, XXVII (1949), 305–10.
[2] Peter Blau, *The Dynamics of Bureaucracy* (Chicago: University of Chicago Press, 1955).
[3] Adapted from Dwaine Marvick, *Career Perspectives in a Bureaucratic Setting*, Michigan Governmental Studies, No. 27 (Ann Arbor: Bureau of Government, Institute of Public Administration, University of Michigan, 1954), *passim*.
[4] Donald C. Pelz, "Some Social Factors Related to Performance in a Research Organization," *Administrative Science Quarterly*, I (1956), 312.

[The Professional Service type is oriented toward the profession.] His main job problems and frustrations can be interpreted in terms of a conflict between the requirements of the job (and/or the values of union officials), on the one hand; and a professional ethos—expressed in a desire to render competent, efficient, objective, technical service of which professional colleagues outside the union would approve —on the other.

[The Careerist type is] highly identified with the hierarchy of his union and is oriented towards a career within it. He has . . . very little if any professional identi-fication. His job satisfactions center around the chance for social mobility via the union career.

What is unique in [the Politico's] role orientation is a basic preoccupation with the political process. . . . The Politico strives for influence and power as ends in them-selves.

The Missionary is oriented in his job towards some more abstract concept of the labor movement; he is highly identified with an outside political or religious-political group. [He is not closely identified with either the organization or his field of specialization.][5]

Gouldner,[6] Caplow and McGee,[7] and Lazarsfeld and Thielens[8] have distinguished between professional and organizational orientations among academic men. Borrowing Merton's terms, Gouldner refers to these two types as "cosmopolitans" and "locals":

Cosmopolitans: those low on loyalty to the employing organization, high on commit-ment to specialized role skills, and likely to use an outer [professional] reference group orientation.

Locals: those high on loyalty to the employing organization, low on commitment to specialized role skills, and likely to use an inner [organizational] reference group orientation.[9]

Evidence collected on the faculty members of a small liberal arts college shows that the criteria (organizational loyalty, reference group, commitment to skill) for differentiating the two types are related in the predicted direction.[10]

These several typologies may be summarized according to the distinctions they make between the professional orientation (*P*) and the organizational orientation (*O*).

This typology of orientations can be used to analyze two kinds of prob-lems. One concerns the individual: how he comes to adopt one orientation rather than another, how he changes his orientation, and the consequences of his orientation for his personal career and other aspects of his life. The other treats these orientations in their significance for work establishment and

[5] Harold L. Wilensky, *Intellectuals in Labor Unions* (Glencoe, Ill.: Free Press, 1956), 129, 145, 153, 114.
[6] Alvin W. Gouldner, "Cosmopolitans and Locals: Toward an Analysis of Latent Social Roles," *Administrative Science Quarterly*, II (1957–1958), 281–306, 444–80.
[7] Theodore Caplow and Reece McGee, *The Academic Marketplace* (New York: Basic Books, 1958).
[8] Paul F. Lazarsfeld and Wagner Thielens, Jr., *The Academic Mind* (Glencoe, Ill.: Free Press, 1958).
[9] Gouldner, *op. cit.*, 290.
[10] *Ibid.*, 294.

profession. This interest leads to analysis of the *distribution* of orientations within work establishment and profession.

	Type I P O + −	Type II P O − +	Type III P O + +	Type IV* P O − −
Reissman	Functional bureaucrat	Job bureaucrat	Specialist bureaucrat	Service bureaucrat
Marvick	Specialist	Institutionalist		Hybrid
Wilensky	Professional service expert	Careerist		Missionary, politico
Gouldner	Cosmopolitan	Local		

* Type IV has two subtypes: those who identify with a third group, such as a social movement (e.g., the "missionary" and the "service bureaucrat"); and those who, for opportunistic reasons, avoid close ties to any group (e.g., the "politico" and the "hybrid").

There is a strong tendency in the literature on personal orientations and social structure to argue for the differential significance of only one type of orientation for a given social structure. For example, it is postulated that a "democratic type" is required for a "democratic polity." This approach is useful mainly in its power to show the dominant psychological aspect of a social system. It is weak, however, in ignoring two obvious facts: (1) there are multiple types of orientation in any complex social system; and (2) there are multiple functions in any complex social system. In order to take account of these facts, we shall assume that *a complex system depends for its effectiveness on a certain distribution of types of orientation*, rather than on only one type. Specifically, we shall argue that three of the types of orientation designated above make *distinct* contributions to a work establishment, each by facilitating the contributions of the others. Our premise is that the division of labor in an organization calls for a diversity of work orientations.

There are at least three major functions to be performed if a professional specialty is to make a satisfactory contribution to the larger enterprise of which it is a part: (1) *production* of technical results (e.g., scientific research); (2) *administration* of the conditions under which technical results are produced; (3) *application and communication* of technical results. Correlatively, it may be hypothesized that those who have a predominantly professional orientation tend to be strong producers of technical results; those who have a predominantly organizational orientation tend to assume administrative responsibilities; and those who seek to combine orientations to both organization and profession are especially capable of facilitating the utilization of technical results. The rest of this section presents evidence for this proposition. Numerous studies are cited because the agreement among them makes it possible to place considerable confidence in the results in spite of the qualifications that must be attached to each.

In a liberal arts college, Gouldner found that faculty members who were strongly oriented to their profession but not to the college were more likely to be researchers than teachers or administrators; those who were strongly committed to the college but not to their profession were more likely to be administrators than teachers or researchers; and those who were committed to their profession but also to the college were as likely to be teachers as researchers, less likely to be administrators.[11] ...

In a government medical research organization, Davis found that scientific performance was closely related to a professional orientation, but not to an organizational orientation or to a mixed orientation. In a military research agency, Marvick found that the professionally oriented wanted the agency to emphasize basic research, whereas the organizationally oriented favored research administration as "the main thing the agency should be doing." Those who were "hybrids" favored application (military research) as the major function.

In industrial research organizations, we find a similar pattern of career orientations among scientists and engineers, corresponding to their primary functions of production of new research, administration of research, and application of research through development and technical service. One of the firms we studied has formalized these career orientations by establishing three ladders of promotion in the research organization: one for researchers, another for supervisors, and a third for technical service people. Interviews with several members of each ladder show that those on the research ladder are strongly oriented toward advancement in their fields of specialization, those on the administrative ladder are primarily identified with the company, and those on the technical service ladder are likely to have a more mixed orientation.

This same study further subdivided the 622 scientists and engineers, none of whom occupied positions in higher management, into two groups on the basis of their job assignments: those engaged primarily in scientific and engineering work, and those in supervisory or administrative work. It will be shown later that despite considerable variation, depending upon the importance of research to a firm, the balance of incentives in industry as a whole is generally heavily weighted on the organizational rather than the professional side. Normally the highest rewards go to those who assume administrative responsibility. In consequence, because of the increasingly large numbers of technical professionals in industry, many are doomed to disappointment even when they lean toward an organizational orientation, given the limited number of managerial positions. Those who have a strong professional orientation are subject to a different kind of frustration, for their opportunities to gain high rewards *without* undertaking administrative tasks are even more limited. Here lies a clue to the relatively high level of job dissatisfaction expressed by industrial scientists and engineers. In the total

[11] Gouldner, *op. cit.*, 454–55.

sample of 622 scientists and engineers, only one-third stated that they were "very well satisfied" with their present jobs. Other studies show that this figure is low compared to other nonmanual groups in industry, including office employees, office supervisors, sales personnel, and foremen.

Compared with research scientists and engineers who do not have administrative duties, scientists and engineers in administrative positions are somewhat less dissatisfied with their jobs, more satisfied with their pay, more optimistic about their chances for advancement, and have more favorable attitudes toward their company. The higher morale of the administrators is solidly based in reality, for many more of them earn high salaries, have had a recent promotion, and participate in decisions affecting their work assignments. ...

Only insofar as there are different types of incentives to link appropriate orientations to the several functions of a research organization can it command satisfactory levels of participation from its members.

ORGANIZATIONAL CONTEXTS OF INCENTIVES

If the work establishment permits its professional employees to be identified solely with the profession, and to treat the organization merely as a place of work, then it will not be able to motivate sufficiently its professional people to help achieve the goals of the organization. In consequence, professional contributions to men will be small and turnover high. If on the other hand the organization seeks to stress organizational incentives at the expense of professional incentives, then it will not be able to acquire a satisfactory professional performance from its specialists. In short, the work establishment faces the dilemma of seeking too much integration of its professionals into the organization and thereby losing their professional worth, versus granting them too much autonomy and thereby weakening their contribution to the organization.

Now the manner in which an organization faces this dilemma depends on the type of organization. At one extreme, the organization whose primary goal is the provision of a professional service contains specialists with stronger professional orientations than does an organization whose primary product is not professional. Therefore, the university can permit the relevant professions to define the status and reputation of its professional employees to a greater extent than can the business or government establishment. The latter, in turn, will rely more on organizational incentives to motivate their professional employees. We will show this by comparing universities, industrial firms, and government agencies in their systems of incentives.

University, Industry, and Government

The university, industrial firm, and government agency vary in the emphasis they give to basic research, application, and administration, and therefore in the use of professional and organizational incentives. The university encourages its scientists to do basic research by giving primacy to the standards and judgments of the scientific community. Industry, on the other hand, relies on an incentive system in line with its economic purposes to motivate its scientists and engineers for research application. Since the government has a greater diversity of functions than either the university or industry, including contributing to the public health, safety, and prosperity, it tends to use more professional incentives than industry but less than the university; and more organizational incentives than the university but less than industry. The university provides greater opportunities to conduct and publish research free from restrictions, and to win appointments and promotions on the basis of professional reputation and accomplishments, whereas industry and secondarily government provide greater opportunities for high salaries and for advancement into executive positions.

Perhaps the single most important professional incentive is freedom to pursue one's own research. . . .

Where the university offers freedom in work as a primary incentive to pursue basic science, industry offers large resources as an inducement (as well as means) to work in commercial applications of science and freedom from teaching. . . .

A second line of evidence that professional incentives are stronger in the university, and organizational incentives are stronger in industry, concerns the bases and kinds of rewards. . . .

Generally, appointments and promotions in the university are based to a considerable extent on professional reputation. Not one of the industrial research establishments we investigated indicated that promotions were made on the basis of reputation in the field. Universities, on the other hand, do not provide strong organizational or economic incentives. The salary scale for scientists and engineers is lowest in the university and highest in industry, with government in a middle position, in spite of the fact that the quality of scientists is higher in the university. . . .

To summarize the argument to this point, we first distinguished between organizational and professional *orientations, functions,* and *incentives.* The appropriate incentives link the functions with the corresponding orientations. Then we showed the greater importance of professional orientations, incentives, and functions in the university compared with industry and government, and in the research-minded faculty compared with the teaching-centered institution. In the following section, we shall examine variations among industrial organizations in the emphasis they give to organizational and professional incentives for their scientists and engineers.

Industrial Contexts

By and large, industry tends to slight professional incentives in favor of organizational incentives and rewards, even for its research scientists and engineers. Industrial establishments tend to stress organizational incentives for at least two reasons. Long and satisfactory use of organizational incentives for other job categories leads organizations to resist changing the structure of incentives to accommodate professional employees. Second, the incentive system is not merely a means for eliciting desired contributions; it also embodies the organization's values, so that different (e.g., professional) incentive systems are viewed as competing sources of loyalty. . . .

This statement fails to recognize the several sources of constraint on the research worker to de-emphasize professional concerns in favor of organizational concerns. One major pressure stems from the dependence of the industrial researcher on management for promotions in the research department. Consequently, even when the individual's primary interest is in his profession, his path of advancement is most immediately through the organization. The dependence of research workers on management for advancement is like that of "staff" on "line," as described by Dalton[12] and others.

A second major pressure on scientists and engineers to respond to organizational cues stems from the widespread practice in industry of using the research and engineering departments as sources of recruitment for other parts of the company. All the establishments we studied use their research departments in this manner. . . .

Many companies now have training programs to help engineers become managers. Another device with the same objective is job rotation to acquaint engineers with all major aspects of company operations. Often engineers are sent back to the university to take courses relevant to management activities. "Technical forums" sponsored by the company are used to give managers the opportunity to look over engineers as potential managers. In light of this stress on advancement of engineers and scientists into management, small wonder that many people originally recruited into research come to aspire to management positions. . . .

The distribution of orientations is also related to career stage: as those on the lower status levels advance to higher posts, there is a corresponding change in orientation. Professional people in industry (and government) are attracted to administrative posts not only because the extrinsic rewards are greater there than in technical work. Managerial responsibilities also may appear to be more challenging than professional work. It may sound paradoxical to say that managing may appeal to scientists and engineers as promising greater scope to their creative energies than does research and development. But the paradox is resolved once it is realized the great extent to which the operations of an industrial work establishment typically limit the scope for creative work on the part of professional people. Work often tends to be of a routine character that technicians could and do perform; controls tend to be tight; opportunities to develop new ideas and skills often

---

[12] Melville Dalton, "Conflicts between Staff and Line Managerial Officers," *American Sociological Review*, XV (1950), 342–51.

are limited; the chance to write and publish research findings usually is restricted; time to keep up on new developments in the field by reading and talking with colleagues is small; and so forth. In study after study, scientists and engineers in industry indicate that they think their special competence is not adequately utilized. . . .

Interviews show that the main orientation of the supervisory staff is toward the organization and advancement into higher management; the main orientation of men on the professional ladder is toward basic science and advancement within the profession; and the main orientation of members of the technical-service staff is toward application and utilization of research results, and advancement in both organization and profession. In other words, organizational incentives are more important for research supervisors, professional incentives for researchers, and the two types of incentives are of roughly equal significance for those in technical services and development work.

CONCLUSION

Professions and organizations are effective in achieving their goals only insofar as they can induce and sustain satisfactory levels of participation. However, they differ in the kind of participation each needs to realize its objectives. The need for participation, and for appropriate incentives, depends on the kind of work to be done and on the nature of the standards to be upheld.

An important aspect of this problem is the potential incompatibility of requirements for participation. For example, business firms seek to increase the commitment of their participants, so that the individual's main orientation, including his hopes for advancement, lies within the establishment. If, however, these participants are scientists or engineers, they also face demands for loyalty from their professions, which need member commitment in order to protect their own values and standards. As a result, interaction between professions and organizations produces competing orientations, career lines, and incentive systems.

Unless scientists are primarily concerned with their professional allegiance, they will be less likely to uphold scientific standards or to aspire to scientific excellence. Where scientific standards and aspirations are weak, the quality of scientific performance will not be high. Hence, where industry dampens the motivation of scientists to participate in outside professional activities, industrial research suffers.

At the same time, specialized organizations have their own needs, which cannot be served by professional competence alone. Industry, for example, requires coördination and utilization of a given expertise with other aspects of the firm. Hence, it needs other kinds of participation by scientists in addition to research excellence. Some scientists (and engineers) must be capable of lending administrative direction to research consistent with the firm's goals, while other technical specialists are needed to help bring research results to operational fruition. But insofar as research administration and utilization are stressed, research creativity and the professional commitment upon which it depends are weakened. Thus the tension between profession and organization becomes a tension within the organization itself.

One major area of conflict and accommodation lies in the relation between professional and organizational incentive systems. The scientific profession seeks contributions to knowledge by soliciting research papers for professional meetings and journals, and by rewarding intellectual excellence with honors and esteem. The industrial firm seeks contributions to production and sales by soliciting new or improved devices, and by rewarding commercial success with promotions in a hierarchy of status, income, and authority. The strain between these incentive systems may be counteracted in various ways, depending on the importance of excellence in research for the commercial achievements of the particular firm, and on the technical competence of the particular professional group. Where research is of great significance to the firm, it generally acquires a high-quality technical staff, which in turn exerts pressure on the company to provide opportunities for professional achievement. Thus we find in the first-rate industrial research organizations increasing use of professional incentives in combination with established organizational incentives. These adaptations of industrial firms to professional demands include time off for attendance at professional meetings sponsored by professional associations, as well as at additional meetings provided by the company itself; payment of professional dues; tuition refunds for further professional training; more liberal publication policies; professional ladders of advancement, which grant greater freedom in research rather than greater administrative responsibility; and so on. Professional people in turn have adapted to organizational demands by conforming to industrial routines; accepting responsibility for seeking commercially feasible devices; frequently assuming administrative positions; working closely with operations; and so on.

By means of these and other accommodations on both sides, the strain between professional and organizational requirements for participation is mitigated. The underlying conflict remains, of course, and is a continuing source of frustration on both sides.

11

Military Career Motivations

MORRIS JANOWITZ

The shifting career motivations of people in an organization may at times account for a historical shift in the characteristic motivation of its organizational leaders. In the army, we have witnessed a change from a career based on missionary zeal before World War II to the recent growth of careerism—the evaluation of the conditions of employment, not the goal of the organization. Professor Janowitz discusses the change in motivations for the selection of a military career and the implications of this change for the intelligence or competitiveness of those who choose military careers.

Given the prevailing emphasis on commercial values and business success in the United States, selection of a military career is often believed to be a weak career choice. Among segments of the civilian public, entry into the military is often thought of as an effort to avoid the competitive realities of civil society. In the extreme view, the military profession is thought to be a berth for mediocrity. Contrariwise, many a military officer sees his career as filling some special mission, rather than as just a job. Since civilian society and its political leaders must rely so heavily on the advice and competence of professional soldiers, these conflicting images are a source of extensive tension.

The selection of a military career, like the selection of any career, represents the interplay of opportunity plus a complex of social and personality factors. In one sense, to say that the military is a mediocre career choice is an expression of a liberal ideology which holds that, since war is essentially destructive, the best minds are attracted to more positive endeavors. Even the more judicious statement that the military has not been able to attract its share of alert minds, is almost a truism. All elite groups could make use of more effective personnel. The military profession has produced individual leaders of great stature, and after twenty years of public neglect—between World War I and World War II—the number of outstanding officers who were available was quite remarkable.

In assessing the selection of a military career, two rather specific empirical questions could be investigated. First, is it true that during the period in which the 1910–50 leaders were recruited, the military profession attracted persons whose basic intelligence was not equal to the intelligence of those in

Excerpted, with permission, from *The Professional Soldier* (New York: Free Press of Glencoe, 1960; pp. 104–24).

other professions? Second, is the issue perhaps not mainly one of sheer intelligence, but of motivation? Could it be that the underlying motivation for a military career is an expression of "careerism," whereby a person seeks what he believes to be a noncompetitive and protected route to the achievement of limited ambitions?

Only a partial answer can be given to our first question as to the intellectual level of officer candidates. For the Army, recruitment into the top military leadership until World War II was overwhelmingly through entrance into West Point. By 1950, however, the concentration of West Point graduates in the Army leadership group had decreased to about one-half, plus another 10 per cent from those selected military schools whose graduates were eligible for direct commission. In 1950 the concentration of West Pointers in the Air Force leadership group was roughly the same as in the Army. By contrast, recruitment into the Navy via Annapolis has been, and remains, almost exclusively the general rule.

It is insufficient to focus merely on intellectual skills and academic performance. Success in middle- and top-level assignments in the military, or for that matter in any bureaucratic organization, requires intellectual skills and training different from those which the colleges afford. The fact that follow-up studies in the military demonstrate a low correlation between academic performance and career advancement is inconclusive, since this would be typical of many other professions, and certainly of the development of elite leadership.

With regard to our second question, the evidence contradicts civilian assumptions concerning career motives of the professional soldier, especially for the first quarter of the century. Up to the period of 1950, the meaning of career choice for the military elite suggests the following hypothesis: While for many persons, and perhaps even for a majority, the military career represented the pursuit of a relatively secure, safe, and promising prospect, more or less similar to other professions, for a substantial minority, at least, the choice of a military career was a strong decision. To speak of a strong career choice means that a person feels that a particular occupation is singularly important to him, since he believes that it will give him the rewards and gratifications he wants.

For such persons, the military career had overtones of a "calling," with a sense of mission. It represented a deliberate rejection of what was believed to be the prosaic and limited horizons of the business world. In the urban commercial centers the selection of a military career was frowned upon. Yet, through their families many urban candidates were exposed to an atmosphere in which being a soldier was thought to be honorable. But it was the rural background that gave special meaning to, and legitimized the military career. In the hinterlands the notion still persisted that there was glory other than that to be gained from profits in the market place. The virtues of physical prowess, social protocol, and a general ideal of service to the community were still valued. The military career offered the strong-willed an opportunity to achieve these values; and, in turn, such career motivation made it possible for the armed services to perpetuate the martial spirit.

THE EXPRESSION OF MISSIONARY ZEAL

Four motive patterns, singly and in combination, were of consequence for those who rose to the level of general or admiral by 1950: tradition, or more precisely family and social inheritance; sheer desire for education and social advancement, with or without a career commitment to the military; experience in a military setting; and "boyhood" ambition. The potential officer's career choice was further influenced not only by his feeling that the armed forces had a vital function, but by the fact that the military had offered an adequate and respectable level of personal security in peacetime. Nor should one overlook the intermingling of these motives with a diffuse desire for an active, athletic-type career.

While the relative importance of different motives is difficult, if not impossible, to reconstruct, one can infer that the effects of tradition and social inheritance were very widespread among those who entered the military profession before 1920. . . .

Social inheritance meant, first of all, having a father who was a professional soldier. Social inheritance also meant having relatives who were military officers, and family tradition. Often, family traditions were transmitted via uncle, cousins, or other relatives. In each case a personal relation between an officer and the youngster had been at work. One is struck by the number of officers who report that stories by and about their grandfathers helped influence them decisively. . . .

In the broadest sense, social inheritance could be based on regional factors alone. . . .

Responses demonstrated a typical mixture of motives, and especially the difficulty of separating out the educational attraction of the service academies. The questionnaire study of West Point graduates reported "educational opportunities" as the second or third reason listed most frequently for attendance at West Point. Clearly, these opportunities were factors in attracting young men in the past. Until the growth of the outstanding civilian technical institutes, the military academies offered as good an education in engineering as was available anywhere. But there were relatively few among those who entered the academies before 1920 and attained high rank who in retrospect claimed that they "went for a good education," with little or no interest in a military career. This theme became frequent among those who entered after 1930—in the period of the depression. Instance upon instance, these older generals and admirals, who came from upper middle-class families, elected deliberately to attend a service academy, rather than to study medicine or law or enter the clergy. Often, this required that they have sufficient funds to enroll in one of the preparatory schools with a reputation for preparing a boy to pass the specialized entrance examinations which the academies administered. The conspicuous minority from the lower middle and even the working classes, for whom an appointment was the only possibility for higher education, had to prepare by their own efforts, or with the assistance of local public school teachers.

For a number of Army and Air Force leaders, military experience during World War I, rather than attendance at West Point, supplied an entrance to a military career. For them, it was the experience of military life that generated the desire to make it a career. Among these, for example, are officers such as General Bedell Smith, for whom military service was the first occupational experience. Others, such as General L. K. Truscott, Jr., had already started on a civilian career as a country school teacher in Oklahoma.

Finally, a small minority revealed that the decision stemmed from a boyhood dream or ambition, a pre-adolescent fantasy, which in some cases could even be established as having formed by the age of ten. Such boyhood dreams can be generated without direct family contact with military tradition. . . .

But any of these responses—social inheritance, educational opportunity, military experience, boyhood ambition—can have an ambiguous meaning. Each response could have meant either that the person had followed through on a career which he had felt he strongly wanted and would pursue with zeal, or that he had embarked on a career which was one among many he could choose from, and had selected it without a consciously purposive decision. These intensive interviews produced data which indicated the relative power of career choices. . . .

To follow a tradition, if one has been coerced, often leaves a residue of dissatisfaction, a feeling that no choice was ever really made. Acting on tradition and social inheritance can mean mere compliance without personal convictions. . . .

In contrast, the memoirs of General Matthew Ridgway indicate how tradition based on positive parental identification can operate to produce a sense of dedication appropriate for a strong leader. . . .

To have been attracted to the service academies because of the superior education they offered could also involve a variety of psychological motives. For the son of a prosperous professional, who had the continuous benefit of family support and an adequate secondary school preparation, especially in mathematics, the selection of West Point or Annapolis was hardly an index of a strong personality. It was merely a sound step in his struggle to advance himself in the professional world. But for the son of a less privileged family, coming from a background which was socially atypical, preparation for West Point or Annapolis could be the expression of great personal drive. This might be the kind of strong career choice which foreshadows determination to perform some sort of mission rather than to merely serve in a post. ...

Case history evidence abounds to identify those officers who entered the military with a powerful sense of zeal and mission, For some, even boyhood ambition, which psychologists might argue is merely fantasy, proved to be an index to the strength of their decision. George C. Marshall was scarcely in his teens when he decided to become a soldier. Because of his family and social environment, as well as the letters he received from his older brother already enrolled at the Virginia Military Institute, the imaginary battles with his boyhood friends had a strong element of reality. Claire Lee Chennault, in his memoirs, did not hide his desire to excel. ...

Military officers frequently made reference to linkage between their profession and the ministry. One Army colonel, when asked about the gratifications of military life, said: "It is not too different from priesthood or ministry in serving a cause." ...

It has not been unusual for a young man to have to make a decision as to whether he would enter the ministry or the military. In the United States, and more often in Europe, sons of clergy have frequently taken up a military career. Conversely, officers who resigned from the military have found in the clergy an expression of their desire to "do service and to perform in the name of a great cause."

Finally, the desire to excel usually expresses itself in high school. The appointment system to the academies tended to recruit students who had attracted some recognition in high school because of scholarship, athletic success, or because of their personal qualities. ...

On the basis of self-selection, appointments went to the energetic and ambitious students, and not to those who were indifferent to their status in society.

For many of those in the military profession who had entered the elite by 1950, available data clearly establish that the military was more than an occupation. It was, in fact, an opportunity to satisfy strong motivations. These observations are more often than not based on those who have been successful. But this is precisely the issue. Not only is the choice of a military career a strong choice for an important minority, but, as in any social institution, the stronger the motivation, the more likely is the possibility that the person will rise to the top. The sense of mission has been strongest among the elite nucleus—the minority of prime movers on whom the success or the failure of the military establishment has depended. But when, as in the case of General "Billy" Mitchell, missionary zeal oversteps ultimate organization forms, the individual runs the risk of expulsion or internal exile. Has this sense of mission been diluted as a career motive among those who are in the potential military elite, and among the contemporary cadets?

THE GROWTH OF "CAREERISM"

The events of the depression of the 1930's marked a transformation of American social structure, and among these changes was the recruitment pattern of the military. The immediate effect was an increased interest in the free education available at the service academies. Applicants and aspirants were no longer limited to members of service families and to those social circles which carried military traditions. Many who won entrance had little or no interest in the military, although the impact of military indoctrination and the outbreak of World War II subsequently influenced a number of them to make the profession a career goal:

I decided to go to West Point in high school but not to become a professional officer. This was in 1932–3 and I didn't have enough money to go to college. I did the necessary studying and took the examination to go to West Point with no intention of staying in the Army. I felt I would be happy to stay in the three years but then get out and teach. . . . After two years I had decided not to stay in. I found the common run of officers was not too impressive and decided to get out in three years. But I graduated in 1938 and would have gotten out in 1941 but the war started and I had to stay. Now during the war I had opportunities which I wouldn't have elsewhere. Also during the war I had a good group of commanders and also I had the rank and career ahead of me when it would have been silly to get out.

The phrase "silly to get out" betrays a careerist orientation based on the evaluation of the conditions of employment, rather than any sense of calling or missionary zeal.

Economic pressures were but one dimension in the larger organizational revolution that was going on in American society with particular consequences for the military profession and its system of recruitment. The older patterns of informal and interpersonal connections guiding the selection system could no longer operate. . . .

The expansion in the size of the military, as well as the large and heterogeneous base from which recruits must be drawn, requires formal and bureaucratic techniques of selection. The organizational revolution thus weakened the older system, based on tradition, interpersonal connections, and private cram schools.

Some effects of the transformed selection system can be seen in the career motives of potential members of the military elite. Those who see the military profession as a calling or a unique profession are outnumbered by a greater concentration of individuals for whom the military is just another job. . . .

The important minority who selected their careers for traditional reasons, or because of social inheritance, is still clearly present. While the number interviewed and the basis of selection limits generalizations, it can be noted that about one-quarter of the Army and Navy officers fell into this category. However, among the Air Force, the influence of tradition was not very widespread. Again and again, Air Force officers indicated that the educational opportunities of the service academies, or the support for education from college reserve programs, had attracted them to Air Force careers. This motive pattern was prominent for about one-half of the Air Force officers.

So pronounced were careerist aspirations, and so legitimate is the expression of such aspirations, that for a sizable minority—about 20 per cent, or one out of every five—no motive could be discerned, except that the military was a job. For these persons, the choice of a military profession constituted weighing the advantages and disadvantages of such a career against what they could, or thought they could, attain in other jobs. Many of them continued their military career simply because they had accumulated so much seniority that they felt they could not cut their investment. Undoubtedly, this type has always been found in the military, as in all bureaucracies. Such officers make little pretense or effort to hide their motives. . . .

The reserve system, with its unpredictable career consequences, fosters a careerist orientation, although it is difficult to separate reality from rationalization. . . .

Among careerists, the importance of public service is reduced from an end-in-itself to one factor to be weighed with other factors in judging the worth of the military profession. . . .

Apart from the careerists, there is a minority who seemed never to have made any decision, but who just drifted into the military. Having had some previous military experience, such as college reserve training or membership in National Guard Units, they felt little concern with the career aspects of their work, but had found life in the military satisfactory. . . .

The questionnaire study of West Point graduates indicates that in recent years there has been an increase in the percentage of military cadets who have had previous military experience and college education. Such trends do not necessarily imply greater career commitment or stronger career motives. On the contrary, many of these men have drifted into the military as a result of immediate experience and available opportunity. . . .

The organizational revolution has not, however, eliminated the presence of those who attest that boyhood "ambition," based on pre-adolescent fantasy, conditioned their choice. The desire to be a great general or a famous admiral still persisted in the post-World War I period. Perhaps it was the absence of great flying generals in the story books of that time that accounts for the absence of any Air Force officer who would admit motivation from such boyhood images.

There is always the danger of imputing more complex motives to our subjects than were actually at work. In the vast military establishment, membership in the potential military elite is open even to those who were motivated by sheer adventure. This is especially the case for Navy and Air Force personnel, although Army officers spoke of the opportunities for outdoor life and for hunting. . . .

Original career motives aside, what commitments has professional experience created among the members of the potential elite? Although all

113 members of the sample have some potential for promotion, obviously, those most likely to rise are the men with the strongest commitment to the military profession. The mechanisms of promotion, whatever their defects, operate in this direction.

When confronted with the question. "If you had an opportunity to do it over again, would you choose another profession?," more than 80 per cent were unequivocal in their positive response. Only an isolated case expressed fundamental antagonism; the remaining minority revealed realistic indecision. . . .

There is initial evidence for an ever-recurring theme—the effectiveness of the military indoctrination system.

The officer indoctrination system involves more than service academies and schools of higher military education, although they are central. The daily routine of military existence is part of the indoctrination system. Whether one enters the military because of a sense of mission or for careerist reasons, constant preoccupation with combat engenders a distinctive self-conception. The fact that the professional soldier considers himself distinctive explains why, in a society in which the military is held in doubtful esteem, social inheritance of the profession—whether coerced or voluntary—takes place at all.

All professions are faced with competition in the recruitment of personnel, and seek to attract those who are dedicated, or who can be indoctrinated with zeal. Similarly, all professional leaders decry the diminishing of career commitments among their new recruits. The development of strong career commitments is a real problem for any profession, and especially for the military. The staffs of the military academies admit privately that, although the intelligence level of new recruits rises year by year, there is no concurrent increase in the sense of career commitment. To judge from the number of junior officers who resign after completing their required services, the contrary is clearly the case. . . .

The service academies no longer provide the best available technical education; those who select them are not following strong desires for technical and scientific education. Except in special cases, congressmen no longer take a personal interest in their academy appointments, or in using them as political patronage. Instead, it is easier, and politically more useful, to announce a public examination and choose successful candidates on the basis of academic achievement, thereby avoiding the charge of favoritism. The new system may be fair, and may even produce more intelligent cadets, but it hardly guarantees the selection of those who are strongly motivated toward a military career. The older informal system was undoubtedly more effective in this respect. An occasional congressman has gone so far as to use personnel selection tests, but there is no valid scientific procedure for selecting heroic leaders or for screening military strategists.

Thus, it is understandable that the academies seek to reserve openings for those who have demonstrated "leadership" ability in high school athletics and student life, and to de-emphasize academic achievement. It is also understandable that the academies seek to draw on the sons of military officers. Private cram schools have declined, and the services now operate their own preparatory schools where those with appropriate background are specially prepared. Increased selection from the enlisted ranks also represents a search for persons with strong career commitments and a heroic outlook. Yet, even those who come from military families seem to be acting less in terms of tradition and more in terms of the rational calculation that an education at military academies and at government expense is the "smart" gambit. Like medical school deans, academy commandants have become deeply concerned about the number, quality, and the commitment of applicants.

In 1955 the United States Naval Academy launched an "Operation Information" to recruit more acceptable candidates. . . .

Recruits who have been attracted to the military profession by "public relations" require the most intensive indoctrination, and the service academies deem themselves well equipped for this task.

12

Career Development of Scientists

SIMON MARCSON

The shifting of career motivations varies closely with the
stages of one's career and the alternative career routes at
each stage. Professor Marcson analyzes this "acculturation"
process in terms of the scientist's learning about the
organization, its desired goals, and the different colleagues
involved at each career stage.

Although the scientist in industry is an employee, presumably as a scientist
he enters the industrial laboratory with a professional self-image. Thinking
of himself as a scientist, the recruit is at the same time faced with the problem
of undergoing adaptation in which his professional self-image changes as he
assimilates the variety of career lines available to him as an employee in an
industrial laboratory. . . .

Once the recruit is in the laboratory he is wittingly or unwittingly faced
with a number of problems regarding his future career. What shall he do
about the career goals and expectations he has brought over from his
training? Is he capable of independent research that the laboratory will find
useful? Is the administration of research a more rewarding career both
professionally and financially? These are some of the questions he must ask
himself. The answers that he works out to these questions as he goes about
his work will affect the type of career line he will follow. At the same time he
is working out answers to these questions he is experiencing and undergoing
change as he comes in contact with the various facets of life in the laboratory.

ACCULTURATION

In the contact between the professional workers and the organization,
each has an impact on the other. Each learns from the other, each engages
in attempts at change, and each accomplishes a measure of change in the
other. In the course of this process each perceives to some extent the changes
wrought and adapts to them. This process may be termed "acculturation."

The acculturative process is clearly evident in the Pacific Electronics
Company laboratory. In bringing in a new member, the laboratory organization attempts to ease the recruit gently into his new role. It is cognizant of
the university recruit's background.

The physicist is imbued during the period of his training with interest and concern of a scientific character, which means that he is interested in making scientific contributions and not contributing to a particular corporation by way of inventions and devices.

Laboratory management is aware that the recruit has research expectations that will have to undergo change if he is to be adequately utilized by them.

However, the recruit, imbued with his graduate training values, remains devoted to them and attempts to give them expression. In turn, the laboratory organization responds to the recruit's behavior in the following manner:

The problem of the laboratory is to recruit individuals and try to broaden them to the interests and point of view of P.E.C. The basic problem of the laboratory is the attitudes the laboratory research people have about themselves with respect to their work. They come into the laboratory wanting to engage in research which would involve them in some tremendous basic discovery, and the problem is to involve them in work which is of just as much interest, and just as much moment as anything else he could be involved in.

The laboratory attempts to pull the recruit into its value system and redirect his research interests. It is concerned about the recruit's attitudes towards the industrial laboratory, but tends to view the cause of them as someone else's fault.

I think the university training could develop a greater respect for the industrial laboratory, as compared to the attitudes with which individuals approach the industrial laboratory. The problem is one of how to make them proud of working in the industrial laboratory and working for P.E.C.

From the point of view of the laboratory, the problem is to broaden the interests of the recruit and to develop within him a devotion to the goals of the laboratory organization. From the point of view of the recruit, the problem is to broaden the interests of the laboratory and to have it develop a devotion to the goals of science. Both the laboratory and the scientist eventually and inevitably affect and change each other.

In the P.E.C. laboratory, the recruit working under a group leader develops a reputation. Because his future with the laboratory and his work satisfactions are bound up with this group, the individual develops loyalty to it.[1] He forms alliances and personal friendships within the working group and within his section. At times the network of relationships cuts across groups to include individuals in other sections and other laboratories.

For instance, one luncheon group at P.E.C. consists of three members of the same section (not the same work group), and a member of the patent department. On the other hand, numerous work groups are also luncheon groups.

[1] It should be emphasized that the norms of the work group differ from the norms of the laboratory organization. The work group serves as a means of conveying selected norms of the laboratory. Laboratory organization norms are identifiable with top laboratory management. The work group member's identification is with his colleagues. This identification restrains the member of the work group from taking over norms which would clearly identify him with top management ("the Boss"). These restraints, in turn, serve as sifting mechanisms for the norms that are taken over by the work group. The result is that the work group member remains loyal to his group, but this loyalty is frequently defined by management as organizational disloyalty.

The new laboratory member is constantly evaluating and ranking all those in his network of relationships. He not only ranks the others, but he also seeks some measure of his own ranking. In doing this he is engaged in *internalizing the norms* of his working group and the norms of the P.E.C. laboratories. As a new research member explained:

Research in one's principal area of interest is partially possible. It is stressed to recruits that it is possible, and, as a matter of fact, it is stressed to recruits that there isn't much difference between industrial research and academic research. One learns, however, in the industrial situation that there is a continuing interest in application.

The new staff member becomes aware of the norms of the laboratory, and how they differ from his own.

TYPES OF CAREER GOALS

The recruit in the P.E.C. laboratory becomes a member of a work group and proceeds along one of four career pathways. First, he may remain devoted to research and a scientific professional career and shape his career goals in this direction.[2] This goal, however, may undergo change as to whether the research involved is applied or basic in character. Second, he may become interested in administration and try to steer his career up the administrative ladder. Third, he may be interested in research but turn to administration because he sees a limited financial and status future for himself in research. Fourth, he might turn to administration because he cannot compete in research with his colleagues. All four types are to be found in varying degrees in the P.E.C. laboratory.

Research Career Goals

In his early years in the laboratory the scientist remains devoted to the scientific career goals which he acquired as a graduate student.

Being an administrative person is not really a sought job. We're all scientists basically. We judge men not on position but on scientific ability. Our goal is not to make a lot of money or boss people around but to become competent scientists.

The scientist in this instance continues to be attached to research, but this does not mean that his conception of desirable research work areas does not undergo change as he internalizes the laboratory's norms.

I worked a couple of summers while I was going to school in an industrial research laboratory and developed my interest in industrial research application. I still feel that basic research is important, but I am interested in application and that is well known by the laboratory.

---

[2] See A. W. Gouldner's analysis, "Cosmopolitans and Locals: Toward an Analysis of Latent Social Roles," *Administrative Science Quarterly* (December, 1957–March, 1958), 281–306, 444–80.

Another scientist explained this process of change in the following manner:

After four or five years the problem solves itself in that there are inherent factors which change and broaden the individual. For one thing, he brushes against practical problems and, therefore, cannot help become interested and involved in them. Secondly, we try to communicate to the individual that he is essentially working on what he is interested in.

The research staff member now begins to accept the laboratory's definition of broadened interests. What is more, the laboratory attempts to convince him that what he is now doing is what he really wants to do. For his own ability to function effectively it is important that he internalize an approximation of the view that he is working on what he really wants to. The change in definition of desirable research areas does not of itself lessen the individual's devotion to research. The largest number of P.E.C. scientists are in this category of research career goals.

Administrative Career Goals (Type A)

After the research scientist has been at work in the laboratory for some time, he realizes that he is no longer in a colleague situation but in an employee one. There is a whole ladder of superiors over him, both administratively and in scientific accomplishment. First, he seeks to reduce his anonymity in the laboratory organization. He then proceeds to join professional societies, deliver papers, and publish reports. For selected members of the research staff, administrative opportunities compete with research as a career goal.

After I began my work it tended to expand and I acquired a group. Still later I was called upon for more and more help by my section leader with various types of administrative work, so that I was gradually pulled more and more into administrative work. I feel that I permitted this to happen, that I allowed myself to be interpreted as being available for administrative work, and that this is one way in which an individual can express ambition.

The administrative ladder becomes increasingly important to a large number of staff members, and they center their ambitions on gaining a rung on it. In this manner a type emerges within the laboratory whose careers are centered on rising in the laboratory organization.

The career-minded scientist concentrates and specializes in a career in the P.E.C. laboratory. He is, as we have seen, enamored of the administrative ladder and works to qualify for such a position. In doing so he does not concentrate on acquiring a status in his profession. This is the concern of the scientist who is interested in this irrespective of the particular organization which employs him. He is less concerned with the administrative ladder in the laboratory.

The factors at work in successfully affecting the adoption of administrative goals by the scientist may be seen in the following statement.

They begin to see themselves in a 9 to 5 kind of a job for P.E.C. and are not willing to give up time from their family and their outside interests. As a matter of fact, they begin to see themselves no longer in terms of a professional in their relations with the professional world, but more as P.E.C. employees.

Another scientist stated:

When I tried to form a journal club about 15 people turned out, although it was open to all 270 members of the laboratories. I did succeed in forming a small informal group in our common field of research for which 8 people turned out for a meeting about every other week. But after a while the meetings began to fall off and the group died.

The self-conception that emerges is of themselves as P.E.C. employees rather than as scientists who happen to be stationed at the P.E.C. laboratory. It is a conception of themselves as employees on the bottom rungs of the administrative ladder.[3] Their career goals of administration have been influenced by the laboratory's conception of success. And this is much desired by the laboratory for it needs administrators.

Administrative Career Goals (Type B)

If the P.E.C. laboratory scientist is devoted to research and remains loyal to it, he is rewarded financially. As a matter of fact, his salary (at present) may go over $20,000 per year. However, once he reaches about $15,000 a year his increases become painfully slow.[4] It is at this point that some scientists begin considering an administrative career, where they may go to $50,000. The scientist realizes the financial and prestige ceiling and sees administration as a way out.

Accepting a supervisory position is a way of moving within the company. It is also a change from the frustration involved in scientific work, but that's not the reason I took this job. An opening takes place, and there's a need for someone to fill a management spot. Many times individuals are talked into taking this kind of job against their will or better judgment.

Administrative positions open up new opportunities in the company, and a more accessible ladder of financial and prestige rewards. Once on the ladder, the scientist's perspective changes and he becomes more involved with the laboratory's organizational apparatus.

Once having made the break, I feel I have started up the ladder. When you are at the bottom, this ladder does not bother you. Once you are on it, it becomes a very important piece of equipment.

Now the problem becomes one of moving up the ladder.

---

[3] See the analysis of self-conception among engineering administrators in Simon Marcson, "Role Concept of Engineering Managers," *IRE Transactions of Professional Group on Engineering Management*, Vol. EM-7, No. 1 (March, 1960), 30.

[4] There is some evidence to the effect that industrial scientific personnel receive about two thirds of their salary increases in the first third of their career, and the other third in the last two thirds of their career.

There is always someone ahead of you. You are able to move up when the spot becomes vacant. In this eventuality you place yourself in the best kind of position by making it obvious that you are the most qualified individual to assume this post. This is true in any organization. In order to do this, one may have to be a little immodest. If you are going to advance, it is foolish not to propagandize. This must be done in not too obvious a manner, however.

On the administrative ladder the scientist becomes an acute strategist in his concern for administrative success.

Administrative Career Goals (Type C)

A third administrative career type is the individual who moves over into administration when he realizes that he can no longer compete in research. A member of the professional staff stated the characteristics of this type in the following manner:

I enjoy my work, and I am rewarded well, perhaps more than my work is worth. The only reason I would consider moving out would be if I felt that the new crop of people were more adequate than I am. I don't want to live a life of quiet desperation, hoping that no one will find out that I am really not producing.

The individual who might be in this position is more reticent about betraying his motives for moving into administration than the individual who can as yet contemplate such a possibility objectively.

The fact that this administrative career type exists is revealed more by the comments of colleagues than by the individual himself.

X is a fair scientist. He is not a top-level one. He is extremely ambitious and wouldn't take second place in research. He was able to sell himself, and to exploit all the necessary circumstances to advance himself administratively. In his present position he doesn't provide scientific leadership but he certainly is a boss.

In a situation calling for individual productivity and creativity, competition will inevitably be present. Just as inevitably will there be individuals who have difficulty in maintaining the competitive race and so seek other avenues of success. Of course, in developing such other avenues, they must change their conceptions of success. One of these changes is in the direction of administrative goals.

In the process of acculturation, then, the scientist develops a number of career goals in research and administration. He also develops a variety of avenues to these goals that serve to change his conception of himself and of his career goals.

13

Careerist Types

HAROLD L. WILENSKY

Professor Wilensky analyzes the "careerist" type of motivation in organizations which is so prevalent in America today. The "careerist" seeks only to reach the top of the hierarchy, as constituted, as fast as possible, in order to have power and control and to improve his social class.

The Careerist is highly identified with the hierarchy of his union and is oriented towards a career within it. He has no ideological motivation, no dilemma-producing nonorganizational goals, and very little if any professional identification. His job satisfactions center around the chance for social mobility via the union career; his job frustrations, if he has any, stem from anything that stands in the way of that career. He is a man with few conflicts in loyalty, and tends to feel that the union has treated him well.

The dominance of middle-class mobility strivings in his role orientation is reflected both in his present appraisal of his job and the circumstances surrounding his entry. He expresses his chief job satisfactions in terms of any or all of the following: (1) Money—the job pays well and thus permits a good life, time with the family, etc. (2) Opportunity for promotion—the job has brought increasing responsibilities, broader experience; it may even be a means for a better job outside the union. (3) Security—in the form of retirement benefits, a steady salary, etc. When he reports these job satisfactions, it is often in the context of a description of thwarted mobility strivings on previous jobs.

"Here you have opportunities you wouldn't have in a company. A man can come out of the shop and up through the union. How often would a man out of the shop be picked up to an executive position—unless he has a pull? In a union if you have ambition and knowledge you can get ahead. . . . In a company, junior executives are given titles of assistant to the assistant to the assistant—but only a few cents in salary increase. Here ability and ambition are recognized." . . .

Much of the Careerist's job satisfaction stems from the process of prestige-borrowing or -lending. His union job means a chance to bask in the reflected glory of great men. Or he enjoys making the union respectable in the public eye—looking after status for the union and hence for himself as an employee of the union. The first satisfaction is especially apparent in this case:

Excerpted, with permission, from *Intellectuals in Labor Unions* (New York: Free Press of Glencoe, 1956; pp. 144–53).

Case 107: It is a pleasure to travel with [top officer]. When he steps into a room you know you're with an important guy. . . .

As this suggests, "career" for this type (in contrast to the Professional Service expert) typically has a broad, community-at-large focus. The coercive comparisons of income and prestige are made with reference to the dominant respectable groups in the community—of which a professional colleague group, if included, is only one, a relatively minor one. If he has any professional identification—and this is rare—its main significance is in terms of the central focus on income-prestige mobility. Case 107, for instance, adds that he gets along very well with certain industry people—but not just his counterparts among company staff experts. His social life does include participation in a profession-connected social club. . . .

But he goes on to explain that it's the same with other high status groups in the community: "When I go to a doctor, he's interested in what the organization is and my job. Labor is getting pretty respectable and it's only right it should." He adds that it's a source of satisfaction to him that when he has come in contact with the rank and file in his union, he's found little difference between his "economic level" and theirs. "These workers are homeowners who send their kids to college."

The broad, respectable community reference comes out again in the job frustrations this type cites. Many complain of a loss of community prestige because of the labor tie. Case 110, for instance, who moved to a new upper-middle-class suburb as his union career developed, is eager to make the union acceptable: "I don't want my kids growing up in an atmosphere that can label a man a radical or a racketeer just because he works for a union." Other complaints, where they do not cross-cut all our role-orientation types, center again on the income-prestige issue: the salary is insufficient, promotion chances are limited, etc.

Confirming this interview picture of mobility striving are three correlates of the Careerist orientation: the "objective" indices of social origin, religion, and associational memberships. The men who entered as Careerists have the largest proportion of wage-worker fathers; they are typically upwardly mobile in terms of inter-generational comparison. Answers to a question on religion can also be taken as a clue to aspirations for community status. Not one of those who entered as Careerists answers "none" on religion; all but one (who says he's an inactive Protestant) mark "some religion." Perhaps more significant is the great number of "respectable" nonprofessional affiliations the Careerist group lists: churches, fraternal orders, alumni associations, the American Legion, the YMCA, the Boy Scouts, even businessmen's clubs, country clubs, the Republican Party, etc.

Though he may see his job in terms of its effect on his income and his income in terms of its uses in raising his community prestige, the Careerist, in contrast to the Missionary or Professional, is oriented inward in his work role—he tends to have a strong identification with the incumbent leadership of his particular union. When he describes his work, he shows no interest in policy impact in the nonbargaining, nonadministrative areas. When asked about his job problems, he reports few difficulties. Several Careerists—even after considerable probing—articulate no job frustrations at all, either because they have none or because they do not want the boss pictured in a bad light (this in itself may reflect their identification with the union hierarchy).

Consistent with this inward orientation is his pattern of colleague contact. Like the Party Missionary, but for different reasons, he is typically isolated from other staff experts in the labor movement, and has little contact with outside professionals. As might be expected, he has no research product. He attaches little importance to such contacts and activities. How could they help in his career within the Gadgetworkers Union? On the other hand, he typically cultivates the off-the-job own-union staff and line contacts necessary to boost his promotion chances and security within his union.

The Careerist's union identification may not imply hostility to the values of the business community (e.g., enemy targets in his work are very minor or nonexistent, and many cases describe fraternization with management). If he has a positive view of straight trade-union goals it is coupled with a feeling that what helps the union helps his career, and helps the community, including the business segment of the community. It is suggestive that proportionately more Careerists report job offers from business-industry, as well as government, than any other main type. On the assumption that job offers are in part a product of cultivation—are themselves a consequence of a man's role orientation—this suggests a willingness to contemplate eventual company employment with some favor, given superior career possibilities. Analysis of other dimensions of his role orientation—the respectable community-at-large focus of his mobility strivings, his associational memberships, etc.—would also point to this conclusion.

Of the thirty-five cases who entered as Careerists, twenty-eight remain so; six became Technician Professionals, one a Politico. Of the 126 cases typed by present role orientation, thirty-two are Careerists. All thirty-two fit the above delineation of Careerist, but important differences in the routes by which they have moved up suggest a subdivision which puts the label "Outsider Careerist" on eighteen of them, Rank-and-File Careerist (or "Porkchopper") on fourteen of them. A brief account of the consequences and correlates of their different occupational origins follows.

The Rank-and-File Careerist

This type got his start as a rank-and-file worker and union activist. Like the Party Missionary, he typically came to the attention of union officials through (1) general activity as a functionary in a local union; (2) demonstrating loyalty to such officials in the early struggles of the union; (3) demonstrating special "technical" skills in union work (e.g., editor of local paper, member of job evaluation committee or compensation committee). His transition to the staff expert job was typically accompanied by a (sometimes large) increase in annual salary and by an effort at self-improvement through reading, night school, correspondence school, or apprenticeship to incumbent experts. By 1951 the Rank-and-File Careerist group was making a median salary of $7,000—just under the overall median of $7,500, much under the $9,500 of the Outsider Careerist, but much more as a rule than they had made as wage workers. The Rank-and-File Careerist, while he feels he got a good break in moving up to the staff job, may find the current disparity between his salary and the outsiders' annoying: "When a professional [a staff expert hired from outside] goes in to the President and asks for a raise," one complains, "he doesn't give him any song and dance about loyalty to the organization, but when I go in I get, 'After all, it's your organization as well as mine.' He can't tell the outsider that. It's either yes or no."

Another consequence of his occupational origin—and confirmation of his union identification—is the high valuation he puts on "practical experience." In his concept of the Ideal Expert the Porkchopper stresses (1) knowledge of the craft, trade or industry gained through actual working experience and/or (2) practical experience as a rank-and-file member or leader in a local union. One Professional Service expert comments, "These 'experts' who've worked their way up from the rank and file are very proud of their knowledge and will not hesitate to tell you about it." Such comments as well as first-hand observation suggest that this type is most likely to exaggerate what is an occupational characteristic of all experts—the anxious effort to preserve the mysteries of the trade.

Having come from the ranks, the Rank-and-File Careerist may still retain in his vocabularly the phrases of dedication to service for the common man: "I like the feeling I'm helping someone else who hasn't had the chance I've had." "I have a warm feeling towards the working class of people." The reference, however, is to an entity he is glad to move away from. Scratch the surface a bit and you get an upward salary transition, a steady career climb, plus comments like the following (from the man with the "warm feeling"):

> You couldn't get a better job as far as liking the work goes. As far as union beliefs, I believe unions are cold, hard, business propositions. Still, underlying it, I believe that they do good. I got no religious tendencies but . . . I want to contribute my part toward evening the struggle up. . . . Also, I'll be frank. I don't know where I could get a salary like this. I'm making a lot more than I'd be making in the plant.

Occasionally this type shows a budding professional orientation, though this rarely blossoms forth full-blown. The effort at self-improvement may lead him to an exposure to academe. His "technical" job exerts pressure for the development of specialized skills, and his association with more highly trained experts in his union may nurture professional aspirations or pretensions. At the same time, the Rank-and-File Careerist wants to enjoy the fruits of a union career—money, good suburban residence, etc.; he may sharply separate work and nonwork spheres ("I'd like to study at X University. . . . But when I get through here at night . . . I want to spend some time with the family").

His occupational history, his relatively uncomplicated outlook and career aspirations, probably put the Rank-and-File Careerist closer than any of my role-orientation types to the thousands of full-time functionaries in the labor movement who carry such titles as Organizer, or International Rep. The label these men often apply to one another, "Porkchopper"—Porkchops symbolizing food on the table—captures one important motivational pattern among them.

THE OUTSIDER CAREERIST

This type contrasts sharply with the Porkchopper in occupational origin, salary transition, and present salary level.

The men who entered as Outsider Careerists typically came from nonlabor, nonideological occupations usually relevant (but sometimes irrelevant) to their first union jobs—such occupations as commercial advertising or newspaper work (no Guild activity), industrial engineer in a company, management consultant, private law practice, and civil service unconnected with the New Deal. Though most of them took a salary cut or stayed on the same level when they made the transition to Labor, this was often a necessary or calculated risk in the interest of long-run earning power. Thus, the median figure of $9,500 puts the present Outsider Careerist group at the very peak of the staff expert salary scale. As one of the transitional salary-cut cases said, "Now I'm getting a good salary, but at the time I came I could have got more outside. I won't kid you, though. It was not much of a sacrifice to come." Several cases felt that they had climbed to the top in their previous occupation and the union, whatever the starting salary, offered a situation with high growth potential. Several others were either unemployed or facing a job loss when the chance for a union career opened up.

Aside from occupational history, salary transition, and present income, there is some contrast with the Rank-and-File Careerist in the way the basic own-union identification is expressed. Like the Technician Professional, the Outsider Careerist tends to be means-centered in describing his work—indifferent to any goals, straight trade union or otherwise. The Rank-and-File Careerist, however, speaks in terms of policy impact on bargaining or administrative issues. This appears again to some extent in the concept of the Ideal Expert: several Outsider Careerists feel the compulsion of specifying as a needed qualification belief in or loyalty to the union worked for, its policies in general, or its policies in the area of the expert's specialty. The Rank-and-File Careerist seems to take this for granted—perhaps on the assumption that the possession of the practical wisdom that comes from rank-and-file shop and union experience automatically produces the proper own-union loyalty. With his previous professional experiences, the Outsider Careerist may be more conscious of the possible range of loyalty conflicts, though such conflicts seldom plague him except in very minor degree.

14

Prestige Grading:
A Mechanism of Control

CARL DREYFUSS

Dreyfuss explains how an artificially created hierarchy can control its members' motivations to work hard and to move up in their career. This control forestalls the constant tendency for career motivations to shift out of organizationally approved channels.

My discussion of the social relations among the employees in the commercial department will have as its basis the rank order of the organization. . . .

This gradation furnishes the main principles of division for my observations; social influences, relations, and reflexes are due to and shaped by this setup.

In the enterprise, the line of demarcation between management and employees is by no means distinctly drawn. The hierarchy is a highly differentiated structure. Its rank gradations are marked by various characteristics: first, by the individual's actual or usurped power to issue orders and to demand obedience; second, by the responsibility which an individual has or believes himself to have—in other words, by his independence, or the degree of his dependence on a superior; third, by his real or fictitious participation in the management of the enterprise or the department; fourth, by his representation of the firm in public, either in purchases or sales or by signing the firm's papers or letters.

A broad power to command and issue orders always carries with it a wide responsibility; conversely, it is possible for an employee to occupy a responsible (that is, a confidential) position which gives him no authority to issue orders yet makes him feel that he participates in the management. . . .

THE INTERESTS OF THE EMPLOYER

The employer is fundamentally interested in preventing the employees of his enterprise from confronting him as a homogeneous group. He attempts to undermine and split their strength through minute subdivision and differentiation. Furthermore, the employee's intense yearning "to be somebody" in the enterprise is not to be underestimated; it has its effect upon the shaping of the rank order. Not only is the outer form of the organization greatly influenced by this motive, but also the formation of its inner structure; a

Excerpted from *Occupation and Ideology of the Salaried Employee*, translated by Eva Abramavoitch (New York: Works Progress Administration and Department of Social Science, Columbia University, 1938).

multitude of departments and gradations strengthen the self-respect of the employer and his ambition to be the head of an important organization. The gradation, however, extended far beyond the technical necessities and requirements of the organization, effects a social and psychic equalization within the rank order for the economic exploitation of the employees. Exaggerated differentiation causes the employees to forget their dependence and stimulates the illusion of the possibilities of promotion. The small power in the hands of some of the employees in the system, even though it is illusory, makes them tolerate their many hardships. Thus the system of gradation, as shown in subsequent discussions, becomes of great ideological importance.

THE INTERESTS OF THE EMPLOYEES

The rank order gives the employee his definite and fixed position within the organization. This position confers upon him rights and duties and determines his technical function. It also decides whether or not the employee, in his occupational activity, can satisfy his urge for social recognition and such impulses as in the ordinary course of his life remain unsatisfied. This opportunity, however, exists to a far greater degree under the system of "artificial" differentiation than under one in which "artificial" influences are eliminated and the gradation is made according to the strict requirements of the organization. (By "artificial" differentiation we mean the gradations of the hierarchy caused by social and psychic factors, in contrast to the "real" differentiation which is determined by the technical requirements of the work.)

If he holds a position which at least affords him the illusion of superiority to some of his coworkers, the employee is enabled to attain a degree of social recognition within the organization as compensation for economic need and social oppression outside it. Such a position is seemingly of higher rank, and in the detailed organism of the artificial setup it stands, in fact, somewhat apart from other positions. This has its effect upon the social circumstances of the employee outside the enterprise; conversely, the desire for such a position in the establishment is due to social differentiations existing outside the establishment.

It is, however, mainly through psychic motives that the employee consents to and collaborates in differentiations of the rank order not based upon technical necessities. The force of impulses and drives is of the greatest influence upon the gradations of the business ladder.

The sadistic inclination inherent in many individuals finds an opportunity for satisfaction in the artificial setup wherever an individual holds a position of power, either actual or apparent. This opportunity exists for almost every employee, because even the lowest rungs of the ladder always offer possibilities for the illusion that the employee has some power to issue orders, although this power may be exercised only over apprentices, office boys, or messengers. Sadistic impulses, especially when coupled with a strong craving for authority, often render an employee a very undesirable coworker or superior, as he is always anxious to exercise and to overreach his power of command and to torture and harass his coworkers.

Another powerful impulse, narcissism, helps along the recognition and formation of the artificial gradations. Narcissism is part of the make-up of every individual, although, of course, its manifestations are not of equal force. An individual holding a job in a business craves satisfaction of this impulse all the more as the work itself and the economic and social position of the employee alone do not satisfy it. Narcissistic individuals, therefore, welcome the artificial differentiation and complication of the business gradation and grasp the chance of exercising even the smallest power of command, despite the fact that the authority bestowed on them may be only fictitious. Some promotions—to manager of a sub-department, to a semi-independent post, or to representative of the firm—afford the employee deep satisfaction and flatter his pride to an extent not justified by the importance of such events from an organizational and economic standpoint. A position which enables the employee to shine in the outside world is the most desirable of all. The positions of traveling salesman, buyer, and sales-girl—as we shall see further on—are desired chiefly because they offer opportunities for the satisfaction of narcissistic urges. Often the most superficial signs of priority are sufficient to satisfy the narcissistic individual: a word of recognition from the employer, praise from a superior, or an office somewhat better equipped than others. The narcissistic desire for authority is intensified by considerable resentment in all those cases, where, through pauperization and loss of class, former independent employers, army officers, or public servants have been forced to become employees.

Jealousy and envy among employees of the same rank or among those just one step higher or lower in rank are incited and inflamed by the continuous struggle for promotion due to the employer ideologies of employees. The fear lest they lose their position and thereby all source of income aggravates the struggle. Thus arises that type of employee described by the term "scorcher" or "slave-driver." Such an employee identifies himself intensively with the executive powers that be, with the superior and the employer; and, although an individual part of the organization, he considers himself a powerful representative of the present system.

The Influence of the Employer

The disturbance of the solidarity of the employees is intensified by the efforts of the employer to prevent, from the beginning, a too close relationship among his employees. In many establishments, for instance, there is a rule forbidding the employees, in their conversation among themselves, to use the familiar "Du" (thou) instead of the more formal "Sie" (you). A similar order states that friendly relations among the employees are to be avoided as much as possible, as they interfere with the normal conduct of business. These rules exemplify the effects made to disrupt the solidarity of the employees by a multiplication of the business gradations.

The arguments offered in defense of these regulations and wishes are not very plausible. An article on this question published by the house organ of a department store includes the following comment: "A particular reason why the too familiar form *du* should be avoided is the fact that one of the employees may be promoted and so become the superior of his former colleagues. In such case, perhaps for the very reason that formerly he was a colleague, it is imperative for him to maintain a certain distance between himself and his subordinates. To term such an attitude highhatting would by no means be justified. Now, if the new superior continues to use the informal *du* with his former co-workers he will certainly find it difficult to maintain that degree of authority which his new position requires of him. If, on the other hand, in his relations with his former colleagues he changes immediately after his promotion from the familiar *Du* to the formal *Sie* he will lose a considerable amount of sympathy, and a smooth cooperation will be made difficult. . . . But, all other considerations aside, the use of *du* is offensive to many customers. The standing of the business, and consequently that of the employees, suffers. For it cannot be denied that persons of good breeding usually preserve a certain distance and use the familiar *du* only in addressing those with whom they actually have narrower bonds of sympathy." Even the *Book of Etiquette* suggests that, though friendliness and courtesy should prevail among employees, too great familiarity is not to be encouraged. Especially in the office and places of work, *du* should be avoided. The rules of an Austrian provincial bank contain the following: "Section 28. The management looks unfavorably upon personal social relations of its employees outside the Bank."

Salary Groups Among the Employees

The principles of division in the official salary schedule of employees are symptomatic of the artificial structure of the rank order. In these schedules we still find differentiation long since discarded in practical business; the so-called occupational and business groups have in part been done away with through the process of rationalization and mechanization. For these theoretical groupings the desire for manifold differentiations is also decisive, and illusions of "higher" positions and of possibilities of promotion are of far greater influence than the conditions actually existing in the establishment, in spite of the fact that in the rationalized establishment these various classifications have, as such, long ago been abolished. Just as the various functions of organization have already become specialized in the management, so the work of individual departments is thoroughly divided. In the large modern establishment we no longer find the correspondent and accountant with their wage-scale tag as described above. If the stenographer handles foreign correspondence, then she is a specialist in one particular language in which she takes dictation and transcribes on the typewriter. The accountant who, without any degree of independence, operates the bookkeeping machine or who performs other special work, is now tied to standardized or routine work.

It is true that in a large establishment there are more rank than salary gradations, but even the latter exceed the number of groupings actually required from a technical point of view. It is interesting to note what one of the largest German publishing houses has to say on this point: "in the case of commercial employees, the regulation of the position in the business by salary agreement has not been successful in the long run. The mere fact that the salary schedule enumerated fifty-four different categories of employee groups was proof that the situation of the employees was unsuited to a collective regulation; furthermore, these fifty-four groups did not include all groups necessary for a complete classification of the employees. This attempt to bring a large number of different individual performances within one scheme of salary schedule resulted in the injuring and restricting of a majority of employees working independently and in the permitting of a minority of subordinate employees to profit at the expense of the others."

PSYCHOLOGICAL OBSERVATIONS

The psychological expert gives an interesting confirmation of artificial division in the rank order of the establishment. Psycho-technical investigations, conducted by experimental psychologists in a large Berlin office of the electrical industry, indicated that the differentiation made by the personnel staff as to the work of the employees had no justification in fact. After a close examination, the psychologists reduced to three groups the twenty-five declared by the management to be the ultimate number of technical and functional groups necessary for the proper working of the establishment. ...

"BUREAUCRATIZATION" OF THE COMMERCIAL DEPARTMENT

The artificial complication of the rank order, which permits numerous employees to feel that they hold higher positions and are to a certain extent independent, is, with its unwarranted differentiations, telescoped positions, and ramifications, diametrically opposed to efforts of rationalization. ...

The cause of "bureaucratic" rigidity, which turns to loss the very process of rationalization established for the express purpose of profit, is not the process of rationalization, the division of the work functions resulting from it, or the structure of the establishment shaped to suit the requirements of that process; the cause is rather the artificial differentiation of the rank order, which by far exceeds the gradation warranted by the technical requirements of an establishment.

15

Aspirations of Telephone Workers

JOEL SEIDMAN *et al.*

Another way to control and stabilize potential shifting in career motivations is to make clear to a potential employee at the time of recruitment that he will remain at one organizational level with only slight salary increases and limited promotions. From the start, aspirations for advancement are cooled off. Professor Seidman and his associates show how this practice affects telephone workers.

Though the telephone workers generally lacked strong ties to their work and to their occupational group, almost all who considered themselves permanently in the labor force expected to remain with the company until retirement. They most often emphasized the possibilities for advancement in a large and complex company, the assurance of continued and regular employment, and satisfaction with their jobs. There was some regret, especially among the younger operators, that they had not chosen employment of a more glamorous nature or more in accord with middle-class values. Those who planned to leave were for the most part single women who disliked the hours or planned to get married, or married women who were needed at home or whose earnings were less necessary now that their families were grown.

Without exception, the men who were interviewed expected to remain. Indeed, they had little choice, since their training and experience as equipment technicians were so highly specialized as to afford little opportunity for alternative types of employment. With few exceptions, however, they liked their work and could think of no other employment they would prefer. The women, mostly operators at a lower level of skill, had less to lose by changing occupations and more reason to hope for certain improvements, notably in discipline and hours. Yet the great majority of the married and widowed women, and many of the single women as well, planned to stay permanently. Like the men, they saw the telephone company as a desirable employer, one that treated them fairly, assured them regular employment and economic security, and offered them opportunities for promotion. Nowhere was there the fear of layoff or of arbitrary discharge so frequently found among factory workers.

The telephone workers looked forward to promotion. . . . This was understandable in view of the variety of jobs available in telephone service and the company's policy of filling many of the more desirable positions by promotion from its own ranks. The equipment technicians in particular looked forward to a variety of opportunities for promotion. The operators also had good opportunities, at least up to the position of service assistant. Beyond this the prospects thinned out, however, since relatively few could expect to be made assistant chief operator or chief operator. Nevertheless, vacancies, when they occurred, were filled from the next lower rank, rather than by hiring outsiders. There were, moreover, a limited number of clerical positions which operators might hope to get.

The great majority of operators believed that the company selected employees for advancement according to impartial, objective standards, including ability, performance, and length of service. Only occasionally was there a charge that favoritism was a factor. Those who felt they had no chance for promotion usually pointed to their age or their record of absences; some who thought they would be offered promotions, however, intended to decline either because they did not want to change their working schedules or because they did not want the additional responsibility. Many of the leaders of the local believed that their union activity, far from hurting their opportunities for promotion, improved their chances of being offered supervisory positions. A successful union officer or active member, it was pointed out, demonstrated an ability to handle people, a quality important to the company in its appointment of supervisors.

While equipment technicians, with few exceptions, preferred their work to any other, most of the women specified other more desirable occupations. Those mentioned included airline hostess, receptionist, secretary, nurse, and teacher—all secure middle-class positions carrying prestige and, in some cases, glamor. Yet many of the operators were as much concerned with working conditions, as in the case of the nineteen-year-old who said: "I guess I'd like to be a secretary. You got your own desk and nobody to bother you. Nobody interrupts your work and you do the work you want to." A middle-aged operator made a somewhat similar point: "If I had it to do all over again, I would get business training and go into office work. The people are just as nice where I work now, but it would not be so nerve-racking. We don't have too much time to make acquaintances." Many women, however, obtained satisfaction from their work or at any rate did not prefer other employment. With some it was simply lack of knowledge about other jobs: "I don't know; I've had no other jobs. It never occurred to me what I'd like."

Telephone employees do not look to the union as an avenue for advancement. Full-time union positions are very few in the Communications Workers of America, and only for the top leaders of the local was such a position even possible. For the average worker, however, it was not even attractive. Most of the women, in addition, did not care for the unpaid job of union steward, usually asserting that they lacked the time. Unlike factory workers, very few doubted their ability to fill the post satisfactorily, suggesting either that telephone workers felt more confidence in their abilities, or that they attached less importance to the steward's position and did not believe that it required any special skills. . . .

Telephone workers were far more willing than factory workers to have their children follow them in their employment. All of them wanted their sons and daughters to have an education first, and there was some hope that they might achieve the professional status so highly valued in our society. Yet the great majority either wanted their children to work for the company or had no objection to such a possibility, again illustrating their liking for the company and the prestige they associated with telephone employment. If their children did so, however, most workers hoped that they would have better positions than they themselves had achieved. Many said that they would like their sons, but not their daughters, to work for the company, reflecting the more desirable position of the skilled equipment technician as against that of the less-skilled and more closely disciplined operator.

Telephone workers evidently have a high regard for their employer. . . . Assurance of permanent employment, relative insulation against the layoffs accompanying even minor business recessions in other industries, wages matching those available elsewhere for comparable skills—these are among the advantages associated with telephone employment.

In addition, the Bell System has made a conscious effort to be a benevolent employer; it has been concerned with a pension system, vacation and sick-leave provisions, good treatment by supervisors, attractive restrooms and lunchrooms, recreational facilities, and the like. It has provided opportunities for advancement by its policy of promotion from within the industry, and has tried to sell itself to its employees and to the general public as a progressive, if not a model, type of employer.

Yet there are important sources of employee dissatisfaction and important functions for the union to perform; otherwise the union would never have developed to its present size and strength. . . .

As seems to be the case, telephone employees regard their company more highly and their union less highly than most manual workers.

16

The Chronology of Aspirations of Automobile Workers

ELY CHINOY

Professor Chinoy describes how organizational conditions affect the paring-down of career ambitions as automobile workers advance in age and seniority. In the beginning, aspirations flounder. The workers have no clear picture of the possible organizational career. Later, workers give up trying to advance in the organization and turn their ambitions toward outside goals. Career motivations are thus shifted by time and continuing in an organizational status.

Despite the cultural admonition to pursue large ambitions, automobile workers focus their aspirations on a narrow range of alternatives. They do not aspire to the top levels of business and industry; they want to become skilled workers, to gain promotion to supervision, to engage in small-scale farming, to open a retail store or a small service establishment of some kind. Since even most of these alternatives entail serious difficulties, however, comparatively few workers persist in hope, remain strong in intention, or persevere in effort. But desire frequently survives.

The varied patterns of desire, intention, plan, and effort revealed by the workers interviewed in Autotown must be seen as only in part the reactions of workers with different personal and social characteristics to similar concrete circumstances. To some extent, these varied patterns of aspirations with regard to both advancement in the plant and out-of-the-shop goals constitute a series linked in time; the same worker may change from one pattern to another as he moves through his occupational career. Indeed, the following hypotheses which have already emerged from our analysis suggest the existence of a more or less typical chronology of aspirations among these workers in a mass-production industry.

1. Many young men who come to work in the factory define their jobs as temporary; they do not expect to remain in the ranks of factory labor.

2. Workers with the most clearly defined out-of-the-shop goals are married men in their late twenties or early thirties who have not acquired substantial seniority.

3. Workers are most likely to develop or sustain hope for promotion to supervision if while still relatively young they gain some form of advancement as wage workers, that is, if they secure jobs at the top of the hierarchy of desirability or if they move from nonskilled to skilled work.

4. The longer workers remain in the plant, the less likely are they to muster the initiative to leave, even if they continually talk of doing so.

5. As their seniority increases, workers can look forward to the possibility of individual wage increases (however small they may be) and of transfer to more desirable jobs.

6. The weight of increasing or already heavy family responsibilities keeps men with long seniority from seriously considering out-of-the-shop goals.

7. Workers who do not gain promotion to supervision before the age of forty or thereabouts quickly lose hope because of management's preference for younger men.

8. After workers reach the low wage ceiling at the top of the hierarchy of desirability, they may be satisfied with what they have achieved or, alternatively, they may become bitter and frustrated because of their inability to go further.

9. Some workers, as they approach the age of retirement, may become interested in out-of-the-shop goals as sources of income for their remainnig years. . . .

From these propositions it seems clear that workers' aspirations emerge from a process in which hope and desire come to terms with the realities of working-class life. But this process is not one which sees simply the gradual dissolution of originally large expectations as obstacles to advancement become evident. Instead we find that workers must repeatedly accommodate new desires generated by fresh stimuli to the concrete circumstances they face at different stages of their occupational careers.

The changing patterns of workers' aspirations therefore bear little resemblance to the popular stereotype of single-minded striving toward ambitious goals. It may well be that the rational tradition in our culture has continually overplayed man's singleness of purpose, that, encouraged by the pioneer ethos of self-help, we have overstressed the power of individual effort against the press of circumstances. It is quite likely that finding oneself vocationally involves in most cases considerable floundering among available alternatives, that few men exhibit the terrible tenacity of Henry Ford or the elder Rockefeller. It seems altogether possible that for men on the level of wage labor, the period of floundering lasts longer, perhaps indefinitely, as they pitch such ambitions as they muster against the limited opportunities available to them.

The process of reconciling desire with reality begins early for industrial workers. In the public schools, if not at home, the working-class youth is repeatedly exposed to the values of success, the belief in the existence of opportunity for all, and the varied prescriptions for getting on in the world. . . .

But as soon as he leaves school, or even before, the working-class youth must come to terms with a world of limited opportunity where there are few chances. Lacking financial resources, he cannot look forward to the possibility of professional training, or even to four years of college which would widen his perspectives and increase his skills. He cannot step into a family business or acquire easily the funds with which to launch one of his own. As soon as his education ends, he must find some kind of job. And in Autotown even a large proportion of high-school graduates will probably become factory workers. . . .

Many working-class boys therefore give up dreams of a rich and exciting occupational future—if they ever have such dreams—even before taking their first full-time job. . . .

Some working-class boys, particularly those without academic aptitudes or interests, may quit school as soon as they are able to secure a job since they feel that they will find themselves in the factory eventually, even if they do graduate from high school. They can no longer do as their parents might have done in the past, leave school in order to learn a trade, since admission to formal apprentice training for any trade now usually requires a high-school diploma. The jobs they find, therefore, promise little for the future. Many working-class boys only come to grips with vocational reality when they finally graduate from high school. Stimulated to a high level of aspiration by the mass media, encouraged by parents and, sometimes, by teachers, they entertain inflated ambitions until the time when they must choose a definite course of action. . . .

The quick surrender by working-class youth to the difficulties they face is not necessarily forced or unwilling. Although they are encouraged to focus their aspirations into a long future and to make present sacrifices for the sake of eventual rewards, they are chiefly concerned with immediate gratifications. They may verbally profess to be concerned with occupational success and advancement (as did fourteen working-class boys who were interviewed), but they are likely to be more interested in "having a good time" or "having fun." . . .

The concern with immediate gratifications unrelated to one's occupation is encouraged by prevalent values in American society. The massed apparatus of commercial advertising incessantly stimulates the desire for things which are immediately available—on the installment plan, if necessary. Together with movies, television, radio, and magazines, advertising sets up attractive—and expensive—models of leisure and recreation. . . .

In a long-range sense, the pecuniary animus of the culture backfires among working-class youth, for the desire for maximum income, when linked with an emphasis upon immediate satisfactions in the sphere of consumption, leads to decisions which virtually eliminate the possibility of a steadily increasing income in the future. . . .

Since "fun" in this world of commercialized entertainment requires money, the immediate objective becomes a well-paid job, a goal most easily achieved by going to work in an automobile plant. Within a few months the son of an automobile worker who goes to work in the factory may be earning as much as his father, who may have been there for twenty years.

Despite the low status of factory work and the hope frequently expressed by automobile workers that their sons will not follow in their steps, many boys head for factory personnel offices as soon as they are old enough or as soon as they finish high school. And others find themselves seeking factory employment after having tried other, less remunerative jobs.

Many of these young workers are aware of the dead-end character of most factory jobs. "You don't get advanced by going in the factory; there's no future there," said one high-school senior whose father had spent his entire adult life in the city's automobile factories. When they do go into the factory, they therefore define their jobs as temporary, particularly if they have earned a high-school diploma. They say that they intend to stay in the factory only until a promising opportunity comes along. In this fashion they can maintain the impression, both for themselves and for others, that they still intend to get ahead, that they are still ambitious.

Because the first job is frequently on the assembly line, these young workers do not quickly become satisfied. They soon seek ways of gaining a more desirable job in the factory. But beyond that limited goal they pay little attention to the possibilities of advancement. They are too young to expect promotion to supervision. They are unwilling to undertake apprentice training, in part because they would have to accept lower wages temporarily, in part because they may not possess the necessary aptitudes or education, in part because they may define factory work itself as temporary. Even if these young workers say that they intend, eventually, to "go into business," they make no definite plans. Their main interests lie in the things they do in their leisure hours. . . .

It seems a tenable hypothesis that this pattern of youthful aspirations represents a modal type which applies to a substantial proportion of working-class youth, as well as those lower-middle-class boys who become nonskilled factory workers. The chief deviation from this pattern is the youth who decides early to become a skilled worker, or who decides after a short tenure in the factory to apply for apprentice training. His ambitions do not focus on rich images of success, but on the promise of a reasonable income, a respected status in the community, and a job which provides interesting work.

These latter values conflict, however, with the immediate gratifications which can be gained by going to work in the factory as a nonskilled laborer. The teen-age working-class youth is not likely to make the sacrifice of present satisfactions unless his aspirations gain support from a personally significant model or are encouraged by persons whom he respects, admires, or loves. . . .

The typical attitudes of young nonskilled workers toward jobs, advancement, and the future persist until marriage or, perhaps, parenthood. With the assumption of family responsibilities, workers tend to become actively concerned about the possibilities of advancement. . . .

By the time these workers marry and have children, however, they have already made decisions which limit the alternatives open to them. Some left high school in order to take jobs which offered little prospect of advancement; others went willingly into an automobile plant after graduating. Now they find that they lack the training which is requisite for advancement in the corporate hierarchy. They have gained no skills which can be used outside the factory. They have not added to their scanty knowledge about the prerequisites and potentialities of alternative jobs. Nor, in their concern with buying a car or having a good time, have they tried to acquire the resources which might enable them to buy a profitable farm or start a successful business. . . .

As unmarried men without responsibility, these workers were careless about the future; now they are forced into taking a defensive stance toward the future despite the stimulus to aspiration and effort. There is no change, therefore, in the pattern of life to which they have been accustomed; life's rhythms of tension and release remain short, from week-end to week-end, from one good time to another. Life may occasionally be pointed toward a vacation a few months ahead, toward Christmas or Easter, toward a birthday or some other family celebration. But long-run desires and expectations are avoided as both past and future are minimized and life is compressed into the week's routine.

Lacking occupational skills and financial resources, most workers confine their aspirations to the limited array of alternatives we have already examined. Since they are unwilling or unable to plan for the long future, they see these goals as isolated small moves rather than as part of a long-range plan. Only one worker, a would-be businessman, talked of becoming rich. He was a twenty-nine-year-old toolmaker who was about to open his own tool-and-die shop. Only the two young workers who intended to go to college could see in their plans the beginning of a career. Unlike the professional or the salaried officeholder, the factory worker does not see his present job as part of a career pattern which channels his aspirations and sustains his hope. Unlike the businessman, he has no ever-beckoning goal of increasing sales and expanding profits to stimulate his efforts.

Hope for one or another of the alternatives on which workers do focus their aspirations may, for a while, run high. Despite the obstacles in their path, some workers are determined and purposeful. The period shortly after marriage when workers become concerned with their future, when they are at or near their physical peak, when family responsibilities may still serve as a stimulant to ambition and effort rather than as a brake, is probably the time of maximum ambition and of greatest expectation, for skilled as well as nonskilled workers. . . .

But many workers see little reason for hope when they assay the possibilities of advancement in the factory and examine the problems and the risks inherent in business or farming. If they have not already gained some advancement on the level of wage labor, they are not likely to see any prospect of promotion to supervision. Indeed, if they have not had an opportunity to learn how to carry responsibility and exercise authority, they are not likely, even if offered promotion, to be willing to take on the problems which they know are inherent in the foreman's role. . . .

Workers who feel impelled to seek advancement despite the limited opportunities in the factory and the risks inherent in leaving tend to dilute their aspirations to a loose welter of hopes and a medley of alternative plans. And workers whose insistent hopes and positive efforts do not bear quick fruit give up their ambitions after a while and cast about as vaguely and uncertainly as the others. Without a "life-plan" which commits them to follow a series of more or less recognized steps, workers simultaneously entertain alternative goals, or they continually shift their attention from one goal to another, usually without investing much hope or effort in any particular one.

While waiting for advancement in the factory which may not come and, in any case, is largely contingent upon forces over which they have little or no control, workers frequently consider the possibility of going into business or buying a farm, as twenty-three of the sixty-two workers interviewed were doing. Even those who are hopeful about advancement in the plant recognize the uncertainties involved and may therefore look elsewhere at the same time. . . .

Interest in out-of-the-shop goals usually represents, as suggested earlier, the desire for escape from the factory rather than a positive search for success. Such interest is, therefore, particularly susceptible to changes in workers' job status and the conditions of work. These changes bear no positive relationship to the objective possibilities of success or failure in business or farming or to the nature of workers' resources or skills. Interest and, in some cases, action may therefore be stimulated—or inhibited—at the wrong time.

Thus business and farming ambitions are frequently whipsawed by changes in general business conditions. In the upward phase of the business cycle, when production is being maintained at a high level or is increasing and workers are regularly employed, the desire to leave the factory is at a minimum even though opportunities for small business may be at their best. When production falls off and temporary layoffs and short workweeks occur, interest in out-of-the-shop goals increases even though workers' resources are being rapidly drained away and the chances of business failure are especially high. Interest in out-of-the-shop goals, as well as hope for advancement in the factory, may also fluctuate with variations in workers' feelings that occur without reference to changes in their jobs. . . .

In a moment of hope, stimulated by some unexpected suggestion, workers may undertake a correspondence course in salesmanship, in automobile repairing, in accounting, in foremanship. . . .

In a moment of discouragement, the course is dropped, the money invested in it lost completely. . . .

At a time when things in the factory seem to be at their worst, workers may look into farm prices, search for a small business of some kind, perhaps answer advertisements for salesmen or look for other factory jobs. But as their mood changes, the search is ended, negotiations that may have been begun are broken off, workers fail to follow up the steps they have already taken.

It seems likely that interest in out-of-the-shop goals may be endlessly renewed by the constant turnover among workers, some of whom do go into business, farming, or white-collar jobs. (The weekly newspaper published by the Autotown C.I.O. Council frequently featured stories about union members who had gone into business for themselves.) But interest, when unsupported by knowledge or resources, rarely remains focused on one particular objective for very long. Since many workers plan to do "something" "as soon as things get better," "if I can save up a few hundred dollars," or "when I get straightened out," they entertain in usually disorderly succession various out-of-the-shop goals which are critically scrutinized and rejected as impractical or are mulled over, dreamed about, vaguely examined, and eventually permitted to fade away. . . .

The pattern of shifting goals and tentative plans may persist for the major part of a worker's occupational life. Occasionally plans congeal into positive action under the impact of a particularly strong stimulus or under the cumulative pressure of a series of events. Frequently these actions are abortive. . . .

A bitter disagreement with the foreman, an unresolved grievance, a job assignment to which he objects, these and many other specific occurrences can provoke a worker into quitting, even though he must start looking for another job without much likelihood of gaining any basic improvement. He may, as many have done, find himself back eventually at the same kind of work in the same plant.

The longer workers remain in the plant, the less seriously do they consider the possibility of leaving, even though they recognize that they are probably going to remain on the level of wage labor in the factory. Eventually they cease to entertain out-of-the-shop goals, accept the fact that they will remain in the factory, and confine their aspirations to a better job in the plant. This shift does not occur at any particular age; it may take place when a worker is thirty, it may not occur until he is fifty or even older. In some instances, of course, it may never occur. And a last burst of interest in business may appear as workers approach the age of retirement when, bedeviled by the economic problems of old age, they seek methods of supplementing whatever pension they are entitled to.

Workers give up their desire to leave the factory as they come to realize that they are not likely to be successful in business or farming and are not likely to gain much merely by changing jobs. At the same time they come to place a heavy stress upon the security provided by long seniority in the plant. This disappearance of ambition does not necessarily mean disappointment or frustration, however. Skilled workers, for example, may never consider any other alternative to their factory jobs, although many do in as amorphous a manner as do most nonskilled workers. They can count on a comparatively good income with a measure of security from a relatively interesting and satisfying job. . . .

Even nonskilled workers who manage to secure jobs at the top of the informal hierarchy of desirability may be reasonably satisfied, particularly if their ambitions were not set very high at the outset, if they have not felt pressure from their families to go into business or see a better job elsewhere, or if they have not been stimulated by the example of friends or relatives who have done well economically.

Some workers, scarred by experience, resign themselves to a future in the factory without satisfaction, but without resentment. They no longer demand much of life except for some kind of job and some assurance that they can keep it. . . .

But if workers come to feel that they must stay in the factory because there is no opportunity in business or farming, if they do not have desirable jobs in the plant, if they began their careers with large ambitions and high hopes, or if they have seen relatives or friends "get ahead in the world," then their acceptance of a future in the factory is accompanied by bitterness and resentment aimed at themselves, at others, or at the world in general.

Part IV

Loyalty and Commitment to the Organizational Career

As we have seen in the last section, there is one type of organizational career motivation that has received considerable attention in research and theory development—the person's loyalty or commitment to the organization. This loyalty is profoundly affected by how he perceives the organization as a base for his career. The following articles present some of the research and theory development on this subject.

Several conditions affect the person's loyalty to his organization. One major condition is whether the person is an expert or professional who is motivated to have a career as such among colleagues, such as a career "in science" or "in law." The problem then becomes to what degree, if at all, he is devoted to his current organizational base and its career. Some experts or professionals may feel no loyalty or commitment to the organization, so devoted are they to a professional career which transcends the boundaries of all organizations. They are called "cosmopolitans," in distinction to "locals," who are devoted mostly to the organizational career (Gouldner). The organization may need such experts and simply put up with their lack of commitment and turnover, knowing that, as they get older, more of them will be likely to become involved in their particular organizational career.

Many structural conditions, however, engender a "local-cosmopolitanism" among organizational experts—those devoted to both organizational and professional careers. One is how many alternatives they have for moving to other organizations. Only by having opportunities to move to other organizations of equal or higher caliber can an expert be oblivious in commitment to his current organizational career. Without these opportunities he cannot realistically transcend his organization's boundaries in pursuing a career. Lack of alternatives elsewhere becomes a condition for developing loyalty to an organization and commitment to a career within it. This condition obtains even though groups of colleagues elsewhere are still used as reference groups on matters of profession. Two conditions restricting opportunities for other organizations are: (1) the fact that there are no better or more prestigious organizations to move to at the expert's level of career; and (2) the fact that the expert's performance would not allow a move to an equal or better organization with an advance in rank.

The former condition particularly applies to people in the top levels of their career in the "best" of the organizations available. Moving elsewhere becomes a moot question. Their local-cosmopolitanism is usually focused on empire building and running their current organization to suit their needs for compatible working conditions (Glaser). These people have been rewarded for successful work at several stages of their career by their current organization; and they have overcome several organizational obstacles to reaching the top of their career (Grusky). For these career rewards they have provided the organization with hard work and prestige by their expertise. The result is a "deepening involvement" process, by which a cosmopolitan becomes a committed local as he grows within the organizational career.

The latter condition—where performance does not warrant an advantageous move—arises for experts that are in the beginning or middle stages of their careers. For them to move may easily involve a loss in organizational prestige and perhaps a loss in career level. They must work hard to stay where they are and hold their own in competition for advancement. Thus their cosmopolitanism becomes readily infused with local commitment because this is how they have to "make it," unless they change their type of work or go to a less prestigeful organization.

Another condition making cosmopolitans into local-cosmopolitans is the normal acculturation processes of learning to work in the organization (Avery, Marcson, in Part III). As the beginning expert tries to learn what is expected of him in practicing his expertise, he starts focusing on organizational goals and problems: he learns to do what will be locally rewarded; he learns how an expert in his field makes it in the organization; and he starts enjoying organizational career rewards. As a result of this continuing process of partially working on organizational goals, and consulting with others more devoted to the organization than he, he is brought around to organizational thinking without realizing it and becomes a local in this measure. If the organization's goals are divergent with the expert's professional goals, the expert is clearly developing a commitment to both a professional and an organizational career, with some ensuing built-in conflict. If the organization's goals are the same as the professional goals involved, then the expert's organizational career is "the" way of having a professional career. And though we may view him as a local-cosmopolitan, he may simply feel that he is only professionally oriented—a cosmopolitan—and that loyalty to the organization which provides a synonymous professional and organizational career is part of this professional orientation.

In the study of loyalty and commitment to organizations the sociologist should always be sensitive to what level(s) of the organization the person is committed or loyal (Glaser, Bennis). To focus only on the total organization as the unit of loyalty is to neglect those who are loyal only to particular work groups, departments, wards, branches, institutes, or other units within the organization, while feeling no loyalty (or even antagonism) to the organization itself. From the point of view of the total organization, it might not matter to which and how many levels of its structure a person is loyal. Loyalty to one level may be enough to ensure hard work and striving for the appropriate organizational career. Further, these structural levels of focus for loyalty are bound to change as the person rises in his career.

The non-expert in an organization may appear after more research to be a somewhat simpler case of loyalty to the career. Not having any strong occupational reference groups outside the organization, he will probably be a devoted local working his way up in the organizational career. If not, he will be either oblivious to his possible career within the organization or looking for a change to another organization for personal preferences.

Also an employee's career, if at the lower levels of the organization, may require little in the way of loyalty except responsible attendance and continued employment to prevent the organizational headache: "turnover." Then the less loyalty, the better for the organization when it must, according to changing conditions, lay off, demote, or discard workers. Loyalty to lower and middle levels by non-expert employees seems to take a temporal form. The organization requires them to speak and work in the interests of the company against all possible intrusions merely while on the job—for example, the sales lady, clerk, or secretary.

Obviously the following articles indicate a narrow view of research to date on loyalty and its relation to organizational careers—narrow in the sense of problems posed and an over-focus on experts. We need a more general approach in research to generate a grounded theory of loyalty to the organizational career.

17

Cosmopolitan and Locals

ALVIN W. GOULDNER

Some experts or professionals may feel no loyalty or
commitment to their organization, so devoted are they to
a professional career transcending all organizational
boundaries. They are called "cosmopolitans," in distinction to "locals," who are devoted mostly to an organizational career. Professor Gouldner spells out various
dimensions of each type.

As Chester Barnard, Herbert Simon, and others have indicated, the recruitment of technical experts is no more necessary for organizational survival
than other conditions, one of the most important of which is "loyalty" to
the organization and to its mission. In general, however, Max Weber's
theory of bureaucracy seems to have taken as given, and therefore neglected,
the role of loyalty needs as functional requisites of modern bureaucratic
groups. For such needs are not distinctive of these groups; they are common
to other and earlier patterns of administration and are thus not focused on
in his ideal-type bureaucracy. It cannot be supposed, however, that a bureaucracy operating in an environment which is dangerous to it or is regarded as
such, which is surrounded by earthly foes or perceives itself as encircled by
dangerous supernatural forces, will give the recruitment of expert personnel
a more salient place than the reinforcement of loyalty.

Every social system, the modern organization included, requires that its
members have some degree of loyalty to it as a distinctive social structure.
This would seem all the more likely if the organization operates in a threatening environment. Weber's theory of bureaucracy tended to overlook the
implications of this. He tended to assume that the more expert an organization's personnel, the more efficient the organization, and therefore the greater
its stability. But if, as Saint-Simon long since saw, those who are expert are
also "cosmopolitan" in outlook and if, as our own analysis suggests, they are
less loyal to their employing organization, then organizational survival may
be threatened by a recruiting policy which attends solely to the expertise of
the candidate. In short, there seems to be some tension between an organization's bureaucratic needs for expertise and its social-system needs for loyalty.
The need for loyalty sets certain limits within which the need for expertise
is pursued and vice versa.

In terms of the considerations presented here, however, the inhibition of

Excerpted, with permission, from *Administrative Science Quarterly*, 2 (December, 1957–March,
1958): 446–50, 465–67.

expertise by loyalty considerations is a variable, changing with the extent of the threat, real or perceived, to which the organization is exposed. Organizations presumably place less stress on loyalty when their mood is one of self-confidence and security, and when they are on the rise vis-à-vis their competitors. They seem likely to concern themselves less with the expertise of their personnel, and to give smaller rewards for efficiency and skill, when they feel themselves challenged and when they face rising antagonists. In short, as Saint-Simon long ago suggested, the full development of modern patterns of administration, with their characteristic stress on expertise and scientific knowledge, appears to be contingent on the decline of conflict.

The distinction between cosmopolitans and locals seems particularly promising because it focuses attention on the tensions between the modern organization's needs for loyalty and expertise. It suggests that certain types, the dedicated, the elder, the true bureaucrat, and the homeguard locals subserve the group's need for loyalty, while the cosmopolitans function to satisfy the group's need for expertise. Moreover, the cosmopolitan-local distinction appears to be potentially fruitful for the study of organizational dynamics and especially of intraorganizational tensions and conflicts.

In studies of industrial or factory bureaucracies many cleavages and conflicts are organized around the manifest roles and are too evident to be missed. Studies of other kinds of bureaucracies, however, have yet to develop stable conceptual tools for identifying the lines of conflict within them. It may be that the study of the relations between cosmopolitans and locals in modern organizations can provide clues for the analysis of conflict within educational, governmental, hospital, and other bureaucracies.

THE LOCALS

The Dedicated

These are the "true believers" who are identified with and affirm the distinctive ideology of their organization. Here, in particular, they are those who stress the distinctive educational philosophy of the college. They are deeply committed to their organization—and to it as a whole—on the grounds that it embodies unique values which they regard as important. They are concerned that those within the organization support this ideology, believing that community agreement is more important than the acceptance of individual differences. They are also more likely to insist that their colleagues possess certain local value orientations rather than technical competencies.

They reveal themselves as a type of local, having stronger commitments to their organization than to a distinctive professional role within it. In this context they are those who support programs for interdisciplinary education rather than those organized along traditional departmental lines. (These men are likely to be the "deployables," who accept transfer from job to job or

department to department and are more likely to think of themselves
as members of Coop College—"Coopians"—rather than as economists,
psychologists, or geologists.) Their focus is on the maintenance of internal
organizational cohesion and consensus rather than on the pursuit of occupational specializations, which they may think of as having divisive and disper-
sive effects on the group. They are likely to be thought of as the loyal and
reliable members of the group, as pillars of its ideological purity. Theirs is
an inner reference group, focusing on the college and its distinctively embodied values.

The True Bureaucrat

These, too, are a type of local. For example, they opposed establishment
of an American Association of University Professors chapter on the grounds
that it was controlled by "outsiders" or was an outside organization. They
did not regard then-current investigations of communism in colleges as
having any effect on their own local campus. But their commitment to Coop
College is basically different from that of the dedicated locals in that their
loyalties are much more particularistic. They are loyal not so much to the
college's distinctive values as to the place itself. They are distinguished, for
example, by their orientation to the town in which their organization is
located and their sensitiveness to the criticisms that townspeople level at the
college. In effect, they are a dissident group of locals who seek to adjust their
organization's values to those in the immediate environment. Unlike the
dedicated locals, they are not advocates of internal consensus but are willing
to engage in internal conflict in order to adjust the group to external pressures.
Thus, far from upholding the organization's traditional values, they may
actually contribute to their subversion. Their concern about outside criticism
leads them to seek changes in the traditional institutions and values of the
organization; e.g., they seek greater control over student behavior and call for
more supervision of students, they are somewhat critical of conscientious
objectors for whom the college had long provided something of a haven,
and they express the belief that it is important to remember that they live in a
community which believes in segregation, although the college itself has long
been firmly antisegregation.

Like other locals, they are committed to Coop College, as indicated by
the fact that they would recommend it as a place for a young teacher to begin
his career and that they do not regard their salaries as too low. There is also
some indication that they are locals in that their professional role commitments
are not salient for them, as suggested by their beliefs that teachers should not
have greater influence in the organization as a whole and that they would not
prefer to have their loads lightened to allow more time for their own research
or writing. If the dedicated locals can be said to be concerned about the
integrity of the organizational values, the true bureaucrat locals are concerned
about the security of the organization. This they seek to accomplish by

installing more authoritarian and formal regulations to control the behavior of others. It is because of this last propensity that we term them "true bureaucrats."

The Homeguard

These locals have the least occupational specialization and commitment; they have little or no advanced college training, write little or nothing, and attend few or no professional conventions. Unlike the dedicated locals, they are not characterized by a commitment to the distinctive values of the local organization; nor, for that matter, are they especially oriented to the local community. There is reason to believe that the organizational subgroup membership of these locals is of distinctive importance in characterizing them. One of the highest factor loadings, for example, is for their department; they tend to be neither full-time researchers nor teachers, but rather administrators.

It is most likely also that they do not occupy the highest administrative positions but the second-rung ones; this is suggested by the loading on the sex factor, which indicates that they are likely to be females. They seem to be bound and loyal to the organization for peculiarly particularistic reasons, especially because they themselves were likely to have studied at the college, or to have married people who had, or both. In short, they are the second-generation "Coopians," people who came back to live and work at their Alma Mater. They are people whose personal history is intimately interwoven with the organization. There are some indications that they use an inner rather than an outer reference group orientation. However, their inner reference group orientation seems likely to be focused on a distinctive part of the whole organization, namely, the middle administrative echelon.

The Elders

These locals are characterized by the fact that they tend to be the oldest people in the group, as well as those who have been with the organization for the longest time. Like other locals, they are characterized by a deep commitment to the organization, intending to remain with it indefinitely. Their commitment to the organization and their older age are likely to be connected. That is, they are likely to be in part constrained to this commitment by their age and imminent retirement; conversely, they may have remained for so long in the group because they were committed to it. They are also probably committed to the organization on the particularistic grounds of their involvement in its informal group structure; they know the largest number of other faculty members.

Their older age may distinctively influence their reference orientations in at least two ways: (1) it is likely that they are oriented to an informal peer group, those as old as themselves and those who came into the organization at about the time they did; (2) having been with the group for a longer time than most others, they are likely to evaluate its present in terms of its past. In other words, their reference orientation may be distinguished not only by a special reference group, other elders, but by a concern about a special or earlier time period.

THE COSMOPOLITANS

The Outsiders

These cosmopolitans have relatively little integration in either the formal or informal structure of the organization. They are not close to students, nor do they know many faculty members well. They have relatively low participation and influence in the formal structures of the organization, nor do they wish more. In a sense they are "in" but not "of" the organization. They have little loyalty to the organization and do not intend to remain with it permanently. They would not stay if their salary was lowered, and they would leave to take a job at Harvard or Princeton even at a lower salary.

They are cosmopolitans also in that they are more highly committed to their specialized skills; for example, they tend to be against interdisciplinary education. Like cosmopolitans in general, they tend to be oriented toward an outer reference group, feeling, for example, that they do not get adequate intellectual stimulation from their Coop College colleagues and that they get more intellectual stimulation from colleagues elsewhere. These cosmopolitans tend to define their role in ways more in keeping with traditional academic conceptions than in conformity with the distinctive Coop College ideology.

The Empire Builders

These faculty members believe that their employment opportunities outside of the college are good, and thus their college commitment is tempered by a sense of economic independence. There is an indication that they are not entirely satisfied with their career possibilities within the college and are likely to be keeping an eye on outside possibilities. Their commitment to their specialized roles is suggested by their feeling that there is too much demand made on them to participate in extracurricular activities. In short, they manifest cosmopolitan orientations.

But they are cosmopolitans of a distinctive stamp. Above all, they are committed to their specific academic departments, particularly in the physical sciences and the creative arts (which were especially strong and cohesive on this college campus). This departmental commitment is suggested, not only by the way in which it turns up on the factor, but also by their expressed feelings that there was too much thoughtless criticism of departments and their members. They seem to have a strong pull toward increased departmental autonomy. For example, they tend to resent the student rating system and to feel that power is too concentrated in the administration's hands. Unlike the outsiders, these men are integrated into the college structure, but primarily into its formal organization. For example, while they will see students fairly frequently concerning their work, they will not invite students to their homes for a class.

18

Reference Groups and Loyalties in the Out-Patient Department

W. G. BENNIS, N. BERKOWITZ,
M. AFFINITO, and M. MALONE

In the study of loyalty and commitment to organizations, the sociologist should always be sensitive to understanding the level or levels of the organization to which an employee is committed or loyal. To focus only on the total organization as the unit of loyalty is to neglect those who are loyal only to a particular work group. Professors Bennis, Berkowitz, Affinito, and Malone discuss the correlates of loyalties of nurses and analyze the work groups toward which nurses feel loyal.

Anyone who has worked within the hospital setting does not have to be told that one of the chief problems facing directors of nursing and hospital administrators is the high turnover of nurses in supervisory, head nursing, and staff nursing positions. Among the causes usually mentioned for the shortage of nurses and nursing turnover are physicians' treatment of nurses, marriage, poor housing, poor working conditions, poor recruitment practices, heavy work schedules created by the shortage of help, and lack of marriage possibilities.[1] Our natural proclivities as social scientists led us to question whether or not these "obvious" factors were the critical determinants of the rapid turnover and mobility.

For one thing, we wondered whether mobility and turnover were not related to factors involving group membership and reference group behavior. It has been shown, for example, that secure anchorage in a primary group that supports the beliefs, feelings, and ideas of members tends to create a cohesiveness usually defined as "the resultant of all the forces acting on members to remain in the group."[2] It is also widely acknowledged that identifying with groups—both membership and nonmembership—tends to shape behavior either toward or against the reference groups. The following questions were then raised: To what groups were nurses loyal? How would nurses rank the various groups of which they were members? Would they tend to rank those groups highest to which they were closest, i.e., their own work group over the medical field? What are the correlates of their loyalties

Reprinted, with permission, from *Administrative Science Quarterly*, 2(4) (March, 1958): 482, 496–500.

[1] Chris Argyris, *Diagnosing Human Relations in Organizations: A Case Study of a Hospital* (New Haven, 1956).

[2] Leon Festinger, "Informal Social Communication," in D. Cartwright and A. Zander (eds.), *Group Dynamics* (Evanston, Ill., 1953), 194.

in terms of age, background, personality characteristics, attitudes toward work? . . .

On the basis of these initial data we had to abandon some of our original hypotheses as not particularly relevant to the nursing situation. For one thing, our local-cosmopolitan data demonstrated some interesting inversions from initial predictions. The cosmopolitans did not refer to an external group, did maintain high in-group loyalty, and were motivated toward organizational commitment. The locals, on the other hand, were interested in external groups (nursing associations), showed lower loyalty than the cosmopolitans to the work group, and were less interested in developing professional skills. . . .

The basic distinction between the nursing profession and other organizational settings lies in the nature of the profession and how it is viewed by its membership. For the majority of nurses the profession is an idealized image, something vaguely equivalent to a personal identity. It represents a symbol, internalized by the individual nurse, which stands more for a way of life than a codified body of knowledge. The nursing profession is not the professional nursing associations: only 41 per cent of the 186,000 nurses belong to the American Nurses Association. Thus we are not here dealing with one group striving for achievement and recognition within the broader professional field and one group vieing for local power. Essentially, the group that would gain recognition within the broader professional field must do so through advancing within the administrative or educational areas in the local nursing situation.

For the nurse there are two major areas of success. By and large the nurse who would rise in terms of recognized titles of success and in terms of financial reward must rise through administrative or educational positions. For the nurse to be promoted beyond a certain stage, she must change her role from that for which she was trained to that of the administrator or educator. In general this is true, not only for those striving for success within the local situation, but also for those striving for recognition by the nursing profession at large. The other path of success is a static one devoid of the usual institutional symbols but deriving recognition and praise from colleagues for performing necessary functions skillfully. Upward mobility in the OPD, as our other data show, is limited by two factors: One has a personal motivation: nurses select nursing as a career partly to avoid supervisory responsibility. Data gathered by Argyris[3] and Marion Pearsall[4] also indicate that nurses do not aspire to administrative posts. In the cancer hospital he studied, Argyris found, for example, that only 24 per cent of the supervisors wanted to be supervisors; 6 per cent of the head nurses wanted to be supervisors, and no staff nurses aspired to a supervisory position. The other factor is based on institutional constraints: there are now no institutional means for

[3] *Op. cit.*
[4] Marion Pearsall, *Nursing Supervisors: A Social Profile* (Boston Univ., June, 1957; mimeo.).

mobility other than the administrative path. How do we reward individuals who increase the domain of skills in which they were trained and for which they receive gratification? Scientific laboratories face this very problem. Such large and progressive laboratories as General Electric and Bell are attempting to solve this dilemma by creating a hierarchy of what Barnard would call functional skills by setting up a lattice of reward systems parallel to the administrative hierarchy. Because of the nurses' disposition to avoid supervisory positions and the lack of a specialized skill hierarchy, the nurse neither aspires to nor even desires advancement.

Essentially, these two factors lead to a case of role conflict. The nurse who wishes to perform nursing functions cannot expect recognition by the larger professional group. The nurse who seeks recognition by the larger professional group must lay aside her nursing functions in favor of administrative or educational positions. In general, the solution to this conflict must lie in the choice of one area of activity over the other.

We have, then, four groups of nurses; two who have solved the conflict inherent in the situation and two whose solution is ambiguous:

1. That group whom we have inappropriately labeled "cosmopolitans" consists of those people who have abandoned efforts toward recognition by the larger field in favor of performing the functions for which they were trained and in favor of increasing their own skills in this area. Although they cannot hope for prestige in the larger group, they can look for praise and recognition from those who see them perform from day to day; hence they express a higher loyalty to their own particular work groups. These findings from our data require further investigation.

2. That group whom we have inappropriately labeled "locals" consists of those people who have made the decision to accept the role of administrator in the effort to obtain recognition by the larger professional field, abandoning the role for which they were trained. This group, competing with their colleagues for the recognition necessary to start them up the administrative ladder, express for this reason a low degree of loyalty to their own particular work groups. Again, further investigation is required.

3. That group of nurses whom we have labeled "interested" may perhaps be the group that has not yet resolved the conflict. Being interested in both the traditional nursing role and the administrative role as a means of gaining recognition, its members are in an impossible position. As a result, nursing service, perceived as the source of their frustration, receives little loyalty. This hypothesis, however, must be considered with extreme caution in the light of our data. It is also this "interested" group which is significantly more "personal" than the uninterested group. This suggests that we may be dealing here with a group which is simply enthusiastic about everything, including people, and find their enthusiasm limited, perhaps by nursing service.

Our findings of an apparent lack of any tendency toward dissatisfaction with supervisors, the representatives of nursing service, were based on items not specifically designed for this purpose, and caution is suggested.

4. Our fourth group, tentatively labeled "uninterested," represents, we suspect, those people who are simply satisfied with a steady, secure job. These people represent those who are striving in no direction relevant to our discussion.

We suspect that the low degree of loyalty to nursing service might be related to the tendency of some nurses to move freely from one hospital to another. If this is so, administrators might find it useful to find some means of promoting a higher degree of loyalty to nursing service. Although our crude measure of mobility does not support this notion, we suspect that it may merit further investigation.

What statement can we now make about the application of local-cosmopolitan theory to the nursing situation? Are we now in a position to state some of the conditions under which the theory will make useful predictions? We can now list at least three properties of reference groups wherein the original local-cosmopolitan dimension may not hold: (1) where the main body of the membership perceives the profession chiefly as embodying ultimate values rather than criteria for skills, research, and the development of a body of knowledge; (2) where the organization goals are fuzzy and inoperable rather than clearly delineated; (3) where the organization is not substantially indispensable for individual success. (We would predict, for example, that Gouldner's concept would be more appropriate for the American Medical Association or American Sociological Society than for professional nursing associations.)

Before we can make accurate predictions about behavior based on reference group theory, we have to make some effort to define more specifically the relevant conditions. It is apparent in the present case, for example, that differentiating the dimensions and properties of reference groups could be critical in determining their effects. In his recent essay[5] Merton advances our present state of knowledge by describing twenty-six of the properties along which reference groups may vary.

Another qualification of the theory would present itself where a local subunit has also attained a reputation in the professional field. Membership in the Bell Laboratory, which has established itself professionally, or in a famous eye-and-ear clinic may have both high professional commitment as well as high loyalty to the local structure.

The theory has proved useful in showing how idiosyncratic data spotlight basic organizational dilemmas. In this case, we have seen how organizational loyalty and professional skills diverge: as one becomes more committed to nursing functions, loyalty to the local hospital ebbs. The basic problem is to preserve loyalty as well as to improve job skills. Unless nursing, as well as other professional groups, can develop an organizational hierarchy which

[5] R. K. Merton, *Social Theory and Social Structure* (New York, 1957), 310–326.

will create reward systems for pursuing those functions for which one is trained, we will see a dysfunctional cycle of gaining job specialization, low commitment to the local structure, and high mobility and turnover. The challenge for nursing is to develop a system where loyalty to the hospital is compatible with performing nursing functions.

19

Enculturation in Industrial Research

ROBERT W. AVERY

Several conditions of working in an organization may turn a potential cosmopolitan into a local-cosmopolitan. Professor Avery discusses one such condition—the normal acculturation processes of learning to work in the organization and learning what is expected of the person.

Enculturation seems an apt term to refer to the social process whereby the young technical man becomes transformed, or transforms himself, into an established industrial researcher. As he begins his career, he is not merely confronted with technical problems awaiting solution. He must define and solve these problems in ways which are appropriate to the culture of the industrial laboratory. Part of his task, then, is to learn his new culture. . . .

When we say that the researcher becomes enculturated, then, we refer to the fact that he undergoes a learning experience wherein he connects his technical competence to the needs of his employer so that both he and his company may benefit. In our usage, enculturation is not intended to carry either a derogatory meaning or the reverse. We use it in a neutral sense.

The industrial laboratory has occasionally been portrayed as a scene of unresolvable conflict between the contradictory demands of science and those of the profit-making enterprise.[1] Without denying that severe conflicts do occur, we suggest that this characterization requires modification. The conflict is most apparent when extremes are compared, but very many, perhaps most, researchers cannot be placed at either extreme. The "local" who is indifferent to science and technology outside his company may be almost as rare as the "cosmopolitan" who regards his contributions to his company as "accidental by-products,"[2] and no more.

Most researchers, we think, are oriented in both directions, although in time they may tend to favor the interests of one somewhat more than those of the other. This defines, we think, the crux of enculturation. The career question confronting the technical man is not, typically, whether to commit himself wholly to localism or cosmopolitanism. Rather he is likely to be constrained to try to extract advantages from both sources.

Excerpted, with permission, from *IRE Transactions on Engineering Management*, 7(1) (March, 1960): 20–24.

[1] H. A. Shepard, "Nine Dilemmas in Industrial Research," *Administrative Science Quart.*, I (December, 1956), 298. Among his nine dilemmas, Shepard includes the scientist's "choice" between "advancement in the company" or "success as a member of his profession." He epitomizes this dilemma in the query: Scientist: local or cosmopolitan?

[2] This phrase is from Shepard, *ibid.*

   This view precludes the use of the more conventional categories of work which are exemplified in the titles men bear. The pure researcher, the applied researcher, and the design engineer all face this central question of enculturation, but their differences may be regarded as ones of degree rather than of kind. Both the pure scientist and the engineer share the general task of capitalizing upon their talents to the ultimate advantage of their employer. The fact that the scientist may be enjoined, for a period, to explore the validity of general principles without explicit attention to their utility, while the engineer is designing and testing manufacturable hardware, does not mean that their interests are completely disparate. Employers do not instruct pure scientists to ignore potential applications any more than they prohibit engineers from suggesting the investigation of the ranges and implications of newly discovered phenomena. The accommodations which scientists and engineers strike will diverge, but they are not necessarily incompatible.

   A further reason why the familiar categories of work are not useful in the present discussion lies in their ambiguity. While they may be defined so that their abstract meanings are relatively clear, they often obscure, rather than clarify, when they are used to characterize the activities of individual researchers. This obscurity arises in part, we think, because the categories themselves are not mutually exclusive. A single project, even a single experiment, may contain both pure and applied aspects. To simplify a complex matter, the logic of science induces researchers to seek the limits of generality of particular theories, while the logic of business enterprise requires specification of sufficient conditions under which a dependable (and potentially profitable) effect can be produced. One or a few experiments can, in principle, be addressed to both of these ends simultaneously. Both orientations share a common interest in the dependable effect. Once the effect has been isolated, a conflict can occur if a scientifically minded researcher seeks the most parsimonious explanation for his observations while a company-oriented manager urges immediate investigation of feasibility under given restrictions of dimensions, cost, etc.

   Here again, except in extreme cases where one orientation excludes the other, the conflict can be too sharply stated. The scientist, as he investigates the total range or variability of conditions sufficient for the dependable effect, may possibly isolate some conditions which can be more efficiently provided than those initially discovered. The manager, for his part, is not interested merely in any conditions which will work. He also places a high premium upon finding the most efficient conditions. The parallelism of scientific and company interests, then, may extend well beyond the single experiment which begins to explain a phenomenon at the same time that it feeds the enterprise with an innovation. Moreover, as particular theories gain generality through strategic experiments, they may become more powerful predictors. Predictions deduced from powerful theory are usually more economical paths to the discovery of further dependable effects than is the sometimes necessary practice of exhaustive experimentation, performed in the absence of theory.

For these reasons, our exploratory study of enculturation in industrial research does not discriminate sharply between individuals with different titles. We acknowledge that enculturating experiences may vary a great deal along the continuum from science to engineering but we are reluctant to impose cutting points. As we have argued, basic research at some points may be identical with applied research. At other times one man's work may carry him imperceptibly from basic to applied, or from applied to basic. The distinction between applied research and design engineering is similarly imprecise. Though our description of enculturation pertains more to men and activities near the middle of the continuum than to those at either end, some portions of the following account may have somewhat broader pertinence. . . .

One of the frequent recollections of the researcher is the initial sense of "feeling lost." Whether his initial assignment was to extend his graduate thesis in a direction which might be interesting for his company, or whether he was attached to an existing group or project, he still required some period of time before he could begin to determine what was expected of him. Parenthetically, it might be remarked that in one sense this is a most suitable introduction to industrial research. The work itself, by definition, involves a probing of the unknown and uncertain, and the consequences of one's work are usually not accurately predictable. Perhaps it is functional for the new man to become accustomed to uncertainty at the very outset of his industrial career.

The sense of being lost may be accentuated for another reason. His years at the university have taught the graduate how to ascertain what is technically sound in his field, and he has become accustomed to making his judgments mainly on technical grounds. As he enters the laboratory for the first time, he usually is not committed to the illusion that only technical soundness will count in his new work. He knows that the principal reason for his laboratory's existence is to enhance the profitability of his company. What he does not know is exactly how he can begin to contribute to this goal. His first ideas about how his technical field might best be exploited in his company's interest are likely to have occurred to others before him. He becomes aware, perhaps after one or two false starts, that his laboratory has a history which he can absorb by talking to people who have long experience in the organization and by painstaking search through records of abandoned ideas and terminated projects. Also, he gradually recognizes that his laboratory is intimately connected to many other sectors of the company, and that these ties place some limits upon the work he can properly undertake. If he commences a line of work which leads to an output that the operations department is not equipped to manufacture, or that salespeople are not prepared to carry into the market, he will experience the frustration of having to terminate a technically promising endeavor because its ultimate product would have no place to go. By trial and error he learns what these other departments are most anxious to see done in his laboratory. As he gains more experience, he discovers that he is not a passive object in this matter. He may have some room to exercise initiative and to persuade others, when he thinks he has proven an idea which others in the company ought to want to develop, make, and sell.

Before he does very much of this, however, another task confronts him. As he comprehends what kinds of ideas are suitable for eventual use in his company, and as he begins to produce these in modest quantities, he must know how to convince his supervisor and his managers that these ideas deserve his time and the company's money. It is significant that, when researchers discuss this task, they talk about the importance of "selling an idea." They use the language of the marketplace and they emphasize that the young graduate must become fluent in two slightly different languages. The enculturated researcher reserves the esoteric vocabulary of his field largely for use with his colleagues. When he seeks to persuade his more business-oriented managers that they should share his enthusiasm for his projected work, he translates his technical abstractions into words that are less exact but more compelling to men who are not immersed, as he is, in the subtle problems of one narrow specialty. Especially he stresses the economic potential of his idea, however remote it may be. . . .

There are a few men who cannot comfortably absorb the role of "idea salesman" into the repertoire of roles which they play in the laboratory. For them an ethical problem intervenes to inhibit their capacity to translate their ideas into nontechnical language. As they see it, any representation of their work which does not include all the technical distinctions and qualifications which they believe are important actually constitutes a misrepresentation. This in turn implies a dilution of their own integrity, and makes the task of selling ideas morally difficult. There is irony in the situation of the technical man who is inhibited from selling his ideas or who cannot do this convincingly. His ideas lack validity until he can secure approval to test and use them. Progress in the sense of scientific advance depends in some measure upon the scientist's proficiency in nontechnical activities.

As a summary of what has been said so far, we may say that an important component of the work of the technical man is the assumption of organizational responsibility. His obligation extends well beyond the solution of technical problems or the planning and execution of experiments. Even before he begins to direct the work of others, he affects the work of others, both positively and negatively. The speed with which he learns how to produce ideas which his competence permits him to investigate and which capture the enthusiasm of managers will determine how soon his efforts will begin to have ramifications in many distant places—in his factory, in salesrooms, in customer satisfaction, and in his company's profit and loss statement, to name a few of these. This idealized sequence of events depends at the very beginning on the researcher's capacity to create usable ideas.

It seems to make a difference—and this is our own interpretation because no person in any of our interviews put the matter quite this way—how the technical man psychologically defines his job. If he draws an imaginary line around his strictly technical function and says in effect, "This is the domain of my work and all else are hindrances and barriers," he may be restricting both his visibility and his possibilities for action so greatly that he can assume relatively little organizational responsibility. By this we mean that he may not actively and continuously assess how his work might contribute to the work of others or how it might ultimately benefit his company. . . .

There is a psychologically different way to define the job of the technical man, and many to whom we have talked have done something like this. Instead of viewing the panorama of external departments, service groups, managers and executives, etc., as obstacles to be surmounted, they may be regarded as opportunities for extending one's knowledge and for creating possibilities for idea-production which otherwise would have been unnoticed. The man who does this finds that he is becoming more sophisticated about economic problems, and he begins to talk knowledgeably about costs and prices and maybe even about return on investments. He learns a good deal about how to deal with people effectively. He recognizes that, as his stature as scientist or engineer increases in the eyes of others, he acquires what might be termed a modicum of legitimate influence. This, in turn, he can use as leverage when problems arise which might interrupt or terminate what to him is a promising line of investigation.

It is almost as if the researcher were expanding the definition of any particular technical task to include the social or organizational factors which affect, or may be affected by, his technical activities. Thus, availability of funds and other resources; attitudes of colleagues, managers, and others; expectations from one's profession-at-large; cost estimates and anticipated returns; personal career chances and preferences; possible or probable actions of competing firms; patentability; actual or potential demands for the ultimate output in the marketplace; consonance of the work with laboratory and company objectives; and other impinging circumstances may be seen as variables in an encompassing system of which a technical experiment or project is one component or subsystem. The success of the technical endeavor, then, does not depend simply upon the elegance of the purely technical solution. It rests as well upon the ease with which the technical solution fits into the superordinate system. Success is achieved when the solution permits a technical output which is feasible within the constraints imposed by the larger system and also enables the system as a whole to function more efficiently and economically. . . .

The situation of the individual researcher, of course, varies from this analogy in the respect that the entire organization (as it affects him and his work) cannot be programmed and divided into manageable components as the complex systems project can be. His surroundings cannot be highly systematized. Ordinarily his specifications are more flexible than those which are generated by the known requirements of a planned system. He may be able to set and alter specifications on his own judgment within rather broad (or fairly stringent) limits. Limits do exist, however. The problem lies in identifying them and ascertaining, when necessary, whether they are alterable through judicious persuasion. Of course these limits are typically uncertain and only measurable in a gross or relative sense. Sometimes they seem to be set arbitrarily, or they may suddenly shift without visible rationale. Occasionally they may close in to leave no room for work at all, as when a project with supreme priority forces lesser efforts to be placed on the shelf or cancelled.

Despite the intangibility and uncertainty of this welter of factors not integral to the task at hand, researchers, in varying ways and degrees, do try to make their organizational environment as predictable as possible. In some fashion every researcher gradually constructs what might be called a mental map of his organization. In this map he includes such organizational considerations as seem to be important to him. Some regions of the map, particularly those closest to him, are sketched out in more detail than other regions. Certain areas are almost completely unexplored. Some maps do not stop at the boundary of the organization but are extended to incorporate, *e.g.*, one's professional colleagues or the situations of customers who use the company's products.

The map in turn serves several purposes for its owner. It reminds him where to find information of various kinds. It tells him where he has access to people and departments and where he does not. It distinguishes official channels from those informal arrangements which often facilitate work. It identifies people or departments whose cooperation or approval is frequently welcome. As the map becomes more detailed and comprehensive it enables the researcher to understand more completely how his organization as a whole operates. Such knowledge is always far from perfect, but it may be sufficient to permit a researcher to anticipate fairly well how certain segments of the organization will respond to his actions. Knowing this, he will also learn where and how it is possible for him to elicit desired responses from his organization by arranging his own activities appropriately. . . .

In this occasional preoccupation with matters which equip him to carry out his organizational responsibilities, he does not lose sight of his technical role. This still stands at the center of his definition of his job. He does not let his organizational education interfere with his technical work. Unless he produces results from the bench which attract respect, he is not likely to have the chance to use his stock of knowledge about his company. Technical growth and enculturation seem to go hand in hand, each benefiting the other but neither sufficient by itself.

20

Career Concerns and Footholds in the Organization

BARNEY G. GLASER

This article, like the previous one, analyzes the focus of loyalty on various levels of the organization. It shows how this focus varies with the stage of organizational career.

Usually, authors state that the scientists about whom data will be presented work in a research organization or in a university department. This statement can be an oversimplification for studies of professional careers. When the scientist affiliates with an organization, he does so within a *set of concentric social units or groups* of which the organization is just one. By joining an *organization*, he locates himself in a *community* of science. The communities of science (clusters of similar research contexts) are roughly graded by scientific prestige and in turn locate the scientists in the *world* of science.[1] Within the organization, in this study, the scientist is placed in another location group, an *institute* focused on the study of a particular disease or family of diseases, which itself is well known in the community of science. Within the institute he joins a *laboratory* and works in a *section*. Within the section he becomes part of an *informal work group* of professional associates.

During the typical recruitment process, the scientist is introduced to the concentric groups within the organization by meeting and talking with future co-workers and the heads of the section, laboratory, and institute. His decision on affiliation, as well as the decisions of recruiting agents, will usually take into consideration both his potential for fitting into each organizational level and the particular community of science. Once the scientist is affiliated with the organization, the concentric groups within it become potential bases of operations to which he can refer himself for various purposes; particularly, all or any one of the groups could become useful as footholds in getting on with a career in the organization and in science. The purpose of this chapter was to show . . . *where* at each stage of a career validated scientists—scientists with professional recognition—are mainly integrated into the organizational structure, and to try to indicate *why* this is so. . . .

As investigators go through the organizational career, they tend—*as validated scientists*—to choose as bases of operations in the organizational

Excerpted from *Organizational Scientists: Their Professional Careers* by Barney G. Glaser (pp. 85–6, 95–7). Copyright © 1964 by The Bobbs-Merrill Company, Inc. Reprinted by permission of the College Division of The Bobbs-Merrill Company, Inc.

[1] This is neatly illustrated by Caplow and McGee's discussion of major, minor, and bush leagues and the problems of changing leagues as having career implications of great magnitude. *Academic Marketplace* (New York: Basic Books, 1958), 147–55.

structure those different footholds that are best suited to resolving typical career concerns.[2] Juniors focus on all three work groups as loci for guidance and support and as bases for establishing themselves as scientists. Once established, the investigators turn to developing a following of potential subordinates among close professional associates. At this stage they also make the crucial decision to commit themselves to the organizational career, because of their chance to make supervisor, because of their research independence, and because they judge the organization to be a prestigeful location in the scientific world. After achieving a supervisory promotion, they tend to settle down for the remainders of their careers among the largest group of professionals in their discrete field.

This chapter demonstrates another property of vertical mobility within organizations. The property is this: *At each stage of a career a person chooses a different primary base of operations among concentric organizational groups for the resolution of his typical career concern.* This property, like that of becoming integrated with different members of one's role-set, is a by-product of having to face different typical concerns at each career stage. Integration into these footholds in the organization is facilitated if one has given evidence of ability to achieve the goal shared by the group. Evidence of ability—in this study professional recognition—helps solve career concerns (1) directly, through its consolidation and advancement effects; and (2) indirectly, through effecting integration among particular members of the scientist's role-set and with particular concentric organizational groups. The integration effects are part of the processes that lead up to and facilitate the consolidation and advancement effects of evidence of ability on resolving career concerns. The over-all effect is the successive deepening of the scientist's involvement in a stable organizational career.

A practical feature of this property of careers is that it clarifies for administrators of research organizations, whose job it is to worry about it, a way of considering the loyalty of the organization's professional personnel. Typically, professionals are perceived merely as either loyal or not loyal to the organization. A more discriminating view would be to consider the professional's stage of career, the problems he must solve at this stage, and those groups within the organization that best help him solve the problems. These will be the groups on which loyalty is mainly focused—as it is not necessarily focused upon the organization itself. Thus, when an administrator is considering loyalty as a determinant of potential turnover of mature senior investigators, it would be easier to predict what is going to happen not by guessing or by asking how firmly committed they are to the organization as a whole, but

---

[2] For a somewhat similar finding on the support of occupational ideologies by different social bases, see James W. Carper and Howard S. Becker, "Adjustments to Conflicting Expectations in the Development of Identification with an Occupation," *Social Forces*, XXXVI (October, 1957), 55. Physiologists find their support in a "close-knit clique"; engineers find their support in the "work world"; and philosophers find their support in an "abstract intellectual world." Their choices depend on "who else" understands their "career problems."

by finding out whether or not they are bothering to develop a following among close professional associates as a strategic step in developing an organizational career. In short, administrators should take a detailed career *process* perspective when viewing problems of personnel management and predicting either turnover rates or individual moves.

21

The Expansion Orientation of Supervisors of Research

BARNEY G. GLASER

When a cosmopolitan reaches the upper stages of a career in the "best" of the organizations available, then moving to another organization becomes a moot question. He has become a local-cosmopolitan, and tends to focus his attention on running his current organization to suit his needs for compatible working conditions and a compatible organizational goal.

Thus far, this report has evidenced two historical themes. One has been related to my discussion of the scientist's career. I have noted that many properties of the organizational career (especially career concerns) change for investigators as they are promoted. Also, as scientists advance, these changes of career concerns, research conditions, strategic personnel, and organizational footholds, effect and indicate a successively deepened involvement of the scientist in the organizational career. These changes and the increasing involvement are based on a snowballing accumulation of rank and recognition. In short, the analysis of a career pattern is the analysis of a historical pattern for the career occupant. At the career's end, the supervisors with adequate professional recognition are thoroughly involved in the organization and committed to its career (their staying-on concern is, for the moment, resolved). This peak in involvement and commitment is a historical result. The second historical theme in this report is that this career is located within an organization that has been expanding and will continue to expand. Thus, the history of individual careers is linked with the history of the organization.

The question therefore arises: At what point do these two histories meet with some consequence? I shall demonstrate in this chapter that a significant interception occurs at the supervisory stage of a career. That is, the people most involved in the organization and most deeply committed to the organizational career are those who are involved most in the organization's expansion. Its expansion impinges on the supervisors. Therefore, their problem becomes one of managing the end stage of a career within this historical context; that is, one of dealing with their concern over remaining in an expanding organization. Their solution is to adopt, for the time being at least, an expansion orientation relevant to guiding the organizational growth. This solution is a distinctive type of local-cosmopolitan orientation; it exists both under the specific historical conditions mentioned (expanding organization and end of a career) and under two further conditions (a satiated current need for professional recognition and a fairly satiated opportunity to better one's position in the world of science). . . .

I suggest that the supervisors with high recognition are oriented primarily to managing the expansion of their organization. And this orientation is a result of the intersection of the histories of the supervisors' careers and of the organization's development. Ninety per cent of the successful supervisors have linked their careers firmly to the organization; thus, they turn to managing a vested interest in their location within the scientific world. While they reported themselves just as "worried that people with clinical backgrounds may have considerably more weight in deciding scientific policies that affect [their] institute" with the advent of the clinical program, they, more than senior investigators or supervisors with low recognition, are in a better position (and can get in better positions) to take action to prevent this potential encroachment on basic research. They are not in current need of more professional recognition to stabilize their careers; they can devote their efforts to controlling the inevitable organizational growth in a manner that *will* benefit, not harm, basic research. In the short run, this expansion orientation would seem to override concern about any dissonance with their high motivation to advance knowledge and any adverse consequences to their basic research, or about worthy clinical goals and organizational prestige. Thus, they support actions toward the clinical goal in order to control and protect in the long run the primacy of the goal of advancing knowlege.

The expansion orientation of supervisors—determined by their position, career concern, and high recognition—is in sharp contrast to the feelings of senior investigators with high recognition who also have their career concern well in hand. These senior investigators feel more worried and less pleased over the prospective change in emphasis on goals. They have little need to share their time for basic research with clinical research. At their stage of a career, a promotion to supervisor of research depends upon recognition for advancing knowledge. Further, this change is incompatible with a goal that 67 per cent are highly motivated to fulfill. Therefore, while they give lip service to long-range goals, they do not support the more immediate actions toward these goals that might interfere with their current basic research and needed original achievements. Thus, the process of advancing from senior investigators to supervisors is linked with a distinct change in perspective toward a major issue, an issue involving the very goals of their research and their organization.

The supervisors with low recognition appear to be at an intervening stage in this change process. Because of their lack of recognition, they seem to have a foot in both camps, as it were. They are supervisors, but they lack the expansion orientation of validated supervisors because of their personal lack of recognition; hence, they lack resolution of their career concern. In line with this deficit, or perhaps because of it, they still retain the perspective of senior investigators with high recognition. They tend to respond to the potential consequences of the coming applied research center with concern about the threat to basic research, from which they require recognition to link their future firmly to the organization's future. Since they are likely to be involved with planning and decisions, they may offer considerable contrast in opinion and influence to the validated supervisors. But, it may be anticipated that upon acquiring recognition for advancing knowledge—hence, resolution to their career concern—they will change to embracing the expansion orientation, regardless of its consequences.

On a more general level, these data indicate another property of vertical mobility within organizations. *As one advances in the organization, the perspective that one has toward important changes and issues that influence the main goal of the organization will change.* This perspective is affected also by the degree of success attained at each career stage. A career perspective would seem important to consider in studies of organizational goals. Given this property, it would seem that the differential perspectives of goals by the organizational members vary not only by organizational levels, such as lower participants, lower elite, and elite,[1] but also by the career stage one is in (or career stages one is between) at each level.

LOCAL-COSMOPOLITAN THEORY

In a previous chapter, I demonstrated that a general orientation of the scientists in this study was one of local-cosmopolitanism. This orientation occurred within the context of an organization whose goal is the same as the institutional goal of science (advancing knowledge), and it applied to the scientists highly motivated to fulfill this goal. The criterion for local-cosmopolitan orientation was the direction of the scientist's work effort. Highly motivated scientists did more, both for basic research and for the organization. These people were termed "basic research local-cosmopolitans" and contrasted with the "applied research local-cosmopolitans." The latter scientists, in accommodating themselves to an organization whose applied and development goals are different from the institutional goal, were oriented to both the organization and the profession in their effort to facilitate the utilization of basic research results.

... I am now in a position to attempt to specify variations that are linked with career stage in the local-cosmopolitanism of the present investigators. These variations are another property of vertical mobility within organizations. It is important to keep in mind that the variations occur in a research organization whose prime goal is advancing knowledge and that is undergoing a general expansion, a strategic part of which is the development of a clinical program and an emphasis on applied research.

[1] Cf. Amitai Etzioni, *A Comparative Analysis of Complex Organizations* (New York: Free Press of Glencoe, 1961), 75–76, 93–94.

Both the junior and senior investigators with low recognition have indicated a partial retreatism from advancing knowledge by an increased interest in applying knowledge. This change will not be difficult to accomplish, as they have indicated little motivation to advance knowledge. In redirecting some research to the application of basic results, their efforts will be oriented both professionally and organizationally. (Perhaps some men also have the medical profession in mind in focusing on applied research. However, the object of cosmopolitanism discussed here is the scientific profession.) In short, some of these people may become *applied research local-cosmopolitans* with the advent of the clinical program. They may be recruited both from basic research cosmopolitans who have lost their high level of motivation and recognition and from locals who will now be provided with a goal that can link them again to their profession.

The junior and senior investigators with high recognition and the supervisors with low recognition are clearly the *basic research local-cosmopolitans.* They are devoted to advancing knowledge while doing more than their share of general organizational duties to maintain the location of their careers. Lastly, the supervisors who have high recognition have become *adaptive local-cosmopolitans.* The differentiating factor between them and the basic research local-cosmopolitans is the locus of their strongest efforts. Both are devoted strongly to basic research and to the high-prestige organization whose prime goal is advancing knowledge. The investigators with high recognition and the supervisors with low recognition put their strongest effort into basic research. The successful supervisors, not currently requiring professional recognition, now put their strongest effort into managing the organizational growth. They switch the balance in strength of effort from the "goal-attainment" to the "adaptive" requirement of the organization—that is, to "accommodating the system to . . . reality demands."[2]

This is the way in which the successful supervisors round out their professional careers as high-prestige people in top positions in a high-prestige organization in the world of science. Given this high degree and level of rank consistency in their positions in science, their adaptive orientation can be seen also as a response to a fairly saturated opportunity to better themselves in their community of science. Scientists in universities with this degree and level of rank consistency may also be adaptive local-cosmopolitans, if, as Caplow and McGee suggest, "In a handful of great universities, where many of the departments believed to be the best in their fields are found, a merger of orientations is possible. There many may simultaneously serve an institution and a discipline and identify with both."[3]

[2] Talcott Parsons, Robert F. Bales, and Edward Shils, *Working Papers in the Theory of Action* (New York: Free Press of Glencoe, 1953), 183.
[3] *Academic Marketplace* (New York: Basic Books, 1958), 85.

22

Career Mobility and Organizational Commitment

OSCAR GRUSKY

Professor Grusky's work adds to the previous article by showing some processes by which a person becomes committed to an organization as he advances in his career.

Organizational commitment refers to the nature of the relationship of the member to the system as a whole. Two general factors which influence the strength of a person's attachment to an organization are the rewards he has received from the organization and the experiences he has had to undergo to receive them. People become members of formal organizations because they can attain objectives that they desire through their membership. If the person discovers that he cannot obtain the rewards he originally desired, he either leaves the organization and joins another; or if this is not feasible, he accepts those rewards which he can obtain and, we suspect, at the same time feels less committed to that organization. On the other hand, obtaining the rewards sought, operates to further his felt obligation to the organization, and his commitment is strengthened. The expectation of reward operates in a like manner. Strength of commitment to an organization should be positively related to the strength of conviction that one will be rewarded by the organization. The nature of one's commitment to an organization may undergo radical change depending on the relationship between belief and reality.[1] Convergence of belief and reality would tend to strengthen commitment, while divergence should cause a decrease in commitment.

Whether one must overcome hurdles in order to obtain the rewards of the organization may be another important factor in determining one's commitment to the organization. If the rewards are readily obtained, one's obligation to the organization is likely to be weak; one becomes convinced that it was his attributes rather than those of the organization which provided the rewards. On the other hand, if one obtains great rewards despite apparent obstacles (such as starting out with a low status in the organization), commitment should be strong. This study examines evidence for the following two general hypotheses.

Excerpted, with permission, from *Administrative Science Quarterly*, 10(4) (March, 1966): 489, 490, 497–502.

[1] Goffman has stated a related hypothesis: "Persons at the bottom of large organizations typically operate in drab backgrounds, against which higher-placed members realize their internal incentives, enjoying the satisfaction of receiving visible indulgences that others do not. *Low-placed members tend to have less commitment and emotional attachment to the organization than higher-placed members.*" (Italics added.) *Asylums* (New York: Doubleday and Company, 1961), 201.

188

Hypothesis 1. All else equal, the greater the rewards an individual has received or expects to receive from an organization, the greater will be the degree of his commitment to the system.

Hypothesis 2. All else equal, the greater the obstacles the individual has overcome in order to obtain the organization's rewards, the greater will be the degree of his commitment to the system. . . .

MOBILITY AND COMMITMENT

Considering the findings, one can draw the following conclusions: (1) In general, strength of organizational commitment was positively associated with seniority. (2) Managers who experienced maximum career mobility were generally more strongly committed to the organization than were less mobile managers. (3) Managers who were moderately mobile did not show any uniformity in their pattern of commitment that distinguished them from the less mobile managers. This latter finding may be due to differential mobility expectations. Managers receiving some promotion may have felt a weaker commitment when their rewards proved smaller than anticipated.

A note on causality is appropriate. The data do not permit one to ascertain whether career mobility produced strong organizational commitment or vice versa. Nor does common sense permit one to make a judgment on the causal relationship. Expressions interpreted as evidence of loyalty to the firm may very well be a condition favoring movement upward in the hierarchy. One could assume that these two variables exercise a reciprocal influence upon each other.

OVERCOMING OBSTACLES TO CAREER MOBILITY

. . . Two barriers to upward mobility in the company are considered: (1) formal education, which is an achieved characteristic; and (2) sex, which is ascriptive. Specifically, it is hypothesized that within each career mobility level, managers who had overcome a barrier would be more fully committed to the corporation than those who had not. Therefore, less educated managers should show greater commitment than managers possessing more formal education, and female managers should be more strongly committed to the organization than male members. . . .

The hypothesis was supported in eight of the nine comparisons; in each of these cases, managers with a high school education showed a stronger commitment to the organization than did managers with college experience. In one instance, level of education did not differentiate: managers with a high school background and those who went to college who experienced moderate mobility demonstrated a similar strength of commitment on the index of general satisfaction with the company. Also, it should be noted that with but one exception, if each educational group is examined separately, there is a positive relationship between level of upward mobility and strength of commitment. . . .

Female managers were more strongly committed than male managers on each of the three indexes, within the two mobile categories. In the minimum mobility category the average percentage difference was 13 per cent, while in the moderate mobility group it was almost 18 per cent. Moreover, in the minimum mobility category, the seniority variable operated against the hypothesis. Although only 45 per cent of the female managers had been with the company ten years or more, 72 per cent of the male managers in this group had equivalent seniority. In the moderate mobility category, the distributions were similar: 74 per cent of the males compared to 75 per cent of the females had been with the firm at least ten years. Seniority it appears was a more critical factor in upward mobility for females than for males.

These findings can be interpreted in terms of reference group theory. Managers compare their progress up the ladder with others who presently occupy and who have occupied similar positions in the corporate hierarchy. They are aware that being male and having a college background influences promotion opportunities in the firm. Hence, the female manager and the manager with only a high school education or less who find themselves promoted rapidly or on a level with managers of higher status (male, college-educated managers) feel strongly obligated to the firm, because the rewards they have received have been greater relative to the others. Strong commitment is also encouraged by job opportunities. The male manager and the college-educated manager have considerably more desirable job opportunities elsewhere than do female managers and those with only a high school education or less. The lack of available opportunities at a similar status level should function to promote strong commitment to the company.

Part V

Sources and Strategies of Promotion

The idea of the successful individual as an independent entrepreneur has changed. Today it refers to the person who has reached the top levels of an organizational career. "Getting ahead" refers now to a process of advancement in an organizational context of associates, superiors, and rules of promotion in a hierarchy (Mills). Further, this success, achieved by the "bureaucratic crawl," can by itself never end up in the person being among "the very rich" (Mills). Thus, in deciding upon an organizational career, a person must consider how rich he wants to be. Perhaps the top salary of an organizational career is enough. If more is desired then the person must choose an organizational career that raises the probability of providing the person, on the side, as he moves up, with an accumulation of advantages that he can parlay into a fortune. The long crawl, then, pays off only if it is transformable at some point into the "big jump" to riskless fortune-making.

For most people, however, this extreme form of success is not the goal. For them it is reaching the top, which boils down to how to be continuously promoted as long as possible. This question leads to another: What accounts for promotions at each stage of an organizational career? Organizational rhetorics usually state that promotions are made on the basis of some combination of ability, competence, merit, and/or seniority. Everyone suspects, however, that also other informal processes and factors are involved. To put it in Mills' terms: "now the stress is on agility rather than ability." He was emphasizing "personality" factors, which is partially a correct emphasis, as the several articles in this section indicate. Let us consider some of the social structural sources and strategies of promotion brought out in these articles that are of major relevance for a formal theory of promotion in organizational careers.

One organizational condition affecting advancement is how many different career lines are offered a person at his stage (Martin and Strauss). Any one stage of a career may be considered a "testing point" for the person to see which of the next career lines he might be ready for (Roth). The test may be considered to last for years, requiring this experience in a position; it might be scheduled as a formal examination or some combination of knowledge, experience, and performance, and so forth. The testing becomes one source of whether the person is ready for a promotion and for which career line. This readiness is one aspect of the timing of promotions. Another temporal aspect is whether the organization requires that the person be moved up after a certain time in his present position irrespective of readiness. The "up or out" rule of academic life, airlines, and law firms, for example, forces either advancement or departure from the organizational career in many instances (Caplow and McGee). The larger the organization, usually the more complex the timing and alternative career lines for advancement.

Another prominent source of promotion in organizations is the processes, both ordered and unordered, of selecting persons for promotion. Large organizations may have elaborately ordered processes for considering each man routinely when he is ready—has been in a position a prescribed length of time (Janowitz). This routine appraisal is usually based on performance, merit, and seniority. However, with these ordered procedures may be juxtaposed, unordered, informal processes which become more elaborate and decisive of promotion as one nears the top of the career. For example, in the army, as one advances the "tapping system" becomes more important for the next step. An officer is tapped for advancement by superiors because of his outstanding accomplishments, his unconventionality, and his ability to fit personally into the next highest group of colleagues.

The formally ordered procedures are fairly well known to the people in the organizational career. They may even be printed in handbooks. Besides being routinely considered, the person may have to receive evaluations or recommendations from certain superiors, some of whom may be informal sponsors and others whose favor must be won by strategies varying from "buttering them up" to shows of high-quality work. Standardized procedures allow people some expectation as to the inevitability of their next promotion. These procedures specify how much control people might achieve over their promotions through gaining information and through indicating points in the structure of the process to exert pressure on those involved in the procedures. Indeed, using controls allowed by the ordered procedures is a test in itself on ability to advance. For example, sometimes attending a transitional school is necessary for the next promotion (a war college, graduate work, flight school, and so forth (Roth)). The test, then, is on the person's ability to achieve an assignment or entry to this school, as well as doing qualifying work once in it. The resort to strategic sponsors and their power is an important strategy here. Learning how and when during his career to apply for the school assignment is vital also. Achieving a skip in stages of career may also be necessary sometimes to be in an advantageous position for a crucial promotion. Being at the right place at the right time, knowing of this place and how to get there again may be necessary for a promotion.

Ordered promotion procedures are liable to change by several contextual conditions. Changing race relations in the community may have changed the requisite composition of various races of ethnic groups at some levels of the organizational career. Perhaps more Negroes must be in the upper levels of the union (Kornhauser) or army. Perhaps law firms have started to hire more Jewish lawyers and then to take them into partnership. The police force may be required to hire any nationality. Also the changing size of the organization shifts conditions for advancement. Expansion creates positions, making advancement easier. Cutting back the size freezes many who might otherwise advance. How many different sites the organization has may affect advancement. It may be hard to promote a man to a level where others feel he is not their equal, even though he is ready to be advanced. If, as in the case of the army, large industries, government, or banks, the promotion can be combined with a move to a new site, formal advancement is less liable to being blocked.

At the other end of the continuum from ordered procedures are ad hoc, unordered promotion processes. Patterns, ordered only by the changing conditions of people and organizational life, of course, may be seen within these processes. The law firm, for example, would appear to use a very flexible process of elimination (Smigel). There are several facets to this process. The person does not really know what will happen to his career until it is about to happen. Promotion does not occur as a discrete jump up in rank but as a growing process of excellence in work and involvement in the firm so that it becomes the natural step to move the man into an associate position or partnership. This natural move up may take years, but usually not more than ten for partnership. It also becomes a natural occurrence that others are eliminated or leveled off, so that when partners are finally chosen, only a few of an initial group of recruits remain to choose from.

Another unordered process is clique system advancement (Abegglen). The clique may be composed of family, friends, or close classmates from a school. The informal reciprocal obligations existing between members of the clique require that they all (eventually) advance together in relative position. If one advances, he pulls the others along with him. Sometimes sectors of the clique advance and the rest are soon brought up. Other times the clique moves up *in toto*. Outsiders to the clique have little chance in rising on the organizational career line taken over by the clique. This clique system may overlap processes of elimination or of sponsorship, but it tends to be broken down by a formally ordered system of advancement, unless it controls this order. For example, cliques in law firms may be obvious because of the homogeneity of the ruling partners on several dimensions, such as religion, social class, and law school. Family and social class cliques used to run the army, but this is a thing of the past, due to both the increased size of the army and the formal promotion procedures causing great heterogeneity among officers. Cliques typically survive best in small organizations, with their reduced requirements of providing careers for large numbers with diverse expertises.

Sponsorship is also another unordered process of achieving promotions. It tends to exist alongside any other type of ordered or unordered process of promotion. It is usually very effective, since people with power can find ways of bringing up others they are sponsoring, whether using formal procedures, informal strategies, or combinations of both. Sponsorship, however, can break down in organizations where merit or seniority is of such high importance that to merely suggest advancement for a private or particularistic reason is to be liable to favoritism, which might hurt a candidate's chances of winning in the competition for a promotion. Another condition hindering sponsorship is when the sponsor himself looses power or position. Those persons he is sponsoring may be carried away with him, loosing out to people sponsored by those in power. Other properties of sponsorship varying a person's chances for promotion are how many sponsors one has and whether they are within the organization or important people outside of it (a dean, a client, or a politician, for example). Sometimes sponsorship dominates all promotion procedures (Hall). This domination creates some codification of its criteria and boundaries of effectiveness among sponsors. However, since sponsorship tends to occur in a closed awareness context,[1] candidates usually never know what will happen or how to achieve advancement except by orders from their sponsor. Several articles in this section discuss other properties of sponsorship, such as how people control the organization by it (Kornhauser), or the reciprocal obligations and mutual needs of sponsors and their candidates (Hall).

No matter what promotion process or combination thereof is operating, sociological researchers have discovered a strong emphasis on promoting the "right" man for the job: a vital condition for many a person's advancement. The image of the right man may be based on idealized reasoning about who is best for this job or stage of career, or it might be based on clear-cut personal attributes and achievements of the candidates. Usually, but not always, these properties of the person become deciding factors for picking a person from a group of candidates that have an adequate level of ability for the job. These attributes may be age, sex, religion, ethnicity, family background, wife, political preference, or club affiliation. Patterned clusters of these attributes

---

[1] Only the sponsor and a few strategic others know what is going on. See Barney G. Glaser and Anselm L. Strauss, *Awareness of Dying* (Chicago: Aldine Publishing Company, 1965).

develop for levels of the organizational career (Collins, Dalton). To violate them by promoting the wrong type of person can cause troubles for the organization, as strikes, walk-outs, factional fights, or low morale. The organization usually adheres to these clusters unless itself and its context change sufficiently that contrary promotions are not damaging to the organization. Individuals try to break through these patterns by working excessively hard so they will be advanced irrespectively (for example, Jewish lawyers in Gentile firms, or an Admiral Rickover type). They then become the token breakdown of the pattern, the exception that proves the rule for the stage of the organizational career in question. Another tactic is for a person to get behind a man soon to retire so he is the only effective successor and will have to be advanced although not the right type.

Clearly this is a well-studied area of organizational careers, because of its central importance to the notion of careers as an advancement process. But, clearly also, we need more generation of formal theory on promotions which can be accomplished by comparative analysis of our current substantive theories and knowledge, combined with studying the many other kinds of organizational careers yet unresearched. (See also Part VII on succession for other categories and properties of promotion.)

23

Success

C. WRIGHT MILLS

In this article, Professor Mills discusses "getting ahead" as currently referring to advancement in an organizational context, as opposed to previously referring to being a successful independent entrepreneur. Thus, current ideology supports striving for promotion in the organizational career.

The idea of the successful individual was linked with the liberal ideology of expanding capitalism. Liberal sociology, assuming a gradation of ranks in which everyone is rewarded according to his ability and effort, has paid less attention to the fate of groups or classes than to the solitary individual, naked of all save personal merit. The entrepreneur, making his way across the open market, most clearly displayed success in these terms.

The way up, according to the classic style of liberalism, was to establish a small enterprise and to expand it by competition with other enterprises. The worker became a foreman and then an industrialist; the clerk became a bookkeeper or a drummer and then a merchant on his own. The farmer's son took up land in his own right and, long before his old age, came into profits and independence. The competition and effort involved in these ways up formed the cradle of a self-reliant personality and the guarantee of economic and political democracy itself.

Success was bound up with the expansible possession rather than the forward-looking job. It was with reference to property that young men were spoken of as having great or small "expectations." Yet in this image success rested less on inheritances than on new beginnings from the bottom; for, it was thought, "business long ago ceased to be a matter of inheritance, and became the property of brains and persistence."

According to the old entrepreneur's ideology, success is always linked with the sober personal virtues of will power and thrift, habits of order, neatness, and the consitutional inability to say Yes to the easy road. These virtues are at once a condition and a sign of success. Without them, success is not possible; with them, all is possible. . . .

The entrepreneurial pattern of success and its inspirational ideology rested upon an economy of many small proprietorships. Under a centralized enterprise system, the pattern of success becomes a pattern of the climb within and between prearranged hierarchies. Whatever the level of opportunity

Excerpted from *White Collar* by C. Wright Mills (pp. 260–65). Copyright © 1951 by Oxford University Press, Inc. Reprinted by permission.

may be, the way up does not now typically include the acquisition of independent property. Only those who already have property can now achieve success based upon it.

The shift from a liberal capitalism of small properties to a corporate system of monopoly capitalism is the basis for the shift in the path and in the content of success. In the older pattern, the white-collar job was merely one step on the grand road to independent entrepreneurship; in the new pattern, the white-collar way involves promotions within a bureaucratic hierarchy. When only one-fifth of the population are free enterprisers (and not that many securely so), independent entrepreneurship cannot very well be the major end of individual economic life. The inspirational literature of entrepreneurial success has been an assurance for the individual and an apology for the system. Now it is more apologetic, less assuring.

For some three-fourths of the urban middle class, the salaried employees, the occupational climb replaces heroic tactics in the open competitive market. Although salaried employees may compete with one another, their field of competition is so hedged in by bureaucratic regulation that their competition is likely to be seen as grubbing and backbiting. The main chance now becomes a series of small calculations, stretched over the working lifetime of the individual: a bureaucracy is no testing field for heroes.

The success literature has shifted with the success pattern. It is still focused upon personal virtues, but they are not the sober virtues once imputed to successful entrepreneurs. Now the stress is on agility rather than ability, on "getting along" in a context of associates, superiors, and rules, rather than "getting ahead" across an open market; on who you know rather than what you know; on techniques of self-display and the generalized knack of handling people, rather than on moral integrity, substantive accomplishments, and solidity of person; on loyalty to, or even identity with, one's own firm, rather than entrepreneurial virtuosity. The best bet is the style of the efficient executive, rather than the drive of the entrepreneur.

Circumstances, personality, temperament, accident, as well as hard work and patience, now appear as key factors governing success or failure. One should strive for "experience and responsibility within one's chosen field," with "little or no thought of money." Special skills and "executive ability," preferably native, are the ways up from routine work. But the most important single factor is "personality," which "...commands attention...by charm...force of character, or...demeanor....Accomplishment without ...personality is unfortunate....Personality...without industry is... undesirable."

To be courteous "will help you to get ahead...you will have much more fun...will be much less fatigued at night...will be more popular, have more friends." So, "Train yourself to smile....Express physical and mental alertness....Radiate self-confidence....Smile often and sincerely." "Everything you say, everything you do, creates impressions upon other people . . . from the cradle to the grave, you've got to get along with other people. Use sound sales principles and you'll do better in 'selling' your merchandise, your ideas, and yourself."

The prime meaning of opportunity in a society of employees is to serve the big firm beyond the line of a job's duty and hence to bring oneself to the attention of the higher-ups who control upward movement. This entails dependability and enthusiasm in handling the little job in a big way. "Character . . . includes . . . innate loyalty in little things and enthusiastic interest in the job at hand. . . . In a word, thoroughly dependable and generally with an optimistic, helpful attitude."

"Getting ahead" becomes "a continual selling job. . . . Whether you are seeking a new position or are aiming at the job just ahead. In either case you must sell yourself and keep on selling. . . . You have a product and that product is yourself." The skillful personal maneuver and the politic approach in inter-organizational contacts, the planful impressing of the business superior become a kind of Machiavellism for the little man, a turning of oneself into an instrument by which to use others for the end of success. "Become genuinely interested in other people. . . . Smile. . . . Be a good listener. . . . Talk in terms of the other man's interest. . . . Make the other person feel important—and do it sincerely. . . . I am talking," says Dale Carnegie, "about a new way of life."

The heraldry of American success has been the greenback; even when inspirational writers are most inspirational, the big money is always there. Both entrepreneurial and white-collar patterns involve the remaking of personality for pecuniary ends, but in the entrepreneurial pattern money-success involved the acquisition of virtues good in themselves: the money is always to be used for good works, for virtue and good works justify riches. In the white-collar pattern, there is no such moral sanctifying of the means of success; one is merely prodded to become an instrument of success, to acquire tactics not virtues; money success is assumed to be an obviously good thing for which no sacrifice is too great.

The entrepreneurial and white-collar ways of success, although emerging in historical sequence, are not clear-cut phases through which American aspiration and endeavor have passed. They now co-exist, and each has varying relevance in different economic areas and phases of the economic cycle. Each has also come up against its own kinds of difficulty, which limit its use as a prod to striving. In a society of employees in large-scale enterprises, only a limited number can attempt to follow the entrepreneurial pattern; in a society that has turned itself into a great salesroom, the salesman's ways of success are likely to be severely competitive, and, at the same time, rationalized out of existence; in a society in which the educational level of the lower ranks is constantly rising and jobs are continually rationalized, the white-collar route to the top is likely to come up against competition it never knew in more educationally restricted situations.

24

The Accumulation of Advantages vs.
the Bureaucratic Crawl

C. WRIGHT MILLS

Professor Mills indicates that success in the "bureaucratic crawl" can itself never result in becoming very rich. Thus, in deciding upon the organizational career, a person should consider how rich he wants to become.

The rise into the very rich stratum seems to involve an economic career which has two pivotal features: the big jump and the accumulation of advantages.

1. No man, to my knowledge has ever entered the ranks of the great American fortunes merely by saving a surplus from his salary or wages. In one way or another, he has to come into command of a strategic position which allows him the chance to appropriate big money, and usually he has to have available a considerable sum of money in order to be able to parlay it into really big wealth. He may work and slowly accumulate up to this big jump, but at some point he must find himself in a position to take up the main chance for which he has been on the lookout. On a salary of two or three hundred thousand a year, even forgetting taxes, and living like a miser in a board shack, it has been mathematically impossible to save up a great American fortune.[1] . . .

2. Once he has made the big jump, once he has negotiated the main chance, the man who is rising gets involved in the accumulation of advantages, which is merely another way of saying that to him that hath shall be given. To parlay considerable money into the truly big money, he must be in a position to benefit from the accumulation advantages. The more he has, and the more strategic his economic position, the greater and the surer are his chances to gain more. The more he has, the greater his credit—his opportunities to use other people's money—and hence the less risk he need take

[1] If you started at 20 years of age and worked until you were 50 or so, saving $200,000 a year, you would still have, at a rate of 5 per cent compound interest, only $14 million, less than half of the lower limits we have taken for the great American fortunes.

But if you had bought only $9,900 worth of General Motors stock in 1913, and, rather than use your judgment, had gone into a coma—allowing the proceeds to pile up in General Motors then, in 1953, you would have about $7 million.

And, if you had not even exercised the judgment of choosing General Motors, but merely put $10,000 into each of the total of 480 stocks listed in 1913—a total investment of about $1 million—and then gone into a coma until 1953, you would have come out worth $10 million and have received in dividends and rights another $10 million. The increase in value would have amounted to about 899 per cent, the dividend return at 999 per cent. Once you have the million, advantages would accumulate—even for a man in a coma.

in order to accumulate more. There comes a point in the accumulation of advantages, in fact, when the risk is no risk, but is as sure as the tax yield of the government itself.

The accumulation of advantages at the very top parallels the vicious cycle of poverty at the very bottom. For the cycle of advantages includes psychological readiness as well as objective opportunities: just as the limitations of lower class and status position produce a lack of interest and a lack of self-confidence, so do objective opportunities of class and status produce interest in advancement and self-confidence. The confident feeling that one can of course get what one desires tends to arise out of and to feed back into the objective opportunities to do so. Energetic aspiration lives off a series of successes; and continual, petty failure cuts the nerve of the will to succeed. . . .

Most of the 1950 very rich who are related to the very rich of earlier generations have been born with the big jump already made for them and the accumulation of advantages already firmly in operation. The 39 per cent of the very rich of 1900 who originated from the upper classes inherited the big jump; and a few of them, notably the Vanderbilts and Astors, also inherited the positions involving the accumulation of advantages. J. P. Morgan's father left him $5 million and set him up as a partner in a banking firm connected with financial concerns in both Europe and America. That was his big jump. But the accumulation of advantages came later when, in his capacity as financier and broker, J. P. Morgan could lend other people's money to promote the sale of stocks and bonds in new companies, or the consolidation of existing companies, and receive as his commission enough stock to eventually enable his firm to control the new corporation. . . .

No man, to my knowledge, has ever entered the ranks of the great American fortunes merely by a slow bureaucratic crawl up the corporate hierarchies. "Many of the top executives in some of our largest corporations," Benjamin F. Fairless, Chairman of the Board of U.S. Steel, said in 1953, "have spent a lifetime in the field of industrial management without ever having been able to accumulate as much as a million dollars. And I know that to be fact because I happen to be one of them myself." That statement is not true in the sense that the heads of the larger corporations do not typically become millionaires: they do. But it is true in the sense that they do not become millionaires because they are "experts" in the field of industrial management; and it is true in that it is not by industry but by finance, not by management but by promotion and speculation that they typically become enriched. Those who have risen into the very rich have been economic politicians and members of important cliques who have been in positions permitting them to appropriate for personal uses out of the accumulation of advantages.

Very few of those who have risen to great wealth have spent the major portions of their working lives steadily advancing from one position to another within and between the corporate hierarchies. Such a long crawl was made by only 6 per cent of the very rich in 1900, and 14 per cent in 1950. But even these, who apparently did move slowly up the corporate hierarchy, seem rarely to have made the grade because of talents in business management. More often such talents as they possessed were the talents of the lawyer or—very infrequently—those of the industrial inventor.

The long crawl comes to a pay-off only if it is transformed into an accumulation of advantages; this transformation is often a result of a merger of companies. Usually such a merger takes place when the companies are relatively small and often it is cemented by marriage—as when the du Ponts bought out Laflin and Rand, their largest competitor, and Charles Copeland —assistant to the president of Laflin and Rand—became assistant treasurer of du Pont and married Luisa D'Anbelot du Pont.

The slow movement through a sequence of corporate positions may also mean that one has accumulated enough inside information and enough friendship to be able, with less risk or with no risk, to speculate in the promotion or manipulation of securities. That is why the generation of 1925 contains the largest proportions of the very rich making the long crawl; then the market was open for such profits and the rules of speculation were not so difficult as they were later to become.

Whatever type of venture it is that enables the rich man to parlay his stake into a great appropriation, at one point or another the "bureaucratic" men have usually been as much "entrepreneurs" as were the classic founders of fortunes after the Civil War. Many of them, in fact—like Charles W. Nash —broke out on their own to found their own companies. Once the crawl was made, many of these men, especially of the 1925 set, took on all the gambling spirit and even some of the magnificence usually associated with the robber barons of the late nineteenth century.

The economic careers of the very rich are neither "entrepreneurial" nor "bureaucratic." Moreover, among them, many of those who take on the management of their families' firms are just as "entrepreneurial" or as "bureaucratic" as those who have not enjoyed such inheritance. "Entrepreneur" and "bureaucrat" are middle-class words with middle-class associations and they cannot be stretched to contain the career junctures of the higher economic life in America.

The misleading term "entrepreneur" does not have the same meaning when applied to small businessmen as it does when applied to those men who have come to possess the great American fortunes. The sober bourgeois founding of a business, the gradual expanding of this business under careful guidance until it becomes a great American corporation is not an adequate picture of the fortune founders at the higher levels.

The entrepreneur, in the classic image, was supposed to have taken a risk, not only with his money but with his very career; but once the founder of a business has made the big jump he does not usually take serious risks as he comes to enjoy the accumulation of advantages that lead him into great fortune. If there is any risk, someone else is usually taking it. Of late, that someone else, as during World War II and in the Dixon-Yates attempt, has been the government of the United States. If a middle-class businessman is in debt for $50,000, he may well be in trouble. But if a man manages to get into debt for $2 million, his creditors, if they can, may well find it convenient to produce chances for his making money in order to repay them.

The robber barons of the late nineteenth century usually founded or organized companies which became springboards for the financial accumulations that placed them among the very rich. In fact, 55 per cent of the very rich of 1900 made the first step to great fortune by the big jump of promoting or organizing their own companies. By 1925, however, and again in 1950, only 22 per cent of the very rich made such a jump.

Very rarely have the men of any of these generations become very rich merely by the energetic tutelage of one big firm. The accumulation of advantages has usually required the merging of other businesses with the first one founded—a financial operation—until a large "trust" is formed. The manipulation of securities and fast legal footwork are the major keys to the success of such higher entrepreneurs. For by such manipulation and footwork they attained positions involved in the accumulation of advantages.

The major economic fact about the very rich is the fact of the accumulation of advantages: those who have great wealth are in a dozen strategic positions to make it yield further wealth. Sixty-five per cent of the very richest people in America today are involved in enterprises which their families have passed on to them or are simply living as rentiers on the huge returns from such properties. The remaining 35 per cent are playing the higher economic game more actively, if no more daringly, than those who used to be called entrepreneurs but who in later day capitalism are more accurately called the economic politicians of the corporate world.

There are several ways to become rich. By the middle of the twentieth century in the United States, it has become increasingly difficult to earn and to keep enough money so as to accumulate your way to the top. Marriage involving money is at all times a delicate matter, and when it involves big money, it is often inconvenient and sometimes insecure. Stealing, if you do not already have much money, is a perilous undertaking. If you are really gambling for money, and do so long enough, your capital will, in the end, balance out; if the game is fixed, you are really earning it or stealing it, or both, depending on which side of the table you sit. It is not usual, and it never has been the dominant fact, to create a great American fortune merely by nursing a little business into a big one. It is not usual and never has been the dominant fact carefully to accumulate your way to the top in a slow, bureaucratic crawl. It is difficult to climb to the top, and many who try fall by the way. It is easier and much safer to be born there.

25

Patterns of Mobility within
Industrial Organizations

NORMAN H. MARTIN and ANSELM L. STRAUSS

One organizational condition affecting advancement is how
many different career lines are offered a person at his
particular career stage. Which career lines are chosen or
available often depends on the action of a sponsor,
especially at high levels. Professors Martin and Strauss
describe how career lines tend to become stabilized in an
organizational structure and how individuals can take
advantage of developed channels of mobility.

The organizational structure of an industrial enterprise has dual and inter-related functions. From the standpoint of management, it provides for an orderly hierarchy of responsibility and authority—a division of work rationally planned to meet the objectives of efficient operation. Vertical and horizontal movement of personnel through the various positions making up the organization is executed so as to make certain that competent men get in the right places at the right time. From the standpoint of the individual member, on the other hand, organization provides a stable set of expectations as to how they, as well as others, should act. Of equal importance, it provides a number of channels through which mobile individuals can move to realize personal objectives. . . .

THE DEVELOPMENT OF CAREER LINES

Over time, the paths of movement of personnel through the system of positions making up a company's organization structure tend to become more or less stabilized. Patterns of vertical and horizontal movement evolve, to form various types of career lines which terminate at various levels of the management hierarchy. These career lines, which are somewhat analogous to the trunks and branches of trees, provide escalators for mobile individuals.

The majority of these lines are minor and terminate at lower executive levels; others move beyond these positions and branch off into middle management; a few major lines lead to the top. A typical career line consists of a series of vertical and horizontal movements from position to position, i.e., vertical movement from section leader to department head within a given division; horizontal movements from department head to department head in different divisions; following this, vertical movement to division head; and so on. Ideally, horizontal mobility—the movement of an individual laterally along a given level of management—gives that person breadth of experience.

Excerpted, with permission, from *Journal of Business*, 29(2) (April, 1956): 101–110.

Vertical mobility, of course, is movement of an individual up or down in the management hierarchy and consists of shifts from one level of responsibility to another.

Within the total complex of positions, certain ones operate as critical junctures or testing points. The performance of the individual at these crucial points determines the type of career line along which he will move—whether he moves on along a line to intermediate or higher management, horizontally to other line or staff jobs, or terminates his career at the level involved.

Typically, these turning points are quasi-training positions. For example, in the production division of one large company, the positions of assistant division manager and plant superintendent serve this function. Management can directly observe the individual being considered for higher management. They can determine his capacity to handle complex human relationships, to assume the initiative in unstructured situations, to handle responsibility, and to be adept at long-range decision-making—all of which are characteristic situations confronting higher management. If his performance is judged to be satisfactory, he moves into a line of progression leading to higher management; if it is somewhat less than satisfactory, he may be moved horizontally for further testing and training, or he may be moved into the next highest position, to remain there for the duration of his career.

At any given level in the executive hierarchy alternative channels of potential movement are present. In some instances these channels are multiple; the individual may move in any one of several directions—vertically or horizontally. In other instances the alternatives are more restricted and may even be closed. They are dead ends. This frequently happens in highly specialized types of jobs. In the case of those positions which function as critical turning points, numerous alternative paths of movement exist. This is necessary so that management can protect itself in cases where they have mistakenly judged the competence of an individual.

In order to make certain that competent and trained individuals move into the right places at the right time, more or less exact and differential training is provided at the various positions. At certain levels this takes the form of highly technical training in specific functions and areas; at others it is oriented toward the development of breadth of experience. This locus is related to a number of variables: the technological requirements of the industry, the type of organization, and the mobility structure.

For example, in one organization with a complex technology and division of labor, the pattern of movement of mobile personnel through lower levels of management is primarily vertical. Little horizontal movement occurs. Training is highly specialized. A primary concern of the management is to make certain that its first-line supervision is technically specialized. Interdepartmental coordination consequently becomes a primary function and the responsibility of middle management.

In contrast, another organization with a relatively simple technology has developed a mobility pattern in which a high degree of horizontal mobility exists at the lower executive levels. The aim of training here is to achieve a variety of experience in first-level supervision and, by so doing, to localize responsibility for coordination well down in the management hierarchy. Its organization structure is relatively flat. In both instances, therefore, a relationship holds between mobility structure, technology, organization philosophy, and type of training. It becomes a major problem in management to achieve the right blending of these components.

The speed at which individuals move along specific career lines tends to follow fairly identifiable timetables. Acceptable age ranges are identifiable for the various strata. While these age ranges are not usually defined explicitly, they nonetheless exist in terms of some of the criteria used by management in determining who moves and who does not. A given individual being considered for advancement may, for example, be passed over because he is "too old" or, less frequently, "too young." If an individual does not move out of a given position and into another by a certain age, there will be a high probability that he will never move farther. He will, in a sense, have his mobility terminated at that level.

The existence of these career timetables enables individuals to assess their mobility prospects and even to predict their chances of advancement to higher levels. A person who does not progress in accordance with these age timetables may know, therefore, that his potential for higher levels of management has been judged unfavorably.

In general, individuals who ultimately reach higher levels in the management hierarchy tend to move rapidly along specific career lines leading to the top. Warner and Abegglen in their studies of occupational mobility in American business and industry note: "Within fifteen years of becoming self-supporting, more than half of the men studied were major executives and a quarter were minor executives."

In order to facilitate the progression of men into higher executive levels and still achieve requisite competence, a skipping of levels may frequently be observed. An individual moves in an orderly manner from one position to the next and from level to level up to a point. He then moves around a given layer of management to a higher position in the hierarchy. In this manner relatively young men assume top-management responsibilities.

Horizontal and vertical movements, therefore, mesh and mutually support each other. On the one hand, horizontal movement may be thought of as being in the service of the vertical in the sense that a company is concerned with training and educating people and testing potential executives. They are also finding terminal places for mediocrity and taking care of those who were misjudged or who faded out. Gaps created by unforeseen circumstances must be filled by trained individuals with a minimum of delay, trouble spots taken care of by shifting versatile men along the line. On the other hand, although perhaps in a more minor sense, we may conceptualize the vertical system as being in the service of the horizontal. It is essential that the executive positions in all the various divisions of a company be staffed by competent and trained personnel. Major and minor career lines exist. These lines siphon off executives into the various levels and divisions. Thus there must be more or less permanent works managers and division superintendents; likewise there must be general foremen and plant superintendents. These people come from off the major vertical ladder—either on their way up or on their way off; others move directly into these positions via subsidiary and more minor career lines. From the standpoint of the student of organization, all these interlocking horizontal and vertical movements add up to an organized system.

At this point it may be well to cite a concrete illustration of some of the already made points. Our example is a large, multi-plant industry engaged in the production of automobile parts. Movement of personnel through the lower levels of the management hierarchy is almost exclusively vertical. Little or no horizontal mobility exists at these lower levels. When it does occur, it tends to be limited to movement within one plant and between departments and is an indicator of unsatisfactory performance.[1] The position of general foreman (the top position at foremen levels) is the initial juncture or crossroad for mobile personnel. Individuals whose performance is highly satisfactory move on into superintendencies or may even jump beyond into higher positions. Those judged to be less competent may be shifted horizontally or may stay where they are.

Considerable horizontal movement of personnel occurs at the middle management levels. Indeed here, in contrast to lower levels, failure to move horizontally is an indicator of only mediocre performance. This horizontal mobility occurs not only within the various departments and divisions of a single plant but also between plants. It brings about breadth of experience and also enables management to judge the potential of the men and to decide whether they should be moved into branch lines terminating in middle management or into career channels leading to top executive positions. This level is therefore a second critical juncture. At the higher executive levels the pattern of movement again tends to be primarily vertical.

Identifiable timetables of progression exist. Individuals must have moved through the foreman ranks and be ready for middle management at latest by the time they are around thirty-five years of age. Otherwise they tend to remain in lower-management positions. Between the ages of thirty and forty, they perform at middle-management levels and are seasoned, as it were, by a variety of experience. Upward movement out of this level must generally occur before the individual reaches forty or, at a maximum, forty-five.

In the company being discussed the main career line to the top centers in the largest of the plants. Most top executives have received the bulk of their

---

[1] The situation is analogous to that frequently encountered in officer candidate schools during World War II. A candidate about whom there was some doubt as to capacity was given a series of trials in various positions. Horizontal mobility was an indicator of possible failure.

training here. From the standpoint of the mobile individual it becomes imperative that sooner or later he get into the career lines of that plant. The characteristics of this career line, therefore, are quite specific: movement up is relatively rapid and clearly defined; youthful age limits circumscribe times by which movement must be made; horizontal mobility at certain crucial junctures is well planned to insure adequate training and testing; the final sequence of positions centers within the largest of the several plants.

In addition to this main career line, branch-off lines lead to middle-management positions. Movements along these lines are not so rapid as that characterizing those who move higher. At some point or other along the career line a faltering or a stumbling occurred, with the result that extra horizontal mobility was necessary. Sometimes these men were held at a given position well beyond the critical age range; at other times they were blocked by competitors who were more powerfully sponsored. On the other hand, some of these career lines are purely local. Movement is confined to one of the smaller plants.

THE MOBILITY STRUCTURE FROM THE STANDPOINT OF THE INDIVIDUAL

From the standpoint of the mobile individual—the person ambitious to move ahead and up—the established patterns of movement in an organization present avenues of advancement. The perceptive individual can, for the most part, determine the channels through which he must move in order to realize his personal ambitions. Cues by which he can assess his own position and his potential for future advancement exist in a variety of forms.

One fundamental cue is the pattern of advancement already established—the complex of vertical and horizontal movements leading to specific levels of management. This, coupled with the timetables setting the ages at which movement must take place, enables him to judge his own progress. Given a stable organization, he can frequently do this with considerable accuracy.

Other cues are more subtle. At times it is difficult to determine whether a movement is a promotion or a demotion. This is especially true when we realize that too much horizontal mobility may actually act as a demotion unless it is coupled with ultimate vertical movement. The individual is growing older, and his mobility potential thereby becomes more limited because of the existence of timetables of advancement. In some industries this is so clearly realized that young executives refuse to accept more than one or two horizontal movements.

A similar comment is applicable to movements into staff positions. These positions are frequently filled by individuals who have not "made the grade" in the line. Such personnel, however, are mixed with others who are definitely competent and are there for clear reasons of function. It requires considerable discernment on the part of the mobile individual to determine the category into which he falls.

From the standpoint of pure tactics, the mobile individual would do well to become attached to a sponsor—an individual in a superior position who can pull him along. Over and beyond this, he must also acquire the ways of behavior acceptable to higher management. This means that he must, in a sense, secede from the ways of thinking and behavior of the management level in which he holds membership and adopt, instead, the norms and orientation of the level to which he aspires. A sort of "anticipatory socialization" must occur; the values of the higher group are taken as a fundamental frame of reference by the mobile person. This process, however, is not without its difficulties. Merton brilliantly characterizes the difficulty as follows:

What the individual experiences as estrangement from a group of which he is a member tends to be experienced by his associates as repudiation of the group, and this ordinarily evokes a hostile response. As social relations between the individual and the rest of the group deteriorate, the norms of the group become less binding for him. For since he is progressively seceding from the group and being penalized by it, he is the less likely to experience rewards for adherence to the group's norms. Once initiated, this process seems to move toward a cumulative detachment from the group, in terms of attitudes and values as well as in terms of social relations. And to the degree that he orients himself toward out-group values, perhaps affirming them verbally and expressing them in action, he only widens the gap and reinforces the hostility between himself and his in-group associates. Through the interplay of dissociation and progressive alienation from the group values, he may become doubly motivated to orient himself toward the values of another group and to affiliate himself with it. There then remains the distinct question of the objective possibility of affiliating himself with his reference group. If the possibility is negligible or absent, then the alienated individual becomes socially rootless. But if the social system realistically allows for such change in group affiliations, then the individual estranged from the one group has all the more motivation to belong to the other.[2]

SPONSORSHIP

Progression of individuals along given career lines is not only a result of technical competence and of being available and trained at the right time. A major influence determining who moves and how far is the action of a sponsor. In many instances, and especially at higher levels, this is almost a necessary condition for mobility.

The relationship of sponsor and protégé tends to be a reciprocal one of mutual benefit and occurs for a variety of reasons: the protégé may complement his superior by being strong in an area of activity where his sponsor is

[2] Robert K. Merton and Alice S. Kitt, "Reference Group Theory and Social Mobility," in Reinhard Bendix and Seymour M. Lipset (eds.), Class, Status, and Power: A Reader in Social Stratification (Glencoe: Free Press, 1953), 409–10.

weak; he may serve in a role as detail man, adviser, or confidant. Regardless of reasons, when the sponsor rises, the protégé moves with him. From the standpoint of the protégé, therefore, he benefits by being pulled up in the hierarchy.

A given sponsor may have a cluster of protégés surrounding him. Ties of loyalty as well as need compel him to push for advancing "his men" as he moves up. As a result, top-management echelons of many companies are made up of interlocking cliques—certain powerful sponsors and their adherents. The mobility patterns in any organization are, therefore, to a considerable extent influenced by the phenomenon of sponsorship.

Such arrangements are not without merit. From the standpoint of efficiency, it is possible for work to get done in an easy manner. Many smoothly working teams of executives evolve. Solidarity is high; common values and styles of action make for consistent behavior. On the negative side, however, the play of "internal politics" can create conflicts and anxiety. Executives who are not members of the cliques may be short-circuited and even undermined. Organizational efficiency may suffer. Serious problems develop when protégés lose their sponsors either because they are dropped or because the sponsor himself loses power because of shifts within the organization. The organization is then faced with the problem of working with individuals who no longer have a place within the scheme of things.

The existence of systems of sponsorship and resultant problems have been well documented in the histories of large companies. . . .

The vice-president in charge of sales of a large industrial concern resigned his position for personal reasons. During the course of his career, he had sponsored several individuals into positions as department sales managers. While these managers were competent enough and remained in their positions, it soon became apparent that the new vice-president was not going to move them higher into zone and district positions. Their techniques of operation did not fit into his philosophy and strategies. Other individuals were promoted around them. Their reactions varied: one became passive and did only the minimum work required; another began to build a little empire of his own, communicating with associates and higher management only when required; others became hostile and aggressive. In brief, they became problems for management. . . .

It would appear that the organizational structure of any concern is a result of the interplay of several factors. Ideally, such a structure should be the result of rational planning and should be developed in accordance with an over-all theory of management and policy. Actually, however, other factors, e.g., individual personalities, play a decisive role. Executives become concerned with developing their own positions and extending their power; positions are created; power struggles evolve. While this is not a universal phenomenon, it is of sufficient generality to be reckoned with. It comes directly to the fore in the activities of sponsors. Here the power structure is superimposed upon the rationally conceived organization. Career lines are frequently affected, causing changes which have an impact both upon management objectives of achieving an orderly and effective system of executive development and upon the mobility aspirations of conscientious and ambitious personnel.

26

Military Tactics of Promotion

MORRIS JANOWITZ

Large organizations may have elaborately ordered processes
for considering each man routinely for a promotion based
on merit and seniority. However, behind these ordered
procedures may be informal processes more decisive of
promotion when one nears the top, such as "tapping" in
the army. Professor Janowitz describes the importance of
such informal processes in determining advancement in the
military.

Even when the military profession was small, homogeneous, and governed
by seniority rules, informal lines of communication and personal reputation
were important in molding an officer's career. As the military profession
became more and more managerial, those who wanted to rise had to establish
a reputation based on their skill or on their heroic qualities. In building a
reputation, each younger officer has the task of coming to the attention of
important superiors. Similarly, superior officers were continuously concerned
with discovering those officers whom they wished to have serve as their sub-
commanders and their staff officers. Before 1941, senior officers, including
General George Marshall, kept such lists of men who they had personally
observed, or who were reputed to have the qualities for important commands.
The process could best be described as a system of "tapping," by which men
were recognized as potential members of the elite.

As a result, the military profession is today engaged in a continuous
process of informally rating their superiors, peers, and subordinates. The
system of peer rating, which the psychologists thought they were introducing
in Officer Candidate School, has been a long-standing informal selection
procedure. Before World War II, mutual contact among officers was widespread since the profession was small, and therefore the informal system was
completely pervasive. The officer had to establish his individuality, but within
the confines of narrow and acceptable limits. The result was to reinforce
conformity in social behavior, for excessive individuality would injure one's
reputation. Because of its growth alone, the military establishment has been
forced to erect an elaborate and formal personnel system to control promotions and career development. But for a realistic understanding of career
development, it is impossible to separate the formal procedures from the
elaborate informal screening that goes on simultaneously. As the size of the

Excerpted, with permission, from *The Professional Soldier* (New York: Free Press of Glencoe,
1960; pp. 145–48).

professional officers' corps has grown, and as the system of promotion by seniority has weakened, there has been a corresponding growth in the complexity of official record-keeping. When official personnel records were first collected, before the War of 1812, commanding officers were brief and perhaps overly forthright. It sufficed to record in a man's dossier, "A good man, but no officer," or, "A knave, despised by all."

Army regulation number 600–185, issued on June 16, 1948, which governs the filing of officer efficiency reports, is a formidable document. In addition to describing the officer's last job in detail, supervising officers are obliged to estimate the officer's capacity along nine dimensions using a five-point scale. His job efficiency is recorded according to nineteen factors; twelve of these are on the basis of "forced comparisons" with all officers in his unit, and seven are determined by means of a ten-point scale. Furthermore, his job evaluation requires the judgment of eighteen personal qualities; twelve of them are made on the basis of "forced comparisons" with all other officers in the unit, and six are on a ten-point scale. This makes possible, presumably on the basis of machine tabulation, a three-digit over-all score. It has been unofficially reported that under such a system justification of promotions can involve differences of one point in the third digit. When, at the close of World War II, the Air Force was faced with the task of selecting fourteen thousand officers, it signed a contract with the American Institute of Research, under the direction of Dr. John Flanagan, and produced an elaborate technique based on the so-called "critical incident" device.

Most responsible social scientists would claim that there is no theoretical or empirical justification for such elaborate personnel testing devices, and that they have come into being only because of the organizational necessity for some manageable criterion. It is understandable that there is widespread unfavorable criticism of the efficiency report system. In reality, the efficiency report and a suitable dossier are merely additional barriers or handicaps that must be surmounted in the race for career promotion. By the same token, it is understandable that elaborate informal devices persist to make such cumbersome systems workable.

The informal "tapping" system continues to operate in the contemporary military establishment, even at the lower levels. At the bottom, where the processing of service records proceeds on a mass basis, the young officer hopes that some higher officer will take a special interest in him and will make an entry on his record, or informally report some meaningful comments beyond the formal ratings. By the time a young officer is a captain in the Army or Air Force, or a lieutenant in the Navy, he may have already established a reputation as an "up and coming" officer, and this reputation is communicated both to him and to his superiors. The search for talent is as intense in the military as it is in any other profession, and to be a sponsor for an outstanding young officer is to the advantage of the more established professional.

At the middle levels, where careers are made or broken, informal networks of communications operate in the context of the activities of official promotion committees and personnel officers. The aspiring officer retains considerable initiative in directing his career, and he seeks out those assignments which are reputed to be part of the successful career. Early in his career he learns that the road to the top, at least to the level of one or possibly two stars, is not through assignment to the specialized technical services, but by being an unrestricted line officer. In the Army the Corps of Engineers occupies a special position. It has high prestige, offers interesting work in peacetime, selects the top graduate from West Point, and enables an officer to find increased employment opportunities after retirement. While the Corps of Engineers has supplied generals who served as administrators and military technologists, it is not a major route to military leadership. Instead, the aspiring officer believes that the prescribed career is in the combat arms, although the fortunes of particular weapons systems change with technological progress. He believes it is important to have command duty, and to be involved in operations when assigned to staff duty. Informal communications play an important role in the allocation of these desired assignments, especially for the middle-level officer who has built a reputation for his skill and potentiality for promotion. At the highest levels, of course, colleague reputation and informal contacts outweigh personnel records as the basis of making assignments.

Practices vary among the services, but it is in the Air Force, strangely enough, that informal contacts are the most crucial in counterbalancing personnel record-keeping. This is due, in part, to the greater mobility of the Air Force officer who has an opportunity to maintain wide contacts, and to literally shop around for his next assignment. In general, until recently, the expanding horizons of the Air Force gave each officer greater latitude and greater power over the management of his career.

In each service, personnel officers and selection boards have more or less clear-cut images of what constitutes the ideal career for the aspiring professional officer. More often than not, these images are firmly rooted in past experiences. The events of each war have weakened them, but they continue to operate with powerful effect in peacetime. What evidence exists to indicate that in the past selection boards and personnel officers have had special talents in estimating the future needs of the military profession? To describe the prescribed military career does not fully encompass the life history of that smaller segment within the military elite who in effect transformed the profession during the last half century.

27

Selecting Law Partners

ERWIN O. SMIGEL

At the other end of the continuum are unordered promotion
procedures. These are patterned only by the changing
conditions of people and organizational life. The law firm,
for example, as described by Professor Smigel, would
appear to use a very flexible process of elimination and
the clique system.

PARTNERSHIP—EXCEPTIONS TO THE RULE

Before investigating the interesting process by which some associates stay
on and come up through the ranks to become partners, another avenue
toward partnership must be mentioned, for there are three exceptions to the
rule of promotion from within. The first involves leading politicians or public
figures. Generally, partners selected from the outside are either famous,
though often defeated candidates for high office, former cabinet members, or
other important government officials. A firm may have a number of reasons
for making this kind of choice—usually, because these people can attract
important clients. Unlike the young associate, the contacts of prominent
men are far-reaching and significant to a law office. Sometimes new leadership
is required and a respected lawyer from the outside is chosen to put an end to
severe internal squabbling, or simply because members of a law office admire
the outsider as a person and a lawyer. Some are chosen for all these
possibilities. . . .

The second exception to promotion through the ranks occurs either when
a firm needs a specialist in an established field or when a firm decides to
expand into another branch of the law. Law firms entering tax law for
example, brought in as highly placed associates or partners, men who had
been trained by the tax department in Washington.

A third exception occurs when two offices merge or when a large firm
takes over the main clients of a smaller one (a large bank provides one
example), bringing some of the lawyers from the smaller firm with them. If
they are particularly important to the client and his work, such lawyers are
then appointed partners.

UP THROUGH THE RANKS

Partnership is a sign of occupational success for the associates. Richard
Powell's hero, in his novel *The Philadelphian*, after being warned by the senior

Excerpted, with permission, from *The Wall Street Lawyer* (New York: Free Press of Glencoe,
1965; pp. 90–109).

partner of the difficulties he is likely to encounter on the road to membership in a large law firm, replies: "The way I look at it . . . in a big firm it's a tough climb to the top, but a mighty nice view if you can get there. I don't want to get to the top in a small firm and find I still can't see over the heads of the crowd. I'll take my chances in a big firm." . . .

The attorney who is offered a partnership is an individual who in the judgment of the firm is worthy of sharing assets and liabilities with them and is worthy of signing the firm's name. In many ways becoming a partner is equivalent to an enlisted man becoming an officer. In both instances few do, and in both instances, these few have passed an important work and social barrier.

It is interesting to note that few associates know the exact meaning of partnership. They know it is an important award. They think it will mean more independence, that the work will be of greater interest and excitement, and that they will have more money and respect. In most of these beliefs they are right. On some points however, they are sometimes incorrect. This is especially true of the new associates, but even the senior associate is not always correct in his judgment about what a partnership really means. For example, they do not know how much money they will be making as partners. The subject of percentages and salary is particularly "hush, hush"—the image about money is unclear. It is unusual for people to work long hours for nine or ten years for an occupational position for which they can set no definite monetary value. Brand new partners are usually given a salary until a proper percentage can be worked out for them. One man was eight thousand dollars off his estimate of what he would earn as a partner. He had guessed twenty-two thousand dollars a year—he started with thirty. Some associates are unrealistic about the amount of additional independence they will have when they first become partners. The new associate just beginning the long path to partnership often does not realize that he still will have to work for someone even when he becomes a partner (even at forty, he is considered a young man by senior partners). When he "arrives," he is just putting his foot on a new ladder, and the struggle up to an even more important position in the firm is also a difficult and hazardous one.

How Long Does It Take?

It is not an easy task to become a partner. Very few do. Those who do generally take between nine and eleven years. This figure differs by firm. . . .

In some offices, mainly the very social, nepotistic ones, two patterns are seen: (1) some lawyers become partners quickly, in fact, 25 per cent of the partners in one "social" firm reached this position by their eighth year of practice with the firm; and (2) at the other extreme, 34 per cent spent thirteen or more years as associates with one man waiting thirty years before he became a partner. Despite this, the average time it took to become a partner in the law office was 11.7 years. . . .

What must an associate do before he is invited to be a partner? What steps does he go through before this happens? What do the firms look for in a partner? To answer these questions it may be profitable to trace the general career patterns of ten imaginary apprentices hired from the class of 1951. The firm usually considers this lawyer with the class that graduated before him and with the one that graduated after. Probably only three men from these three classes will eventually be invited to join the firm. When they first arrive, little overt competition is found. The pay scale is about the same for all beginning lawyers and remains so for the first three years. They start out in a pool or doing research on a variety of subjects and are on general call. They have similar interests and tend early in their careers to form close ingroups. This pattern was intensified when early marriage was not as prevalent as it is today. After approximately the third year, individuals begin to specialize and are distributed among the various departments and work for different partners. As this specialization occurs some colleagues begin to leave the firm for the various reasons previously described, until in the eighth year only two or three of any "vintage" are left. It is from among these attorneys, and those left from the classes immediately before and after, that the firm at that time chooses its partners.

COMPETITION

Competition among associates at this point is at its height. Competition, however, started earlier and plays a part in the selecting-out process. It is rarely, especially at the beginning of their stay, severe and usually covert. Its existence, however, is recognized. Sixty members of the sample were asked about competition among associates. Fifteen per cent denied its existence, most giving *esprit de corps* as the reason. The others felt that competition did exist, as evidenced by (in order of the frequency with which the specific reasons were given) (1) efforts to do better work than the next man; (2) seeking of additional work and responsibility; (3) the taking on of additional night work and the showing of excessive drive; (4) miscellaneous intangible ways; (5) efforts to work for important partners; and (6) the need to take risks. Sixteen per cent who felt that competition existed cited its bad aspects, calling particular attention to "knifing," the harming of reputation, and, finally, to wives' campaigns at social affairs. Ten per cent felt that some competition existed but maintained that it was not extreme; they did not offer illustrations. . . .

In general, competition between associates shows up in the amount of work they are willing to take on and in the time they are willing to spend on it. It may appear in the quality of production and have some effect on obedience to minor house rules. Many associates claim that competition is impersonal and that the associate really competes against himself, as you can in golf. Those who try the more obvious approaches of flattery are in danger of losing more than they could possibly gain. Competition among associates is based mainly on competence and perseverance. It rarely becomes conflict, partly because even serious contenders for a partnership usually do not work on the same matter. In fact, competition throughout the firm is kept down because people of different ages work on different levels, on different matters, in different departments, and because overt extreme competition is not considered professional. This relative lack of severe competition, as we shall see later, is important because it has implications for professions and professional organizations.

Competition nevertheless exists and its effect as a selective agent depends in part upon the personality of the participants. Some lawyers leave because they cannot stand or do not like the competition. In a way, what those who leave for this reason say is that they feel they do not have the competence or that they are not willing to work hard enough to make the grade; others report that they find the competition so minor that they can say the atmosphere in their law office is relaxing. By the time a man is ready to be considered seriously for a partnership, those who found the competition too severe, or did not like it, have left.

The senior associate who is up for consideration for partnership has survived many tests. He has ignored the call of immediate riches ("I damn near left three times. One job was many times my salary"); judged correctly the managing partner's mention of a position with a corporation ("I was asked once if I wanted to take a job. I remember I was upset because I thought this an invitation to leave"); stuck it out when it did not look as if an opening existed in his field ("When after I had worked for eight years in the tax department, they asked me to change to corporation law, I did not know what to make of it, but I changed. They had an opening in this other department and were trying me out").

In terms of work, the associate who started out as the broad researcher and postgraduate student gradually finds that he is a member of a department and a specialist. As this narrowing process takes place, so does the final weeding out occur. Members of his class have left or were asked to leave and only three or four people from his group remain. These few who have survived face still another test, despite the fact that they have been under observation for at least eight years. They now begin to receive assignments from most of the main partners, instead of just from members in their department. This new work pattern functions in two ways—it tends to broaden the attorney and it gives an opportunity to the senior partners, who may not know the associate's work in detail, to judge him. For two or more years these senior associates will be under tremendous pressure to pass the test of working for the most powerful partners. At the end of this period one of the class of 1951 will probably have been made a partner. . . .

What Qualities Are Needed To Become a Partner?

Associates, partners, and lawyers who had worked for the various large firms studied were asked: "What can an associate do to further his ambitions for a partnership?" and "What does the firm look for in a partner?" Table 1 lists the attributes mentioned in order of frequency.

Table 1—What Can an Associate Do to Help Himself Become a Partner?

Techniques to Partnerships	Associates		Partners	
	(N)	(%)	(N)	(%)
Be a good lawyer, work hard	33	18.8	32	24.0
Bring in business	23	13.0	19	14.3
Maintain good relations with client	21	11.9	12	9.0
Have proper social background and contacts	20	11.5	7	5.3
Obtain sponsorship	18	10.2	6	4.5
Have proper personality	14	8.0	14	10.5
Have luck	13	7.4	12	9.0
Fulfill needs of the firm	6	3.3	7	5.3
Become indispensable to firm	5	2.8	4	3.0
Choose right department	3	1.7	0	0.0
Take responsibility	3	1.7	4	3.0
Go to right schools	3	1.7	0	0.0
Engage in outside activities	2	1.1	2	1.5
Don't know	2	1.1	1	0.8
Have leadership ability	0	0.0	3	2.3
Other	10	5.7	10	7.5
Total	176*	100.0	133*	100.0

* Totals more than the lawyer sample since multiple answers were given.

It is interesting to note that both partners and associates agree that hard work is one of the keys to partnership. Proportionally, however, partners mention it more often. Associates and partners do not agree on the role of sponsorship, good relations with clients, the importance of social background, proper connections, and right school. In all these instances the associates believe these items play a larger role in selection than do partners. Partners believe that the personality of the candidates, needs of the firm, luck, and ability to take responsibility are more important in choosing firm members than do associates.

Most answers contained a combination of techniques which might help the associate to become a partner. Hard work and ability, however, even when not specifically mentioned in answer to the question, were assumed by the great majority. In fact, these two attributes were thought of as minimum requirements. Those who survived eight years of observation could most assuredly claim both ability and hard work among their traits. But these two attributes are not considered enough. A former associate who had been passed over, and who now is a partner in a smaller firm, thought client-getting and client-keeping a surer road to partnership. . . .

An associate in a large office claimed he did not know how to become a partner but knew how not to be one.

You won't be a partner: (1) if you don't have awareness of interpersonal relationships on the partnership level—and poor relations with the client doesn't help either; for example how you dress is a factor; (2) if you're married to a girl with no money or client contact; (3) if you're a man trusted to do a job by the top people in the office, think you can do a job, and then don't do it well; (4) if you're not one of those fellows who are reaching out and looking for work. . . . One thing I do know: if there is anything that typifies these downtown firms it is thoroughness. If you're sloppy in the clutch, you're in deep trouble. . . .

PARTNER SPONSORSHIP

While a number of people thought partner sponsorship was important, others felt that it could do an associate some harm. A partner states this position:

Seeking sponsorship is a mistake I think some associates may make. Partners resist someone who is being sponsored solely by one man.

There is a great deal of debate among associates about the advantages and disadvantages of sponsorship. Some argue that it is best to have a senior partner's endorsement because he has the power. Others believe that this is not so good, for many older partners do not feel they should pick the men the younger partners will have to live with. Some suggest that the older members of the firm may not be as aggressive as a young partner on the make. . . .

Whether sponsorship is or is not the best way to attain partnership, such situations do exist. They grow out of the intimate work associations which occur in law firms where the partner is dependent on the associate for certain kinds of information and service and the associate is dependent on the partner for advice and protection. In firms where associates work mainly for a single partner or a few partners, and are highly regarded, this reciprocal relationship is bound to occur. Since it occurs for a number of associates at the same time, however, the question remains which partner's sponsorship means the most. Associates often try to place themselves so that they can be in a position to work for the partner who they think can do them the most good.

Many other bromides are offered. An attorney more sophisticated than most in the ways of the large law firm decided to specialize in trust and estate work. . . .

He planned to get into a department where there would be a partner who would be retiring ten years later, when the associate estimated he would be ready for partnership. Whether such long-range planning is feasible seems doubtful.

CLIENT SPONSORSHIP

Others think that client sponsorship is the sure path to success. "The best way to become a partner is to work for clients who contribute substantially to the firm, so that eventually they call directly and begin to depend on you and you become more and more important." Others feel the same way. One associate testifies: "Sometimes you can be made a partner when a corporation says, 'We think a partner should be handling our work.' They are really recommending the associate who is working for them." . . .

Both associates and partners, when asked specifically about the influence of the client on the law firm, thought that the client could not make a man a partner but that he could help him become one. Clients of those firms who were interviewed agreed. The large law firms, they felt, resent pressure from their clients and in most instances are able to withstand it. The client knows this. . . .

Additionally, (1) most clients feel that an attempt to insist that a man be made a partner might spoil their relationship with their law firm; (2) clients' contact with the associate, especially on high levels, is limited—the more important executives do not know the associate well enough to go all out for him; (3) the law firms are very proud of their independence and, in periods of prosperity at least, feel that they do not have to make this kind of concession; (4) partnership is very important to the firms—it would take a great deal of pressure before they would be willing to take on a man as a member of their organization whom they do not think should be a partner. . . .

There is no doubt, however, that the client has some influence in the decision to make a man a partner. Influence is not used here in the derogatory sense. It means that the law firms want and seek out the opinion of the clients and weigh it with other factors. All three parties (clients, partners, and associates) know this and take it into account.

SOCIAL BACKGROUND

Many young lawyers mentioned social background as a help toward partnership. That this is important was shown in the figures on the number of members who are in the *Social Register*, although it is true that some lawyers were listed in the *Social Register* after they became partners. An associate from a large firm believed that proper social background was "a plus if you have it, but it is not a minus if you don't." A partner from the same firm, when asked specifically what part social background and contact plays, stated, "For us it won't produce much because in the long run what pays off is work." . . .

MUST WORK HARD

Social background does help and in some firms it is a necessary condition for membership, but even in these law offices ability and "hard, hard work" are musts for the associate if he expects to become a partner. Weymouth Kirkland, head of Kirkland, Ellis, Hodson, Chaffetz & Masters, the largest law firm in Chicago, when asked by a reporter from the *Chicago Daily News* (May 31, 1958) what advice he has for the new men his firm takes on every year, replied: "Just work—all the advice on earth is no good without that." There is a great deal of evidence obtained from the sample indicating the importance of hard work and long hours. . . .

Not only do some associates show off by working at night, but some of their wives when the opportunity presents itself show off for them by talking about it to impress senior partners. Hard work seems to be part of the tradition of the law and if we look back at the lives of successful lawyers, we see that they took hard work for granted. . . .

While it is no longer the custom for people to work as long as they once did, lawyers in large law firms still put in long hours working some nights and weekends. It is true that some of this "overtime" is unnecessary, and that some are trying to impress the partners; that some stay downtown and eat supper on the client; that others have nowhere else to go or are in the habit of working nights; still, most of it is necessary and due to the demands of their practice and of the law. There are very few people in the large law firms who will not agree that hard work is one of the major requirements an associate must fill if he expects to become a partner.

PERSONALITY

Do attorneys take personality into consideration when they choose their new partners? What exactly do they look for? As in the reasons for recruitment choice, partners found it difficult to answer this question succinctly. While they want similar attributes in a partner as they looked for in associates, they have higher standards for their future peers. The attributes they want in the recruit must now have been developed. The difference in choosing a lawyer just out of school and a partner is that the latter has been under observation for at least eight years. Now the firm knows what it is getting. . . .

A man's usually here eight to ten years. We have that time to watch him. Still, what we want gets down to intangibles. Some of the best technically equipped lawyers we did not take because of personality difficulties, primarily because we did not think they could inspire confidence in clients. Our big job is to keep the client. Bringing in work is no longer important. A man has to be technically capable, get along with lawyers, and get along with clients. He should have the quality of leadership and be able to inspire people, make people have confidence in him.

When pressed for the qualifications an attorney needed to be a partner, one member of a law firm listed the following: He must (1) be able to see all the angles of a problem; (2) be painstakingly careful; (3) have a legal sense of the law; (4) have ability to get along with people, which includes patience and tolerance; and (5) have ability in the field of negotiation in order to try to get the best possible deal for his clients. All this adds up to being an able lawyer. Most partners insist that their future co-participators must have these qualifications. However, some members of a firm have different concepts of what makes an able lawyer. . . .

What these partners and others have said is that they want able lawyers with whom they and their clients can get along. They recognize that this is not enough, however, and that they need more. What this "more" is they can't specifically say. However, they do know what they want and often can pick a man long before he has developed into the kind of lawyer they will choose for a partner. . . .

The heirs apparent are usually known throughout the firm and they are obvious. Even when interviewing, it was possible to pick out the men who would (on the basis of personality, social background, and ability to answer questions) probably be chosen as the next partners. The chosen people are treated like heirs and the quality of their work is held up as a model. As one partner said, "If we have such a man we will take him on, opening in the firm or no opening." When there are a great many golden boys or when there are none currently on the horizon and a firm needs a partner, or when a number of partners are needed, the choice is more difficult. Generally, in a situation involving two or three men of equal ability, personality, social background, or the strength of the sponsoring partner would tip the scale in favor of one candidate or the other.

The process of selection is similar for all the firms in this study. However, different law offices stress some different aspects of lawyer's background when they make their choice. While there is some variance in taste, it is only a question of degree, and the Wall Street lawyers comprise a very homogeneous group. . . .

28

The Airline Pilot's Career Timetable

JULIUS A. ROTH

Like Professors Martin and Strauss, Professor Roth picks
up the idea of "testing points" for promotion and analyzes
how a person may exert control over testing points to
keep his promotion timetable or schedule.

The career bench marks and testing points of the airline pilot were the subject
of a study by L. Wesley Wager.[1] Some of these career contingency points, as
Wager calls them, are administratively standardized and come at regular intervals—for example, the monthly reports on copilots and the quarterly
flight checks for captains. Some are an inevitable part of the career but not
so precisely timed—transition schools, upgrading schools, change from flying
reserve to a regular schedule. In such cases, the pilot—like the hospital patient
or business executive—is faced with the task of trying to figure out when each
of these points in his career should be attained and what it means when a
given point is reached much earlier or much later than expected. Finally,
there are the contingency points that are rare and unexpected (except perhaps
in an actuarial sense) and therefore cannot be anticipated and planned for—
the "technical emergencies" and "irregularities." The way in which a pilot
handles an emergency or the nature and seriousness of an irregularity for
which he is responsible is evaluated by his superiors (if they know about it)
and may be entered into his company record and thus affect future assignments and promotion, or, in a serious case, cause him to be suspended or
discharged.

As in the case of the business executive, the company conceives of some
of the contingency points as testing points. The transition schools, where the
pilot is trained and tested in a type of aircraft that he has not yet flown, are
used this way, especially for the junior copilot. Every pilot is expected
eventually to become a captain capable of flying all the different kinds of aircraft used by the company. If, therefore, he is unable to master satisfactorily
the control of any type of aircraft, he has no future with the company and
may be discharged. The transition school is especially crucial for the first-year
probationary pilot, who may be discharged by the company for any cause

Excerpted from *Timetables* by Julius A. Roth (pp. 85–8). Copyright © 1963 by The Bobbs-
Merrill Company, Inc. Reprinted by permission of the College Division of The Bobbs-Merrill
Company, Inc.

[1] "Career Patterns and Role Problems of Airline Pilots in a Major Airline Company"
(Ph.D. dissertation, University of Chicago, 1959). I have added my own interpretation to some
of Wager's information.

and is likely to be dropped after any failure without being given another chance.

There are important differences, however, between the ways in which the testing points are used for business executives and for pilots. In the case of the executive, it is usually not a question of complete success with promotion or complete failure with discharge. The executive who does not win the confidence of his superiors may be "cooled out" in various ways, even being promoted another step before being shelved in a fairly high-level, but dead-end, position. He may be transferred to a less important location, given a non-crucial staff position, given a raise and higher-sounding title without corresponding authority or responsibility—but he is still a business executive even though no longer moving up the ladder. The career of the pilot does not offer these alternatives. The pilot *must* keep moving up the ladder until he eventually becomes a senior captain—or flunk out along the way and cease to be a pilot. Airline piloting apparently has no chronic sidetrack for the unwanted. It is a matter of "up or out," with no euphemisms to protect the failures.

This is not to say that the pilot has no control whatever over his career timetable. Wager points out a number of ways in which a pilot may slow down or speed up certain career phases. He can put off transition schools or upgrading schools for a time by claiming that he is not ready. (However, he cannot stall such school assignments very long and he must always consider whether his temporary refusal makes a poor impression on his superiors.) The copilot can make himself ready for upgrading more quickly by getting himself assigned to captains who are more generous in giving their copilot an opportunity to fly the plane. He can select a domicile (home airport) that has relatively few pilots with higher seniority and therefore a better chance for faster promotion (or do just the opposite if he feels unready for upgrading). He may control the adverse effect that irregularities may have on his career timetable by covering up the irregularities whenever possible.[2]

In order to exercise such control, however, the pilot needs information. If he wants to manipulate domicile assignments, he must know what the seniority lists for the various domiciles are, what their schedule of operations is, how the local managers handle requests for changing the schedule of schools and captain-copilot assignments, and so on. To decide whether or not he should try to delay a given transitional school, the pilot must know what kind of performance the school requires, whether it will be held against him if he has insufficient practice, what will happen if he does not pass the test the first time, and so on. In fact, pilots are *not* well informed on such matters. They are not, like the hospital patient, surrounded by sources of information. Their work schedules are such that they see very little of their colleagues—especially those colleagues who are closest to them in their career timetable.

[2] Wager points out that it is a general belief among pilots that irregularities will be interpreted against the pilot by airline officials even when there is good evidence that the pilot was not at fault, and, therefore, pilots tend to say as little as possible in their flight reports and especially to keep details about rule violations, irregularities, and emergencies to a minimum.

They are largely removed from the scene of operations about which they must make predictions, again unlike the TB patient who learns much about his own future by just keeping his eyes and ears open. The junior copilot, who has the greatest need for such information, usually has the least access to it. Wager points out that an important function of the transitional schools is to bring together groups of pilots at about the same career stage in one place for a number of weeks where they can spend some time in informal exchange of information about the planes, the company, the captains, the flight managers, the domiciles, the rules and their evasion, and the other conditions of work, and thus return to their job somewhat better equipped to predict and control their career.

The change in the career timetable norms, which has occurred in TB treatment as a result of changes in treatment methods, can be illustrated even more dramatically in the airline pilot's career. Because of rapid changes in the size and nature of the airline industry, the changes in rules controlling aircraft operations, and the repeated introduction of new types of aircraft, the timetable of career phases has undergone some marked shifts through the years. Wager dealt directly with this issue by dividing his pilot subjects into groups which started their airline careers before 1939, 1939–44, 1945–49, and after 1949 and collecting information on such matters as how long they were copilots on reserve, captains on reserve, and copilots before upgrading, and how much time elapsed between transitional schools. The interested reader may find the details in Wager's dissertation. It is sufficient here to note that the earlier phases of the career are being stretched out. Thus, the pilots starting with the company in the 1950's take longer on the average to make captain than those who started in the 1930's. Almost all the other career phases have been lengthened in the same way. For example, while the majority of those starting with the company in the 1930's was flying a regular monthly schedule in less than a year after being upgraded, those starting with the company in the late 1940's in almost all cases needed more than three years after upgrading to achieve such a schedule.

Wager did not deal directly with the actual process of developing timetable norms and using them for predicting and controlling one's own timetable. However, we may speculate about the effect that the stretching out of contingency points and the paucity of information about career contingencies may have on prediction and control. The new junior copilot has the greatest opportunity for collecting information about the career timetable from the captains with whom he flies, but the experience of these captains, who started five to twenty years earlier, may be quite inappropriate to his own case. When he hears these captains tell of being upgraded in less than two years and flying a regular schedule shortly after, the new-generation pilot may wonder what is wrong when he is still flying copilot four years later. He may even wonder whether this is a reflection on his own competence. And what does the older captain think of these younger men who still have not been upgraded three, four, or five years after beginning their airline careers?

If the matter were simply a contrast between the twenty-year men and the newcomers, the timetable changes would be readily recognized and corrections made. However, when you have all the intermediate groups with progressive changes throughout the years, it may be difficult for a group at any particular point to know what expectations are reasonable for *them*. Under such circumstances it is probably difficult to develop stable norms of a career timetable. I suspect that the newer pilots—insofar as they are able to obtain relevant information—tend to use the group just a little ahead of them as a reference group to develop their own norms. If so, they are likely to believe that their own timetable is lagging behind the norm.

29

Publish or Perish

THEODORE CAPLOW and REECE J. McGEE

> One aspect of testing points for promotion is that at a
> particular career level a man must perform as prescribed
> in an allotted time before the next promotion comes due.
> If he does not perform adequately, then in lieu of a
> promotion, he may be asked to leave or edged out of the
> organizational career to make room for others. Professors
> Caplow and McGee discuss conflicts between the criteria
> for evaluation of performance and other aspects of role
> performance in the academic professions.

For most members of the profession, the real strain in the academic role arises
from the fact that they are, in essence, paid to do one job, whereas the worth
of their services is evaluated on the basis of how well they do another. The
work assignment, for which the vast majority of professors are paid, is that of
teaching. There are a few—a very few—who are supported by full- or part-
time regular research appointments, but their number is insignificant compared to the vast majority who are hired to teach, and in whose contracts no
specification of research duties is made. Most professors contract to perform
teaching services for their universities and are hired to perform those services.
When they are evaluated, however, either as candidates for a vacant position,
or as candidates for promotion, the evaluation is made principally in terms
of their research contributions to their disciplines. The following quotation is
an interesting case in point; note the aftereffects on the peers.

"Among other things, he coached the student group. He got canned by an
ad hoc committee which split 4 to 3 in his favor, but it was decided to can him on the
basis of the split. Some of us feel that this was a case of real campus politics.
It may have been honest and it may not, but it was clear that his really tremendous
work with this student group hadn't been weighted at all in the consideration of his
promotion. He did a really tremendous job. It caused the rest of us to decide that
if this kind of activity was not what was honored—and he'd led them to several
national recognitions—then we'd do what was honored—namely, sitting in the
library and writing weighty papers, and let their goddamned student group go to
hell, which it has."

It is neither an overgeneralization nor an oversimplification to state that
in the faculties of major universities in the United States today, the evaluation
of performance is based almost exclusively on publication of scholarly books
or articles in professional journals as evidence of research activity. Out of 371

Excerpted, with permission, from *The Academic Marketplace*, by Theodore Caplow and Reece
J. McGee (pp. 82–5). Copyright © 1958 by Basic Books, Inc., Publishers, New York.

responses to the question, "Do you think he has reached the peak of his productivity as yet?" 122 respondents define "productivity" unmistakably as research, or publication of research; only 14 refer either directly or indirectly to the teaching of students; and 11 of these 14 qualify the importance of teaching in some way. The other 235 responses are so worded that it is impossible to state what criteria are being used for productivity. Throughout the interviews, however, departures from the publication formula for productivity are rare indeed. The explicit definition of publication as the criterion of productivity is very common. In addition, respondents often specifically exclude from consideration other activities, such as teaching, administration, creative artistry, public service, or internal service to the university.

"Yes, he's getting involved with administration there, and that's the kiss of death for any research." . . .

"She hasn't been in positions where productivity was demanded or even permitted. She's always been a practicing clinician; in her current job there's no time for research. I would say that if this goes on, her peak has been reached." . . .

It has been suggested that the recent emphasis on team research in the social and physical sciences may be, in part, a protective device for the non-research-minded professor and for his counterpart who can do research but finds it difficult to put his results in publishable form. There is some evidence, of an admittedly speculative character, to support this contention. It appears that research teams are usually composed of one strong research worker, or "idea man," and a number of less brilliant colleagues working more or less under his direction. It is also commonly alleged that team research is somehow identified with qualitatively inferior work. These are only assertions, however, and there are many instances of brilliant results attributable to teams, and of research situations (*e.g.* high-energy nuclear physics) which require team effort. Certainly a team *may* provide the protection of joint publication for a man who would not otherwise see his name in print. Until quite recently, no such recourse was available, but, on the other hand, teaching had greater importance. . . .

It is interesting, after this echo of an older ethic, to realize that the criterion of publication is rationalized today by the argument that research activity is essential to effective teaching. Formerly, it was possible to make a career either in the university *or* in the discipline, and the man who chose a local career sustained himself through service to the institution and personal relationships in the faculty. The campus elder statesman is still a familiar figure on American university campuses, but it would seem that, as the present elders retire, there will not be many of a younger generation to take their places.

Today, a scholar's orientation to his institution is apt to disorient him to his discipline and to affect his professional prestige unfavorably. Conversely, an orientation to his discipline will disorient him to his institution, which he will regard as a temporary shelter where he can pursue his career as a member of the discipline. And he will be, as a matter of course, considerably more mobile than his institutionally oriented colleagues. In a handful of great universities, where many of the departments believed to be the best in their fields are found, a merger of orientations is possible. There a man may simultaneously serve an institution and a discipline and identify with both. But tensions exist between the two orientations everywhere. It is worthy of note that the publication requirements in the highest ranking departments are the most rigid, so that the men they select have already met the requirements imposed by the discipline.

Several respondents referred to the "guild aspect" of certain disciplines—especially mathematics and physics. Their comments seem to assert that, in these fields at least, for the successful professor the institutional orientation has entirely disappeared.

30

Informal Factors
in Career Achievement

MELVILLE DALTON

Once a group of persons have proven themselves adequately
skilled for a higher level job, then informal factors come
into play, when choosing who will get the promotion. At
each level of the organizational career, clusters of informal
factors operate to effect selection. Professor Dalton
discusses the relationship between informal criteria of
success and the perpetuation of discriminatory practices.

The means by which individuals rise to higher positions in the organizations
in which they work out their careers has long been a matter of dispute. At
least in the United States the belief is common that personal relations are
important in occupational promotion.

Some students of business and industry have stated that "pull," "connections," "family contacts," etc., are important in success. At least one high
industrial executive has echoed this with emotion, and another declares that
such factors as "race, nationality, faith, politics, sectional antecedents, . . .
etc.," are important criteria of selection in all organizations, probably less so
in industry than in political, church, and academic bodies.

However, there is a dearth of objective evidence to support the view either
that measurable attributes believed essential for functioning in given organizations are not used in the selection of candidates or that specific informal
criteria, not necessarily related to the attributes presumably desired, are used
to a significant degree.

The problem here is to learn what factors were at work in the selection
and advancement of individuals through the managerial hierarchy of a factory
and to evaluate, as objectively as possible, the relative influence of these
criteria in the careers of the managers. . . .

The problem of how individuals were selected and advanced through the
hierarchy was first attacked by study of formal statements in the managerial
handbooks. These manuals gave no pertinent information on this subject.
They merely indicated that "ability," "honesty," "co-operation," and "industry" were the qualities essential for promotion. Formal statements from
high responsible officers were similar. But these official expressions were con-
fidentially challenged by numerous informed, reliable officers throughout the
hierarchy who declared that other factors were often of much greater importance in achieving success. . . .

Age, service, and schooling all showed such irregularities that neither the

Excerpted, with permission, from *American Journal of Sociology*, 56 (March, 1951): 407–415.

maximum nor the minimum of any were criteria of promotion. This is not to deny that vague, unformulated criteria of "ability," such as those earlier noted, were used with varying degrees of effectiveness to assure minimum performance in office, but to say that the precise nature of such criteria and the extent of their application was uncertain and was intermingled with the functioning of other more objective factors that were clearly important as selective criteria.

INFORMAL CRITERIA OF SUCCESS

Covert charges are made in the plant among lower and middle officers that higher officers advance because of conforming to unofficial and irrelevant requirements rather than by "ability." Undoubtedly personal jealousies and failures had a part in these charges, but major attention here will be given to the designated factors instead of attitudes toward them.

The alleged influences were (*a*) being a member of the Masonic Order; (*b*) not being a Roman Catholic;[1] (*c*) having an ethnic background largely Anglo-Saxon and Germanic; (*d*) being a member of a local yacht club; and (*e*) being affiliated with the Republican Party.

Masonic Membership

Most Protestant non-Masons and Catholics alike declared that being a Mason was a prerequisite to advancement in the plant.

Some non-Masonic Protestants praised the organization but declared that the local Masonic lodges contained "too many social climbers who are ruining things by getting in just to get a good job instead of helping the organization."

The younger Catholics complained that "95 per cent of management belong to the Masons" and that Catholics, who are a majority in the community, were not properly represented. An older Catholic staff officer expressed the belief that the Masons were "getting too strong in the plant." He declared, however, that in recent decades there had been two Catholic general managers who "appointed Catholics to good jobs when it was convenient, but not as much as the Masons do now." He also alleged that officials of the central office were aware of this Catholic-Masonic struggle and nullified its effects by replacing a retiring general manager with one lacking the pertinent characteristics of the majority group of then current subordinates. Data were lacking to support or refute this statement.

Even intimates among the Masons in higher positions would say no more than that "being a member doesn't hurt" and that "you always know you can get service and help from each other." . . .

---

[1] This dichotomy of Catholic-Mason is introduced because Catholics considered themselves ineligible for Masonic membership in view of church restrictions on the taking of certain oaths required of Masons. The latter declared that no individual was barred from the organization because of being a Catholic.

Here it will be seen that together the Catholics and the neutral group were only 31 per cent of the managers against 69 per cent who were Masons. . . .

This gives a highly significant difference, suggesting, with the other data, that participation in Masonry was, indeed, an informal criterion of success.

It will be noted that the managers of highest status, the superintendents, were 78 per cent Masons. One might expect the next highest concentration of Masons to be among the general foremen rather than the first-line foremen. That the reverse was true may have been in part due to frustration among first-line foremen, who recognized the symbol and pursued it in the same way that some of their members changed their names to escape rejected ethnic categories (see below) or dropped Catholicism as they groped to find the avenues to advancement.

That the staff group had the fewest Masons may have resulted from functional and other antipathies between staff and line that rendered staff personnel less acceptable.

Ethnic Composition

The name-changing just referred to, caustic remarks among lower managers of Central and South European extraction that "you've got to have the right complexion to get anywhere around here," and the general use of opprobrious epithets all indicated a high level of ethnic consciousness among the managers.

Respective ethnic origins of the 226 managers were determined by personal knowledge, by checking with intimates concerning others, by free interviewing, and by reference to personnel files.

It will be observed that Anglo-Saxons constituted at least half of each managerial group, that Germans were next in number, and that the superintendents were entirely Anglo-Saxon and German. The proportion of this ethnic combination will be seen to vary inversely with rank in the line hierarchy. That is, the general foremen, second in rank, were 93.5 per cent, and the first-line foremen 74.1 per cent, Anglo-Saxon and German. . . .

The staff group, unique in having the lowest percentage of Anglo-Saxons and the highest percentage of Germans, lay between the two lower line strata with 83.4 per cent.

Some of the interstrata differences are supported statistically and leave little doubt concerning the selective force of ethnic condition. . . .

The significance of ethnic selection among the managers was sharpened by examination of the community's ethnic pattern. Using the city directory, and employing surnames as a criterion of ethnicity, a random sample showed that Anglo-Saxon ethnics constituted about 26 per cent, and German ethnics about 12 per cent, of the total population. Data from the 1940 census indicated that the community had a large foreign-born population, of which those from Germany and the British Isles together were less than 15 per cent.

Membership in a Yacht Club

Gossip in the many offices of the plant suggested that social activities and friendships in the local yacht club, in connection with other criteria, might be important in the selection and promotion, or at least the continuance in office, of numerous individuals.

A survey showed that 114 officers of the plant were members. This figure included 14 superintendents (one of whom was president of the club), 24 general foremen, 29 first-line foremen, and 47 staff officers. Among the latter were 33 lower supervisory and non supervisory personnel not included in the sample, and 14 officers from the sample.

While these proportions are smaller than those of the two preceding items, interviews among members, together with casual but revealing comments, indicated that activity in the club and freely given effort to increase and maintain its physical plant and accessories won favor with higher officers that was probably very helpful when candidates for promotions were being considered.

Political Affiliation

Presumably all the managers were members of the Republican party. This was suggested (*a*) by statements by men of all strata; (*b*) by the apparently universal practice among the managers of reading only an avowedly Republican newspaper in the plant; (*c*) by the fact that discussion favorable to policies of the Democratic party was in all detectable cases covert and occurred chiefly among first-line foremen; and (*d*) by the fact that in the few cases in which officers had earlier served as public political incumbents they did so as members of the Republican party.

In presenting these data, the aim is not to imply that the managers needed only to meet the indicated criteria in order to rise and that "natural" capacity was negligible in success. It is assumed that an aspirant meeting the unofficial criteria but lacking minimal aptitude to function would almost never be deliberately selected for advancement. Rather the point to be stressed is that managerial aptitude might or might not be encompassed by the process of informal selection. Absence of a sharply defined mode of ascent encouraged the managers to search for more subtle means of elevating themselves. As is probably true in most organizations, and even to some extent where promotional processes are well formulated, the managerial search for mobility ladders sharpened their sensitivity to the attitudes and attributes of superiors and induced competition to please. Functional requirements frequently became secondary in the concern to adopt currently acceptable social attributes and to meet the personal wishes and tacit expectations of superiors (themselves often concerned to have subordinates of like traits) with the hope of making a good impression.

Such skill in pleasing appeared frequently to cause superiors not to see, or to overlook, other qualities among aspirants and in some cases to appoint individuals who later failed to perform as expected. Once such persons attained office, their superiors could not admit errors in judgment or renounce the personal claims that had been built up. Hence failures were usually protected by creating new offices (sinecures) for them, or appointing them "assistants to," which were often inconstant positions of little responsibility from which they could be dropped, as convenient. Officially, "changing conditions" or "production demands" required the new appointments. While holders of these offices[2] were usually referred to in gossip as having "fouled out," the positions were also sometimes given to very aggressive and capable officers (who approximately met the unofficial criteria) as a reward when higher posts were unavailable.

SUMMARY AND CONCLUSIONS

The data on occupational experience showed no definitive formal procedure for selection of the managers. In the absence of such a method, selection to a large extent was carried on informally, with personnel rising from lower strata by conforming to social characteristics of personnel in upper strata, the chief criteria (varying as dominant groups of personnel changed through time) being ethnicity, religion, participation in specific out-plant social activities, political affiliation, and membership in accepted secret societies. Evidence showed no necessary relation between these criteria and capacity to forward plant goals.

The data suggested that unrestricted informal behavior may in some cases initiate and perpetuate conditions termed by the larger society as "discriminatory" and "undemocratic."

There appears to be a growing gap between career practices and our insistence that status may be earned by adhering to formal procedures, that vocational training will prepare an individual for executive positions, etc. Drives for career success seem inevitably to color the carrying-out of official duties, so that neither, as was indicated in earlier papers, can follow specific lines. Hence it appears more realistic in most cases to regard status achievement in hierarchy as subject to many influences and earnable only to a degree. This appears due largely to (a) our valuation of personal success—and the consequent struggle to attain it; (b) the limited number of positions; (c) the loose and shifting character of our society which makes difficult the formation of fixed lines of ascent and inclines personnel to evade such lines as do arise; (d) the almost unavoidable intrusion of personal sentiments into the

---

[2] The existence of such offices suggested either that whatever formal criteria were used for selection were frequently invalid or that if valid formal criteria existed they were often overlooked in the play of personal relations involving informal criteria. Informants estimated that the number of "good" sinecures varies from fifteen to twenty-five, while those of lesser value might fluctuate to forty-five or more.

professional functioning of interacting officers; and (*e*) the conflict, in most large organizations, of individual and group interests which further reduces the weight of formal techniques in career perfection and allows increasing opportunity for the rise of nonfunctional criteria of selection.

31

Sponsorship and Rejection

ORVIS COLLINS

Like Professor Dalton, Professor Collins analyzes how
clusters of informal factors affect promotions among
people with equivalent skills. He indicates that these
informal factors are made viable criteria for promotion
through sponsorship.

It is one of the shibboleths of modern management that advancement from
job to job must be based on efficiency. By "efficiency" is meant the capacity
to do work. Management argues that, if an institution is to continue to
function, the majority of its members (in this case job-holders) must have at
least a minimum capacity for performing their individual functions. Within
the factory such attributes as physical strength, education, and age are all at
one time or another implied by the term "capacity to do work." To a production engineer a division of labor is necessary, since, for one reason, a 200-
pound male can perform certain work more efficiently than a 110-pound
female; a man of thirty is able to perform certain physical tasks too great for
the strength of the average man of sixty-five; and a graduate of an engineering
school can perform work involving mathematics quite beyond a person who
left school in the eighth grade.

Once, however, several candidates are admitted to possess the technical
efficiency required for performance of the work, other qualifications become
important. And at Somerset, a New England factory, the most important of
these is the ethnic identification of the individuals involved. In this factory individuals must be ethnically qualified to hold certain jobs, a circumstance
which has resulted in the development of a pattern of ethnic job expectations,
sponsorship, and rejection. This paper is an analysis of the system in operation, with a description of the maneuvers which accompanied attempted
promotions on the part of one group and those which accompanied successful
or unsuccessful attempts to reject these promotions.

I gathered the information which will be used to demonstrate the presence
and functioning of this system during two years while employed as a workman
at Somerset, a management-owned industry employing a labor force which
varied between 1,800 and 2,000. . . .

I soon became aware of an ethnic structure within the factory; among my
fellow-workers expression of this fact was often made. A Negro friend remarked, "You got to be a Mason or a Catholic to get anywhere around here."

Excerpted, with permission, from "Ethnic Behavior in Industry: Sponsorship and Rejection in a
New England Factory," *American Journal of Sociology*, 51 (January, 1946): 293–98.

When I asked about one of the Irish foremen, a fellow-worker said, "With a name like Collins you'll fit with him all right." Later it became apparent that there existed at Somerset a clearly definable system of ethnic sponsorship in matters of promotion. The proposition here will be that, whatever other considerations may have been involved in the promotion of employees, one of the key issues was always the ethnic identification of the individual proposed for promotion. Nationality or race was almost never explicitly declared to be a consideration in these situations but was always present.

It should be pointed out that in such an urban-ethnic area family names are important as one of the most obvious ethnic symbols, but they are not always reliable as such. A newcomer to any group is immediately placed by his name. Later other factors may qualify or even nullify this early judgment. For this reason anyone who has lived in a New England urban area learns a new respect for the adage, "What's in a name?" . . .

During my stay at Somerset there were three members of lower top management whose names seemed to indicate that they had other than good English blood in their veins. No matter, however, what may have been the indiscretions of their ancestors, Holzer, O'Brian, and Orlando had adopted all the Yankee symbols. . . .

Furthermore, wherever an ethnic status system develops, there is likely to develop a pattern of name-changing. During my stay at Somerset I think I heard this story, or variations of it, at least half-a-dozen times:

> You know the ditty,
> "Here's to Boston, the land of the bean and the cod
> Where the Cabots speak only to Lowells
> And the Lowells speak only to God."
> Well, Judge So-and-so after a hard day at the bench during which he had taken care of numerous pleas by various foreign gentlemen came home and said to his wife:
> "Here's to Boston, the land of the bean and the cod
> Where the Cabots have no one to speak to,
> The Lowells speak Polish, by God."

. . . Such a story illustrates the feeling entertained by individuals of English-speaking stock about the "borrowing" of one of their most prized symbols by individuals socially subordinate but upwardly mobile.

But the same Yankees who defend this name symbol through ridicule at one time forced English names on newcomers to New England. Industrial organizations, and Somerset was very much among them, went in heavily during one period for what was called "hiring off the dock." Through the merits of this system the newly arrived European found himself possessed of (or by, if you choose) an already prepared lodging, a job, and a new name pronounceable by English tongues. The employers in turn obtained a new workman whose peasant soul had not been besmirched by the Irish heresies of wages, hours, and working conditions. Tony Taylor, Joe Brown, and Chris Cook were typical recipients of such New England generosity. . . .

JOB-ETHNIC HIERARCHY

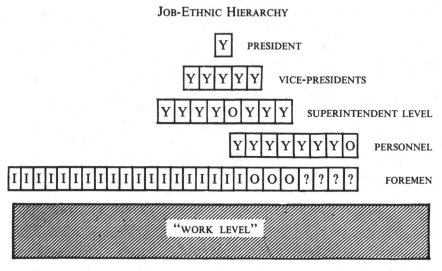

Y = Yankee; I = Irish; O = Other than Yankee or Irish; ? = Not identified. The non-Yankee at the superintendent level is a testing engineer. The non-Yankee member of the personnel group is a young Italian who does safety cartoons and acts as general errand boy.

The chart indicates not only that certain jobs were held by the ethnically acceptable but that large areas of the plant hierarchy are almost completely occupied by members of one ethnic group. Jobs of managerial type are held by individuals of native or Yankee stock, and jobs of supervisory nature are held almost exclusively by Irish. "He is a foreman, although not Irish," is a succinct and commonly made statement of a Somerset pattern of expectation: the exception calls forth comment. One can see also that a member of top management, a superintendent, for example, can be expected to be a Yankee and that the personnel department is Yankee-monopolized.

If, then, the Irish- and Yankee-held positions as shown by the chart are separated by encircling, two sharply defined areas are set up. These areas quite clearly coincide with the management and with the supervisory areas of the factory structure. In the remaining portion of the chart are the individuals at the working level. As they are represented, they appear to be an un-differentiated mass. If, however, it were our purpose here to examine them more closely, we should find that there also are certain structures of job occupancy among the worker group.

Because this ethnic pattern of job occupancy has existed so long at Somerset (the company was established about 1890), an ethnic pattern of expectation has developed . . . a person of certain identification will be promoted to fill a vacancy or a newly created job. In other words, this is a social, as distinct from an individual, expectation.

Since most of the foremen at Somerset are Irish, both Irish and non-Irish have come to expect newly appointed members of supervision to be Irish. This does not mean that all individuals in this position must be Irish, but it does mean that, when management appoints a non-Irish person to a supervisory job, it should be very sure that it has an especially good reason for making the appointment.

Since members of both management and labor have learned to recognize this system of ethnic job expectations and know fairly well how to adapt themselves to it, promotions are made year after year without, in the majority of cases, conflicts developing. But, when the pattern is violated, there is usually trouble.

Management, of course, has the formal prerogative of selecting whichever individuals it feels are capable of filling openings, and this is explicitly recognized by the union. Any action, therefore, which develops in opposition to a promotion is highly informal, as the following illustrates.

In the spring of 1942 the subforeman in charge of one of the special-treating work groups decided to go into the armed services. Sullivan had been "Old Country" Irish and was exceedingly popular with his men. When he left, the management announced that a Yankee by the name of Peters was to replace him. Peters had been in the department a considerable length of time and seems to have been well liked by the other men. But, when I came to work on the second shift, I heard that there had been a threat of a walkout in the special-treating department. I do not recall the exact conversation, but most of the discussion was centered around Donovan, another employee of the department, who the men seemed to think should have been given the job. A walkout materialized and lasted for one shift. . . .

A formal grievance was lodged with management charging that Donovan had been discriminated against. Obviously the local did not have a legal leg to stand on, since the right of promotion is vested in management. I do not know that either side took the grievance statement seriously. The filing of the grievance merely served as an excuse for the men to return to work while the local handled matters through regular channels. But social pressure within a tightly integrated work group is terrific. Several days later Peters, the Yankee, failed to come to work, the report was circulated that he was ill, and management selected a man named Murphy to take over for him. Peters did not return to work, and Murphy was later made subforeman. . . .

The group rationalization seems to have been: It has always been the duty of the foreman to help choose his subforemen, but management appointed a subforeman, a Yankee, without consulting the foreman under whom he was to work. If Conner had not been cheated of this privilege, he would have insisted upon an Irish assistant. Donovan is Irish and the leader of the gang; therefore, it is up to us to see that Donovan gets the job by inducing the Yankee, Peters, to leave. But if Murphy gets the job that's all right because he is Irish, too. That is the sort of situation which arose when management failed to promote in accordance with the expectations of the individuals involved. In this instance the labor group clearly demonstrated its ability to reject a promotion which did not fit into the ethnic pattern. . . .

It is significant, however, that no opposition is given to Yankees promoted to fill jobs within the area of the hierarchy dominated by Yankees. At Somerset staff jobs of a certain type are distinguished by the term "administrative." Personnel jobs are always spoken of as "administrative," and jobs of this sort are pretty well monopolized by Yankees. Accordingly, when wartime expansion made necessary a series of new administrative posts, the management without exception selected Yankees to fill them. . . .

Sometimes, when a new job is created, the people involved are not sure whether it is a supervisory or an administrative position. This does not often happen, but I was able to observe one such incident. . . .

This new department was to be known as the "Central Janitor Service," and the janitors from each department were to be reassigned to it. . . .

This was an explicit but verbal agreement between management and labor. At first blush it seems impossible that a misunderstanding could arise. But the project immediately hit a snag. The labor members insisted that the choice of a "janitor foreman" was in line with the other duties of the safety and health subcommittee. Management was indignant: its prerogatives were being encroached upon. But after several caucuses management agreed that if labor would have candidates submit their names, management might select the new janitor foreman from among them. The labor nominations were, with one exception, both workingmen and Irish. Management rejected all of them.

Several days later management posted notices that applications for "Sanitation Engineer" would be accepted and immediately chose Roundtree, who was Yankee and a plant guard.

The repercussions were violent, but the appointment "stuck." By changing the title of the new job from "foreman" to "engineer," management had removed the job from *supervision* to *administration*. It was clear that if the job could be placed under administration, it was entirely different from what labor had conceived it to be. Through the mechanism of a change of title, management had upset the social logic by which labor had concluded that the job was supervisory and should be secured for an Irishman. Labor's argument had lost its force. . . .

This analysis of three situations has illustrated the functioning of a system of ethnic sponsorship and rejection in one New England factory. The system is part of the social matrix in which it appears and not an isolated phenomenon.

32

Sponsorship in the Medical Profession

OSWALD HALL

Sometimes, when sponsorship dominates all promotion procedures, it then generates some codification of its criteria and boundaries of effectiveness among sponsors. Professor Hall describes the operation of this mechanism in the medical profession.

It is a characteristic of our own type of society that a person chooses his doctor in large part on the basis of characteristics which are irrelevant to the competence of the practitioner. In general when one chooses a doctor he selects a person who is white, male, Protestant, of upper class tastes and standard of living. In a given community certain doctors are chosen more frequently than others merely because they are popular, or fashionable, or associated with a successful doctor. None of these characteristics has any direct bearing on the competence of the doctor chosen. However, it is just such choices that build up a substantial clientele for a doctor. It is not argued here that persons in need of a doctor's services consciously check such a list of characteristics before making a selection. All that is contended is that persons carry about with them preferences and biases of which they may be largely unaware, but which influence profoundly the careers of the medical practitioners in the community concerned. In the jargon of sociology, the status ascribed to a doctor determines the status he achieves as doctor.

These apparently extraneous factors influencing a doctor's career are not mere fortuitous circumstances. In so far as the doctors of a given community are established, and possess relatively loyal clienteles, they form a system. This system can effectively exclude the intruding newcomer. On the one hand they have control of the hospital system through occupying the dominant posts therein. On the other hand they tend to develop, in the course of time, through association, a sort of informal organization. Rights to position, status, and power become recognized and upheld; mechanisms of legitimate succession and patterns of recruitment become established. . . .

The title of this paper calls attention to a neglected feature of professional life, and offers a basic concept for the study of professions. It is presumed here that the *established* members of the profession will in the course of time develop a sort of organization which functions to provide order, to ascribe and maintain status, to control the conduct of the members, and to minimize competition and conflict. In other words they will develop an orderly manner

Excerpted, with permission, from "Informal Organization of the Medical Profession," *Canadian Journal of Economics and Political Science*, 12 (February, 1946): 31–33, 40–44.

of incorporating new members into their community, of repelling the un-wanted and the intruder, of allocating rights and privileges, of distributing clients among colleagues, of applying sanctions and penalties, and preserving their status.

To call such an organization "informal," implies that it does not originate by establishing a constitution. Actually it may possess no formal constitution. In this case the activity precedes the recognition of a purpose, and the group may have a well-defined pattern of action without an official apologia. It is an assumption of this paper that the working constitution of any established profession is something that has to be discovered. Moreover it is very likely to deviate significantly from the formal constitution. The latter is likely to present an idealized picture of what the members would like outsiders to believe, and should not be accepted uncritically as a description of the work-ings of the professional group. . . .

In this paper the informal organization of the medical profession is referred to as the "inner fraternity." The name connotes that the group has some of the characteristics of the secret society, some of the features of the primary group, and that the relationships are closer and more inclusive than those of sheer colleagues.

While the inner fraternity influences the practice of medicine in diverse ways it has one dominant method of functioning. Its basic activity is referred to here as "sponsorship." By sponsorship is meant simply that established members of the inner fraternity actively intervene in the career lines of new-comers to the profession. By so doing they influence the careers of those selected. The intervention may continue over very long spans of time and relate to many features of the professional career. Sponsorship is a dual process. It facilitates the careers of those selected, and relegates those not so selected to a position where they compete under decidedly disadvantageous terms. In this way it tends to keep the inner fraternity a stable, self-perpetuat-ing group, and maintains its control over the profession in general.

Much of the assistance given by the sponsor to his protégé is of an in-tangible sort. It may be as nebulous as the help of an older person who encourages a younger person to define himself as a potential colleague. Since the professional ambition is, in its early stages, a fragile affair this aid is very important. However, the aid may be much more substantial. It may mean smoothing the path to easy acceptance to the right training school; it may mean appointments to positions within the appropriate institutions; it may mean deflecting clientele from the sponsor to the protégé; it may mean designating the protégé as successor to the sponsor.

Such sponsorship is not necessarily a one-sided process. It permits the newcomer to share in the established system of practising medicine, but it also imposes responsibilities upon him. It obligates him to fulfil the minor positions in the institutional system. Where he needs expert advice or assistance it obligates him to turn to his sponsor. And if he is designated as a successor to an established member of the profession he necessarily takes over the duties and obligations involved there. Hence the protégé is essential to the continued functioning of the established inner fraternity of the profession.

The assumption of the inner fraternity provides a frame of reference for observing the conduct of the members of the profession. It provides a sort of lens for drawing into focus types of facts which would otherwise escape the notice of the enquirer. . . .

In the interviews quoted there is abundant evidence of the existence of an inner fraternity—in other words an informal sort of organization. It is not identified in this fashion. Different doctors pick out different aspects of it, and they view it in varying lights. Some see it as the stranglehold of an ethnic group. Others look upon it as control of the profession by a group of specialists. Some allude to it as a spatially segregated group. Others look upon it as a homogeneous religious group of practitioners. Still others look on it as an integral part of the profession, a control group necessary to administer the institutions and safeguard the ethics of the profession. Some see mainly the presence of disturbing cliques within the profession. They all agree in recognizing the existence of a group, one whose bonds and functions appear extraneous to the practice of medicine, but one which exercises a profound influence upon their careers.

In order to test the validity of this hypothesis a study was undertaken to discover whether or not there was a group, spatially segregated, homogeneous as to religion and ethnic characteristics, limited to the more important types of specialties, commanding the important hospital posts, and integrated into a system in which its members exchanged substantial favours. These five points will be considered in turn.

THE DISTRIBUTION OF DOCTORS

Spot maps were prepared to determine the spatial distribution of doctors within the community studied. Two heavy concentrations of offices appeared, comprising about one-third and one-sixth of the doctors of the community respectively. The rest of the doctors were distributed in random fashion throughout the remainder of the community. Interestingly enough there were very few doctors' offices in the central business section. Their absence from this area poses an interesting problem in human ecology. The smaller concentration of doctors' offices occurs in a low rent residential area, while the larger concentration occurs in the highest rent residential area of the city.

The offices in the area of heaviest concentration are unique in that doctors have grouped themselves in buildings housing from two to eight. A couple of the buildings involved were commercial ventures built especially to accommodate the medical or dental profession. In the main what has occurred is that one doctor has acquired a large residence and transformed it into a set of offices and gathered around himself a set of congenial colleagues. In general it can be argued that the spatial relationships of these doctors are an index to their technical relationships. Those with offices in the area of densest concentration are welded into a set of close working relationships, while the individual groups of doctors occupying the multiple offices discussed above maintain an even closer set of relationships.

ETHNIC AND RELIGIOUS COMPOSITION OF THE PROFESSION

The most important dividing lines in the medical profession in the community studied were ethnic and religious, and not technical. The large general hospitals can accommodate any type of case from maternity to brain surgery. The specialists in all the varied fields are able to work together to provide the range of services which a general hospital offers. However this is true only within the limits of separate ethnic groups and religious communions. By and large, Jewish, Catholic, and Protestant doctors are attached to hospitals of their own group. Unfortunately for purposes of research the lines of demarcation found in the profession are largely disregarded in official statistics. Locally the most important distinctions in the population concern four groups: the Old Yankee, the Irish, the Italian, and the Jewish. The first and the last are utterly disregarded in census figures, while only the first generation Irish are distinguished.

When spot maps were prepared of the ethnic distribution of doctors' offices it appeared that the small area of concentration was almost entirely Italian, the Irish doctors were scattered at random throughout the city, while the Yankee and Jewish doctors each had about half their numbers in the large area of dense concentration. The Italians and Irish had almost no representation in this area. Inspection of the multiple offices showed that each was restricted to one ethnic group.

SPECIALIZATION

Information on specialization can be found in the Medical Directory. By and large specialization is restricted to the Yankee and Jewish groups. Moreover the specialists have gravitated to the area of heavy concentration, the East Side. The multiple offices discussed earlier house specialists almost exclusively. It is fairly clear that the minute division of labour involved in specialization requires close spatial relationships in order for the specialist to deal effectively with his patients and colleagues.

HOSPITAL CONNEXIONS

It was indicated earlier that hospital connexions are almost essential to the present day practice of medicine. This is particularly true of the practice of a specialty. Information was obtained on all the hospital connexions of all the doctors of the community. These hospital connexions were classified in order of their importance. In the community studied the hospitals were almost all of the closed type—that is, doctors can practice only on the invitation of the men already on the staffs. Hence the doctors holding the positions of importance in the dominant hospitals of the community wield a peculiarly important type of power. Moreover the newcomer entering medicine is extremely dependent on the selection policy of those in positions of authority.

The hospital positions are of three main types: internships, externships, and positions on the active staff. Internships permit the young doctor to carry on his education under practical working conditions. It is in the hospital that one learns medicine. However internships do not give the young doctor access to paying patients. Externships permit the young doctor to carry on his education in the charity clinics of the hospital. While he may at the same time be accumulating patients in his private practice, the position as extern does not aid directly in accumulating a clientele. The positions on the active staff permit the doctor to take his patients into the hospital. This is the key privilege as far as hospital connexions are concerned. Until a doctor has this privilege he is seriously limited in the things that he can do for his patients.

The main hospital system of the community comprises about ninety positions above the rank of assistants. Of these approximately two-thirds are held by Yankee specialists occupying multiple offices in the area of concentration on the East Side. The heads of departments are still more heavily concentrated in the above group. The composition of the controlling group in the main hospital, the Staff Association, is more heavily weighted still.

The group of Yankee, East Side specialists occupies a position of pivotal importance. They are spatially homogeneous. They belong to the democracy of first names. They practice integrated specialties, and thereby share clienteles. They can designate the appointees to positions on the hospital system. By continually recruiting young men to their offices they maintain the stability of their group through time.

THE SYSTEM OF REFERRING

The practice of specialized medicine hinges around the referral system. No doctor can succeed unless he gets incorporated into the local system. One of the first questions that a specialist asks a new patient is "Who referred you to me?" Among specialists it is, of course, a reciprocal system, one on which they are mutually dependent. Moreover it is an autonomous system, and once established is secure from any competing group. Disloyalty to such a group by its members would be very costly. The rules of the referring game are unwritten, but extremely important in the eyes of those involved. Some measure of their importance can be gathered by noting the amount of emotion generated by such activities as "fee-splitting." The latter practice substitutes a monetary relationship for the established system, and in that sense constitutes a threat to the very system itself.

There are two types of referring. General practitioners find it necessary to send their difficult cases to the specialists. The latter have no occasion to send patients in the opposite direction, though they are under obligation to refrain from tampering with the loyalty of the patient to his general practitioner. On the other hand specialists are continually sending patients with an ailment outside their competence to other specialists. These favours are reciprocal. Hence there is a tendency for the inner fraternity to gather ever new elements to its collective clientele, and to preserve and maintain that clientele. Its members are thereby sheltered in the competition for patients in the practice of medicine.

The material gathered on the referring process was collected from a small group of patients who could recall their relations with different doctors. The evidence pointed clearly to the fact that the inner fraternity referred always towards its own members, and never toward outsiders. Outsiders were frequently obliged however to refer patients to the inner fraternity because of the concentration of important specialists within that group.

The above materials document the existence of an inner fraternity within the medical profession, a spatially segregated group, homogeneous with respect to ethnic and religious affiliations, involved in the lucrative specialized fields of medicine, occupying the dominant hospital posts, and having preferred claims on the good paying clienteles of the city. It maintains its existence, and controls the practice of medicine, by sponsoring new members.

The interview materials exhibit the ramifications of the sponsorship process. Six distinctive activities are worthy of note. (1) The selection of recruits to the profession. The members of the inner fraternity exercise an indirect control over the selection policies of medical schools by their recommendations of students. No significant studies have been made to date of the manner in which medical schools recruit and select their students. (2) The selection of interns. His internship is one of the most important status badges that the doctor wears. It can never be discarded, and serves immediately to categorize the doctor. It constitutes a persisting judgment on the young doctor, and represents a crucial turning-point in his career. By their institutional positions the inner fraternity control the allocation of the better internships. (3) The appointment of externs. An externship is the legitimate avenue to progress in the hospital system of the community. It obligates the doctor to work in the charity clinics. It involves a heavy tax on time and energy. It is an index that the incumbent is in earnest about his medical career. The inner fraternity controls the allocation of these. (4) Appointment to staff positions. These are an indication that the doctor has "arrived." Externships are both, sifting devices and periods of probation. The inner fraternity decides which externs will be selected for staff positions, and how long the periods of probation will be. (5) Incorporation into the office practice. The durable medical practices of the community persist beyond the lives of the founders. The latter can invite younger men to share and inherit such practices. Such an invitation carries with it the prestige associated with the office itself, and with the name of the established doctor. It carries the endorsation and certification of the established doctor. The members of the inner fraternity have a monopoly over such favours. (6) Incorporation into the system of referrals. The practice of medicine is synonymous with the acquisition of a clientele. The chief vehicle for acquiring patients is the referral of another doctor. There is no speedy route to this goal. One must traverse the designated stages, and be vouched for at each stage by an established member of the fraternity. One maintains his position in such a system by remaining personally acceptable to the membership of the inner group. . . .

The concepts of the inner fraternity and the sponsoring process seem to offer a particularly fruitful lead to the study of any profession. They are useful tools for tracing the stages in the professional career, for understanding the mechanisms of control within the profession, and for interpreting the milieu within which professional life is carried on.

33

The Negro Union Official:
A Study of Sponsorship and Control

WILLIAM KORNHAUSER

Sponsorship of the "right" people in promotions becomes
a means that sponsors use to control their organization
and its relation to the community. In Professor Kornhauser's case study, those in high positions needed a few
Negroes in union office to control the Negro members
and to provide an approved image of membership composition to the surrounding community.

Selection of some and exclusion of others to fill positions in a trade-union,
as in other organizations, are aspects of the control of the organization for
those in authority and determinants of personal career for those aspiring to
union office. Therefore the processes of selection of new personnel reveal
aspects of the ways in which unions function, the ways in which personal
careers in unions develop, and the manner in which the two are related.

The bases of selection involve positively and negatively evaluated social
categories of people available for recruitment. A person may be selected for
advancement because the way in which he is categorized has strategic significance for the organization from the point of view of the leadership. This is
illustrated by the manner in which a Negro becomes an official in a union
with a predominantly white membership. Selection of a Negro for union office
involves recognition by white leaders of the expediency of his advancement
within the organization. When this recognition occurs, the white officials may
sponsor a Negro for union office—since it is through such a mode of selection
that those in authority may single out persons possessing the desired attributes—and use their personal power to encourage and advance them in the
organization. Such a system of selection impinges upon vital interests of the
union leadership, as well as upon the different interests of the sponsored. The
following examination of instances of selection of Negroes for (higher) union
office relates these two sets of interests to personal careers and the functioning of the union within which they are carried out. . . .

CONDITIONS LEADING TO SELECTION OF
NEGRO UNION OFFICIALS

Size and importance of Negro membership

The Negro's chances for entrance into and advancement within the union
hierarchy are related to the size and importance of the Negro membership in

Excerpted, with permission, from *American Journal of Sociology*, 57(5) (March, 1952): 443–53.

his local and in the international and to the significance of race relations for the position of the union in a given situation. Where Negroes are numerous in the international, they often will be successful in pushing one of their local leaders into a high position in the union. This is supported by observations that where Negroes are scattered through white locals and therefore have more difficulty in acting as a unit, they usually will fail to develop their own strong leadership. White union officials commented that they "cannot find Negro leaders to push in the union." The reasons may include those identified by one of these officials, namely, either the whites keep the Negroes from becoming leaders on a local level (where most union careers begin) or/and Negroes develop a sense of inferiority and futility in predominantly white locals and consequently keep quiet. Where the national union's membership is solely or largely Negro, there develops the strongest, most outspoken Negro labor leadership. . . .

But there are cases in which a sizable and vocal Negro membership has not led to selection of a Negro for high union office. . . .

Hence, the "push" that a Negro union leader, or would-be leader, receives from Negro members is not sufficient for his selection as an official in a union in which Negroes are in a minority. There must be a "pull" from the white leadership of the union to put him in office above the local level.

Conflict situation facing union leadership

To stay in power, the union leadership must be able to (1) win union members in competition with employers, other unions, and antiunion or apathetic workers; (2) gain union members' support in conflicts with other unions seeking to win over its membership; and (3) hold union members' loyalties in conflicts with other persons and groups seeking to take over the union leadership. These three types of conflict situations, as defined by the to union leadership, are the three major kinds of conditions under which Negroes are selected for union office.

1. Many unions, primarily industrial types, have faced the continuous problem of organizing Negro workers for the following reasons: they often found Negroes in large numbers and strategically located in their jurisdictions, they met employer attempts to divide the work force along racial lines, they faced other unions which used the race issue against them, and they found a good deal of white-worker hostility against organizing Negroes and distrust of the union on the part of the Negroes. Of the thirty-four unions studied, half have been confronted with all or most of these conditions. All seventeen of these unions have selected Negroes as organizers in situations in which a sizable number of Negroes have been involved and in which special appeals of this sort to the Negro workers have been considered expedient. Furthermore, where an initial organizing effort is being made, a majority of these unions often manipulate the newly formed local's elections to get Negro representation among its officers. This tactic is employed to increase the

likelihood that the local will stay organized and not split along racial lines. It has been used principally in the South, less frequently in the North. White union leaders volunteered cases of their selection of Negroes under these conditions of initial organization of a local.

2. A Second type of conflict situation facing the union leadership is that of jurisdictional strife with other unions. Under these conditions, the leadership must be able to build up and hold the allegiance of the membership. Where a strategically significant number of Negroes is involved, the leadership will be likely to make special appeals for their support, employing such means as the sponsorship of a Negro member for high union office.

3. The third type of conflict situation facing the union leadership, or would-be leadership, is an internal struggle for power. Again, where Negroes are numerous in the union, special appeals will be made to them to get their votes, and here, too, sponsorship of a Negro for high office is effective. In the following case political gains were made by a faction within the union through such sponsorship efforts even though sponsorship itself failed. . . .

In summary, the conditions underlying the selection of a Negro for higher union office are twofold: (1) the "push" of a sizable Negro membership in the union and/or in the union's jurisdiction; and (2) the "pull" of white leaders faced with a conflict in which their sponsorship of a Negro promises to have tactical advantage. The sponsorship is, in part, an anticipation or recognition of the power of Negroes as a group in the outcome of the conflict. Hence, careers of Negroes in unions are tied to the position of Negroes as a group in the work force and union, where that position is defined as important by those in power in the union—for those in control are the sponsors (actual or potential) of Negro officials, and sponsorship is the crucial means by which Negroes get into union office.

THE PROCESS OF SELECTION OF NEGRO UNION OFFICIALS

Sponsorship

The modes of recruitment of people to fill positions in an organization vary from impersonal and formal processes to highly personal and informal ones. Systems of sponsorship approach the latter pole, since sponsorship involves the use of personal power by some to pick others for entrance into and advancement within the hierarchy.

Sponsorship in unions usually takes one of two paths. Either a person is chosen for nomination on the administration's or opposition's slate of candidates for elective offices or, if the position is appointive, he is put directly into office. Who does the sponsoring and how it is done vary widely from the very nature of such an informal and personal process. Sponsorship by white leaders of Negroes for office illustrates this point. Generally, when certain white leaders decide they want a Negro elected to office, they take into consideration the sentiments of the Negro members, usually by choosing a Negro officer or informal leader of a local with a large Negro membership. That is what happened in case 3: The white official approached the informal leader of the Negro members of the local as a potential candidate for a local office. When sponsorship is for a national office, the Negro selected almost always is already an officer of a local or a member of the national staff. . . .

Career lines

Up to this point, selection of Negroes for office has been discussed from the perspective of the sponsoring white leadership. From the point of view of the sponsored Negro, patterns of recruitment appear as career lines and contingencies. The generalized pattern consists of (1) a large and strategically important Negro membership in the union which exerts more or less pressure on the union leadership to recognize it by placing one or more of its group in office; (2) a conflict confronting the union leadership, involving another union, a faction within the union, management, or some other group; (3) a decision on the part of the white leadership to sponsor Negro leadership in light of the particular conflict; (4) the selection of the Negro by the white leaders, the choice usually being a leader of a local with a large Negro membership; and (5) the appointment of that Negro to a position on the national staff or his nomination on the slate of national officials. In all cases examined the career line of the Negro leader in a union with Negroes in a minority began in his being active in a local, usually in an office of the local; then came his appointment to a staff position or election to a national office, or his appointment came first and then his election to national office. . . .

FUNCTIONS OF SELECTION OF NEGRO UNION OFFICIALS

One would expect the system of sponsorship to have consequences defined as tactically advantageous by the white sponsors and as more or less problematic for personal careers by the sponsored Negroes.

Symbolic function

To win and keep Negroes as union members and as supporters of their actual or proposed administration, those in power or aspiring to it often will sponsor one or more Negroes for union office, particularly when there is an immediate contender for the Negroes' allegiance. The sponsors expect that the Negro in office under their auspices will serve as a symbol of the union, or faction within it, to the Negroes whose allegiance is sought. This *symbolic* Negro official, defined on the basis of the manifest function for the sponsors, probably typifies the majority of national Negro officials in predominantly white unions. . . .

In general, the rationale of the sponsors is that, by taking the initiative in giving the various groups in the union representation among the officials of the union, those in control can stay in control or those aspiring to power can gain power. . . .

In summary, then, the symbolic leader is expected by the sponsors to win the support and confidence of Negro members for the union and/or a particular faction within the union, first, because his very presence in office is a symbol of the union leadership's professed interest in championing Negro rights and, second, because his actions in office also are a symbol of the supporting and protecting of Negro interests. . . .

Liaison function

A second type of Negro union leader is the "liaison" man. He may be distinguished abstractly as a separate type, but actually all Negro officials more or less share his qualities. . . .

The Negro union leader in a predominantly white union acts as a liaison man between the union leadership and the Negro rank and file. . . .

Thus, the Negro official in the predominantly white union typically is given authority primarily over Negro members. Particularly in times of racial conflict he is expected to "straighten things out" by "dealing with his own people." This is the case even though the formal constitution dictates that all union offices have control over areas of activity rather than over racial or ethnic membership groups. Thus, the presence of a Negro in office initially tends to redefine the function of that office. That is, the office comes to involve expectations on the part of the white leadership that the Negro official will act as a representative and leader of Negro members, serving as a link in the hierarchy of communication and control.

The liaison function of Negroes in official capacities means that they have an integrative role in the organization. But what does "integration" mean? In part, it refers to the day-to-day structure of action in the union and to its system of communication and control, in which the Negro leader is a sort of transmission belt of directives downward and collective demands upward. But in part, too, it refers to a public relations function of the union, where the audience is the Negro membership, plus other groups involved in a given situation. At this point, the liaison type of Negro leader merges with the symbolic type. . . .

A Negro union leader made a more bitter appraisal of the functions of Negro officials:

> Some unions have a Negro on the staff, or a committee to deal with these matters [of race relations]. But they have no power! Their only function is to *take care of* the Negroes, and they don't do that! Having a Negro on the staff is *just a show* for most unions!

This is not to conclude that Negro officials have no influence on union actions. Frequently they do not; "liaison" is not a particularly creative function. But at times they do become active factors in union race relations— less frequently in other areas. The prime example has been Randolph's actions inside the AFL, a continuous pressure on the Federation to take a stand in favor of civil-rights legislation and, less successfully, to take a stand against its own affiliates which discriminate.

Consequences of sponsorship for Negro officials

From the point of view of the Negro official in a paid capacity the system of sponsorship is a bread-and-butter proposition as well as a series of problems for his ideal goals. Caught between a Negro membership to which he generally owes his primary allegiance and a white leadership to which he probably owes his position in the union, with both making often conflicting demands on him, the Negro union official will tend to see his role as "ambassador" of the Negro members, winning as much as possible for the group while at the same time keeping the good will of the white leadership. As a consequence, occasionally the Negro officer will develop a vested interest in the separate organization of Negroes inside the union.

Nevertheless, there is evidence to indicate that, once a Negro gets into a high position in the union, by means of small day-to-day acts he sometimes is able to change his initial role of sharply circumscribed functions to one covering wider and wider areas of action commensurate with that of the white man filling a formally equivalent office. For example, two Negro officials are known to have moved into active participation in union-management negotiations, although continuing to perform symbolic and liaison functions as well. Thus, in spite of his initial role, the Negro union official occasionally moves into areas of activity in which he drops the racial functions and assumes those inherent in the office as such.

If this shift should come to characterize more than a few scattered cases of Negro leaders, it would indicate, as Professor Hughes pointed out with reference to the Negro personnel man, that the race line in industry was disappearing.

CONCLUSIONS

The color of a man's skin may lead to his sponsorship for or exclusion from a job. Therefore it is a career contingency for him. The color of a man's skin may have power or status or other functions for an organization or looser work group. Therefore, it is a control contingency for those in power. . . .

But a person's racial identification is not the only type of social category which serves as a basis of selection or exclusion. In this respect the member of a minority who is recruited for office on the basis of that membership is no different from the doctor who is sponsored for his "family name" by the "inner fraternity" of medicine or the lawyer sponsored for his "contacts" by the law firm. In all such cases the sponsors' expectations for the role of the sponsored, and the manner in which that role is supported and modified by the latter's conduct, reveal aspects of the dynamics of the group as a whole.

Therefore, it is suggested that, by investigating the social characteristics imputed to and sought in new personnel by sponsors in various occupations, the conditions under which such attributes are singled out, and, finally, the functions of the sponsored for the organizational or work-group leadership, a more adequate picture of interrelations between personal careers and the institutions within which these careers are carried out may be drawn.

34

Advancement in the Japanese Factory

JAMES C. ABEGGLEN

While the clique may have effects on promotion choices in any organization, in this article Professor Abegglen shows how the clique may take over the organizational career completely in the Japanese firm, presenting great barriers to advancement to those not in the clique.

This discussion of the relationships between the formal organization and the career of the employee is not meant to imply that informal factors play no part in careers or career opportunity. Some of the informal factors have been pointed out in foregoing sections. For example, nepotism plays a definite role in the basic recruitment process. In addition, the literature on Japanese society makes reference to a special kind of informal relationship, known as the *oyabun-kobun,* or parent-child relationship, that should be briefly considered here. It is an explicitly recognized set of reciprocal obligations between senior and junior that have been observed and delineated for certain kinds of Japanese work relationships. In the course of this study some attention was paid this kind of relationship. On the whole it appears justified to report that the *oyabun-kobun* relationship in its true form does not exist in the large firm. Certain kinds of industry, especially stevedoring and construction work, retain this form of organization, however, and it is a conspicuous feature of the considerable gambling and entertainment industry of Japan. Apart from these semi-legal and illegal areas, it is interesting to note that the relationship survives most strongly in those industries which, in the United States at least, are most heavily ridden with racketeering; and the system has real parallels to American racketeering. It does not seem accurate to describe the relationships between people in the large Japanese firm in these terms.

It is quite true to say that relations between younger and older, superior and subordinate individuals often have a heavy component of what we might call paternalism, which has close parallels to the father-son relationship. Thus, for example, the Japanese foreman feels responsible for the well-being of his workers, quite outside the work situation. Family problems, death in the workers' family, illness, quarrels between workers on a personal level, the well-being of the worker in the community—all of these have been in the past and even now are important parts of the foreman's responsibility. However, this is not the kind of formal and organized relationship that is implied in the *oyabun-kobun* terminology.

Excerpted, with permission, from *The Japanese Factory* (New York: Free Press of Glencoe, 1960), pp. 90–93.

255

Looking at the present situation, and thinking in terms of management relations especially, a more important term than *oyabun-kobun* is the word *batsu*, or clique. In the discussion of recruitment procedures it was noted that groups of young men entering *shokuin* status together in a given year are recruited from a limited number of universities, which means in practice that a given age group on entry into the company's employ has had some previous interaction and intimacy. This intimacy from college years is maintained in the company by dinners, parties, and other informal activities. Further, a senior member of management, usually a graduate of the same university, will often become familiar with and associated with the careers of such a group of younger men. On the basis usually of common university experiences and background there develop in the large firms distinct cliques that play a very considerable though informal part in career progress and success. It is this factor that helps account for the frequency with which graduates of foreign universities have real career difficulties in Japanese firms.

The role of a senior member of management in these clique structures underlines the importance of such a person in the training system of the Japanese firm. The elaborate methods used in American firms to train employees at all levels for their jobs is in little evidence in the Japanese company. Training is largely a matter of on-the-job training, learning from seniors and superiors. Thus the new factory hand is placed in an apprenticeship system and his learning is derived only in small part through formal schooling. Job learning takes place in the shop and, remembering that the vocational school or commercial or industrial curriculum is not part of the Japanese school system, it is the responsibility of the senior worker to teach the new worker the methods of the plant. This situation is no less true of management. The absence of formal training operations in the Japanese firm adds to the close relations between worker and superior and increases the ties that knit the worker to the company in an essentially paternalistic relationship.

These ties, established within the sprawling formal organization, parallel closely the kind of relationship indicated in the small textile factory between the owner and his workers. While the size of the organization precludes the intimate knowledge of and interaction with superiors that is the central force in the operation of the small workshop, two types of relations which parallel the system of the small shop may be seen in the large firm. The first is the strong tie between the company and the worker described earlier, the lifetime commitment of worker and firm to each other, and the elaborate system of extra-monetary obligations and rewards that have been developed in the large plant. The second is the intrafirm relationship between superior and subordinate developed in the clique system at the management level and in the apprentice-teacher and worker-foreman relationship in the factory itself.

To present fully the close parallels between the small Japanese factory and the large one in terms of social organization, it is necessary to move beyond the formal system and look at the role of the company in the worker's total life activity. The interpenetration of job with other social activities that is so striking in the small factory may be seen also in the largest Japanese factories. The large factory, like the small twenty-worker operation, is an organization which has its involvements with the whole range of the worker's life, an involvement expected and accepted by the workers and one which bears on such important questions as the role of the trade union in the Japanese factory.

Part VI

Managing
Demotion

Promotion is the successful aspect of being moved through an organizational career. However, as we have said, not all movement is up; some is down and is likely to be awkward or painful to the demotee and the organization. Thus, one central problem arising for a theory of demotion in organizational careers is how a demotion is managed by both the organization and the person and his associates. This problem breaks down into two aspects. How can people ascertain that a demotion has in fact occurred; and once sure of it, what are the strategies for coping with its consequences?

We are fortunate to have More's article, which sets down eleven different empirical forms of demotion, as a starter on how to define demotion in organizational careers. To be sure, these are not the only forms, as indicated in the articles by Martin and Strauss, Goldner, and Dalton. They are only the more clearly definable ones. Many organizations will purposely try to obscure demotions to prevent the strains it is likely to produce in the person and his associates. Whatever the degree of clarity or obscurity, demotions occur in three general forms, singly or in combination. A person may be demoted through a change in his job, in his relative position within the organizational career, and in his current organization.

Job refers to the performance required, working conditions, salary, and other benefits and deficits associated with the job. Demotions of this nature can be very obscure and subtle, as well as quite clear.

Relative positions within the organizational career

refer to the number of its stages and the number of people at each stage. Demotions of this sort, if the hierarchy itself is clear, are usually clear. They can be obscured with several organizational tactics, however, such as by adding new positions over a person, so that while he is being promoted it is actually a demotion, by obscuring advancement criteria, by horizontal mobility (Martin and Strauss) with subtle changes in job content and/or honorary rewards, by sinecure positions (Dalton) which can be established for either high or low competence people, by "zig-zag" mobility (Goldner) which combines demotions and subsequent promotions to the point that the person is not sure where he is relative to others nor where he started, and by filling similar positions with both successes and failures. A clear strategy used by organizations is to elaborate harmless positions and even promote people into them (Abegglen). This is used by organizations which cannot fire people because it has given life commitments or tenure.

Changing a person's current organization can be a clear demotion based on the differential organizational prestige or benefits resulting from the change. Some changes are initiated within and by the organization to different sub-organizations, such as in the army and large banks. Others are initiated by the person, such as going from a top university to the "bush" leagues, or going to work in a low-prestige restaurant (Whyte). In some cases of changing organizations, the demotion is relatively lower but still respectable; in other cases a lowly evaluated organization may itself indicate outright failure for the person.

Besides degree of clarity, another aspect in defining a demotion is the *relative* failure which it indicates. A clear demotion might have occurred, but the person might not have lost much relative to his previous position or others' positions (for example, the promotion sideways or upwards to a harmless position). This demotion, then, is only a slight comparative failure, which can be easily overlooked, and more easily so if it has been obscured. Another kind is being passed up by others moving up or by not achieving levels which favored models have arrived at. The clearer these forms of comparative failure, the more painful they are likely to be. However, they may indicate nothing more than the lack of outstanding success, while still indicating moderate success (Glaser). Also slight comparative failures are likely to be differentially perceived by many demotees, ranging from some feeling distraught and some feeling that they have actually been promoted. The range of perceptions varies with the degree of clarity of the demotion and the possible interpretations of relative failure (Smigel). In contrast to slight changes the relativity of demotion in some cases is a clear failure to perform adequately or a loss of a prestigeful position and job. People in these circumstances approach absolute failure in their own minds and those of others.

The relativity and clarity of demotions is born from the balance of pressures the organization is under to obtain levels of excellence or adequacy of performance and people's desire to achieve or rest at such levels. Linked with this balance is that of the relative degrees of security or insecurity in a position which the organization provides for stimulating the appropriate level of performance. Then, when a change in the person's position, job, or organization occurs, he and others may judge by the established balances whether a demotion has occurred. These balances on performance and security stimulate people to compete in certain ways for promotions and for avoiding demotions by, for example, taking risks with innovations, putting out careful, routine work, and so forth.

Once a demotion is defined and its relative failure calculated, how is it handled by the demotee and organization? Some people, of course, desire it, especially older people who no longer want to work so hard to compete and would rather relax in an easier job with adequate salary. Others rationalize with a "peaking out" theory: they have peaked out in ability to compete for positions in the organizational career and now they only can stay put or move down. This theory can be normalized by the organization for all its members, so all expect to "peak out" and demotion therefore is accepted as an inevitable part of the career (Goldner). Others say demotion is the "price one pays" for going too high in the career. Obscured demotions may simply be never mentioned by people, since they are the easiest for a person to deny, especially if the organization is providing fringe rewards (for example, trips, salary increase, and so forth) at the same time. They may devote themselves to a family or leisure pursuit to the neglect of further "making it" in a career.

Demotion can be a stigma for a person when it is clear enough to ascertain and the relative failure indicates the person's organizational career is blocked forever or downwardly mobile. Under this condition the stigma spoils the organizational identity and career of the person.[1] In some careers, such as nursing, people can go down or up as often as they desire with no stigma; it is merely accepted as taking another job. In other careers, such as academic, the stigma of loss of position is strong—indeed it may seldom happen for this reason, as suicides may result. Organizations will endeavor at times to cover the stigma by various strategies, such as by normalizing the final stages of career with a demotion, as we have said. The organization may retrain them for a "new" job, principally to build up confidence, self-esteem, engage them in educational programs and seminars to show them the vital "relevance" to the organization of their new work, and so forth. These organizational responses to the stigma of demotion (see More, Martin and Strauss, and Goldner for other responses) may be summed up in trying to "cool-down" (Glaser) the unfortunate person to a level of self-appraisal and career expectation commensurate with his career movements. Cooling-down the person is necessitated by the strong responses of depression, apathy, hostility, irritability (see Whyte), withdrawal, and so forth, with which many persons meet a stigmatizing demotion. When not cooled down, the person is likely

[1] Erving Goffman, *Stigma* (Englewood Cliffs, N.J.: Prentice-Hall, 1963).

to be a disruptive force in the organization, making trouble, avoiding cooperation, and exercising undue influence or authority over others.

Some of our best theory on organizational careers has been written for the problem of demotion. But it is only a beginning in the study of this, often subtle, type of relative organizational failure; it is only a beginning for the comparative analysis necessary to generate a formal theory of demotion in organizational careers.

35

Consequences of Failure in Organizations

NORMAN H. MARTIN and ANSELM L. STRAUSS

Organizations may engage in many obscure forms of
demotion to avoid openly confronting a person's failure.
Professors Martin and Strauss discuss responses to the
"cooling out" strategies an organization may use to
effect a subtle demotion.

The meshing of horizontal and vertical movements of personnel is not always
perfect. Individuals are moved into positions prematurely, sponsors drop
protégés, and miscalculations are made. Problems are therefore created which
must be dealt with. Incompetent individuals have to be moved into positions
where they cannot do serious damage but where their experience can still be
used; frustrated mobility drives must be diverted into harmless channels. In
any organization such malfunctioning and changes are inevitable.

The correction most obviously takes the form of firing, but more subtle
means are frequently used, such as open or concealed demotion and arrest
of further promotion, which common parlance refers to as "kicking a man
upstairs," "shunting him to another department," and "banishment to the
sticks." Indeed, unless an organization is willing openly to remove personnel
from important positions by outright firing or demotion, it must resort to less
blunt tactics.[1] These techniques are well worth studying, for they are related
to organizational functioning in determinable and important ways. Why a
man is demoted or blocked, how, when, and what are his responses, may be
fateful, or at least significant, both for the person and for the organization.

Unless the incompetent individual is fired, he frequently is not told bluntly
or directly that he is being removed from a position because of failure in
meeting company requirements. The typical procedure is simply that the man
receives his orders from an appropriate superior, usually without much choice
of alternative, and must shift to the new position within a matter of days. He
may know or guess that he has failed, but there are hedges for his hurt ego in
so far as he is shunted or promoted rather than openly fired or demoted.

Such removals from positions have been termed "cooling out" by one
sociologist, Erving Goffman,[2] who has borrowed the term from the con man's

Excerpted, with permission, from W. Lloyd Warner and Norman H. Martin (Eds.), *Industrial
Man* (New York: Harper, 1959).

[1] The recent *Fortune* magazine article on "How to Fire an Executive" (October, 1954), by
Perrin Stryker, suggests that expulsion of top personnel is neither a simple matter nor necessarily
the method of demotion most practiced.

[2] Erving Goffman, "On Cooling the Mark Out: Some Aspects of Adaptation & Failure,"
Psychiatry, XV (1952), 451–63.

vocabulary. There it refers to the psychological disturbance which arises when the "mark's" ego is hurt after he discovers that he has been "taken" by the con man; therefore, the latter usually provides a mechanism whereby the victim will be cooled out; otherwise he will go to the police or create other embarrassing disturbances. Like the con man, any organization, Goffman suggests, must protect itself against the consequences of demoting its members by seeking to minimize humiliation and loss of self-esteem.

There are numerous organizational methods for cooling out, but any given organization cannot make casual selection among them. These methods flow both from the organizational structure and from accepted ways of behavior. If horizontal movement, for example, is used, then a flexible organization structure must exist. Otherwise there would be no place to shunt these men. Assigning them to staff positions requires the practice of a staff philosophy of management. Movement per se, indeed, must be a part of the accepted ways of behavior.

Thus in one concern studied—an organization with a broad and flexible system of positions—horizontal shunting, either within branches or between branches, is combined with honorific or terminal promotions. Occasionally, and especially at the upper ranks, a relatively functionless post is created to slide a man into. Staff positions, therefore, frequently function as receptacles for incompetency. These methods of removing men are closely linked with the nature of the vertical and horizontal mobility routes in the company.

Among other methods for cooling out, we might mention the following: use of seniority to slow up promotions, destruction of mobility drives, forcing of resignation, open demotion, bribing the failure out of the organization, progressive down-grading by merging departments, continual and rapid transfer from one branch to another, and continual bypassing. In some instances an organization has occasion to cool out men temporarily, often with the tacit or overt understanding that the move is not permanent. Sometimes this happens when a man is promoted too rapidly to be competent at handling his post. He is then shunted to another department or division at the same rank. If he fails again, he is given a terminal promotion.

RESPONSES TO BEING COOLED OUT

There are both short- and long-range responses to the cooling-out process. The former are probably less important, both for the men themselves and for the company. Some men, as we have pointed out, temporarily withdraw, become hostile, apathetic, and morose. Overt hostility seems to be more characteristic of men at lower levels; higher up, there appears to be an attempt at covering up, carrying on, and putting a good public face on the matter. The long-range responses are more serious. We have already pointed out some of these in our illustration of the effects of sponsors dropping protégés. At lower levels, supervisors may become antimanagement in orientation. They may strongly identify downward, turning, as it were, to face-to-face relationships with employees for their chief work satisfactions. At higher levels executives may become increasingly intractable and develop a tough, hard-boiled quality and an individualistic philosophy which makes them treasure autonomy. They may come to look upon their departments or divisions as private baili-wicks and develop possessive attitudes toward them. Along with this goes a rationale or myth of indispensability. Superiors find them unduly centered upon their own departments and complain that communication between themselves and these department heads is poor. They tend not to delegate authority properly, gathering control into their own hands. This means that they provide inadequate training for rising subordinates.

Such long-range effects of personal failure within the organization call forth answering responses from the organization. We might visualize this as a series of gestures taking place over a lengthy period of time. The company makes judgments upon men, cools out those who fail in specific ways, is met with answering responses from the men, and in turn must respond to their responses. The company has to set some of its internal policy, therefore, to take into account such untoward and unforeseen eventualities as the intract-ableness of executives who have been cooled out.

There are several approaches which companies use in responding to such situations. Training programs and seminars frequently are useful in broaden-ing the perspectives of these men. Attempts are made to build up their self-esteem by broadening their responsibilities and giving them special assign-ments. In still other instances companies respond by formalizing channels of communication—by forcing such executives to make periodic reports. Frequent horizontal shifting tends to break down departmental thinking and possessiveness and to nip in the bud any potential collegueship of these executives stemming from their similar predicaments. From the standpoint of organization structure, it may even be necessary to create staff positions to house those who have been kicked upstairs.

Thus the organizational strategies for handling partial or complete failures of personnel are many and add up to a complex system of policy acts. Such a system for handling failure is integral to getting men allocated, jobs done, and administrative leaders, high and low, picked, trained and developed.

A stable organization and a systematic meshing of methods of cooling out thus go hand in hand. A system of mutually supporting methods wherein those methods do not run excessively afoul of one another cannot exist when the organization is undergoing great policy changes or has just terminated a major power struggle. Major organizational changes eventuate not merely in the supplanting of old demotional procedures by new ones but in the piling-up of old. The picture is further complicated because in large organizations shifts of power go on continually with different degrees of speed and intensity in the several component divisions. These may be expected to affect, directly or indirectly, the cooling-out procedures of each. . . .

The systematic procedures for cooling out can also be viewed from the social-psychological or career perspective. To ask what happens to a man as he moves through these successive positions is equivalent to asking what effects his occupation has upon him both sequentially and in the long run. It is no easy matter to pin down the steps in the psychology of his change. Psychologists usually are content with characterizing the personalities of executives either without saying much about how the person got that way or speculating fairly generally about the social context within which personality is affected. The impact of occupational position upon personality can be studied more pointedly by tying the psychologist's kind of research into organizational and career investigation. It is just here that further studies of the effects of demotion and the arresting of promotion should prove most valuable. The crucial periods in a man's life are frequently associated with private and public recognition of failure. In so far as the type of failure and the handling of it are not unique but are common and related to organizational structure, there is the possibility of determining and studying the crucial turning points in personality development within occupational worlds.

36

Demotion in Industrial Management

FRED H. GOLDNER

Some organizations may make demotion socially acceptable as a stage of career where a person normally "peaks
out." These organizations may also follow through, as do
other organizations where demotion is unacceptable, by
obscuring the acceptable demotion in a good deal of
ambiguity to cope with potential strain. One tactic of note
is "zig-zag" mobility which combines demotion with
promotion. Professor Goldner discusses some of the
various means by which organizations make demotion
socially acceptable.

Organizations, like societies, face a problem of maintaining standards of
behavior without destroying motivation or causing alienation. They must
balance the inducement[1] offered by the promise of success through upward
mobility against the fear of failure invoked by the threat of downward
mobility. Discussions of mobility in society have treated success and failure as
separate issues, emphasizing on the one hand the functions of stratification
systems in motivating people to fill important roles,[2] and, on the other, the
role of downward mobility, uncertainty of success, and failure to reach culturally defined goals in producing deviant behavior.[3]

But in analyzing organizations, if not societies,[4] success and failure cannot
be treated separately. The narrower boundaries of organizations and the
precariousness of their existence make more crucial the problem of maintaining standards of behavior without alienating participants or destroying their
motivation. One organizational incumbent frequently succeeds at the expense

Excerpted, with permission, from *American Sociological Review*, 30(5) (October, 1965): 714–24.

[1] For a discussion of such inducements, see James G. March and Herbert A. Simon, *Organizations*, New York: John Wiley, 1958, 99.

[2] Kingsley Davis and Wilbert E. Moore, "Some Principles of Stratification," *American
Sociological Review*, 10 (1945), 242–49. For later versions of this argument see Wilbert E. Moore,
"But Some are More Equal Than Others," *American Sociological Review*, 28 (1963), 13–18, and
Melvin Tumin, "On Inequality," *American Sociological Review*, 28 (1963), 19–26.

[3] Robert K. Merton describes the deviance produced by failure to reach culturally defined
goals in *Social Theory and Social Structure*, Glencoe, Ill.: The Free Press, 1957, Ch. 4. For discussions of the relation between politically deviant behavior and downward mobility or uncertainty
of success see Daniel Bell (ed.), *The Radical Right*, Garden City, N.Y.: Doubleday Anchor
Books, 1964, Chs. 1–4, 13, 14. Bruno Bettelheim and Morris Janowitz relate downward mobility
to other types of deviant behavior in *Social Change and Prejudice*, New York: The Free Press of
Glencoe, 1964, 29–34.

[4] For example, people are assigned responsibility for managing systems of stratification in
organizations but not in societies.

of another.[5] And to maintain standards of performance organizations occasionally must eliminate incompetent incumbents through such mechanisms as discharge and demotion.[6]

Unless organizations can legitimize failure, then, or at least a significant proportion of it, they risk deviant acts of withdrawal on the part of the participants. My purpose in this paper is to explore some of the ways in which organizations make demotion socially acceptable. The materials are drawn from a case study of the management of a large, rapidly growing industrial organization (currently over 50,000 employees) with facilities throughout the country in manufacturing, research, and sales. . . .

OPPOSING PRESSURES

To meet competition, organizations must establish standards of performance. And the pursuit of excellence tends to create an intense internal competition in which each manager and executive must continually compete for his position with those below him. Under this system, merely adequate performance is insufficient. As one executive[7] put it: "We have a problem with people who are adequate, when you have others who could do an outstanding job." Carried to an extreme such a system results in insecurity and high turnover.

The pressure toward intense competition among the members of the organization produces a counter-pressure—the need for stability and security —which increases with the average age and length of service of managers and executives.[8] Management generally, and in this firm in particular, is

[5] The bulk of the work previously devoted to career mobility within organizations has dealt with problems of turnover or succession and not with patterns of mobility or associated organizational adaptations. Among the exceptional attempts to deal with career mobility rather than succession are: Bernard Levenson, "Bureaucratic Succession" (despite its title) in Amitai Etzioni (ed.), *Complex Organizations*, New York: Holt, Rinehart and Winston, 1961, 362–95, and Norman H. Martin and Anselm L. Strauss, "Patterns of Mobility Within Industrial Organizations," in W. Lloyd Warner and Norman H. Martin (eds.), *Industrial Man*, New York: Harper, 1959, 85–101. Examples of studies of succession include: Alvin W. Gouldner, *Patterns of Industrial Bureaucracy*, Glencoe, Ill.: Free Press, 1954; Oscar Grusky, "Corporate Size, Bureaucratization, and Managerial Succession," *American Journal of Sociology*, 67 (1961), 261–69; and Robert H. Guest, "Managerial Succession," *American Journal of Sociology*, 68 (1962), 47–54. Space limitations preclude consideration here of the important issues pertaining to strivers vs. non-strivers. See, for example, Charles H. Coates and Roland J. Pellegrin, "Executives and Supervisors: Contrasting Definitions of Career Success," *Administrative Science Quarterly*, 1 (1957), 506–17.

[6] For a list of various kinds of demotion see Douglas M. More, "Demotion," *Social Problems*, 9 (1962), 213–21. Levenson, *op. cit.*, also deals with this issue. Demotion has received little attention although most case studies that deal with management include references to demotion. Gouldner, *op. cit.*, 61, discusses the demotion of Bill Day. See also Melville Dalton, *Men Who Manage*, New York: John Wiley, 1959, 170–72 and 65. Evidence of demotion in Russian industry is provided by Joseph S. Berliner, *Factory and Manager in the USSR*, Cambridge: Harvard University Press, 1957, 48, and Theodore Caplow and Reece J. McGee discuss it in a non-industrial setting in *The Academic Marketplace*, New York: Science Editions, 1961, 51–52.

[7] I shall use the terms "executive" to refer to those at headquarters operations involved in the decision-making process as it affects large segments of the organization, and "manager" to refer to those located in the field.

[8] The organization is a relatively new one that has grown rapidly. Only recently have older men become a significant portion of management.

inclined to take care of those who have contributed so much to the organ-ization in the past. Given some minimal degree of efficiency, this pressure tends to produce a situation in which managers are permitted to remain as long as they perform adequately. . . .

A harder line is taken by those starting out in management and by those at the top, who are under heavy pressure to maintain specific profit levels.[9] Those on the way up soon become dissatisfied with low rates of demotion, as one such manager indicates:

The main complaint I have with the division at the branch and district manager level is we have less adequate management than we could have. You have to lay the blame on headquarters. In the other division they cut throats as fast as they turn around. This is the way it's going to have to be in this division.

Perhaps the classic example of the open and continuously competitive type of system to which this man refers is in professional athletics. The boxer must meet all challengers. The football player's job is threatened by each new crop of recruits. But even here, mechanisms are developed to protect the in-cumbents. The champion boxer may be able to stall for such long periods of time that boxing associations find it necessary to issue ultimata. Veteran football players devise ways to put rookies "in their place."

Movement in the direction of relying solely on criteria of excellence creates a number of problems for the organization. The harder line adds a burden of personal risk and pressure to higher positions that must be com-pensated in some manner, to enhance managers' willingness to assume the responsibilities of certain positions. Perhaps the greatest threat to organiza-tional effectiveness in this type of structure is that it will create an atmosphere of fear, leading decision makers to prefer conservative alternatives.

Movement toward accepting "adequate" performance at the expense of excellence also creates problems for the organization. Not only is efficiency apt to decline, but dissatisfaction may spread among those in the lower echelons who resent the lack of opportunities to move up, especially when those above are thought to be inferior. As one executive put it:

If there is someone in management who isn't pulling his weight, then it is unfair to the multitude of people. There are so many people vying for so few jobs.

In the context of these opposing pressures—one favoring a competitive system based on the norm of excellence and the other favoring criteria of adequate performance—the organization must cope with failure and the task of maintaining efficiency.

This company rarely exerts its right to discharge management personnel relying instead on the less severe mechanism of demotion. Not one of our

---

[9] A similar conflict is taking place in the society at large, between the need for a higher economic growth rate, which requires acceptance to all technological innovations, and the conse-quent displacement of employees. Technological innovations seem to have been given priority, so that dissension is primarily between the private and public sectors of the economy with respect to responsibility for retraining and reallocating the displaced workers.

respondents ever indicated a fear of being discharged from the company, although many were concerned about their positions within it. Demotion, in turn, is made more tolerable because a second company practice is to promote from within. These managers and executives had already performed satisfactorily, or better, at a lower level in the organization. One executive offered: "Having been successful enough to get the job, I wouldn't feel I was an utter disgrace for having failed on the job." A manager summed up a more general feeling:

No one is getting fired if his intent is right. This is damn important. We are all stockholders and all of us have chosen this company as a career company and some of us have passed a point of no return. If we get fired, where do we go?

I have no firm evidence, but comments like these suggest that extreme anxiety is alleviated by combining employment security with uncertainty of position, while at the same time personnel are motivated to produce, to remain flexible, and to innovate. If employment security were at stake the pressure would be to work hard but also to "play it safe," and security of both employment and position would weaken incentives to produce and innovate.

The point of balance between security and efficiency required in this kind of profit-seeking industrial firm is different from that required in other kinds of organizations or even in some of the professional units within this organization. For example, universities explicitly provide tenure and do not have a complex series of officers within which to move faculty members. Since personnel are expected to "produce" innovative and challenging research, which may threaten the status quo, the balance point must be such as to provide as much security as possible to the incumbents. Thus, having proved his competence a man does not have to compete with these below. Without this security, researchers, teachers and scholars might find it difficult to hold ideas at odds with those currently fashionable or to develop new ones.[10]

ACCEPTING DEMOTION

One of the most important findings in this study was that these management employees accept the real possibility of a demotion in their career. They saw demotion as a normal part of their future. They envisaged a fairly standard mobility curve that ascended, leveled off for a while, and then descended slightly. One statement by a manager illustrates this view:

If I don't move up I will eventually move backward. There is no standing still. Someplace along the line the curve is going to start downward—of effort and productivity on my part. . . .

Those in sales management, still compensated by some form of commission plan, are in an especially difficult situation. Their earnings curve may decline

---

[10] For a fictional account of the results of a system where professors, to hold their positions, must periodically meet any challenger from below in a competitive examination see George J. Stigler, "An Academic Episode," *AAUP Bulletin*, 33 (1947), 661–65.

sharply at its end, since commission earnings generally exceed the straight salary earnings of others in management.[11]

Most important, the culture of the organization encompasses a belief in the normality, almost the inevitability, of demotion. Sixty-three per cent of the executives who were interviewed at headquarters foresaw the possibility. Their attitude is best expressed by the one who reported:

In my circumstances, you have to be stupid not to look to the future and not to have a philosophy about it. For a man to be in it and not develop a philosophy about moving up or down—he would be a nut.

The view of headquarters from the field reinforces this image. Witness this observation by a field manager:

I like this job and realize it isn't a lifetime one and I will have to go either up or down. From what I gather in looking at [headquarters'] assignments, you have every opportunity to peak out at 45 to 50. You have every opportunity to fall on your head. Realistically for 99 per cent it does peak out.

. . . Even managers who are certain they will continue to move up become strangely ambivalent over the possibility of going the other way:

Your replacement is always around the corner. You can't just sit back but have to stay on the stick. I've never thought of going downward. I certainly realize the possibility always exists but I have no intention of going in that direction.

or:

Leveling off hasn't entered my mind. I don't feel I have reached the limits of my abilities or desires. It will be reached some day but not necessarily. Our corporation is not famous for letting people grow old in their job.

The interviewees also point out that a belief in the possibility of demotion makes individuals within the organization more flexible and consequently more inclined to take risks. . . .

Somewhat surprisingly, the questionnaire data indicate no clear relation between perceived chances of promotion and those of demotion. Individuals who see no chance of being demoted and individuals who see a good chance of being demoted do not differ in the chances they see for a promotion in the near future. The absence of an inverse relation between perceived chances of promotion and demotion is further evidence that acceptance of demotion is culturally supported, making it possible to entertain simultaneously the possibilities of future success and failure.

Acceptance of demotion is due largely to mobility patterns throughout the organization, and these patterns, in turn, arise from a number of organizational and personal conditions. Some may be unique to this organization or at least to its present situation. I shall deal with these conditions in the remainder of this paper.

---

[11] Careers with early peak earnings are also exemplified by professional athletes who must enter another field before 40 and thereafter seldom equal their earnings as athletes. A crucial difference between sports and business, however, is that athletes expect their earnings to peak out early. In addition, when an athlete enters a new field his reference group changes. No stigma is attached to the loss of a physical ability through age.

Organizational Adaptations

Mechanisms for obscuring demotions

One of the chief devices by which the organization copes with the potential strains of demotion is to cloak the demotion in a good deal of ambiguity. By reducing the visibility of demotions the organization softens their potentially disruptive features.[12] Contributing to this ambiguity is constant movement through positions (especially lateral movement) which prevents individuals from clearly identifying a move as a demotion.

... Data show that managers and executives are just as prone to expect lateral movement as promotion. Guessing whether a move was a demotion, a promotion, or a lateral is one of the common forms of gossip in this company. A move that caused a great deal of discussion involved a high executive who was replaced, given a temporary assignment, and a few months later assigned to a position that reported directly to his successor. The discussion centered upon the novelty of such an obvious demotion, and the conjecture among discussants was that the individual must have requested the move. "The company wouldn't force such a thing."

Some moves are so ambiguous that observers mistakenly interpret them as demotions, or the "demoted" man may fail to recognize his loss of status or that others define his move as a demotion. This ambiguity was vividly demonstrated during a discussion between myself and a company executive. The executive received a phone call from a recently demoted friend who sought advice. After closing the call he turned in astonishment: the caller had said he was asking for advice because he knew the executive had been through a demotion. The executive then recounted all his moves, maintaining that none of them was a demotion as far as he was concerned.

Organizational participants recognize this pattern of ambiguity. In the words of one manager who was afraid he might soon be demoted:

If it broke over [a particular issue] they would demote me and I would take it and go along with it. I wouldn't like it. It would be a bitter pill wouldn't it? I'll say one thing. There is no set pattern [of demotion] in this company. That is for sure. I think this is good. I think it is real flexible.

The ambiguity of moves is in part due to the changing structure of large American industrial corporations generally. In many organizations clear-cut lines of authority no longer exist, nor are positions arranged in a clear hierarchical line that leaves no doubt of the status of each one. Boundaries of responsibility overlap and are in a constant state of flux.[13]

---

[12] For a discussion of functionally optimum degrees of visibility see Merton, *op. cit.*, 341–53.

[13] Seventy per cent of the survey respondents responded in the 6–10 range on a 0–10 (extremely false to extremely true) scale to the statement, "There is much overlapping responsibility in the company." An account of these conditions as encountered in the study of one particular management function is presented in Fred H. Goldner, "Industrial Relations and the Organization of Management," unpublished Ph.D. dissertation, University of California, Berkeley, 1961, 13–51.

Ambiguity is fostered not only by diversification but also by company growth resulting in the creation of many new jobs and positions, and in most divisions of this company growth has been considerable. In divisions that have not grown, managers feel more insecure about their future. One manager posed the problem in referring to the opportunities in another division:

No one has told *me* what will happen [in my future] just like I can't tell the salesman. We don't have the laterals the other division has.

Growth may be encouraged in the first place by attempts to deal with demotion. Organizational expansion occurs not only to meet production or profit goals, but also to meet personnel "needs." Providing for employees' ambitions and cushioning the failure of those demoted leads to the creation of new positions in the organization. An executive brought this out in discussing the reasons for the search for new products:

In broadening the base there will be places for men who can no longer run as salesmen or manager but who have something to contribute. There are many branch managers in the other division who moved into staff jobs. They are paid fine salaries but not the pressure of a branch office. Now in our division we don't have this.

Organizational expansion in response to the motivational needs of personnel might be called personnel-directed growth, or better still—*organizational "lebensraum"*—as distinct from market directed growth produced by increased demand for the organization's goods and services and from diversification prompted by financial stability.

If the number of available positions ceases to grow, alternative mechanisms for creating ambiguity about moves are still available. Moving managers who are obviously "on the way up" into the same jobs as persons who are thought to be on the way down increases ambiguity. As a result the job itself offers no cue to onlookers as to the incumbent's true status.

One division of the company had utilized one of its geographical locations to "retire" men who could no longer meet the standards of excellence, only to run into trouble when it became known as a "dumping ground." The effectiveness of that operation was essentially destroyed until the organization started to send men on the way up to the same location, mixing them in with those who had been demoted.[14] An old-timer who is sent there now may recognize this as a demotion, but at least it is an effective operation, not one where everyone has given up. Thus, filling similar positions with both successes and failures creates an intermediary level and cushions the shock of demotion. It provides a substitute for the special positions that might be available in a growing and complex organization.

[14] Although this operating division of the company was growing in size it still was less complex than other divisions and had no opportunity to create special positions. The location in question lent itself to experimentation because its market characteristics distinguished it from the others. Highly competent employees shunned it until it was made a distinct step toward promotion. Here the ambiguity was a function of executive decision and not inherent in the nature of the work involved.

Other techniques have also been used to create ambiguity.[15] Actions typically seen as rewards for success are also sometimes used to compensate for demotion, e.g. a "trip to Europe." Managers sent for training outside the company included those being prepared for greater responsibilities and those who required a period away from the company to adjust to disappointments. Money is also used: "Some people are doing just as well in money so it [their demotion] is not so bad."

Another major technique used to create an atmosphere of ambiguity and uncertainty might be called "zig-zag" mobility. This is the combination of a demotion with a subsequent promotion.[16] The possibility of subsequent promotions makes the adaptation process much easier for a demoted individual. Belief in the "zig-zag" pattern and acceptance of it has become part of the organizational value structure: over half (51 per cent) of the managers and executives surveyed saw more than a fair chance (5 to 10 on the 0–10 scale) of moving back up for someone in their position who had been demoted. More important, this pattern helps set the climate for risk-taking. A manager who had undergone this kind of mobility related his experience:

I never agreed it [my demotion] was a fair thing to begin with. I defended myself too strongly perhaps. The thing that bothered me was there was no good reason. It was quite a decision to stay in the company. I pushed it all aside and five years later made District Manager.

This "zig-zag" mobility is a natural phenomenon in a widely-dispersed diversified organization that contains many lines of "skill" and authority as well as a social acceptance of demotion.[17]

Acceptance of decline as inevitable may be conditioned by the presence or absence of a base to which the incumbent can return. As Weber pointed out, it is easier for a lawyer to risk defeat in politics than it is for a large-scale entrepreneur.[18] It is to this lack of a base that a group of managers, discussing demotion, referred when they mentioned the insecurity felt by specialists who go into general management. With the rapid advances being made in most

[15] Some writers have taken strong issue with the presence of ambiguity in promotional systems. For a list of recommendations to reduce ambiguity in academic mobility, see Caplow and McGee, *op. cit.*, Ch. 11.

[16] Professional baseball offers a clear example of zig-zag mobility. Even though the teams are in constant contact with one another it is not unusual for a player to fail on one team and succeed on another. Players may also shift back and forth between the major and minor leagues. The position of team manager is most comparable to those in this study. A team manager released from one club is seen as a likely candidate for other teams, even those who finished higher in the standings.

[17] March and Simon, *op. cit.*, 99, cover one aspect of this point in their proposition that "the larger the organization, the greater the perceived possibility of interorganizational transfer, and therefore, the less the perceived desirability of leaving the organization." They conclude by claiming that "a substantial amount of what would be called turnover in smaller firms is classified as 'interdepartmental transfer' in larger firms."

[18] Max Weber, *From Max Weber; Essays in Sociology* (trans. and ed. by Hans H. Gerth and C. Wright Mills), New York: Oxford University Press, 1946, 85. The attempts of defeated union leaders to avoid the decline in status implied by such a defeat are treated by Seymour Martin Lipset, "The Political Process in Trade Unions: A Theoretical Statement," in Monroe Berger, Theodore Abel, and Charles H. Page (eds.), *Freedom and Control in Modern Society*, Princeton, N.J.: D. Van Nostrand, 1954, 82–124.

fields today a prolonged stay in general management leaves the ex-professional at a severe disadvantage if he must return to his specialty.

The vagueness of criteria for advancement

The various mechanisms that obscure demotions, and so cushion their shock, also contribute to the vagueness of criteria for promotion. The absence of firm guides to advancement has both negative and positive consequences for the organization. One demoted executive, looking back on his demotion, commented on this vagueness:

The problem with him [the boss] was learning what he wanted. Personally, I don't look at this as a failure. I am learning how big business operates at this level [said sarcastically]. If I had it to do over, I would not have been so free with information. Each time I gave them some information it gave them the opportunity to ask another question and put you on the defensive. *Now I give them nothing unless I have to.*

Thus the uncertainty generated in a subordinate can have the negative consequence of motivating him to create ambiguity for those above. Withholding information from superiors certainly is a dysfunctional consequence of the ambiguity surrounding criteria of advancement.

Criteria for advancement become increasingly vague the higher the position in the organization.[19] And at the same time, the possibility of demotion increases. According to one high executive:

The fellows right below this level recognize the possibilities of slipping [and know it when it happens. But] at this level and above you can stub your toe without being aware of it.

Those who are demoted or who are forced to anticipate it want to know why. As one executive said:

They [should] recognize that when we get to this level we are big boys now and can take it. They should level and say why—we are prepared for it.

But offering reasons for demotions when the criteria are vague poses a difficult problem for those above. Some executives in the organization have raised the question of whether individuals should be informed of all the reasons for their demotion. This led to an interest in, as one executive put it: "The art of managerial control without heartbreak or ruin to the individual."[20] Management wanted to avoid forcing a superior to defend his judgment by using all the ammunition available to justify his decision. As Goffman describes the process in a mental institution, the man's record is searched for errors that

---

[19] For one account of the kind of criteria used at the top of an organization see Chester I. Barnard, *The Functions of the Executive*, Cambridge: Harvard University Press, 1938, 224.

[20] This conception is strikingly similar to Erving Goffman's use of the term "cooling out" in "On Cooling the Mark Out: Some Adaptations to Failure," *Psychiatry*, 15 (1952), 451–63. Clark used the same concept in a slightly different way, dealing with the function of an institution in the cooling out process. The analogous process in the present study involves the large number of career paths that may be sought and achieved, including that of professionalization within the organization. Burton R. Clark, "The 'Cooling Out' Function in Higher Education," *American Journal of Sociology*, 65 (1960), 569–76.

will justify the action taken against him: "This dossier is apparently not regularly used, however, to record occasions when the patient showed capacity to cope honorably and effectively with difficult life situations. Nor is the case record typically used to provide a rough average or sampling of his past conduct."[21] In a mental institution, however, the authorities want the patient to accept not only his confinement but also his "sickness," while industrial managers want a demoted individual to accept his demotion without resenting it to a degree that would reduce his effectiveness in another position. To cite only negative incidents from a man's record would undermine this objective.

Additional considerations inhibit disclosure of all the reasons for demotion. As Barnard has noted, the criteria for executive performance may refer primarily to ability to "fit in" with other executives.[22] Trying to make "fitting in" explicit is not only difficult but can also be embarrassing. So vague a criterion also increases the possibility of error, for the lack of fit may not be the individual's fault, or the present composition of the executive group may change.[23] *An organizational structure that permits zig-zag mobility has more opportunity to rectify such "mistakes."*

PERSONAL ADAPTATIONS

Up to this point I have been discussing organizational arrangements that exist independently of particular individuals. A number of them make it easier for the "demoteds" to protect their pride and maintain their commitment to the organization. Regardless of what the organization does, however, many adaptations are worked out by individuals for themselves.[24]

The key to a demoted individual's ability to maintain his personal effectiveness lies in the process of self-redefinition—an adaptation that may occur in anticipating demotion as well as after the event.[25] An important prior adaptation is to emphasize the long hours and pressures required as one goes up the ladder. Although most are willing to pay this price, they constantly refer to it. As one manager put it:

After having been exposed to the constant turmoil and problems connected to a growth business as rapid as ours is growing, I think there is a little more to life than what you have to give up to go into that echelon.

A higher management executive expressed his attitude even more specifically:

---

[21] Erving Goffman, *Asylums*, Garden City, N.Y.: Anchor Books, 1961, 155.

[22] Barnard, *op. cit.*

[23] An attempt to handle the notion of "fitting in" is made by the development of a concept of "person-set" in David Caplovitz, "Student-Faculty Relations in Medical School: A Study of Professional Socialization," unpublished Ph.D. dissertation, Columbia University, 1961, Appendix F.

[24] One conception of forms of individual adaptation to the similar phenomenon of blocked mobility in society is developed by Merton, *op. cit.*, Ch. 4. For accounts of personal adaptations to blocked mobility in organizations see Levinson, *op. cit.*, and Goldner, *op. cit.*, 203–12.

[25] See Goffman, "On Cooling the Mark Out," *op. cit.*

I'd be an SOB if I would want to be general manager. It is the worst job I have ever seen in my life. It's unbelievable. He is twisted and torn and works from 8:00 A.M. to 11:00 P.M. all the time. Imagine having a job where your job is on the line on a problem and you have no time to think about it because you are on another problem.

Making comments on the "price" one must pay for moving up the career ladder makes it much easier to accept lack of mobility or demotion.

Anticipatory adaptations may be triggered by the demotion of an acquaintance:

[He] had thought it never could happen to him. He wasn't mentally prepared. So I said I should [be]. If it happens what are you going to do? So every city I go to I make sure I make some friends and nice business contacts.

These prior or anticipatory adaptations will obviously be utilized by many in the organization who will never be demoted. The more such behavior takes place the greater the danger of a self-fulfilling prophecy. And as individuals stop exerting themselves to succeed or begin refusing to take risks, the organization loses some of its power. Such possibilities enhance the importance of the organizational mechanisms discussed above.

A common method of adaptation used by the respondents was to shift their attention to another "self." A man engages in a number of activities, of which his work may be only one. To compensate for a defeat in any one of these spheres of activity he may increase his investment in another sphere.[26] This is one of the chief reasons why many managers consider the West Coast and other "desirable" geographical assignments as ideal places to go after being demoted. Such locations afford special opportunities to shift attention to family and leisure activities.

One manager described the reaction of a subordinate manager he had demoted:

There are a lot of ramifications in a demotion. [Before his demotion he] was critical of two other men who had been demoted with salary reductions and when they moved had bought more expensive homes—and yet he also did it. It was sort of an appeasement to the wife.

A shift of attention often requires a joint adaptation by the individual and his family. One executive said that he had to bring his wife into his plans only when he got to a higher management position, where the future was uncertain:

All our wives are given this philosophy and share it. I never brought my wife into the business until I got this job. At [the previous job] I didn't have the responsibility. She knows the good things about it—that I like it and the prestige and I work for the family's future. The money, and pressures, and time away are not her ideas of the good things about it.

[26] For an account of some of the shifts between work and other alternatives see Harold L. Wilensky, "Work, Careers, and Social Integration," *International Social Science Journal*, 12 (1960), 543–60.

A similar adaptation is to shift one's interest to community activities. Sales managers, for example, not only shifted their interests to the community but also argued that other managers should do the same thing, and that the company ought to supply more of the funds necessary to belong to community organizations. This proposition was usually couched in terms of increasing sales, but the men who offered it were those who were not going anywhere in the company.

The most difficult part of an individual's adaptation has to do with the people he must face. As one manager said about a demoted colleague who was scheduled to take a company-sponsored trip with a group of managers: "If I were him I wouldn't go. Everybody was ducking him."[27] Bystanders are frequently embarrassed in the presence of an acquaintance after his demotion, and unsure of how to approach him. One present manager who had been demoted[28] recognized this embarrassment on the part of others, even though he was satisfied with the demotion:

The only thing that bothered me is that when I left none of the people called me in to talk to me. I had the feeling it was a hush-hush thing, [and it was as if they were saying] quote: He is leaving headquarters and don't say anything, unquote. I don't want anybody to feel sorry for me but glad, because I certainly was.[29]

The organization is large enough to be able to move demoted individuals to other parts of the country. This facilitated adaptation by permitting demoted individuals to avoid encounters with those who knew them in their former capacity. This post-demotion adaptation, however, conflicts with one form of prior adaptation, for an individual who anticipates demotion and shifts his attention to the community faces the additional problem of withdrawing if he is subsequently demoted and sent elsewhere.

SUMMARY

Patterns of mobility within an organization, including demotion, are a crucial part of its structure. I have described some aspects of the relations between demotion and the organizational need to maintain standards of competence as well as individual commitment in one large business firm. The willingness of managers and executives to accept demotion has enabled this

---

[27] For an account of the relation between demotion and paranoia see Edwin M. Lemert, "Paranoia and the Dynamics of Exclusion," *Sociometry*, 25 (1962), 2–20.

[28] In this and the case mentioned above, the demotions were fairly obvious to others familiar with the individuals in their previous status. Not *all* moves are ambiguous; they vary from complete clarity of implication to total obscurity. But the ambiguous ones determine the organization's culture. Even in clear-cut cases like this one, demoted individuals were frequently sent to other locations. A separate study of specific moves is needed, to develop an index of ambiguity and to document the effects of different degrees of ambiguity.

[29] This individual was happy because the demotion took him out of a situation that was ruining his health. An often-quoted study of the relation between striving and ulcers in Jurgen Ruesch, *et al.*, *Duodenal Ulcer*, Berkeley: University of California Press, 1948. The study shows that patients with ulcers were more likely to be climbers than statics or decliners. Unfortunately, no adequate comparisons were made with a normal population.

organization to move them around to suit its productive needs without destroying individual commitment to the organization.

The potential dysfunctions of demotion tend to be minimized by organizational arrangements that make personnel movement ambiguous, by new positions created largely to fulfill the "ego needs" of personnel, and by the pattern I have identified as "zig-zag" mobility. Ambiguity regarding the meaning of moves has been enhanced by an absence of clear lines of authority which is characteristic of contemporary industrial organizations.

In addition to these structural arrangements for softening the blow of failure, various individual adaptations permit the demoted person to save face. One personal adaptation is, paradoxically, provided by the strong competition for higher management positions. This competition makes it necessary to spend so much energy and time on the job that an individual may find it relatively easy to forego the rewards offered at such a high price and thereby satisfy another culturally-endorsed value—spending time with one's family.

The possibility that alternative goal systems are commonly developed and substituted for the conventional goal of occupational success needs investigation, as does the evolution of conventional definitions of success and failure.[30] If all societies—and organizations—require some system of stratification, to place and motivate individuals, then consideration of the dysfunctions produced by stratification may suggest that alternative *unstratified* systems are also necessary. Perhaps all social systems necessarily include areas of endeavor that are unstratified, thus providing alternatives for those who cannot or do not wish to succeed in the stratified areas, yet must be kept within the system.

[30] One such investigation deals with downward mobility and work careers, in an attempt to explain the optimism of the downwardly mobile. See Harold L. Wilensky and Hugh Edwards, "The Skidder," *American Sociological Review*, 24 (1959), 215–31. Another important attempt to understand the process whereby success is defined is David C. McClelland, *The Achieving Society*, Princeton: D. Van Nostrand, 1961.

37

Comparative Failure in Science

BARNEY G. GLASER

Besides degree of clarity, another aspect of a demotion is
the relative failure which it indicates. The clearer the
forms of comparative failure, the more painful they are
likely to be. However, a certain degree of failure may
indicate nothing more than the lack of outstanding
success, while indicating moderate success.

A perennial problem for some scientists is their *feeling* of *comparative failure*
as scientists. This problem becomes clearer if we consider two major sources
of this feeling that are inherent in the very nature of scientific work. (*i*) In
science, strong emphasis is placed on the achievement of recognition; (*ii*) the
typical basic scientist works in a community filled with "great men" who have
made important and decisive discoveries in their respective fields; they are the
acknowledged guiding lights. These esteemed scientists, who have attained
honors beyond the reach of most of their colleagues, tend to become models
for those who have been trained by them or who have worked under them.
As Eiduson has put it in her recent psychological study of basic research
scientists "Scientists: are idols-oriented."

To take these honored men as models is important for training as well as
for a life in research. During training, one learns to think creatively. Emulation of these models results in the internalization of values, beliefs, and norms
of the highest standard. This emulation of the great continues and guides the
scientist in his research work, however individual in style his work may be.

But it is precisely here that a feeling of comparative failure may arise. In
emulating a great man the scientist tends to compare himself with the model.
He estimates how closely he has equaled his model in ability to adhere to high
standards of research, to think of relevant problems, to create "elegant" research designs, to devise new methods, to write clearly, to analyze data. In
addition, because of the strong emphasis on attaining recognition for research
contributions, the scientist perhaps will compare his own degree of success
with his model's to gauge how he himself is doing. In using the great man's
achievements and the recognition accorded him as criteria, the scientist may
be motivated to strive continually and unremittingly toward greater heights. On

Excerpted, with permission, from *Science*, 143(3610) (March 6, 1964): 1012–14. Copyright ©
1964 by the American Association for the Advancement of Science. The section, "Research on
Comparative Failure in Science," is from *Organizational Scientists: Their Professional Careers*,
by Barney G. Glaser (pp. 122–26). Copyright © 1964 by The Bobbs-Merrill Company, Inc.;
reprinted by permission of the College Division of The Bobbs-Merrill Company, Inc.

the other hand, he may see himself, over time, as a comparative failure for not having attained a comparable amount of recognition.

Eiduson brings out the dynamics of this problem for scientists:

The model, then, is the ego ideal figure, who represents the ultimate position, and in fact, defines what a scientist should do, how he should think, how he should act. *By comparison, everything else is inevitably of lesser worth* [italics mine]. We have seen the way the scientists in this group rebuke themselves as they become old, distracted, sit on committees or government advisory boards, or become administrators—and thus move away from the ideal. From this picture it is obvious that the scientist is hard on himself. He has a built-in, clearly marked scalar system, along which attitudes and kinds of performances are measured. When he moves away and deviates from the pattern, he becomes a maverick, or a person who has tossed aside the flaming torch.

AVERAGE SUCCESS

With this problem in mind, I recently made a study of the organizational careers of basic research scientists, one purpose of which was to ascertain the consequences, for the scientist's career, of receiving or not receiving an average amount of recognition: At the time of the study, these scientists were employed in a government medical research organization devoted to basic research. This was a high-prestige organization from the standpoint of scientists and was run much as though it were a series of university departments. The study is relevant to this discussion in showing something of the career history of basic research scientists, who are today in increasing proportions leaving the university setting to become affiliated with high-prestige organizations devoted to basic research. In these contexts organizational scientific careers are still primarily dependent on professional (not organizational) recognition.

By "average amount of professional recognition" I mean supervisor's favorable evaluation of the quality of the scientist's current research, and proper credit, through publication and through acknowledgment in the publications of others, for his contribution to the cumulative knowledge in his field. This definition gives the three major sources of recognition within reach of the typical scientist; references from superordinate colleagues, publication, and publication acknowledgments in the work of others. This "average" degree of professional recognition is attained by most of the country's scientists at any one time and by practically all scientists at one time or another. This degree of recognition is in marked contrast to the highly regarded, and restricted, high-prestige honors (in the form of awards, prizes, grants, lectureships, professorships, and so on) that are part of the professional recognition accorded those scientists who make great and decisive discoveries—the "great men."

Three general aspects of scientists' careers were studied: performance; security in, and advancement of, position; compatibility with others, and satisfaction with one's location in science. With respect to performance, an average degree of recognition was found basic to high performance. That is, recognition maintained high motivation to advance knowledge, and high motivation resulted in the scientist's devoting more of his own time to research; this, in turn, resulted in high-quality scientific performance, as judged by the researcher's closest professional colleagues.

Since, of course, such performance on the part of many individuals is the basis of organizational prestige, it was not surprising to find the organization providing, in return, a stable scientific career for a scientist who received average professional recognition. The scientists accorded this degree of recognition, in contrast to those accorded less, felt more satisfaction in their jobs and salaries. They tended to be more optimistic about their chances of promotion, and their rate of promotion was higher. With respect to the conditions for research—a most important consideration for basic-research scientists—they fared considerably better than scientists not accorded average recognition. They had more freedom to work on their own ideas, had more chance for originality, had more chance to use their current abilities and knowledge as well as to gain new abilities and knowledge, and had generally better research facilities and supplies. In sum, the "average" recognition accorded them was sufficient to give them security and advancement in their scientific careers.

Lastly, with average recognition, the high-quality performance and steady advancement could be achieved in a setting that provided personal satisfactions. The scientists accorded average recognition, again in comparison to those accorded less, were more content with their research and non-research colleagues. More of them felt intense interest in working with close professional associates. They were more satisfied with their assistants and with the other scientists, the organization leaders, their own supervisors and the directors of their particular institutes. They felt strengthened through belonging to work groups, such as sections and laboratories. They depended more on personal contacts for scientific information, both inside and outside the organization. They participated more in seminars, meetings, and the activities of professional clubs and other small groups.

Closely linked with this compatibility with their associates was a satisfaction with their location in the community of organizations of science. The scientists accorded average recognition, in comparison to those accorded less, felt strongly attached to their respective institutes and organizations. Indeed, they were more satisfied with the organization's reputation in the scientific world, and more of them felt that a sense of belonging to an organization which had prestige in both the scientific and the general community was of utmost importance. In comparing their own organization (from the standpoint of what job factors they deemed most important) with the "best" of universities, hospitals, industrial research organizations, and government research organizations, more of them consistently reported that their organization was generally better. In sum, the context of their careers in science was highly favorable.

Together these findings suggest that an average amount of recognition has a generally stabilizing effect for the careers of the scientists within the high-prestige organization of the study. (Even for individuals who received little or no recognition, the pressure on careers was not so great as to cause an exodus from the organization or from science itself. The great majority of these men thought the lack of recognition was only temporary and planned to continue in the organization, trying to advance knowledge.)

These findings suggest that career stability based on average professional recognition is probably found in other organizations similar in nature to the basic-research organization of this study, and that in organizations of lesser standing even less recognition may assure career stability.

In the light of these findings it appears that the feeling of comparative failure that may result when the average scientist judges his lesser success by the considerable success of his "great man" model tends to occur in many instances within the context of a stable, promising career. Further, most scientists can gain, if they do not have it currently, the degree of recognition necessary for a stable career. Comparative failure, then, is an evaluation resulting from a social comparison. It is not to be taken as absolute failure (loss of position as a scientist). A comparative failure can still be successful; an absolute failure is through.

THE SCIENTIFIC CAREER: A CARNIVOROUS GOD?

Comparisons with great men are, however, taken not as comparative but as absolute failure by Kubie in his famous article "Some unsolved problems of the scientific career." Kubie warns future scientists of the perils ahead when devoting themselves to that "carniverous god, the scientific career." His criteria in warning of potential failure, are absolute (not comparative) judgments, based on the careers of the more notable great men of science. For example, he talks of the "ultimate gamble which the scientist takes when he stakes his all on professional achievement and *recognition* [italics mine], sacrificing to his scientific career recreation, family, and sometimes even instinctual needs, as well as the practical security of money." Implying again that the scientist whose success falls short of the great man's is an absolute failure, he characterizes the young scientist as having "a self deceiving fantasy: that a life of science well may be tough for everyone else, but that it will not be for him," and as having "ambitious dreams; unspoken hopes of making great scientific discoveries; dreams of solving the great riddles of the universe."

Kubie states that the young scientist "dreams unattainable dreams." More directly relating his judgments to great men, he cautions against choosing science as a career, because of the "many failures it took to make one

Pasteur." He states that most young scientists, in using great men as models, unwittingly set themselves up to become failures: ". . . most young men view their prospect solely by identifying with their most successful chiefs, never stopping to consider how many must fail for each one who reaches this goal." Without making the distinction between absolute and comparative failure, this last statement clearly implies the former.

Admittedly, from this standpoint many must fail and few will attain the stature of their models, but this is hardly a reason for dissuading young men from becoming scientists. The chance is slight that they will equal or surpass their models, but they should be informed that most can gain the fundamental degree of recognition indicated in my study as necessary for a promising career in science. Surely the career to which they commit themselves need not be, as Kubie says, "devoid of security of any kind, whether financial or scientific."

Furthermore, these young men should be encouraged to enter science and take great men as their models, for most will be the artisans who do the commendable, but not earth-shaking, research which accumulates to form the foundation for future decisive advances. Kubie himself has recently, although somewhat ambivalently, recognized this, in comparing the typical scientist with the internationally famous scientist. "These little known and unrewarded men are the expendables of science. They are no less essential than are the few who reach their goals. Therefore, until many years had passed it would be hard to weigh which of these two men had had the more profound impact on scientific knowledge."

Perhaps my discussion draws the kind of "implication" from "statistics" that Kubie is looking for in future research when he says in his article on the scientific career: "It is the . . . duty of scientists and educators to gather such vital statistics on the life struggles of a few generations of scientists and would-be scientists and to make sure that every graduate student of the sciences will be exposed repeatedly to the implications such data may have for his own future." Career decisions are perhaps among the most important determinants of a man's fate, and anything which contributes to an understanding of the career in science may help people make these decisions more wisely.

RESEARCH ON COMPARATIVE FAILURE IN SCIENCE

While it is possible to be a comparative failure in virtually any occupation, the chances of becoming one are built directly into the occupation of scientist. Yet little or nothing is known about this area of comparative failure. Therefore, I wish to discuss a few of the properties of comparative failure that may be useful for guiding exploratory research. To be sure, the most important and meaningful properties of this problem area are yet to be discovered.

Since comparative failure is based on some social comparison, statements about it must always take into account a reference criteria. In this study the reference individual is the "great man" model in science, and comparisons are based on his degree of success. The criteria for this invidious comparison must be established empirically for any occupation within its particular situational context. The problem of comparative failure may be seen as a specific one within the more general area of comparative reference group theory.

The relative nature of comparative failure is in marked contrast to the absolute nature of failure wherein one cannot hold an occupational position and therefore must leave it. Comparative and absolute failure vary independently. A person who is an absolute failure may or may not be a comparative failure. It is true that a scientist forced out of science because of mediocre work will probably feel himself a comparative failure with reference to his many former colleagues and models. However, if he can leave these comparative reference individuals behind during the "cooling-out "process attached to his loss of occupational position, he may not at all feel himself a comparative failure. More simply, if he realizes from his absolute failure that he was not cut out to be a scientist, then evaluations of comparative failure become superfluous and may not persist. Again, comparative failure can unnecessarily cause absolute failure, that is, cause a scientist to leave his profession or to stumble along feeling that he is an absolute failure.

Comparative failure takes on more strategic meaning when no absolute failure is involved. A major source of comparative failure is, of course, demotion or downgrading of one's rank in the occupation. This topic has been analyzed quite nicely for business and industrial organizations. It has yet to be considered for scientists. Another general source of comparative failure appears when an important reference individual outstrips the scientist. Statements about colleagues, such as "He advanced very quickly," can mean that the speaker was probably left behind with a lesser degree of success. Practically all scientists have classmates and colleagues who have been far more successful.

Another interesting and significant source of comparative failure was brought out in this volume. With reference to the "great man" model, the typical scientist can have an objectively satisfactory career and yet feel a comparative failure! If this feeling persists, he may be oblivious to the stability of his promising career. If he actually lacks the fundamental range of recognition and, further, feels that his chances of gaining some recognition are hopeless when compared to his model, in focusing on the unattainable he is likely to ignore the general possibility of having a fruitful (if lesser) career by achieving the degree of recognition within reach of his ability.

The adjustment to comparative failure involves a "cooling down" of aspirations for success so as to be in accord with one's research ability and career prospects (rather than a "cooling out," as Goffman has described it for absolute failure, when one must give up all those aspirations linked with an occupation or position). The scientist as a comparative failure does not have to go through the often very painful process of giving up commitment, involvement, and investment in his chosen profession. He need only set his achievement and career sights at a lower level than those of his models. Indeed, his models, who provide the basis for an unfavorable comparison, also provide a perspective on just where to set hopes for a career in science. This perspective is denied the absolute failure, since he is going nowhere.

Various aspects of both the scientist and his "great man" model will affect judgments of comparative failure. Aspirations for a success similar to the model's probably are highest immediately after graduate school, but they diminish as the scientist takes his own and his model's measure during the years of research maturity that follow. This change most likely will vary according to the age at which the model did outstanding research; in some fields, great men appear at an earlier age than in others. If he is in a field in which great discoveries come early, the scientist may feel that he is "through" soon after he has begun. If the discoveries come late, then he may believe he has ample time to equal his model—and his feelings of comparative failure may emerge much later.

The type of models that a scientist takes will also vary according to his age. The young scientist usually is focused on his classmates, equal colleagues, teachers, his work supervisors, and current great men in his field. Hence, he has many reference individuals on which to base a feeling of comparative failure before he cools down his aspirations. In later years, as these models no longer loom so large, the more successful scientist may switch to the non-living immortals of his field. Indeed, although a scientist may have become a great figure, he may still evaluate himself strongly as a comparative failure, judging himself in relation to the immortals he aspires to equal. Notwithstanding the many useful consequences of taking immortals as models, it is quite possible that comparative failure can be even more intense for a contemporary great man whose aspirations (in contrast to those of the typical scientist) may have been sharpened, not dulled, on the grindstone of experience. In other words, not only may a comparative failure be successful, but the most successful scientist may be the most intense comparative failure. Thus, comparative failure may be more pronounced among beginning scientists and current great men than it is among others.

It should be noted also that I have dealt only with comparative failure as self-evaluation, not as other-evaluation. The latter also represents an area for research in the sociology of science. For example, a strategic aspect of advancement in the scientific career is the comparative evaluations given by the scientist's referees.

These are speculations. Only future research can tell us of the processes leading to comparative failure; of its incidence at various stages of an objectively successful career; of the "cooling down" mechanisms by which scientists cope with such a feeling and are helped by others to cope with it; of its effect on creativity, motivation, and partial retreatism; and of its effects on absolute failure and organizational turnover.

38

Demotion

DOUGLAS M. MORE

Professor More introduces his article on the forms and
consequences of demotion quite well in the first paragraph.
In reading this piece, the reader must remember that these
forms and consequences vary by the clarity of the demotion
and its relative failure.

Our purposes in this paper are: (1) to lay out a scheme of the forms of demotion that we have observed; (2) to indicate the conditions which increase the
likelihood of demotion being used as a business process; and (3) to analyze
the consequences of demotion on the individuals demoted and on the company organizations in which this takes place. . . .

One or more of the forms of demotion classified below occurred with
sufficient frequency to constitute a company-wide phenomenon of note and
importance. In the former group, the lack of demotion as a phenomenon can
be attributed in most cases to consciously adopted policies of dismissing a
man after he has been found wanting in a position, rather than demoting
him to a lower level job. Such companies make this policy because they feel,
and often state, that it is more detrimental to company morale to demote a
person from a management position than it is to dismiss the individual involved and to seek a replacement for him. . . .

Before proceeding to a consideration of the forms of demotion, it is
necessary to define the term in a general sense. We consider it as a process in
business and industry in which an individual is reduced to a lower grade or
classification of function, or has his relative position in the hierarchy decreased as a result of surrounding forces. Both promotion and demotion are
results of external forces, or authorities, acting on individuals. A man cannot
be promoted to a higher position or demoted to a lower position by his efforts
alone, but must be acted upon by some other person who has this authority.
Demotion in this sense includes a wide range of changes of behavior or status
within a company, all the way from those which imply minimal change up to,
but not including, outright dismissal from the company.

THE FORMS OF DEMOTION

The forms of demotion we have observed are:

1. *Lowered job status with continuation of the earlier compensation.* This is
the case when a man is demoted from a position of general foreman to line

Excerpted, with permission, from *Social Problems*, 9(3) (Winter, 1962): 213–21.

foreman in the department but, at the discretion of the president of the company, earns the same amount of money at the lowered status.

2. *Lowered status with decreased compensation.* This particular form of demotion seems to be the most characteristic one to define the term itself. We doubt, however, that it would be the commonest form, if it were possible to achieve an accurate count. As an example, we have noted the situation in which a general superintendent, paid at the rate of $13,500.00 per year was demoted to the status of a divisional superintendent with a cut in pay to $10,800.00 per year. As an interesting sidelight, it was found necessary to raise the salary of a parallel divisional superintendent from $9,600.00 per year to $10,800.00 per year when this move was made, in order that the two men should have the same compensation on the same level.

3. *Retained status with decreased compensation.* Strictly, perhaps this should not be considered a form of demotion because the individual involved retains the same level of prestige and functional authority that he previously had, but is merely being paid less to do the job. We include it here for completeness, but would not insist on maintaining this form in our over-all scheme. It is not common except with men of advanced years who are "semi-retired."

4. *Being "bypassed" in seniority for promotion.* Although in this kind of case there is no objective change in an individual's status, there is apparently a loss in a person's reputation and his strength to influence operations within a company. In a very obvious sense, to anyone who knows the situation this can be seen as a "slap in the face." Commonly we note that men in this category seem to give up hope for promotions in the age range from 50 to 55 years.

5. *Change of job to a less desirable function.* A particular instance we observed recently involved this form of demotion for a chief engineer in the company. Originally he was in charge of an engineering development group. When the project his group had been assigned bogged down and he seemed incapable of moving ahead with it, the project was reassigned to another engineering group. The engineer in question was removed from his position and, without change of level in formal company status or compensation, was moved to a position in charge of plant maintenance engineering, while one of his former subordinates was promoted to the position he had vacated.

6. *Maintained formed status with decreased span of control.* An example is of a single individual who had general charge of market research, marketing programs, advertising, and the sales force. In a subsequent period he retained line direction of the sales force, another individual, reporting to the President, was named Director of Marketing.

7. *Exclusion from a general salary raise.* In the past several years our expanding economy and increased inflationary pressures have produced several rounds of salary raises in most large firms, especially for important executive

positions. From time to time we have observed instances in which particular individuals have been excluded from a general salary raise often with a side comment running somewhat as follows, "Everybody is getting a raise this year end, but we just can't see giving Joe Smith a raise at this time. We currently are paying all we can for the job he is doing."

8. *Increased steps in the hierarchy above given position.* This phenomenon frequently occurs in small to medium sized companies that are expanding rapidly. As the complexity of the company's operations increases with increasing size, the necessity for greater diversification of management talents and specialization by departments increases. Technological advances have made impossible further honoring of the maxim to promote from within. Frequently, new positions are created in the managerial hierarchy, particularly at intermediate levels, so that such departmentalization can proceed smoothly. Everyone below the position created may be considered as having had a demotion, in the sense of being removed one further step from possibly moving to a very high position in the company. Such instances should be considered important demotion phenomena when it is apparent that a position has been created in the company hierarchy to prevent the advance of certain key people at lower levels.

9. *Movement from line to staff authority, but with the same compensation.* Generally such moves in a company are tantamount to demotions in the sense of removing the individual from the possibility of advancing in the power hierarchy of the company. In many modern organizations which are strongly research-oriented and research-directed, this may not be the case.

10. *Retention of the same job level, with same compensation, and carrying with it equal authority and responsibility, but transfer out of direct line of promotion.* This is distinguished from the preceding statement, because there is no implication that the person has changed his job function. We have in mind the case that we observed recently of an individual who was moved from being a general manager of a major metal fabricating plant in close connection with the main offices of the company to a position in charge of an even larger branch plant in a distant rural area. He was effectively severed from informal, social relationships with people in powerful positions in the home office, and consequently had his chances of advancement through such informal processes severely decreased.

11. *Position elimination and reassignment.* This kind of demotion occurs most commonly in major company reorganizations. These are frequently a consequence of management efficiency studies and the like. It is found that certain positions in the firm are totally unnecessary. Because the individual occupying such a position may have considerable tenure in the company, it frequently is deemed possible to reassign him to another job. The course of reassignment in which this connotes demotion is such that the person is moved into a department with a loss of senior rank or a decreased level of function within the company power structure.

Conditions Increasing the Likelihood of Demotion

We have assembled, in the following, those conditions we have found in a variety of businesses to be associated with demotion as it has been outlined above. . . .

1. *Extreme paternalism as the company "climate."* This is a frequently observed feature of companies in which demotions are common. Paternalism is not simply an attitude of management; it also reflects acceptance on the part of lower levels of management and workers of a filial role toward the parental head of the company. It is precisely this emotional acceptance of the paternalistic image that permits the punitive practices of demotion to occur and to be accepted by the management and worker groups.

2. *Seductive benefit programs.* In many companies, although benefit programs seem to operate to the direct benefit of the employee, it is possible for an individual to accrue a considerable retirement benefit with a company after he has been with it a number of years. This tends to increase the likelihood that a person will accept a change of status downward in order to remain with the company to be able to participate to the full in his anticipated benefits. Especially is this true when he would receive only a percentage of final benefits were he to leave the company prior to full retirement age.

3. *Scarcity of positions outside the company to which men might move.* Demotion can occur in instances such as this when a company controls virtually all the jobs of importance in a given area. When this is the case, if a worker leaves a company, he is put to considerable hardship to move himself and his family some distance from his present location in order to find work concomitant with his level of training and ability. This increases the possibility that a company may be able to deal with its workers in an arbitrary way.

4. *High average age in supervisory personnel.* Above age fifty foremen, supervisors, and others in the company middle management levels find it relatively difficult to move from a job in one company to a similar or better position in another company. Although a person may be well qualified for a job, companies, as much because of the folklore of employment practices as anything, exhibit reluctance to employ people over age forty. This is so severe a question that some states have legislated against employment discrimination toward a senior citizen. When high average age among supervisors occurs in a firm, it is possible for the company to demote individuals without them feeling that they have any chance of moving elsewhere. These men seem to feel that they have to take it as it is dished out to them.

5. *Sharply fluctuating work load.* This is a condition that tends to permit demotion, particularly in industries that are strongly influenced by seasonal changes, because of varying contractual loads as is the typical case of the job shop. A job shop is dependent on contracts from clients, and when it doesn't get them, it is forced to lay off workers and often to decrease the size of the supervisory staff. During such a layoff, persons at one of the higher super-

visory levels may be stepped down to jobs at lower levels, at least temporarily. The way this process increases the likelihood of demotion is that certain individuals the company may have decided to cut back need not be promoted back to former levels of authority when there is the next major buildup in employment.

6. *A company condition of loss or non-profit.* This condition frequently necessitates a reduction in management overhead. As the phrase goes, men who have been "taking it easy behind the desk" may have to roll up their sleeves and get back to work.

7. *Mergers producing an over supply of managerial personnel to staff the available positions.* This often occurs in mergers of companies of approximately equal size in the medium to large ranges. In such conditions, unless there is a clearcut continuation of a division of products and services, the merged company does not need, for example, two vice-presidents in charge of sales. After mergers there is commonly a great deal of loss of morale in middle management ranks, as the two companies who have been merged begin to shake down. Everyone seems to be watching closely to see who it is that is going to move into a position or retain his former position, and which members of the two company managements are going to have to take a back seat.

8. *Belated recognition that certain men have been promoted beyond their capacities.* This often results in what business has come to phrase as "restructuring of job content," in which the expectations of the company toward the man in a position are realigned to be more realistically in accord with what the person can do. Whenever there is an intensification of specifications laying out the duties inherent in a position, this tends to remove authority and responsibility from the position itself. For a company to have to spell out a man's job for him in considerable detail, means that it has removed from him the possibility of exercising independent judgment, initiative, or discretionary behavior.

9. *Broad company reorganizations of management structures and functions.* Demotions occur in these instances because company officials come to realize that management efficiency may have to be improved. Such management improvement programs often result in decreased need numerically for managers as such. When meaningful studies of efficiency are completed it is often found that there are individuals in the group who are in non-functional, or at least minimally effective, positions. Demotions and reassignments frequently follow.

10. *Position obsolescence.* This often occurs as a consequence of mechanization or automation. In these instances, companies—since warm-heartedness rather than cold-heartedness seems to be the current business philosophy— often tend to try to "make" positions in order to retain people on the staff, to avoid creating economic hardship among employees who have been with them some time. The fact is, however, that these men must be seen as demoted as regards their actual levels of functioning in the company.

11. *A contracting economy in the company's area of activity.* In a rapidly changing economy there are many entire industries that are decreasing while others increase. Frequently this happens as new inventions and new methods make possible the displacement of them in the market. For example, extruded and molded plastics are rapidly displacing many items that formerly were produced in the glass and metal industries. Those segments of the glass and metal industries, in proportion, exhibit a contracting number (or proportion) of management jobs available. The status of a contracting aspect of an industry complex tends to decrease vis-a-vis other parts of the same industry complex. As its status decreases, the amount that a company is willing to allocate to executive salaries in that area of its operation correspondingly is constricted. Railroading, and those companies supplying to the railroads, present this feature rather clearly at this time, and have over the past decade.

CONSEQUENCES OF DEMOTION

In this section we wish to take the third step in our analysis of demotion in two respects. First, we consider the way demotion affects the individual demoted, and then the effects of demotion on the company as a whole.

When a person is demoted, this generally is the result of a negative evaluation of him or his job by his superiors. Such an implicit or explicit negative evaluation tends to increase the individual's feelings of anxiety about his job, to lead him to question his own worthfulness. The person may show, as a consequence, increasing negativism, bitterness, resistance to direction within the firm, and may go so far as to express a defeatist attitude with respect to his total life goals. Frequently we have noted demotion to result in widespread lethargy in a person's behavior, almost amounting to an inability to function. Often, individuals who feel especially bitter toward their companies for having demoted them show tendencies toward sabotage, in an effort, in effect, to get even with the company for the hurt and damage it has done to them.

The above are rather blatant results. In our experience there is often a more subtle effect of affective withdrawal of the person from group contacts. While the person may continue to work, and work well, at his job, this withdrawal process results in a kind of non-communicative blandness in social contacts in the work situation. Psychologically speaking, this may result because the individual feels he must maintain self-esteem by withdrawing from any contact in which he might be subject to further negative interpersonal evaluations. It may also represent a retreat into a wishful fantasy life, a la Walter Mitty, rather than a concentration on the objective requirements of the work role.[1]

---

[1] Martin and Strauss suggest that class background of the demotee strongly influences the type of negative reaction, lower class people more prone to act out and higher class men more apt to withdraw.

Although negative effects of demotion are probably more pronounced, in a significant minority of cases there are definite positive effects. The demotion can act as a spur to work hard to recapture former status, resulting in increased effort and output. The man may become more realistically self-critical and may drive himself toward more thoroughness and perfectionism. He may readjust his aspirations to more realistic levels, and, as a result, improve his functioning to the point that he can be promoted back to former status.

In a third group there appear to be feelings of contentment. This most often occurs to men who have been demoted from positions which were extremely burdensome to them, given their abilities and talents. The demotion represents to them a release from tension-producing burdens of authority and responsibility they were unable to handle. These men express a sense of comfort at being able to return to familiar, easier tasks. In retrospect we learn that these are the men who have expressed at the time of their promotions some resentments against the company and their superiors for having pushed them into positions they felt they were unprepared to handle.[2]

There are levels of negative and positive effects to be distinguished. Quite commonly we note an intensification of the "climate of authoritarian paternalism" and the implied consequences of such a system. With increased authoritarian paternalism we often find an increased cohesiveness in the worker groups at the bottom of the company, and consequent increased conflict between worker groups and management. Top management tends to lose bargaining power, in part because it loses the loyalty of middle management. Foremen may become unwilling to "administer" a labor contract. This trend also leads to placing greater burdens of decision making and communication on one or a very few people at the top of the firm. This can easily decrease the over-all efficiency of the company organization.

Another effect on a company as a result of established demotion practices is a loss of morale in all levels of management below the very top. Specific effects that we would lump under this general term are:

1. Decreased individual productivity.
2. Decreased creative efforts from men in positions that require creative work.
3. Loss of loyalty to the company, a feeling that the company no longer deserves the emotional attachment the person had given it earlier.
4. An increase in turnover in middle management and in supervisory positions.
5. Increased chronic illnesses and absenteeism, as a result of the unwillingness of people to come to work, because they feel that the work is not worthy. Interestingly this may be seen as actual chronic illness, or merely reported chronic illness.

[2] The extent to which a sample of demotees contains a high percentage of these "contented" ones may be involved in the conclusion that downwardly mobile people exhibit low frequencies of mental disturbance. Further studies of emotional adjustment as related to vertical mobility probably should attend to some classification, such as we suggest, into reaction types.

6. Increase in abuse of privileges—tendency to stretch out the lunch hour, rest periods, and coffee breaks to unreasonable length; decreased attention to the work itself; increases in petty theft; use of the company's facilities for personal interests.

7. Moonlighting. In companies that have a history of demotion, and in which the process of demotion is well-established, it is our impression that, except in those companies that rigidly restrict the workers' right to work anywhere else, there is a high frequency of outside work and outside business interests. Men often will give more time or energy to such interests than they will give to their main jobs.

8. Formation of protective power cliques. The *informal* structures of supervision tend under demotion to become more and more rigid as subgroups coalesce in an attempt to secure sufficient power for themselves to insure personal continuance as small, entrenched enclaves in the management hierarchy.

Some results of a system of demotion may be seen as positive. There may be a clear gain in morale, rather than a loss, when the persons demoted are individuals who are responsible for major problems in the company. If the manager demoted was one who was unable to make decisions, or to institute action, and his replacement can do so, there is a sharp increase in morale. This results in better definition of work roles, decrease of confusion resulting from ambiguity. Few things are more destructive of morale than a vague, diffuse, and ambivalent definition of the work situation. Corresponding to such gains in morale there may be gains in efficiency and productivity throughout the firm.

Another kind of gain that may occur under demotion depends on the prior establishment of a well-publicized promotion-demotion system. This permits moving men up to positions temporarily for training purposes, then demoting them to former jobs. This allows a company to develop a body of trained managers on which to draw for expansion or replacement when needed. For this to have positive effects, it must be recognized and accepted in middle management, and there must have been time for the men involved to see that the system does indeed operate to create opportunities within the company. To be realistic a company must make it clear that these are trial or training assignments, not final promotions. Demotion out of the position, then, is not seriously taken, and perhaps should not be seen as fitting into the broad picture of demotion as we have outlined it. . . .

Any further development toward a theory applicable in this area will have to be integrated, in our opinion, with general theory of vertical social movement. Demotion must be seen only as a special instance of downward social and occupational mobility. The total theory will have to take into account the economics of the firm, the labor market, and other general changes in the occupational system.

39

Moving Up and Down in the World

WILLIAM FOOTE WHYTE

Change in a person's organization to one of lesser grade can
be a clear demotion even if his career in the new organization is successful. Professor Whyte discusses the case in
which the downwardly mobile person is likely to have
problems adjusting to his new organization and work
which may further hinder his career.

The attitudes of the worker toward his job and toward his fellow workers
depend in large measure on his social position in the community. This social
status is constantly subject to change. In a society such as ours, where class
lines are not insurmountable barriers, there are always some who are moving
up in the world and others who are dropping down.

Of course, this condition is not peculiar to the restaurant industry.
Whatever the industry, there are always people in it whose social status is
continuously fluctuating, as well as those whose status remains fairly constant.
The worker's job performance, the incentives he has for working, and his
relations with fellow workers and with management are all influenced by his
status and by the direction of his mobility. . . .

As I have pointed out, the restaurant industry has provided some of its
business leaders of today with the opportunity to rise from the smallest
beginnings to positions of wealth and social prominence. For a few who have
outstanding business judgment and who are willing to work hard and make
sacrifices toward the future, the road to the top is still open.

People of this type have made important contributions to building up the
restaurant industry, and yet we must recognize that, while there may always
be room at the top, the higher you go the less room there is, so that it is unrealistic to expect most restaurant workers to be motivated by ambitions that
can be fulfilled by only a very few of them.

The owner who assumes that any large proportion of his workers is
aiming for the top will be sadly disillusioned, but if he keeps his eyes open
for more modest ambitions, he will find what he is looking for. Take the waitress, for example. Only a few waitresses rise through hostess positions to
dining-room management. Most of them are unwilling to sacrifice their tip
money in order to become hostesses, and yet the waitress position may be a
means of moving up in quite another way.

Of course, the waitress who works in a low-standard restaurant is not moving up, nor is the married woman who is working to support an invalid husband or to care for children left to her upon the death or divorce of her husband, even if she works in a restaurant of refinement.

For the young girl from a lower class city or rural home who goes to work in a restaurant of high social standing, the situation is quite different. Our study indicates that a large proportion of city waitresses have come in from rural areas. The restaurant becomes for them a foothold in the life of the city, and it may also make it possible for them to rise in the world. . . .

The individual who has come down in the world presents his own peculiar problem of adjustment, in any industry. This is the picture we find among some of the restaurant industry's personnel.

The problem of adjustment is by no means confined to the workers. For example, Mr. Harris, a restaurant supervisor, had once owned a small factory, but the depression ruined him, and he was forced to start over. Getting into the restaurant business, he learned the technical side of the work well and showed enough intelligence and initiative to win a supervisory job. However, he was not able to reconcile himself to his fall in status, and his attitudes toward restaurant work and workers reflected this difficulty. This was the way he talked:

"I stood for that nonsense as long as I could, but I bawled her out good this morning. She probably hates me, but I don't care what they think of me. I don't care for any of them. . . ."

As will be emphasized later such expressions of hostility are not objective comments on the restaurant industry. They are, rather, expressions of the maladjustment of the worker who has come down in the world.

The depression also served to bring Sheila De Winter down in the world. She had been married to a prosperous small-town businessman, and she had held a prominent position in the social life of the town. The crash wiped her husband out, and shortly after that he died. Sheila came to Chicago and settled down in a rooming-house district, with her daughter. There she got a cashier's job in a small, family-owned restaurant.

Her work was unsatisfactory from the beginning. She had little contact with her fellow workers, and the owners suspected her of undermining morale by criticizing management, telling people they were working too hard, complaining of favoritism, and so on. Our observations indicated that at least some of these charges were justified. . . .

Martha and Jane, both downward mobile, prepared chicken pies, hamburgers, and stuffed peppers. While working with great speed, they carried on audible conversations criticizing the work of the rest of the kitchen force. These they accompanied with sneering looks. After the two women left for lunch, we began to get the reactions of other workers. One of them said, "I'm sure glad I don't have to work with them any more. They sure try to run you, don't they?" . . .

The chef was very sensitive about his fall in status. He could not get along with anyone who jibed him about it or who acted superior in any way. When Mary and Elsie did not prod him on his mistakes or remind him of his fall in the world but simply accepted him as an equal, he became a cooperative worker—at least for them.

This indicates that, while the downward mobile worker will always present a problem of adjustment, his reactions will vary widely according to the way other people behave toward him. . . .

This discussion should not leave the impression that a fall in status by itself accounts for all the behavior of the downwardly mobile worker. Nevertheless, in case after case, we find that the people who have the most difficult problem of adjustment have one experience in common: they have fallen in status. We are therefore justified in giving special emphasis to this factor and exploring means for dealing more effectively with the problems it creates.

We should not hold out hopes that, given skillful supervision, *any* downwardly mobile worker can make a happy adjustment. There are some people who have become so basically maladjusted to the world around them that no supervisor can expect to fit them harmoniously into the organization. That is probably the case with Martha and Jane—although both were highly efficient workers in handling their own individual jobs. When working with a congenial crew, Joe, the chef at the Lentz Lunch, performed adequately enough to meet the low standard of that restaurant, but he continued with his heavy drinking and shortly thereafter left to take another job. It is no easy task to provide stability for a worker who has been seriously maladjusted for a number of years.

While the problems of each individual will present their individual characteristics, there are certain points to be borne in mind by the supervisor who seeks to understand workers who have moved up or down in the world. First, these three status questions need to be answered:

1. Where is the worker now?
2. Where has he been?
3. Where is he going—or trying to go?

Finding the correct answers to these questions will help explain the worker's attitudes toward his job and his fellow workers. . . .

Management faces a problem in the case of certain downwardly mobile workers. They are not necessarily inefficient and shiftless. In fact, several of those we have been discussing were extremely conscientious and efficient in their own particular jobs. They created problems simply because they could not get along with their fellow workers.

The man who has come down in the world is likely to create such disturbances because he finds it difficult to accept fellow workers as his equals. Thinking of his past position, he looks down upon other workers. Having no loyalties toward the other workers, he does not hesitate to criticize them to management. There is nothing that can do so much damage to teamwork among employees as this sort of criticism.

The worker who has come down in the world tends to have hostile attitudes toward his work and toward fellow workers. The supervisor cannot act with skill unless he understands the meaning of these attitudes. When the worker says that the restaurant industry is a place for people "with strong backs and weak minds," or speaks of other workers as "trash," the natural tendency of the supervisor is to react with wounded pride and condemn the worker. Instead, he should recognize that the attitudes do not refer to the restaurant industry, except incidentally. The worker is talking primarily about himself. He is saying, in effect, "I have come down in the world, and I resent it. I used to have a position of much higher prestige." . . .

Supervisors should also understand the worker's motivations in talking about his former status. The worker who has come down is likely to make exaggerated claims for the position he once held. For example, Martha's claim that she once had four servants is probably an exaggeration. If the supervisor sees through such stories, he may be tempted to say, "Who do you think you're kidding?" Such a reaction would be disastrous. It would make the worker hostile to his supervisor and even more aggressive in his social claims. . . .

That is, the person may exaggerate his former standing, but this in itself shows the anxieties and insecurities he feels in his present position. . . .

Skill in dealing with the downwardly mobile is not easy to acquire. In order to be effective in this area, supervisors need first to overcome attitudes that are deeply ingrained in our American society. We are brought up to believe that this is a society in which any man with ability and drive can get ahead, and there is an element of truth in that belief. Certainly our American society presents greater opportunities for mobility than most societies of the world, and thousands of people are at this very moment in the process of climbing the social and economic ladder. As they are successful, we applaud them and reward them.

In fact, we put so much emphasis upon upward mobility, that we are inclined to overlook the fact that a man's upward movement takes place in relation to the rest of his society. This means that, wherever people are moving up, there is also a large body of people who are standing still and a number of people who are dropping down. This last group we tend to overlook entirely or to look at only in a moralistic manner. Successful upward mobility comes to be identified with all the virtues of ambition, conscientiousness, clean living, and so on, whereas downward mobility is thought of as indicating irresponsibility, shiftlessness and so forth.

The feeling that downward mobility is tied up with low moral character is so deeply ingrained that the supervisor will find it difficult to look upon those who have come down without prejudging their cases. It should be noted that some of these individuals may have lost their once higher positions through depression, business reverses, or other circumstances over which they had no control. Even when this is not the case the individual may still be a useful citizen.

The restaurant supervisor is by no means unique in making unfavorable judgments upon downwardly mobile people. This is a problem of our American society that is faced by all industry. Students of social problems have as yet given far too little attention to the difficult adjustments that must be made by those who have come down in the world. . . .

40

Incompetence in the Japanese Factory

JAMES C. ABEGGLEN

A strategy that may be used by organizations that cannot
fire people to obscure many demotions is to elaborate
harmless positions and promote people into them. Professor
Abegglen discusses the operation of this system in the
Japanese factory.

The second area of special interest in an examination of the formal organization of the factory is the relationship between the organizational system and
the careers of the employees. The organization comprises two distinct parts
for the employee. The first is that portion of the hierarchy, accessible to
graduates of the old-system higher primary schools and present-day middle
schools, which extends from apprentices through workers and group leaders
to foremen. These employees are *koin*; and the calculus of their careers is a
separate matter from that of graduates of other levels of schools for whom
there extends, at least in theory, the remainder of the organization to the top-
most positions. In fact, career progress is more circumscribed for high school
graduates than university graduates; but leaving this aside the careers of the
better educated persons take in these upper ranks.

There seems no question that the elaboration of positions in the upper
reaches of management is partly caused by the extreme difficulty encountered
in attempting to demote or fire employees and the need to offer title and rank
to compensate for the limited flexibility of the wage system. Recalling the
discussion of recruitment and compensation, it is clear that if an error is made
in recruitment into the *shokuin* group some internal mechanism must be
available to minimize the error. If a man is not an able factory hand he is not
fired, but he can be shifted to some routine and harmless position without
damaging the firm. Similarly, a man who enters the company from college
cannot be demoted or fired. The need for some system of relatively harmless
positions for the *shokuin* who prove incompetent appears to account for some
of the elaboration of positions and titles. It is necessary to find a niche for a
man of insufficient capacity where he can perform minor functions without
too greatly harming the over-all effectiveness of the plant and without
damaging the prestige of the individual.

In addition to providing a safety valve for errors in recruitment, the multiplication of positions also makes it possible to reward individuals with
tangible evidence of career progress within the confines of a single firm. The

Excerpted, with permission, from *The Japanese Factory* (New York: Free Press of Glencoe, 1960;
pp. 86–90).

problem became especially acute following the war and during the period of postwar adjustments in those companies which had considerably expanded their work force during the war. They found themselves and still find themselves heavily overstaffed at the management level. To compensate for temporary losses of personnel to the armed forces, recruitment into management ranks had continued during the war, but both wartime and prewar personnel were entitled to positions following the end of the war. This fact alone made for a generous staffing at the *shokuin* level. Later, although this kind of war-expanded firm did cut back sharply its factory force during the 1949–1950 period, it was not able proportionately to reduce its management staff. Finally, the large company, while willing to cut off entirely the recruitment of additonal laborers at the present time, feels that it must continue to recruit college graduates, at least in reduced numbers. The result of these factors is the presence in most Japanese firms of a very large number of management and staff personnel proportionate to those in laboring and clerical positions.

The net effect has been to retard sharply career progress among company executives, particularly since the retirement age of 55 is seldom observed in the upper reaches of management. The positions of deputy and assistant managers of sections especially make it possible for the company to offer some career recognition to men who would not otherwise achieve the advancement to which their seniority entitled them.

Apart from the need to reward able individuals, the pressure to provide career recognition is a function of two very general considerations. It will be recalled that wage differentiation is limited, and a title and the appurtenances of formal office are of course an alternative to increased wages in rewarding employees. Parenthetically, too, it might be noted that where one firm (or military organization or government agency) employs many titles and ranks, firms and organizations working in relation to it must also use a similar range of titles to facilitate communication.

More important by far is the second consideration in the use of title and position as career reward—the part played by age and age-grading in the Japanese company. The relationship between age and rank is a very close one in the Japanese firm. It can be generally stated that it is not possible to promote a man to a rank where he will be in authority over persons substantially senior to himself. By the same token it is necessary to promote a man to some extent when he reaches a sufficient chronological age. (Of course, since workers do not move from one firm to another length of service and age are directly connected.) This general rule about seniority and promotions is true in both broad groupings within the plant, among laborers as well as staff workers.

Thus, for example, a group leader in a plant will have at least 10 and the foreman of the group 20 years of service. Progression within the management hierarchy is no less regularized by age. Age will not ensure progress beyond a certain point, but its lack will ensure that a man does not progress until his allotted years are fulfilled. Thus a college graduate will not achieve branch-chief status until he is about 30 to 35 years of age. He will be 35 or 40 at his next promotion, perhaps 40 or 45 at the next, and will become a department chief as he nears 50. Not all will go so far, but age forces promotion within broad limits. No college graduate could remain without some rank indefinitely nor, conversely, of course, could he be promoted as superior to older men.

Because of the overstaffing of *shokuin* in many plants, this general rule of governing promotion by length of service exerts continued pressure to have available positions that are at least formally higher in the company hierarchy. The deputy and assistant posts have been devised to meet this demand, but to say that these positions are therefore non-functional in plant operations is not to say that the men holding them have no authority. They represent, rather, a further division of authority and a further dilution of the decision-making function, which worsens the already present shortcomings of the Japanese organizational system.

41

"Failures" Who Stay with the Law Firm

ERWIN O. SMIGEL

In this vignette, Professor Smigel shows how achieving tenure, yet being passed over for promotions, combine to indicate a person's clear, relative failure to his colleagues.

Not all men who stay with a firm become partners. Some who stay remain as permanent associates. Many of these—but not all—are regarded as failures by the younger lawyers. Thirty-one members of our sample were asked to describe the rule of these associates. The descriptions, listed in order of the frequency with which the role was performed, were: handles routine matters (blue sky or everyday banking matters); has specialized knowledge (immigration law or labor law); gives assistance and comfort to young lawyers; and completes work which involves limited responsibility. Because most of these jobs involve routine work and because implicit in these roles is the knowledge that these associates have been passed over, colleagues consider them failures. The fact that they stay on reinforces the judgment. They are examples of potential defeat to the young associates. Nevertheless, the average permanent associate is financially secure—some earn as much as twenty-five thousand a year, and in a very few instances, even more, although this is unusual—and most perform useful functions. Generally, they are asked to stay because the firm needs them. Even those offices which have an "up-or-out" rule occasionally find it advantageous to break it. These "failures" are useful because they do not often make mistakes, are usually specialists in narrow areas of the law, and are willing and able to take on jobs the young associates on the make prefer not to do.

Excerpted, with permission, from *The Wall Street Lawyer* (New York: Free Press of Glencoe, 1964).

42

Demotion and Sinecure Offices

MELVILLE DALTON

Adding to strategies set forth in the previous articles are
Professor Dalton's findings on how demotions are
obscured by organizations.

Little attention has been given to the fall of individuals in organizations.
Possibly as a status tragedy, the whole subject has been shunned, except for
superficial post-mortems on "reasons for failure," which usually skirt the
errors of status-givers, the validity of criteria used in selection, and the social
factors in organizational defense tactics.

Demotion from failure is typically disguised to protect not only the individual ego and the organization's investment in him, but also his original
sponsors. If the demotee has high status, a post is created for him, or he is
made an "assistant-to," where "his skills will be most helpful to the company," or he is fitted into a staff "to round out his experience," etc. He retains his previous salary.

B. Schwann was Rees' second assistant. We saw how Rees sought to hand
down unofficially official decisions to strengthen first-line foremen. When
Rees was visiting the Central Office or busy with other things, much of this
work fell to Schwann. At other times Schwann was expected to "trouble-
shoot" and aid in nipping developing grievances by keeping Rees informed
on shop affairs. At all times he was expected to have on tap a supply of
effective suggestions. Because he was always available, hard-pressed executives
called on him more and more for informal suggestions which were treated as
decisions by line chiefs—at their wit's end, or eager to involve the staff in
trouble. Son of a school teacher, Schwann had little background for making
potentially hazardous decisions. He took a degree in education, and in his
own words, "led a soft life in college." He then taught in a small high school
for several years, became "disgusted" with the work and pay, and took a
job as timekeeper in industry. From there he entered Milo by personal connections. He moved to second assistant in five years and was transferred two
years later to a newly created clerical office with routine functions in the same
staff, "where we can make better use of his psychology." But according to
superintendent Meier:

Schwann was eased out because he couldn't do the job. He'd complain of his
stomach hurting him. Right in the middle of a meeting with a dozen people sitting
around a table, he'd jump up in pain and run out into the hall to get a drink of

Excerpted, with permission, from *Men Who Manage* (New York: John Wiley & Sons, 1959;
pp. 170–73).

water and come back with tears running down his cheeks. He knew of the relation between nervous strain and stomach ulcers so he'd pretend he had indigestion. Hell, we all knew he had ulcers. His nervous system just couldn't stand up under that sort of strain.

You'd go up to his office for an answer on some squabble you were in with the union. He'd listen and tighten up all over. Then he'd squirm and twist and strum his fingers on the table. Finally he'd give you an answer and say, "How's that? Is that about right? What do you think?" Well, hell! That's no answer! You go in to see him because you don't know what to do, and then a guy shows you *he* doesn't know what to do! You want a quick, decisive answer and no beating around the bush—something sharp and final, the way Rees hands it out. You're usually holding up things waiting for that answer.

Well, you know what happened. Schwann had to give up. He was too soft. He didn't have the nervous system to take it. . . .

SINECURES AND COMPETENCE FOR OFFICE

Thinking of sinecures as flexible offices with pay but few if any fixed duties, we can see that the office of "assistant-to" was frequently a sinecure. In addition to the functions of "assistant-to" that were summarized in Chapter 3, sinecures were used to accelerate and bolster careers. They could be created at nearly any level, be dropped arbitrarily, or they could be semipermanent and be succeeded to. But not all posts of "assistant-to" were sinecures, nor were sinecures confined to this office. Whether to reward those who were failing but had served well, or as a substitute for unavailable higher posts, to protect an overrated person from claims beyond his revealed strength—as in the case of Schwann, as an inducement, to cover errors in judgment of appointing officers, or when given in rare instances just as a favor, in all cases sinecures could have the dignity and façade of any office. For example, the formal organization chart shows that superintendent Ruf had a first-line foreman reporting directly to him. Informants said this foreman had no "real" responsibilities, but was only a "stooge." The same statement was made of the similarly-placed foreman in the charted department between Geiger and Meier. The chart also shows at least a dozen general foremen without first-line foremen. Some of these offices were clearly more than sinecures, though several of them had few routine duties, and all the occupants received the pay of general foremen for no more than the duties, without the pressures, of first-line foremen. Confidential complaints by some foremen and "authentic" general foremen indicated that several of the offices were given as direct rewards for various reasons. And during reorganizations some had been preserved for morale purposes or to hold highly competent general foremen who might have quit if demoted. Like that of "assistant-to," use of these offices had followed expediency and social demands more than economic logic. However, it is likely that the long-run gains of Milo were greater than if rigid formal theory had been followed.

Never referred to as such, sinecures were common enough to be talked about a great deal at Milo. Informants estimated that the number of "good" sinecures, including those in the staffs, varied from fifteen to twenty-five, while those of less value might fluctuate to forty-five or more. The failures who held sinecures were spoken of as persons who had "fouled out" or who "couldn't cut the buck." Others were "just on the payroll" for unexplained reasons, or were "fair-haired boys," or possessed "flashy personalities," or had "a lot of get-up and go."

Attitudes toward sinecures were by no means always unfavorable. Much like our senators and their attitudes toward lobbying, few officers, including those at top levels, could be sure that changing conditions or ill-health would not at some time find them glad to be protected or rewarded by a similar post. However, there was resentment in some cases because the real nature and operation of sinecures could not be publicized. Hence some persons mistakenly regarded them as permanent positions and grew embittered after hungering for one specifically only to see it remain vacant for months, or even die. The unofficial existence of sinecures was obviously contrary to organizational theory as well as the ideal in American business and industry that measurable contributions and reward should clearly match in all cases.

VARIATIONS OF INCOME

Salary variations inside specific limits were officially thought to be natural if not inevitable because of tacitly recognized differences in seniority, experience, etc. However, as with other features of planned action, various conditions intrude to produce unplanned results. Set up in part to protect morale, the limits for a given salary range are overstepped to (a) encourage the nearly indispensable person to whom material reward is uppermost; (b) correct negative errors in appraisal and protect the appointing officer by allowing the granted status to stand, but with reduced salary; (c) lift the spirit of certain persons during presumably temporary reorganization by lowering their rank without salary change, as with demotion of assistant superintendents to general foremen; and (d) induce an officer to submit to being "loaned" to another department where his title will continue unchanged to conceal the salary increase and prevent disturbances. . . .

Part VII

Organizational Succession

What is a career movement, from the point of view of
a person, is, from the point of view of the organization, the succession of people into and between positions. Thus, in managing promotions, demotions,
simotions (horizontal mobility), and recruitment of
individual careers, the organization is managing its
succession requirements and problems, and in so doing
it is creating much interdependence of organizational
careers. Organizational succession refers to the flow
of people into, through, and out of the organization
at all levels. Succession to top leadership has always
been a well-publicized and studied (but special) problem for people inside and outside of organizations,
particularly large ones. The organization, however,
must manage problems of succession at all levels,
which are perhaps not as crucial as succession to
leadership, but are nevertheless quite important. In
some cases the public can also become quite concerned
with succession problems at lower levels of careers,
such as with the turnover rate of nurses in hospitals,
layoffs resulting in unemployment problems for a
city, or shortage of blue and white-collar workers.
The following articles indicate the substantial amount
of work on this aspect of organizational careers. But
this work is a mere beginning for generating a dense,
inclusive formal theory of succession by comparative
analysis. It is also over-focused on professionals and
executive upper ranges of organizations. It seems
sufficient, however, to provide us, upon analysis, with
the beginning formulation of a general process of
succession which, in turn, can theoretically guide

further research for generating of grounded theory on this dimension of organizational careers.[1]

The general process of succession would appear to have three stages. First, a vacancy occurs. Second, the organization fills the vacancy by a replacement. Third, there is a take-over of the position by the replacement. At each stage there are sub-processes. A small organization may undergo this process infrequently. A larger organization may be continually and multiply undergoing this process with many people at many levels. The process may be planned and routine or serendipitous and unplanned for all levels or only particular levels of the organizational career and for either or all stages of the processes. The planning may be designed for individual successions or continual, multiple successions of large numbers of people. Individual succession occurs mainly in line-succession: people in relative order can only move up on one hierarchical line of, say, one administration or one department. Continual, multiple successions are typically planned for echelon-succession: people are moved to the next career stage on schedule, irrespective of their current hierarchical lines. Examples of echelon-succession are found in the civil service, army, banks, and academic organizations. Hierarchical lines, thrown out of order by such promotions, simotions, or demotions, may be brought back to order by moving people between different hierarchies after or during the move. Now let us consider some of the major properties and sub-processes of each stage of this process of succession as grounded in the following articles.

Vacancies of career positions occur in two essential ways: voluntary or involuntary departures by a person (see, particularly, Caplow and McGee, Smigel and Dalton). Voluntary vacancies mostly occur from promotions and resignations for health, current interpersonal incompatibilities, early retirement, travel, occupational drift, and better or "unbeatable" offers for organizational careers elsewhere. Involuntary vacancies occur from routine retirement, demotions, simotions, death, routine rotations, "weeding out," or elimination processes, dismissals, and layoffs for poor performance or lack of business, operations, or funds. No matter how well-planned succession may be, there are still several serendipitous sources of both individual and multiple vacancies on voluntary or involuntary bases. Thus, replacement, no matter how well-planned and anticipated, can pose crucial problems for the organization when vacancies in strategic positions come as a surprise. The timing of vacancies can either generate or eliminate problems of replacement. Vacancies can also occur when new positions are created during organizational expansion or change.

Replacement for a vacancy can be a most crucial decision for the organization. In multiple vacancies and replacements at lower levels of careers this step may be highly planned and not organizationally significant, even if ad-

[1] See Barney G. Glaser and Anselm L. Strauss, *The Discovery of Grounded Theory* (Chicago: Aldine Publishing Company, 1967), Chapter 3, "Theoretical Sampling."

versely affecting the local work force (for example, the building trades). But even in these routinized replacements, hidden troubles for the organization may be brewing, such as when the "wrong" man is made a foreman, head clerk, or supervisor, causing disruption and morale problems among workers (see Part V). Sometimes replacement is avoided by doing away with a position vacated by an individual. This may create consternation among one or two other people who perhaps had wished to move up to this position.

Replacement is crucial because three vital organizational conditions are at stake: organizational stability and change (Gouldner, Gusfield), interdependence of organizational careers (Levenson, Gusfield), and the social-psychological processes of position-holding at stages of a career (Strauss, Dalton). Questions of organizational change and stability or continuity are a direct concern in choosing a successor or planning for multiple routine successors. The desire to avoid change, provide continuity, or institute change in a preferred direction at whatever level of the organization is a significant factor in making appointments. The person is judged on how he will handle the take-over and manage a change or the stability of his sector of the organization. This judgment is based on his experience, his clique affiliations, his education, personality, influencibility, political preferences, and so forth. Indeed, the wish to institute organizational change is often implemented not by changing social structure or systems but by replacing people in strategic organizational positions.

The interdependence of organizational careers involved in choosing a replacement or a series of them is a touchy problem for the organization with hierarchical lines. One promotion to a vacancy can set off a chain reaction of necessary successions all the way down the line, generating intense competition between contenders for the vacancies that occur. Planned succession for hierarchical lines is an effort to reduce the disruptive consequences of such chain reactions. Sometimes a replacement bypasses several others on the line who, say, are not sufficiently competent or too old for the vacancy. These others may feel thereby a deep sense of demotion and cause trouble. Also the whole sentimental order supporting the career for the hierarchy in question may be challenged, causing trouble and disenchantment with the career, resignations, and organizational ineffectiveness (Trow).

Impending vacancies and choices of a replacement engenders what Levenson has called "anticipatory succession" among people lower in the hierarchy. This occurs less in organizations with echelon-succession since they can move up irrespective of mobility in their current hierarchy. In anticipation of who will get the appointment, potential successors compete with each other, debate, wager, guess who will be appointed, form cliques of support for candidates, and temporarily take over the vacancy to show ability. The interdependence of careers is clearly indicated in all the maneuvering. Once a successor is chosen, interdependence takes on other dimensions. Some people behind the promoted person move up themselves or realize that they are behind moving channels of mobility. They are promotable in time. Others stuck behind a person who did not get the position realize that they may be blocked from moving up, unless they are good enough to bypass a superior. They become for the time being non-promotables and perhaps disillusioned with their career. Others, after a series of successions, will not know how promotable they are in the future; their careers have now become interdependent with new people. People start maneuvering to get from blocked to open hierarchical lines. Each line also has its range of possible promotions, some making the upper management a possibility and others only middle or lower. In small, family-owned organizations no one may ever reach the top except a family member. The interdependence of careers signified in sponsorship processes also figures into who is chosen as successor and who might be left behind.

The motivational aspects of being a successor generate social-psychological problems and processes when changing positions. Some people eager to move up have virtually given up their present position before leaving it by their zealous anticipatory succession for the next position. The organization may have a problem in keeping them patient and doing a good job until the succession occurs. Another organizational process is to "groom" people beforehand for succession by providing them broad or focused experience, schools, and indoctrination. Also they may require being trained in different demeanor and loyalties for the new position. Some people will not be severed from their old position; they are too satisfied with their career and work. The organization must either coach or coerce them to give up cherished activities and move up. They may be persuaded to succeed with realizations that they cannot remain in one place because they are not getting any younger, that the organization needs their expertise in higher level capacities, that it "does not look right," that they or their work may be outmoded soon anyway or that they could be fired, that they may never have another chance to rise, and so forth. Once advanced they are given tolerance periods to readjust their identity and learn the new job. Also their new subordinates or equals who were formerly equals or superiors respectively must have time to adjust to new relationships.

Since the foremost consequence for an organization when a successor (or series of them) takes over a position is organizational change, stability, or continuity, the succession process must be watched closely by organizational members in top administration. Through succession an organization controls potential change or stability. The closeness of watching varies with the increase in size, complexity, and decentralization of an organization and with its rates of successions (Grusky). Control is initially achieved through bureaucratic routines for succession and ultimately through delicate decisions on how specific replacements will act when they take over. How will these people's loyalties, motivations, ability to supervise and work, and social life change or affect the new position and ultimately the organization?

People are asked or made to take over positions for essentially two reasons of control: (1) changes must be made on some organizational dimension (Gouldner) or changes must not be made; and (2) continuity must be maintained or social order must be perpetuated (Gusfield). These changes or continuities refer to such dimensions as goals, morale, staff problems, effectiveness, values, work loads, and so forth, of the sector of the organization involved.

A condition that generates a need for change and a successor who can handle it is a desire for improvements, such as more efficiency, effectiveness, or profits; better service; different management-worker relations; aggressiveness; and so forth. Doing away with waste, unofficial reward patterns, graft, and other kinds of "takes" stimulate the need for improvements in the operation of the organization. In Gouldner's case the successor used the strategy of "strategic replacements" to gain control for changes. He started a chain reaction of succession. While some improvements resulted, his changes, especially in the unofficial reward system, were so drastic as to generate a strike. A successor must be chosen according to his ability to make changes paced temporarily in a reasonable way to allow others in the organization to change accordingly.

A condition that generates a need for continuity and stability is the need on leadership's part to perpetuate its regime and underlying values (Gusfield). This leadership may take on an age-graded generational stand against a new one moving up in the organizational career with different life experiences, education and values. Large unions, corporations, and voluntary organizations often experience this conflict between generations. Two frequent strategies to perpetuate the regime are rigged, controlled, or fixed elections and "pipe-line succession." The latter refers to successors being picked years in advance and then put in positions that legitimately guarantee their takeover of leadership positions when the time comes, however serendipitous. This strategy can occur as far down the levels of the organizational career as top leadership deems necessary. It can take many years to break through this resistance to change, as we often see in political organizations.

In summary, the following articles, as discrete efforts to study and theorize about organizational succession, upon comparison integrate into a beginning formal theory on the process of succession in organizations. This theory is very useful for continued thoeretical sampling in research for generating more theory on this area of organizational careers.

43

The Problem of Succession in Bureaucracy

ALVIN W. GOULDNER

Professor Gouldner's article considers facets of the replacement and take-over stages of the process of succession in organizations.

Classical political scientists, attuned to the vicissitudes of crowns and courts, have, in their concept of succession, left a residue of observation and analysis that bears reexamination by modern social scientists. Limiting their attention to the highest authorities of government, they have noted that replacement of an old by a new ruler was often attended by public crises. "Such periods have frequently been characterized by bitter conflicts occasionally developing into full-fledged wars, of which the Spanish, Polish, and Austrian wars of succession are outstanding examples."[1] Political scientists have conceived of the method of succession as "one of the principal factors determining the stability of any given form of government" and have therefore used it as an attribute for the classification of types of government.

However, modern sociologists, far from being influenced by these judgments, have almost entirely ignored the phenomenon of succession. It is possible that the political scientists' association of the concept of succession with problems of the most supreme authorities may partially account for this, for modern sociology is largely secular in outlook and, carrying the stamp of disenchantment common to our age, looks to "pedestrian" things for enlightenment.

The sociologists' neglect of the concept of succession becomes acutely problematical if account is taken of the pivotal role it acquired in the work of Max Weber. Insofar as Weber had a theory of historical change, his major analytical categories posited an alternation of charismatic and bureaucratic or traditional modes of authority. These rotations were conceived of as cyclical fluctuations within a trend which moved toward increasing rationalization of social action.[2]

Excerpted, with permission, from Alvin W. Gouldner (Ed.), *Studies in Leadership: Leadership and Democratic Action* (New York: Harper, 1950; pp. 339–51).

[1] Frederick M. Watkins, "Political Succession," *Encyclopedia of the Social Sciences.*

[2] Cf. Introduction by H. H. Gerth and C. Wright Mills (editors), *From Max Weber: Essays in Sociology* (New York, 1947). My late colleague, Jeremiah Wolpert, suggested that continuing rationalization increasingly delimits the possibility of traditionalistic authority and also radically modifies the nature of charismatic authority, so that the latter's traits may be deliberately manipulated. This type is perhaps more accurately characterized as pseudo-charismatic, according to Wolpert.

Charismatic authority, involving the acceptance of a ruler because of his singular personal attributes, was held to disrupt the process of rationalization when existing routines proved inadequate. Hostile to workaday procedures, a charismatic movement is alienated from economic and familial institutions and supports itself irregularly. Charismatic authority is, then, ephemeral to the extreme. Ordinarily, its instability provokes insecurity among the charismatic leader's staff and followers, who seek to safeguard their material and ideal interests. Their anxiety, Weber states, is brought to a climax by the problem of succession.

Weber proposes that the methods used to secure a successor result in routinizations which, depending mainly on the economic context, move in either a traditionalistic or bureaucratic direction. To Weber, then, the problem of succession is the umbilical cord which connects charisma to its heir. Succession is the key concept which in his analysis bridges the polarized modes of authority. Yet despite this concept's analytically strategic role, Weber fails to give a coherent picture of its content and its function in his system of theory. Exactly how succession leads in the one case to bureaucratic, and in the other, to traditionalistic, authority is unclear.

More recently, some of the problems attendant on succession in a bureaucracy have received comment from Arnold Brecht[3] and Marshall Dimock.[4] Both Brecht and Dimock have focused on the problem of "bureaucratic sabotage," the resistance of the "permanent" staff of a bureaucracy to the policies of their superior, especially when he is new to office. Dimock attributes this conflict to a short circuit in communication between the successor and the old staff who, over the years of their association, have developed subtly expressed understandings of which the successor is ignorant. Why the communication failure occurs, and in particular its institutional conditions, is not considered in any detail. While noting that the successor is primed for change, Dimock gives no explanation of the circumstances which engender this attitude.

In actuality, empirical studies of the process of succession and its concomitant problems are practically nonexistent. In the following discussion, observations will be drawn from a study of an absentee-owned factory near Buffalo, New York. This factory, which combines both mining and surface processing operations, is located in a rural community into which urban characteristics are only slowly seeping. These observations are offered with the following intentions: (1) To suggest and provide a warrant for certain hypotheses concerning the interrelations between succession and the development of bureaucracy, (2) To outline a theoretical context in which one commonly noted industrial phenomenon, "strategic replacements," may be usefully fitted, (3) To illustrate the potential utility of employing a "secularized"

---

[3] Arnold Brecht, "Bureaucratic Sabotage," *Annals of the American Academy of Political and Social Science*, June, 1937.

[4] Marshall E. Dimock, "Bureaucracy Self-Examined," *Public Administration Review*, Summer, 1944.

concept of succession in the study of organization. By a "secularized" concept of succession is meant the replacement (for any reason) of an individual in a strategic position in any formal or informal group, without prejudice as to whether this group is large or small, autocephalous or heterocephalous, of broad or narrow jurisdiction and composition. Such a concept of succession would, it seems, escape the Carlylean implications of that employed by political scientists.

CASE HISTORY OF A SUCCESSION

At the time we began our study two things were at the center of the plant personnel's attention: first, an accelerating degree of bureaucratization and, second, a series of replacements among foremen and supervisors.

Among many evidences of growing bureaucratization was an increasing separation between the company's and worker's property, the company having begun a stricter control over its machinery, raw material, and finished product, making these less accessible to workers for personal use than formerly. The old personnel manager, an informal, community-conscious man with little formal education and a "dislike of paperwork," was replaced by a rule-sensitive, company-conscious man with some college education. The number of paper reports required from supervisors was being increased; a formal, printed "warning" notice used for disciplinary purposes was introduced. The no-absenteeism rule was being strictly enforced; new modes of punching in and out were promulgated; the supervisory staff was being extended and divided into two groups—"know-how" and "do-how" foremen. The characteristic impersonalized "atmosphere" of bureaucratic structures began to pervade the plant.

These innovations, it is crucial to observe, began shortly after the arrival of a new plant manager, Vincent Keat. The correlation between succession and crystallization of bureaucratic trends was striking. Shortly after his arrival, Keat began to remove some of the old supervisors and foremen and to bring in new ones. Four replacements were made with men in the plant. The new personnel manager was brought in from the plant at which Keat had formerly been manager. (It had been a smaller and less important factory.) Several new foremen's positions were opened up and promotions made to them. This rapid change of supervisory personnel following a succession is so familiar in an industrial situation that it deserves a distinctive name and in this paper has been called "strategic replacement."

What is there about the role of a successor that conduces to increased bureaucratization and strategic replacement? The problem may be separated into two parts: (1) The frame of reference of the successor and the definitions of his situation to which it disposes; and (2) the objective attributes of the factory situation.

The successor's frame of reference

In this case, succession involved advancement for Keat, the new plant manager. The main office personnel who determined his promotion reminded Keat of his predecessor's inadequacies and expressed the feeling that things had been slipping at the plant for some while. They suggested that the old plant manager, Godfrey, was perhaps getting overindulgent in his old age and that he, Keat, would be expected to improve production quotas. As Keat put it, "Godfrey didn't force the machine. I had to watch it. Godfrey was satisfied with a certain production. But the company gave me orders to get production up." With the pressure of renewed postwar competition things would have to start humming; traditionalized production quotas were to be rationalized.

Keat, grateful for his opportunity to ascend in the company hierarchy, of course, heeded the main office counsels. It may be emphasized that a "briefing" does more than impart technical data; it also functions to structure attitudes toward an assignment. Keat, therefore, came to his new plant keenly sensitive to the impersonal, universalistic criteria which his superiors would use to judge his performance. He knew his progress would be watched; he desires also to express his gratitude and is, consequently, anxious to "make good." As a member of the main office administrative staff commented: "Keat is trying hard to arrive. He is paying more attention to the plant. But he lacks Godfrey's [the old plant manager's] personal touch. Keat will follow along organizational lines, while Godfrey handled things on the personal basis."

There is, however, a second and apparently conflicting element in the new plant manager's frame of reference. On his way up, he may have made friends whose loyalty and help expedited his ascent. Since the time of succession is often a time of promotion and enhanced power, it may be the moment of reckoning awaited by the friends when their past favors to the successor can be reciprocated. There seems little question, however, that this particularistic element in the new plant manager's frame of reference is a minor one. For if worse comes to worst, he may evade the old obligations, since he is now no longer among those to whom he owes them. Or, more likely perhaps, he may interpret fulfillment of old particularistic obligations as a means of securing personnel which would enable him to guarantee successful accomplishment of his new mission and of the abstract, impersonal goals to which he is mainly oriented. This need evoke no conflict of values within the successor, for one's friends are most often viewed as "competent" people, and in the case of a highly placed individual there are reasons why this is very probable.

Thus, even before setting foot into the plant, Keat had a notion of the kinds of things which needed "correction" and was tentatively shaping policies to bring about the requisite changes. He defined the situation as one calling for certain changes, changes oriented to the abstract, rational standards of efficiency. Because he is a successor, new to the plant, a stranger among strangers, as yet untied by bonds of friendship and informal solidarity with the people in his new plant, both his perceptive and executive capacities may be relatively devoid of nonrational considerations.

The factory situation

Oriented toward efficiency and the minimization of nonrational aspects of the factory organization which would impede it, the new plant manager entered the factory. He found that to which his frame of reference has been sensitized. Inevitably, a factory, like any other social organization, reflects a compromise between formal and informal organization, between rational and nonrational norms. Keat found that workers "borrowed" tools from the plant for their own personal use, that they have customarily helped themselves to raw materials and even finished products for use about their homes, workshops, and farms. He found that some workers preferred to "punch in" early and accumulate a little overtime, or "punch out" early on special occasions. The miners, far from eager to conform with Protestant norms of regular work, believed that a certain amount of absenteeism was one of their traditional prerogatives and a normative way of manifesting that "down here, we are our own bosses." The new plant manager's expectations were confirmed: the plant was in "evident" need of specific changes to heighten its efficiency.

Whom could Keat hold responsible for this "lax" state of affairs? Oriented to formal and individualistic diagnoses, he tended to place responsibility on the old supervisory staff, and indicated that he considered it their duty to remedy the situation along lines he suggested. At this point he encountered his first sharp resistance. "Every foreman had set ways," explained Keat. "When I wanted to make some changes the supervisors told me, Godfrey used to do this and that. . . . I didn't make many changes and I'm satisfied with the changes I've made. The foremen are getting smoothed off now. [You had some difficulty with the supervisors . . . ?—interviewer.] Yes, I had some trouble in straightening our shirkers. Some of them thought they were going to get fired. I could work on these guys. But others, who didn't expect to get fired, were. Each foreman is just a little bit on edge now. They don't know whether they're doing right. . . . A new plant manager is going to make some changes—to suit my own way. I had to watch them. I made those changes."

Thus among the things the new plant manager resolves to change, when he encounters their resistance, are the old supervisory personnel. But why is it that the old supervisory staff resists the new manager's plans?

A new manager is faced with a heritage of promises and obligations that his predecessor has not had an opportunity to fulfill. These old obligations are most important when made to the old supervisory staff, or to others constituting the old plant manager's informal social circle. For, placed as they often are in powerful positions, they may be able to mobilize sentiment against him or use dilatory tactics to impede his efforts, unless he fulfills his "inherited" obligations.

An interesting illustration of this at the plant involves the present union president, Ralph Byta. Byta was a neighbor of Godfrey and had been induced by him to come to work at the plant. Godfrey had made Byta some promises which he was unable to meet, due to his sudden death. Some four months after Keat's arrival, Byta ran for and was elected president of the local union. Byta's new position was now much more invulnerable than those of the other "old lieutenants" who held supervisory positions. He could not be replaced or fired and had to be "dealt with." As Byta put it, "The good men know that a union's the best way to get ahead. You can't walk into the company and ask them for a raise for yourself. It's different, though, if you represent 150 men. Then, too, if the company sees you're a leader (and the company sees it!) well, maybe you can get yourself a raise."

Nor was Byta's expectation a fanciful one; it had solid justification in the company's previous actions. As a member of the main office administrative staff told an interviewer: "Some of our foremen are ex-union presidents. . . . The union can pick out a good man for president. If you want a good man pick the president of the union. If you have good morale, the men elect responsible people to the union leadership." At first Byta played the role of a "militant" and was characterized by management as "bitter." Months after his election, the new plant manager had a "man to man" talk with him, and Byta is now viewed by management as much more "reasonable" than when newly elected. Byta's case is an example of the problems with which a new manager is confronted through the old lieutenants and members of the old informal group.

Resistance to a new plant manager by the old group of lieutenants may be provoked for reasons other than the former's reluctance to acknowledge the old manager's obligations. The new manager, for example, may not be viewed as a legitimate successor by the old lieutenants; they may consider one of their own group as the legitimate heir. In this company, the supervisor of ——— building is customarily viewed as "next in line" for promotion to manager. It seems significant, then, that Keat was most hostile to the supervisor of ——— building, considering him to be the "least strict" of all the supervisors. On one occasion Keat had to be hospitalized during a siege of heated wage negotiations. The supervisor of ——— building became acting plant manager. From management's point of view, he played an extremely ineffectual role in the negotiations, not attempting to "handle" or "control" the situation when it headed toward a strike.

In general, the annoyance of the old lieutenants is sharpened when they find their once-favored status incompletely understood and perhaps ignored by the successor. The old lieutenants' resistance to the new manager finds its counterpart among the rank-and-file operatives when measures planned to foster efficiency are initiated. The operatives resist because they resent the infringements that these make on their established prerogatives. That an increase in efficiency often means greater work effort on their part without

compensatory rewards is viewed as unjust. They may also, like the supervisors, question the legitimacy of the new manager. Whether or not this
occurs depends in part on the specific yardsticks used by a particular group of
workers to evaluate a manager's "right" to hold his job. The point to be
underscored is that succession provides an occasion when questions about
the legitimacy of a manager will be considered most permissible.

The manner in which a manager gets his position may be one of the criteria
of legitimacy. For example, "coming up from the ranks" may be a criterion
of legitimate authority among workers in present-day industry. The way in
which the manager exercises his authority may be another measure of his
legitimacy. If, for example, he recognizes workers' traditional rights and
"does not act superior," the workers in this plant are likely to consider his
authority legitimate. These workers also think a manager should "stand on
his own feet" and not be meticulous about clearing problems through the
company's main office.

Sensitized, however, as he has been by his main office briefing, the successor is quick to define some of the workers' customary rights as impedi-
ments to efficiency. Again influenced by his status as a successor, he will
tend to await main office dispositions of problems, thus irking operatives
who still think of a manager very much as an independent entrepreneur. As a
main office staff member recognized, "A new plant manager is more prone
to lean on the top administration than is a more experienced one."

An index of the degree of rank-and-file resistance to a new manager is
the prevalence of what may be called the "Rebecca Myth." Some years ago,
Daphne DuMaurier wrote a book about a young woman who married a
widower, only to be plagued by the memory of his first wife, Rebecca, whose
virtues were widely extolled. The idealization of the absent is a well-known
phenomenon. One may suspect that almost every former plant manager is to
some extent idealized by the workers, even though he may have been disliked
while present.

It was precisely such a situation that confronted Keat. Workers' reminis-
cences about the regime of "Old Godfrey" are scarcely less than a modern
version of "Paradise Lost." The workers' comments spontaneously contrast
and compare, playing the old manager off against the new. The social function of the Rebecca Myth seems plain enough. By attaching themselves to
Godfrey's memory, the workers can, in his name, legitimate their resistance
to changes planned or implemented by Keat.

The new manager was, therefore, faced with two interrelated problems.
First, how to implement the efficiency goals he had set himself. Second, how,
as a necessary condition for solution of the first problem, to eliminate the
resistance to his plans by workers and supervisors. In addition, Keat was
enmeshed in a problem on a totally different psychological level. This is the
problem of coping with his own mounting anxiety which, aroused by the
definition of his promotion as a "test," is further accentuated by the resistance

he meets. He has two major tactics of solution available to him: (1) the technique of informal solidarity and/or (2) the technique of impersonal routinization or other changes in the formal organization. . . .

BUREAUCRATIZATION AND STRATEGIC REPLACEMENT AS PROBLEM SOLUTIONS

The successor can attempt to arouse informal solidarity and group sentiment, harnessing them to his goals. Such an approach might be exemplified by the appeal: "Let's all pitch in and do a job!" The use of *gemeinschaft* or, more properly, *pseudo-gemeinschaft* as a tactic for promoting his ends is employed by Keat within the limits permitted by his personality. He has, for example, taken pains to get to know the men. "I talk with them," he says, "I congratulate them about births and things like that, *if I can only get an inkling of it*. Personal touches here and there help." But *pseudo-gemeinschaft* is an inadequate means to the manager's ends because it premises two things not always available.

It requires, first, a greater consensus of ends and sentiments between management and workers than exists. As an obvious example, Keat (like most managers) was primarily concerned about meeting his production quota and keeping costs down. The workers are, however, much less interested in these. It is difficult to maintain, to say nothing of creating, informal solidarity in pursuit of ends which are differentially valued by group members.

Second, the successor wise to the ways of *pseudo-gemeinschaft* would require knowledge of the informal networks and the private sentiments they transmit, if he were to manipulate them successfully. But because he is a successor and has little "inkling" of the subtle arrangements and understandings comprising the informal structure, these are inaccessible for his purposes. As already indicated, he even has difficulty with the informal group nearest his own level, the old lieutenants. The successor is, therefore, impelled to resort to tactics more congruent with his role: impersonal techniques, formalized controls, and strategic replacements.

The problem of disposing of the old lieutenants takes time. A new manager cannot, and often will not, act too hastily for fear of precipitating a conflict for which he is not yet prepared. He does not wish to be accused of failing to give the old lieutenants a "chance," nor of seeking to install his favorites with indecent haste. He spends some time "sizing up" the situation, looking for possible allies and lining up replacements.

In the meanwhile, however, the manager has no social "connective tissue," that is, an informal group structure between himself and the lower echelons. Relatively isolated at this point, he receives mainly formal and technical communications. His anxiety is channeled into suspicion of what is happening below. One worker sized up the situation as follows: "When Godfrey was here, it was like one big happy family. Keat is all business. Why, Godfrey could get on that phone, call up the foreman, and have the situation well in hand. Keat has to come around and make sure things are all right. Maybe that's why he's bringing in his own men."

In the absence of a position in the well-developed system of informal relations within the plant, and because he cannot be everywhere at once personally checking up, the new manager begins to introduce rules and emphasize adherence to them. He elaborates a system of "paper reports" which enable him to "keep his finger on things." Observing informal gatherings of workers chatting, he is somewhat upset, not merely because of what they are not doing, but also by what they may be saying and doing. He is therefore attracted to a "make work" policy and seeks to keep the men busy, perhaps acting on the Protestant precept that the "devil finds work for idle hands."

When he considers the moment judicious, he begins to make the strategic replacements, spinning out a new informal group that will conform to his needs and support his status. Through this network he can guarantee that the meaning or "spirit" of his orders will be communicated. This last point deserves emphasis, for, no matter how model a bureaucratic structure he may mold, its formal rules will be enmeshed in and in need of reinforcement by a framework of non-rational values.

The technique of strategic replacements obligates the new lieutenants to the successor, establishing extra-formal ties between them, which the manager may draw upon to implement his goals. The degree to which this technique does obligate the new lieutenant to the successor was observed in an interview with a newly appointed foreman. Unlike his references to the preceding managers, this foreman called the new manager by his first name, was very reluctant to give voice to the near-universal references to Keat's strictness, and fantasied that Keat is better liked than Godfrey. Thus changes in the occupants of formal statuses, strategic replacements, have consequences for informal organization which are functional for the successor.

To summarize this discussion of the interplay of succession, bureaucratization, and strategic replacements: It should be clear that, since this was a plant with a history of some twenty-five years as part of a large, expanding company, it was far from innocent of bureaucratic intentions prior to his arrival. There was no such pure case available for study. On the contrary, the plant had experienced a degree of bureaucratization, and the new manager was oriented to values which might have led him in a bureaucratic direction, regardless of the circumstances of succession. The point, here, however, is that the role of a successor apparently involves the occupant in certain problems which, from his viewpoint, are conditions of his action. These conditions conduce to the same process of bureaucratization as do the new manager's company-structured values. The existence of the conditions concurrent with succession make bureaucratization functional to the successor. Put in another way, it is the emergence of the problems of succession which require that the successor learn and use bureaucratic methods. The presence of these conditions exerts pressure on the successor to organize bureaucratically. *He organizes bureaucratically, not only because he wants to or because he values these above other methods, but because he is compelled to by the conditions of succession—if he wishes to maintain his status.*

In this plant there were about six managers from the time of its inception: an average of about one for every five years of its existence. This suggests that it is necessary to consider another specific dimension of succession, the rate of succession. When contrasted with comparable institutions of societies antecedent to our own, the rate of succession in the modern factory seems "high." The modern corporation, one of whose manifest functions is to enable business organizations to persist beyond the life of their founders, is an institutional condition for this high rate. Another institutional condition is, in one of its facets, absentee ownership or, more fundamentally, private ownership of large-scale means of production.

In such a situation authority becomes something of a commodity handed back and forth under certain general conditions. Like a commodity, it can then only rarely be custom-tailored, fitted to size, and it tends to be standardized to facilitate its transfer. Where authority may have to be transferred frequently, personalized loyalty to those who wield it may impede its mobility. It is therefore functional for the mobility of authority to attach workers' loyalty to the rules, not to the plant manager. Thus bureaucratization is functional for an institutionally conditioned high rate of succession, while, in turn, a high rate of succession operates as a selecting mechanism to sift out a bureaucratic mode of organization.

Reference to authority as a "commodity," while somewhat inexact in the above paragraph, nevertheless calls attention to some distinctive dynamics of certain modern forms of social control. In modern business-industrial societies, as in all their Western European predecessors back to the epoch of tribal disintegration, property is a basis for the acquisition of authority, prestige, influence, and power. In itself, "property" connotes the superiority of those who have specific rights in a valuable object as against those who do not—at least, insofar as these valuable objects are concerned. Thus the factory owner, by virtue of his ownership of a specific property form, is simultaneously endowed with authority over his employees. In current business societies, authority is a concomitant of ownership of means of production.

Insofar as production property is involved in a market and can be bought and sold for cash and credit, so too is the correlate authority. If modern property forms are distinguished by the extent of their involvement in a market, so also are modern means of social control, including authority. The high rate of succession in the economy has, therefore, as a further institutional condition, a market for production property. If the problem of succession is translated into the economist's terms, "labor turnover" among strategic personnel, another of the institutional conditions for a high rate of succession emerges: a free labor market. There seems reason to believe that a high labor turnover on any level would disrupt informal group systems, deteriorate non-rational consensus, and impede integration of worker and job. The careful specification and delimitation of functions and the emphasis on rule-oriented behavior—both crucial aspects of bureaucratic organization—may serve as functional equivalents for disorganized informal patterns.

Informal organization and consensus is not, of course, disrupted solely by succession or labor turnover. Other crucial sources of their disorganization, which cannot be developed here, would include cleavage along status lines. Moreover, it seems uncertain whether the conclusions tentatively presented here would apply, on the same level of abstraction, to other institutional spheres such as political parties and governmental organization. It may, however, prove fruitful to examine the differential degrees of bureaucratization manifested by the Democratic and Republican parties on the one hand and small radical parties on the other. Despite the greater size of the former (and this should seem crucial to those who consider size a compelling determinant of bureaucratization), they have only recently begun to develop in a decidedly bureaucratic way.

The tiny groups of the left, however, are far more advanced in this respect. Whether the persevering traditionalistic loyalties to the larger parties, creating a low degree of succession and turnover, and the much-remarked-upon high turnover among radical groups, are related to their differential bureaucratization is a hypothesis worth investigation. In a similar area, the history of the Russian Bolshevik party is rich with data suggestive of the role played by rapid succession in fostering bureaucratization. Lenin's definitive defense of his bureaucratic conception of party organization (*What Is to Be Done?*) is largely oriented to the problem of maintaining "continuity of organization" and the need to cope with repeated police arrests of "leading comrades." The history of the development of civil service in the United States (or elsewhere) would also appear to contain data for evaluating the hypothesis presented here. Two aspects of succession in this area apparently deserve close study: (1) the high rate of succession among elected or appointed departmental heads, which is institutionally conditioned by periodic elections; and (2) the "spoils system" with its rapid "rotation in office," as the historical antecedent of American civil service.

It may be well to close this section with a caution: No systematic theory of bureaucracy is here intended. All that has been suggested is that a high rate of succession is one mechanism, among others, apparently functional for the development of bureaucratic organization. Deserving of more positive emphasis, however, is this: Since groups possess forms of stratification, it can not be tacitly assumed that all individuals, or all positions, in the system of stratification exert equal influence on those decisions from which bureaucratization emerges as planned or unanticipated consequence. Bureaucratic behavior must be initiated by the manager or, in any event, finally ratified by him or by his superiors. What has here been essayed is an analysis of some institutionally derived pressures that converge on certain strategic industrial positions, compelling their occupants to behave in ways which make them initiate or accept bureaucratic patterns.

44

Regularized Status-Passage

ANSELM L. STRAUSS

Convincing people to be replacements or stemming their
over-zealous drive to be replacements are social-psychological problems that organizations must face in relation
to the timing of successions throughout the organizational
structure and the timing of appropriate career moves.

Membership in any enduring group or social structure inevitably involves
passage from status to status. In order that a group persist and flourish, each
status must be filled, jobs must be done. The incumbents of positions die,
retire, leave, fail, and sometimes betray the organization. New kinds of goals
develop and so new positions are created. Other positions get sloughed off,
and persons who previously filled them must shift or be shifted elsewhere.
Lengthy retention in a given status may hide a genuine shift of social position,
as old duties and prerogatives are dropped and new ones accrue. Unless a
group were to be wholly undifferentiated, its members necessarily have to
move up, down, and sideways.

Many passages of status are highly institutionalized, so that individuals
move through them in orderly sequence. Professorial ranks in colleges and
universities are an instance of such a step-by-step progression; but so is the
normal movement from bride to wife to expectant mother to rearer of children. When movement is thus regularized, there must be predecessors and
successors: people have been there before and will follow you. This gives
continuity not only to the group or organization, but also to personal experience. In a host of ways, you are prepared for what is to come, are made
aware of the immediacy of the next transition, are reminded that you have
just now made a passage. The attainment of status may require that you have
certain experience, and meet certain standards of conduct and performance;
these, myth and story, example and direct instruction, are indispensable. The
more subtle aspects of preparation include forewarning you that certain
things will soon happen, that you will experience certain experiences, and feel
certain feelings; and when you do, certain predecessors will stand ready with
interpretations of such predicted events. Their interpretations embody the
special language of the group. Ex post facto explanations are also at hand, so
that when a person encounters situations for which he has no definitions, he
will be offered ready-made ones. "We all went through this." "At your age,
that happened to me too. It means that. . . ."

Excerpted, with permission, from *Mirrors and Masks* (New York: Free Press of Glencoe, 1959; pp. 100–109).

Providing that the definitions offered are not too many and too divergent, you are thereby moved along an orderly line of development. By organizing your action in terms of preferred rationale, you thereby confirm their usefulness and validity. I say validity because your action then can be easily named by other people, and familiarly, even comfortably, responded to. Merton in another connection has called this the "self-fulfilling prophecy"—although I am emphasizing here primarily the continuity that an acceptance of rationale affords. Thus, advice given within an occupation to incoming personnel about clients serves to perpetuate certain relationships and experiences with the clients.

If conflicting rationales leave a person in definitional confusion, or if for other reasons he reaches novel interpretations of his experience, the regulated chain of status-progression is threatened. However, alternative explanations of given events may traditionally exist within a single institution, so that the acceptance by a novice of one or another explanation sets immediate conditions for the pursuit of alternative career routes. This, indeed, is true not merely at the inception of a career but at any point along it, providing that unexpected situations and experiences are traditionally rationalized. Thus a young professor who discovers that he has neither the ability nor the incentive for genuinely excellent research can find institutional sanction and rationale for devoting himself to building a reputation as an outstanding teacher of undergraduates.

When positional mobility follows known sequences, different motivations frequently become appropriate at each successive status. Passage from one to another involves not only changes of action and demeanor, but of the verbalized reasons that are associated with them. Indeed, the stability of a given social structure rests largely upon a proper preparation for these sequential steps. Motivations appropriate to earlier—and usually lower—status must be sloughed off or transmuted, and new ones added or substituted. This necessity is marvelously illustrated in a description by Arensberg and Kimball of family transition in Irish peasant families. At the time of the son's marriage, a series of cognate changes in status, act, and motivation are intended to occur simultaneously. The father must yield control of family policy and cease active work; the son must assume responsibility and ardently wish to do so; the mother must become a household guide and teacher to her son's wife; and the latter must remain temporarily subservient. But the younger woman must also be properly motivated to leave her own family, physically and psychologically, and to become a mother as quickly as possible. When her child is born, the young mother must enthusiastically assume full household responsibility. Simultaneous with this momentous event, the old couple pass to a status of old age. This latter change carries with it an organization of perspective and activity that can be called "making ready for death," the next—and last—status. At any step of this complicated drama of progression, things will go awry if the actors lag behind or speed up unduly in their action or rationale.

And, in fact, the strains in family and community life fall exactly at those points where the speed of transition gets out of alignment.

Even in relatively stable structures, where career paths are regular and well regulated, there always arise problems of pacing and timing. Ideally speaking, successors and predecessors should move in and out of offices at equal speeds, but they do not and cannot. Persons who are asked to move may be willing to do so, but must make actual and symbolic preparation to leave. Meanwhile, a successor may be waiting impatiently to take over. In status-passage, transition periods are a necessity, for people often invest heavily of themselves in a position, come to possess it as it possesses them, and it is no easy matter for them to sever themselves from it. If the full ritual of leave-taking is not allowed, a person may be for some time only partially in his new status. On the other hand, the institution stands ready with devices to make him forget, to plunge him into the new office, to point out and allow him to experience the gratifications accruing to it, as well as to force him to abandon the old. Where statuses pyramid so that each is conceived as the logical and temporal extension of the last, severance is not such a disturbing experience. But even here if a person must face his old associates in unaccustomed roles, problems of loyalty become knotty. For this reason, a period of tolerance immediately after formal admission to the new status is almost a necessity. This tolerance is rationalized with phrases like "It takes time," "He is not quite yet in it," "We all make mistakes when starting, until we learn that. . . ."

But people not only drag their heels, they may be too zealous, too eager. Those who are new to a position often commit the indelicate error of taking formal promotion or certification much too literally, when actually there exist intervening informal stages that must be traversed before the full prerogatives of position are attained. This passage may involve tests of loyalty as well as the simple accumulation of information and skill. These informal status grades are referred to in the special language of rankings: "He's a *new* lieutenant" or "That board member is one of the old-timers." An overeager person may be kept in line by all kinds of controlling devices; for instance, a new sales manager discovers that it will take "just a little while" before things can be arranged so that he can institute the changes he envisages in his department. Even a newly appointed superior has to face the resentments or cautiousness of personnel who have preceded him in the organization; and he may, if sensitive, pace his "moving in on them" until he has passed unspoken tests.

When a man is raised to the rank of his former superiors, an especially delicate situation is created. Officially he is now equal to, or like, his former teachers and elders. But equality is neither created by that official act nor, even if it were, could it come about without a certain akwardness. Imagery and patterns of responses must be rearranged on both sides, and strong self-control must be exerted in order that acts be kept appropriate—even to the self-conscious use of first names, often violating an outmoded but still strongly operative sense of propriety. Slips are inevitable, for although the new status may be fully granted, proper situational identities may be temporarily forgotten to everyone's embarrassment. The former subordinate may come eventually to command, or take precedence over, someone toward whom he previously looked for guidance. At the very least, the colleagues may have to oppose each other over some crucial issue which arises and divides people of the same rank. When former sponsors and sponsored now find it necessary to array themselves differently on such issues, recrimination becomes overt and betrayal explicit. It is understandable why men who have been promoted often prefer to take office, or are advised to do so, in another agency or organization or branch office, however great their desire for remaining at home.

The problems attending the speed of status-passage are merely part of the larger organizational problem of recruiting members for various posts. Recruitment is generally thought of only in connection with bringing newcomers into the structure; but insofar as replacements must be found for each position, on every level, personnel either must be brought in from the outside or trained in other internal positions. In both cases, persons must be induced to give up current endeavors and commitments in order to move onward and, usually, upward. Within the organization, certain persons must be deterred from aiming too high, but others must be induced to cease practicing prized skills and to give up clear satisfactions in exchange for the presumed rewards of the next position. If the latter rewards seem great enough, candidates for each position will be found; but if they are improperly motivated to move to the new position, they will experience considerable strain in transit. Until engineers become used to the idea that their careers frequently involve beginning as engineers and ending as administrators, they experience severe shocks to personal identity when as administrators they cease practicing their engineering skills. E. C. Hughes has recounted the story of one engineer who dreamed a nightmare in which he had lost the capacity to operate a slide rule. In social science research nowadays, it has become necessary for some research professors to spend time and energy finding research money for their junior colleagues. "I spend my time on this. I'm always working on it, I spend my evening writing letters, seeing people, telephoning. I have to make sacrifices in my own research, of course." The Harvard professor from whom this quote is taken must be ready and willing to append "of course" to his sacrifice of research and its satisfactions; otherwise his personal dissatisfactions will outweigh the benefits, accruing to his juniors and to the department, of his contribution toward the common organizational task of raising necessary funds.

Indeed, at every level of an organization, personal stress can arise if motivations are inappropriate for further passages. Self-conceptions may mesh with or grate against institutional arrangements for sequential movements.

At Harvard University, few assistant professors can expect to attain the tenure ranks; most anticipate going to other colleges and universities after a maximum of five years. If an assistant professor regards his years at Harvard as stimulating and prestigeful preparation for a better post elsewhere, he is relieved of many strains of competition. But he must guard himself—and some do so insufficiently—against putting down roots into the community and prevent himself from hoping, however vaguely, that he will be extended tenure. Harvard is able to recruit its assistant professors so effectively— from its own graduate schools as well as from other universities—only because this rank is an early step of a career that is completed elsewhere.

When occupancy of a status is accompanied by acute strain, there is an enhanced possibility that the regular or institutionalized sequence of steps will be abandoned. At these points, people break away in desperation or with defiance, leaving their occupations, families, social classes, and other such organizing frameworks of commitment and loyalty. If recruits are plentiful and not too much time, effort, and money have been expended upon them, their loss may be regarded as minimal. Otherwise steps must be taken to prevent such defection. The conditions that are causing personal stress must be examined, greater rewards offered, in order that stress can better be endured; and alternative career paths must be opened up, or at least seem to aspirants to have opened up. However, the occurrence of stressful situations may not force a man entirely out but merely lead him to aim at a different career within the organization or establishment, causing him to abandon the greater effort necessary to reach the top ranks or to shift his aspirations to other channels. Some choices of specialty and vocation involve this kind of shifting, as when one abandons a line of occupational endeavor but uses it or its skills to make the shift. Hence, in certain specialties, until the routes of entry become institutionalized, recruits are drawn from many fields, often from their failures or their rebellious members. This means that these men are embarked upon an uncertain though not necessarily hazardous future, since the sequences of status-passage have not yet been precisely laid down and sanctified by tradition.

When organizations and institutions are expanding, forming, disintegrating, or in any way changing radically, the personal lives of their members are rendered more tortuous and uncertain and at the same time more dangerous and more exciting. The opportunities for power and personal advance in expanding social structures are obvious, but even when the latter are disintegrating, some clever or fortunate people forge new career opportunities. The dangers of rapid organizational change—whether of expansion or contraction —can be illustrated by what happens to old-timers who reach high positions only to find these no longer carry distinctive prerogatives and honors. Danger also dogs the novice who blindly follows old career models, for a model always is in some significant regard out of date unless the times and the institutions are relatively stable. During periods of great institutional change, the complexities of career are further compounded by what is happening to the careers of those orders with whom one is significantly involved. The ordinary ties of sponsorship weaken and break because those in positions to sponsor are focusing upon matters more immediately germane to their own careers. The lower ranks feel the consequences of unusual pressures generated among the ranks above. People become peculiarly vulnerable to unaccustomed demands for loyalty and alliance which spring from unforeseen organizational changes.

Insofar as careers can be visualized and implemented because of the relative stabilities of those social structures within which one has membership, the continuity and maintenance of identity is safeguarded and maximized, and methods of maintenance and restoration are more readily utilized and evolved. However, the movement from status to status, as well as the frustration of having to remain unwillingly in a status, sets conditions for the change and development of identities. Although my examples have been chosen mainly from work organizations, this way of looking at adult development is not at all restricted to occupational life. The lives of men and women can—theoretically, at least—be traced as a series of passages of status. Insofar as this is so, we most heartily agree with Erikson's striking statement that a sense of identity "is never gained nor maintained once and for all. Like a good conscience, it is constantly lost and regained. . . ."

45

Vacant Position and Promotion

MELVILLE DALTON

Professor Dalton takes up the sources of vacancies of
position—the first stage of succession processes—and
then, as does Professor Strauss, considers the social-
psychological processes of replacement—the second stage.

Inconsistencies about the official route upward naturally provoked fears,
speculation, and search for unofficial routes. Vacation of an office by the
advancement, death, or transfer of its occupant was followed by a period of
silence and suspense as to who the successor would be. Except in case of
sudden death, there had usually been some planning for the vacancy, but this
was often vague even to those who counted themselves as likely candidates.

At Milo a small group of superiors, which included Hardy, conferred and
prolonged the suspense by delays of one to three weeks in naming a successor.
Importance of the office was naturally a factor. Sometimes it was allowed to
die, but no notice would be given of this intent. Assuming the office would
continue, the field was left open for specualation on the criteria that would be
used.

The behavior of both those with and without hope of being chosen showed
conviction that personal factors would decide, and that the choice would
have personal consequences for subordinates. During this period, subordinates who professed to have excellent grapevines would slight their duties
to impress others with their knowledge of what candidates were most in favor.
Wagers were made with odds given and taken on two or more possible
candidates. At the same time there was debate as to who *should* have the
office with expressed fear and hope as to the consequences. While supporters
of a candidate pointed to his favorable qualities such as age, experience,
education, personality, influence, and family conduct, others noted cases
where these factors meant nothing. Some of those fearing a certain appointment, assured the group they would transfer or quit "rather than work under
him."

Unexpected appointments or promotions brought exicted analyses of the
selection. In some cases personal competence as a factor was never mentioned,
though theorizing about the matter might recur for months.

The assumption that all members of a firm perpetually crave to move
upward, and that only the aggressive can rise, has noteworthy exceptions.
The case above of Perry could have been multiplied several times, even up to

Excerpted, with permission, from *Men Who Manage* (New York: John Wiley & Sons, 1959;
pp. 167–70).

the divisional level. The mere wish not to go higher in the ranks, as in Perry's case, did not prevent the person from rising. Though some individuals successfully declined invitations to take higher office, others were coerced into entering management, or into taking higher supervisory posts.

The case of Evans illustrates successful rejection of higher rewards and the variations of upward drive in one individual. Despite the fact that he denounced the conduct associated with success, and that he "raised hell" with his superiors when he "was passed up three times in favor of somebody else," he recently declined the assistant superintendency when it was offered to him. His explanation to me:

> Goddamn the job! When I was younger and needed the money, I couldn't have it. Now that my kids are all grown and nearly through college the old lady [his wife] and me can get by without it. It would have been damn good ten years ago to have a little extra cash. But I'm fifty-three now and I don't have the expense I used to have. There's a lot more hell goes with the job than used to. I don't mean to be catching hell the last twelve years I'm here. Some guys'd sell their souls to be a superintendent, but not me.

Some workmen of great skill and technical grasp were encouraged by Milo managers to enter the ranks, and in some cases were forced to.

L. Jackson was one of these. As a practicing Fundamentalist from a farm community he possessed certain presumed virtues for ascendancy. His habitual hard work, reliability, and often stated belief that "man was meant to earn his bread by the sweat of his brow," were not lost on H. Warren, general foreman of that area. Warren was convinced that "Jackson is a man you can trust when your back's turned." He asked him to accept a foremanship. Jackson declined. Warren offered uncommon privileges, including the right to select individual members for his work crew. Jackson still refused and explained that he was "not qualified to be a boss." Accustomed to bitter rivalries for foremanships, Warren was delighted and redoubled his efforts. Just before taking his vacation, Jackson again declined. Returning on Monday two weeks later, Jackson was approached by a work crew who asked for assignments. He responded with "Why ask me?" They quoted Warren as having ordered them the preceding Friday to report Monday to their new boss, Jackson, and they referred him to the bulletin board for proof. Jackson tore the notice from the board and went to Warren's office where he also found Warren's chief, O'Brien. They both apologized for their action, and explained that they were "on the spot. Please help us. There's not another man we value as much as you. We've got to get the work out and nobody else but you can do it." Jackson accepted, but rejected the position in less than three months. Division chief Springer had complained to Warren over some production detail in his province. When Warren conferred with his foremen and found that one of Jackson's men was responsible for the difficulty, he spoke sharply to Jackson. Jackson quit his job and went home. Warren and O'Brien drove over to see him that night and explained that they meant nothing "by bawling you out. That's part of the job. We have to do that to make things look right upstairs. You know there was nothing personal meant. Won't you reconsider?" Jackson refused to return except to his old job as workman.

When Warren was later made top manager of one of the corporation's smaller units he again turned to Jackson, and this time asked him to come and head a department. Jackson declined. His case shows that Milo directors were concerned to reward some kinds of ability.

The division chief, Revere, took that office under protest. Starting at the bottom at age twenty-two, he climbed to department head in twenty-two years. After ten years there he was asked to take his present position. He declined and gave bad health and diminished family responsibilities as reasons. However, his reluctance was based less on these considerations than on status and income factors. After having been department head for four years, Revere had seen Hardy take over this very division at the age of twenty-nine. Informants said Revere wanted the job at that time and was bitter over Hardy's getting it. And Hardy's moving into his present post six years later did not soften Revere's feelings. As division head Hardy had received $17,500 as compared to the $12,500 received by Revere when he took over the office. Although this was an increase for Revere of $3700 over his salary of $8800 as department head, it was still $5000 less than a rival had received. The gain of $3700 did not cover the injury to Revere's feelings and had to be supplemented by the command that he take the vacated position or retire.

The cases of Jackson and Revere point up both the complexities of career motivation and the play of personal relations in planned organizations.

Barnard's discussion of leadership continues to be one of the most penetrating. He is concerned with the executive's problem in making personnel changes. Any change is likely to bring demand for more change when individuals and groups are competing for advantage and reward on the assumption that all are equally able and deserving. Dealing with the democratic situation, in which subordinates have the right to talk back and to do something about their dissatisfactions, requires political skills in addition to formal competence. However open discussion of differences in this respect is taboo because of potential discord, loss of confidence among members, etc.

. . . Nevertheless higher officers must consider the capacity of competing candidates to utilize and aid necessary cliques, control dangerous ones, etc. Too often the search for men who combine formal competence with this unspecified skill throws a top officer into despair. He is likely to put a premium on "loyalty" in terms of the candidate's seeing the job as he does. Wittingly or not, he begins to look for attitudes like his own as assuring a basis for understanding and cooperation. But he knows the difficulty of getting at the disposition and probable behavior of untried and artful people, however overwhelming their credentials. Hence at varying levels of conscious purpose, the appointing chief gropes for more valid marks of loyalty. This does not of course mean that he does not value subordinates who on occasion differ with him.

With considerable scientific support, his search moves on the assumption that those with qualities and interests like his own will think as he does. Hence in his quandary he finds it good that the prospective candidate is also Irish, went to such-and-such a school, came from a "good" family (socio-economically like his own), and has civic activities and recreational tastes similar to his own. These likenesses would naturally not be advanced as proofs of fitness in general discussion, but tacitly or unconsciously they pre-dispose judges to see the prospect as one with a "good job outlook" and readiness to act jointly on critical issues. Moved by these pleasing character-istics, the desperate personnel assessor may easily overlook other qualities. He receives every encouragement from the ambitious and "highly visible" subordinate who is probing for ways to please, and for marks he can copy to show the chief how much they have in common. This aggressive self-advertisement and social mimicry may quite naturally be interpreted as a sign of the desired political skill. Certainly it indicates strong desire and a will to succeed which can push the inert excellence of other candidates out of the picture. But such behavior is not a guarantee of executive finesse, and may well indeed conceal the lack of it as well as other necessary qualities. It is thus quite possible for the highly visible appointee to be attitudinally out of step with his sponsors, and yet misleadingly appear to have been lifted by favoritism based on his successful mimicry. He may of course fit both the formal and informal tests and still fail if the official criteria are not based on what is needed in the executive role.

Willkie, however, fears that all such aping is likely to get out of control. The "powerful executive" surrounds himself with "a corps of hardened yes-men . . . who pick up ideas from their superior, amplify them, and parrot them impressively. . . ." In industry an "unconscious conspiracy" develops "a strong, secret, and tacit organization which maintains itself by accepting only those with similar ideas, or those friends, relatives, and class-conscious equals who can be counted on to support the hierarchy."

Without being an apologist, one must note that this condition is the ultimate consequence of selection purely on the basis of social traits; it is not true of all industry, nor confined to industry, nor inevitable. As a "rebel," Willkie is of course overstating what has always been present in varying degrees in most organizations in the more complex societies. It is pedantic even to mention that this can be documented voluminously by various students. Obviously an industrial firm is fossilizing when selective criteria—as any set of attitudes and characteristics—become ends in themselves. However when concern with social traits is limited to avoidance of what would be blatantly negative items to most members, the threat to the organization is much less than the other extreme of focus on purely formal qualifications. A fetish of formal tests can lead to their use as a blind to prevent charges of favoritism. Employed with this intent, status-givers may still (*a*) select with attention to formal and social skills as without the test; and at the same time (*b*) adoitly inject various personal, cultural, and ethnic preferences to maintain a "balance of power" among two or more factions. Here, as elsewhere, men can decide what they want and then willfully reason their way to a conclusion.

Those concerned to avoid this might first limit the pool of candidates to the technically fit, so that the final focus can identify those most able to deal with internal tensions and the more subtle phases of group actions.

This dual focus promises (*a*) more judgment and less moral anguish in those who must communicate things forbidden to the dignity of formal channels; and gives (*b*) some assurance of the approximate homogeneity basic to ready cooperation.

Despite mountains of print on the subject, there are still no generally accepted indexes of competence in office. We cannot say how much of what develops after a decision is the result of the decision maker's insights, and how much arises from unassessed factors in the ongoing complex. Some executives see the situation as so ambiguous that "most people don't live long enough to get blame or credit" for their decisions, and that one's decisions may never be proved wrong. . . .

Since higher officers eventually move, die, or retire, obviously no specific social earmarks can be fixed, however much a given set may be the focus of imitation today. Given the internal struggles that play around every important replacement, there is each time some unavoidable departure from the current balance of formal and informal factors. As at Milo, gradual changes over thirty years converted the item of a Catholic majority to a minority and a Masonic minority to a majority.

In terms of democratic theory, any set of informal requirements may become discriminatory. And when they are made ends in themselves, they certainly become undemocratic. But when controlled, they are likely to form a basis for cooperative effort. Men need not like each other to cooperate, and people with similar characteristics may dislike each other. But mutual liking—which is more probable when key characteristics and viewpoints are similar—assures a cooperative tie that formal selection and guidance, with all its merits, cannot guarantee. . . .

46

How Vacancies Occur in Academic Careers

THEODORE CAPLOW and REECE J. McGEE

In this article, Professors Caplow and McGee consider the vacancy stage of the succession process, bringing out the crucial distinction between voluntary and involuntary vacancies.

We may now attempt to answer a more pressing question: *Why* do academic men change jobs?

INVOLUNTARY TERMINATION

The involuntary termination, because it is dramatic in a feeble sort of way, is perhaps more interesting than the voluntary resignation. [In the sample,] there were 36 firings—that is to say, dismissals admittedly involuntary. The reader is again reminded, however, that, of the 123 cases labeled as resignations, some were probably dismissals disguised by the common administrative practice of allowing a faculty member to resign and "keep his record clean."

Examination of the data discloses a number of reasons for involuntary termination. Perhaps the most common and widely recognized cause is the "up or out" system. This policy is standard in the major universities, although the ruthlessness with which it is enforced seems to vary considerably. The basic formula is as follows: A staff member is employed by the university for a maximum number of years (commonly five, six, or seven). At the end of that period, he must either be promoted "up" to tenure status, which usually comes with the rank of associate professor, or his employment is terminated and he goes "out." Almost everywhere, the severity of these rules is mitigated by provisions for granting tenure to assistant professors who are unable to meet promotion requirements, usually for lack of the doctorate, but who are on other grounds, such as excellence in teaching or possession of special skills, worthy of permanent appointment. Such exceptions are routine in some institutions and extremely rare in others. The criteria by which men are evaluated for tenure appointments are many and varied. . . .

Dismissal may result from such perceived traits as simple incompetence, social ineptness, or a quarrelsome disposition. Judgments of "immaturity" appear with some frequency. Evaluations of this kind also appear in many cases of voluntary termination in our sample. Accidental superfluity also

Excerpted, with permission, from *The Academic Marketplace*, by Theodore Caplow and Reece J. McGee (pp. 46–80). Copyright © 1958 by Basic Books, Inc., Publishers, New York.

places a small number of men from the major universities on the job market each year. Terminations for this reason reflect no discredit on the individual, and the department may express considerable regret about his loss. Again a quotation from an interview may be illuminating.

> He was a gifted painter, but we also had one in an associate professor who was a better teacher. There isn't any doubt about his technical competence, but his promotion was blocked by this other man. The chairman felt it was unfair to hold him back from promotion. The decision to let him go was made in January.

A closely related reason for termination is the insufficiency of institutional resources when a man is favorably regarded but the budget does not provide funds for his permanent appointment. . . .

Another form of involuntary termination, more common than professors like to admit to themselves, is firing by the administration. These cases often become *causes célébres*, and academic men have their folklore about the local incidents on their campuses and are made familiar with the major national ones by the *A.A.U.P. Bulletin* and the press. The Loyalty Oath controversy of 1949–52 at the University of California is an example in point. . . .

Dismissal sometimes takes the form of a refusal to grant leave. Since this often results in resignation, the termination is technically voluntary. Nevertheless, the refusal of leave, although fairly rare, is a most effective device for accomplishing the removal of a professor with tenure.

Termination on prejudicial or discriminatory grounds, usually those of race or sex, seems to be rare, and our sample includes no cases in which a department member admits that a colleague was dismissed on this basis. Discrimination of this kind is far more likely to occur in hiring, and it is plain at a few of the departments studied that "only white Protestant males need apply."

Our sample does not happen to include any dismissals for political belief or affiliation, but these do occur and are well-documented in the literature on academic freedom.

Rules about "inbreeding" and "outbreeding" also account for a fair number of involuntary terminations, the former being far more common than the latter. "Inbreeding" refers to the hiring of graduates to teach in the same department in which they obtained their training. It is commonly disapproved but widely practiced. "Outbreeding" is characteristic of only a few of the nation's great universities and is a sort of mirror image of inbreeding. It consists in hiring the graduates of other institutions for junior posts only, so that tenure appointments may be reserved for one's own graduates after they have been seasoned elsewhere. It is usually defended by the theory that having held even a temporary position in so eminent a faculty will be an asset to a man throughout his career. That this makes for high mobility among assistant professors goes without saying.

Nonpromotion as a cause of involuntary termination is similar in effect to the refusal to grant leave. Among tenured associate professors, it often results in resignation. Unlike the refusal to grant leave, however, where administrative considerations may be the major issue, it operates solely through psychological mechanisms. The associate professor who was one of four assistant professors promoted at the same time is unlikely to remain in the department when the other three are given further promotion and he is left behind. . . .

Even more subtle than nonpromotion, as a device for getting rid of unwanted department members is the "sale down the river," in which a department arranges an outside offer for one of its own members and then persuades or subtly forces him to accept it. This device also functions by pressure on the professional ego, to which most professors are extremely sensitive. A man will seldom linger in a department whose members are unanimously urging him to go elsewhere. A sale down the river lies behind most department efforts to inform a member about other positions, regardless of the altruistic, morale-centered explanations that are offered. . . .

The essential elements of a sale down the river are an unusual degree of initiative on the part of the department and the presentation to the helpless candidate of a *fait accompli.*

Scandal is another familiar reason for involuntary termination, but only two cases were reported in the sample, although several others were discussed. If the small talk of the profession is to be believed, scandals resulting in terminations almost always involve sexual offenses against undergraduate students. (Graduate students presumably are able to take care of themselves.) Although there are stories on every campus about the professor (of either sex) who seduces his students (of either sex), there are few tales told of the professor who patronizes call girls or is "repeatedly" arrested for disorderly conduct.

In connection with involuntary terminations, we should distinguish two kinds of dismissal in terms of their outcomes. These are dismissal from the profession, which results in the choice of a different career by the person dismissed, and dismissal from the major universities, which means exile to the academic Siberia of minor colleges and universities, from which few men return. . . .

VOLUNTARY TERMINATION

Resignations or voluntary terminations accounted for 57 percent of the total mobility in the sample. As with involuntary terminations, the data show a variety of reasons for such terminations. The reader is again reminded that these are rough categories and are not presented as exhaustive or absolute. In general, it may be said that voluntary terminations occur: (1) because of discontent and discord within the department, (2) upon the reception of an unbeatable offer, (3) through a "drifting away" process, and (4) for non-academic, personal reasons.

The theme of discontent and discord is a common one in the academic profession—so common that departmental feuds are regarded as normal and one does not have to pry very far into the history of almost any department to find one. Feuds frequently result in individual mobility—if not a general exodus from the department as the wounded and vanquished leave the field.

... The unbeatable offer appears in three themes or variations: (1) the Bound to Rise theme—the subject outgrows his university to the point where his own prestige overshadows that of any position which may be offered to keep him there, (2) the El Dorado theme—some special factor, such as climate or cultural setting, assumes such importance to a man that he will make any sacrifice to attain it, and (3) the Silver Cord theme—the university at which the subject took his degree has the power to recall him at any time, often at some material loss to himself. The Silver Cord is, apparently, one of the marks of a *great* university; no man in the sample heeded the call back to Sleepy Hollow State College, but there were numerous instances of men being drawn back to Chicago, Columbia, and Harvard. Such a man returns, apparently, not because he is lured by money or prestige but because the university to which he goes is the one where he was trained and feels most at home and where he can fulfill the ambitions he held in graduate school. The three themes are about equally common. . . .

Another cause of voluntary termination is "drifting away" from the department—the situation in which a man's ties with his colleagues become more and more tenuous as he becomes psychologically, and almost always physically, estranged from it, until one day there are no ties left. This drifting away is characteristic of: (1) men doing research which takes them away from their home bases for periods of years; (2) ex-administrators who attempt to return to their pre-administrative scholarly pursuits to find themselves unknown in their old departments (and often unwanted as well); and, (3) men who drift upward into administration, first serving on advisory committees, then acting as consultants, and finally becoming full-time officials.

A final category of voluntary terminations involves personal motives and covers a variety of situations—common and uncommon, comic and tragic—often so inextricably entangled with one another that specific instances become difficult to categorize. Some 22 percent of all the voluntary terminations in the sample involved personal elements.

The Lure of Money

When the interview reports are analyzed thematically, the appearance of salary themes exhibits a curious pattern: Only 18 percent of the departed men were reported to have been dissatisfied with their salaries when in place, but 58 percent of them were reported to have been attracted by a better salary in the new position they accepted elsewhere. Similarly, only 21 percent of the replacements are reported to have been dissatisfied with their former salaries, but 48 percent of them are said to have been attracted by the offer of a better salary.

THE OUTSIDE OFFER

One further element in the story of how vacancies occur calls for comment here—namely, the availability of offers from other institutions—since mobility is obviously a function of the opportunity to be mobile. . . .

Men at lower prestige levels obtain offers in many ways. They register with placement bureaus, they write to their friends, and they "establish contact" with institutions where they think they would like to teach. On the middle levels of prestige, offers may not be sought, but they do tend to come when a man is known to be unhappy in his position. . . .

My experience has been definite: when I'm unhappy, I get offers. I get out and prod around, make my availability known, make myself attractive. The guys that I know that are getting offers are the guys that are looking for them. Now this isn't true for the people with real prestige; they get them anyway. . . .

As this quotation suggests, men at higher prestige levels do not have to let their availability be known. People inquire about them and offers seem to come to them in every mail. The prestige system, however, works in wondrous ways. The men at the very top of a discipline may receive no offers at all because their prestige is too high. It is assumed that their salaries and working conditions are not as good as they should be (for men of such eminence) but are the best which the institution can afford. Most departments will hesitate to make an offer to them, since any offer would be presumably inadequate and, therefore, insulting. If an offer should be received, however, the greatly eminent scholar cannot demand that its terms be met by his own institution, since his prestige requires the assumption that his institution is already doing everything possible for him.

HAZARDS OF INTERACTION

An academic organization, like any other, must maintain a certain minimal level of sociability among its members, but it is possible for a professor, regardless of his own status or prestige, to come into conflict with persons anywhere within the institution. Opponents arise at all levels. . . .

Similarly, the category of personal reasons for termination includes many interactional nuances. The following quotation refers to a professor who resigned his position for "personal" reasons.

I think he was deeply hurt over being relieved as chairman. He resented the choice of a man who was not an acceptable successor to him. This was an element in his leaving. He had administrative talent his successor didn't. . . .

Another situation in which a man's associates are responsible for his mobility is that of rivalry. Many departments are not large enough to contain two strong men, and the one whose prestige is overshadowed or threatened may leave. . . .

The characteristics of students may also become a major source of dissatisfaction. Consider the following, for example:

He was extremely critical of the mediocrity of a great many of his students. He was heartily disliked by some—many—students, and worshipped by some others. . . .

One cause of dissatisfaction which is difficult to classify is the "historical accident." Often concealed under some other label, historical accidents account for a small but significant number of terminations. The category is best defined by illustration.

For a long time before he became a professor, he was irked by the slowness of promotion. And it was slow for the same reason that has been true in many large departments since the war. . . .

It seems to be generally the case that a man's peers are more aware of his dissatisfactions than his superiors. . . .

A professor will generally complain to his chairman only about matters which are beyond the latter's control, for to complain about a matter within the chairman's scope is to challenge his authority. Thus complaints about the chairman will be made to peers, one of whom will carry the tale to the chairman. In this way the status of the peer is enhanced, since the act of making the complaint to him implies that he can do something about it. The peer, in turn, is able to confront the chairman because the complaint is not his own. As an intermediary, he is not challenging the chairman's authority and will not fear retaliation.

It is this interplay of statuses which best explains why each status level is more friendly toward the next lower adjacent level than toward lower nonadjacent levels. Thus, the dean feels closer to the chairman than to other professors, and the president feels closer to the dean than to chairmen; the situation being always structured in such a way that the chairman carries the complaints of other professors to the dean, and the dean carries the complaints of chairmen to the president. Since status considerations do not permit the complainer to present the criticism as his own, he must play the role of sympathetic intermediary. In effect, he identifies himself with the higher adjacent status level, reassuring his superior of identification with *him* and not with the rabble he is forced, by the nature of his position, to represent. . . .

In summary, . . . the "push" of academic migration is stronger than the "pull." The majority of vacancies cannot be attributed to the lure of opportunities elsewhere but to dissatisfaction—either the failure of the incumbent to please his associates or their failure to please him, or both. . . .

47

Weeding Out Lawyers

ERWIN O. SMIGEL

Professor Smigel, like Professors Dalton, Caplow, and McGee, considers the many facets and sources of vancancies and brings out the combined effects of voluntary and involuntary pressures to vacate.

The weeding-out process does not stop with recruitment but continues after a lawyer is initially selected by a firm. The turnover is heavy, and men leave for a variety of reasons long before they are ready to be considered for a partnership. Although most associates want to become partners, others know when they enter, or decide soon after, that they do not want to stay.

An important reason for accepting a position with the large firms is the desire for the postgraduate education they provide. If the apprentice comes only to be educated, he leaves when he has finished his "internship" and learned the basic ingredients of large office practices and techniques.

FINANCIAL CONSIDERATIONS

Some lawyers use the large law offices as stepping stones to positions with big business. They leave the law firms as opportunities present themselves and accept positions as "secretaries," house counsel, or corporation executives. A significant number of lawyers take these corporate jobs because they pay more. Some, in fact, leave because they cannot afford to stay with the law firm. They often have large families and their desired standard of living is high. When a good position in a corporation comes along or is sought after and found, and offers a pension plan, methods of reducing immediate income tax, and a substantial increase in pay, these lawyers feel they have to accept the offer. Many an important executive position is filled by the alumni of these firms. . . .

One complaint lawyers sometimes make is that they find it difficult to do their jobs well and spend what they consider to be enough time with their family. Some of these men value family over firm and leave the large law office. . . .

Since hard work and long hours are important for the success of both man and firm, default by men who do not want to meet these requirements is generally welcomed by the large firms. It eliminates a type of lawyer they cannot use.

Excerpted, with permission, from *The Wall Street Lawyer* (New York: Free Press of Glencoe, 1964; pp. 74–85).

341

Dislike for Large Law Firm Practice

Another category of associates separate themselves from the large firms because they do not like what they are doing. They feel they are not aiding "people" or that they are really not functioning as lawyers in the sense of going to court, solving clients' individual problems, working on a great variety of "human" matters. In contrast, those who stay say that what they are doing is operating at the summit of law practice. ("We are working on the very heart of the law—where else can a young associate work on problems involving such vast sums and such important people?") The associates who want to stay are impressed with the importance of the legal issues, the money, the clients, and the general significance—or power—involved in some of their duties. The men who go are nevertheless impressed with what the large law firm does but feel that other aspects of law are also important. One man who had been an associate in a large firm and who is now a professor of law presents additional reasons for breaking with a large law office:

At the professional level the job was nearly perfect. The only real shortcoming was that it did not teach all phases of the law. In terms of operation I felt inhibited in not being able to have my own clients and I wanted to find out what the rest of practice was like. . . .

On the other hand, a number of lawyers who stay with the big firm chose it because it already had its clients—this too is a selective factor. Then there are those who say about the people who go into the large law firms or stay with them that they have no initiative or that they are seeking the security of the "womb." These conjectures will be discussed later. For the moment it is sufficient to surmise that differences in attitude serve their function in the weeding-out process. This self-selecting-out functions so well for the firm that when associates are being considered for a membership, the firm need not be concerned about dissident attitudes; the dissidents will already have left.

Employment "Agencies"

The "up-or-out rule" is designed to insure that lawyers who are not going to be made partners leave the firm, permitting a constant flow of new talent into the organization. This rule (not all firms have it) also has the side effect of counteracting the complaint that "you never know how you're doing." It requires that eventually (usually within a ten-year period) associates be informed that they are not going to be partners. (This same rule can be found in most major universities except that the period a professor must wait before he gets tenure is shorter.) Some offices therefore function as employment centers, with a threefold aim: to give security to their associates, to demonstrate their own view that it is not "professional" (or at least not "nice") to fire a lawyer, and to provide their corporate clients with good legal and executive talent. Generally, the managing partner solicits jobs and suggests associates from his firm to fill them. Some offices cultivate this function more than others and can provide excellent employment opportunities for their future alumni. While not every man can become a partner, very few leave the firm without a good position—often one paying a higher salary than the partnership they did not get. The firms which best provide employment outlets win the reputation of "taking care of their men."

"Failures" Who Leave

In addition to those who do not want to stay, there are also those lawyers who fail. Failure may be evident at the very beginning of a man's career because he does not fit in, is unwilling to work, is incapable—any number of reasons which indicate that he is not good for the firm. On the other hand, excellent lawyers may be considered unsuccessful even after ten years of satisfactory practice if they are not chosen for partnership. There are, then, different levels and reasons for failure. Failure itself is carefully disguised by the firms with the knowing help of their members and associates. Because of the widespread feeling that it is not professional to fire a lawyer, termination of employment often is a long, drawn-out affair. Usually failure is so well disguised that only the expert and educated eye will recognize it. The difficulty in discerning failure is compounded because some potential successes choose to leave and some of those who stay have settled for inferior positions without much hope of advancement. It is difficult also because the men involved—both the judges of success and the candidates—often do not label lack of success as failure. The firm often gives ego-saving reasons to men who have to leave. And, when they first accept positions with giant law firms, associates start preparing themselves for the possibility of not being taken into a partnership. They tell themselves and others that only a very few can make partner, or that it is just a matter of luck—for example, so-and-so who left was a topnotch lawyer but the firm had no opening for him—or that jobs in big business offer greater challenge and opportunity.

Some of this rationalization is true. The difficulty of determining what is failure or who is the failure thereby increases. It is further compounded because failure is redefined by the experienced attorney. There are many types of failure—failure to get the legal job done correctly or the social failure to get along with colleagues or clients. Most men have to be able to handle these functions adequately if they are to become partners. And partnership is the sure indicator of success.

When Do They Leave?

It is difficult to estimate exactly the timetable on which associates decide to leave the large law firms. It differs by firm, and records generally are hard to obtain. The first real movement away from the law offices coincides with the completion of postgraduate training. Though this period is flexible, such internships last no longer than three years. At Simpson Thacher & Bartlett, another firm for which records are available, slightly more than half (22) the associates who entered the firm in 1945 or after and who left by 1959, left in the first three years; all but three left in the second and third years.

At this time the young lawyer can still go home, especially if home is not a metropolis, and open his own office, for his contacts and those of his parents are still available to him. Equally important, he has not yet become so specialized in big business law that his training has incapacitated him for general practice.

One assignment partner, however, claims:

They won't leave us in the first three years unless they don't work out. In fact, they don't start to leave us until after the fifth year. They know that when they get out they're either going to another law firm [small one] or into the corporate field and they are not going to change that decision unless they did not make the right decision in the first place. . . .

The fifth and sixth years are important ones in terms of deciding whether to stay, not only because competition is becoming more clearly defined but also because client and colleague contacts have come to play an increasingly important role in career opportunities. Many associates begin to investigate these job opportunities seriously at this time, particularly because they are better able, after five years, to evaluate accurately their chances with the law firm.

The longer an associate stays, the greater the necessity for him to decide whether he has a real chance of being asked to join the firm. If he feels his chances are poor, he must ask himself when is the best time to leave. It is generally agreed that this period must come before the lawyer loses his attractiveness to another law firm or to a corporate client, and before his colleagues feel he has been passed over. An outside position must, therefore, be found before the tenth year with the firm, depending of course on how long it customarily takes to become a partner in a particular law office. . . .

One middle-ranked partner from the sample of lawyers interviewed provides additional reasons for this time unit:

In the pre-war days, there used to be a standard theory that a man should stay for ten years. Then the firm would decide to keep him or place him somewhere. Things have speeded up a great deal now. Our feeling is that finding a permanent place should start after six or seven years. This is partly due to economics. If a man stays here for ten years, his salary is so high that what the corporations can offer him is not so desirable, though it is more than the firm pays. The corporation wants a man earlier, partly because of economics, but partly also because they can train him to fit into their organization.

The lawyers who gamble on the chance of being made a partner and lose, try to leave soon after they know they have been passed over. In firms where there is no "up-or-out" rule, they can spend a longer time looking for a job, but men who were in serious competition for a partnership find it uncomfortable to remain with the firm, and try to leave. They usually go to the client corporations or to smaller law firms as partners. Although they, and their immediate colleagues, feel such men have failed, the larger world may consider them successful. Their salaries are higher and their power appears, on the surface at least, to be greater. Many who did not want to leave, as well as those who had planned to, become successful in the law and in business. This, of course, is true of lawyers in general.

Difficulty of Determining When to Leave

It is not easy to know when to leave; the decision involves a formidable test of judgment—judgment which depends upon being able accurately to measure one's progress. An associate, when asked how he knew where he stood, replied:

It's awfully hard to get a commitment. If you ask, and you usually do not, they say "I think you are doing well." This is only a hint, but enough; by a process of osmosis you get to know. I think I have great possibility. I've decided to take the risk and stay on and see. You feel it in the air if you are going places. One way of telling is the responsibility they give you. But anyone is foolish to think it's in the bag.

The earliest, most enduring, and continuous signs come in the form of the work assigned. If a man receives the more difficult of more desirable work, he can usually estimate that he is making more progress than the others in his vintage. If not, he has to decide whether this is due to chance and if it will change. If he decides it will not change, then he must consider leaving unless he is willing to stay on as a perpetual associate. He has, it is true, any number of clues, but these often are not definitive. Probably the most extreme use of work as an indicator of progress or lack of it, occurs when a firm wants to fire someone. A female associate who has been with a law office for eight years reports that she is being eased out. "They feel it is not professional to tell you officially to leave so they punish you by taking away work. It is the classic way of firing someone. I know this is happening because I was told by my immediate partner that the senior partner did not like me. I did a small job for him and he thought I didn't do it well."

It is customary around the Christmas season for the senior partners or the partner in charge of a department to distribute a bonus, if there is one. While it is not proper and not generally considered "good form" to ask how salaries compare, it is considered acceptable to ask how bonuses compare. Usually it is not necessary, for the distributing partner will tell a man as he comes around with the firm's "gift," "You have done as well as anyone." This indicates that the associate is still in the running. If he is told, "You did the best in your group," then he knows he is ahead. The responses become standardized and so this particular indicator is regarded as a good one.

It is true that occasionally an associate is told that he has no future in a firm. One partner reported: "We generally tell people we dont' want, or can't keep, 'See if you can't get located by the end of the year; if you can't, see me.'" An associate also often receives hints and suggestions from friendly partners who insist they are not speaking for the firm. Generally signs are not so clear and an associate has to decipher them himself. One of the most difficult clues to interpret develops when the law office offers an associate a position outside the firm. Is he to feel that the firm does not want him, or simply that he is being offered an opportunity to decide his future for himself? There is evidence that both possibilities exist. The lawyer who does not receive the outside job offer through the firm feels he has the edge. One associate reportedly slated for partnership states a little proudly:

I have never had an outside job offered to me by the law firm or a client, but have had some from outside the firm. I know that clients have asked about talking to me— the firm tells them that they can't talk to me, that I am not interested. About two or three months later someone in the office will casually say that T asked about me and was told that I was not interested. It clearly means that my efforts for the firm are satisfactory and that there is a possibility of a partnership.

A managing partner was asked if it were true that if an associate was offered a job it meant that the firm did not want him. He states:

No. If we want a man but are not sure if he will make it here we have to tell him this does not mean that he has to leave. We tell him that this does not indicate his future. However, if we offer him a great many jobs, this may be taken as an indication that we do not want him.

One of the clearest indicators that an associate must leave is the announcement that other lawyers who graduated when he did have been made partners. Unless specifically told that this was an exceptional situation and that he is still being considered, an attorney must then recognize that he has been passed over and look for another position. . . .

The associate's dilemma grows as he nears the date when his partnership should be announced. In some offices the time spent with the firm is the best index of when to leave. One associate who had carefully examined this process in the Wall Street community reports: "Sullivan & Cromwell is the guide to use as far as time is concerned. They have a system there. When you are about thirty-five or thirty-six years old, you come up for your first year of eligibility. Somehow you know this is your year—if you miss it that year and someone in your class makes it, and if you miss two years, then you know you haven't made it—then they try to get you a job in two years. At S & C this is a conscious process—not so here. In addition, the age for partnership here is about thirty-eight or forty years. That includes the difference made by going into the service." . . .

The rules concerning permanent tenure in large law firms are not clear and it is considered in poor taste to ask about them openly. Some also consider it bad strategy. As one associate put it, "I don't ask them because to do so would be a sign of weakness and of lack of confidence." In the final analysis, the employee lawyer is reduced to interpreting a difficult set of clues. This holds true for all except the obvious failures and the obvious successes.

48

Bureaucratic Succession

BERNARD LEVENSON

Professor Levenson rather neatly analyzes the interdependence of careers and "anticipatory succession" involved in the replacement stage·of succession.

For several centuries, the word succession has been used to refer to the process by which one religious or political leader replaces another. When the word was converted into a sociological concept, chiefly by Max Weber toward the beginning of this century, it retained the historically ingrained emphasis upon the replacement of men in the higher reaches of institutional life. So it was that Weber discussed succession as part of the routinization of charisma, centering upon the consequences that follow the death of a particular kind of leader. Later, when Alvin Gouldner studied succession in an industrial organization, the emphasis on change in top management was still there.[1]

When the focus of inquiry is only on changes in top leadership, succession tends to be viewed as sporadic, turbulent, often as disruptive. And it tends to emphasize cases in which organizations are largely ill-prepared to cope with succession, cases in which the successor learns his role only after he assumes the position. Thus the personalities of the aspirants, their informal relations, their manipulative prowess, and the process by which the new leader, once selected, stabilizes himself in power become the foci of analysis. Once the successor is secure in his position, the succession as a process is assumed to be completed.

Succession to office at the top, of course, is sometimes accompanied by explosive changes in organizational structure and policy. But the viability of an organization requires that vacancies be filled on *all* levels, not merely on the top level.[2] That succession is a normal and continuous feature of organizational life leads directly to the concept of *anticipatory succession*. By this, I refer simply to the circumstance that personnel are trained for higher-level jobs while those jobs are occupied by other people. The occasions contributing to anticipatory succession are familiar enough: the incumbent of a position is absent—because of illness, jury duty, vacation, or whatever—and

[1] See *From Max Weber: Essays in Sociology*, H. H. Gerth and C. Wright Mills (trans. and eds.) (New York: Oxford, 1946), 262 ff.; Alvin W. Gouldner, *Patterns of Industrial Bureaucracy* (Glencoe, Ill.: Free Press, 1954).

[2] Sociologists refer to succession on lower levels by the negatively toned term "turnover," a conceptual distinction which this paper proposes to dispel.

one or another subordinate temporarily fills this position. Anticipatory succession is evidenced not only through this "pinch-hitting" role but also through the preparatory "coaching" of subordinates and through the informal delegation of tasks by the immediate supervisor.[3]

Moreover, the obvious fact that bureaucratic positions are hierarchically connected points up the artificiality of studying top positions apart from lower-level types. Replacement on a higher level necessarily sets off a chain reaction in the organization. When a successor is recruited from a lower level within the organization, the change at once creates the problem of filling the position which he vacates. Succession does not involve a single personnel transaction but rather a chain of transactions.

In the following discussion I shall try to work out the implications of a broader conception of bureaucratic succession. The first section examines anticipatory succession from the vantage point of middle-level supervisors. In particular, I shall argue that anticipatory succession decisively influences styles of supervision—and consequently affects the opportunities of subordinates. The second section views succession from the perspective of subordinates with the aim of showing how their differential opportunities pressure them to behave differently. The final section considers succession from the viewpoint of management and discusses some devices for dealing with obstructed channels of mobility.

ANTICIPATORY SUCCESSION

A frequent approach to the analysis of supervisory practices starts with the *leadership traits* of individuals occupying supervisory positions. But these same supervisory practices can also be seen as consequences of anticipatory succession.

To clarify the important distinction, consider a hypothetical case. The manager of a company intends to retire soon and begins in earnest to appraise his lieutenants in order to select and train one as his successor.[4] On all social and technical criteria, his lieutenants are highly competent and not measurably different. The selection narrows to evaluating them on such leadership traits as the following: ability to deal informally with subordinates; willingness to delegate tasks to them and train them for higher-level positions; allowing them latitude and autonomy in their work instead of stifling them with supervision.

In such a case, the lieutenant who manifests these traits to the greatest

---

[3] In this discussion, "supervisor" will refer to an employee who has authority over subordinates. "Superior" will refer to an employee who has authority over supervisors.

[4] Managers, particularly of small companies, often are too preoccupied with daily activities to think of their company's future management. External forces frequently exert pressure on them to lengthen their time perspectives. Banks and suppliers represent such forces. Before extending appreciable credit, they usually must be satisfied with a company's plans for succession. See C. Roland Christensen, *Management Succession in Small and Growing Enterprises* (Andover, Mass.: Andover Press, 1953), Chap. 5.

extent may be selected as "next-in-line." There is evidence that the subordinates of such supervisors generally have relatively high morale and
productivity. In general, the "trait approach" to supervisory behavior
searches for traits of leadership, such as those just mentioned, that make for
promotability within an organization.

But supervisory behavior which appears to stem from deep-seated
personality dispositions may sometimes be a consequence, not a cause, of
promotability. Suppose, for example, that the lieutenants are equal in all
respects. Nonetheless, to ensure the uninterrupted functioning of company
activities and the orderly transfer of status the manager must select someone.
By a feat of imagination, let us suppose that unable to choose among them
in a more rational way, he makes his decision by the throw of a die.

This done, a particular lieutenant is signaled that he is the anticipatory
successor. Thereupon his behavior toward subordinates may well undergo a
change. Whatever his personality traits, the supervisor who knows himself
to be next-in-line may become motivated to adopt leadership practices such
as those described above. His structural situation makes it a matter of self-
interest.

The promotable knows that after he is promoted the position he has
vacated will have to be filled. Delay in filling it will mean more work for the
people under him. Since the one who fills his job will be supervised by him,
more than likely he will want to train one of his own subordinates: they
already know what to expect of him and he of them. However little zeal a
promotable may have for coaching, his failure to train a successor to his old
position may later compel him to fill it with a subordinate who owes loyalty
to another sponsor.

Furthermore, the anticipatory successor will be pressured to delegate
many of his present duties, in order to have enough free time to learn the
duties of his next job and to pinch-hit for *his* superior whenever his help is
enlisted. But this, in turn, has consequences for the network of relationships
in the company. Having less time to police his subordinates, he will be
obliged to give them more information and autonomy.

An anticipatory successor need not worry that informing subordinates
about the details of his current job will lessen his indispensability. Quite the
contrary; if he is too "security-minded" and does not tell them just what they
would need to know to fill his job someday, he might become indispensable,
in a pyrrhic sense, by being regarded as essential in his *current* job. Anticipatory successors are, undoubtedly, apt to sense all this as a result of the
exigencies of their situation.

These observations suggest that morale and productivity of work units
may *lessen* following the replacement of a supervisor who has himself just
been promoted. Usually this is interpreted as resulting from the circumstance
that the replacement has not yet "learned the ropes." This of course is often
so—but it may also result from the replacement's having no prospects for

immediate promotion. Since he is not likely to be promoted again for some time, his style of supervision may be quite different from that of his predecessor. Consequently his subordinates may be less likely to cooperate as closely with him as with their previous supervisor. If this hypothesis has any merit, we should find that work units exhibit cycles of high and low productivity and morale depending upon the promotability status of the supervisor.

It cannot be assumed that supervisors uniformly know their prospects for advancement. The cues by which this information is ferreted out are important themes for organizational research. As I have implied, occasions of anticipatory succession in which people are called upon to substitute in performing the roles of absent or otherwise occupied higher-level personnel are apparently prime sources of such information. Whatever the sources, the awareness of the degree of promotability (whether accurate or imagined) may account for much of the difference in supervisory behavior among those occupying the same formal position.

Sometimes management may adopt the policy of obscuring the promotability of personnel in order to spur aspirants to competitive, and thereby presumably peak, effort. One way of implementing such a policy is to postpone the selection and training of successors until supervisors have vacated positions. To prevent anticipatory successors from emerging will require that pinch-hitters for temporarily absent supervisors be recruited from the *same* level rather than *below*.[5] In so far as there has been no opportunity to train or test replacements prior to promotion, organizations that adopt this policy run the risk of promoting the "wrong" people. (The final section of this paper discusses the difficulties of reversing such "mistakes.")

Management can also obscure promotability, not by failing to train anyone for a position, but by training many aspirants. Anticipatory succession, however, involves costs. There is, first, the time and effort expended by higher-level personnel in training. There is, second, the cost of the sometimes expensive errors made by neophytes before they have acquired a command of the higher-level job. And, third, there is the hidden cost resulting from the loss in productivity while trainees are absent from their usual jobs. Moreover, the time will come when someone must be selected to fill a vacancy. The successor may then experience difficulty in maintaining authority over a group of subordinates who have received virtually the same training and experience as he has. The company may discover that its resources had been spent in developing people for employment elsewhere—inasmuch as many of those trained for higher-level positions who turn out to be also-rans may seek higher-level employment in another company.

Thus dilemmas will confront every organization when it seeks to ensure continuity in succession to positions. In addition to its particular goals,

---

[5] Instead of lateral pinch-hitters, higher-level personnel can substitute for lower-level absentees. *Downward substitution*, however, is often perceived as an indicator of unpromotability. Hence, while the action would serve to obscure promotability status on one level, it will reveal unpromotability on a higher level.

every organization has the implicit goal of survival. If it over-ensures survival by having anticipatory successors two or three deep, it may, in effect, be operating a training school which services the needs of other organizations. Contrastingly, the organization which pays little heed to continuity of succession may become too unstable to achieve its principal objectives.

ADAPTATIONS OF SUBORDINATES TO
UNPROMOTABLE SUPERVISORS

Whether promotability has its source in the leadership traits of a supervisor or whether promotability itself evokes the practices of leadership, it is evident that subordinates of highly promotable supervisors are in greatly different situations from those of subordinates of less promotable supervisors. Whatever their abilities, their structural location makes them either beneficiaries of their supervisor's success or depressed shareholders of their supervisor's immobility.

From the subordinate's viewpoint, the unpromotable supervisor[6] restricts his opportunities. As Merton has pointed out, marked discrepancy between culturally emphasized goals and socially structured opportunities for realizing those goals generates pressures toward deviance.[7] Merton's paradigm, though exemplified by a discussion of mobility in the larger social system, can, with appropriate modifications, be used to analyze mobility within a single organization. In fact, it would seem that the student of deviant behavior should find the organization a strategic site for investigating the social genesis of deviance, its control, and structural rearrangements aimed at mitigating its effects.

In the remaining part of this section, Merton's paradigm will be utilized to analyze the behavior of subordinates to unpromotables.

WITHDRAWAL

One way in which the subordinate of an unpromotable supervisor can come to terms with his situation is by leaving. Viewing his opportunities as limited, he may decide that chances for success will be greater in another organization. "Withdrawal" is analogous to Merton's category of "retreatism." The subordinate who quits a job does not withdraw from society, as Merton's retreatist does, but he does abandon the success goals and the means for realizing them held out to him by the organization he leaves behind.

Whether the subordinate of an unpromotable adapts in this way rather than another will depend in part on his status-set and on other aspects of his situation, outside the organization. It might be conjectured, for example,

---

[6] As used here, unpromotability refers to "dead-end" personnel occupying particular positions as distinct from the familiar notion of the "dead-end" position.

[7] Robert K. Merton, "Social Structure and Anomie," in *Social Theory and Social Structure* (rev. ed.; Glencoe, Ill.: Free Press, 1957), 131–60.

that the subordinates who are comparatively young, unmarried, or endowed with savings will to a greater extent than the rest choose to leave. The conjecture might also be advanced that although the subordinates of unpromotables will tend to leave an organization in greater proportion than the subordinates of promotables, the latter, when they do leave, are more likely to obtain higher-level positions, whereas the former are more likely to take positions at the same level as those they have quit. These observations may be enough to suggest how the conceptions under review could be fruitfully applied to problems of organizational turnover.

Ritualism

Employees who do not have the economic leverage or the physical vitality to start anew may resign themselves to the fact that they have reached a "point of no return." Aware that they must remain in their job despite blocked mobility, they may gradually lose interest in their work and settle down to a minimum level of performance. In short, by abandoning ambition, their adaptation corresponds to Merton's "ritualism."

Innovation

Subordinates who neither withdraw nor slip into ritualism but persist in their efforts to advance are perhaps more interesting sociologically. They provide clues to a major source of organizational change. An employee may continue to conform to the organizational norm of seeking advancement, but in trying to overcome his relative deprivation he may be impelled to innovate.

The innovation may take the form of "public relations" to attract the notice of promotable supervisors, who may subsequently recruit him, and the notice of his supervisor's superiors so that they may come to know of his performance and abilities. The employee may become assertive at meetings; he may invent occasions for interacting with those who can facilitate his recognition; or he may write numerous memoranda proposing organizational improvements. As a way of accelerating advancement which might otherwise come slowly, if at all, public relations may be quite legitimate; often as it forwards the employee's personal goals, it also enhances his contribution to the organization.

If the actions designed to by-pass the immediate unpromotable supervisor and to attract the favorable notice of higher officials are executed in a brash or ostentatious manner they will, of course, defeat their purpose. The immediate (unpromotable) supervisor and the promotable supervisors, as well as their superiors, will be alienated. For these actions deny, in effect, the legitimacy of the hierarchic structure. Subordinates of promotables do not have to engage in such attention-getting activities to the same extent; they already have access to a relative influential in the organization and through him have comparative opportunity for being observed by superiors. The structural context rather than personality traits may thus frequently account for "pushy" or aggressive behavior.

In the effort to impress superiors and focus attention upon himself, the subordinate of the unpromotable may take imprudent risks; if he seeks, for example, an overly lucrative contract, his company may lose a valued customer. In other cases, risk taking may be coupled with departures from organizationally prescribed behavior: duties or staff may be opportunistically inflated; functions may be "pirated" from other units; competent rivals may be eclipsed by dubious means.

Rebellion

When an organization makes a supervisor unpromotable, an unintended consequence may be to encourage his subordinates to scrutinize his assumptions and procedures of work. A subordinate who wants to advance would understandably try to discover what superiors expect. Knowledge that a supervisor is unpromotable may be interpreted to mean that he is not fulfilling the expectations of his superior. The subordinate may conclude that such a supervisor is not a model to be emulated and that advancement in the organization will presumably not be achieved by replicating his behavior. Re-examining a supervisor's mode of work in this way may generate new ideas which may provide the impetus for eliminating inefficient procedures.

Carried out extensively, however, this form of innovation may undermine a supervisor's authority. This situation will occur especially when a subordinate holds the supervisor responsible for his immobility and acts aggressively toward him. This typically results in "staging a showdown." An occasion is selected when the supervisor is demonstrably in error and the intervention of someone superior to them both is required to resolve the conflict. The superior, while he may conclude that the subordinate is indeed more clever and capable than his immediate supervisor, may have little taste for being thrust into such an explosive situation and regard the behavior as little more than here for rebelliousness.

Merton's rebel seeks to bring into being a new social structure; rebellion here is far more restricted, being directed mainly against the authority of the unpromotable supervisor.

In discussing adaptations of subordinates located behind unpromotable supervisors it has not only been taken for granted that the subordinate is motivated to achieve success in the organization but it has also been assumed that he knows the promotability status of his supervisor. This, of course, varies empirically. Adaptations of subordinates will be contingent upon the degree to which the promotability of supervisors is visible and the extent to which the perceptions of subordinates are accurate. There is ample room here for distorted perceptions.

The ways in which promotability status of supervisors is communicated to subordinates may be similar to the ways in which supervisors learn about their own chances. Of primary importance, I believe, is the phenomenon of anticipatory succession. Situations where one or another supervisor is called upon to substitute frequently for a superior—and in turn calls upon one of his subordinates to substitute for him—may heighten the observability of promotional prospects.

Another source may be supervisors who know themselves to be "next-in-line." They will often communicate their prospective advancement to subordinates, sensing that this will enlarge their capacity to elicit cooperation. Correspondingly, unpromotable supervisors will be motivated to obscure their dim prospects, although with time their unpromotability becomes increasingly difficult to hide.

And even where direct communication does not occur, ambitious subordinates will have their antennae out for indicators of promotability. By comparing the characteristics of those who have been promoted with those who have not, inferences are bound to be made concerning the technical capacities, interpersonal skills, and social characteristics essential for advancement in a particular organization. Those who have been with the organization for some time, for example, may observe that above a certain echelon no position is occupied by a woman; if their supervisor happens to be a women, they may conclude (perhaps mistakenly) that organizational policy discourages her upgrading.

The literature on personnel and administration devotes considerable attention to assessment of employees by their supervisors. As the foregoing discussion suggests, important complementary processes are at work: lower-echelon employees continually assess the mobility chances of their supervisors. "Who is going where?" comprises a large share of employee conversation and thought, and research on these complementary evaluations would undoubtedly contribute much to organizational sociology.

MANAGERIAL ADAPTATIONS TO BLOCKED CHANNELS OF MOBILITY

The social unit analyzed by Merton in his theory of deviant behavior is the total society. When the theory is applied to smaller social structures such as a single bureaucracy, a difference soon becomes apparent: the structural sources of deviance are more visible and more modifiable. The political administrator may be persuaded that crime, suicide, or mental illness stems from limited access to legitimate means of achieving success. But changing structural conditions to make means and ends more congruent is a problem so complex that except perhaps in monolithic societies, political action tends to be directed more toward the control of deviants than toward social change. In an organization, however, identifying and removing pressures toward deviance does not present as formidable a task. To the extent that the blocking of mobility channels by unpromotables generates deviance, there are numerous ways for management to come to terms with the problem. This last section considers a few of these.

Two classes of organizational devices for clearing blocked channels can be provisionally identified: (1) removing an unpromotable from his position; and (2) changing the nature of the position itself.

Removing the unpromotable from his position

It might seem that removing an unpromotable from his job is a simple managerial task. But the expense, effort, and subterfuge that frequently accompany attempts to dislodge presumably incompetent staff from their jobs show that it is anything but simple.

If the problem is defined as removing an unpromotable from his position, there are four types of "solution": he can be fired; he can be moved laterally within the organization; he can be demoted; or he can be promoted, to an innocuous and seemingly honorific position. Each of these solutions entails costs as well as gains for the organizations. The frequency with which one or another of these solutions is employed, as well as the conditions disposing management to use one rather than another, is a matter of no small interest for future investigation.

In discussing the strains involved in discharging personnel, Goffman has stressed the psychic damage to the people who are fired. He has noted that some managers, aware of these adverse effects, look for alternatives to this means of ridding themselves of a man judged unsuitable or incompetent. But other considerations—apart from altruism or compassion—make separation unsatisfactory as a solution. For one thing, the judgment that he is incompetent will embarrass not only the man being fired but also the superior who had sponsored his appointment or earlier promotion. To discharge a protégé is to administer a managerial rebuke to his sponsor; in effect, it proclaims to others within the organization his incapacity for judging ability. For this reason, we would expect that firing an unpromotable will less often be adopted when the sponsor is still with the organization—unless he himself is the actual target of the firing. Furthermore, if discharge or forced resignation is often used as a device for removing roadblocks to mobility, the system of succession may be damaged. Others in the organization might be made insecure, sufficiently so to be alert for positions in other organizations which do not rely on such harsh personnel techniques.

As has been noted, another technique for clearing blocked channels is to move the unpromotable to a job on the same level of status and authority, but with differing responsibilities. This technique, too, sometimes has not altogether intended consequences. If it is to be effective, presumably the reason for the transfer must be hidden; the alleged need to give the horizontally mobile man breadth of experience can at best veil the real aim. Since the veil is thin, the real reason can easily be discerned. If it is not, the danger arises that such horizontal movement will be perceived by others as a normal step in the organizational career line. When management blurs lateral "promotions" with horizontal shunting there is always the chance that promising people will be shunted into dead-end jobs.

The most difficult and perhaps the least satisfactory solution is demotion. Copeland has put the matter well, explaining why its secondary effects preclude widespread use:

... long before a mistake in promotion has become so apparent that corrective action is warranted, the misfit's former position ordinarily will have been filled, and a whole chain of promotions and shifts in personnel will have taken place. The misfit cannot be returned to his old job without upsetting these new arrangements, thereby causing disappointments, resentments, and even feelings that there has been a lack of good faith. It is almost axiomatic in business administration that a mistake in promotion, particularly in the higher administrative echelons, cannot be corrected by demotion. . . .[8]

In passing, it might be noted that the chain of consequences which Copeland ascribes to demotion probably parallels the consequences of filling a higher-echelon vacancy by an "outsider." The person within the organization who anticipated being the successor often experiences failure to move into the vacancy as being equivalent to demotion. Moreover, if knowledge of the vacancy is widely known throughout the organization, it is possible that a chain of anticipatory successors has crystallized, each member of which experiences the event as virtual demotion.

A fairly common solution to the problem of blocked channels of mobility is to install the unpromotable in a higher-level honorific position, often one created especially for him. The existence of quasi-functional positions to allow for the practice of "kicking a man upstairs" cannot be accounted for adequately without a general conception of succession as a social process. Weber, for example, maintains that bureaucracies require individuals to be qualified to fill the positions they hold. Creating a job to fit a particular individual—especially where he will contribute little to the organization— appears hardly rational. Although honorific jobs may seem nonrational in a short-run reckoning, they are probably functional in the long-run if by clearing blocked channels they facilitate the effective flow of personnel within the organization.

Clearing blocked channels by honorific promotion poses its own problems. If the position is manifestly functionless, it may not serve its purpose of providing a dignified resting place for an employee who has reached "executive menopause." Neither the employee himself nor others will be convinced that it is more than retirement on the job, a sinecure imposed upon the recipient. If, however, its true nature is screened, the honorific position might become imbedded permanently in the organizational structure instead of being merely a transient arrangement to accommodate a single loyal employee. After the unpromotable retires, others might be sought to occupy the position;

---

[8] Melvin T. Copeland, *The Executive at Work* (Cambridge, Mass.: Harvard, 1955), 126.

and unless appropriate functions are added to the position, the process of utilizing honorific positions may prove partly self-defeating.

Modification of job content

When it becomes apparent that a "job is too big for a man," a solution might be to tailor the job to fit the man rather than to remove him. Since mistakes in succession are not easily reversible by restoring the promoted man to his previous position, the blocked-channels situation sometimes signals management that the duties of the position are too demanding for the abilities of the typical occupant. By subdividing a job, the range of competence needed to perform it is reduced. And at the same time that the promotable is made more effective in this less demanding job, a new channel of mobility is created. In short, the existence of unpromotables in organizations can catalyze the process of bureaucratization and can result in the expansion of an organizational structure.[9]

CONCLUSION

In extending the concept of succession to cover replacements throughout organizations rather than only in high-echelon positions, I have tried to take seriously two characteristics of bureaucracies: continuity and the hierarchical interdependence of roles. The first requires that personnel be trained for higher-level positions *before* vacancies occur. This aspect of organizational life has been designated by the concept of anticipatory succession. The second directs attention to the effects upon subordinates of the differential promotability of their supervisors. The fruitfulness of this more general approach to succession is exemplified by the light it sheds upon such seemingly diverse organizational phenomena as styles of supervision, deviant behavior, and organizational change.

[9] It can also lead to contraction. By merging two units, a post occupied by an unpromotable can be eliminated. Reorganizations that seem dictated by market conditions or by efforts to increase efficiency sometimes have their source in the need to eliminate the organizational stasis produced by an unpromotable.

49

The Problem of Generations in an Organizational Structure

JOSEPH R. GUSFIELD

In this article, Professor Gusfield relates the interdependence of careers operating at the replacement stage of succession to the reasons and requirements of the take-over stage.

Conflicts of power and policy between age-groups are a common feature of many organizational structures. Factories, churches, labor unions, and political parties often distribute power, prestige, and income along an age-grade hierarchy. The existence of "old guard" and "young Turks" is found in many areas of society other than the specifically political. This paper examines some sources of age-graded power and their consequences for organizational stability in the Woman's Christian Temperance Union.

A depiction of the age-grade problem as one of culture conflict points to the difficulties age differences entail for organizational unity. Given such variables as rapid cultural change and competing cultural authorities, conflict between age-groups may be anticipated. Karl Mannheim has pointed out that the existence of generational differences leads to divergent political and social styles and modes of thought which greatly influence the character of public issues.[1] When two or more generations appear within the same organization we may consequently anticipate factional conflict.

In the Woman's Christian Temperance Union differences between generations have been most marked since repeal of the Eighteenth Amendment.[2] In pre-prohibition periods the WCTU functioned as part of a general reform movement with humanitarian aims. Its major interests and activities manifested a concern for the plight of lower-income groups. The central mission of the organization, total abstinence from use of all alcoholic beverages, was viewed as a solution to problems of poverty. In this period WCTU doctrine was the outlook of a socially secure Protestant middle class. Post-prohibition doctrine and activity of the WCTU has tended to express

Excerpted, with permission, from *Social Forces*, 35 (May, 1957): 323–30.

[1] "The fact of belonging to the same generation or age-group and that of belonging to the same class, have this in common, that both endow the individuals sharing in them with a common location in the social and historical process, and thereby limit them to a specific range of potential experiences, predisposing them for a certain characteristic mode of thought and experience, and a characteristic type of historically relevant action." Karl Mannheim, "The Problem of Generations" in *Essays on the Sociology of Knowledge* (London: Oxford University Press, 1952), 291. It should be pointed out that the crucial factor, as Mannheim saw it, was the common experience of the age-group, rather than the fact of age *per se*.
[2] Joseph R. Gusfield, "Social Structure and Moral Reform: A Study of the Woman's Christian Temperance Union," *American Journal of Sociology*, LXI (November, 1955), 221–32.

moral indignation toward contemporary American middle classes, rather than a concern for "uplifting the down trodden." Study of the socio-economic composition of WCTU local leadership revealed a decline in the socio-economic status of local leaders since repeal in 1933. The loss of prestige of WCTU membership has thus been a key problem within the WCTU.

RESPONSES TO ORGANIZATIONAL CRISIS

The repeal of the Eighteenth Amendment reflected a basic change in the reception of temperance doctrine by the American public. Temperance organizations now faced a more hostile public than at any time in their history. We are interested in the reaction of the organization's tactics to this crisis. Our general analysis of the generations problem leads us to see older generations as less willing than newer members to change tactics and past policy.

Within the WCTU two differing responses to the crisis of repeal were advocated at the time we studied the organization, 1952–54. One type of response we shall call "conviction-oriented." This type emphasized the continuance of the tactics and goals of the prohibition period. Even though public accessibility is made more difficult, convictions must be maintained. The second type of response we shall call "public-oriented." Those who advocated this approach wished to substitute the primacy of educational and persuasional aims for those of less respectable legal and political measures to restrict the sale of liquor. The fact that this issue still existed indicates the unsettled nature of WCTU reaction after twenty years.

The conviction-oriented employed a tactic of rectitude. They refused to accept immediate organizational influence as justification for change in existent policy. This was especially stressed in their support of the prohibition doctrine and in refusal to cooperate, in campaigns against alcoholism, with organizations not in sympathy with the WCTU stand of total abstinence. . . .

While conviction-oriented members were unconcerned about the impact of their actions on public acceptance and access, the public-oriented members advocated tact. These members argued that the prime objective of the organization should be moral suasion. They advocated a de-emphasis of the prohibition issue, which they saw as unworkable and a source of public antagonism. This type of adherent was fearful of the possible impression some WCTU members might have on public attitudes. Several told stories critical of individual members whose dress or eccentric behavior sustained the image of the temperance reformer as a "crackpot" or a "bluenose." . . .

In concrete instances, of course, these two types overlapped frequently Nevertheless, they gave tone and direction to specific policy that differed considerably. Conviction-orientation led to the maintenance of the prohibitionist cause and to an attitude of tactical rigidity. Public orientation led to tactical flexibility and weakening of prohibitionist fervor. . . .

In the twenty years between 1933 and 1953 the policies and activities of the WCTU have been closer to those of the conviction-oriented than to the policies and tactics of the public-oriented. Only with the ascension of a new president in 1953 has the WCTU seemed to be moving toward measures to enhance the organization's access to the public.

Within the WCTU, many persons interviewed spoke of the past administration as the "old-guard" and of the conviction-oriented as the "die-hards." Despite the changed environment resulting from Repeal, the WCTU maintained continuity with past doctrine. This cannot be explained by uniformity within the organization since, as we have seen, the outlines of factionalism existed. How were the "old-guard" able to keep control of the organization for a generation?

SOURCES OF GENERATIONAL POWER

The organizational power of the older generation may stem from the mechanisms which maintain the incumbent in positions of power. Given the rigid nature of a past commitment, the maintenance of incumbency power reduces the capacity of the organization for change. We can imagine a system in which older members respond to new situations by advocating organizational change as do younger members. Also, we can imagine a system in which older members resist organizational change, but the mechanisms of power distribution do not give them great opportunity to implement their commitments. Accordingly, our analysis of the WCTU's relative organizational rigidity focuses on the power and transformation of the office holders. . . .

Organizational oligarchy

Like most American voluntary associations, the formal charter of the WCTU enunciates a system of representation and diffusion of power in which the rank and file possess great influence in making policy. As is often true in such a situation, the WCTU has developed an informal structure which places power in the hands of an "active minority" and acts to perpetuate incumbents in office.

One factor explaining the power of the incumbents on the national level is the scarcity of the skills and resources requisite for holding office in a woman's reform organization. Those who operate the organization in its day-to-day routine must be able to live near the national headquarters. In a woman's organization, availability of leaders is influenced by the husband's occupation. Where he is unable to leave a place of business, occupancy of a national office by the wife may entail a marital crisis. The constitution requires the president, the corresponding secretary, and the treasurer to be in residence at headquarters. This restricts the offices to those who live nearby, are widows, or single, or have retired husbands. Both the costs of movement and the relatively low salaries ($3600 for the national president in 1952) further restrict the jobs to wealthy members. The general status of women and the relatively low level of personal commitment require that husband and wife both be able to take the position. This was shown during the study when the corresponding secretary resigned her position because her new husband's parish was not in the Chicago area.

Leadership in the day-to-day operation of an organization is of crucial importance in regulating control of policies. In the WCTU this fact makes the role of the national president immensely important. Through her control of the office at headquarters she leaves her "touch" on many avenues of WCTU activity. She reads the WCTU journal before it is printed each week and exercises considerable editorial power. The literature printed by the WCTU is chiefly made up at headquarters. Even the librarian pointed out that the library is run differently under different administrations. The "headquarters gang" thus has responsibility for the communications received by the local leaders and members. Further, the "headquarters people" travel among the local and state WCTUs very frequently, working as speakers at WCTU events. Consequently they are in communication with local areas. In these ways, the official positions are not nominal but really entail power.

Oligarchy and self-succession

One of the most significant ways in which the incumbent remains in power, however, is through the manipulation of the formal charter. This is most apparent in the incumbent's ability to be reëlected to office.

The nomination and election of officers takes place at the annual convention. Persons are nominated by write-in votes of delegates. If a majority is not achieved on the first ballot by any one candidate, a second ballot is held with candidacy limited to the two receiving the highest votes on the first ballot. This procedure might be expected to result in frequent turnovers of office and numerous second ballots. Indeed, it would seem that this procedure would make nomination and election very difficult and prevent the existence of a power-holding minority with lengthy tenure. The facts are otherwise. Since the organization of the WCTU in 1874 there have been 330 separate elections for various national offices. A second ballot has been necessary in only 15 cases, approximately five percent of the times.

It seems highly unlikely that such unanimity could be obtained on the first ballot without some prior guidance to convention delegates. Indeed, the national officers and the executive board often functioned informally as a nominating committee. This was evident from the accounts of newly-elected national officers. One said that she had to decide in one month whether or not she wished to take the office, "when the committee asked me if I'd take it." Neither she nor the committee felt that this procedure was unusual or that there would be any difficulty in securing election. Another newly-elected officer explained that she got the position because someone on the executive board knew her and knew she had the needed skills for the job. "The former person in this office wasn't too satisfactory and they asked me." In this manner the group at the top manages to control the selection and succession of officers.

Succession rules: the "pipeline"

The issue of succession is a crucial question for any ongoing organization. Methods of life tenure and of hereditary succession have often been advocated as ways of solving the destabilizing effects of frequent change in officers and leaders. The "democratic mold" has been advocated as a means of insuring changes in policy and as a means to obtain both knowledge of the wishes of the rank and file and their loyal support of the leadership. While the democratic method operates to gain stability through obtaining assent, it leaves the organization open to frequent internal factionalism. Many American organizations have developed traditions which regulate succession in such fashion that the succession is decided by a set of norms which dictate the democratic selection.

One such tradition common in many American voluntary associations is that of the "pipeline." In this system, persons move up the ladder of offices in some regular order. In the WCTU, the presidency, when it becomes vacant, regularly goes to the vice-president. This system insures orderly succession. But such a system requires two things if it is also to insure flexibility of policy: (1) The office must be a "real" and not a nominal one; and (2) there must be some traditions which enforce vacancy and limit the tenure of the incumbent. The inconsistency in this system should be apparent. If an office is more than nominal, it creates power and necessitates experience in its work. Therefore, the second element is difficult to obtain. It is hard to get people out of office, because they have the power to stay there and because it takes time to learn the job.

The "pipeline" tradition is thus least apt to produce strain where the office is essentially a distributive good bestowing honor but not power. In some organizations, like the American Sociological Society, the offices may be chiefly honorary. In an organization like the American Legion the "power" tends to reside in the secretariat.

In the WCTU the "pipeline" system operates to prevent policy changes. The existence of the powerful president who really runs the organization gives the presidency a lengthy tenure. Since the vice-president proceeds to the presidency, the effective choice of the president is made long before the situation in which she functions as president. In the past four presidencies the organization was being led, at the conclusion of the president's stay in office, by women whose selection had been effectively made approximately twenty years before. A consequence of this is to perpetuate older generations in power.

Incumbency and the sentiment against ego-loss

Once established, a rule tends to be maintained by the power of the rule maker. It is also maintained by the sentiments which may be violated by breaking it. One of the most significant of these sentiments operative in the WCTU is the sentiment against inflicting aggression. Because a rule is stated in impersonal terms, applicable to all within its categories, departures from the rule have personal connotations. Thus, if the incumbent were to be turned out of office, the implication exists that she was so inept that, even given the tradition, the group could not accept her.

Erving Goffman has pointed out the difficult problem posed for social systems by the necessity to inflict defeat and failure on some persons.[3] In American culture, removal from office tends to be a blow to the ego of the officeholder. Consequently, the action of members to bring about such loss of ego is an aggressive act. Since the rules lead the officeholder to anticipate incumbency *as long as he is acceptable to the members,* turnover in office can hardly be kept from being a punishing action.

In organizations such as political parties, labor unions, or businesses, the pressures of financial commitment and career contingencies may act to balance the norms against inflicting ego-loss. The attitude that "business is business" implies the impersonality of the act and the consequent immunity of the power-holder from the imputation of aggressiveness. Even so, such organizations are often deeply troubled by the necessity for firing employees and officials.

In the WCTU, positions do not bring great tangible rewards for the officeholder. The salary is minimal and few have made a professional career out of the WCTU. This may be one factor in explaining the reluctance of members to break the norms of lengthy tenure. People feel guilt if they act to expel an incumbent from office or move ahead of her in the line of succession. The action is seen as one of hostility, disturbing to "good feelings." . . .

Efforts to utilize potential power to bring new persons into office are thus frustrated by the norm of kindness to the incumbent. As a result, officers can achieve long tenures in office. In one of the large states, WCTU members had suggested that the incumbent president retire. She had felt "very hurt" and the movement to defeat her was discontinued. . . .

The behavior contemplated in one state illustrates the lengths to which the group will go to maintain "good feelings." In this case, the state president had held office for more than thirty years. . . .

In this fashion, the norm against aggression becomes a means for the maintenance of the incumbent and the continuance of tenure traditions. Once established, the rule is supported by the weight of the interests of the

---

[3] Erving Goffman, "On Cooling the Mark Out," *Psychiatry,* XV (1952), 451–61. Also see Erving Goffman, "On Face-Work: An Analysis of Ritual Elements in Social Interaction," *Psychiatry,* XVIII (1955), 213–31.

officeholder and the sentiment of the non-officeholder against disturbing the incumbent's ego.[4]

ADAPTIVE STRUCTURES

The response types discussed earlier are not the only elements operative in structuring the approaches of the members and officers to WCTU policy. Certain consequences of these positions are not easily ignored. Other values than those encompassed in the response types are at work. The effort to realize contradictory values operates to produce what Talcott Parsons has called "adaptive structures." . . .

One of the imperatives of organizational existence is the continued recruitment of new personnel. As long as incumbent personnel are committed to organizational continuity they must face the problems of recruitment. "Adaptations," in the sense of changes in policy, are not a solution to the value conflict between the conviction-oriented and the public-oriented. This latter conflict is an argument about the ethics and strategy of "adaptation." Adaptive structures would rather be ways in which the value positions of the incumbents were not changed but the structure of the organization permitted new personnel in key posts.

Our previous analysis of the forces maintaining the structure suggests that two structural types might be solutions to the problem: (1) ways of ejecting incumbents which do not lead to loss of ego; and (2) ways of letting new persons into positions of power without disturbing incumbents. Such adaptive structures have appeared in the WCTU.

The tension between response types is also a tension between age groups. The power of the older group in the WCTU has been felt to repel younger members, people between 35 and 50. In the literature and in the interviews there was concern expressed that the WCTU was "top heavy" with old people. "We must do something to attract the younger member" was a common statement. In this manner recruitment becomes an "exigency" or constraint on the behavior of the incumbent and acts to develop adaptations such as the following:

"*Easing off*" *processes*

Many sociologists and anthropologists have called attention to the important function played by ritual and ceremony in the transition from one role to another. Erving Goffman has shown the need for social devices to forestall the potential hostility of persons subjected to rejection, defeat, or failure. The WCTU has attempted to ease retirement from office by the development

---

[4] It is worth noting that this often leads to a change in the function of the rule or tradition. The system of "pipeline," for example, was originated after the death of a strong president who had nominated her own vice-president. It prevented a re-occurrence of such presidential power. Also, coming after a strong president, it prevented the election from being too critical for WCTU unity.

of fictional roles which enable the retiring incumbent to veil the rejective aspect of removal.

One such form is the office of Member Emeritus. This device, most prevalent in academic circles, is appearing more frequently in other organizations, such as churches and labor unions. In the WCTU, a member is eligible for the title if she has served on the executive board for 15 or more years. Such persons are listed in the annual convention report, written about in the WCTU journal, and introduced to the convention at annual meetings. In this way the guise of the "elder statesman" is maintained by a fiction which minimizes the finality of the rejection and enables the incumbent to preserve "face."

Another variant of this device is the practice of movement to an allied organization. This was used by several national presidents on retirement. The World Woman's Christian Temperance Union is an organization of prestige but little day-to-day work. WCTU presidents hold an office in it. Either through becoming president of that organization or by the mere official position they hold there, the national president can use this both as a tangible position of prestige and as an "excuse" for retirement which still minimizes ego-deprivation. . . .

"Separate but equal"

To some extent, conflict between groups is avoided by prevention of contact. In an effort to recruit younger people, give them some voice in the organization, and prevent tension between age groups, separate units of the WCTU were formed in 1933. These groups, known as Iota Sigma units, meet in the evenings rather than in the afternoons, as regular WCTUs do. Program materials speak of them as "open to business and professional women and to young matrons." The national corresponding secretary, who is in charge of recruitment, explicitly viewed the Iota Sigma as a way to meet the age-group conflict through separation. . . .

The impact of the "pipeline" on policy continuation is strikingly seen in the case of the last WCTU president. Early in her life, during her college days, she became deeply identified with the prohibition movement and the Prohibition Party. Her husband was one of the leading figures in the Prohibition Party, and once was its presidential nominee. She was a prominent leader in the WCTU and in 1933 was elected vice-president. In 1944, according to the traditional norms of succession, she was elected president. Her position epitomized the point of view of the conviction-oriented in the WCTU. It would have been extremely difficult for her to reverse the commitment of 40 years of agitation and assume a more flexible policy.

Tenure traditions

The modes of succession are not the only forces operating to keep older people in office. In general, it is difficult to get people out of office, once they have been installed.

Rejection of an incumbent is rare. Of the eight instances occurring in this time span, only two might be considered true rejections or turnovers. In two cases the incumbent moved up to a higher office, thus leaving a vacancy. The two higher offices were vacated because of poor health, a reason which was validated by interviews and by our knowledge of the hospitalization, in the previous year, of one of the officers. In another case, the officer had been the Washington lobbyist for WCTU for many years. The failure of her successor in this job forced her to return to it. In another instance, already mentioned, marriage necessitated resignation. Of the two cases of turnover, one resulted from executive committee action. The incumbent was not put up for reëlection because she seemed to lack the skills necessary for the job. Nevertheless, she had held the post for six years. In the last case, the officer was not reëlected by the convention.

Why is it so difficult for the WCTU to change officers? Politics often witnesses the casting aside of the old leader when a change seems called for in the interests of party victory. While we have shown the existence of tenure and succession traditions, we have not indicated how these are maintained.

Such efforts have not proved very successful in attracting membership. They must be limited to cities large enough to sustain two units. After twenty years, neither the total membership nor the annual increase in Iota Sigma units is reported in WCTU documents, although all other sub-units, such as children's and adolescent's branches, are reported.

"Seduction of the innocent"

The perfect mode of adaptation to this problem of transmission would be one which insured recruitment into positions of power for younger members and still did not lead to the rejection of older members. This is possible in one type of situation. When a new office is created or when, for some unique reason, there is no successor for a vacant office, an opportunity appears to place younger members in power. In such instances, higher officers attempt a deliberate form of what Selznick calls "coöptation." Authority is given to the younger person, so as to insure greater representation. However, it is also given as a means to develop activities through which the new member or officer can develop a deeper commitment to the WCTU. For example, in upstate New York, county and state organizers initiated a unit in 1951. When they found a woman aged 35 interested in WCTU they offered her the first presidency, although there were other, older women there who had previous experience in WCTU in other towns. This coöptation was possible since there was no vested interest in the office dictated by any clear tradition. In another case, a local unit decided to organize a children's branch. The president chose a somewhat marginal member as the director. As the president explained it, "She's a woman in her forties, and we'd like to get her more in the WCTU."

The neutrality of rules

In some state units, the WCTU is beginning to define the tenure of office by a rule which limits it to a specified term. In one state the term has been set at eight years. The rule is an impersonal form. Because it is stated in universalistic rather than in particularistic terms, rules limiting tenure are able to provide the ego protection necessary for the incumbent to accept gracefully removal from office. The limited use of this technique, however, suggests that it is not feasible to introduce it while offices are being filled. In one state it came into existence during an interregnum period with an acting president.

The adaptive problem

In the long run, the WCTU is changing toward a more flexible organization bent on increasing its access to the general public within the framework of its present mission as a critic of deviation from older, middle-class standards. Newer and younger persons are succeeding to office. Death and illness, twin assistants to organizational change, are also constraints to which organizations are heir.

The problem of transmission, however, is a problem to which the entire organization is sensitive. As long as members and officers are committed to the perpetuation of the organizational mission, they are alive to this problem. Consequently, the tendencies toward incumbency power are somewhat reduced.

People who become committed to a cause and to a set of doctrines do not give up the fight easily. Like the cowboy hero, they prefer to "die with their boots on" rather than "hang up the spurs" and capitulate to the rustlers. The problems of organization, however, aggravate the conflicts created by generational diversities. The rules and traditions of succession may operate to accentuate the role of the older generation through maintaining the incumbent in power. The power of the opposition to remove the incumbent is limited by the norms against aggressive actions. Necessities of organizational transmission spring from the member's concern for its mission. These necessities leave the organization open to needs for recruitment of younger members and thus the needs to remove older persons from power. Some devices have arisen which permit graceful exits and which may assure quicker entry into power positions. Nevertheless, the movement toward tactical and strategic change has taken a generation in the WCTU.

50

The Effects of Succession:
A Comparative Study of Military and
Business Organization

OSCAR GRUSKY

The closeness of control exercised over how a person takes over his new position varies with the increase in size, complexity, and decentralization of the organization, and with its rate of succession. Professor Grusky discusses the effects of succession in military and business organizations.

The problem of succession is the organizational equivalent of the larger societal problem of generations. The replacement of personnel in complex organizations is a continuous process, just as the cycle of life and death is an inevitable feature of human existence. This study is concerned with a comparative analysis of the effects of succession on a military installation and a large business firm.

The study of succession, sometimes called occupational or administrative succession, has been pursued from two vantage points. One approach locates the problem exclusively at the top of the organization hierarchy. Such a viewpoint offers the distinct advantage of a focus upon those elites that are generally most accountable for the direction and implementation of organizational objectives. A second approach emphasizes that the proper study of succession should be broadened to include the effects of personnel circulation through positions at all levels in the hierarchy. By this approach the concepts of occupational mobility and administrative succession tend to be fused and career mobility in an organizational setting is seen not only as essential for leadership development, but, at the same time, as creating problems of organizational continuity in the performance of its critical functions. Succession, as we shall use the term, is meant to refer to the processes associated with the movement of members out of the organization and their replacement by new members.

Comparative analysis of military and industrial organization suggests that military organization has reached a stage of bureaucratic development which seemingly anticipates the future movement of other complex systems. Concepts now commonly applied in industry, such as line of command, staff-line, the development of oral briefing, and others, were derived from military experience. It is already evident that the highly bureaucratized patterns of career succession in the military have spread to large industrial corporations. Still, the degree of bureaucratization of careers is greater in military than in

Excerpted, with permission, from *The New Military* (New York: Russell Sage Foundation, 1964).

business organization. Four factors have contributed to the extensive organizational control of the military over officer career patterns: the nature of its mission, its size, complexity, and geographical dispersion. The intense political and social implications involved in the management of violence require careful control over the training particularly of those in executive positions. The distribution of goods and services for profit does not require the same degree of close control. The sheer size of a centralized military establishment necessitates control by extensive rules and regulations. There were about 2,450,000 men under arms and 343,000 officers on active duty in 1962. Research indicates that large size in itself may not require an unusually large administrative apparatus, but size is positively related to complexity of organization and the more complex the system the greater the demand for a large administrative staff. The many component parts of the military mission and the related necessity for locating military units all over the world combine to emphasize the overall complexity of the United States military establishment. However, it should be kept in mind that because the military is both a unified and highly centralized system it is not strictly comparable to business organization. Rotation in the military is from one unit to another within a single establishment. The business executive may either transfer from one unit to another within the corporation or move to another firm. Hence in business two different modes of succession exist whereas there is one in the military. We have assumed arbitrarily that the military base may be considered to be equivalent to the business firm. We justified this decision on the grounds that both units of study have clear and, we think, parallel organizational identities within their respective institutional contexts as well as within the local community in which they are situated. Interdepartmental transfers, either in the military base or business organization, were not considered in this study. Instead, our focus was on movement into and out of the military base and the business firm.

Assuming that "Military career lines are highly standardized, as compared with other professions," and some comparative data will be presented to test this contention, what are the effects of this bureaucratization? Two independent studies have shown that large, and therefore more bureaucratized, organizations have greater rates of executive succession than small organizations. Kriesberg has pointed out that this may mean that career patterns are different in the small and large systems. The small organization is more likely to be manned by "homeguards" or "locals," whose careers are characterized by relatively little movement from place to place. Larger organizations are more likely to be dominated by executives who are "itinerants," moving frequently from organization to organization. Military systems are of theoretical significance to organization theory because all those of executive rank are, of necessity, itinerants. Thus military systems are desirable objects of investigation for the student of succession because they represent a relatively extreme career situation. Military rotation policies require officers to change their assignments after a given period of time. This period may be one year in hardship areas, but more typically two, three, four, and at times, five years. Hence executive succession at all military installations is highly routinized and frequent.

A number of studies of small organizations have indicated that succession is disruptive, typically producing low morale and conflict among the staff. It is likely that in highly bureaucratized organizations such as the military where succession is closely regulated, these disruptive responses are muted. By standardizing career experiences the organization systematically prepares the manager for future moves. Comparisons of business firms and military installations facilitate the study of the effects on succession of differential degrees of organizational control.

Three problems formed the central interest of our study. First, we were concerned with the structural context in which succession takes place. What are the organizational correlates of the two types of succession, bureaucratic and less bureaucratic? Second, we were interested in the consequences of succession for organizational commitment. How does rotation influence the orientation of the military officer to his present organizational assignment? Third, we were interested in adjustment to community life. How does the military officer adapt to the transient nature of his family life? Is he truly "rootless" or does his behavior reflect an alteration in the conventional patterns of integration found in stable settings? . . .

Rapid succession is associated with greater homogeneity among organizational members. Bureaucratic control involves the widespread application of rational, universalistic criteria in dealing with members of the system. Hence general indexes of bureaucratization are the extensiveness of rules, the degree of hierarchicalization, impersonality, and the focus on managerial expertise. The opposite type of control, the nonbureaucratic, implies the absence of those factors. In the less bureaucratic form, social control is more personal and the uniqueness of the organization and its chief administrators is paramount.

The more rapid succession of officers at the military installation meant that the range of executive experience in the organization was much less among this group than among the business managers. Most of the officers at the Air Force base had two years or less experience, while most of the business managers had at least five years' experience in the organization and almost half of the top level managers had at least fifteen years. Therefore it appears that a concomitant of rapid succession may be decreased executive homogeneity with respect to experience in a particular organizational setting. But the military officer rotates through an establishment which has a basic format and a high degree of organizational standardization. At the same time, the socialization for higher position of all managers, business and military, requires constant exposure to a large number of organizations. The crucial difference would seem to be this: The business executive is more likely than his military counterpart to be able to count on staying with an organization for a long enough period to implement major innovations.

In general, rapid succession encourages executive homogeneity with respect to universalistic criteria. Data on age and seniority may be cited illustratively. . . .

A comparatively slow rate of succession in the business firm studied seemed to function to produce homogeneity through shared experiences in the organization. The significance of leadership homogeneity for administration has been noted by Selznick: "Another developmental problem is that of creating an initial homogeneous staff. The members of this core group reflect the basic policies of the organization in their own outlooks. They can, when matured in this role, perform the essential task of indoctrinating newcomers along desired lines. They can provide assurance that decision-making will conform, in spirit as well as letter, to policies that may have to be formulated abstractly or vaguely. The development of derivative policies and detailed applications of general rules will thus be guided by a shared general perspective." Such functions, essential to business organization, ostensibly are replaced in military systems by bureaucratic forms.

The high rate of succession in the military installation militated against the creation of homogeneity through shared experiences in the particular organization of which the officer is a part. Instead, the bases for homogeneity would seem to lie with the similarity of the officers' military training, social values, the hierarchy of authority, age, sex, and other nonparticularistic factors. In the military, the nature of the particular installation is less important to administration than the fundamental similarities of each base. Rapid succession may be both a cause and a product of organizational uniformity.

Rapid succession is associated with limitations on executive control. It is frequently argued that in an organization where few executives can anticipate long periods of service and most can look forward to relatively short tenures in that particular organization, the ability of the executive to implement major policy changes is greatly weakened. By contrast, failure to rotate creates powerful barriers to innovation by entrenching traditionalistic perspectives. Continuous rotation clearly fashions the pattern of organizational innovations in military systems, especially at the operational level. All too frequently, the first year of a three-year tour of duty is spent familiarizing oneself with the idiosyncrasies of the base, the second in implementing a number of relatively limited rule changes, the third in setting the base in order in anticipation of departure. Moreover, where civilian employees have long tenures and military officials are frequently rotated, we would expect the former group to tend to absorb a disproportionate amount of influence on the implementation of policy and policy-making. Nor is such a situation conducive to identification with the commanding officer of a military base. The performance of General Curtis E. LeMay in welding the Strategic Air Command into a highly effective and adaptable force was undoubtedly related to the fact that he was left in command for over eight years rather than the normal shorter tour of duty.

When asked: "What officer of General rank, past or present, do you admire most?" the 497 military officers who responded selected 118 different generals. Less than one per cent selected their own commanding officer. For these officers, the system of rotation produced attachments not so much to one well-known leader but to one of many lesser known leaders. It is only in the small unbureaucratized organization or in the large complex system unified through a single overriding objective, as in combat, that a specific leader is closely identified with the organization as a whole.

Summary

We have assumed that bureaucratic career patterns were more typical of military than business organization. And we did find that rapid succession, typical of highly bureaucratized systems, characterized the military installation to a much greater extent than it did the business firm. Moreover, not surprisingly, we found consistent evidence of greater hierarchicalization in the military site.

It was the consequences of rapid succession, however, which concerned this exploratory study most of all. How do organizations and their members respond to highly routinized and rapid succession? The limited evidence was examined in four problem areas: executive homogeneity, control, commitment, and community involvement.

Because bureaucratic control necessitates the extensive application of rational criteria for selection and promotion of personnel, homogeneity among executives with respect to numerous social characteristics tends to result. Accordingly, we found at each rank level greater uniformity in age, length of time in the organization, and seniority among the military officers than among business managers.

Routinized succession conditions the exercise of organizational control. Rapid succession in the military inhibits strong identification with the chief executive. The data collected for this study indicated that length of tenure at the military base increased the perceived authority of the officers, including those at the highest ranks. Length of tenure also increased perceived authority in the business setting, but not at the top ranks. Thus it appears that in the military, bureaucratic forms of rotation, regardless of the organizational objectives they serve, weaken personal executive power and encourage the development of a general orientation toward organizational authority. . . .

More favorable orientations toward the organization and the specific department were found in the military setting than in the business organization. In the military system, and unlike the business firm studied, length of experience in the particular installation was not systematically related to the strength of these attitudes. Instead, the more favorable orientations to the organization and the subunit could be seen as tied closely to the greater standardization of assignment and greater strength of professional commitment in the military.

Evidence supporting the hypothesis that frequent succession inhibits extensive participation in community life was not found. Instead, the opposite pattern prevailed. Military officers, despite their short time in the community, were found more likely to be members of various community voluntary associations than were business managers. The findings were viewed as suggestive of a pattern of adaptation to bureaucratic succession. Military officers, knowing full well that their assignment to a given base was temporary, apparently responded by rapidly integrating themselves into the local community through memberships in numerous voluntary associations.

51

Executive Succession in Small Companies

DONALD B. TROW

When a replacement bypasses several others on his way up, the whole sentimental order supporting the organizational career may be challenged, causing trouble and disenchantment with the career. Professor Trow discusses the factors involved in management succession.

This secondary analysis of data collected about management succession in a sample of over one hundred small- to medium-sized manufacturing companies has indicated the following:

1. The median length of service of the company presidents is about 20 years. It is somewhat higher than this for founders of companies and lower for nonfounders, and it is still lower (about 14 years) for managers who were not principal owners.

2. There is a strong association between planning for succession and subsequent profitability: companies in which a successor had been chosen and trained appear much less likely to have suffered a period of financial difficulty while the new president learned to manage.

3. The size and growth of the management group and the pattern of company ownership are associated with planning for succession. In the cases studied prior to succession the smaller, stable, family-owned companies tended not to have chosen and trained successors; when succession had actually occurred, however, there was no difference in planning between these companies and larger, growing, publicly owned ones. The difference is attributable to later planning in the smaller companies.

4. Management ability appeared to have two different effects on the succession process. In companies in which the manager's son was the potential successor, a low level of competence on his part seems to have delayed both planning for succession and the succession itself. Secondly, among all companies in which an unplanned succession occurred, subsequent company profitability appears to be associated positively with the successor's ability.

These results largely support the conclusions of the original study. In addition, however, they suggest a change of emphasis in the conclusions concerning the effects of company size, growth, and ownership upon succession planning: these factors appear to affect the timing of planning rather than its likelihood. In addition, the analysis indicates that management ability plays a larger part than was suggested in the original study. While it is hardly

Excerpted, with permission, from *Administrative Science Quarterly*, 6(2) (September, 1961), 237–39.

surprising that managerial ability is found to be related to company performance, the analysis goes beyond this in revealing the particular ways in which
ability interacts with the succession process to produce its effect.

The general pattern of the succession-planning that appears to underlie
the results is that of a decision problem extending over time. During the latter
part of the manager's career, succession begins to loom as a problem requiring
action. If there is a son (or son-in-law or nephew) of the principal owner, then
he is the first possible successor considered. If he appears to be interested
and competent, then action is taken to assure his succession and to see that
he gets adequate training; that is, a plan (in the sense used in this study) is
formulated.

If there is a son, but he is too young, is not interested, or appears to be of
borderline ability, then a decision is postponed to see whether he will become
interested and/or whether further experience in lower management positions
will increase his competence sufficiently for him to be the successor. In the
meantime, however, the company is without a plan, and if the death or forced
retirement of the manager brings about succession anyway, then the son is
likely to be the successor. If there has been no change in his level of interest
or competence, then he is not likely to have the full support of other organization members. Because of this problem or because he makes poor decisions
the profitability of the company is likely to decline.

If there is no son, then present members of management are considered
as possible successors. Here, the likelihood that there will be someone of
sufficient ability to be considered as a successor is greater in larger, growing
companies where there is a level of management between the president and
the shop foreman; therefore a plan can readily be formulated. ...

Finally, if there is no one within the company who can be considered for
succession, then an outsider is sought, and the same factors—size, growth,
and ownership—influence the attractiveness of the position and hence the
amount of delay in getting a plan for succession formulated. Smaller family-
owned companies find greater difficulty in attracting managers from outside
and because of the high cost of a successor-designate may tend to delay even
seeking one.

Although this general pattern of the succession-planning process serves
to link together the factors and relationships that this analysis has shown are
involved, the pattern does not of course convey a picture of the variety of
ways in which the succession problem is handled by individual companies.

Part VIII

Moving between Organizations

•

At first thought it might seem that moving between organizations is a fateful career step, perhaps requiring changes of great moment to the person. This may easily be the case, but it is not necessarily so. The move may also come as a matter of course in a routine career pattern. A useful way to begin analysis of the significance to a person's career of a move between organizations is to classify it as one of four general kinds of moves. Does the move entail a change in type of organizational career and does it entail a change in organizations or in sub-organizations of a parent organization?

CLASSIFICATION OF MOVES BETWEEN ORGANIZATIONS

		Type of Career	
		Same	Different
Parent	Same	1. Least Change	3.
Organ-			
ization	Different	2.	4. Most Change

In the above chart of this classification, we have shown the probable relative amount of change involved for the person. This relative amount of change does not necessarily indicate the degree of impact nor the dimensions of change for the person. This question, as yet, lacks grounding in research for generating formal propositions. Let us consider examples we have for each cell.

Changing only sub-organizations (Cell 1) is a characteristic of organizational careers in large complex

377

organizations, such as the armed or civil services, school systems (Becker), banks, large industrial organizations, and so forth. A person can put in for a transfer in order to change his working conditions (such as Becker's school teacher) or geographical location, and this change can mean very much to the person. These volitional transfers are likely to be either horizontal, as with teachers, or vertical, as in the army or banks. Organizations may decide on these transfers as part of their work requirements, or for advancing or demoting a person. Routine transfers can occur every few years as an organizational policy (for example, in the army). Thus, the main factors in perhaps making this a change of great importance to the person are different working conditions and/or geographical location or a demotion.

The same career but in different organizations (Cell 2) we would judge as having relatively more impact of change on the person than Cell 1. Still pursuing his career, his move, if volitional, is likely to be linked to an equal or advanced career level. The prestige of the new organization may be a factor in this calculation. However, now he must adjust not only to new working conditions, but also to new organizational policies influencing his work and career, and, perhaps, to a new geographical location. If the move is the result of a well-calculated career plan, the adjustment to the new organization is probably a welcome challenge and not too bothersome a change, such as with the academic career pattern of "outbreeding," or with scheduled student careers (Glaser). This welcome change is particularly the case with executives of technical firms such as IBM, who take jobs in business or industry running a technical department for more money, higher rank, and better working conditions. This type of fruitful move of experts is a typical pattern. Nurses, as we see in Pape's article, engage in "touristry" as a career plan in the early stages of their careers. Touristry is moving between organizations for the purpose of travel to different parts of the nation or world while pursuing a career in organizations whose conditions facilitate this mobility.

While the changes may be welcome if the person moves between organizations as part of his own plan, it can be a most unwelcome change if the organization gets a person a job elsewhere in order to get rid of him. The move might entail a demotion as well as subtle discharge. However, it might entail a promotion, but in a lower prestige organization (for example, to a "bush-league" college), so while his career is ostensibly advancing, he is on balance going down. Calculation of the career changes in these moves is up to the people involved, and differential calculations of the same move are prevalent.

Changing sub-organizations and type of career (Cell 3) may entail a complete career change within the organization by the person starting afresh in a different sub-organization. This may occur, for example, in switching from staff to line or from enlisted to officer corps. The person obtains a new start from the organization among people who do not know him nor can easily associate him with his previous career motivations, identity, and competence. The person may request this fresh start or the organization might consider it the most advisable way to save or help him in starting out again. Besides coming as a planned new start, a complete change in career may necessitate a change in sub-organization, come with this change, or be forced on the person by the organizational change. It also might come at a normal stage in a person's present career where he has the option to change or go on as he is; for example, researcher-scientists reach a point where they decide to stay in research for the remainder of their careers or switch to administration. In any case, it seems that the impact of this change is greater than Cell 2, because a new career, sub-organization, and working conditions must be adjusted to, even if the general organizational policy is the same.

Changing one's career within the organization may be an advantage offered by a large organization that becomes part of a person's career plans. But also it is a function of the alternatives the person has for moving to new organizations (Wilensky). If the person has no alternatives elsewhere for his new career, he is "locked in" the current organization and must continue "as is" or try for a new career in a new sub-organization. And unless he has some type of tenure, he is likely to be quite dependent on his current organization's desires as regard whether he can switch, and if switching whether he will be better off. His ability to negotiate his changes depends in part on his ability to move to another organization, and to have this ability known. This latter ability will vary strategically with his age, training, and competence, and the prestige of his current organization. His satisfaction with his current type of career is also relevant. Some people who realize that they should change organizations or sub-organizations, which might require a new career, cannot make the change because of "love" for their work.

Changing both career and organization entails, on the face of it, the most changes in store for the person. These changes may be "drastic" for the person and take a long time to adjust to if they were not desired or planned for. Sometimes people never adjust to them. If desired and part of a career plan, they are likely to be met with a welcome challenge to make good in a new alternative to work life. Indeed, when these changes are made as careful career planning, we must look at the underlying sociological changes involved, for they may not be as great as the apparent changes. For example, Etzioni shows that in their changing careers and organizations, army officers going into private organizations as executives choose the same type of "compliance structures" they were used to in the army. Thus, on this important organizational dimension, there tended to be no change.

A central category from the person's point of view in these four types of moving between organizations are his career plans. Glaser presents one useful scheme for their analysis. In this scheme it is important to include with "3—influences upon the actor," the organizational conditions under which moves are facilitated or hindered. Some organizations, such as educational institutions, make moves automatic between organizations or sub-organizations. Others facilitate moves, as by the standard employment practices of hospitals and the licensing of nurses. Others hinder moves as much as possible through union requirements, blackball lists, promises to never rehire a person, and so forth. In "2.a—motivations of the actor," it is important to specify his intentions with regard to staying with the organization and its career. Does the person intend to stay for a long time or for a short, necessary experience? Is he using the organization as a stepping stone to another in his career? If so, is this an open or closed maneuver? Is the organization a formal stepping stone, such as a hospital for interns? Is the person passing through the organization on the way down, up, or just drifting?

A central category from the point of view of the organization pertaining to moving between organizations is that this provides a type of interdependence between them. This interdependence is probably most relevant with people staying in the same career but applies to all four types. Once in the new organization the person can give away secrets of the old organization, or he can be used as a future contact or liaison man with his former organization. If he can keep some foothold in the former organization, as with friends or holding a nominal position, the person can also interlock the organizations, such as on the directorates. This moving may also indicate a "raiding" relationship between organizations. The raiding of scientists between government, industry, and university organizations carries with it the potential impact of a linkage of some sort for the benefit or deficit of either or both organizations.

52

The Career of the Schoolteacher

HOWARD S. BECKER

Changing sub-organizations is a characteristic of careers
in large, complex organizations such as the army, school
systems, or banks. Professor Becker analyzes facets of this
career move for a school system.

The concept of *career* has proved of great use in understanding and analyzing
the dynamics of work organizations and the movement and fate of individuals
within them. The term refers, to paraphrase Hall, to the patterned series of
adjustments made by the individual to the "network of institutions, formal
organizations, and informal relationships" in which the work of the occupation is performed. This series of adjustments is typically considered in
terms of movement up or down between positions differentiated by their
rank in some formal or informal hierarchy of prestige, influence, and income.
The literature in the field has devoted itself primarily to an analysis of the
types, states, and contingencies of careers, so conceived, in various occupations. We may refer to such mobility through a hierarchy of ranked positions,
if a spatial metaphor be allowed, as the *vertical* aspect of the career.

By focusing our attention on this aspect of career movement, we may
tend to overlook what might, in contrast, be called the *horizontal* aspect of
the career: movement among the positions available at one level of such a
hierarchy. It need not be assumed that occupational positions which share
some characteristics because of their similar rank in a formal structure are
identical in all respects. They may, in fact, differ widely in the configuration
of the occupation's basic problems which they present. That is, all positions
at one level of a work hierarchy, while theoretically identical, may not be
equally easy or rewarding places in which to work. Given this fact, people
tend to move in patterned ways among the possible positions, seeking that
situation which affords the most desirable setting in which to meet and grapple
with the basic problems of their work. In some occupations more than others,
and for some individuals more than others, this kind of career movement
assumes greater importance than the vertical variety, sometimes to such
an extent that the entire career line consists of movement entirely at one level
of a work hierarchy.

The teachers of the Chicago public schools are a group whose careers
typically tend toward this latter extreme. Although it is possible for any
educationally qualified teacher to take the examination for the position of

Excerpted, with permission, from "The Career of the Chicago Public School Teacher," *American
Journal of Sociology*, 57(5) (March, 1952): 470–77.

principal and attempt ascent through the school system's administrative hierarchy, few make the effort. Most see their careers purely in teaching, in terms of movement among the various schools in the Chicago system. Even those attempting this kind of vertical mobility anticipate a stay of some years in the teacher category and, during that time, see that segment of their career in much the same way. This paper will analyze the nature of this area of career movement among teachers and will describe the types of careers found in this group. These, of course, are not the only patterns which we may expect to find in this horizontal plane of career movement.

.   .   .   .

The positions open to a particular teacher in the system at a given time appear, in general, quite similar, all having about the same prestige, income, and power attached to them. This is not to deny the existence of variations in income created by the operation of seniority rules or of differences in informal power and prestige based on length of service and length of stay in a given school. The fact remains that, for an individual with a given amount of seniority who is about to begin in a school new to her, all teaching positions in the Chicago system are the same with regard to prestige, influence, and income.

Though the available teaching positions in the city schools are similar in formal characteristics, they differ widely in terms of the configuration of the occupation's basic work problems which they present. The teacher's career consists of movement among these various schools in search of the most satisfactory position in which to work, that being the position in which these problems are least aggravated and most susceptible of solution. Work problems arise in the teacher's relations with the important categories of people in the structure of the school: children, parents, principal, and other teachers. Her most difficult problems arise in her interaction with her pupils. Teachers feel that the form and degree of the latter problems vary considerably with the social-class background of the students.

Without going into any detailed analysis of these problems, I will simply summarize the teacher's view of them and of their relation to the various social-class groups which might furnish her with students. The interviewees typically distinguished three class groups: (1) a bottom stratum, probably equivalent to the lower-lower and parts of the upper-lower class, and including, for the teacher, all Negroes; (2) an upper stratum, probably equivalent to the upper-middle class; and (3) a middle stratum, probably equivalent to the lower-middle and parts of the upper-lower class. Three major kinds of problems were described as arising in dealings with pupils: (1) the problem of *teaching*, producing some change in the child's skills and knowledge which can be attributed to one's own efforts; (2) the problem of *discipline*, maintaining order and control over the children's activity; and (3) the problem of what may be termed *moral acceptability*, bringing one's self to bear some traits of the children which one considers immoral and revolting. The teacher feels that the lowest group, "slum" children, is difficult to teach, uncontrollable and violent in the sphere of discipline, and morally unacceptable on all scores, from physical cleanliness to the spheres of sex and "ambition to get ahead." Children of the upper group, from the "better neighborhoods," were felt to be quick learners and easy to teach but somewhat "spoiled" and difficult to control and lacking in the important moral traits of politeness and respect for elders. The middle group was considered to be hard-working but slow to learn, extremely easy to control, and most acceptable on the moral level.

Other important problems arise in interaction with parents, principal, and colleagues and revolve primarily around the issue of authority. Parents of the highest status groups and certain kinds of principals are extremely threatening to the authority the teacher feels basic to the maintenance of her role; in certain situations colleagues, too, may act in such a way as to diminish her authority.

Thus, positions at the teaching level may be very satisfactory or highly undesirable, depending on the presence or absence of the "right" kind of pupils, parents, principal, and colleagues. Where any of these positions are filled by the "wrong" kind of person, the teacher feels that she is in an unfavorable situation in which to deal with the important problems of her work. Teachers in schools of this kind are dissatisfied and wish to move to schools where "working conditions" will be more satisfactory.

Career movement for the Chicago teacher is, in essence, movement from one school to another, some schools being more and others less satisfactory places in which to work. Such movement is accomplished under the Board of Education's rules governing transfer, which allow a teacher, after serving in a position for more than a year, to request transfer to one of as many as ten other positions. Movement to one of these positions is possible when an opening occurs for which there is no applicant whose request is of longer standing, and transfer takes place upon approval by the principal of the new school.

The career patterns which are to be found in this social matrix are not expected to be typical of all career movements of this horizontal type. It is likely that their presence will be limited to occupational organizations which, like the Chicago school system, are impersonal and bureaucratic and in which mobility is accomplished primarily through the manipulation of formal procedures.

The greatest problems of work are found in lower-class schools and, consequently, most movement in the system is a result of dissatisfaction with the social-class composition of these school populations. Movement in the system, then, tends to be out from the "slums" to the "better" neighborhoods, primarily in terms of the characteristics of the pupils. Since there are few or no requests for transfer to "slum" schools, the need for teachers is filled by the assignment to such schools of teachers beginning careers in the Chicago system. Thus, the new teacher typically begins her career in the least desirable kind of school. From this beginning two major types of careers were found to develop.

The first variety of career is characterized by an immediate attempt to move to a "better" school in a "better" neighborhood. The majority of interviewees reporting first assignment to a "slum" school had already made or were in the process of making such a transfer. The attitude is well put in this quotation:

When you first get assigned you almost naturally get assigned to one of those poorer schools, because those naturally are among the first to have openings because people are always transferring out of them to other schools. Then you go and request to be transferred to other schools nearer your home or in some nicer neighborhood. Naturally the vacancies don't come as quickly in those schools because people want to stay there once they get there. I think that every teacher strives to get into a nicer neighborhood.

Making a successful move of this kind is contingent on several factors. First, one must have fairly precise knowledge as to which schools are "good" and which are not, so that one may make requests wisely. Without such knowledge, which is acquired through access to the "grapevine," what appears to be a desirable move may prove to be nothing more than a jump from the frying pan into the fire, as the following teacher's experience indicates:

When I put my name down for the ten schools I put my name down for one school out around——["nice" neighborhood]. I didn't know anything about it, what the principal was like or anything, but it had a short list. Well, I heard later from several people that I had really made a mistake. They had a principal there that was really a terror. She just made it miserable for everyone. . . .

Second, one must not be of an ethnic type or have a personal reputation which will cause the principal to use his power of informal rejection. Though a transferee may be rejected through formal bureaucratic procedure, the principal finds it easier and less embarrassing to get the same result through this method, described by a Negro teacher:

All he's got to do is say, "I don't think you'll be very happy at our school." You take the hint. Because if the principal decides you're going to be unhappy, you will be, don't worry. No question about that. . . .

Finally, one must be patient enough to wait for the transfer to the "right" school to be consummated, not succumbing to the temptation to transfer to a less desirable but more accessible school:

When I got assigned to——[Negro school], for instance, I went right downtown and signed on ten lists in this vicinity. I've lived out here, so I signed for those schools and decided I'd wait ten years if necessary, till I found a vacancy in the vicinity.

The majority of teachers have careers of this type, in which an initial stay in an undesirable "slum" school is followed by manipulation of the transfer system in such a way as to achieve assignment to a more desirable kind of school.

Thirteen of the interviewees, however, had careers of a different type, characterized by a permanent adjustment to the "slum" school situation. These careers were the product of a process of adjustment to the particular work situation, which, while operating in all schools, is seen most clearly where it has such a radical effect on the further development of the career, tying the teacher to a school which would otherwise be considered undesirable. The process begins when the teacher, for any of a number of possible reasons, remains in the undesirable school for a number of years. During this stay changes take place in the teacher and in the character of her relations with other members of the school's social structure which make this unsatisfactory school an easier place in which to work and which change the teacher's view of the benefits to be gained by transferring elsewhere. Under the appropriate circumstances, a person's entire career may be spent in one such school.

During this initial stay changes take place in the teacher's skills and attitudes which ease the discomfort of teaching at the "slum" school. First, she learns new teaching and disciplinary techniques which enable her to deal adequately with "slum" children, although they are not suited for use with other social-class groups. . . .

Further, the teacher learns to revise her expectations with regard to the amount of material she can teach and learns to be satisfied with a smaller accomplishment. . . . She thus acquires a routine of work which is customary, congenial, and predictable to the point that any change would require a drastic change in deep-seated habits.

Finally, she finds herself explanations for actions of the children which she has previously found revolting and immoral, and these explanations allow her to "understand" the behavior of the children as human, rather than as the activity of lunatics or animals. . . .

At the same time that these changes are taking place in the teacher's perspectives, she is also gradually being integrated into the network of social relations that make up the school in such a way as to ease the problems associated with the "slum" school. In the first place, the teacher, during a long stay in a school, comes to be accepted by the other teachers as a trustworthy equal and acquires positions of influence and prestige in the informal colleague structure. These changes make it easier for her to maintain her position of authority vis-à-vis children and principal. Any move from the school would mean a loss of such position and its advantages and the need to win colleague acceptance elsewhere.

Second, the problem of discipline is eased when the teacher's reputation for firmness begins to do the work of maintaining order for her: "I have no trouble with the children. Once you establish a reputation and they know what to expect, they respect you and you have no trouble. Of course, that's different for a new teacher, but when you're established that's no problem at all."

Finally, problems of maintaining one's authority in relation to parents lessen as one comes to be a "fixture" in the community and builds up stable and enduring relationships with its families: "But, as I say, when you've been in that neighborhood as long as I have, everyone knows you, and you've been into half their homes, and there's never any trouble at all."

The "slum" school is thus, if not ideal, at least bearable and predictable for the teacher who has adjusted to it. She has taken the worst the situation has to offer and has learned to get along with it. She is tied to the school by the routine she has developed to suit its requirements and by the relationships she has built up with others in the school organization. These very adjustments cause her, at the same time, to fear a move to any new school, which would necessitate a rebuilding of these relationships and a complete reorganization of her work techniques and routine. The move to a school in a "better" neighborhood is particularly feared, desirable as it seems in the abstract, because the teacher used to the relative freedom of the "slum" school is not sure whether the advantages to be gained in such a move would not be outweighed by the constraint imposed by "interfering" parents and "spoiled" children and by the difficulties to be encountered in integrating into a new school structure. This complete adjustment to a particular work situation thus acts as a brake on further mobility through the system.

Either of these career patterns results, finally, in the teacher's achieving a position in which she is more or less settled in a work environment which she regards as predictable and satisfactory. Once this occurs, her position and career are subject to dangers occasioned by ecological and administrative events which cause radical changes in the incumbents of important positions in the school structure.

Ecological invasion of a neighborhood produces changes in the social-class group from which pupils and parents of a given school are recruited. This, in turn, changes the nature and intensity of the teacher's work problems and upsets the teacher who has been accustomed to working with a higher status group than the one to which she thus falls heir. The total effect is the destruction of what was once a satisfying place in which to work, a position from which no move was intended. . . .

Ecological and demographic processes may likewise create a change in the age structure of a population which causes a decrease in the number of teachers needed in a particular school and a consequent loss of the position in that school for the person last added to the staff. The effect of neighborhood invasion may be to turn the career in the direction of adjustment to the new group, while the change in local age structure may turn the career back to the earlier phase, in which transfer to a "nicer" school was sought.

A satisfactory position may also be changed for the worse by a change in principal through transfer or retirement. The departure of a principal may produce changes of such dimension in the school atmosphere as to force teachers to transfer elsewhere. Where the principal has been a major force upholding the teachers' authority in the face of attacks by children and parents, a change can produce a disastrous increase in the problems of discipline and parental interference. . . . This problem is considered most serious when the change takes place in a "slum" school in which the discipline problem has been kept under control primarily through the efforts of a strict principal. Reactions to such an event, and consequent career development, vary in schools in different social-class areas. Such a change in a "slum" school usually produces an immediate and tremendous increase in teacher turnover. A teacher who had been through such an experience estimated that faculty turnover through transfer rose from almost nothing to 60 per cent or more during the year following the change. Where the change takes place in a "nicer," upper-middle-class school, teachers are reluctant to move and give up their hard-won positions, preferring to take a chance on the qualities of a new incumbent. Only if he is particularly unsatisfying are they likely to transfer.

Another fear is that a change in principals will destroy the existing allocation of privilege and influence among the teachers, the new principal failing to act in terms of the informal understandings of the teachers with regard to these matters. . . . On the other hand, the coming of a new principal may be to the great advantage of and ardently desired by younger, less influential teachers. . . .

Any of these events may affect the career, then, in any of several ways, depending on the state of the career development at the time the event occurs. The effect of any event must be seen in the context of the type of adjustment made by the individual to the institutional organization in which she works.

This paper has demonstrated the existence, among Chicago schoolteachers, of what has been called a "horizontal" plane of career strivings and movements and has traced the kind of career patterns which occur, at this level, in a public bureaucracy where movement is achieved through manipulation of formal procedures. It suggests that studies of other occupations, in which greater emphasis on vertical movement may obscure the presence and effects of such horizontal mobility, might well direct their attention to such phenomena.

53

Touristry: A Type of Occupational Mobility

RUTH H. PAPE

Mrs. Pape's article deals with the motivation behind the changing of organizations, but not the career, and the conditions which foster this kind of mobility.

Every year millions of working Americans are on the move. Summer only brings an increase in the year-round tide of vacationers who travel within the confines of their two, three or four weeks off from the job. Only the very wealthy can maintain a permanent vacationer status, although the retired or unemployed may be able to cover as much territory while bumming around.[1] Besides the vacationers, however, there are travelers who are making more or less permanent migrations in search of a better job, a better climate or a better neighborhood. Some also are following migratory jobs, as in agriculture, or intermittently migratory ones, as with lumbering or construction work. There are even some occupations into which travel is built as a requisite feature, as in the transportation industry, the Foreign Service and the military. But this is hardly voluntary mobility for, when the Navy invites a young man to see the world, the itinerary is hardly of his own choosing.

But there is a group of people who do work, who travel more or less where and when they please, who seem never to have been described or analyzed in the literature of geographic or occupational mobility. Well-known to despairing employment agencies and employers, these people are practicing what I choose to call "touristry," a form of journeying that depends upon occupation, but only in a secondary sense in that it finances the more primary goal, travel itself. Performing a highly-demanded service which is easily documented, either by a transferable license or by relatively simple tests, they are able to spend a longer time at touring than a simple vacation would allow by merely taking a job in the area they wish to sample and keeping it only as long as features unrelated to the job continue to be attractive.

It is this form of mobility that I wish to delineate in this paper. I shall discuss the factors which permit touristry not only within nursing but also in a wider social context. From the structure of nursing, I shall derive general characteristics for the pattern of touristry, apply these against various occupational situations, and try to demonstrate its probability as a future part of certain occupational types, especially among the growing groups of technicians.

Excerpted, with permission, from *Social Problems*, 11(4) (Spring, 1964): 336–44.

[1] Theodore Caplow, "Other Mobilities," *The Sociology of Work* (Minneapolis: University of Minnesota Press, 1954), 88–98.

Certain characteristic conditions for touristry lie outside the specific dimensions of nursing. Work, for example, plays a secondary part in the life expectations of American females despite the growing numbers who work. Although a girl's education may include quite lengthy preparation for a formal occupation, unquestionably her main anticipation is of marriage and the adult role of wife-homemaker-mother. Until this event, however, she must pass the interim in a socially appropriate manner.

Completion of schooling, however prolonged, tends to represent a transition from dependent child to semi-adult. To maintain an otherwise normal offspring in dependent status after this point is not usually possible. Although there may be an interval of job-seeking, it cannot be unduly protracted without increased social pressure. The first "serious" job confirms the transition toward adulthood and the general expectation is that economic and social independence will follow until the time of marriage.

Since marriage is, generally, the prime goal of the young female, any job she holds is seen as only an interim position, not the ideal. As she awaits this prized status, it is expected that she is practicing the business of domesticity as she manages her own miniature household. Many working girls do remain at home but some payment for board and room is generally expected, even if it is of a token nature. Apart from maintaining an appropriately decent level of living, little other responsibility is ordinarily put upon her. In fact, there even seems to be a social mandate to act irresponsibly, to sow the feminine equivalent of wild oats short of grave moral errors that would jeopardize marriage.

Except for maintenance and, perhaps, an occasional obligation to give some financial aid to her family, the new working girl, at least of the middle-class, has great freedom to use her salary as she pleases, usually for those things a dependent child was never given within a family budget. Future need and security do not fit within her life view, so long-term savings or insurance policies are not typical spending objects. Acquisition of home furnishings seems to fall within the aura of marriage or at least settling down and thus is viewed as inappropriate until then. The usual purchases may be characterized as luxury goods and services of a personal nature, such as clothes, cosmetics, a car: all items directed toward social improvement. Any savings would tend to be toward vacations, travel and the larger luxuries, although the self-restraint needed for this is largely mitigated by current credit practices.

TOURISTRY IN NURSING

Historical aspects

Probably from the very start of nursing as a distinct occupation in the United States, there have been some practitioners who realized that, with this skill, it would be possible to travel wherever they wished. Perhaps this was the feminine form of the old-time wanderin' man. Answering the call of alien places has traditionally been viewed as a curse by the solid citizen, but the possibility has been a correlative attribute of nursing for so long that its existence has come to be taken for granted by nurses and those who must employ them. Nurses, in fact, seem never to have viewed this possibility unfavorably and rather consider it one of the definite advantages of their occupation. Others, however, see it from a different perspective. Even as early as 1928, when hospital nursing had hardly become recognized as an occupational entity, vigorous complaints were heard from the proprietors of nursing registries that one of their major and recurrent problems was the "tramp nurse" who was "more a roving spirit and cannot be relied upon," who "stream by, stopping over to work for [a] short time." A physician diagnosed it as a "strange pathological malady—itching foot" from which these early nurses suffered. Even now when professionally committed physicians focus on this pattern as a problem of direct significance, they tend to be irritated, if not shocked and irate, at this unorthodoxy within nursing professionalism.

Present employment conditions

Nurses who wish to travel now have many alluring choices. Air and ship-lines, the Peace Corps, and the armed services all stress exotic foreign service. But for those less willing to submit to the accompanying time restrictions and commitments, there is still the self-planned and self-limited route of touristry. It is true that there are some countries where it is not possible or desirable to work (so that nurses would wish to save for a *bona fide* vacation to go there), but more and more nurses are finding ways to extend their touristry even beyond national boundaries.

That nurses turn their licenses almost directly into travel tickets may be seen in the recruiting advertisements in almost any nursing journal. Beside the usual details of salary, installation description and fringe benefits, may be found frequent references to the local attractions either present or within easy range.[2] Whether these are effective or not, hospitals in metropolitan areas are often largely staffed by nurses who come not only from other locales but other states and countries as well.

For many years it has been common knowledge that there is an almost universal shortage of nurses. Hawaii is presently the only state that does not need, in various stages of desperation, every nurse that can be attracted. California, for example, must recruit roughly 75 percent of its work-force from nurses trained outside the state. It is no wonder then that the process of establishing licensure has been made as efficient and painless as possible, reportedly making it possible for a nurse with sufficient and adequate docu-

---

[2] "Living is Fun in Southern California!" and "(X Hospital) means the center of things and the best of everything for you!... more satisfaction in work and at play than you ever dreamed possible." These appeared as facing ads in *The American Journal of Nursing*, 63 (#6, June, 1963), 146–47.

ments to begin work after only "a few minutes" at the office of the California Board of Nurse Examiners. Even those whose transcripts must be sent for may work in the interim with an easily obtained temporary license. Within nursing, California, along with New York, is noted for having the most stringent requirements for graduate nurses.

Employment, too, has become a simplified process, especially in stress times resulting from great turnover and short staffing. Although two weeks, notice is the polite expectation in leaving any job, nursing directors are only too willing to offer an immediate starting date and often suggest that they cannot really wait for proper notice to be given and fulfilled. Job requirements are also minimized, often demanding no more than proper licensure and the appearance of stamina to do the job. References, when checked, are usually returned with vague, polite phrases unless there has been highly unsatisfactory service. So few nurses write ahead to secure a job that it becomes apparent that staff-level jobs are believed to be always available. And the fact that they are seldom disappointed not only proves the truth of their prediction but also reinforces the high estimation of the widespread shortage of nurses.

Thus it may be seen that one of the permeating characteristics of the nursing job market is the scarcity of practitioners. Among the consequences are expeditious credentialling and the minimizing of requirements for the lowest level positions, which only ease the process of getting a job and, hence, of leaving one.

Touristry and the Nurse

Nursing, as it is taught and officially projected, is supposed to have elements of devotion and dedication with humanitarian and/or professional characteristics. Even though nursing as an occupation has incorporated the mobility factor, recruiting literature tends to assume the existence of a regular career-escalator pattern, even while being forced to acknowledge the vast corps of nonemployed married nurses. Certain of my data suggest that orientation to nursing as a primary focus is tied to the passage of time, and "career-nurses" are only to be found in a higher age bracket as well as in higher administrative and educational echelons than are the newly graduated staff nurses being considered here. The latter, rather, consider their nurse-role as only a part of a more generalized life-pattern, and usually only a very minor part. Thus I am not using the word, career, in its more general sociological sense of temporal and status passage between positions, but to define the orientation the nurses themselves hold to the position that work plays in their overall life expectations. Nonetheless, even a relative lack of emphasis on the work-role can also be viewed as a definite stage within the pattern of nursing, since some older career-oriented nurses recount having passed through or having known of this stage in comparable age groups.

Occupational conditions

Besides being young, more or less occupationally educated and middle-class, the newly graduated nurse finds herself with the added advantage of possessing an eagerly sought trade. Although salaries are generally felt to be disproportionately low to the amount of prior training, the newest graduate is still able to step into a basic hospital staff position at a rate considerably above other beginning jobs for women, especially the unskilled or semi-skilled ones which most take. This salary rate also often ignores a lack of prior experience, maturity or career commitment. Added to this is the widespread knowledge that she will be able to get a job almost anywhere in the country.[3]

This makes it easier for her to indulge in that other luxury that has enjoyed rising popularity with the middle class in proportion to the decline of isolationism, especially since the end of World War II: the exploration of different geography, tourism. Certainly vacation travel has been made increasingly easy with the advent of the "fly-now-pay-later" concept, vacation bank loans and economy plans for trips and tours all over the accessible world. But vacations generally occur within the confines of a job's annual leave system, during a special leave of absence or between positions and are generally predetermined and limited by the funds and time saved for them. But, by setting up a new base of operations, financed by a local job, the young nurse, among others, is able to enjoy the merits of any particular region at her own pace and for just as long as she wishes.

Initiation of the touristry pattern

Although nursing students do not often give it as a reason for going into nursing, possibly the easy transferability of practice may be one of those secondary selling points that draw a large number of travel-minded girls into nursing schools. As graduation approaches, among the growing and sharpening fantasies of goals for the students are the shared dreams of where they will go. The potential tourists become aware of mutual interests and thus may band together to prepare for their trip. At graduation, the girls are restrained only by the need to take and pass their licensing examinations, then to earn enough money to get wherever they plan to go and pay a month's rent when they get there. Whenever this is accomplished, the touristry-bent nurse bursts onto the employment market in earnest, not only ready to leave her childhood status but also her childhood neighborhood, at least as far as the years in the schooling area have made this represent it.

The rates and timing may vary but graduation usually sees a number of newly married girls who have gone directly on with the traditional feminine mode, thus skipping over the interim of independence and irresponsibility.

---

[3] "Where do you go from here? After graduation, almost anywhere you please. So, please keep (X Hospital) in mind." Full page ad in *The American Journal of Nursing*, 63 (6), (June, 1963), 162.

At this stage, few girls plan to remain unmarried, unless they are committed to religious goals, are far older than the usual, or are settled into a pattern of deviance that does not include marriage. Many young graduate nurses report, however, that although they fully expect to marry, it is not part of their immediate plans and they can well imagine working the two years that statistically fall between a girl's coming onto and leaving the labor market for the first time.

These are the girls who say they are not yet ready for marriage, who want to see something else before they settle down, but who are also willing to admit that marriage may come along any moment and change those ideas. These are the nurses who may be seen working in many of our metropolitan hospitals with only a few months' working experience behind them, usually at their training hospital. They have come in groups of two or more, located a furnished apartment, sharing costs and chores, and then gone looking for a job, usually intent on all working together too.

Touristry in operation

What makes them different from workers migrating in search of greener job pastures is that, for them, a job is merely the way to support themselves decently while they see the sights, sample the social life, have a bit of fun and then move on. These nurses do not follow any orientation to work as a central focus of living; their attention is directed to values outside the job environment and they use their work as a means to other, unrelated ends.

Thus the standards they do use in evaluating a job seem unrelated to those used by career oriented nurses or any who would try to apply professional standards. In touristry, pay is naturally the prime consideration since this is the man reason for working at all. Nurses from the East and South are attracted to the higher pay offered in the West without taking into account the comparably higher costs of living there. But pay schedules are fairly standardized within a region and there is no tradition of individual negotiation. Immediately after salary comes a concern with hours. Hospital-scheduling, as for any 24-hour institution, conflicts with the work-day that most of the American public puts in. The lack of predictable days off also interferes with any attempts at long-range planning. Another consideration of high importance, that euphemistically masquerades under the heading of "social opportunities," is the quantity of available young men in the immediate and surrounding areas. One factor that bears most directly on quitting, but also figures in job acceptance, is the strenuousness of the job. There are few nursing jobs nowadays that are routinely exhausting, but these girls insist on enough energy after work to engage in the social activities that are their prime interest. Thus it happens that whenever the turnover of staff becomes exceptionally heavy, a certain portion of those remaining will soon quit because the added work they must do leaves them unable to lead their non-work lives as they would wish.

Termination of touristry

Just as surely as it can prevent touristry, so marriage will put a stop to it as a pattern. The irresponsibility interim of the young girl's life can also be closed by a call to return home to attend to family crises, such as illness or death. Of course, returning home may also mean that the girl, without considering settling down, has found touristry to be unsuitable for her personally. Some find that they are greatly disappointed with what they meet in travel, that things are not so much better than they were at home. Others may rapidly find that they are frankly homesick and were never cut out for touristry.

There are a certain number of working nurses who, with the passage of time and the approach of their thirties, begin to suspect that marriage may not be as inevitable as they had expected at twenty-two. Among other reactions may well be the appearance of concern for an occupational future and such attendant factors as advancement and security. These nurses may travel again, but their moves are then more likely to have a direct relation to the more classical forms of work oriented mobility.

The "permanent" tourist

A very few nurses may find travel so entrancing that they will continue it even as a prime pattern. In my sample group, there were two staff nurses who realized that they were fairly well past the age of inevitable marriage, who had considered settling into a career commitment pattern but had given this up. One had already applied to the U.S. Foreign Service and was only awaiting acceptance before quitting. The other had only vague ideas of when and where she would be next but characterized herself as "one of the movers." Both fantasized the ideal husband as one whose job required extensive travel. Although neither were actually settled into an orientation toward future security, there is probably a point where it is simpler and less risky to combine touristry with occupation in one of those fields or agencies where travel is a necessary characteristic.

Consequences for the employer

Nurses afflicted with touristry have various effects upon their employing agencies. They add, of course, to the turnover problem which seems to plague the metropolitan areas especially. Although they may depart at any time during the year, it may be that the onset of summer brings "itching feet" into a full blown rash. Talk of travel among the departing tourists seems to stir longings to join the migrant flock, sometimes even sooner than the girl herself had planned.

Many nursing directors have learned not to assign the members of one household to a single service or even a single shift. Some directors, if they have any choice, even prefer not to hire more than one member of such a group. From hard experience they have learned that there is, indeed, a flock phenomenon and a single decision to move on could strip a service of much of its staff. Sometimes these preliminary precautions are not enough, for the touristry group often changes its configuration; one roommate may drop out of the pattern and be replaced by a new member locally recruited, often from among co-workers on the unit.

Problems may arise when the touristry oriented nurse must be dealt with by nursing directors and supervisors who, at this stage in their lives, have assumed a career commitment. Those of the latter who are perturbed by high staff turnover rates may try to find a solution within their own perspective without realizing that factors in the work situation are usually irrelevant to the tourist's decision to quit. Thus the nursing office may strive to adjust the work load or the constitution of the ward. Attempts may be made to institute social gatherings among the staff nurses of the entire hospital without realizing that it is not more female company these young women are seeking.

It is possible, however, that these seem plausible corrections when the reasons given at the time of resignation are used as the basis for planning. Although the touristry pattern is well known, it is not viewed as truly legitimate and more socially acceptable reasons are usually given. Then too, the young nurses may not be wholly aware of how the lures of touristry operate to make their current job seem suddenly so dissatisfying.

However, it is apparent from talking with those who must hire young nurses, that touristry is an expected factor and personnel directors, although hardly happy about it, are simply resigned to it as a pattern of work. In fact, they sometimes entertain the wistful hope that theirs will be the institution in which these young nurses finally decide to settle down.

DISCUSSION: TOURISTRY AND TECHNICIANS

Up to this point, we have been considering touristry as it appears in one specific group, nurses, who represent the model *par excellence* of touristry. I would like now to apply this pattern onto various other occupations to illustrate what factors operate to restrain and permit this as a way of life for others, as well as suggest where further expansion of touristry could be expected.

Touristry is not generally possible within the traditional professions or the occupations that follow their structure. Jobs which depend on a personal clientele or reputation demand time, concentration and stability. And even though teachers step into ready-made school classes, they are bound by contracts and their notorious traveling must occur during vacations.

As for the job scarcity factor, the U.S. Bureau of Labor Statistics reports that currently the jobs in electronic engineering, physics and chemistry are most difficult to fill. But these are male occupations and are most frequently linked, like those in universities, to the more usual career-making, and touristry would interfere with advancement. The Bureau spokesman confirmed this by noting that, even though these applicants may pick their own geographical location to begin with, they somehow do not move around as would happen in touristry.

However, there are occupational groups other than nurses for whom touristry is possible and whose employers are beginning to complain of their transiency. Within the health professions, medical technologists, X-ray technicians and dental hygienists have already made reputations as migrants. The Bureau of Labor Statistics also added that stenographers are in such short supply that they can and do travel anywhere they wish with the assurance that a job will be waiting for them.

There are even certain jobs open for men who would pursue a touristry pattern at the expense of job advancement or marriage. Journeyman-printers can support themselves in traveling wherever unionization and scarcity assure them jobs. Groups of homosexual males are reportedly utilizing the still scarce occupation of data processor to tour around their specialized circuits.[4]

Far from presenting a solution to this "problem," I would suggest that touristry will not only increase but will also spread to other occupational groups. The fantastic proliferation and expansion of the sciences and professions in recent decades have created a special and relatively new category of worker, the technician, whom I wish now to consider. According to the U.S. Department of Labor, technicians can be defined as "skilled workers with training beyond the high school level, but not usually with a college degree. . . . Most technicians have some theoretical knowledge of their specialization, together with an understanding of the practical application of the theory."

For example, medical advancement and specialization have so complicated individual practice that physicians have been forced to relinquish many tasks to subordinate or technical personnel. Eventually new occupational groups have become formalized around a set of tasks and strive to establish requirements for admission to this status. Medical technicians have well established task training programs which are progressing toward an academic orientation. They have also started a move toward licensure, at least in California. However, it is still possible for an informally trained person to qualify for licensure and it is also possible for an unlicensed technician to work, even though some hospitals have set licensure as a criterion for employment. It is clear that this group has some feelings of cohesion but still has no clear mandate to define their own territory.[5]

For many reasons, the actual numbers of either technicians or women working as technicians is unknown, but all predictions point to marked

[4] Little material is available on current activity in "Hobohemia" that was so thoroughly studied in the past. Surely many factors have acted to diminish the number of old-style vagrants and bums, but I cannot imagine that unemployed travel has completely vanished.

[5] E. C. Hughes, "License and Mandate," *Men and Their Work* (Glencoe, Ill.: The Free Press, 1958), 78–87.

increases of both. Certain Civil Service classifications, excluding the health and biological sciences, showed greater concentration of women technicians than others, ranging "from 2 percent of the engineering aides to 75 percent of the mathematical aides." Whenever these specializations become standardized, it is likely that some will be categorized as "women's jobs." There is already a tendency to consider some areas in the electronic and chemical laboratories, for instance, as particularly suitable for women. A government report on the biological sciences reports that, "in fact, women are often preferred as supporting personnel to higher scientists because of their careful handling of detail and their patience, dexterity, and reliability."

As the prerequisite training moves away from plant experience into junior and community college curricula, larger numbers of young, middle-class girls will be influenced to prepare themselves for such technical positions. The pressures that have created these jobs will undoubtedly increase so that various qualified technicians will be at a premium for a long time. This sets up all the necessities for a seller's market within which touristry can flourish.

54

Compliance Specialization and Executive Mobility

AMITAI ETZIONI

Changing both organization and type of organizational career may, on the face of it, seem a sharp change for a person. But Professor Etzioni shows that, if the underlying organizational dimensions, such as compliance structures, are similar, the change may not be a dramatic one.

To underscore further the significance of the differences in compliance which distinguish organizations from one another and separate subunits within organizations, we examine the effect of shifting from one compliance type to another on a central organizational process, namely that of executive mobility.

EXECUTIVES AS COMPLIANCE SPECIALISTS

We began this chapter with a review of three approaches to the study of control specialization. Applied to the study of intra-organizational and inter-organizational mobility of executives, the following three alternative propositions can be formulated:

(a) An executive will be most effective if he holds positions in which the same or similar types of performance are supervised, and the same basic knowledge and skills are required. Division of labor and technology are believed to determine the scope of effective horizontal mobility. . . .

(b) An executive controls people, and since this is the basis of all organizational control, effective horizontal mobility is virtually unlimited. Dubin represents this alternative position. He asserts:

. . . Inevitably, every executive and administrator gets "minded" in accordance with the values of the organization for which he works. I submit, however, that the *educated executive is one who can operate effectively in different kinds of organizations having different values and objectives.* . . .

The "universal" approach to the functions and characteristics of executives is clearly dominant in the literature. Barnard studies the functions of *the* executive, just as students of organization, we saw earlier, study *the* bureaucracy, not particular types. Lists of qualities of executives are typically lists of qualities every person should be blessed with (such as capacity, knowledge, courage, "quality") and those required of every officer (effective use of time, perspective, judgment, self-control) or leader (personal power, sensitivity). . . .

Excerpted, with permission, from *Complex Organizations* (New York: Free Press of Glencoe, 1961; pp. 271–77).

Some exponents of the universal approach imply that profit-making organizations supply a model for the administration of all types of organizations. Business methods and business personnel are seen as best fitted to run any organization, whether a school, a hospital, a church, or a community chest. . . .

Ministers frequently complain about the lack of insight into the differences between a church and a business which businessmen reveal when they assume that every organization can be run in basically the same way—their way. . . .

The high representation of business leaders and the low representation of labor leaders on the boards of hospitals, schools, colleges, universities, voluntary associations, and other nonutilitarian organizations in the United States reflects in part the political reality of the communities in which these organizations operate and which they serve. But to some degree it also reflects the assumption that every organization can be run like a business.

(*c*) Our position is that the effectiveness of the mobile executive is limited to compliance areas rather than administrative or technological boundaries. As long as mobility takes place between positions in organizational units or organizations which have a similar compliance structure, we would expect comparatively little loss of effectiveness. If, on the other hand, mobility requires transfer from one kind of compliance structure to another, considerable changes in behavior, orientation, or effectiveness of the executive are to be expected. An executive who was highly effective in running a steel mill may be quite ineffective in running a professional organization, such as an engineering firm, and an executive who was quite ineffective in running a steel mill may prove to be just the man for the engineering position. Many officers who are quite effective in running production will do much less well in running a public relations department.

Since we did not find any data directly bearing upon our proposition, we attempted to collect some of it. The names of thirty-two members of organizational elites who had previously held positions in military organizations, were picked at random from daily newspapers. Their military positions were classified as "combat" or "desk" positions. Their subsequent civil positions were classified as "externalists" or "instrumentalists." "Externalist" positions require handling external relations of the organization, such as public relations, labor relations, and serving as contact man in Washington; they also include the top positions in universities and voluntary associations provided the main task is external (e.g., raising funds). "Instrumentalist" positions include only direct administration of production and expert staff positions in production, finance, marketing, and the like.

Combat posts, we suggest, require more normative power than desk posts, and externalist roles require more normative power than instrumental roles. Hence we expected that military commanders who had made their career and gained their reputation mainly as combat leaders would be more likely to become externalists than instrumentalists, and that military leaders who had mainly desk posts would be more likely to become instrumentalists than externalists. Note that unlike most studies of inter-organizational mobility from one type of organization to another, we examined mobility from one type of *sub*organization to the *same* analytical subunit in *another type* of organization. This enables us to control for compliance differences in each organizational type.

MOBILITY FROM MILITARY TO CIVILIAN POSITIONS

Past Military Posts	Present Civilian Posts	
	Externalists (*High Normative*)	*Instrumentalists* (*Low Normative*)
Combat (High Normative)	11	1
Desk (Low Normative)	4	8

Of the 32 persons, 24 were classified as either externalists or instrumentalists in their present position, and as either combat leaders or predominantly desk men in terms of their military career and source of reputation. As Table 1 shows, those who held combat positions were much more likely to hold externalist rather than instrumental civilian positions. This finding is in line with our hypothesis, since combat and externalist positions have similar compliance requirements; both require more normative power than desk and instrumentalist positions, which give comparatively less weight to normative controls and greater weight to utilitarian controls. As we would expect, then, those who had a desk position in their military career were twice as likely as combat officers to hold a less normative, more utilitarian position in their civilian career. Five had such a mixed military career that they were classified as "compound" types. All of these five also had a compound civilian career—that is, they moved back and forth between instrumentalist and externalist positions in civilian life. These cases also support our hypothesis concerning the relationship between compliance specialization and mobility: Less specialized actors are better able, both in the military and the civilian domain, to move from one compliance structure to another. For three cases the post-military career could not be determined with sufficient precision to allow classification. This limited material seems to illustrate our hypothesis and to lend to it some support. . . .

In sum, the first approach we have described sees executives as "specialists," the second as "generalists" in knowledge about a particular type of organizational output. We suggest that most top executives are generalists in the performances they can supervise, but specialists in the type of compliance they utilize in doing so. In other words, it seems to us that *most executives are more effective in one type of compliance structure than in the other two.* It may be true that all executive positions require the ability to work "through" people, but there are different ways of doing that—differences in the appeals which can be made to lower participants, and in the sanctions which can be applied to them.

Compliance specialization of executives is less apparent than performance specialization, in part because there are only three common types of compliance structure while there are many hundreds of performance specializations. An executive can move among positions and cross many administrative boundaries without changing to a different *type* of compliance structure. In this sense the specialization of control agents, of executives, is broader— permits more horizontal mobility without loss of effectiveness—than does the performance specialization of skilled workers and experts.

55

Security and Alternative Career Possibilities in Other Organizations

HAROLD L. WILENSKY

Changing one's career within an organization may be an advantage, offered by a large organization, that becomes part of a person's career plans. But Professor Wilensky shows that it is also a function of the alternatives the person may have for moving to new organizations.

The final paradox in the process of building confidence concerns the matter of loyalty and the expert's dependence on the boss. Personal loyalty to the boss is an imperative of survival for all the experts. In those experts who do not achieve an inner circle role, this imperative often makes for a "yes-man" mentality rooted in complete dependence on the boss for security and prestige. The really successful experts, however, are those who have not only demonstrated their loyalty, but have maintained enough independence to permit disagreement and objectivity. The components of this independence are complex. In part it consists of the mere weight of inside information: "He's taken me into his confidence so much," said one expert, "he's told me so many of his dreams, plans, his opinions of everyone—that he simply can't push me around too much. Besides, I tell him off." Inside knowledge is a help, but in the absence of some solid sense of security, the expert is not likely to "tell the boss off" so easily. For inside knowledge becomes relatively harmless if, by getting fired, the expert is removed from the political process.

SECURITY AND THE EXPERT'S DEPENDENCE ON THE BOSS

An expert's sense of security in an organization with no system of tenure, such as a union, is in part dependent upon his alternative employment opportunities, the replaceability of his skills, and his "connections" or "base" in or out of the organization. If these objective factors contribute to a sense of security, and if a sense of security is related to influence, we would expect the High Influence experts to be in a favorable market position.

A few of the High Influence experts (and several of the important ex-experts) clearly have acquired a "base"—a political following within the organization that could be mobilized in support of their continued service. Frequently, the rank-and-file base of the High Influence expert rests either on (1) his job functions; or (2) his political affiliation with a party or faction with strength in the union.

Excerpted, with permission, from *Intellectuals in Labor Unions* (New York: Free Press of Glencoe, 1956; pp. 226–30).

As for "connections" outside the union and replaceability of skills, there are two statistical clues to their relation to influence. The first is the predominance of Contact Men among those who rate high on influence. The second rough clue is in the data on how the experts got their first union jobs. The number using job-getting methods which involve outside contacts increases in direct proportion to increases in influence ratings. About three-eighths of those rated Low on influence, one-half of those rated Medium, and three-fifths of those rated High had government, business, newspaper, independent consultant, or labor relations specialist contacts who helped them to get their union jobs.

Finally, there is the question of alternative employment opportunities. Mobility-wise, many of the experts are locked up in the labor movement. Limited data on what became of 112 predecessors of the incumbents studied, suggest that it has not in the past been easy to move directly from a union to industry, business, universities, or commercial publications. Almost half of the predecessors died on the job, retired, or moved to another labor job. Many of those in private consulting depend in good part on a union clientele; several of those who went to government and elsewhere have jobs which are filled by union nominees or which depend on Labor support. The engineers, lawyers, and pension experts find it easiest to move on to jobs in no way dependent upon Labor.

Assuming there is a lack of alternative nonlabor job possibilities, how would this be reflected in the mentality of the staff expert? A typical comment illustrates the sense of insecurity of many (in both stable and unstable unions).

> You become labeled as a union [expert], a union partisan. Your flexibility does decline. Your skills become bound up with the particular organization you're attached to and the range of alternative job possibilities narrows. . . . Hell, you never know what the future holds. I could get the axe next year.

The sense of insecurity this respondent feels might continue, even if there were considerable chance to move into the nonunion world at comparable salaries in similar jobs. In fact, there is some evidence that the present incumbents do have plenty of opportunity to sever the labor tie. Data show that the staff experts in the Main Sample have received a large number of industry-business and government job offers. Many of the experts are evidently confined to the labor movement by a self-imposed rule. They find the prospect of cutting themselves off from the labor movement distasteful; the offers from industry, business, nonlabor consultant firms, government agencies, etc., are unacceptable. A few cases—especially among the Missionaries and Program Professionals—not only do not see any job outside the labor movement (save going into a plant, or back to college), but they also cannot see working for any union but the one they are in.

In terms of this analysis of alternative job chances as a factor in expert influence, what is significant is the picture of who admits to no job offers at all. Only one in sixteen High Influence cases admits he has had no job offers since he has been working for a union, but six in twenty-one of the Medium Influence cases and twenty-five in seventy-two (over a third) of the Low Influence cases so indicate. The proportion of all cases in the Main Sample who specify receipt of at least one job offer goes up as influence ratings go up —from about 57 per cent of the Lows to 71 per cent of the Highs.

Why this should be so is suggested in several interview comments. A staff expert describes a very High Influence colleague's opening speech to the Board as "a masterpiece":

> He said, "I want it clearly understood that I'm in a position to leave any time I want to." . . . He said, "You are my client and I'm your lawyer and I'm here to serve you in that capacity."

The expert who made this speech—a Professional Service type—explains his conviction:

> The greater degree of independence a top man can feel the better—he can speak up and offer his honest independent judgment. There's much too little of that. Staff people are too dependent on their jobs. The ideal situation is where you have staff people who know they're wanted and are in demand. They can then have security and be independent. Too great a dependence on the officer affects your judgment—no question about it.

Lack of acceptable alternatives, both cause and consequence of long immersion in a particular organization, appears to account for the middling influence (as well as middling salaries) of some old-timers of the "right" functional type (Contact Man), whose demonstrated loyalty is unquestioned. They have some security; they've become "fixtures around the place." But they are still very dependent upon the boss. One said:

> I could go to work for the X industry tomorrow . . . for twice as much as I make here. But my heart wouldn't be in it at all. . . . I've been offered jobs with the industry. But when you've got a comfortable spot it's hard to move. I suppose it may affect your willingness to stick your neck out. . . .

56

Internship Appointments of Medical Students

WILLIAM A. GLASER

If a move between organizations is the result of a well-calculated career plan, adjusting to the new organization is likely to be a welcome challenge. Professor Glaser also presents a very useful scheme for analyzing the process of moving between organizations as a career plan.

Within an occupation people move in a patterned series between jobs and between locations. Many of these status sequences result in work with increased responsibility, authority, and technical complexity. In the professions which are based on very complex knowledge and whose grave responsibilities can be entrusted only to expert practitioners, aspirants must first pass through a series of increasingly demanding educational organizations before they are permitted to enter the statuses reserved for those who are fully qualified. Recently occupational sociologists have begun to identify some of the alternative career lines to be found within any occupation or profession. This paper attempts to carry forward this work by showing how certain combinations of conditions in the occupational structure itself govern the movement of one type of person along one career line, while another type of person follows a different career line.

This paper discusses the process by which personnel flow from one status to the next in an organized occupational system. First, we set forth a simple accounting scheme describing the conditions determining the particular move occurring in any such status sequence. Second, we present data showing some of the conditions that determine the movement of personnel in the medical profession from the student status to the status following.

ACCOUNTING SCHEME EXPLAINING THE FLOW OF PERSONNEL BETWEEN STATUSES

When occupants of one status move to another, the latter is acquired either by achievement or by ascription, and usually from among alternatives. When movement is voluntary, some kind of decision is made, but the action is not the simple outcome of one determining condition. A complete explanation of the decision process would cover such factors as the actor's knowledge about his present and future needs and opportunities, his motivations and capacities, the influences affecting him, and the actual opportunities and barriers confronting him. If certain kinds of information, motivations,

Excerpted, with permission, from *Administrative Science Quarterly*, 4(3) (December, 1959): 337–54.

influences, and opportunities tend to occur simultaneously, and if they repeatedly bring about sequences between a particular pair of statuses, then the sociologist has succeeded in identifying certain organized channels governing the flow of personnel within the social structure under study.

When attempting to gather sufficiently complete data about an action with many dimensions and to explain the reasons for the action, one should be guided by an accounting scheme.[1] Following is a simple accounting scheme that indicates the relevant aspects of the voluntary movement from one status to another:

1. *Information:* What does the actor know about the opportunities available for achieving his goals in his current status? Which of the possible destinations does he know about? How complete and accurate is his information?

2. *Characteristics of the actor:* (*a*) *Motivations.* What are the goals he seeks to achieve either in his current status or in some alternative status? What immediate gratifications does he expect, and what gains does he foresee as promoting realization of his long-range plans? (*b*) *Capacities and handicaps:* Which of his characteristics will help or hinder him in fulfilling the role expectations in each of the statuses available to him?

3. *Influences upon the actor:* What persons and impersonal media are directing influences upon the actor for or against departure from his current status and for or against entry into other possible statuses? What sanctions can they exercise upon the actor to support their influence?

4. *Ease of entry into the possible statuses of destination:* Among the statuses which the actor might enter, are some scarce while others equal or exceed the numbers of aspirants? Does entry into certain statuses require special qualifications or assistance by influential superiors?

THE PASSAGE FROM MEDICAL SCHOOL TO INTERNSHIP

To demonstrate the uses of the foregoing accounting scheme, we have investigated the status sequence from medical student to hospital intern. This transition is one of the important sequences in the training and movement of personnel in the medical profession. Selection of a particular kind of internship and a particular hospital has life-long consequences for the career of the individual physician[2] and great functional significance for the profession.

The internship is a one-year postgraduate period, spent training in a hospital after graduation from a medical school. Internships in American

---

[1] For explanations and illustrations of the use of accounting schemes or paradigms in research, see Paul F. Lazarsfeld and Morris Rosenberg (eds.), *The Language of Social Research* (Glencoe, Ill.: 1955), sec. v; Robert K. Merton, *Social Theory and Social Structure* (2nd ed.; Glencoe, Ill.: 1957), 13–16, 50–55, 460–61; and the sources listed in Charles Kadushin, "Individual Decisions to Undertake Psychotherapy," *Administrative Science Quarterly*, 3 (December, 1958), 383 n. 5.

[2] Oswald Hall, "The Stages of a Medical Career," *The American Journal of Sociology*, 58 (March, 1958), 329–32; "Types of Medical Careers," *ibid.*, 55 (November, 1959), 246–50.

hospitals are taken by nearly all alumni of American medical schools and by many graduates of foreign medical schools. The training consists of in-service clinical work in the hospital, supplemented by some didactic instruction. After internship the young physician may take further postgraduate training in the form of a hospital residency, or he may enter general practice.

Selection of an internship requires two major decisions. First the medical student elects either a rotating, straight (hereafter called specialized), or mixed internship—except in a few states, where only a rotating internship is acceptable for licensing. A rotating assignment involves spending brief periods of time on each of several services in the hospital; whereas a specialized internship is spent on one clinical service throughout the year. A mixed internship involves long periods of time on a few services. The medical student's other major decision is to list hospitals, showing priorities, where he would like to spend his internship. From this list, his actual assignment is made through the procedures of the National Intern-matching Program.

This paper will examine the choice between rotating and specialized internships, since the alternatives represent distinct status sequences from the common starting point in medical school, and present two different kinds of training that may lead into different career lines. Generally this choice lacks some of the complexities specified in our accounting scheme. For example, while differential knowledge about available opportunities may affect choice during their careers, usually senior medical students have already learned all they need to know about the nature of rotating and specialized internships. While barriers restrict entry into many statuses, rotating internships are easily available and a specialized internship usually can be secured by anyone urgently wanting one. For many other kinds of status sequence, an elaborate decision analysis is needed to identify the motivations and influences involved, but the analysis of motivations and influences in the student-intern sequence is greatly simplified because some of the decisions are virtually automatic. After successfully completing the four-year medical school course, the student automatically graduates; by law or by custom all American physicians take an internship; consequently the only problematic decision is the type of internship chosen.

The data were gathered from all members of the three most recent graduating classes at one medical school by administering questionnaires to the students at the end of each one of their four years in medical school. The responses used in this paper were given at the end of the fourth year, shortly after their internship appointments were announced. This paper correlates these responses with the actual assignments. The type of internship a medical student receives is nearly always the kind he requested, but some fail to get assigned to the kind of *hospital* they preferred. Our correlations between fourth-year questionnaire responses and postgraduate appointments resemble the correlations between questionnaire answers in earlier years and the internship *plans* which the same medical students expressed at those times.

MOTIVATIONS AND CAPACITIES OF THE MEDICAL STUDENT

Career Plans

Because the internship is one stage in a long-range chain of statuses, the medical student's choice is determined in part by the expectations and career plans he developed during his undergraduate medical education. Some medical students plan to become specialists, while others expect to become general practitioners. Among these same students, the plans of some are definite, while those of others are tentative and subject to change.

As postgraduate training, rotating and specialized internships would seem to possess different attractions and benefits to medical students according to the direction and certainty of their plans. A rotating internship gives a varied training which can prepare the individual for different kinds of practice and permits explorations of the various fields; a specialized or mixed internship focuses narrowly on one or a few fields. Internship appointments are related to ultimate career plans in the expected way. Those planning to enter general practice tend to take rotating internships. Among those planning for a more specialized practice, the less certain the plans are, the higher is the proportion of rotating internships.

When career plans are specified more exactly, expectations or preferences ultimately directing the medical student's career toward specialization or academic medicine also bring about high rates of specialized internships. Plans to enter medical school teaching or research are regularly associated with selection of specialized internships; rejection of such work is correlated with rotating appointments. In addition, if the student expects to locate his office in a medical school, he tends to choose a specialized internship, whereas those who foresee practice in a group clinic tend to choose rotating appointments.

Since choice of internship correlates with the medical student's ultimate conception of his practice, it is also closely related to the intervening statuses leading to his destination. For example, the type of internship selected depends in part on whether or not the medical student expects to continue his postgraduate education in the form of a hospital residency. Plans to enter general practice immediately after the internship are strongly correlated with the choice of rotating appointments. Because a rotating assignment gives the intern a series of brief experiences in all the important services of a hospital, it is a good rehearsal for the varied patient problems that the general practitioner encounters. Among those who intend to take a residency, those less certain about this stage (and therefore considering possible immediate entry into general practice) take the more flexible rotating assignments more often than their classmates whose residency plans are definitely fixed. Since a residency is specialized training usually leading to specialty practice, students who are very certain of taking a residency have the highest frequency for taking the specialized internships. . . .

For interning, the specific field chosen depends on the area in which the medical student expects subsequently to take his residency. (Some of our other research shows that residency field, in turn, is a rehearsal for the next and final step in the sequence, that of actual practice in some special field.) . . .

When no such specialized internship is available in a field, its future practitioners secure appointments in related or more general medical areas. For example, half of the twelve future psychiatrists secured medical internships.

While most specialized internships tend to be selected only by future specialists in the field, this is not true of the medical internships. Half the medical internships are secured by students planning to continue work in internal medicine during their residencies, but half are chosen by those planning to concentrate in other fields. Elsewhere we have found that tentative choice of internal medicine plays an important part in the crystallization of the undergraduate medical student's career plans while he is still in medical school; similarly, a medical internship (like a rotating internship) functions not only as a preparation for concentration in internal medicine, but serves also as a switching point into other specialized fields of practice.

According to the data, certain typical sequences exist between internships and residencies. The two most all-embracing programs—a rotating internship and a residency in internal medicine—tend to follow each other. A medical internship precedes a residency either in internal medicine or in some other specialty. A specialized internship in any other field is usually followed by a residency in that same field. The principal sequences are summarized in Table 1.

PRINCIPAL SEQUENCES BETWEEN INTERNSHIP AND RESIDENCY

Internship	*Residency*
Rotating	⎧ Internal medicine ⎨ Field other than internal medicine ⎩ None, i.e., general practice
Medical	⎰ Internal medicine ⎱ Field other than internal medicine
Surgical	Surgery
Pediatrics	Pediatrics

Incorporation of the values of the medical profession

. . . Previous research tentatively suggests that specialized internships have higher prestige within the medical profession than rotating assignments. A specialized internship shows an early and firm intention to specialize, and specialization best embodies the medical profession's goals of expert command over advanced knowledge and skills. Faculty members in medical schools value specialization highly; they sometimes define specialized internships as the desirable first step, and they often encourage favored students to follow career lines directed toward specialization. Consequently, the more strongly a medical student has internalized the values of the profession, the more likely he will be motivated to select a specialized internship, the more likely he will be exposed to faculty influence, and the more likely he will be to get faculty recommendations to support his application for such a scarce and highly prized appointment.

Capacities and handicaps

Rotating and specialized internships are statuses which present different benefits, deprivations, and risks to the medical student. A rotating internship is a flexible program which can be the stepping stone to a wide choice of career lines, including immediate entry into general practice or continuation of training in a specialty. Usually it is readily available at those hospitals which pay large salaries to their resident staffs—although, of course, this is not true of every rotating internship. A specialized internship is often the first stage of many years of specialized training, perhaps all of them spent on the resident staffs of famous teaching hospitals carrying high professional prestige but paying low salaries.

The need to maintain flexibility in career planning, capacity to postpone entry into private practice, and financial status are variables which govern the kind of internship the medical student elects. If he is young, single, financially secure, and thus able to commit himself to many years of low-paid post-graduate education, he selects a specialized internship more frequently than do his classmates. But if he is older than his fellow students, head of a family, financially insecure, and thus not sure that he can risk an early commitment to a long period of specialty training, he takes a rotating internship.

INFLUENCES UPON THE MEDICAL STUDENT

So far we have concentrated on one aspect of the decision process; namely, some of the important predispositions which determine entry into one or another kind of internship. In a full explanation another dimension is the influence upon the medical student of his personal associates and other sources.

The data available do not permit a complete reconstruction of all the relevant influences affecting the choice of internship, but the questionnaires do permit inferences about the influence which may be the most important one—the medical school faculty. When medical students seek advice about career plans and other professional problems, they rely upon the faculty for advice more often than upon other sources. . . .

The type of internship the medical student receives is related to the type of faculty member upon whom he relies for guidance. Such a result is related to the inclusion in the faculty of physicians exemplifying different kinds of practice and different career lines. The full-time faculty member is usually a specialist in one of the basic sciences or in a field of clinical medicine, and sometimes he is a nationally recognized authority. The part-time faculty member spends most of his time in private practice in the community, usually his practice is more varied than that of the full-time faculty member; sometimes he is a general practitioner, and sometimes his personal and professional values and goals differ from those of the full-time faculty member. If a medical student is oriented primarily to the influence of the full-time faculty he is more likely to secure a specialized internship, but if he is oriented primarily toward the part-time faculty usually he will secure a rotating assignment. Among students who give equal ratings to both types of staff members equally, a strong dependence upon the full-time staff will produce a slightly lower rate of rotating assignments than occurs when such reliance is weak.

EASE OF ENTRY INTO TYPES OF INTERNSHIP

For many status sequences the flow of personnel into new statuses is fundamentally affected by whether the opportunities are scarce or plentiful, whether special qualifications must be met, whether personal influence is needed, and so forth. Such barriers restrict medical students' entry into the limited number of appointments at the high-prestige eastern teaching hospitals; and at the same time the shortage of applicants with respect to openings makes entry very easy into the many hospitals with less prestige. The barriers are much fewer for these types of internship. Usually a rotating or a specialized appointment can be secured somewhere, and the medical student's principal maneuvering to anticipate, avoid, and overcome barriers concerns his choice of hospital.

In a few cases, however, the appointment to a type of internship may be affected by whether this type is scarce or plentiful at the hospital where the young physician succeeds in securing his appointment. For them the opportunity for an unplanned change in status sequence may have appeared. Once they gained entrance to a teaching hospital, they may have seen that specialized appointments are easily available in such organizations. . . .

Most medical students receive the kind of appointment they expected. Among those who do not, changes in hospital exceed changes in type of internship, a plausible result in view of the barriers which restrict chances of appointment to the most desirable hospitals.

Part IX

Executive and Worker
Career Patterns

Career pattern is a broad general category which describes a person's career or a type of career. In our case, a career pattern occurs within an organizational structure which sets limits to its requirements and is a partial determinant of it. Organizational career patterns may be contrasted to the general notion of occupational career patterns, which may or may not be organizationally bound for periods of time. Much of what we have discussed in the previous eight introductions provides the elements of organizational career patterns. These elements may be brought together under two dimensions of career patterns—shape and time. Further, we have presented in this section articles on executive and worker career patterns which are usually considered in writings as "extremes" of a range or as "very" different. In comparing them on the various elements of shape and time, the reader will see that these patterns can be quite similar in many respects, even if different on the level of social prestige with which each is generally held. Indeed, some variations within types of executive or worker career patterns may be far greater than between them.

The shape of an organizational career pattern can be described by two properties—length and direction. Length refers to where it begins and where it ends on the organizational hierarchy, and how many positions there are in between terminals. Length, then, specifies the type of career hierarchy involved and the sector of the organizational hierarchy the length covers. Thus, for example, some organizational careers of manual workers (Harper and Emmert, Blauner, Chinoy in Part III) have only one or perhaps two positions and are at the bottom of the organizational hierarchy, such as auto, postal, and textile worker careers. However, some manual careers, such as chemical workers, may have an elaborate set of positions to advance through, as many executive patterns have. However, it is usual to find that the higher up on the organizational hierarchy, the more the number of positions in a career pattern.

Where the career begins in the organization depends on the tributaries to recruitment (Mills), such as education, friendships, experience, apprenticeship, and so forth, as well as processes of recruitment. Where it ends depends on its ceiling within the organizational hierarchy and retirement requirements. From the point of view of the person terminating his career passage, ending a career pattern depends on his capabilities and age, and the various factors we have discussed which account for promotion and demotion. Ending an organizational career is a dimension upon which we have no body of focused research or theory; otherwise it would have been an important topic to include as a section in this reader. Like recruitment, and movement within the career, it is necessary to study the organizational processes and conditions of terminating or retiring from a career. Our discussion of demotion and dismissal touches only a few properties of ending a career.

The second property needed to describe the shape of an organizational career pattern is the direction of its movement. Demotion, simotion, and promotion combine to generate a career pattern. These movements may account for several shapes in direction of movement, besides the classic image of a direct line up to the ceiling of the pattern. There may be reversals in direction when the career "peaks out" and moves down. There may be repeatable movements as a career goes up and down with promotions and demotions. There may be plateaus accounted for by horizontal mobility. The shape may have a tree image, when at critical points alternative career lines may be equally well chosen. The direction of movement may be not to the top but away from the organization to private practice (Strauss and Cohen).

The shape of a career pattern may be prescribed and standardized by the organization, thus providing members a clear, concrete image of the path to success (Janowitz). However, the same organization, along with these conventional careers, may also allow unconventionally shaped careers which are developed out of the adaptive capacities of persons molding a new form of career for themselves. These adaptive career patterns, it would appear from the Janowitz and Mills articles, are developed by people who are determined to reach top leadership and who, in their self-made quest and by the sponsorship of other top leaders, jump over many of the conventional positions. The two main sources of prescribed career patterns are the organization's type of work or production and the requisit division of labor. Adaptive career patterns tend to ignore the requirements of these sources.

To graph an organizational career pattern one needs to know, besides the length and direction of its shape, the temporal aspects of its movement. These aspects include length of time in a position, rate of advancement between positions, duration of the whole career to various retirement points and transitional periods such as schooling, temporary positions, or coasting through preparatory jobs. Transitional periods are provided for by transitional statuses which structurally block out a portion of time for the person. For example, training periods provide a "student's" status, or temporary positions provide an "acting" status.[1]

Temporal aspects of career patterns may be handled in many ways by the organization. They may vary on the degree they are routine and scheduled as we have seen in promotion. They may vary on the degree they are well ordered so that the movement of one person through a career pattern is temporally articulated with the movement of another person at a different stage of the same career. The interdependence of personal careers within the same pattern, when temporally articulated, will not be likely to disrupt the organization, as we saw in the discussion on succession. Temporal movements, such as advancement, demotion, or retirements may be formally, privately, or secretly announced, or never mentioned. For example, a life insurance organization uses secret phone calls to a person to announce the timing of impending career moves. Secret or private announcements may easily change the behavior of a candidate at his current work, resulting in clashes with former associates that are inexplicable to them because they are unaware of their causes. Temporal aspects of career patterns are also deduced by people from various kinds of signs or cues left by the organization about impending movements.

The organization may provide either or both a lifetime career pattern or a passing-through career pattern. The latter has a built-in expectation or intention that the person will move to another organization after a specified time (for example, internship or residency in a hospital). Passing-through career patterns may and may not be articulated with the career patterns of other organizations. They are for hospital organizations, being scheduled on a yearly basis. This articulation results in a system of career patterns between hospitals from studentship, through internship and residency, to practice.

Organizational career patterns change in shape and temporal aspects throughout historical time (Mills and Warner and Abegglen), because of changing social conditions of education, employment, and technology, and because of changing organizational structures. For example, executives now tend to start with higher education at middle levels of the organization compared to thirty years ago when they tended to leave high school or grammar school and start out as laborers and become "self-made" men. Thus a specific career pattern for an organization is liable to continual modification

---

[1] On transitional statuses see Barney G. Glaser and Anselm L. Strauss, "Temporal Aspects of Dying as a Non-Scheduled Status Passage," *American Journal of Sociology*, 71 (July, 1965): 48–59.

by the pace of history. For example, the recruitment of army officers has continually changed from drawing upon upper-class sons to candidates from any social class or race who can cope with the changes in technology, required expertises, and organizational complexity. Also, recruitment is affected by changing social and race relations and by new patterns of upward mobility through education. The current multiplication of "professionals" and their changing patterns of work within and outside organizations has generated new organizational career patterns. Automation has, with its development and spreading use, generated new organizational career patterns. It remains to accomplish the necessary study and research for generating theory on the trends of changing organizational career patterns.

57

The Chief Executives

C. WRIGHT MILLS

Where a career pattern begins in an organization depends on the tributaries to recruitment as well as on the processes of recruitment. Where it ends depends on its ceiling within the organizational hierarchy and retirement requirements. Professor Mills discusses the criteria for success in the higher corporate world.

On the middle levels, specialization is required. But the operating specialist will not rise; only the "broadened" man wil' rise. What does that mean? It means, for one thing, that the specialist is below the level on which men are wholly alerted to profit. The "broadened" man is the man who, no matter what he may be doing, is able clearly to see the way to maximize the profit for the corporation as a whole, in the long as well as in the short run. The man who rises to the top is the broadened man whose "specialty" coincides with the aims of the corporation, which is the maximizing of profit. As he is judged to have realized this aim, he rises within the corporate world. Financial expediency is the chief element of corporate decision, and generally, the higher the executive, the more he devotes his attention to the financial aspect of the going concern.

Moreover, the closer to the corporate top the executive gets, the more important are the big-propertied cliques and political influence in the making of his corporate career. This fact, as well as the considerations for co-optation that prevail, is nicely revealed in a letter that Mr. Lammot du Pont wrote in 1945 in response to a suggestion from a General Motors executive that General George C. Marshall be appointed to the board of directors. Mr. du Pont discussed the proposal: "My reasons for not favoring his membership on the board are: First his age [The General was then 65]; second, his lack of stockholdings, and third, his lack of experience in industrial business affairs." Mr. Alfred P. Sloan, chairman of General Motors, in considering the matter, generally concurred, but added: "I thought General Marshall might do us some good, when he retires, following his present assignment—assuming he continues to live in Washington; recognizing the position he holds in the community and among the government people and the acquaintances he has—and he became familiar with our thinking and what we are trying to do, it might offset the general negative attitude toward big business, of which we are a symbol and a profitable business, as well. It seems to me that might be some reason, and in that event the matter of age would not be particularly consequential."

In considering other appointments, Mr. Sloan wrote to W. S. Carpenter, a large owner of du Pont and General Motors: "George Whitney [G. M. director and chairman of J. P. Morgan & Co.] belongs to the board of directors of quite a number of industrial organizations. He gets around a lot because he lives in New York where many contacts are easily and continuously made. Mr. Douglas [Lewis W. Douglas, a G. M. board member, chairman of the Mutual Life Insurance Company, former Ambassador to Great Britain] is, in a way, quite a public character. He seems to spend a great deal of time in other things. It seems to me that such people do bring into our councils a broader atmosphere than is contributed by the 'du Pont directors' and the General Motors directors."

Or examine a late case of corporate machination that involved the several types of economic men prevailing in higher corporate circles. Robert R. Young—financial promoter and speculator—recently decided to displace William White, chief executive of the New York Central Railroad and a lifetime career executive in railroad operation.[1] Young won—but did it really matter? Success in the corporate world does not follow the pattern it follows in the novel, *Executive Suite*, in which the technologically inclined young man, just like William Holden, wins by making a sincere speech about corporate responsibility. Besides the favors of two friends, each a leading member of the very rich, Mr. Young's income, over the past seventeen years—most of

---

[1] Over a luncheon table Young offered White the title of "chief operating officer" and stock options—"an opportunity to buy Central stock at a fixed price and without any obligation to pay for it unless it went up." White refused, announcing that if Young moved in he would give up his contract: $120,000-per-year salary until retirement at 65; a $75,000-a-year consultant fee for the next five years; then a $40,000-a-year pension for life.

Immediately White hired, out of Central's funds, a public relations firm at $50,000 a year plus expenses, turned over the $125 million advertising budget of the Central to the coming fight, and engaged a professional proxy solicitor from Wall Street. From Palm Beach, Young began maneuvering cliques among the rich and among friends with contacts to get control of blocks of the property. His side came to include three important members of the very rich— Allen P. Kirby of the Woolworth fortune; and two men each worth over $300 million: Clint Murchison, with whom Young had previously done business, and Sid Richardson, whose ranch Young had visited. The deal shaped up in such a way that a block of 800,000 shares at $26 a share ($20.8 million worth) was secured. Of course, the multimillionaires did not have to put up the cash: They borrowed it—mainly from the Allegheny Corporation, which Young is presumably able to treat as his personal property and .07 per cent of which he personally owns. And they borrowed it in such a way as to cover all risk except 200,000 shares. They were on the scheduled new board of directors. Young had 800,000 voting shares.

Chase National Bank, a Rockefeller bank, had had the trusteeship of these shares and now had sold them to Murchison and Richardson. John J. McCloy, the Bank's board chairman, arranged for White to meet Richardson and Murchison, who flew up the next day to New York City. The Texans, who now owned 12½ per cent of the New York Central, attempted to arrange a compromise. They failed, and a fight for the votes of the more scattered owners began.

Young's side spent $305,000. (Later the New York Central repaid it, thus footing the bills of both the winners and the losers.) One hundred solicitors for White from coast to coast were reaching stockholders, as well as several hundred volunteer employees of the railroad. Young also engaged a professional proxy solicitation firm; he also had the services of Diebold, Inc., a firm manufacturing office furniture which Murchison owned—250 of its salesmen were hired to solicit proxies. If Young won, the office furniture for New York Central might henceforth be made by Diebold.

it from capital gains—is reported to be well in excess of $10 million. His yearly income is well over a million, his wife's, half a million—and they manage to keep, after taxes, some 75 per cent of it. But then, no fiction known to us begins to grasp the realities of the corporate world today.

When successful executives think back upon their own careers, they very often emphasize what they always call "an element of luck." Now what is that? We are told that Mr. George Humphrey makes it a point to have "lucky men" work with him. What this means, translated out of the magical language of luck, is that there is an accumulation of corporate success. If you are successful, that shows that you are lucky, and if you are lucky, you are chosen by those up the line, and thus you get chances to be more successful. Time and time again, in close-ups of the executive career, we observe how men in the same circles choose one another. For example, Mr. Humphrey was on an advisory committee to the Commerce Department. There he meets Mr. Paul Hoffman. Later, when Mr. Hoffman heads ECA, he pulls in Mr. Humphrey to run an advisory committee on German industry. There General Clay notices him. General Clay naturally knows General Eisenhower, so when General Eisenhower goes up, General Clay recommends Mr. Humphrey to his close friend, President Eisenhower.

There is another item that ties in with the network of friends which people call "luck": the social life of the corporation. It is a reasonable assumption that part of the executive career is spent "politic-ing." Like any politician, especially when he is at or near the top of his hierarchy, the successful executive tries to win friends and to make alliances, and he spends, one suspects, a good deal of time guessing about the cliques he thinks oppose him. He makes power-plays, and these seem part of the career of the managerial elite.

To make the corporation self-perpetuating, the chief executives feel that they must perpetuate themselves, or men like themselves—future men not only trained but also indoctrinated. This is what is meant when it was truly said recently of a man high in the world's largest oil company that he "is really as much a product of the company as are the two million barrels of oil products it makes every day." As future executives move upward and toward the center, they become members of a set of cliques, which they often confusedly refer to as a team. They must listen. They must weigh opinions. They must not make snap judgments. They must fit into the business team and the social clique. In so far as the career is truly corporate, one advances by serving the corporation, which means by serving those who are in charge of it and who judge what its interests are.

The executive career is almost entirely a career within the corporate world, less than one out of ten of the top men over the last three generations having entered *top* position from independent professional or from outside hierarchies. Moreover, it is increasingly a career within one company: back in 1870, more than six out of ten executives gained the top rung from outside the corporation; by 1950, almost seven out of ten did so from within the company. First you are a vice-president, then you are president. You must be known well, you must be well liked, you must be an insider.

Success in the higher corporate world is obviously determined by the standards of selection that prevail and the personal application of these standards by the men who are already at the top. In the corporate world, one is drawn upward by the appraisals of one's superiors. Most chief executives take much pride in their ability "to judge men"; but what are the standards by which they judge? The standards that prevail are not clear-cut and objective; they seem quite intangible, they are often quite subjective, and they are often perceived by those below as ambiguous. The professors of "business psychology" have been busy inventing more opaque terms, and searching for "executive traits," but most of this "research" is irrelevant nonsense, as can readily be seen by examining the criteria that prevail, the personal and social characteristics of the successes, and their corporate style of life.

On the lower and middle levels of management, objective criteria having to do with skillful performance of occupational duties do often prevail. It is even possible to set up rules of advancement and to make them known in a regular bureaucratic manner. Under such conditions, skill and energy do often pay off without what one may call the corporate character having to be developed. But once a man of the lower ranks becomes a candidate for higher corporate position, the sound judgment, the broadened view, and other less tangible traits of the corporate character are required. "Character," *Fortune* magazine observers have remarked, even how the man looks as an executive, became more important than technical ability.

One often hears that practical experience is what counts, but this is very short-sighted, for those on top control the chances to have practical experience of the sort that would be counted for the higher tasks of sound judgment and careful maneuver. This fact is often hidden by reference to an abstract, transferrable quality called "managerial ability," but many of those who have been up close to the higher circles (but not of them) have been led to suspect that there probably is no such thing. Moreover, even if there were such a generalized ability, only the uninformed would think that it was what was needed in high policy office, or that one should go to the trouble of recruiting $200,000-a-year men for such work. For that you hire a $20,000-a-year man, or better still, you employ a management counseling firm, which is what the $200,000-a-year men do. Part of their "managerial ability" consists precisely in knowing their own inabilities and where to find someone with the requisite ability and the money to pay for it. In the meantime, the most accurate single definition of ability—a many-sided word—is: usefulness to those above, to those in control of one's advancement.

When one reads the speeches and reports of executives about the type of man that is required, one cannot avoid this simple conclusion: he must "fit in" with those already at the top. This means that he must meet the expectations of his superiors and peers; that in personal manner and political view, in social ways and business style, he must be like those who are already in, and upon whose judgments his own success rests. If it is to count in the corporate career, talent, no matter how defined, must be discovered by one's talented superiors. It is in the nature of the morality of corporate accomplishment that those at the top do not and cannot admire that which they do not and cannot understand.

When it is asked of the top corporate men: "But didn't they have to have *something* to get up there?" The answer is, "Yes, they did." By definition, they had "what it takes." The real question accordingly is: what does it take? And the only answer one can find anywhere is: the sound judgment, as gauged by the men of sound judgment who select them. The fit survive, and fitness means, not formal competence—there probably is no such thing for top executive positions—but conformity with the criteria of those who have already succeeded. To be compatible with the top men is to act like them, to look like them, to think like them: to be of and for them—or at least to display oneself to them in such a way as to create that impression. This, in fact, is what is meant by "creating"—a well-chosen word—"a good impression." This is what is meant—and nothing else—by being a "sound man," as sound as a dollar.

Since success depends upon personal or a clique choice, its criteria tend to be ambiguous. Accordingly, those on the lower edge of the top stratum have ample motive and opportunity to study carefully those above them as models, and to observe critically and with no little anxiety those who are still their peers. Now they are above the approval of technical ability and formal competence, business experience and ordinary middle-class respectability. That is assumed. Now they are in the intangible, ambiguous world of the higher and inner circles, with whose members they must come into a special relation of mutual confidence. Not bureaucratic rules of seniority or objective examinations, but the confidence of the inner circle that one is of them and for them, is a prerequisite for joining them.

Of the many that are called to the corporate management, only a few are chosen. Those chosen are picked, not so much for strictly personal characteristics—which many of them cannot really be said to possess—as for qualities judged useful to "the team." On this team, the prideful grace of individuality is not at a premium.

Those who have started from on high have from their beginnings been formed by sound men and trained for soundness. They do not have to think of having to appear as sound men. They just are sound men; indeed, they embody the standards of soundness. Those who have had low beginnings must think all the harder before taking a risk of being thought unsound. As they succeed, they must train themselves for success; and, as they are formed by it, they too come to embody it, perhaps more rotundly than those of the always-high career. Thus, high or low origin, each in its own way, operates to select and to form the sound men with well-balanced judgment.

It is the criteria of selection, it is the power to conform with and to use these criteria that are important in understanding the chief executives—not merely the statistics of origin. It is the structure of the corporate career and its inner psychological results that form the men at the top, not merely the external sequence of their career.

So speak in the rich, round voice and do not confuse your superiors with details. Know where to draw the line. Execute the ceremony of forming a judgment. Delay recognizing the choice you have already made, so as to make the truism sound like the deeply pondered notion. Speak like the quiet competent man of affairs and never personally say No. Hire the No-man as well as the Yes-man. Be the tolerant Maybe-man and they will cluster around you, filled with hopefulness. Practice softening the facts into the optimistic, practical, forward-looking, cordial, brisk view. Speak to the well-blunted point. Have weight; be stable: caricature what you are supposed to be but never become aware of it much less amused by it. And never let your brains show. . . .

The criteria for executive advancement that prevail are revealingly displayed in the great corporations' recruitment and training programs, which reflect rather clearly the criteria and judgments prevailing among those who have already succeeded. Among today's chief executives there is much worry about tomorrow's executive elite, and there are many attempts to take inventory of the younger men of the corporation who might develop in ten years or so; to hire psychologists to measure talent and potential talent; for companies to band together and set up classes for their younger executives, and indeed to employ leading universities which arrange distinct schools and curricula for the managers of tomorrow; in short, to make the selection of a managerial elite a staff function of the big company.

Perhaps half of the large corporations now have such programs. They send selected men to selected colleges and business schools for special courses, Harvard Business School being a favorite. They set up their own schools and courses, often including their own top executives as lecturers. They scout leading colleges for promising graduates, and arrange tours of rotating duty for men selected as potential "comers." Some corporations, in fact, at times seem less like businesses than vast schools for future executives.

By such devices, the fraternity of the chosen have attempted to meet the need for executives brought about by the corporate expansion of the 'forties and 'fifties. This expansion occurred after the scarce job market of the 'thirties, when companies could pick and choose executives from among the experienced. During the war there was no time for such programs, which, on top of the slump, made for a decade-and-a-half gap in executive supply. Behind the deliberate recruiting and training programs there is also the uneasy feeling among the top cliques that the second-level executives are not as broad-gauge as they themselves: their programs are designed to meet the felt need for perpetuation of the corporate hierarchy.

So the corporations conduct their raids among the college seniors, like college fraternities among the freshmen. The colleges, in turn, have more and more provided courses thought to be helpful to the corporate career. It is reliably reported that the college boys are "ready to be what the corporation wants them to be . . . They are looking hard for cues." Such "alertness and receptivity may well be a more important characteristic of the modern manager than the type of education he received. Luck obviously plays a part in the rise of any top executives, and they seem to manage to meet luck better than halfway."

The cues are readily available: As corporation trainees, the future executives are detached from a central pool and slated for permanent jobs, "only after they have been given a strong indoctrination in what is sometimes called the 'management view.' The indoctrination may last as long as two years and occasionally as long as seven." Each year, for example, General Electric takes unto itself over 1,000 college graduates and exposes them for at least 45 months, usually much longer, to a faculty of 250 full-time General Electric employees. Many people are watching them, even their peers contribute to the judging, for which, it is said, the trainee is grateful, for thus he will not be overlooked. Training in "Human Relations" pervades the broad-gauge program. "Never say anything controversial," "You can always get anybody to do what you wish," are themes of the "effective presentation" course worked up by the Sales Training Department of the knowledgable corporation.

In this human-relations type of training, the effort is to get people to feel differently as well as to think differently about their human problems. The sensibilities and loyalties and character, not merely the skills, of the trainee must be developed in such a way as to transform the American boy into the American executive. His very success will be an insulation of mind against the ordinary problems and values of non-corporate people. Like all well-designed indoctrination courses, the social life of the trainee is built into the program: to get ahead one must get along, with one's peers and with one's superiors. All belong to the same fraternity; all of one's "social needs can be filled within the company orbit." To find his executive slot in this orbit, the trainee must "take advantage of the many contacts that rotation from place to place affords." This too is company policy: "If you're smart," says one smart trainee, "as soon as you know your way around you start telephoning."

There are many arguments pro and con about training programs for executives, but the Crown-Prince type of program *is* a central argument among the top executives of big corporations. Nine out of ten young men, even today, do not graduate from college—they are excluded from such executive training schools, although most of them will work for corporations. What effects do such programs have among those who have been called to the corporation but are not among those chosen as Crown Princes? Yet there must be some way to inflate the self-images of the future executives in order that they may take up the reins with the proper mood and in the proper manner and with the sound judgment required.

The majority view of one small but significant sample of executives is that the man who knows "the technique of managing, not the content of what is managed," the man who knows "how to elicit participative consultation . . . how to conduct problem-solving meetings . . ." will be the top executive of the future.[2] He will be a team player without unorthodox ideas, with leadership rather than drive. Or, as *Fortune* summarizes the argument: "Their point goes something like this: We do need new ideas, a questioning of accepted ways. But the leader hires people to do this for him. For this reason, then, the creative qualities once associated with the line are now qualities best put in staff slots. The top executive's job, to paraphrase, is not to look ahead himself, but to check the excesses of the people who do look ahead. He is not part of the basic creative engine; he is the governor." Or, as one executive put it: "We used to look primarily for brilliance . . . Now that much abused word 'character' has become very important. We don't care if you're a Phi Beta Kappa or a Tau Beta Phi. We want a well-rounded person who can handle well-rounded people." Such a man does not invent ideas himself; he is a broker for well-rounded ideas: the decisions are made by the well-rounded group.

Lest all this be thought merely a whimsical fad, not truly reflecting the ideological desert and anxiety of the executive world, consider sympathetically the style of conduct and the ideology of Owen D. Young—late president of General Electric—who serves well as the American prototype of modern man as executive. In the early twentieth century, we are told by Miss Ida Tarbell, the typical industrial leader was a domineering individual, offensive in his belief that business was essentially a private endeavor. But not Owen Young. During World War I and the 'twenties, he changed all that. To him, the corporation was a public institution, and its leaders, although not of course elected by the public, were responsible trustees. "A big business in Owen D. Young's mind is not . . . a private business . . . it is an institution."

So he worked with people outside his own company, worked on an industry-wide basis, and laughed at "the fear that co-operation of any kind might be construed as conspiracy." In fact, he came to feel trade associations, in the corporate age, performed one role that once "the church," in a time of small businesses in a local county, performed: the role of moral restrainer, the keeper of "proper business practices." During the war, he became a kind of "general liaison officer between the company and various [government] boards, a kind of general counsel," a prototype of the many executives whose

---

[2] Of 98 top executives and personnel planners recently asked to choose between the executive "primarily concerned with human relations" and "the man with strong personal convictions . . . not shy about making unorthodox decisions," some 63 were willing to make the choice: 40 said the human relations man, 23 the man of conviction.

co-operation with one another during the wars set the shape of peacetime co-operation as well.

His interest in the properties he managed could not have been more personal had he owned them himself. Of one company he helped develop, he wrote to a friend: "We have worked and played with it together so much that I feel sure it is not boasting to say that no one knows the strength and weakness—the good and bad side of this property better than you and I. In fact I doubt if there were ever such a great property which was known so well . . ."

His face was always "friendly and approachable" and his smile, one colleague said, "his smile alone is worth a million dollars." Of his decision, it was said, "it was not logical document . . . It was something his colleagues felt was intuitive rather than reasoned—a conclusion born of his pondering, and though you might by rule and figures prove him wrong, you knew he was right!"

58

Self-Made Men

C. WRIGHT MILLS

In line with the previous article, Professor Mills discusses
adaptive career patterns used by self-made men which
break through standard career patterns provided by the
organization.

Most labor leaders held jobs in the trade or industry with which they were
later to deal as union officials. They do not appear to have taken these jobs
merely to become union members and thus to make their careers in the unions.
There is, however, another career pattern: before they became union officials
of any kind, some labor leaders held jobs, mostly white-collar higher in the
social scale than those organized by the unions they were later to lead. In
both organizations, this white-collar pattern is slightly more frequent among
the state officials than among the officers of the internationals, among secretaries than among presidents. The experience is closely associated with educational struggle and with college education: half of the labor leaders on
national and state levels who were white-collar workers are college men.

This pre-union career involving white-collar jobs and/or educational
struggle may take two formal paths: (1) A man may take a job in a local of
some trade union that has organized workers below the level of his occupation.
Because of union rules, he will usually take a job in the shop in order to have
the employment record necessary to become a union member. This labor link
in his white-collar career is ritualistic. Some younger men who were unemployed white-collar workers during the Thirties took laboring jobs from
need, and then went into labor union work. (2) A man who has been working
as a skilled laborer and has never held any other type of job may struggle to
rise from the ranks of labor into a white-collar position. The years during
which he struggled for education and better jobs, as well as the character
of those experiences and of his occupational origin, do not indicate that he
was bent primarily upon a union career. Yet this upward struggle was eventually channeled into a trade union hierarchy.

BEGINNING POINTS

The labor leader may begin his union career as a business-like man, a
political man, or a disgruntled working man.

Throughout the history of the American labor movement, the third way has been and still is dominant: a man of plain wage-worker origin begins work as a wage worker and rises out of the ranks and up the union hierarchy. He may take this route because of a militancy aroused by frustrated ambition or by an upsurge of indignation. Many of America's older labor leaders, in fact, began their career by being fired for their union ideas. They answered back in the only way open to them during certain economic periods—by fighting for or even by founding local labor unions. But a generalized rebel spirit or an ideological buttress certainly is not necessary to the labor leader's actions. A serviceable ideology can be picked up along the way; often speeches by labor leaders contain much rough-hewn rhetoric and little else.

In the decades before the first World War, and again during the great slump, socialist orientation was an important starting point for many union careers. Ideological adherence to some set of leftward ideas automatically led to a labor leader career; regardless of the brand of political ideas, almost every leftward group has looked upon the unions as instruments of political struggle. In this ideological pattern, a man might enter the shop with the deliberate intention of becoming a leader of its workers; under this impulse, he might either attempt to found a union if none existed or to work his way up in any union already there.

An opposite career-beginning developed perhaps more frequently during the Thirties than previously. Men of some education and background saw the union career as a good proposition. They were white-collar people of various sorts and aspirations, but in the economic squeeze of the Thirties, were forced into shops and factories. Once there, they saw two ways up: the route of the foreman to a management job or the more perilous but in many ways more promising route of the labor leader. Some may also have had ideological convictions, not necessarily more left than those of pure and simple unionism as practiced during the era of the New Deal. There were, in addition, men who raised enough capital to open an office in the union business.

In the reality of given cases, ideological and business motives are always mixed. It is a question of emphasis; in the trade union world there are men who have practical careers in ideology just as there are men who cultivate ambitious convictions. Personal motive and public reason often coincide with opportunity in such a way as to make most difficult any real untangling of the three. David Dubinsky, for instance, or Julius Hochman "went into the shop with the vaguely contradictory ambition of leading the workers toward 'emancipation' while saving enough money to study medicine or law." One thing that Dubinsky didn't want to become—although he had the opportunity —was a small clothing manufacturer.

William Green, whose parents were English miners and followers of Keir Hardie's "Christian Socialism," belonged to the socialist opposition within the AFL before the first World War. He was an organization man, that is, he was part of the miners' organization, which was part of the opposition. His rhetorical talents and this vaguely socialist background undoubtedly increased his motives for becoming a labor leader. After he was in, it has been said, he "rose in the world by standing still." Yet the little motors of ambition are laboring away in the trade union world, as in every other occupational and leadership hierarchy.

Between ideological urge and personal business-like ambition in the career-line of a labor leader, it is not at all unlikely that a shift has occurred, in accordance with the decline of the socialist movement in the United States. Entering the unions out of a belief in some political idea is primarily a nineteenth-century phenomenon, although it carried over into the twentieth. The business-like pattern is probably more typical of the 1932–47 era of union history.

CAREER-LINES

Whatever his original motives, a man may become a leader of some rank by: (1) creating a union himself; (2) being elected by his shopmates to a local union post, either that of shop steward or directly to a local office; or (3) being appointed organizer or business agent by a national or local organization, and from that appointed position climbing up via a series of elections.

The majority of the labor leaders began their union career on the local level, as shop stewards and then local officers, or simply as elected local officers. Only a handful of leaders began their careers in their present offices. ... Most of the leaders on all three levels began as heads of locals or as local committeemen. But a second starting point is important, especially among national and state officers: an appointment to the job of organizer.

On the national level of leadership, 14 per cent of the AFL and 9 per cent of the CIO leaders began in their present rank; a great many of these founded the unions they now head. There does not seem to be much movement from the city and the state lineup to the national. The local is the primary starting point for the city, state, and national hierarchies, but once a man enters the city or state organizations, apparently he is less likely to go on to the national headquarters. These figures correspond to the vocational idea current in labor unions that state offices are often places of derailment. The national leaders either begin nationally or rise from the locals without going through state offices.

More CIO leaders on both the national and state levels began as appointed organizers than did the leaders on the same levels in the AFL. The AFL has a slightly more rigid hierarchy of promotion than has the CIO, and the CIO is a good deal more centralized. In both organizations the career begins at the bottom, but in the AFL it is more apt to follow the route up via elections.

This difference between the AFL and CIO, especially in regard to the proportions who began as appointed organizers, not only reflects the fact that success in the CIO rests somewhat more upon organizing skill, but it also reflects and illustrates the rise of the white-collar career.

In the older AFL unions, only 5 per cent of the leaders with entrepreneurial or white-collar backgrounds began as appointed national organizers as compared with some 16 per cent of those with wage-worker background. In the CIO, however, 26 per cent of the leaders with white-collar jobs prior to their union careers began as national organizers as against 16 per cent of those having wage-worker backgrounds. This is not only a difference between the CIO and the AFL; it is a shift in union career-lines as well. The better-educated man with a white-collar background now tends to enter the field as an appointed organizer. Of course, such power as he acquires through elections is gained by his organizing talents, and in this respect he is just like the other dominant career type: the man who begins by being elected as a shop steward or local officer must also organize in order to win elections.

This shift in the beginning point of union careers, and the increased frequency of a white-collar link in the career of the CIO national leaders, point to the growth of bureaucracy in the labor union world.

Twenty or 30 years ago, the organizer came from the ranks, or was drawn by a national organization from among successful local leaders. Sometimes workers who had been discharged for union activity from jobs in the plants were hired as organizers and placed in other locals. What training the organizer had was empirical or handed down to him as a rule-of-thumb. But during the Thirties, when legal frameworks had to be attended to, organizing problems became more technical; an organizer had to have some training. Lore and simple experience were not enough. Business had its training courses for salesmen; during the Thirties, labor unions began to develop training schools for organizers.

The typical organizer is still of the older sort, however, and his career begins in the local. Unions are still more like patronage machines than streamlined bureaucracies. This fact probably affects the organizers or international representatives more than any other category of personnel. In at least one big union in the CIO, there are three types of organizers:

I. Men to whom a job is given as a political pay-off, usually former local officials who were loyal to the national executive but were ousted from their elected post during a political reshuffle. Quite often these men are rather useless as organizers, and they can only do little jobs for the official to whom they are attached. Yet the official feels a moral political obligation to them even when he cannot depend upon them.

II. The inner circle surrounding a national officer, men who are considered wholly dependable and who form the cadre of the machine of the national leader, promoting his security of position. In unions that are split at the top, each of the cliques may have a set of such organizers. They prepare the vote of the locals assigned to them and do the political maneuvering necessary to keep conventions and appointments in line.

III. Organizers who specialize in initiating and maintaining organizations of various kinds within the union world. They see their job as that of a professional, and often they have salaried professional backgrounds. They may deplore the politics in their work or that of their colleagues, but they will play along when it is necessary. Because unions are not strict bureaucracies, but are run by patriarchs according to patronage, there is a strong tendency for the trained organizer also to become a machine politician.

Virtually all routes to trade union leadership start in the locals; regardless of the particular career pattern which he has followed, the trade union leader is a man who has climbed a long way. Considering his occupational origin and the character and extent of his education, he finds the top-flight trade union post a perch of success. And in the American vocabulary, success means money.

59

The Elite Military Nucleus

MORRIS JANOWITZ

The shape of a career pattern may be prescribed and
standardized by the organization, thus providing members
a clear, concrete image of the path to success. This clarity,
however, allows unconventially shaped careers to be
carefully planned around the conventional. Professor
Janowitz describes the implications of this for the military
organization.

In an organization as large and complex as the armed forces the prescribed
career line gives the young officer a concrete image of the successful military
professional. The prescribed career line further enables the establishment to
develop a cadre of like-minded young men to perform essential functions.
Although for each service the details of a prescribed career become fixed in
the minds of the aspiring officer, the content of this prescribed career is
inevitably based on past experiences. Yet, the military establishment adapts
to change precisely because its most outstanding leaders anticipate future
requirements, and expose themselves to experiences which are outside the
prescribed career. Thus, one of the basic hypotheses for the period from 1910
to 1950 was that prescribed careers, performed with high competence, led to
entrance into the professional elite, the highest point at which technical and
routinized functions are performed. By contrast, entrance into the smaller
group of prime movers—the nucleus of the elite—where innovating perspectives and skills are required, is open to persons with unconventional careers.
Such a proposition seems to have special importance in accounting for
those officers who became involved in politico-military affairs during a period
when these matters were not defined as part of the role of the professional
soldier.

The formulation of Arthur K. Davis in this connection is undoubtedly
correct in principle, but far too extreme: "The effectiveness of military
leaders tends to vary inversely with their exposure to a conventional routinized
military career." Most officers who have entered the top one-half of 1 per cent
of the hierarchy have complied with conventional career forms; but, in
addition, they have frequently had specialized and innovating experiences
which have increased their usefulness to the military profession. Among
these leaders, the men who have been most decisive are characterized by
even more pronounced unconventionality in their career lines.

Excerpted, with permission, from *The Professional Soldier* (New York: Free Press of Glencoe
1960; pp. 150–65).

Leadership Models

The rule-breaking military leader of unconventional background has a long history in American military affairs. In the instance of George Washington it is impossible to unravel reality from myth, yet, he has come to stand for a Cincinnatus—the civilian surveyor and farmer who took up arms, and who in his very person embodied the unconventional genius. During the Revolution, "Mad" Anthony Wayne and "Swamp Fox" Marion established the tradition of the fighting hero, who had the ability to improvise on the spot. Andrew Jackson personified the military leader who was more concerned with the superiority of native American "frontier" skills than with the formalities of the military profession. He made his contribution to the tradition that the combat commander should be "one of the boys."

While the Civil War was the first major armed conflict managed by military professionals, the unconventional type was represented at crucial times. Victory for the North hinged, in no small measure, on the contribution of the untidy figure, U. S. Grant, who emerged gradually from obscurity, and who succeeded where professional soldiers of established reputation had failed. Grant was, of course, a product of West Point, but his career was marginal at best, by professional standards. He spent much of his time in low-prestige quarter-master-type assignments, which were nevertheless appropriate in sensitizing him to the tasks of large-scale warfare. His personal difficulties made him such a problem to the profession that he resigned from military service, until the Civil War reopened his career. The Civil War also produced a plethora of men in the heroic model, with Stonewall Jackson and Jeb Stuart as the prototype of men who were truly maverick individualists and whose strength rested in their passionate dedication to the "cause."

The conspicuous military figure during the Spanish-American War was not even a professional soldier, but a civilian—Theodore Roosevelt. In the years before the outbreak of World War I, Leonard Wood emerged as a prime mover in his effort to convert the ground forces from a collection of Indian fighters into a modern army. Leonard Wood was, of all things, a doctor, and to have a doctor appointed to the post of Chief of Staff during a period of growing professionalization was deeply resented by the insiders. But it required an outsider who was uncommitted to the traditions of the past to serve as a catalyst. Leonard Wood, like John Pershing who was to follow him, maintained the outward facade of the heroic cavalry officer. . . .

John Pershing's career was closer to the professional military formula, but was much more than a prescribed career. While on duty as a junior officer in the Philippines during the period of the pacification, he was almost the only one of the officers of a considerable garrison who became very much interested in the rebellious Moros. While other officers were following the social protocol of an overseas garrison, he was associating with the natives, studying them, and learning their language. Pershing became well known and influential among the local native leaders, and attracted the attention of General George W. Davis, who was in charge of developing a form of civil-military government. Because of his knowledge and experience with the native population, Pershing was placed in an important staff post as the superior of many older officers.

His career, further developed through influential connections achieved by his marriage, demonstrated that he was a military organizer who recognized the administrative dimensions of warfare, although he displayed a warrior demeanor. His network of military associates included others with a managerial orientation: James G. Harbord, who rose from the enlisted ranks to serve as his Chief of Staff, and who left the Army to become president of The Radio Corporation of America, and General Frank Ross McCoy, a West Point graduate, who became central logistical manager and who later served in numerous politico-military posts.

World War I offered Douglas MacArthur his first opportunity, as a brigade commander in the 42nd Rainbow Division, to establish his reputation as an individualist. Even then his costume was as notorious as his tactical skill: a floppy cap, a riding crop, and often a sweater with a huge wool muffler around his neck—all unorthodox, but attention-producing. Another outstanding rule-breaker of World War I was the exponent of air power—William "Billy" Mitchell.

Under democratic political control, as it has operated in the United States, the unconventional military leader represents selection by civilian authorities. Particularly in the Army, because of its greater potential for involvement in politics—both domestic politics and politico-military affairs in war-time—civilian authorities have had a tendency to select those who embody managerial perspectives for strategic positions, rather than those who glorify war-making. The profound popular suspiciousness, or at least ambivalence, toward the professional soldier has helped insure that such atypical soldiers would rise to the top. These innovators, whose perspectives are not captured and blocked by the traditions of the profession, bear the responsibility for adapting the military to new tasks.

In the military establishment the fighter spirit itself tends to become extinguished. Those who make a successful career of seeking to renew it are also innovators, in a sense, although they may draw their stimulus from the past rather than the future. As one advances in the military hierarchy, with its endless routine and prolonged periods of peace, it takes an act of strong assertiveness and individuality to maintain the fighter spirit. A successful military establishment must be run by military managers, but must include in its very elite a leaven of heroic leaders.

In the absence of a crisis, and lacking civilian pressure, the management of the military profession between World War I and World War II reverted to narrow professionalism. Only one of the four chiefs of staff of the Army, Douglas MacArthur (1930–35), could be called a powerfully motivated person, but even his admirers admit that during this period he played a conventional role by his own standards. The other chiefs of staff remain almost completely unknown organization men. This observation could be stated in reverse. The type of leadership of the inter-war years was hardly predictive of what would emerge during war. With the advent of hostilities, dozens, if not hundreds, of ranking officers were pushed aside in the effort to advance younger and more creative officers whose thinking had not been confined by military routines.

The conspicuous leaders in World War II and its immediate aftermath were not representative men, but rather exaggerations of the conflicting themes in the military profession. Regardless of the struggles for glory, the military managers maintained positions of effective authority. The dominant image of the military manager was embodied in such men as Dwight Eisenhower, Omar Bradley, H. H. Arnold, Walter Bedell Smith, William D. Leahy, and Ernest King. These were the men who reflected the technical and pragmatic dimensions of war-making. The heroic leaders who gave dramatic leadership to strategic and operational commands were represented by such men as "Bull" Halsey, George Patton, Jonathan Wainwright, James Doolittle, and Curtis LeMay.

Yet, in World War II contradictory images of the military elite were represented by the contrast between George Marshall, the prototype of the military manager, and Douglas MacArthur, who fused both roles, but who often performed as the heroic fighter. The contrast is more than a contrast in leadership style, for, in the end, each man and his disciples developed a conflicting political outlook which deeply influenced the management of World War II. The reams that have been written about the differences of character, skill and style of Marshall and MacArthur tend, however, to obscure certain crucial similarities. Both men were self-consciously prime movers who were concerned with mobilizing the military profession to achieve national objectives.

Douglas MacArthur was the son of a professional Army officer, who rose to be a general and communicated a sense of mission to his son. MacArthur's powerful ambition and his superior intellect set him apart from the typical professional, although throughout his career he displayed outward conformity to the standards and protocol of the old Army. No simple explanation suffices to account for the detachment that George Marshall was able to develop toward the military profession. Many point to the fact that he attended the Virginia Military Institute because he was refused an appointment to West Point, that his father was a Democrat in a Republican stronghold. . . .

Two incidents—real or mythical—highlight the different use to which these men put their strong personalities and their skepticism of formal authority. MacArthur was concerned with maintaining his heroic self-image; Marshall with developing the concept of the effective military professional. In the words of one of his most ardent admirers, General George C. Kenney, the reputation MacArthur had for "insisting on his rights and incidentally for winning most of the arguments, started almost at the beginning of his Army career." Kenney recounts a characteristic episode at West Point which reveals not only a willingness to take risks, but also a personal definition of honor and obedience to military authority. MacArthur objected violently to a professor because he believed that he had been erroneously put on a list of class "goats" for poor work in mathematics, and because he had been ordered to take additional make-up examinations. He felt that he had met his mathematics requirements, although he had not taken the requisite number of examinations. Challenging a direct order, he is reputed to have stated, "I have not failed my mathematics course and I will not have my name listed with those who failed. Orders can be rescinded and if my name is not removed from that list by nine o'clock tomorrow morning, I will resign." The next day his name was removed and, as the MacArthur story would have it, while his roommate was so worried that he could hardly close his eyes, MacArthur slept through the night soundly. In myth and reality, MacArthur's career was based on a flouting of authority, although he demanded strict obedience from his subordinates. MacArthur resisted military authority when it involved an affront to his honor and, by inference, to his fighting spirit.

The image of George Marshall is formed from episodes which reflect a different attitude toward challenging traditional authority. As an unknown lieutenant in the Philippines, he made a bet with a fellow lieutenant that he could name three trivial faults the inspecting officer would find when he inspected the men on parade. Furthermore, Marshall stated that during field exercises he would commit three grave errors in tactics which would pass unobserved. The bet was accepted, and Marshall listed the three errors on an envelope. Having committed these errors, Marshall observed that no one saw anything amiss, and therefore collected his bet. Such behavior reflected his attitude toward his superiors and his willingness to challenge them for professional goals, rather than for personal honor.

Marshall's two chief subordinates—Dwight Eisenhower and H. H. Arnold—were also unusual officers who did not conform merely to the prescribed model. Contrary to the belief that he did not demonstrate his capacities before 1939, Eisenhower had clearly displayed his skill in representation and negotiation. . . .

Like Marshall, his sponsor, he had a sense of detachment about his profession, and Marquis Child, the biographer, has faithfully recorded his spirit, which was apparent even at West Point:

Eisenhower was a roughneck. He broke the rules just as often as he dared. Law abiding classmates were shocked at his daring. . . . His conduct was that of the tough boy from the wrong side of the tracks, defying the code and yet managing by his resourcefulness to live with it.

Eisenhower did not come from a solid upper middle-class family, but truly from the other side of the tracks. . . .

Arnold's career was launched in a dramatic effort at resistance to military regulation which made him famous even before he joined his first regiment. When he was assigned to the infantry instead of the cavalry, his senator and congressman called on the Adjutant General to effect a change in his assignment to the cavalry. When the Adjutant General refused, reminding Arnold that as a second lieutenant he would do whatever anyone in the Army ordered, Arnold replied, "No, Sir, I am not a second lieutenant in the U.S. Army. I haven't accepted my commission." The senator ushered Arnold out of the room, and a compromise was arranged; Arnold remained in the infantry, but at least he was assigned to the Philippines where his youthful vigor might more easily find expression. . . .

As conspicuous heroes in American history, admirals have conformed more closely to the prescribed model. Of the four leading figures in the emergence of the naval establishment during the period of the Spanish-American War—George Dewey, Alfred T. Mahan, Winfield Scott Schley, and William T. Sampson—only Mahan was a true nonconformist. He falls into the category of the military intellectual, rather than the category of innovating military manager, whose reputation, at that time, resided more in civilian circles than in the naval establishment. The Navy's activities in World War I were routine and were dominated by traditionalists, with the notable exceptions of Admiral Bradley Fiske and Admiral William Sims, the iconoclastic advocate of air power. . . .

The Marine Corps produced its maverick in the person of General Holland M. Smith. By Marine Corps standards, he was a managerial type. Smith prided himself for his hostility toward the Navy and his reckless dissent: "But I was a bad boy. I always have been a bad boy in inter-service arguments and I often am amazed that I lasted so long in the Marine Corps." While H. Smith's career was of necessity filled with troop command assignments, he spent considerable time in planning and staff posts. He was a pioneer in the development of amphibious warfare and wrote the basic manuals for assault landing which later were taken over by the Navy and the Army. As he was prone to point out, these tactics were perfected on purely "theoretical" grounds, since there was no successful precedent in modern times. His career was in essence a fierce struggle to overcome the resistance of the Bureau of Ships in the naval establishment to larger and more efficient landing craft.

But the elite nucleus consists of more than a few conspicuous leaders. In 1943 Walter Millis, the military historian, wrote a perceptive introduction to a book, entitled *These Are the Generals*, whose table of contents could be taken as one indicator of the elite nucleus at the midpoint of World War II. Of this group, the military managers—strategic, diplomatic, and logistical—were in the majority. Partly because the United States had engaged in little prior combat, most of them were without extensive field experience. But, of necessity, the highest posts were of the "staff" variety. Millis points out that only seven of the seventeen commanded troops in battle.

The course of the war revised and enlarged the list. Some men were killed in operational accidents; others had their careers wrecked by military and diplomatic reverses; new names were added as the result of personal achievement or organizational accident. In the end, the American military traditions repeated themselves. The members of the top elite, taken as a whole, do not present a picture of Prussian-type staff officers, but rather of civilianized military managers. The heroic leaders were conspicuous, since opportunities for combat command proliferated, but they were decidedly in the minority. While generalizations about such a relatively small group are hazardous, two observations seem possible. First, more often than not military managers were characterized by a social background at variance with the traditional pattern of recruitment from upper middle-class rural and old family stock. They tended to come from the families of lower sôcial status or more marginal circumstances. Heroic leaders could often be identified with the survival of "aristocratic-like" traditions, if only as perpetuated by service-connected family backgrounds. Second, these men—whether military managers or heroic leaders—were characterized by powerful impulses to dissent and to challenge the structure of military authority as it had evolved during peacetime. . . .

The events of World War II and its aftermath seem to have had the consequence of developing officers, especially in the ground forces, who fused the two styles. First, the opportunity for specialized and politico-military assignments greatly increased. Second, as the analysis of military discipline has sought to demonstrate, this merger was possible because the skills of air staff work and combat tend to overlap in important dimensions, and, as a result, authority comes to involve a decline in domination. A plethora of top leaders emerged whose actual experiences permitted them to present themselves as both military managers and successful combat commanders. General Ridgway's career typifies the pattern of the innovating officer who fused both images, but in which the military manager was ultimately dominant. His professional development was replete with experience which was unusual for an army officer.

Ridgway was born in 1895 at Fort Monroe, Virginia, where his father was a colonel in command of a battalion of field artillery. After graduation from West Point with the class of 1917, he felt that he was off to a good start when he was assigned to the Mexican border with the Third Infantry Regiment, and given command of a rifle company. As rumors were current that his regiment was to go to Europe, he believed that he would have an opportunity for the rapid advancement which combat brought to the professional soldier.

However, instead, he received orders to report to West Point as an instructor and was assigned to teach Spanish, since apparently he had done well in that subject as a cadet. Instead of combat experience, he stayed at West Point for six years, first as a language instructor, then as a tactical officer, and finally as faculty director of athletics. While teaching Spanish at West Point, he was deeply concerned that he might lose contact with his specialty— the infantry. After some garrison service with the Fifteenth Regiment, then on duty at Tientsin, he sought to take up a traditional line of military duty and volunteered for the 1928 Olympic Army Squad. Instead, General Frank McCoy sent for him, and requested that Ridgway accompany him to Nicaragua where McCoy was going to supervise the elections. (In addition to the fact that by this time Ridgway spoke Spanish fluently, he had the personal qualities for such an assignment.) This was the second time he was diverted from traditional activities to opportunities which, in the long run, proved more useful to his career. After Nicaragua, he served once again with General McCoy on the Bolivian-Paraguayan Conciliation Commission.

His next assignment was to the advanced infantry course at Fort Benning, where he came under the influence of General Marshall. By this time, he was clearly designated for a politico-military career. On completion of the course he was sent to Nicaragua again, and then assigned to the Philippines as technical adviser on military matters to Governor General Theodore Roosevelt, Jr. The remainder of the 1930 period was spent at staff assignments, including an assignment to the Army War College in Washington. When war broke out at Pearl Harbor, Ridgway was serving at the War Plans Division in Washington; he had recently accompanied General Marshall to Brazil on a special mission designed to strengthen resistance to the Nazi penetration.

During this entire period Ridgway felt most uncertain about his future career, since he had had no combat experience. "Here at last was my chance to wipe out that blot on my record—or rather fill in that blank on my record where it said 'combat service, none'—a lack that had always made me vaguely uncomfortable in the presence of officers who had been action in World War I." But the administration of the War Department had already tabbed him for higher command. In February of 1942 he was appointed Assistant Divisional Commander under General Bradley, who was then organizing the 82nd Infantry Division. Thus, after having had practically no prior troop experience, he was given a command well above his expectations. The remainder of his career involved rapid advancement, first, through strenuous divisional assignments to higher corps responsibilities, and culminating in assignments as the strategic commander of the 8th Army in Korea, Supreme Commander of SHAPE, and Army Chief of Staff.

The success of the professional officer is not achieved through mechanical compliance with orders from higher headquarters. As the Allied invasion of Italy was being prepared, the Italian government began negotiations for surrender. One aspect of the planning for surrender procedures involved dropping Ridgway's 82nd Air-Borne Division into the Rome area. Ridgway calculated that this was an impossible mission. Yet, the opportunity and the hope for dramatic success in the Italian campaign had led the entire Allied High Command to underwrite this operation. When Ridgway presented his reasons for the impossibility of the operation to General Harold Alexander, he was told, "Don't give this another thought, Ridgway. Contact will be made with your division in three days, five at the most."

Instead of accepting this reassurance from the High Command, Ridgway not only continued to resist his orders, which, as it turned out, would have been disastrous, but also felt impelled to develop some workable plan for resolving the opposed pressures. He proposed to General Walter Bedell Smith, Chief of Staff, that an officer go on a secret mission to Rome to visit with Marshal Badoglio and learn whether the Italians were able to support the landing operation. Consequently, just a few hours before the air-borne operation was to take place, the Allied emissary in Rome, General Maxwell Taylor, was able to report, first-hand, that the mission was impossible. Ridgway's determined resistance to the orders only increased his stature and reputation as a field commander.

The pragmatic concern for innovation which Ridgway represented hardly implies a denial of the special characteristics of the military profession. Ridgway epitomized the fighter spirit and sought to keep it alive for organizational ends, rather than for personal honor. When his division was slated to become the first air-borne unit, he immediately had himself "checked out as a paratrooper." Attached to one side of his parachute harness were hand grenades, and, appropriately for the military manager, a first-aid kit was attached to the other side. Even in his heroic image, he was realistic and pragmatic.

With the introduction of nuclear warfare and guided missiles, a new type of professional has entered the elite nucleus—the military technologist, a conspicuous example being Admiral Hyman Rickover. The military technologist is not a scientist, or for that matter an engineer; basically, he is a military manager, with a fund of technical knowledge and a quality for dramatizing the need for technological progress. As long as the concept of the military generalist predominated, the technologist was excluded from the highest ranks. The promotion of Rickover to a three-star admiral represents departure from this tradition, and is further evidence of the changing composition of the military elite.

As described earlier, Rickover was an outsider in the naval profession, but his personal, social, and professional "marginality" did not bar his making a profound identification with the naval organization. His career was completely atypical, or at best no more than that of a "mere" technical specialist. He worked prodigiously, he commanded the fierce loyalty of his staff members, and he was civilianized to the point of disregarding naval protocol. His continued success was, to a considerable extent, based on outside support from congressional leaders, which support Rickover had the ability to mobilize: Rickover was able to maintain the confidence of congressional leaders when crucial decisions were at stake. When a congressman asked him, "Haven't you prepared for this hearing?," Rickover is reputed to have replied, "Certainly, I shaved and put on a clean shirt. . . . You can't fool a congressman for long. Sooner or later he will find out whether you're telling the truth. If you are, he'll help you. If not, you get the meat ax. . . ."

The three key officers in the military development of guided missiles—Bernard Schriever in the Air Force, John Medaris in the Army and William F. Raborn, Jr., in the Navy—all obviously conform to the managerial type. Schriever, a product of the ROTC and not West Point, received a few years of flight training and then was returned to civilian life. During the war he flew on bombing missions, and in his first post-war assignment he gained a reputation for his criticism of the B-52 program. (He advocated a lighter bomber which could shoot missiles.) By the time the von Neumann Committee in 1954 recommended highest priority for developing missiles, Schriever had identified himself as the Air Force expert and was given the key missile assignment. Medaris, too, had a deviant career by Army standards. He served as an enlisted man in the Marine Corps and became an officer without having attended West Point or any other higher military school. His career involved extensive service in the Ordnance Corps; he also served as Chief of the Military Mission to Argentina. Admiral Raborn followed the prescribed career of the naval generalist, and became involved in missile development late in his career.

60

Organizational Career Patterns
of Business Leaders

W. LLOYD WARNER and JAMES C. ABEGGLEN

This presentation is a series of major findings on the
organizational career patterns of 1952 business leaders.
Professors Warner and Abegglen indicate how organizational career patterns change in shape and temporal
aspects throughout historical time.

OCCUPATIONAL BACKGROUND

No more than 14 per cent of the businessmen studied began their careers
in the "laborer" or "foreman" categories. The office, rather than the shop,
provides the background for most of these executives. It should also be noted
that 1 per cent of the men studied began their careers as owners of businesses.
. . . The general and overwhelming trend is for business leaders to move
through the white-collar groups, with all other occupational categories
decreasing in size rather rapidly. Few of the business elite remained long in
the laboring occupations. Movement out of the lower white-collar positions
is also prompt, and is generally into lower managerial white-collar positions.
Movement out of the professions into business is fairly rapid. Within fifteen
years of becoming self-supporting, more than half of the men studied were
major executives and a quarter were minor executives. . . .

INTERFIRM MOBILITY

Men who worked through their careers in a single firm, and those who
were employed by two or more firms during their careers, experienced the
same general sequence of occupations; and men who began their careers as
laborers were as stable in this respect as men who began their careers as
professional men. In summary of interfirm mobility, the business elite are
highly mobile in this as well as in other ways. Only a fourth of the men studied
worked for a single firm throughout their careers; this mobility from one
company to another took place throughout the business career—after they
became executives as well as earlier. Men from lower status occupational
backgrounds tended to move from one firm to another more frequently than
those from business backgrounds, and college graduates were less likely to
move between firms as they went on to top business positions than men with
less formal education.

Excerpted, with permission, from *Occupational Mobility in American Business and Industry,
1928–1952*, by W. Lloyd Warner and James C. Abegglen (pp. 115–203). Copyright © 1955 by
the University of Minnesota.

LENGTH OF CAREER

The length of the business career before achieving a top business position was longest for the sons of laborers—26 years—and shortest for sons of major executives—20.6 years. Apart from the advantages already noted, in terms of representation in business leadership, the time difference of some five and one half years may be taken as an index of the advantage of birth (and its attendant qualifications for an executive position). In this distribution of the time required to achieve the present business position, the sons of farmers as a group fall closest to the sons of laborers, with a time period of 25.1 years on the average. . . .

Men from higher occupational backgrounds enter business at relatively older ages. They achieve business leadership in relatively less time thereafter than do men from the lower status occupational backgrounds. . . .

EDUCATION

Given the prerequisites to mobility—motivation, skill, opportunity, and the rest of an undetermined complex—the occupationally mobile man may obtain the necessary skills outside the boundaries of formal education. The total time required for this more difficult process does not greatly exceed that involved in the usual conventional approach to training and experience. This is true, of course, only for those rare few with little formal education who filter through and appear in this study. . . .

ORGANIZATIONAL EXPANSION

In the exhortative literature on business success, most notably in commencement addresses, the expansion of American business is treated as an important dimension in occupational mobility. The common phrase "the new frontiers of American business" refers to those types of business and business firms that have in recent years shown most spectacular growth. Whether these rapidly expanding businesses do in fact provide for greater occupational mobility is an unresolved question, and the point admits of argument in both directions. On the face of it, increased opportunity for advancement is offered in a firm where rapid expansion is under way, as new positions are opened. It may be argued, however, that the rapidly expanding firm or industry is one that most needs access to capital offered by men of higher status backgrounds, and therefore can least afford to deny itself the possible advantages of filling executive positions with these men.

Occupational mobility is somewhat greater in rapidly expanding firms than in slowly expanding firms. The differences are consistent but not great. Sons of laborers, farmers, and white-collar workers are present in leadership of rapidly expanding firms in greater proportions than they are in slowly expanding firms. However, the expansion of the type of business in which the firm is located does not appear to be so important a factor . . . as the expansion of the firm. The two factors together do not operate in an accumulative and consistent fashion.

From the fact that only a limited relationship exists between business expansion and occupational mobility, as given by father's occupation, the conclusion should not be drawn that business expansion is an inconsiderable factor in the selection and distribution of the business elite. It is observed that stable firms, and stable types of business and industry, do recruit leaders from all occupational backgrounds in much the same proportions as do rapidly expanding firms and types of business. . . .

From the consideration of the effects of business expansion on the recruitment of the business elite, two general conclusions appear. One, the disadvantaged occupational groups are not represented, on the whole, more frequently in rapidly expanding types of business than in the stable ones. The "frontier" of business, where opportunity is golden, is something of a myth in terms of occupational background. However, when education is considered, rapidly expanding types of business do indeed offer more substantial opportunities to men with less formal education. These men make up a much larger proportion of the leadership of these "frontier" sectors in the business community. . . .

ORGANIZATIONAL SIZE

. . . It would appear that the giant business firms, instead of closing off opportunity for sons of men in lower status occupations, are areas of considerable occupational mobility in American business. It is the smaller, less complex firm where mobility is less frequent. It would appear, however, that the enormous business structures place more emphasis than do the smaller ones on college education as a requisite to business leadership. . . .

The pattern is that occupational mobility takes place from lower status backgrounds at a higher rate into lesser positions, and at a lesser rate into higher positions. . . .

FAMILY AND FRIENDS

There is little or no difference in the time taken by those men with *no* relatives and friends in the firm . . . and by the several types in whose cases personal friends were involved. Briefly, there is little or no difference between the advancement of a man with friends and those without them in his business. The old adage of businessmen that "friendship may get you in the firm but after that you're on your own" seems to be well borne out by the breakdown of the two types of men, those with and those without friends in the organization. . . .

The sons of major executives go elsewhere in increasing numbers for their careers; the sons of owners tend to stay in the fathers' firms. . . .

Clearly circumstances and the nature of the small enterprise seem to foster the "inheritance" of the father's position; conversely, very large enterprises are less favorable environments. . . .

The fact that the smaller of the important firms included in this study are generally characterized by a much higher level of inheritance of position than are the largest business firms in America is a finding of broad significance. It has long been held that the giant corporation, often exercising a near monopoly in its sector of the economy, represents a considerable danger to the democratic recruitment of economic leadership. In this view the giant corporation represents a final form of plutocracy, the control of important areas of the society by a small financial and industrial elite. These data demonstrate the error of this view. It is the smaller firms in which caste-like occupational succession predominates; it is the largest firms in which recruitment to business leadership most frequently occurs from all levels of the occupational system.

The general cause appears to lie in the extent of the trend to rationalization of the giant firm. Recruitment of leadership is rationalized along with production, distribution, and financing. The separation of ownership as represented by stock holdings from the active management of these huge firms, the heightened impersonalization of relationships within the firm, increased specialization of the occupational role at all levels of status in the firm—these and other phenomena of the social organization of the large corporation contribute to the results noted in this study. It is in the less-rationalized smaller firm that familial relationships play a more important role in executive recruitment. Given access to education and training by men from all levels of the society, there is nothing in the nature of the "monopolistic" giant corporation to dictate oligopolistic executive recruitment. On the contrary, the formalized structure and rationalized procedures of these corporations work to accelerate occupational mobility in the business system. . . .

In other words, . . . occupational inheritance is less frequent today than it was a generation ago, insofar as it takes place, the effects are to substantially elevate rank within the business firm. Nepotism is less common than previously but more effective where and when it takes place.

The stronghold of the inherited position in America today is in the smaller enterprises; the freest and most open positions are in the largest enterprises. The bigger the business the freer it is for the ambitious and for those who start from the bottom to seek their fortunes and to make their successful advance into the places of business prestige and power. . . .

Financial Aid

In general the power of money, although very much present in the careers of many men, is of decreasing significance in the competitive world of those who strive for position among the business elite. . . .

The relation of financial aid to the power of close social and family connections in the firm shows several things: (1) that the overwhelming majority of those receiving financial assistance belonged to that category of men with *relatives* in the firm; (2) that friends were of little importance; and (3) that those without friends or relatives received very little monetary aid. Whereas one fourth (23 per cent) of all men with relatives in the firm were aided, only 6 per cent of those with friends and 2 per cent of those with no connections were benefited. Financial assistance and influential connections in the firm go together; yet three fourths of all men with kindred in the same business organization received no direct monetary aid from them. . . .

The special influence of the family and friends of the family is present. Some men are benefited by financial aid. Gifts and inheritance advantage the more highly placed men. The man from farther down has a longer and a harder way to travel than those born to fathers in the business elite. Yet the chronological ages of both groups are very similar despite the fact that those with influential connections take less time. More of the latter start later, having devoted more time to higher education.

Since 1928 there has been a strong trend away from the influences of the family and an increasing emphasis upon competitive achievement. Birth status does not assure a son of the elite permanent position there. More and more the factors involved in achieved status influence occupational succession into the business elite. . . .

Marriage

The time it takes a laborer is almost exactly the same whether he marries a woman from the top or someone of his own class—25.9 years for the former and 26.1 for the latter. Marrying the boss's daughter or someone of equivalent status does not shorten his climb to the top, nor does any other marriage seem to help. The range here is about two years. . . .

Clearly, if there are any advantages in the shortening of time, they do not lie with the man who marries the boss's daughter or someone in the superior economic group. What gains such marriages bring lie in the social rather than in the economic area. These men seem to advance on their merit or through social advantages which are part of the total business situation. American businessmen "do not get places" in business by upward marriage; they get there by "doing things."

61

Career Patterns of Manual Workers

ROBERT BLAUNER

Some organizational careers of manual workers, unlike
executives, have only one or two positions in the organizational hierarchy, and some have many positions, like
executives. In both cases, they are on the bottom half of
the organizational hierarchy. Professor Blauner discusses
career patterns of several different kinds of manual
workers.

THE PRINTER

In many industries, the development of a worker's potentiality is contingent on advancement to work in which the level of skill and responsibility
provides more challenge than the more numerous production jobs. In printing, however, opportunities for growth are present in journeyman status.
Advancement seems less important. In fact, the typical skilled printer is in
an ambiguous position with respect to advancement. On the one hand, he
has already achieved considerable mobility, either through a formal apprenticeship or through on-the-job promotions. And while supervisory positions,
self-employment, or a career in the union are available for a few, for most
manual workers promotion means the upgrading of skill, status, job grade,
and wages within the ranks of blue-collar work.[1]

With 70 per cent of the blue-collar workers in the industry skilled craftsmen or foremen, most printers are already at the top, where there is no
higher to go. This is probably the reason why in the Roper survey only 48
per cent of the printers said that their jobs lead to promotions if they do them
well. This proportion is almost identical with the general sample norm for all
factory workers.

Advancement to more skilled and responsible work is not therefore as
important an element in the development of the printer's potentialities as

Reprinted from *Alienation and Freedom* by Robert Blauner by permission of The University of
Chicago Press (pp. 52–53, 85–86, 112–13, 148–53). Copyright © 1964.

[1] Promotion to foreman is possible for a small number of printers because they, unlike most
blue-collar workers, possess the necessary technical and social skills. Many skilled craftsmen,
however, do not see any advantage in "rising" into supervision: their work, pay, and status are
already sufficiently rewarding. Self-employment is also a realistic avenue for many printers.
Because there is room in the industry for a large number of small shops which require little
capital, a printer, like a building-trades craftsman, is quite likely to start his own business at
some time during his career. If the shop fails or turns out to be "more trouble than it's worth,"
he slips back into the status of an employed journeyman printer without great difficulty. A
union office is another possibility. Printers are more likely to be interested in a union career
than workers in other industries for a number of reasons: their literacy and social confidence,
their high level of participation and interest in the affairs of their local chapel, and the fluid
leadership structure in the union itself.

it is for a semiskilled worker. The skilled printer feels that he has already made it to the pinnacle of the working-class world; and with his strong craft consciousness and satisfying work, the lack of further formal advancement is not felt as depriving. Because his experience and knowledge accumulates, the old printer at the end of his career maintains his usefulness and is often the most respected man in the shop, unlike the old automobile worker, who may skid to the lowest job in the plant hierarchy.

When work provides opportunities for control, meaning, and self-expression, it becomes an end in itself, rather than simply a means to live. For printers, the job means much more than a weekly pay check. Their satisfactions are largely intrinsic, related to the nature of the work itself, rather than extrinsic, or concerned with aspects of the job beyond the actual work. In the ITU study, only 11 per cent gave wages, security, or working conditions as their sole reason for liking printing. In contrast, a study of automobile workers found that such extrinsic concerns as wages and job security were seen as the predominant positive aspects of the job, rather than the nature of the work.

When ITU printers were asked what they liked most about printing, the average respondent offered two reasons. The most frequent response, mentioned by 38 per cent, was that the work was varied and lacked monotony. Almost as many printers, 37 per cent, said that they liked the creativity and challenge of their work. These two intrinsic motivations were followed by an external response, wages and security, mentioned by 29 per cent. Another intrinsic reason, the educational character of the work, was offered by 21 per cent. In addition, 21 per cent were concerned with working conditions and 6 per cent with the prestige of the occupation.

THE TEXTILE WORKER

The textile industry also restricts the development of its employees' potential because of its limited opportunities for advancement. There are few skilled jobs. The occupational ladder is limited, and there is a narrow wage spread. In 1954 about half the workers in the southern part of the industry were earning between $1.00 and $1.20 per hour. Of the major industries, only the wage distribution in automobile manufacturing is more compressed.

As an old industry, textiles has long since passed through the periods of expansion and growth which bring increased promotion opportunities. In the present period of economic decline, textile workers are indeed fortunate simply to hold on to their jobs.

In the Roper study, only 40 per cent of the textile workers say their jobs lead to promotions if they do them well. This is the fourth lowest industrial figure: only the leather; stone, clay, and glass; and automobile industries have lower proportions. Advancement into management ranks is even more unlikely because of the mill hands' low education, lack of social skills, and castelike status. Only 11 per cent thought they had good chances of getting jobs above the level of foreman, considerably less than the 20 per cent so optimistic among the entire sample. . . .

When there are many women in an industry, the advancement chances of the male workers are increased. Women are concentrated in the lowest-skilled jobs which are usually dead ends. In industries such as textiles, where strong traditional attitudes about the relative status of the sexes prevail, women are rarely considered for higher positions. Male textile workers can therefore be somewhat more optimistic about advancement, since they can hope for one of the few skilled jobs or a job supervising the ranks of women. Indeed, more than half of the male textile workers, 53 per cent, said that their jobs lead to promotions; only 16 per cent of the women workers felt this way. In apparel, another industry with a predominantly female labor force, 54 per cent of the men and 33 per cent of the women expected promotions.

THE AUTO WORKER

The lack of advancement

The "massified" wage, skill, and status structure produced by conveyer-belt technology also increases alienation because it reduces the opportunities for advancement. In assembly-line plants there are relatively few skilled jobs toward which low-skilled operatives can aspire. In addition, because skilled jobs often require formal apprenticeships or on-the-job training not easily available to most workers, "there is a deep gulf between skilled and non-skilled jobs." In one auto plant, only 6 per cent of the skilled maintenance workers had started their careers on the assembly line. Another study found that 80 per cent of the unskilled workers were not even actively interested in skilled work.

Blue-collar work in the automobile industry has no natural ladders of promotion, by which each job systematically leads to a higher one, and so on. A man is hired for one job, and he expects to stay on that job. Only 4 of the 47 unskilled workers in Chinoy's sample had the next best paying job in their department or division as a goal. In the Roper study, only 39 per cent of the automobile workers said that their jobs led to promotions, if they did them well. Only two other of the sixteen industries had lower proportions of workers without expectation of advancement. . . .

Only a small proportion of automobile workers want and expect to become supervisors but this situation is not peculiar to the industry. The advancement barrier between the ranks of the blue-collar workers and the supervisory level results not only from the scarcity of higher positions but also from differences in social status and the manual worker's general lack of social and leadership skills. And a considerable proportion of qualified manual workers do not want to leave the solidary relations with their mates and assume the responsibilities and aggravations of foremanship.

A special factor contributing to the automobile worker's high degree of social alienation is the nature of work both off and on the line. Unskilled, repetitive, and stereotyped, it does not permit a man to demonstrate those qualities of skill, initiative, leadership, and resourcefulness which are usually the requirements for a higher position. Often, the worker does not know what to do in order to qualify for promotion. The standards of selection are not clear, and there is a tendency for workers to feel that pull and connection get a man ahead. Automobile workers are particularly likely to be cynical and feel that the advancement pattern is unjust rather than equitable. Workers were asked to choose what "gives a person the best chance to advance in the plant" from among such possibilities as the quality of work, work attitude, length of company service, etc. The proportion of cynical responses, 50 per cent, given by automobile workers was the second highest among the sixteen industries. Only the steel industry had a slightly higher percentage of cynical responses.... In the more highly integrated printing and textile industries, cynical answers were offered by only 30 per cent of the respondents.

Auto workers were considerably less likely than others to feel that the quality of a man's work and his energy and willingness to work were the key factors that contributed to advancement. The generally cynical attitude suggests that there is little consensus between workers and management concerning the standards of distributive justice, a critical aspect of normative integration. It is significant that the three industries which are the most anomic on this point—steel, transportation equipment, and automobiles—are those which have the highest proportions of workers employed in very large factories.

CHEMICALS

Status structure, advancement, and loyalty to company

A fourth factor which influences integration in the chemical industry is its status structure. An elaborate system of superior and inferior ranks supports a normative structure because those in higher positions have presumably internalized the goals of the enterprise and more clearly express its values. The existence of achievable higher positions also serves to motivate those of lower status to accept the goals of the organization and to act in accordance with its norms.

The technological requirements of continuous-process production encourage a finely elaborated status structure, since, as we have seen, a balanced skill distribution emerges, made up of employees at all levels of training and responsibility. This differentiation is further developed within each operating department, where the jobs make up an elaborate hierarchy. A typical operating department consists of seven men in seven different job grades, from a beginning helper to the responsible head shift operator. Each job is a step on a natural ladder of promotion. Workers start in the department at the bottom, and the assumption is that the men will work up, one step at a time, and eventually reach the top position. At each step, there is an increase in training required, job duties (particularly responsibility), pay, and status.

Georg Simmel has written of the "inevitably disproportionate distribution of qualifications and positions" which means that all social organization involves a "contradiction between the just claims to a superordinate position and the technical impossibility of satisfying this claim. . . ."[2] Simmel observes that among the ordinary workers in a factory there are certainly very many who could equally well be foremen or entrepreneurs. The highly differentiated stratification in the chemical plant is possibly one of the best solutions to this problem of the inevitable injustice of all social systems. The elaborate hierarchical arrangement probably allows the maximum number of people to be in positions where there are others below them in rank, and this is another force for social integration.

The high level of advancement which a stratified blue-collar world makes possible is a fifth factor which supports normative integration in the continuous-process industries. The situation differs considerably from that of the automobile, textile, and other industries. Many Bay Company workers commented that in other industries a man is hired to do a particular job and it is assumed he will stay on that job. The job histories of these chemical workers show a great deal of upward movement. Of the twenty-one workers interviewed, twenty had some job advancement; only one had experienced no job change.

A representative case is that of a thirty-three-year-old operator who started with the company thirteen years ago as a bus boy in the cafeteria. After three years he moved into the ammonia plant, where he worked in succession as a janitor, a cylinder painter, and a cylinder-filler. After three years in the ammonia plant, he moved into the methionine plant and began climbing its job ladder. He started as a helper, moved up to finishing operator, then to ion operator, then to mercaptan operator, and finally to his present job as hydantion operator, fifth highest on a ladder of seven jobs. Above him are the acrolein operator and the head shift operator. After reaching these two steps, the salaried position of process foreman is his goal.[3]

In addition, skilled maintenance craftsmen in the continuous-process industries are recruited from the ranks of the less-skilled employees through formal apprenticeship and training programs. In an auto plant studied by

[2] Georg Simmel, *Sociology*, trans. Kurt Wolff (Glencoe, Ill.: Free Press, 1950), 300–3.

[3] All in-plant job careers do not show such neat upward progression, however. Another operator had been on eight different jobs in his four years with the company, and much of this movement was horizontal and some even downward. He began as a laborer in the distribution department and then became a helper in the chlorination plant. This was on the bottom of the ladder, but it held the possibility of upward movement. But the latter plant shut down, which sent him back into the yard pool of unskilled labor. He moved back again into distribution and then worked in an experimental plant called the petroleum pond.

Robert Guest, only 6 per cent of the maintenance craftsmen had started their careers on the assembly line:[4] fully skilled craftsmen were hired from the outside. In direct contrast, at one of the largest oil refineries, 90 per cent of the 1,000 skilled workers in 1937 had originally started in the plant as unskilled laborers.

A study of a major oil refinery similarly reports that "the method of upgrading, whereby all new hires start out in the labor pool and branch out from there into specialties," contributes to general job satisfaction. "After a short stay in the labor gang it is almost inevitable that a worker progress. ... Under this scheme the majority of our long term respondents have experienced considerable mobility in the refinery."

The Roper survey results confirm the superior advancement opportunities in the chemical industry. Seventy-nine per cent of the chemical workers, compared to only 47 per cent of all workers answered that their jobs led to promotions if they did them well. This was by far the highest proportion among the sixteen industries and was exactly twice as large as the proportion of automobile and textile workers who expected promotion. The second highest figure, 63 per cent, was in the petroleum refining industry. . . .

Advancement opportunities for chemical workers exist largely within the blue-collar manual sector; the route into supervision, engineering, and higher management is not as open. However, chemical workers may have slightly better chances of rising out of the blue-collar ranks than workers in other industries because the industry's rapid growth creates more openings.

Jobs in the automobile industry rarely allow a worker to show those qualities of skill and leadership that he may possess. Chemical operating and maintenance jobs not only permit their use; they often develop such potentialities. This fact and the relative lack of a worker-management cleavage in the industry result in greater feelings of equity concerning the distribution of promotion than exist in other industries. The advancement progress of each employee is reviewed periodically in the continuous-process industries, and this means that misunderstandings and resentments about promotions can be "aired out." In addition, such bureaucratic procedures as seniority provisions and the public posting of job openings also diminish the sentiments of injustice and inequity. Although individual workers have their own grievances, there seems to be no general feeling that advancements within departments are awarded unfairly, in contrast to the situation observed by Chinoy at the ABC automobile plant. However, there is considerable dissatisfaction about the age limit which kept middle-aged operators out of craft apprenticeship programs. And resentment against the length of time necessary to transfer from shift work to day jobs appears to be common in many continuous-process plants.

---

[4] Robert Guest, "Work Career and Aspirations of Automobile Workers," in Walter Galenson and Seymour M. Lipset (eds.), *Labor and Trade Unionism* (New York: John Wiley & Sons, 1960), 322.

The high level of integration in the chemical industry is confirmed by Roper statistics which show that chemical employees, along with garment workers, had the lowest proportion of cynical responses to the question on what qualities get a man ahead. Cynical responses were 24 per cent, compared to 39 per cent in the whole sample and 50 per cent in the automobile industry. Sixty-nine per cent of the chemical employees, far more than in any other industry, said that it was one's energy and willingness to work which resulted in advancement. The responses of oil workers to this question suggest considerably less satisfaction with the norms of distributive justice in that industry. Cynical responses were 43 per cent, which is higher than the all-factory average; refinery workers were considerably more likely to stress seniority as the key factor. Forty-nine per cent of the oil workers mentioned this, compared to 28 per cent of the chemical employees and 25 per cent of all workers. . . .

The structuring of advancement opportunities in continuous-process technology enhances the integration and cohesion in these industries; conversely, the high level of integration increases an employee's motivation to advance and is therefore an incentive toward superior performance. An insightful operator, who had worked in four other industries and developed a comparative perspective, makes this point:

> There's more place to advance here than in other places. At the can company I was at the top but there's not much difference between the bottom and the top. In the brickyard there's no difference at all—you stay on the same job all your life. Here the difference between my job and the top job is about $1,200 a year. That makes an incentive to do your best and to get promotions. I guess that's the way the company sees it.

However, I must qualify this highly positive picture. The institutionalization of mobility routes through formal job ladders and the company's encouragement of aspiration and training result, naturally enough, in a high level of expectation of upward movement. In addition, the industry's employment security has been so consistent that workers are not as preoccupied with holding on to their jobs as are the automobile workers and textile workers. When the job is secure, advancement becomes even more important psychically. And since promotions are rarely as rapid as workers would like them, considerably dissatisfaction often results.

The economic downturn of the past few years has decreased the rate of advancements in the industry sharply and thus has aggravated this crisis in expectations. Taking advantage of the general postwar prosperity and its own growth position, the chemical industry expanded very rapidly in the late forties and to a lesser extent in the early fifties. Advancements were quite rapid. When other industries were laying off workers during recent recessions, it was able to avoid unemployment because of its superior economic and growth situation: workers who quit or retired were simply not replaced. However, in this period, advancement has slowed down drastically.

The finding in the 1947 Roper survey that four-fifths of the chemical workers felt their jobs led to promotions would probably not be repeated today: although the superior advancement pattern, compared to other industries, still holds in general. In fact, the very large degree of dissatisfaction with this decline in upward movement is suggested in Davis' 1959 survey. Among eleven characteristics of the job, "opportunity for advancement" was most consistently liked least by the respondents. Yet, 27 per cent of these same respondents admitted that chances to get ahead were better than at other companies.

Despite these recent disappointments, the job security and upward mobility in the chemical industry mean that employment there tends to become a life-long career—in the sense that a white-collar employee or a civil servant has a career. When employment is viewed as a permanent career rather than as a short-term job, loyalty and identification with the organization are enhanced. These attitudes are further supported by the non-manual, clean, and responsible nature of the process operator's work, which gives him something in common with the white-collar employees in his own company and distinguishes him from the mass of factory workers in heavy industries.[5] In short, the conditions of work in the process industries produce a worker who is more middle-class, in situation and perspective, than most blue-collar employees.

We have seen that continuous-process technology results in a distinctive plant social structure, many aspects of which contribute to a high degree of social cohesion and normative integration. It is fortunate that these natural, spontaneous, social processes work in this direction because automated production requires an integrated manual work force for its successful operation. Not only does the responsibility demanded of the operator necessitate more loyalty to the enterprise than when work is standardized, but the constant technological change inherent in continuous-process production also makes an integrated work force essential.

The continuing economic and technical advances in the oil refining and chemical industries would be impossible if workers in these industries were disposed to resist innovation and change, as are many industrial workers. The high degree of integration, the relative lack of conflict, and the high level of job security in the chemical industry provide an atmosphere in which technological change is more accepted by workers and unions than in the automobile industry, where, because of its history of labor-management

[5] A possible consequence of career employment in manual work may be the development of a future time perspective, a trait which has been considered characteristic of the middle class rather than the working class. Many Bay Area plant workers mentioned that they could expect to move up a notch or two at least five years from now because certain top operators were due to retire then.

It is interesting to contrast the end of career lines in the automobile and the chemical industries. Older workers in the automobile industry cannot take the pace of the line and may be forced to take lower-paying jobs such as those of sweepers. The older chemical workers hold down the most skilled and responsible jobs in both the operating and the maintenance departments: younger workers count the years and months until they retire.

strife and its irregular employment pattern, workers are naturally suspicious of the motives and effects of technological innovation.

A study of the Opinion Research Corporation found that automobile workers were more likely to oppose automation and fear its consequences than were chemical workers. Fifty-eight per cent of the chemical employees, compared to 43 per cent of the auto workers, felt that "improved machines" were "a good thing for employees." In addition, a consistently higher proportion of automobile workers felt that their company should neither install faster machines nor move in the direction of more automation. . . .

62

The Career of the Letter Carrier

DEAN HARPER and FREDERICK EMMERT

Professors Harper and Emmert analyze the career pattern of the postman in terms of how it fits both the official and unofficial hierarchies of the organization.

THE SORTING AND DELIVERY OF MAIL

The official job of the letter carrier is to sort incoming mail for those on his route, to deliver it, to collect mail deposited in collection boxes along his route, and to perform various duties associated with these activities. Before describing the official rules which specify how this should be done and indicating how the letter carrier actually performs his duties, a brief description of the typical career of the letter carrier will be given.

The carrier applicant who passes the Civil Service examination and accepts employment is first appointed as a substitute carrier. He is paid on an hourly basis and is assured a minimum of two hours of work a day. His main duties are to serve as a substitute carrier on the route of a regular carrier when the regular carrier has his day off, is sick, or on vacation; in this he will work a number of different routes, moving about the city from day to day. In addition, the substitute carrier works two or three evenings a week collecting mail. He also can on occasion be pressed into work as a distribution clerk. As regular carriers retire or die, routes become available for reassignment. The substitute carrier with seniority is promoted to a salaried regular carrier position and temporarily assigned to the vacant route. Periodically all such vacant routes are bid for by regular carriers; each route goes to the carrier with seniority. There is considerable variability in the recruitment problems of different local Post Offices. In some areas of the country a substitute is able to obtain a regular route of his own after a few months; in other areas it may take him up to three years.

The next step in the career of the carrier, if he is motivated to seek promotion, is to a supervisory position. Those appointed to supervisory positions are selected by each local postmaster from the list of postal employees who have successfully passed civil service tests. A further aspect of the career of some letter carriers is a second job. Since the postal work day of most carriers ends at 3:30, a number of them work at second jobs. . . .

Excerpted, with permission, from *Social Forces*, 42(2) (December, 1963): 217–18, 222–23.

OFFICIAL AND UNOFFICIAL HIERARCHIES

In the official organization of the Post Office there exist several hierarchies, Many statuses are related to each other in terms of an authority relationship; further, one individual may "stand higher" in the hierarchy than another. but yet not have any legitimate direct authority over the other. In addition, there is a reward hierarchy—the pay scale—which is closely correlated with the authority hierarchy.

In addition to the hierarchies which are stated or implied by the official rules and regulations there are also unofficial hierarchies which are supplementary to and grow out of the official hierarchies. These have to do with power, privilege and prestige.

Among the carriers three distinct work statuses will be compared. First, regular carriers can be distinguished from substitute carriers; second, as was indicated, among the regulars there are mounted carriers who deliver mail to roadside mail boxes from their cars and unmounted or foot carriers who deliver mail on foot.

The mounted carrier and the unmounted carrier are at an equal level in the official hierarchies. One does not have authority over the other and, apart from longevity, both receive the same base pay. The regular carrier does not have authority over the substitute except for those specific occasions when a particular substitute is assisting a particular regular carrier. However, since all carriers are promoted from substitute to regular carrier status the latter is higher in the official hierarchy.

First of all, it can be noted that the regular carrier is granted more prestige than the substitute carrier. This is due to the different official rewards which regular status brings, i.e., definite work hours rather than hourly wages, a five-day work week rather than a six-day week and the psychological security of a fixed work assignment. Secondly, prestige differences develop between the mounted carrier and the foot carrier. The mounted carrier receives a car allowance, overtime pay, and help from substitute carriers. Because he receives these things and the foot carrier does not, the mounted carrier is accorded more prestige; in general, a mounted route is valued more than a foot route and those who have them are esteemed. This is an addition to the hostility felt toward the mounted carrier by the foot carrier.

By virtue of the prestige differences, two other hierarchies emerge; these are the privilege hierarchy and the power hierarchy. The substitute carrier is frequently denied certain privileges. Unofficial norms prescribe that no substitute carrier shall leave the station to deliver his mail before all regular carriers have their mail sorted, that substitute carriers will help each other if they have difficulty in sorting mail, that substitute carriers will not have their morning coffee in the "swing room" (the employee's locker room found in most stations) on "heavy mail" days and that on "light" days substitute carriers will not spend as much time in the "swing room" as regular carriers.

The substitute is typically younger than the regular carrier, has been in the postal service a shorter time, and since he may move around from substation to substation in his work assignments, he frequently becomes peripheral to the *unique* informal organization of any substation. Because of these factors the regular carriers are able to exert influence on the substitute and they tend to enforce these privilege differences. As several subs were told by a regular carrier in the "swing room" on a heavy day: "What are you guys doing in here? Why the ink isn't even dry on your applications yet!" Comments such as these from a fairly cohesive regular carrier group are usually sufficient to enforce these privilege differences.

Thus, emerging out of the official authority and reward hierarchies is a prestige hierarchy. Associated with the prestige hierarchy is a privilege hierarchy reinforced by a power hierarchy. These unofficial hierarchies are supplementary to the official hierarchies.

Other studies in industrial sociology have described the emergence of some of these unofficial hierarchies. Cottrell describes a prestige hierarchy among the various railroad work statuses where prestige is correlated with skill required for the job, pay and conditions of work.[1] Roethlisberger and Dickson indicated that in the bank wiring room the wiremen were superior to the soldermen and those who wired connectors were more esteemed than those who wired selectors; these prestige differences were associated with skill required for the job and pay differences.[2]

Whyte has pointed out that distinctions are made among the various jobs in the kitchens of restaurants which partially depend upon the prestige value of the materials used and the position of the job in the flow of work.[3]

[1] See W. Fred Cottrell, *The Railroader* (Palo Alto, California: Stanford University Press, 1940), 12–41.

[2] F. J. Roethlisberger and William J. Dickson, *Management and the Worker* (Cambridge, Massachusetts: Harvard University Press, 1950), 495–96.

[3] William Foote Whyte, *Human Relations in the Restaurant Industry* (New York: McGraw-Hill, 1948), 33–46.

63

From Organizational Career to
Private Practice

A. Psychotherapists

ANSELM L. STRAUSS, LEONARD SCHATZMAN,
RUE BUCHER, DANUTA ERLICH, and
MELVIN SABSHIN

The following two excerpts by Professors Strauss (*et al.*)
and Cohen indicate how the organizational career may,
by conditions, lead to or be a purposeful stepping stone
to establishing a private practice—both jointly with the
career, and then shedding the career.

Most attending men who regularly treat patients at this hospital are ex-
residents who have been graduated from its training program. While the
somaticists are wedded to the institution, the ex-residents are engaged only
temporarily in hospital practice. Most are merely passing through the very
early stages of long careers, stages during which their initial practices are
split between office and hospital. Later they will, for reasons to be spelled out,
virtually cease to have hospital practices.

This group of men numbered about twenty-five at the time of our study.
It consisted of all the recent residents, except those serving in the armed
forces and one who has become an administrator at PPI. There is good reason
for the young psychiatrist to treat some of his patients at the hospital. Most
of his early referrals are patients deemed in need of hospitalization. Like the
somaticist, he frequently first meets his patient only after their actual hospitalization. His former supervisors and his friends among the ex-residents refer
patients whom they are too busy to see or do not wish to treat. Since most
hospitalized referrals do not wish to continue in therapy at his office, the
young psychiatrist can expect to develop his office practice very slowly *via*
this path.

He gradually reduces the number of his hospital visits as his office referrals
increase or as his office schedule becomes tighter because patients persist in
longer therapy. He may also suddenly find his list of hospitalized patients
dropping to virtually nothing because they are all discharged at approximately
the same time. Then, too, if he receives a few office referrals, he will have
correspondingly less time for hospital work. In such ways, he begins to withdraw from the hospital.

Excerpted, with permission, from Anselm Strauss, Leonard Schatzman, Rue Bucher, Danuta
Erlich, and Melvin Sabshin, *Psychiatric Ideologies and Institutions* (New York: Free Press of
Glencoe, 1964; pp. 187–90).

Yet while he is visiting hospitalized patients, the hospital serves him well. Many ex-residents have told us that the early months of practice are a lonely time: The hospital serves to counteract this isolation, affording a locale where they can meet and pass pleasant conversational moments with colleagues and residents. The hospital is also a locale where professional, albeit informal, advice can be had for more puzzling cases.

Once launched into practice, ex-residents are led further and further away from part-time hospital practice. In past years, a majority has entered upon the institutional ladder that leads, by the end of residency or soon after, to the Chicago Psychoanalytic Institute. Such young men have decreasing amounts of time to spend with patients, for the Institute eats up time. (It also has eaten up money, since a training analysis is required before candidacy.) The young psychiatrist begins to discover that office practice is more economical or at least requires less commuting. It he moves to the suburbs, his time becomes even more valuable and the hospital correspondingly less convenient. Beside, he often frankly admits that a hospital practice is something of a drag upon him physically: A hospitalized patient is more likely to phone at night, and hospital personnel can raise bothersome problems. The kinds of referral that he was pleased to get earlier, no longer please him so much. The further he progresses in analytic training, the more he is apt to be attracted, for purely intellectual reasons, by the types of patient seen in office practice.

There is a more important reason for young psychotherapists' abandonment of hospital practices: They have never intended to treat hospital patients past their early careers. With rare exceptions, they entered residency anticipating office practice. Although the first year of residency plunges them into administrative duties and has them treating hospitalized patients under supervision, few residents become permanently interested in administration or in hospitalized patients. Even during that first year, their attention is focused more upon supervision than upon hospitalized patients. During the next two years, they treat mainly clinic patients. After residency, they recognize that a few years must pass until they can manage a wholly office practice. Many also look forward to attending the Analytic Institute and developing concurrently a more psychodynamic practice. Such time as can be spared from practice they may devote to supervising residents, thus following the established pattern of a practitioner who also teaches. Even those ex-residents who do not go on to the Institute or to a more analytic practice conceive of practice mainly as composed of office patients.

Nevertheless, counterpressure and inducements do prevent a few from quickly or completely abandoning the hospital. From time to time, an older psychotherapist will treat a patient there—frequently an office patient who has come to need hospitalization. An occasional ex-resident does part-time research at PPI and finds it convenient to carry a few hospital patients also. In addition, PPI's associate director, who administered the residency program during the period of our research, has attempted to further resident's interest in hospital administration; partly by teaching classes in social psychiatry and also by encouraging residents, as well as recent graduates, to become co-ordinators of PPI's wards.

Whatever impact such programing may have had on the residents' therapeutic notions, it has had only minor impact on their career styles. Hospital administration does not yet command high prestige, and, to follow in the footsteps of PPI's present administrators, one must also possess genuine commitment to research. A psychoanalytic career carries much prestige in Chicago, as elsewhere, and there seems to be no decline of this prestige among these young physicians. Such careers will afford them relatively comfortable livings (although we would be hard put to make an accurate judgment of the relative weights of money and prestige—nor do we care to try). There is also no question that—given the supervision and training that PPI residents receive and despite milieu, transactional, and physiological emphases in the curriculum—the residents are prepared to be psychoanalytically oriented. Most do become analysts, in fact, or at least psychotherapists.

What this orientation means for the hospital, as now constituted, is that it affords a ready supply of young attending men who regularly treat patients there. Each young generation serves its period, often much enjoying its continued contact with the hospital and personnel and the intellectual and emotional pleasures of treating hospitalized patients. When at last these young physicians prepare to leave the hospital scene, another generation stands eager to take their places—for a time.

Speculation about the futures of these men is not too hazardous. Those who become full-fledged analysts probably will never return to any hospital practice. They will follow the more traditional path of supplementing an office practice with supervisory, committee, and occasionally teaching and research activities. For future PPI graduates, other contingencies exist. If the hospital becomes larger, more interest in administration may be generated, possibly abetted by the generally increasing prestige of hospital practice and administration throughout the metropolitan area. Much more likely is that residents may increasingly join the middle group of psychiatrists who are analytically oriented but not actually analysts. These psychotherapists may become interested in schizophrenics and psychotics, and such interest will lead them to remain associated with hospitals where those types of patient can be treated. But such careers belong to the future: Today's PPI resident is destined for private office practice after a brief apprenticeship divided between office and hospital.

B. Social Workers

MICHAEL COHEN

... Another career difference which seemed likely to distinguish among social workers was the type of positions they had held. The respondents were asked whether they had held any of the following types of social work positions: direct-service, supervisory, executive or administrative, teaching social work, consultation, and research. Virtually all of the respondents had held direct-service positions. . . .

There is a significant difference at the .01 level or beyond between the percentages of private practitioners who have held each type of position, except research. These results suggest that those social workers engaging in private practice are also the ones who tend to hold higher level positions in the profession.

Other findings show that private practitioners are older than non-private practitioners and have been in social work longer. Therefore, it was possible that they have tended to hold higher level positions as a result of their longer tenure. To test this possibility, the two groups were compared holding length of time in social work constant. The results of this comparison (not shown here) revealed that, for the most part, this was not the case, those engaging in private practice tending to have held higher level positions than the others regardless of length of time in social work. A comparison of respondents according to position held in 1963, holding length of time in social work constant, showed similar results, suggesting that those engaging in private practice have also tended to move faster into higher level positions than the others.

The data test the hypothesis that social workers who have held higher level positions are more likely to enter private practice than are other social workers, by comparing the private practitioners with non-private practitioners, both those who refused the suggestion to engage in private practice and those to whom private practice was not suggested. . . . These results substantiate the conclusion that those who have held higher level positions are more likely to engage in private practice.

Finally, there is evidence that private practitioners had achieved these higher positions before accepting their first case: 55 per cent reported holding positions removed from direct-service at that time.

The data in this section suggest a distinction among social workers between the more and the less organizationally successful. The former are the ones who tend to enter private practice, and this factor appears crucial.

Excerpted, with permission, from "The Emergence of Private Practice in Social Work," *Social Problems*, 14 (Summer, 1966): 88–89.

461

Index

Printed in the United States
by Baker & Taylor Publisher Services